《视听表演北京条约》立法史料编译

上册

汉英对照版

侍孝祥　唐震　陶冶　林佩瑶／主编

法律出版社 LAW PRESS · CHINA
——北京——

图书在版编目(CIP)数据

《视听表演北京条约》立法史料编译. 上册 : 汉英对照 / 侍孝祥等主编. -- 北京 : 法律出版社, 2024
ISBN 978-7-5197-8860-5

Ⅰ. ①视… Ⅱ. ①侍… Ⅲ. ①世界知识产权组织-知识产权-国际条约-研究-汉、英 Ⅳ. ①D913.4 ②D813.7

中国国家版本馆 CIP 数据核字(2024)第 037792 号

《视听表演北京条约》立法史料编译
(上册)(汉英对照版)
《SHITING BIAOYAN BEIJING TIAOYUE》LIFA SHILIAO BIANYI (SHANGCE) (HAN-YING DUIZHAO BAN)

侍孝祥 唐 震 陶 冶 林佩瑶 主编
丛书编译组 编译

责任编辑 屈 瑶
装帧设计 臧晓飞

出版发行 法律出版社
编辑统筹 学术·对外出版分社
责任校对 张翼羽
责任印制 胡晓雅 宋万春
经 销 新华书店

开本 710 毫米×1000 毫米 1/16
印张 45 字数 761 千
版本 2024 年 6 月第 1 版
印次 2024 年 6 月第 1 次印刷
印刷 北京新生代彩印制版有限公司

地址:北京市丰台区莲花池西里 7 号(100073)
网址:www.lawpress.com.cn
投稿邮箱:info@lawpress.com.cn
举报盗版邮箱:jbwq@lawpress.com.cn

销售电话:010-83938349
客服电话:010-83938350
咨询电话:010-63939796

书号:ISBN 978-7-5197-8860-5
定价(上册):189.00 元

凡购买本社图书,如有印装错误,我社负责退换。电话:010-83938349

编 译 者

（按姓氏笔画排序）

王依劼	王欣玉	卢思元	朱佳平	李兆良
余　熠	汪若蓝	沈敬杰	张　莹	张　敏
陈健淋	邵望蕴	林抒蔚	林佩瑶	罗圣婕
侍孝祥	胡　超	俞　璐	姜广瑞	徐丽红
陶　冶	桑清圆	黄怡宁	程欣怡	谢采洪
鲍依娜				

编委会成员简介

张　斌　上海市高级人民法院原副院长、一级高级法官

王　迁　华东政法大学教授、博士生导师、校学术委员会副主任

丛立先　华东政法大学知识产权学院院长、教授、博士生导师

刘军华　上海市知识产权法院副院长、法学博士

唐　震　上海市松江区人民法院副院长、法学博士

侍孝祥　华东政法大学知识产权学院副教授、澳大利亚昆士兰科技大学法学博士（PH.D）

尹腊梅　华东政法大学知识产权学院副教授、法学博士

陶　冶　上海市浦东新区人民法院知识产权审判庭副庭长、三级高级法官、法学博士

编译者简介

王依劼　华东政法大学法学硕士（知识产权）

王欣玉　华东政法大学法学硕士（知识产权）

卢思元　上海市杨浦区人民法院知识产权审判庭法官助理、法学硕士

朱佳平　上海市高级人民法院知识产权审判庭四级高级法官、法学硕士

李兆良　上海市徐汇区人民法院知识产权审判庭法官助理、法律硕士

余　熠　上海市徐汇区人民法院知识产权审判庭法官助理、法学硕士

汪若蓝　华东政法大学法学硕士（知识产权）、安徽省铜陵市铜官区人民法院法官助理

沈敬杰　上海市杨浦区人民法院知识产权审判庭法官、法学硕士

张　莹　上海市高级人民法院知识产权审判庭三级高级法官、法学硕士

张　敏　上海市徐汇区人民法院知识产权审判庭一级法官、法学硕士

陈健淋　上海市高级人民法院知识产权审判庭法官助理、法学博士

邵望蕴　上海知识产权法院知识产权审判二庭法官助理、法学硕士

林抒蔚　上海市普陀区人民法院知识产权审判庭二级法官、文学硕士

林佩瑶　上海市徐汇区人民法院知识产权审判庭四级高级法官、法学硕士

罗圣婕　上海市宝山区人民法院商事审判庭四级法官、法学学士

胡　超　上海市普陀区人民法院知识产权审判庭法官助理、法学硕士

俞　璐　上海市普陀区人民法院知识产权审判庭法官助理、法学硕士

姜广瑞　上海市浦东新区人民法院审判监督庭（审管办、研究室）一级法官、法学博士

徐丽红　华东政法大学法学硕士（知识产权）

桑清圆　上海市浦东新区人民法院知识产权审判庭二级法官、法学硕士

黄怡宁　华东政法大学法学硕士（知识产权）

程欣怡　华东政法大学法学硕士（知识产权）、上海市杨浦区人民检察院检察官助理

谢采洪　华东政法大学法学硕士（知识产权）、广州市白云区人民法院法官助理

鲍依娜　上海市徐汇区人民法院知识产权审判庭书记员、管理学学士、英语学士

* 注：卢思元、朱佳平、李兆良、余熠、沈敬杰、张莹、张敏、陈健淋、邵望蕴、林抒蔚、林佩瑶、罗圣婕、胡超、俞璐、姜广瑞、桑清圆、鲍依娜为上海法院知识产权对外交流小组成员。

序　一

2021 年 9 月，中共中央、国务院发布《知识产权强国建设纲要（2021—2035）年》，要求“深度参与全球知识产权治理”，提出“扩大知识产权领域对外开放，完善国际对话交流机制，推动完善知识产权及相关国际贸易，国际投资等国际规则和标准”。

《视听表演北京条约》是联合国成立以来首个在我国签订、以我国城市命名的国际知识产权条约，其缔结和生效的意义重大。从国际知识产权保护的角度来看，该条约有效提升了对表演者权利保护的水平，是惠及全球表演者的新起点；对我国而言，它不仅使我国表演者在同属条约缔约方的其他国家和地区获得充分保护，激发表演者的创作热情，促进文化的传播与多样化表达，更是充分彰显了我国深度参与全球知识产权治理，推动完善知识产权国际规则的决心与担当。

本书对 1997 年 6 月至 2012 年 6 月所形成的《视听表演北京条约》立法史料进行了详尽的梳理，内容既包括各国提案、非政府组织发言，也涵盖了历次会议的背景资料以及阶段性成果，忠实全面地展示了视听表演保护问题的谈判过程。本书分为上、下两册，以中英文对照的方式呈现给读者，为深入学习和理解《视听表演北京条约》的立法目的、文本含义及体系逻辑提供了有益的参考。此外，《视听表演北京条约》的谈判历时 16 年，期间争议持续不断，借本书回顾此番缔约过程，也能让我们真切体会到缔约成果的来之不易，感受到推动国际知识产权规则体系建设的筚路蓝缕。

具体而言，本书按照缔约阶段将内容划分为了三个部分：

首先是缔约的准备阶段。本书编译了视听表演议定书专家委员会于 1997 年及 1998 年分别召开的两次代表大会的相关资料，包括各国及地区立法中已有的关于视听表演的规定，世界知识产权组织成员国提交的关于视听表演的信息，来自欧共体、韩国、美国、南非等国家的提案，拉丁美洲和加勒比区域协商会议报告，亚洲及太平洋区域协商会议报告。以上资料就术语定义、未录制的视听表演中的经济权利、保护的受益人等方面进行了讨论。随后，由于世界知识产权组织机构的改革，视听表演议定书专家委员会被版权及其相关权常设委员会（SCCR）所取代。在缔约准备阶段，SCCR 于 1998 年至 2000 年召开了四次会议。从各方提交材料来看，关于视听表演保护问题的观点和立场分歧日益凸显，给条约的缔结带来不小的挑战。

其次是缔约争议阶段。由于 2000 年有关视听表演的外交会议较为仓促，许多问题尚未得到解决。针对相关问题，SCCR 主席编写了《关于拟由外交会议审议的视听表演保护文书的实质条款的基本提案》供各方代表参考和讨论。除此之外，本书还编译了这一阶段国家和区域研讨会的成果总结及立场盘点、关于视听表演国际保护的主要问题和立场的背景文件等材料。

最后是缔约完成阶段。关于保护视听表演的外交会议于 2012 年 6 月在北京召开，本书编译了此次会议的核心文件《视听表演北京条约草案》，内容涉及表演者实质性权利条款、表演者权利行使条款以及与条约有关的程序性事项等。

值得一提的是，本书由世界知识产权组织（WIPO）国际条约立法史料编委会的成员们共同翻校、编汇而成。他们中有来自华东政法大学的知识产权专家学者，也有上海三级法院的知识产权法官和法官助理。这既是上海高院与华东政法大学积极开展知识产权“院”“校”合作的开山之作，也是上海高院努力锻造具有国际视野的知识产权审判队伍的具体举措，应予深化和延续。

值本书付梓之际，受邀作序。一言以蔽之，本书作为官方立法史料的编译之作，无论对于理论研究者还是实务人士都具有较高的借鉴意义。在此衷心地期待本书的出版能丰富理论研究，提高实操水平，为加强知识产权国际保护贡献智慧；更祝愿《视听表演北京条约》的生效为各缔约国的视听产业提供齐全完备的法律保障，促进视听行业的繁荣发展。

是为序。

张　斌
上海市高级人民法院原副院长
2024 年 4 月

序　二

《视听表演北京条约》于2012年6月24日在我国北京举办的世界知识产权组织（WIPO）外交会议上获得通过，并在2020年4月28日正式生效。作为第一个以我国城市命名的国际知识产权条约，它解决了长期以来对以视听录制品录制的表演缺乏充分国际保护的问题，对于维护表演者的权益和完善国际版权保护体系具有重要意义。可以预见，随着条约的生效以及在我国的落地实施，表演者权利的保护水平将得到全面提升，视听产业也将进入高质量发展的快速通道。

然而，《视听表演北京条约》磋商、起草、缔结复杂，其内容具有较高程度的专业性和复杂性。即使从事知识产权保护工作，如果对条约缺乏深入学习，对其内容也难以充分理解。对我国法院审理外国表演者以视听录制品录制的表演案件而言，挑战更为严峻，要求各级司法机关条约更为系统地理解与把握条约内容。在审理有关案件时，法院除了首先要确定原告以视听录制品录制的表演能否在我国获得保护——查询相关外国人的所在国是否已经加入条约，还要了解该表演可在我国获得保护的范围：我国在批准条约时，对条约第11条第1款、第2款，也就是要求向表演者授予专有权利和获酬权的规定声明保留，所以我国没有义务根据条约第11条第1款和第2款的规定去保护表演者的向公众传播权和获酬权。同时，法院还应当注意我国在批准条约时，没有对条约第19条第1款——“时间上的适用范围”声明保留，因此，条约生效之前已经录制成视听录制品的表演仍然受到保护，但根据第19条第3款的规定，在条约对每一个成员国生效之前，他人未经许可对以视听录制品录制的表演利用的行为，即便在条约生效之后应当被认定为侵权，本条约也不能对该行为溯及既往适用。同样可能存在理解偏差的还有港澳台表演者权利保护问题：一方面，港澳台地区不可能成为条约的缔约方，所以法院不能依据条约对此三地表演者以视听录制品录制的表演进行保护；另一方面，港澳台表演者的权利获得保护的根本原因在于表演者属于我国《著作权法》第2条规定的“中华人民共和国公民”，因而可直接根据我国《著作权法》对其表演予以保护。上述事例说明，对条约的理解和把握任重而道远。

为了使人们进一步理解《视听表演北京条约》，本人曾承担撰写《视听表演北京条约》释义的工作，但授人以鱼不如授人以渔，若能对条约相关立法史料进行梳理及翻译，必将为深入学习和理解《视听表演北京条约》提供有益的参考。为此，在上海高级人民法院与华东政法大学牵头组织下，经过世界知识产权组织（WIPO）国际条约立法史料编委会的成员们共同翻校、编汇，《〈视听表演北京条约〉立法史料编译》一书终于问世。

该书将缔约过程分为缔约准备、缔约磋商和缔约完成三个阶段，对 1997 年 6 月至 2012 年 6 月期间所形成的核心立法史料进行了详细梳理。其中，不仅包括历次会议的背景资料以及阶段性成果，还涵盖了各国提案、非政府组织发言，并以中英文对照的形式提供给读者，其全面和忠实程度可见一斑，可以为条约的理论和实务研究提供第一手宝贵资料，助力理论研究者以及实务人士理解和把握《视听表演北京条约》的立法目的、文本含义及体系逻辑。

对《视听表演北京条约》的理解和把握，不能将目光只逡巡于条款本身，不能只见树木，不见森林，必须深入研究条约立法史料，这样才能实现对条款体系化把握，避免机械教条的错误适用带来不利后果。本书正是为了实现该目的而进行的基础工作。

受邀为《〈视听表演北京条约〉立法史料编译》一书作序，我深感荣幸。希望通过本书，读者能乘风破浪，为《视听表演北京条约》在我国的准确实施和我国著作权法的发展做出更大贡献。

王　迁
华东政法大学教授、博士生导师、校学术委员会副主任
2024 年 5 月于上海

Contents

目　　录

VOLUME 1

STAGE 1 THE CONCEPTION OF THE TREATY

上　册

第一部分　缔约准备阶段

第一部分
缔约准备阶段

1.

Committee of Experts on a Protocol Concerning Audiovisual Performances (September, 1997)

Meeting code: AP/CE/I
Date: September 15 to September 19, 1997
venue: Geneva, Switzerland
Meeting Documents URL: https://www.wipo.int/meetings/en/details.jsp?meeting_id=3184

1.

视听表演议定书专家委员会会议

（1997 年 9 月）

会议代码：AP/CE/I
会议日期：1997 年 9 月 15—19 日
会议地点：瑞士日内瓦
会议文件链接：https://www.wipo.int/meetings/en/details.jsp?meeting_id=3184

1.1 Existing National and Regional Legislation Concerning Audiovisual Performances

Document Code: AP/CE/1/2
Language: English
URL: https://www.wipo.int/edocs/mdocs/copyright/en/ap_ce_i/ap_ce_i_2.pdf

Chinese Translation: Not Available.
URL: N/A

COMMITTEE OF EXPERTS
ON A PROTOCOL
CONCERNING AUDIOVISUAL PERFORMANCES
Geneva, September 15, 16 and 19, 1997

EXISTING NATIONAL AND REGIONAL LEGISLATION CONCERNING AUDIOVISUAL PERFORMANCES

Memorandum prepared by the International Bureau

I. INTRODUCTION

1. The WIPO Diplomatic Conference on Certain Copyright and Neighboring Rights Questions which took place in Geneva from December 2 to 20, 1996, on its last day, adopted the WIPO Performances and Phonograms Treaty (WPPT).

2. Among the documents of the Conference had been a “Basic Proposal for the Substantive Provisions of a Treaty for the Protection of the Rights of Performers

1.1 当前各国和地区立法中关于视听表演的规定

文件编号：AP/CE/1/2
文件语言：英语
文件链接：https://www.wipo.int/edocs/mdocs/copyright/en/ap_ce_i/ap_ce_i_2.pdf
中文文本：无
文件链接：无

视听表演议定书

专家委员会

1997 年 9 月 15 日、16 日和 19 日，日内瓦

当前各国或地区立法中关于视听表演的规定

由国际局编制的备忘录

一、介绍

1. 1996 年 12 月 2 日至 20 日，世界知识产权组织在日内瓦举行了关于版权和邻接权若干问题的外交会议，会议最后一日通过了《世界知识产权组织表演和录音制品条约》(WPPT)。

2. 会议的文件包括“关于保护表演者和录音制品制作者权利条约实质性条款的基本建议，供外交会议审议”(CRNR/DC/5 号文件)以及各代表团在会议期

and Producers of Phonograms to be considered by the Diplomatic Conference" (document CRNR/DC/5) as well as a number of relating amendment proposals submitted by Delegations in the course of the Conference. Under some of these documents, or at least under some of the alternatives included in them, the coverage of the rights of performers would have extended to audiovisual performances, the WPPT, however, with the exception of some rights related to unfixed performances, does not cover audiovisual performances.

3. The Conference addressed this issue in a Resolution concerning Audiovisual Performances (document CRNR/DC/99), adopted on its last day with the following text:

"The Delegations participating in the Diplomatic Conference on Certain Copyright and Neighboring Rights Questions in Geneva,

"Noting that the development of technologies will allow for a rapid growth of audiovisual services and that this will increase the opportunities for performing artists to exploit their audiovisual performances that will be transmitted by these services;

"Recognizing the great importance of ensuring an adequate level of protection for these performances, in particular when they are exploited in the new digital environment, and that sound and audiovisual performances are increasingly related;

"Stressing the urgent need to agree on new norms for the adequate legal international protection of audiovisual performances;

"Regretting that, in spite of the efforts of most Delegations, the WIPO Performances and Phonograms Treaty does not cover the rights of performers in the audiovisual fixations of their performance;

"Call for the convocation of an extraordinary session of the competent WIPO Governing Bodies during the first quarter of 1997 to decide on the schedule of the preparatory work on a protocol to the WIPO Performances and Phonograms Treaty, concerning audiovisual performances, with a view to the adoption of such a protocol not later than in 1998."

4. The Resolution (and a Recommendation concerning Databases also adopted in the Diplomatic Conference) was discussed at the thirtieth series of meetings of the Governing Bodies of WIPO, namely the General Assembly of WIPO, the WIPO Coordination Committee and the Assembly of the Berne Union, in Geneva, on

间提出的若干有关修正案。根据其中部分文件，或至少根据其中所载的部分备选办法，表演者权利的涵盖范围将扩大到视听表演，然而，除与尚未录制的表演有关的一些权利外，WPPT 并未涉及视听表演。

3. 会议最后一日通过的关于视听表演的决议（CRNR/DC/99 号文件）中讨论了这个问题，文案如下：

"参加在日内瓦举行的关于版权和邻接权若干问题的外交会议的各代表团：

"鉴于技术发展将使视听服务迅速增长，进而增加表演艺术家利用将由这些服务来传播视听表演的机会；

"认识到为这些表演提供适当保护的重要性，特别是当人们在新的数字环境中利用这些表演，并且有声表演和视听表演的关系日益密切的时候；

"强调迫切需要就新的规范达成共识，以对视听表演进行适当的国际法律保护；

"遗憾的是，尽管大多数代表团作出了努力，但 WPPT 并未涵盖表演者对其表演的视听录制品享有的权利；

"呼吁世界知识产权组织主管理事机构在 1997 年第一季度召开一次特别会议，就 WPPT 关于视听表演议定书的筹备工作安排表作出决定，以期不迟于 1998 年通过这一议定书。"

4. 1997 年 3 月 20 日和 21 日在日内瓦举行的世界知识产权组织理事机构第三十次系列会议，即世界知识产权组织大会、世界知识产权组织协调委员会和伯尔尼联盟大会，讨论了该决议（以及外交会议通过的一项关于数据库的建议）。

March 20 and 21, 1997.

5. The Governing Bodies took, inter alia, the following decisions (document AB/XXX/4, paragraph 20):

"(i) A Committee of Experts on the protocol concerning audiovisual performances will be convened for September 15 and 16, 1997, and an Information Meeting concerning intellectual property in databases will be convened for September 17 and 18, 1997. September 19, 1997, will be reserved for the adoption of the reports of both the Committee of Experts and the Information Meeting.

"(ii) The International Bureau will, separately for each of the two subjects, prepare a document on the existing national and regional laws and regulations. Furthermore, the International Bureau will invite the Governments of the Member States of WIPO and the European Community by circular to communicate to it in writing information on the de facto situation, particularly contractual practices, existing in their respective countries, as well as any statistics."

6. The present document examines the existing and regional legislation in the WIPO Member States, of Cartagena Agreement and of the European Community, with the exception of a few countries where the laws or recent amendments were not available at the International Bureau in any of the working languages of WIPO at the time when the document was prepared. Since the existing international norms may-and in many cases do-have direct or indirect relevance for national and regional legislation, those norms are also reviewed briefly. The information received in answer to the above-mentioned circular is included in a separate document.

Ⅱ. SCOPE OF THE WPPT AND SCOPE OF THIS MEMORANDUM

7. The presentation of national and regional laws and regulations in this memorandum should correspond to the foreseeable coverage of performers' rights in a possible protocol to the WPPT. A protocol to the WPPT concerning audiovisual performances would only have to deal with aspects other than those already resolved in the WPPT. It seems therefore useful to recall to what extent these rights are already covered in the WPPT. For this purpose, it is appropriate to distinguish between moral rights, economic rights in live performances and economic rights in fixed performances.

(a) Article 5 of the WPPT grants performers moral rights, as regards live aural performances or performances fixed in phonograms.

5. 理事机构做出的决定包括但不限于（AB/XXX/4 号文件第 20 段）：

“（i）1997 年 9 月 15 日和 16 日将召开视听表演议定书专家委员会会议，1997 年 9 月 17 日和 18 日将召开数据库知识产权问题信息会议。1997 年 9 月 19 日将专门留给专家委员会和信息会议通过报告。

“（ii）国际局将分别为这两个专题编写关于现行国家和区域法律法规文件。此外，国际局还将以通知的方式邀请世界知识产权组织成员国政府和欧共体成员国政府以书面形式通报各自国家的实际情况，特别是各国的合同惯例以及统计数据。”

6. 本文件回顾了世界知识产权组织成员国、《卡塔赫纳协定》成员国和欧共体成员国的现行和区域立法，但少数国家除外，在编写本文件时，国际局不掌握这些国家使用世界知识产权组织任何一种工作语言编写的法律或近期修正案。由于现有的国际规范可能，且在许多情况下确实与国家和区域立法有直接或间接的相关性，因此这些规范也需要进行简要回顾。所收到的对上述通知的答复资料载于另一份文件。

二、WPPT 以及本备忘录的范围

7. 在本备忘录中提出的国家和区域法律法规应符合 WPPT 可能的议定书中对表演者权可预见的涵盖范围。WPPT 视听表演议定书只需处理 WPPT 中已经解决的其他方面。因此，不妨回顾一下 WPPT 在多大程度上已经涵盖了这些权利，为此，应区分精神权利、现场表演的经济权利和已录制表演的经济权利。

（a）WPPT 第 5 条授予表演者对其现场有声表演或表演的录音制品享有的精神权利。

(b) Article 6 of the WPPT grants performers exclusive economic rights in their live performances in respect of broadcasting and communication to the public. This right extends to both aural and audiovisual performances. The same Article also grants an exclusive right of authorizing "fixation" of unfixed performances, but Article 2(c) of the WPPT defines "fixations" as only meaning "the embodiment of sounds, or of the representation thereof."

(c) As far as performers' economic rights in their fixed performances are concerned, the WPPT covers performances fixed in phonograms only (see Articles 7 to 10 and Article 15).

8. Consequently, the remaining subjects of a possible protocol to the WPPT concerning audiovisual performances appear to be:

(a) moral rights of performers as regards their live audiovisual performances and the audiovisual fixations of their performances;

(b) economic rights of performers in respect of the act of audiovisual fixation of their unfixed performances; and

(c) economic rights of performers in respect of uses of audiovisual fixations of their performances.

9. Each of these three distinctive areas of protection are covered, in the following presentation of national and regional legislations, by a separate chapter.

10. The legislations of the following countries are not mentioned in the following chapters, as they do not contain any provisions on intellectual property protection of performers:*Algeria**, *Andorra, Angola, Bahamas, Benin, Burkina Faso, Burundi, Central African Republic, Côte d'Ivoire, Cuba, Cyprus, Egypt, Gambia, Georgia, Guatemala, Guyana, Haiti, Liberia, Libya, Luxembourg, Mali, Mauritius, Monaco, Morocco, Nicaragua, Saint Kitts and Nevis, San Marino, Senegal, Sierra Leone, Sudan, Suriname, Tajikistan, Tunisia, Turkmenistan, Uganda, United Republic of Tanzania* and *Zimbabwe*.

Ⅲ MORAL RIGHTS OF PERFORMERS AS REGARDS THEIR LIVE AUDIOVISUAL PERFORMANCES AND AUDIOVISUAL FIXATIONS OF THEIR PERFORMANCES

A. International norms

11. There is no provision at the international level on moral rights of

(b)WPPT 第 6 条授予表演者对广播和向公众传播其现场表演享有的专有经济权利。这项权利包括有声和视听表演。该条还授予表演者授权“录制”尚未录制的表演的专有权,但 WPPT 第 2 条(c)款将“录制”定义为“对声音或声音表现物的体现。”

(c)至于表演者在其已录制表演中的经济权利,WPPT 仅涵盖录音制品中的表演(见第 7 至 10 条和第 15 条)。

8. 因此,WPPT 关于视听表演可能的议定书似乎还包含以下主题:

(a)表演者对现场视听表演和表演的视听录制品享有的精神权利;

(b)表演者对其尚未录制的表演的视听录制品的经济权利;和

(c)表演者使用其表演的视听录制品的经济权利。

9. 下文将基于上述三个不同的保护领域,分章介绍国内和区域立法。

10. 下列国家的立法在以下章节中没有提及,因为它们没有任何关于表演者知识产权保护的规定:阿尔及利亚*、安道尔、安哥拉、巴哈马、贝宁、布基纳法索、布隆迪、中非共和国、科特迪瓦、古巴、塞浦路斯、埃及、冈比亚、格鲁吉亚、危地马拉、圭亚那、海地、利比里亚、利比亚、卢森堡、马里、毛里求斯、摩纳哥、摩洛哥、尼加拉瓜、圣基茨和尼维斯、圣马力诺、塞内加尔、塞拉利昂、苏丹、苏里南、塔吉克斯坦、突尼斯、土库曼斯坦、乌干达、坦桑尼亚联合共和国和津巴布韦。

三、表演者对现场视听表演及其表演的视听录制品的精神权利

A. 国际规范

11. 除 WPPT 第 5 条之外,国际层面上没有关于表演者精神权利的规定。

performers, other than in Article 5 of the WPPT.

B. Regional legislation

12. Decision 351-Common Provisions on Copyright and Neighboring Rights-of the *Cartagena Agreement* (to which *Bolivia, Colombia, Ecuador, Peru* and *Venezuela* are parties), recognizes moral rights to performers in respect of their performances and it does not make a distinction between live aural performances and live audiovisual performances, nor between performances fixed in phonograms and audiovisual fixations of performances.

13. The legislation of the *European Community* does not contain provisions on moral rights of performers.

C. National legislation

14. The national laws of the following countries contain no provisions on moral rights of performers in respect of any kind of performance or fixation of a performance: *Australia, Barbados, Canada, Congo, Democratic Republic of the Congo, Gabon, Ghana, Indonesia, India, Iraq, Ireland, Israel, Jamaica, Japan, Jordan, Kenya, Lesotho, Liechtenstein, Malawi, Malta, Namibia, Niger, Nigeria, New Zealand, Republic of Korea, Rwanda, Thailand, Saint Lucia, Saint Vincent and the Grenadines, South Africa, Switzerland, Togo, Trinidad and Tobago, United Kingdom, United States of America* and *Zambia.*

15. Those national laws which recognize moral rights to performers, in general, do not make a distinction between live aural performances and live audiovisual performances, nor between performances fixed on phonograms and audiovisual fixations of performances. This approach is followed by the national laws of *Armenia, Austria, Belarus, Belgium, Bosnia and Herzegovina, Bulgaria, Cameroon, China, Costa Rica, Croatia, Denmark, Dominican Republic, El Salvador, Estonia, Finland, France, Germany, Greece, Honduras, Iceland, Italy, Kazakhstan, Kyrgyzstan, Latvia, Lithuania, Madagascar, Mexico, Netherlands, Norway, Panama, Paraguay, Philippines, Poland, Portugal, the Republic of Moldova, Romania, the Russian Federation, Slovenia, Spain, Sweden, Turkey, Ukraine, Uruguay, Uzbekistan* and *Yugoslavia.*

16. It is recalled that, within this group of legislations, the content of the protection of moral rights of performers varies to some extent from one legislation

B. 区域立法

12.《卡塔赫纳协定》(成员国包括玻利维亚、哥伦比亚、厄瓜多尔、秘鲁和委内瑞拉)第 351 号决定——关于版权和邻接权的共同规定，承认表演者对其表演的精神权利，该规定不区分现场有声表演和现场视听表演，也不区分表演的录音制品和视听录制品。

13. 欧共体的立法中没有关于表演者精神权利的规定。

C. 国内立法

14. 下列国家的国内立法中没有关于表演者对任何类型的表演或表演的录制品享有精神权利的规定：澳大利亚、巴巴多斯、加拿大、刚果共和国、刚果民主共和国、加蓬、加纳、印度尼西亚、印度、伊拉克、爱尔兰、以色列、牙买加、日本、约旦、肯尼亚、莱索托、列支敦士登、马拉维、马耳他、纳米比亚、尼日尔、尼日利亚、新西兰、韩国、卢旺达、泰国、圣卢西亚、圣文森特和格林纳丁斯、南非、瑞士、多哥、特立尼达和多巴哥、英国、美国和赞比亚。

15. 部分国家的国内立法承认表演者的精神权利，且一般不区分现场有声表演和现场视听表演，也不区分录制在录音制品和视听录制品上的表演。下列国家的国内立法采用了上述模式：亚美尼亚、奥地利、白俄罗斯、比利时、波斯尼亚和黑塞哥维那、保加利亚、喀麦隆、中国、哥斯达黎加、克罗地亚、丹麦、多米尼加共和国、萨尔瓦多、爱沙尼亚、芬兰、法国、德国、希腊、洪都拉斯、冰岛、意大利、哈萨克斯坦、吉尔吉斯斯坦、拉脱维亚、立陶宛、马达加斯加、墨西哥、荷兰、挪威、巴拿马、巴拉圭、菲律宾、波兰、葡萄牙、摩尔多瓦共和国、罗马尼亚、俄罗斯联邦、斯洛文尼亚、西班牙、瑞典、土耳其、乌克兰、乌拉圭、乌兹别克斯坦和南斯拉夫。

16. 值得一提的是，在同样的立法模式下，各国关于表演者精神权利保护的内容在一定程度上存在差异。

to another.

17. In the national laws of certain other countries, the following specifications as to the protection of moral rights in respect of audiovisual performances can be noted:

- In *Argentina*, the principal performer of a "musical and/or literary work" has the right to have his name mentioned when his performance is broadcast or transmitted, and on the phonogram incorporating his performance. This protection does not extend to audiovisual fixations, but it seems to cover the audiovisual dissemination of the live performance of a "musical and/or literary work." On the other hand, the performer of a "musical and/or literary work" has the right to oppose the dissemination of his performance on the basis of a reproduction which would cause serious or unjustified prejudice to his artistic interests. In this respect, audiovisual fixations seem to be included.

- In *Brazil*, the publisher of a phonogram is obliged to indicate the name of the performer whose performance is incorporated in the phonogram, subject to contractual arrangements to the contrary. (This provision does not apply to "non-verbal" performances or to performances for advertising purposes.) In the case of this country, performers do not enjoy, in respect of their performances incorporated in audiovisual fixations, moral (or economic) rights.

- In *Chile*, while performers, in general, do not enjoy moral rights, the producer of a cinematographic work has the obligation to record the names of the principal performers on the film.

- In *Guinea*, the principal performers have the right to have their names mentioned in connection with live performances and any public transmissions thereof as well as on phonograms. This right does not extend to audiovisual fixations, while the right of performers to be protected against any distortion is granted without such restriction.

IV. ECONOMIC RIGHTS OF PERFORMERS IN RESPECT OF THE AUDIOVISUAL FIXATION OF THEIR UNFIXED PERFORMANCES

A. International norms

18. Article 7.1. (b) of the *Rome Convention* (the "International Convention for the Protection of Performers, Producers of Phonograms and Broadcasting

17. 在其他部分国家的国内立法中，关于视听表演精神权利保护的规定如下：

– 在阿根廷，“音乐和 / 或文学作品”的主要表演者有权在广播或传播其表演时，以及在其表演的录音制品上提及其姓名。这种保护未延伸至视听录制品，但似乎包括对“音乐和 / 或文学作品”现场表演的视听传播。另一方面，“音乐和 / 或文学作品”的表演者有权反对通过复制件传播其表演，该等传播将会对表演者的艺术利益造成严重或不当的损害。在这方面，视听录制品似乎涵盖其中。

– 在巴西，录音制品的出版者有义务指明录音制品所含表演的表演者姓名，合同另有约定的除外（该规定不适用于“非语言”表演或广告表演）。就该国而言，表演者对其收录于视听制品中的表演不享有精神（或经济）权利。

– 在智利，虽然表演者一般不享有精神权利，但电影制作者有义务在电影中记录主要表演者的姓名。

– 在几内亚，主要表演者有权要求在现场表演和任何公开转播以及录音制品中提及其姓名。这一权利未延伸至视听录制品。但表演者不受任何歪曲的权利则不受此限制。

四、表演者对其尚未录制表演的视听录制品的经济权利

A. 国际规范

18.《罗马公约》[《保护表演者、录音制品制作者和广播组织国际公约》（1961 年）]第 7 条第 1 款（b）项规定，表演者有可能制止在未经其同意的情况

Organizations" (1961)) provides for performers the possibility of preventing the fixation, without their consent, of their unfixed performances, without making a distinction between aural fixation and audiovisual fixation of live performances.

19. Article 14.1 of the *TRIPS Agreement* ("Agreement on Trade-Related Aspects of Intellectual Property Rights" (1994)) also provides for performers the possibility of preventing the fixation of their unfixed performances but it reduces the scope of this right to fixation on phonograms.

B. Regional legislation

20. Decision 351 of the *Cartagena Agreement* and Council Directive 92/100/EC of the *European Community* on rental right and lending right and on certain rights related to copyright in the field of intellectual property grant performers the right to prevent and/or authorize the fixation of their unfixed performances irrespective of whether the performance is aural or audiovisual and whether the fixation is limited to sounds or is audiovisual.

C. National legislation

21. National laws that protect performers rights at all, in most cases also grant performers the right to prevent and/or authorize the fixation of their unfixed performances irrespective of whether the performance is aural or audiovisual and whether the fixation is limited to sounds or is audiovisual. This applies in addition to the national laws of the Member States of the above-mentioned regional organizations (except the laws of *Luxembourg* and *Portugal*), also to the national laws of *Armenia, Australia, Barbados, Belarus, Bosnia and Herzegovina, Bulgaria, Canada, Cameroon, China, Chile, Congo, Costa Rica, Croatia, Czech Republic, Democratic Republic of the Congo, Dominican Republic, El Salvador, Estonia, Gabon, Guinea, Honduras, Hungary, Iceland, Israel, Jamaica, Japan, Kazakhstan, Kenya, Kyrgyzstan, Latvia, Lesotho, Liechtenstein, Lithuania, Madagascar, Malawi, Malta, Mexico, Namibia, Niger, Nigeria, New Zealand, Panama, Philippines, Poland, Republic of Korea, Republic of Moldova, Romania, Rwanda, Saint Lucia, Saint Vincent and the Grenadines, Slovenia, South Africa, Switzerland, Thailand, The Russian Federation, Trinidad and Tobago, Togo, Turkey, Ukraine, Uzbekistan, Yugoslavia* and *Zambia.*

22. The following national laws do not grant such a broad fixation right:

下，不区分有声录制和视听录制品的现场表演。

19.《TRIPS 协定》[《与贸易有关的知识产权协定》(1994 年)]第 14 条第 1 款规定，表演者有可能制止录制其尚未录制的表演，但该条款将这一权利范围缩小到对录音制品的录制。

B. 区域立法

20.《卡塔赫纳协定》第 351 号决定和欧共体第 92/100/EC 号理事会指令，关于出租权和出借权以及知识产权领域中与版权有关的某些权利，授予表演者制止和 / 或授权录制其尚未录制的表演的权利，无论该表演是有声表演还是视听表演，无论录制品仅限于声音还是视听录制品。

C. 国内立法

21. 保护表演者权利的国内立法，在大多数情况下，也授予表演者制止和 / 或授权录制其未录制的表演的权利，无论该表演是有声表演还是视听表演。这一规定除了适用于上述区域性组织成员国的国内法(卢森堡和葡萄牙的立法除外)之外，还适用于下列国家的国内立法：以及亚美尼亚、澳大利亚、巴巴多斯、白俄罗斯、波斯尼亚和黑塞哥维那、保加利亚、加拿大、喀麦隆、中国、智利、刚果共和国、哥斯达黎加、克罗地亚、捷克共和国、刚果民主共和国、多米尼加共和国、萨尔瓦多、爱沙尼亚、加蓬、几内亚、洪都拉斯、匈牙利、冰岛、以色列、牙买加、日本、哈萨克斯坦、肯尼亚、吉尔吉斯斯坦、拉脱维亚、莱索托、列支敦士登、立陶宛、马达加斯加、马拉维、马耳他、墨西哥、纳米比亚、尼日尔、尼日利亚、新西兰、巴拿马、菲律宾、波兰、韩国、摩尔多瓦共和国、罗马尼亚、卢旺达、圣卢西亚、圣文森特和格林纳丁斯、斯洛文尼亚、南非、瑞士、泰国、俄罗斯联邦、特立尼达和多巴哥、多哥、土耳其、乌克兰、乌兹别克斯坦、南斯拉夫和赞比亚。

22. 下列国家的国内立法未规定如此广泛的录制权：

- In *Argentina*, the fixation of a performance ("interpretation") of a musical work on a carrier requires prior consent of the principal performer(s). As this provision is contained in a regulation entitled "Intellectual property in phonographic reproductions," it seems that it is confined to fixations of sounds.

- In *Brazil*, the fixation right of performers is also limited to the fixation in sound recordings.

- In *Portugal*, the consent of the performer to broadcast his live performance implies authorization of its fixation and of broadcasting and reproduction of the fixed performance, unless otherwise agreed. (The performer retains an unwaivable right to remuneration for such additional uses).

- In the *United States of America*, the right of the performer to authorize a fixation of the sounds or sounds and images of his performance is limited to live musical performances.

V. ECONOMIC RIGHTS OF PERFORMERS IN AUDIOVISUAL FIXATIONS OF THEIR PERFORMANCES

A. International norms

23. As far as reproduction is concerned, under Article 7.1. (c) of the *Rome Convention*, performers have the right "to prevent" the reproduction of a fixation of their performances:

- if the original fixation was made without their consent;

- if the reproduction is made for purposes different from those for which the performers gave their consent;

- if the original fixation was made in accordance with the provisions of Article 15 (on exceptions and limitations), and the reproduction is made for purposes different from those referred to in those provisions.

24. The Convention provides that, if performers have consented to broadcasting, it is a matter for national legislation of the Contracting States to regulate the protection against the reproduction of a fixation made for broadcasting purposes (Article 7.2. (1)). The Convention also leaves it to the legislation of the Contracting States to rule on the use of fixations made for broadcasting purposes (Article 7.2. (2)).

– 在阿根廷，在载体上录制音乐作品的表演（演绎）需要获得主要表演者的事先同意。由于这一规定载于一部名为“录音复制件的知识产权”的规章中，因此似乎仅限于声音的录制品。

– 在巴西，表演者的录制权也仅限于录音的录制。

– 在葡萄牙，表演者同意广播其现场表演，意味着授权对其现场表演进行录制以及对已录制的表演进行广播和复制，除非另有约定。（表演者保留对这种额外使用获得报酬的权利，该权利不可放弃）。

– 在美国，表演者授权录制其表演的声音或声音和图像的权利仅限于现场音乐表演。

五、表演者在其表演的视听录制品中的经济权利

A. 国际规范

23. 就复制而言，根据《罗马公约》第 7 条第 1 款（c）项之规定，表演者有权“制止”对其表演的录制品进行复制的行为。

– 如果最初的录制未经其同意；
– 如果复制的目的超出表演者同意的范围；

– 如果最初的录制是根据第 15 条（关于例外和限制）的规定进行的，且复制的目的不同于该条规定的目的。

24.《公约》规定，如果表演者同意广播，则应由缔约方的国家立法规定保护措施，防止为广播目的对录制品进行复制的行为［第 7.2 条第（1）款］。《公约》还规定，缔约方的立法应就为广播目的使用录制品作出规定［第 7.2 条第（2）款］。

25. The Convention does not provide, in favor of performers, for further rights to authorize or to prevent exploitation of fixed performances, and Article 12 of the Convention providing a single equitable remuneration to performers, to producers, or to both, for certain "secondary" uses, only covers phonograms. The rights of performers are subject to certain limitations under Article 15 of the Convention, in particular as regards private use, use of short excerpts in connection with the reporting of current events and as regards ephemeral fixation by a broadcasting organization for its own broadcast as well as use for the sole purpose of teaching or scientific research. Further limitations are allowed paralleling those which Contracting States provide for with regard to the protection of authors rights.

26. However, the right of performers to prevent the reproduction of audiovisual fixations of their performances is subject to the provision of Article 19 which provides that, "once a performer has consented to the incorporation of his performance in a visual or audiovisual fixation, Article 7 [which includes the above-referred provisions on the rights of performers], shall have no further application." As a result of that so-called "cut-off provision," performers lose all protection in audiovisual fixations which are made with their consent.

27. The *TRIPS Agreement* (Article 14.1) only provides for performers rights in fixations on phonograms.

B. <u>Regional legislation</u>

28. Decision 351 of the *Cartagena Agreement* grants performers the right to authorize the reproduction of fixations of their performances and further provides that the Member States may set limits on this right in the cases allowed by the Rome Convention. (However, several Member States of the Agreement grant a more favorable protection to performers).

29. The relevant directive of the *European Community* is dealt with under the title "National legislation," below. The reason for this is double: first, the national laws of the Member States of the European Community cannot be appropriately described separately, and, second, because, it also seems necessary to indicate the differences existing in some Member States in relation to that directive.

C. <u>National legislation</u>

30. The relevant provisions of national laws are described, below, in a way

25.《公约》没有为表演者规定授权或制止利用已录制表演的进一步权利。《公约》第 12 条规定，就部分“二次”使用行为，应向表演者、制作者或两者支付一笔合理报酬，但仅涉及录音制品。表演者的权利受到《公约》第 15 条某些规定的限制，特别是在个人使用、在时事报道中少量引用、广播组织为自己的广播节目短暂录制以及仅为教学或科学研究目的使用等方面。对于作者权利的保护，缔约国可以作出与其国内法同样的限制。

26. 然而，表演者制止复制其视听表演录制品的权利须遵守第 19 条的规定，该条规定，“一旦表演者同意将其表演纳入录像制品或视听录制品中，第 7 条(包括上述关于表演者权利的规定)将不再适用”。根据这一所谓的“权利丧失条款”，表演者对经其同意录制的视听录制品丧失所有的保护。

27.《TRIPS 协定》(第 14 条第 1 款) 只规定了表演者对录音制品享有的权利。

B. 区域立法

28.《卡塔赫纳协定》第 351 号决定规定，表演者享有对复制其表演的录音制品进行授权的权利，并进一步规定，在《罗马公约》允许的情况下，成员国可对这一权利设定限制(然而，《卡塔赫纳协定》的诸多成员国给予了表演者更有利的保护)。

29. 欧共体的相关指令见下文“国内立法”部分。这种情况存在双重原因：第一，欧共体成员国的国内法不能单独加以适当描述；第二，似乎有必要表明一些成员国在该指令方面存在的差异。

C. 国内立法

30. 以下是国内立法的相关规定，立法方式大致相同的国内立法被归为一

that those laws which follow more or less the same approach are grouped together. Unless it is otherwise specified, the provisions discussed extend to both sound fixations and audiovisual fixations.

Protection limited to fixations of live musical performances

31. In the *United States of America*, performers enjoy the exclusive rights of reproduction, distribution and rental in respect of fixations of the sounds or sounds and images of their live musical performances. For any transfer of these rights, written form with signature of the rights owner is required. This recent legislation contains no definition of the notion of "live musical performance." However, the relevant section is titled: "Unauthorized fixation and trafficking in sound recordings and music videos."

Exclusive rights limited to certain uses of an audiovisual fixation made without the performer's consent.

32. In *Namibia, Niger* and *South Africa*, performers enjoy the exclusive right of reproduction, under the condition that the performance was fixed without their consent.

33. In the *Republic of Korea*, performers enjoy, in the case where their stage performance has been recorded without their consent, the exclusive right to broadcast such recording.

34. In *Trinidad and Tobago*, performers are granted an exclusive right of broadcasting, communication by cable and public performance, if the fixation used for these acts has been made without their consent.

Protection confined to certain remuneration rights

35. In *Argentina*, performers enjoy a right to remuneration for the recording of their performances on any medium capable of being used for sound or visual reproduction. A remuneration is also due for the broadcasting or retransmission of the performance. This provision seems to include the exploitation of audiovisual fixations.

36. In *China*, performers enjoy a right in respect of reproduction as well as commercial distribution of fixations of their performances (sound and video recordings). While it is not clear whether the performer has a right to authorize these acts, he is at least entitled to a right to remuneration to be paid by the producer of

类。除非另有规定，否则所讨论的条款既适用于录音制品，也适用于视听录制品。

保护仅限于现场音乐表演的录制品

31. 在美国，表演者对其现场音乐表演的声音或者声音和图像的录制品享有复制、发行和出租的专有权。对于这些权利的任何转让，都需要权利人以书面形式签字。最近的立法没有对“现场音乐表演”的概念作出定义，但相关章节的标题是：“未经授权录制和买卖录音和音乐录像。”

专有权仅限于未经表演者同意对视听录制品的特定使用。

32. 在纳米比亚、尼日尔和南非，在未经表演者同意对其表演进行录制的情况下，表演者享有复制的专有权。

33. 在韩国，在未经表演者同意录制其舞台表演的情况下，表演者享有广播该等录制品的专有权。

34. 在特里尼达和多巴哥，在未经表演者同意对其表演进行录制的情况下，表演者享有广播、有线传送以及公开表演的专有权。

保护仅限于某些获酬权

35. 在阿根廷，表演者有权因将其表演录制在能够用于声音或视觉复制的任何媒介上而获得报酬。表演者还有权因广播或转播其表演获得报酬。这一规定似乎包括对视听录制品的利用。

36. 在中国，表演者享有复制和商业发行其表演的录制品（录音和录像）的权利。虽然尚未确定表演者是否有权授权这些行为，但其至少有权获得录音或录像制作者支付的报酬。

the sound or video recording.

37. In *Paraguay* and *Uruguay*, performers are granted a remuneration right for broadcasting or reproduction of their performance. The laws provide for a mechanism to establish the amount of the remuneration in case where no agreement is reached.

38. In the following countries, national laws correspond to the minimum level of protection prescribed by the Rome Convention: *Canada, Colombia, Dominican Republic, Guinea, India, Ireland* and *Rwanda*. This includes the application of the "cut-off" provision quoted in paragraph 26, above.

39. Some other national laws also apply the cut-off provision, but they, at the same time, grant rights somewhat more extensively.

40. In *Belarus, Kazakstan, Kyrgyzstan, the Republic of Moldova* and *the Russian Federation*, a broadcasting right and a cable transmission right are granted, where the original fixation was made for non-commercial purposes, as well as a remuneration right for private copying.

41. In *Congo*, besides the reproduction right, as regards fixations made without consent or authorized for other purposes, a broadcasting right is also granted, as regards the same kinds of fixations. Both of these rights are cut off in the case mentioned in Article 19 of the Rome Convention.

42. In *Hungary*, the operation of the cut-off provision does not extend to a remuneration right for private copying (levy on recording material) and to a remuneration right for simultaneous retransmission of a broadcast or an original cable program.

43. In *Japan*, in addition to the reproduction right, a performer has the right to authorize broadcasting and original wire transmission if these acts are based on a fixation made without consent of the performer.

44. In *Latvia*, in addition to a right to broadcast or other communication to the public, a right of fixation made for commercial purposes is granted, but is also subject to the cut-off provision for which, in this case, a signed contract with the film producer is required.

45. In *Mexico*, the reproduction right as such is not confined to the cases mentioned in Article 7.1. (c) of the Rome Convention.

37. 在巴拉圭和乌拉圭，表演者享有因广播或复制其表演而获得报酬的权利。两国法律规定了在未达成协议的情况下确定报酬数额的机制。

38. 下列国家的国内立法符合《罗马公约》规定的最低保护水平：加拿大、哥伦比亚、多米尼加共和国、几内亚、印度、爱尔兰和卢旺达。其中包括适用上文第 26 段引述的“权利丧失条款”。

39. 其他部分国家的国内立法也适用了“权利丧失条款”，但同时又授予了在一定程度上更为广泛的权利。

40. 在白俄罗斯、哈萨克斯坦、吉尔吉斯斯坦、摩尔多瓦共和国和俄罗斯联邦，如果原始录制系出于非商业目的，则立法授予广播权和有线传送权，以及因私人复制而获得报酬的权利。

41. 在刚果共和国，对于对未经同意或超出授权目的进行的录制，除复制权外，立法还规定针对同类复制件享有的广播权。在《罗马公约》第 19 条提到的情况下，这两项权利均会丧失。

42. 在匈牙利，“权利丧失条款”不适用于因私人复制而获得报酬的权利（对录制材料征税），以及对广播节目或原始有线节目进行同步转播而获得报酬的权利。

43. 在日本，除复制权外，表演者有权授权广播和原始有线传送，如果该等行为基于未经表演者同意的录制品。

44. 在拉脱维亚，除了广播或以其他方式向公众传播的权利外，立法还授予为商业目的的录制的权利，但也须遵守“权利丧失条款”，在这种情况下，必须与电影制作者签订合同。

45. 在墨西哥，复制权本身并不局限于《罗马公约》第 7 条第 1 款（c）项规定的情况。

46. In *Barbados* and *Saint Vincent and the Grenadines*, broad exclusive rights of reproduction and of broadcasting are cut-off where the performer consents in writing to the broadcaster to make an audiovisual work of the performance.

Protection of rights similar to those granted by the Rome Convention, but without cut-off provision and partly with somewhat wider rights

47. The national laws of the following countries provide for a reproduction right as under the Rome Convention, but without a cut-off provision: *Democratic Republic of the Congo, Israel, New Zealand, Peru, Philippines* and *Thailand*. In *Australia*, performers are protected in addition against distribution, importation, broadcasting and public performance of recordings made without their consent.

48. In *Ecuador*, in addition to an exclusive reproduction right, rights to remuneration are granted for broadcasting, cable retransmission and reproduction for private use.

49. In *Estonia*, in addition to an exclusive right of reproduction, performers have the exclusive right to use the sounds and images of their performances separately, when they have been originally fixed together and form an integral whole, as well as a right to remuneration for private copying.

50. In *Gabon*, performers, in addition to the reproduction right, enjoy a remuneration right for private copying (blank tape levy).

51. In *Iceland*, the reproduction right is not subject to the conditions mentioned in Article 7.1. (c) of the Rome Convention, and in addition performers enjoy a right to remuneration for private use (blank tape levy).

52. In *Jamaica* and *Saint Lucia*, performers enjoy exclusive rights in respect of any use made without their consent as well as in respect of the adaptation of their fixed performances.

53. In *Kenya*, performers also enjoy the right of broadcasting if made from an unauthorized fixation.

54. In *Malawi*, broadcasters enjoy exclusive broadcasting and cable distribution rights, regarding fixations made under the limitations of the law, as well as equitable remuneration for broadcasting and cable distribution of fixations made by broadcasters.

55. In *Zambia*, performers are granted the reproduction right in respect of

46. 在巴巴多斯和圣文森特和格林纳丁斯，如果表演者书面同意广播者就其表演创作视听作品，则丧失广泛的复制和广播专有权。

保护与《罗马公约》所授权利相似的权利，但未适用“权利丧失条款”，部分权利有所扩大

47. 下列国家的国内立法规定了《罗马公约》所规定的复制权，但未适用“权利丧失条款”：刚果民主共和国、以色列、新西兰、秘鲁、菲律宾和泰国。在澳大利亚，表演者还有权制止发行、进口、广播和公开表演未经其同意制作的录制品。

48. 在厄瓜多尔，除了复制专有权外，立法还授予因广播、有线转送和为私人使用目的复制而获得报酬的权利。

49. 在爱沙尼亚，除了复制专有权外，表演者还享有单独使用其表演的声音和图像的专有权（原始录制时声音和图像被录制在一起并形成一个整体），以及因私人复制获得报酬的权利。

50. 在加蓬，除了复制权外，表演者还享有因私人复制而获得报酬的权利（空白磁带税）。

51. 在冰岛，复制权不受《罗马公约》第 7 条第 1 款（c）项规定的条件限制。此外，表演者还享有因私人使用而获得报酬的权利（空白磁带税）。

52. 在牙买加和圣卢西亚，表演者对未经其同意的任何使用以及对其已录制表演的改编享有专有权。

53. 在肯尼亚，对于未经授权的录制，表演者也享有广播权。

54. 在马拉维，广播者对在法律限制下制作的录制品享有广播和有线方式传送的专有权，并对广播者制作的录制品的广播和有线传送享有公平获酬权。

55. 在赞比亚，表演者对经其同意或未经其同意录制的录制品享有复制权，

recordings made with or without their consent and the rights of distribution, rental and importation in respect of unauthorized recordings.

Wider scale of exclusive rights granted in audiovisual fixations irrespective of whether made with or without the consent of the performer, without a cut-off provision.

56. The following legislations are part of this category: the above-mentioned directive of the European Community, the national laws of the Member States of that Community, except those of Ireland, Luxembourg and Portugal, and the national laws of Armenia, Bolivia, Bosnia and Herzegovina, Bulgaria, Cameroon, Chile, Costa Rica, Croatia, Czech Republic, El Salvador, Ghana, Honduras, Italy, Liechtenstein, Lithuania, Madagascar, Malta, Nigeria, Norway, Panama, Poland, Romania, Slovenia, Switzerland, Turkey, Ukraine, Venezuela, Uzbekistan and Yugoslavia.

57. All of the above-mentioned legislations provide for a reproduction right and a distribution right, except the national laws of the following countries which do not expressly provide for a distribution right: Bolivia, Chile, El Salvador, Nigeria, Panama and Turkey.

58. The following legislations mentioned in paragraph 56 provide for an exclusive rental right: the directive of the European Community, the national laws of the Member States of the Community, except those of Ireland, Luxembourg and Portugal, as well as the national laws of Bolivia, Bulgaria, Costa Rica, Honduras, Liechtenstein, Madagascar, Norway, Poland, Romania, Slovenia, Turkey and Venezuela. (It is understood that a number of national laws provide for a rental right in respect of phonograms only; these are not enumerated here). In Switzerland, the rental right, with regard to both phonograms and videograms, is reduced to a right to remuneration, exercised through mandatory collective administration.

Exclusive rights of communication to the public, broadcasting and distribution by cable of audiovisual fixations.

59. Among the national laws mentioned in paragraph 56, a broad exclusive right of communication to the public is granted in Belgium, Bolivia, Bulgaria, Cameroon, Costa Rica, Czech Republic, Denmark, France, Honduras, Lithuania, Madagascar, Malta, Netherlands, Poland, Romania, Sweden and Uzbekistan. In

对未经授权的录制品享有发行权、出租权和进口权。

无论视听表演录制品的制作是否获得了表演者的同意，该录制品上都存在着一些更广泛的专有权，并且不受限于“权利丧失条款”。

56. 下列立法属于这一类别：欧共体的上述指令、欧共体成员国的国内立法，爱尔兰、卢森堡和葡萄牙除外，以及亚美尼亚、玻利维亚、波斯尼亚和黑塞哥维那、保加利亚、喀麦隆、智利、哥斯达黎加、克罗地亚、捷克共和国、萨尔瓦多、加纳、洪都拉斯、意大利、列支敦士登、立陶宛、马达加斯加、马耳他、尼日利亚、挪威、巴拿马、波兰、罗马尼亚、斯洛文尼亚、瑞士、土耳其、乌克兰、委内瑞拉、乌兹别克斯坦和南斯拉夫的国内立法。

57. 上述所有立法都规定了复制权和发行权，但下列国家的国内法没有明确规定发行权：玻利维亚、智利、萨尔瓦多、尼日利亚、巴拿马和土耳其。

58. 第56段提到的下列立法规定了出租专有权：欧共体指令、欧共体成员国的国内立法，爱尔兰、卢森堡和葡萄牙除外，以及玻利维亚、保加利亚、哥斯达黎加、洪都拉斯、列支敦士登、马达加斯加、挪威、波兰、罗马尼亚、斯洛文尼亚、土耳其和委内瑞拉的国内立法（据了解，一些国家的法律只规定了录音制品的出租权，这些法律在此没有列举）。在瑞士，通过强制性集体管理，录音制品和录像制品的出租权限于获酬权。

向公众传播的专有权、广播权和通过有线方式传送视听录制品的权利。

59. 在第56段提到的国内立法中，比利时、玻利维亚、保加利亚、喀麦隆、哥斯达黎加、捷克共和国、丹麦、法国、洪都拉斯、立陶宛、马达加斯加、马耳他、荷兰、波兰、罗马尼亚、瑞典、乌兹别克斯坦给规定了向公众传播这一广泛的专有权。在瑞典和丹麦，向公众传播的权利是向公众提供表演的权利的

Sweden and Denmark, the right of communication to the public is part of the right of making a performance available to the public.

60. In Germany, the exclusive right in this area is confined to broadcasting of unpublished recordings.

61. In Chile, a right of broadcasting and rebroadcasting is granted.

62. In Nigeria, the exclusive right covers broadcasting, inclusion in cable programs and public performance.

63. In Panama, El Salvador and Venezuela, the right of communication to the public is limited to recordings published for non-commercial purposes.

64. In Bolivia, Costa Rica and Honduras, “any other use” of a performance is also covered by an exclusive right of the performer. In France and Madagascar, the exclusive right also covers any separate use of the sounds or images of the performance, where the performance has been fixed as regards both sounds and images.

65. The right of communication to the public is reduced to a right to remuneration in the following cases:

- In Belgium, in case of broadcasting of the audiovisual fixation as well as in case of its communication in a public place, on condition that the performance is not used in an entertainment and that no entrance fee is charged to the public to enjoy the communication.

- In Costa Rica, in case of broadcasting or other communication to the public of a videogram published for commercial purposes, performers enjoy a right to participate in the producer’s remuneration.

- In the Czech Republic, Turkey and Greece, the remuneration right covers any broadcasting of an audiovisual fixation containing the performance.

- In Spain, any communication to the public of a recording is covered by a remuneration right.

- In Bosnia and Herzegovina, Croatia and Yugoslavia, the remuneration right extends to communication to the public other than broadcasting.

- In Germany, such a right applies to broadcasting of a published recording as well as to any other communication to the public of a recording, whether published or not.

一部分。

60. 在德国，这方面的专有权仅限于广播未出版的录制品。

61. 在智利，立法授予广播权和转播权。

62. 在尼日利亚，专有权包括广播权、有线电视节目权和公开表演权。

63. 在巴拿马、萨尔瓦多和委内瑞拉，向公众传播的权利仅限于为非商业目的出版的录制品。

64. 在玻利维亚、哥斯达黎加和洪都拉斯，表演的“任何其他用途”也为表演者的专有权所涵盖。在法国和马达加斯加，专有权还包括对表演的声音或图像的任何单独使用，前提为表演的声音和图像均已被录制。

65. 在下列情况下，向公众传播的权利仅限于获酬权：

– 在比利时，视听录制品的广播以及在公共场所的传播，前提是该表演不用于娱乐，也不向接受传播的公众收取入场费。

– 在哥斯达黎加，出于商业目的广播或向公众传播录像制品，表演者有权参与制作者的报酬分配。

– 在捷克共和国、土耳其和希腊，获酬权涵盖任何对包含表演的视听录制品进行广播的行为。

– 在西班牙，任何向公众传播录制品的行为都属于获酬权涵盖的范围。

– 在波斯尼亚和黑塞哥维那、克罗地亚和南斯拉夫，获酬权扩大到广播以外的向公众传播行为。

– 在德国，这一权利适用于对已出版的录制品进行广播，以及对已出版或未出版的录制品以其他方式向公众传播的行为。

- In Madagascar, a right to equitable remuneration is granted for use of published videograms in non-dramatic public performances, in broadcasting and simultaneous and unchanged cable retransmission.

- In Poland, the right to remuneration extends to any broadcasting of published recordings other than "fiction films."

- In Switzerland, such a right covers broadcasting, rebroadcasting, public reception and presentation of a videogram.

- In Uzbekistan, the right to remuneration applies to broadcasting of recordings published for commercial purposes.

66. It is to be noted that, in a number of national laws of the category mentioned in paragraph 56, as well as under the relevant directive of the European Community, a remuneration right for communication to the public or for broadcasting of a fixed performance is also granted, but limited either to any fixations of sounds or to phonograms published for commercial purposes.

Presumptions of transfer of rights from the performer to the producer of the audiovisual fixation, accompanied or not by provisions securing the remuneration of the performer in case of transfer.

67. Under the directive of the European Community, when a contract concerning a film production is concluded, the transfer of the rental right to the producer is presumed, subject to contractual clauses to the contrary (rebuttable presumption of transfer). In case of transfer, the performer retains an unwaivable right to equitable remuneration for a rental.

68. As an alternative, the directive permits Member States to provide that the signing of a film production contract by the performer has a mandatory effect of authorizing the rental, subject to the condition that the contract also provides for an equitable remuneration of the performer in case of rental of copies.

69. While the choice between these alternatives is free, Member States are not allowed to apply a cut-off provision as under Article 19 of the Rome Convention.

70. Most Member States of the European Community have chosen the first alternative. One group among those Member States (Austria, Denmark, Finland, Spain and the United Kingdom) has implemented the rebuttable presumption of transfer of the rental right only, without extension to any other rights. Liechtenstein

– 在马达加斯加，对于在非戏剧性的公开表演、广播以及同步且不变的有线转播中使用已出版的录像的行为，可享有公平获酬权。

– 在波兰，获酬权延伸到对除“虚构电影”以外的任何已出版录制品的广播。

– 在瑞士，这一权利涵盖对录像的广播、重播、公众接收和展示。

– 在乌兹别克斯坦，获酬权适用于对出于商业目的出版的录制品的广播。

66. 应当指出的是，在第 56 段所述的某些国内立法中，以及根据欧共体的相关指令，还规定了向公众传播或广播已录制表演的获酬权，但仅限于任何出于商业目的出版的有声录制品或录音制品。

推定将权利从表演者转让给视听录制品的制作者，同时附带或不附带保证表演者在转让时享有获酬权的规定。

67. 根据欧共体指令，在订立有关电影制作的合同时，推定将出租权转让给制作者，但须遵守相反的合同条款（可推翻的转让推定）。在转让的情况下，表演者保留对出租公平获酬的不可放弃的权利。

68. 作为一种替代方案，该指令允许成员国规定，表演者签署电影制作合同时具有授权进行出租的强制性效果，但条件是合同还规定，在出租复制件时，表演者享有公平获酬权。

69. 成员国可以在这些备选方案中自由选择，但不得适用《罗马公约》第 19 条规定的“权利丧失条款”。

70. 欧共体的大多数成员国选择了第一个备选方案。其中一组成员国（奥地利、丹麦、芬兰、西班牙和英国）只执行了可与驳回的出租权转让推定，而不延伸到任何其他权利。根据《欧洲经济区协定》与欧共体相关的列支敦士登和挪威适用同一制度。

and Norway, linked to the European Community by the European Economic Area Agreement, apply to the same system.

71. The second group of European Community Member States, namely, Belgium, Germany, Greece and Italy, but also-outside the European Community-Bulgaria, Poland, Slovenia and Ukraine, provide for a rebuttable presumption of transfer of all exclusive rights of the performer, as regards the exploitation of performances included in cinematographic works.

72. In Sweden, a transfer of the right to record the performance on a film includes the right to make the recorded performance available to the public, through the film, in cinemas, on television or otherwise.

73. In the Netherlands, an employer is entitled to exploit the rights of a performer (in respect of all kinds of performances and recordings) where this has been agreed between the parties or derives from the nature of the employment agreement concluded between them.

74. No provision on any kind of presumption of transfer can be found in the legislations of Armenia, Bosnia and Herzegovina, Croatia, Ghana, Malta, Madagascar, Switzerland, Turkey and Uzbekistan.

75. Among the national laws mentioned so far, the following provide for a right to equitable remuneration in the case of transfer of the rental right to the producer:

- The law of Austria provides for an equitable share of the performer in the remuneration which the film producer obtains for authorizing the rental of copies.

- In Belgium, in case of audiovisual productions other than in a non-cultural field or for advertising, performers are entitled to separate remuneration for each exploitation mode.

- In Germany and Spain, performers retain, after transfer of the rental right, an unwaivable right to equitable remuneration for the rental of copies, which is exercised by mandatory collective administration; the remuneration has to be paid by the rental outlets.

- According to the law of Greece, performers retain, even after transfer of rights, a right to remuneration for each exploitation act, in particular an unwaivable right to equitable remuneration for rental.

- In Italy, after transfer of the rental right, performers retain the right to a fair

71. 第二组欧共体成员国，即比利时、德国、希腊和意大利，以及欧共体以外的保加利亚、波兰、斯洛文尼亚和乌克兰，针对电影作品中包含的演出的利用，规定了可予推翻的全部专有权转让推定。

72. 在瑞典，电影录制权的转让包括通过电影、电影院、电视或其他方式向公众提供录制表演的权利。

73. 在荷兰，根据双方约定或双方签署的雇用协议的性质，雇主有权利用表演者（针对所有类别的表演和录制品）的权利。

74. 亚美尼亚、波斯尼亚和黑塞哥维那、克罗地亚、加纳、马耳他、马达加斯加、瑞士、土耳其和乌兹别克斯坦的立法中没有关于转移推定的规定。

75. 在迄今提到的国内立法中，下列国家的法律规定了将出租权转让给制作者时享有的公平获酬权：

– 奥地利法律规定，在电影制作者为授权出租复制件而获得的报酬中，表演者有权获得合理的份额。

– 在比利时，在非文化领域或广告用途以外的视听制品中，表演者有权就每种利用方式获得单独的报酬。

– 在德国和西班牙，表演者在转让出租权后，保留了一项不可放弃的权利，即通过强制性集体管理，获得出租复制件的合理报酬；报酬必须由出租网点支付。

– 根据希腊法律，即使在权利转让之后，表演者仍保留就每种利用方式获得报酬的权利，特别是就出租获得合理报酬的不可放弃的权利。

– 在意大利，在出租权转让后，表演者保留对制作者订立的出租合同获得

remuneration for rental contracts concluded by the producer.

- In the Netherlands, where an employer, according to the rule quoted above, is entitled to exploit the right of the performer, he shall owe to the performer equitable remuneration for each form of exploitation.

- In the United Kingdom, the performer who has transferred his rental right to the producer retains the right to equitable remuneration for the rental. This right may not be assigned by the performer except to a collecting society for the purpose of enabling it to enforce the right on his behalf. The equitable remuneration is payable by the producer or any successor in title.

76. Two further national laws provide remuneration rights for performers: The Copyright Act of Malta provides that performers have the right to obtain an equitable remuneration for the rental of a cinematographic film; this apparently applies in the case of the contractual transfer of the rental right of the performer to the producer. According to the Copyright Act of Turkey, performers may transfer their rights to the producer "against equitable remuneration."

77. The second alternative provided for in the directive of the European Community is chosen by the law of France, which, firstly, provides that the signing of a contract between a performer and a producer for the making of an audiovisual work implies the transfer of the exclusive rights to the producer, and, secondly, prescribes that such contract shall lay down separate remuneration for each mode of exploitation of the work, failing which the amount of remuneration shall be determined in accordance with collective agreements existing in the relevant sector. Furthermore, the responsible minister is empowered to make existing collective agreements compulsory for all parties concerned. This model seems to have been followed by Cameroon, while the law of Madagascar, containing no rule on whether and in which way a transfer of rights is produced, provides that contracts must be written and signed by both parties and must specify a distinct remuneration for each mode of exploitation and that, otherwise, the remuneration will be fixed according to the fees laid down in the respective comparable collective agreements.

Remuneration for private copying

78. Among the national laws mentioned in paragraph 56, the following provide, in favor of performers, for a right to remuneration for private copying through a

合理报酬的权利。

– 在荷兰，如果雇主根据上述规则有权行使表演者的权利，雇主应为每种形式的利用向表演者支付合理的报酬。

– 在英国，当表演者将其出租权转让给制作者时，其仍保留基于出租的获得合理报酬的权利。除将该项权利转让给集体收费协会，由协会代表其行使权利外，表演者不得将该项权利转让给其他对象。该合理报酬由制作者或其继承者支付。

76. 另外两项国内立法规定了表演者的获酬权：《马耳他版权法》规定，表演者有权获得出租电影的合理报酬；这显然适用于以合同方式将表演者的出租权转让给制作者的情况。根据《土耳其版权法》的规定，表演者可以“在获得合理报酬的情况下”将其权利转让给制作者。

77. 法国选择了欧共体指令中规定的第二个备选方案，法国法律规定，首先，表演者和制作者之间签订制作视听作品的合同意味着将专有权利转让给制作者；其次，这种合同应为每种利用作品的方式规定单独的报酬，否则，报酬数额应根据有关部门现有的集体协议确定。此外，负责该事务的部长有权使现有的集体协议成为所有有关各方必须遵守的强制性协议。喀麦隆似乎遵循了这一模式，而马达加斯加的法律没有关于权利转让是否以及以何种方式产生的规则，规定合同必须由双方制定和签署，并且必须为每种利用方式规定不同的报酬，否则，报酬将根据相应的集体协议规定的费用确定。

私人复制的报酬

78. 在第 56 段提到的国内立法中，以下法律规定了表演者通过征税制度获得私人复制报酬的权利，在所有情况下至少对空白录制载体（空白磁带或卡带）

levy system whereby, in all cases, at least blank recording carriers (blank tapes or cassettes) are charged and, in some cases also the recording equipment: Austria, Belgium, Bulgaria, Cameroon, Czech Republic, Denmark, France, Germany, Italy, Netherlands, Nigeria, Poland, Romania, Slovenia, Spain, Switzerland, Ukraine and Uzbekistan. (As indicated in paragraphs 40, 42 and 48 to 51, in the laws of Hungary, Ecuador, Estonia, Gabon and Iceland, there is also such a right to remuneration).

[End of document]

收费，在某些情况下还包括录制设备：奥地利、比利时、保加利亚、喀麦隆、捷克共和国、丹麦、法国、德国、意大利、荷兰、尼日利亚、波兰、罗马尼亚、斯洛文尼亚、西班牙、瑞士、乌克兰和乌兹别克斯坦。（如第 40、42、48 ~ 51 段所述，匈牙利、厄瓜多尔、爱沙尼亚、加蓬和冰岛的法律也有关于获酬权的规定）。

（文件结束）

1.2 Information Received from Member States of WIPO Concerning Audiovisual Performances

Document Code: AP/CE/1/3
Language: English
URL: https://www.wipo.int/edocs/mdocs/copyright/en/ap_ce_i/ap_ce_i_3.pdf

Chinese Translation: Not Available.
URL: N/A

COMMITTEE OF EXPERTS
ON A PROTOCOL
CONCERNING AUDIOVISUAL PERFORMANCES
Geneva, September 15, 16 and 19, 1997

INFORMATION RECEIVED FROM MEMBER STATES OF WIPO CONCERNING AUDIOVISUAL PERFORMANCES

Memorandum prepared by the International Bureau

I. INTRODUCTION

1. The WIPO Diplomatic Conference on Certain Copyright and Neighboring Rights Questions which took place in Geneva from December 2 to 20, 1996, on its last day, adopted the WIPO Performances and Phonograms Treaty (WPPT).

2. Among the documents of the Conference had been a "Basic Proposal for the Substantive Provisions of a Treaty for the Protection of the Rights of Performers

1.2 世界知识产权组织成员国提交的关于视听表演的信息

文件编号：AP/CE/1/3
文件语言：英语
文件链接：https://www.wipo.int/edocs/mdocs/copyright/en/ap_ce_i/ap_ce_i_3.pdf
中文文本：无
文件链接：无

视听表演议定书

专家委员会

1997 年 9 月 15 日、16 日和 19 日，日内瓦

世界知识产权组织
成员国提交的关于视听表演的信息

由国际局编制的备忘录

一、介绍

1. 世界知识产权组织关于版权和邻接权若干问题的外交会议于 1996 年 12 月 2 日至 20 日在日内瓦举行，会议最后一天通过了《世界知识产权组织表演和录音制品条约》（WPPT）。

2. 会议的文件包括《保护表演者和录音制品制作者权利条约实质性条款的基本建议》（CRNR/DC/5 号文件）以及各代表团在会议期间提出的若干有关修

and Producers of Phonograms to be considered by the Diplomatic Conference" (document CRNR/DC/5) as well as a number of relating amendment proposals submitted by Delegations in the course of the Conference. Under some of those documents, or under some of the alternatives included in them, the coverage of the rights of performers would have extended to audiovisual performances; the WPPT, however, with the exception of some rights related to unfixed performances, does not cover audiovisual performances.

3. The Conference addressed this issue in a Resolution concerning Audiovisual Performances (document CRNR/DC/99), adopted on its last day with the following text:

"The Delegations participating in the Diplomatic Conference on Certain Copyright and Neighboring Rights Questions in Geneva,

"Noting that the development of technologies will allow for a rapid growth of audiovisual services and that this will increase the opportunities for performing artists to exploit their audiovisual performances that will be transmitted by these services;

"Recognizing the great importance of ensuring an adequate level of protection for these performances, in particular when they are exploited in the new digital environment, and that sound and audiovisual performances are increasingly related;

"Stressing the urgent need to agree on new norms for the adequate legal international protection of audiovisual performances;

"Regretting that, in spite of the efforts of most Delegations, the WIPO Performances and Phonograms Treaty does not cover the rights of performers in the audiovisual fixations of their performance;

"Call for the convocation of an extraordinary session of the competent WIPO Governing Bodies during the first quarter of 1997 to decide on the schedule of the preparatory work on a protocol to the WIPO Performances and Phonograms Treaty, concerning audiovisual performances, with a view to the adoption of such a protocol not later than in 1998."

4. The Resolution (along with the Recommendation concerning Databases also adopted in the Diplomatic Conference) was discussed at the thirtieth series of meetings of the Governing Bodies of WIPO, namely the General Assembly of

正案。根据其中一些文件或文件中所列的一些备选办法，表演者权的涵盖范围将扩大到视听表演；然而，除与尚未录制的表演有关的一些权利外，WPPT 不涵盖视听表演。

3. 会议在最后一天通过的《关于视听表演的决议》（CRNR/DC/99 号文件）中讨论了这一问题，文案如下：

“参加在日内瓦举行的版权和邻接权若干问题外交会议的代表团，

“鉴于技术的发展将促使视听服务迅速增长，这将增加表演艺术家对借助这些服务传播的视听表演加以利用的机会；

“认识到为这些表演提供适当保护的重要性，特别是当人们在新的数字环境中利用这些表演，并且有声表演和视听表演的关系日益密切的时候；

“强调迫切需要就新的规范达成共识，以对视听表演进行适当的国际法律保护；

“遗憾的是，尽管大多数代表团作出了努力，但 WPPT 并未涵盖表演者对其表演的视听录制品享有的权利；

“呼吁世界知识产权组织主管理事机构在 1997 年第一季度召开一次特别会议，就 WPPT 关于视听表演议定书的筹备工作安排表作出决定，以期不迟于 1998 年通过这一议定书。”

4. 1997 年 3 月 20 日和 21 日在日内瓦举行的世界知识产权组织理事机构第三十系列会议，即世界知识产权组织大会、世界知识产权组织协调委员会和伯尔尼联盟大会，讨论了该决议（以及外交会议通过的一项关于数据库的

WIPO, the WIPO Coordination Committee and the Assembly of the Berne Union, in Geneva, on March 20 and 21, 1997.

(a) fixation;

(b) broadcasting and communication to the public.

5. The Governing Bodies took, *inter alia*, the following decisions (document AB/XXX/4, paragraph 20):

"(i) A Committee of Experts on the protocol concerning audiovisual performances will be convened for September 15 and 16, 1997, and an Information Meeting concerning intellectual property in databases will be convened for September 17 and 18, 1997. September 19, 1997, will be reserved for the adoption of the reports of both the Committee of Experts and the Information Meeting.

"(ii) The International Bureau will, separately for each of the two subjects, prepare a document on the existing national and regional laws and regulations. Furthermore, the International Bureau will invite the Governments of the Member States of WIPO and the European Community by circular to communicate to it in writing information on the de facto situation, particularly contractual practices, existing in their respective countries, as well as any statistics."

6. In harmony with the second part of item (ii) of the above-quoted decisions, the Director General, in a circular dated April 1, 1997, invited the Governments of the Member States of WIPO and the European Community, to communicate to the International Bureau the information mentioned in the said item, by May 31, 1997.

7. By the above-mentioned deadline, the International Bureau had received information from the Governments of the following countries: China, Israel, Kyrgyzstan, Mexico, Norway, Republic of Moldova, Switzerland and Uruguay. That information-as regards audiovisual performances-is summarized in the following paragraphs, whereas the full text of the relevant parts of the countries' contributions is included in the Annex to this document. Information received after the above-mentioned deadline will be made available later.

II. GENERAL INFORMATION ON THE *DE FACTO* SITUATION

8. Each of the responses received from the Governments mentioned in the preceding paragraph refers to the existing national legislation of the country concerned. The responses received from China and Mexico contain the text of the

建议)。

(a)录制;

(b)广播和向公众传播。

5. 理事机构做出的决定包括但不限于(文件 AB/XXX/4,第 20 段):

“(i)1997 年 9 月 15 日和 16 日将召开视听表演议定书专家委员会会议,1997 年 9 月 17 日和 18 日将召开数据库知识产权问题信息会议。1997 年 9 月 19 日将专门留给专家委员会和信息会议通过报告。

“(ii)国际局将分别为这两个专题编写关于现行国家和区域法律法规文件。此外,国际局还将以通知方式邀请世界知识产权组织成员国政府和欧共体成员国政府以书面形式通报各自国家的实际情况,特别是各国的合同惯例以及任何统计数据。”

6. 与上述决定第(ii)项第二部分一致,总干事在 1997 年 4 月 1 日的通知中请世界知识产权组织和欧洲共同体成员国政府在 1997 年 5 月 31 日之前向国际局通报上述决定第(ii)项第二部分提到的内容。

7. 在上述截止日期之前,国际局收到了下列国家政府的资料:中国、以色列、吉尔吉斯斯坦、墨西哥、挪威、摩尔多瓦共和国、瑞士和乌拉圭。资料中与视听表演有关的内容在以下段落中作了概述,而各国提交资料相关部分的全文则列入本文件附件。在上述截止日期之后收到的资料将在稍后提供。

二、关于现实情况的基本资料

8. 上段提到的各国政府的答复中,每一份答复都提到本国的现行国家立法。从中国和墨西哥收到的答复载有国家法律相关条款的案文(这些答复不包含任何进一步的信息),而从以色列、吉尔吉斯斯坦、挪威、摩尔多瓦共和国、瑞

relevant provisions of the national laws (and those responses do not contain any further information), while the responses received from Israel, Kyrgyzstan, Norway, Republic of Moldova, Switzerland and Uruguay sum up the relevant norms. That information is reproduced in the Annex and is also reflected in document AP/CE/I/2 on "Existing National and Regional Legislation concerning Audiovisual Performances."

III. CONTRACTUAL PRACTICES

9. According to item (ii) of the decisions quoted in paragraph 5, above, the information requested on the *de facto* situation was to cover particularly contractual practices. Five of the eight above-mentioned responses contain information on such practices.

10. The response received from Israel refers to the general freedom of the parties concerned to conclude contracts in harmony with the provisions of the law.

11. The information received from Kyrgyzstan, in this respect, states that no applications for registration of contracts of performers of audiovisual works have been filed.

12. The response received from Norway states that no information is available on contractual practices between performers and e. g., producers of films, and it adds that, according to the legal tradition of the country, there is no statutory regulation concerning the transfer of rights from employees to employers in that field.

13. The response received from the Republic of Moldova, in addition to a description of the statutory provisions concerning minimum remuneration to be paid to performers, outlines the collective management system for performers' rights, and deals particularly with the problems relating to the distribution of remuneration.

14. The information received from *Uruguay* refers to some general aspects of the contractual practice and the related jurisprudence, particularly as far as television programs (both broadcast and cable distributed) are concerned. It also mentions that the payments due to performers for their audiovisual performances are collected by a collective management society. In international relations, that society applies the so-called type-B contracts, under which the societies do not transfer payments to each other; the payments received for the members of the other (foreign) societies

士和乌拉圭收到的答复总结了相关规范。该资料转载于附件，并反映在有关“当前各国或地区立法中关于视听表演的规定”的 AP/CE/I/2 号文件中。

三、合同惯例

9. 根据上文第 5 段所引述的决定第（ii）项，要求提供的关于现实情况的资料将特别包括合同惯例。上述八份答复中有五份包含了关于此类惯例的资料。

10. 从以色列收到的答复提到有关各方享有订立符合法律规定的合同的一般自由。

11. 从吉尔吉斯斯坦收到的这方面的资料表明，没有人提出过视听作品表演者合同的登记申请。

12. 挪威的答复指出，没有关于表演者与他人（例如电影制作者）之间的合同惯例的资料；其补充说，根据该国的法律传统，该领域内没有关于将权利从雇员转移给雇主的法规。

13. 摩尔多瓦共和国的答复除了对表演者最低报酬的法律规定的说明外，还概述了表演者权的集体管理制度，并特别涉及与报酬分配有关的问题。

14. 从乌拉圭收到的资料涉及合同惯例的一些概况和相关判例，特别是与电视节目（包括广播和有线广播）有关的内容。它还提到，应支付给表演者的视听表演款项是由集体管理协会收取的。在国际关系中，协会适用所谓的 B 型合同，根据这种合同，协会之间不相互转移款项；为其他（外国）协会成员收取的款项也由收款国境内收取了该款项的协会使用（进行分配或用于集体目的）。

are also used (distributed or utilized for collective purposes) by the society having collected the payments within the country of collection.

IV. STATISTICS

15. In harmony with the relevant part of item (ii) of the decisions quoted in paragraph 5, above, information was requested also on statistics concerning audiovisual fixations; however, none of the responses covered by this document contains any statistics.

[Annex follows]

四、统计数字

15. 与上文第 5 段所引述的决定第(ii)项的有关部分相一致，还要求提供关于视听录制品的统计信息；然而，本文件所涵盖的答复均无任何统计数字。

（后接附件）

ANNEX
RESPONSES RECEIVED FROM MEMBER STATES OF WIPO
(see paragraph 7 of the document)

CHINA

I. Definitions of performance, performer and producer of video recordings

Article 5(2) of the Implementing Regulations of the Copyright Law of the People's Republic of China (hereinafter referred to as "the Implementing Regulations"): performance is the public presentation of a work by performing music or drama, reciting a poem, or doing similar acts, through vocal sound, facial movements and body movements, directly or with the aid of technical devices.

Article 6 of Implementing Regulations:

(6) producer of video recordings refers to a person who makes video recordings;

(7) performer refers to an actor or any other person who performs literary and artistic works.

Ⅱ. Provisions concerning the protection of performers and producers of sound recordings and video recordings

The Copyright Law of the People's Republic of China (hereinafter referred to as the "Copyright Law")

Article 28. Publishers, performers, producers of sound recordings and video recordings, radio stations, television stations and other entities who or which have obtained, pursuant to this Law, the right to exploit the copyright of others, shall not infringe the author's rights of authorship, alteration or integrity, or their right to remuneration.

Article 36. A performer shall, in relation to his performance, enjoy the right

(1) to claim performership;

(2) to protect the image inherent in his performance from distortion;

(3) to authorize others to make live broadcasts;

(4) to authorize others to make sound recordings and video recordings for commercial purposes, and to receive remuneration therefor.

Article 38. When producing a sound recording or video recording the producer

附件
从世界知识产权组织成员国收到的答复
（见文件第7段）

中国

一、表演、表演者和录像制作者的定义

《中华人民共和国著作权法实施条例》（以下简称《实施条例》）第五条第二项：表演，指演奏乐曲、上演剧本、朗诵诗词等直接或者借助技术设备以声音、表情、动作公开再现作品。

实施条例第六条：

（六）录像制作者，指制作录像制品的人；

（七）表演者，指演员或者其他表演文学、艺术作品的人。

二、关于保护表演者和录音录像制作者的规定

《中华人民共和国著作权法》（以下简称《著作权法》）

第28条　出版者、表演者、录音录像制作者、广播电台、电视台等依照本法取得他人的著作权使用权的，不得侵犯作者的署名权、修改权、保护作品完整权和获酬权。

第36条　表演者对其表演享有下列权利：

（一）表明表演者身份；

（二）保护表演形象不受歪曲；

（三）许可他人从现场直播；

（四）许可他人为营利目的的录音录像，并获得报酬。

第38条　录音录像制作者制作录音录像制品，应当同表演者订立合同，

shall conclude a contract with, and pay remuneration to, the performers.

Article 39. A producer of sound recordings or video recordings shall have the right to authorize others to reproduce and distribute such sound recordings or video recordings and the right to obtain remuneration therefor. The term of protection of such rights shall be fifty years, expiring on December 31 of the fiftieth year after the first publication of the recording.

A producer of sound recordings and video recordings who is authorized to reproduce and distribute a sound recording or video recording shall also pay remuneration to the copyright owner and to the performer as prescribed by regulations.

Article 42. A radio station or television station shall, in respect of a program produced by it, enjoy the right…

(3) to authorize others to reproduce and distribute the radio or television program, and to receive remuneration therefor.

The term of protection of the rights specified in the preceding paragraph shall be fifty years, expiring on December 31 of the fiftieth year after the first broadcasting of the program.

A producer of sound recordings or video recordings who is authorized to reproduce and distribute a radio or television program shall also pay remuneration to the copyright owner and to the performer as prescribed by regulations.

Article 45. Anyone who commits any of the following acts of infringement shall bear civil liability for such remedies as ceasing the infringing act, eliminating the effects of the act, making a public apology or paying compensation for damages, depending on the circumstances:

(7) broadcasting a live performance without the consent of the performer.

Article 46. Anyone who commits any of the following acts o infringement shall bear civil liability for such remedies as ceasing the infringing act, eliminating the effects of the act, making a public apology or paying compensation for damages, depending on the circumstances, and may, in addition, be subjected by a copyright administration department to such administrative penalties as confiscation of unlawful income from the act or imposition of a fine:

(4) reproducing and publishing a sound recording or video recording of a

并支付报酬。

第 39 条　录音录像制作者对其制作的录音录像制品，享有许可他人复制发行并获得报酬的权利。该权利的保护期为五十年，截止于该制品首次出版后第五十年的 12 月 31 日。

被许可复制发行的录音录像制作者还应当按照规定向著作权人和表演者支付报酬。

第 42 条　广播电台、电视台对其制作的广播、电视节目，享有下列权利……

（三）许可他人复制发行其制作的广播、电视节目，并获得报酬。

前款规定的权利的保护期为五十年，截止于该节目首次播放后第五十年的 12 月 31 日。

被许可复制发行的录音录像制作者还应当按照规定向著作权人和表演者支付报酬。

第 45 条　有下列侵权行为的，应当根据情况，承担停止侵害、消除影响、公开赔礼道歉、赔偿损失等民事责任：

（七）未经表演者许可，广播其现场表演。

第 46 条　有下列侵权行为的，应当根据情况，承担停止侵害、消除影响、公开赔礼道歉、赔偿损失等民事责任，并可以由著作权行政管理部门给予没收非法所得、罚款等行政处罚：

（四）未经表演者许可，对其表演制作录音录像并出版的。

performance without the consent of the performer.

(Moreover, limitations on rights provided under Article 22 of the Copyright Law shall apply to performers and producers of sound recordings and video recordings.)

Implementing Regulations

Article 44. No time limit shall be set on the term of protection in relation to the rights provided for in Article 36(1) and (2) of the Law.

In the case of the term of protection in relation to the right to remuneration which the performer enjoy by virtue of the second paragraph of Article 39 and the third paragraph of Article 42 of the Law, the first paragraph of Article 39 and the second paragraph of Article 42 of the Law shall apply.

Article 46. Performance by foreign performers taking place in the territory of China shall be protected by the Law.

ISRAEL

1. Contractual practices concerning… the protection of performers in the field of audiovisual performances

In general parties are free to contract as they see fit taking due note, where relevant, of the provisions set out in the Performers' and Broadcasters' Rights Law, the Copyright Law and Ordinance and the Contracts Law.

2. Statistics

To the best of [our] knowledge no statistics are maintained by any governmental institution.

KYRGYZSTAN

Information with respect to the protection of performers in the field of audiovisual performances: On February 20, 1997, the Government of the Kyrgyz Republic approved "The Provisional Regulations on Copyright and Neighboring Rights." Performers of audiovisual works enjoy their rights in accordance with the Part VIII of the Regulations and on the basis of contracts regulate legal relations with authors and producers of audiovisual works.

Unfortunately, no applications for registration of such contracts have been filed so far with Kyrgyzpatent.

（此外,《著作权法》第 22 条规定的权利的限制适用于录音和录像的表演者和制作者。）

《实施条例》

第 44 条　著作权法第 36 条第（1）、（2）项权利的保护期不受时间限制。

著作权法第 39 条第 2 款和第 42 条第 3 款规定的表演者获酬权利的保护期,分别适用第 39 条第 1 款和第 42 条第 2 款的规定。

第 46 条　外国表演者在中国境内的表演,受著权法保护。

以色列

1. 关于保护视听表演领域表演者的合同惯例

一般来说,当事人可以自由地订立合同,并视情况适当考虑表演者和广播组织权利法、版权法和条例以及合同法中的规定。

2. 统计数字

据我们所知,任何政府机构都未保存统计数据。

吉尔吉斯斯坦

关于保护视听表演领域表演者的信息：1997 年 2 月 20 日,吉尔吉斯共和国政府批准了《版权和邻接权暂行条例》,视听作品表演者依照《条例》第八部分的规定,以及在规范视听作品作者与制作者法律关系的合同的基础上享有权利。

遗憾的是,迄今为止,尚无此类合同向该国的国家知识产权和创新服务机构 Kyrgyzpatent 提出登记申请。

MEXICO

[The text of the relevant provisions of the Federal Law on Copyright (published on December 24, 1996), included in the response:]

TITLE III

Transfer of Economic Rights

CHAPTER I

General Provisions

Article 30. The owner of the economic rights may freely, subject to the provisions of this Law, transfer his economic rights or grant exclusive or non-exclusive licenses for use.

Any transfer of economic rights shall be for consideration and temporary. In the absence of agreement on the amount of remuneration or the procedure for setting it, or on the time limits for the payment thereof, the competent courts shall decide.

Acts, agreements and contracts by which economic rights are transferred and licenses granted shall invariably be concluded in writing, failing which they shall be null and void as of right.

Article 31. Any transfer of economic rights shall provide for the grant to the author or to the owner of the economic rights, as the case may be, a proportional share in the proceeds from the exploitation concerned, or a predetermined, fixed amount of remuneration. That right shall be unrenounceable.

Article 32. The acts, agreements and contracts by which economic rights are transferred shall be entered in the Public Copyright Register in order to be binding on third parties.

Article 33. In the absence of any express provision, any transfer of economic rights shall be deemed to be for a term of five years. A term of more than 15 years may only be agreed upon in exceptional cases where dictated by the nature of the work or the scale of the required investment.

Article 34. Future production may only be the subject of a contract in the case of a specific work the characteristics of which have to be laid down in the said contract. The global transfer of future works shall be null and void, as shall any provisions whereby the author undertakes not to create any works.

墨西哥

[《联邦版权法》(1996年12月24日公布)有关条款,列入答复:]

第三部分
经济权利的转让
第一章
一般规定

第30条　经济权利的所有人可以在符合本法规定的情况下,自由转让其经济权利或授予专有或非专有的使用许可。

任何经济权利的转让需有对价且是暂时的。在没有就酬劳数额或确定酬劳的程序,以及支付酬劳的期限达成协议的情况下,管辖法院应作出裁决。

转让经济权利和授予许可的行为、协议和合同必须以书面形式确立,否则,其权利无效。

第31条　任何经济权利的转让都应规定作者或者经济权利的所有人(视情况而定)有权按比例分配基于相关利用产生的收益,或获得预先确定的固定报酬。这项权利是不可放弃的。

第32条　转让经济权利的行为、协议和合同应当在《公共版权登记册》中登记,以便对第三方具有约束力。

第33条　在没有任何明确规定的情况下,任何经济权利的转让应被视为为期五年。只有在工作性质或所需投资规模决定的特殊情况下,才可商定15年以上的期限。

第34条　未完成的成果只能是特定作品合同的标的,且作品特点必须在该合同中予以明确。未完成作品的全球转让无效,作者承诺不创作任何作品的任何规定也无效。

Article 35. Any license affording exclusive rights shall be expressly granted as such and shall give the licensee, where not otherwise agreed, the right to exploit the work to the exclusion of any other person, and also the right to grant non-exclusive authorizations to third parties.

Article 36. The license affording exclusive rights shall oblige the licensee to take whatever action is necessary for the licensed exploitation to be effective, depending on the nature of the work and the customs and practices prevailing in the professional, industrial or commercial activity concerned.

Article 37. Acts, agreements and contracts concerning economic rights that are executed before a notary, public broker or any authenticating official and are entered in the Public Copyright Register, shall be considered properly executed.

Article 38. Copyright shall not be conditional on the ownership of the physical object in which the work is embodied. Unless expressly agreed otherwise, the disposal by the author or his successor in title of the material medium containing a work shall not constitute transfer to the acquirer of any of the economic rights in the said work.

Article 39. Authorization to broadcast a protected work by radio, television or any other similar medium shall not include the right to rebroadcast it or exploit it.

Article 40. The owners of authors' economic rights and neighboring rights may claim compensatory remuneration for any copying or reproduction done without their permission and not covered by any of the limitations provided for in Articles 148 and 151 of this Law.

Article 41. Economic rights may not be either attached or pledged, but the benefits and products derived from the exercise thereof may be so used. [...]

CHAPTER IV

Stage Performance Contract

Article 61. Under a stage performance contract the author or owner of the economic rights, as the case may be, grants to a natural person or legal entity, known as the impresario, the right to perform a literary, musical, literary-musical, dramatic or dramatico-musical, work, a work of dance or a mimed or choreographic work in public against monetary compensation, while the impresario undertakes to effect the performance on the agreed conditions and in accordance with the

第35条　任何授予专有权利的许可均应明确此种专有性质，除非另有规定，应给予被许可人不受任何人妨碍利用该作品的权利，以及给予被许可人授予第三方非专有许可的权利。

第36条　授予专有权利的许可应责成被许可人根据作品的性质，以及相关职业、行业或商业活动中通行的惯例和做法，采取任何必要措施使被许可的利用有效。

第37条　在公证人、公共经纪人或任何认证官员面前缔结且在《公共版权登记册》上登记的有关经济权利的行为、协议和合同，应视为已适当缔结。

第38条　著作权不得以作品所依附的实物的所有权为条件。除非另有明确约定，作者或继受者对含有作品的物质媒介所有权的处置不构成对该作品中任何经济权利的转让。

第39条　授权他人通过广播、电视或任何其他类似媒体广播受保护作品的，该授权不包括对作品转播或加以利用的权利。

第40条　作者的经济权利和相邻权的所有人可以就任何未经许可，且不属于本法第148和第151条规定的限制情形的拷贝或复制行为要求报酬补偿。

第41条　经济权利既不得留置也不得质押，但行使经济权利所产生的收益和制品可留置或质押。……

第四章
舞台表演合同

第61条　根据舞台表演合同，作者或经济权利的所有人（视情况而定）授权一个自然人或法人，即所谓的主办方，无偿公开表演文学、音乐、文学音乐、戏剧或戏剧音乐、作品、舞蹈作品、哑剧或编舞作品，而主办方则承诺根据商定的条件和本法的规定开展演出。

provisions of this Law.

The contract shall specify whether or not the rights granted are exclusive, and where appropriate the conditions and characteristics of direction or performance.

Article 62. Where the period during which the work is to be performed to the public is not specified in the stage performance contract, it shall be understood to be one year.

Article 63. The impresario shall be under the following obligations:

(i) to ensure public performance on the agreed conditions;

(ii) to guarantee access to the performance free of charge to the author, the owner of the economic rights or their representatives;

(iii) to pay the agreed remuneration to the owner of the economic rights.

Article 64. Unless otherwise agreed, the stage performance contract signed between the author and the impresario shall authorize the latter to perform the work throughout the territory of the Mexican Republic.

Article 65. The provisions on publishing contracts for literary works shall apply to stage performance contracts in so far as they are not at variance with the provisions of this Chapter.

CHAPTER V

Broadcasting Contract

Article 66. Under a broadcasting contract the author or owner of the economic rights, as the case may be, authorizes a broadcasting organization to broadcast a work.

The provisions applicable to the broadcasts of such organizations shall apply as appropriate to those effected by cable, optic fiber, electromagnetic waves, satellite or any other comparable medium that serves for the remote communication to the public of protected works.

Article 67. The provisions on publishing contracts for literary works shall apply to broadcasting contracts in so far as they are not at variance with the provisions of this Chapter.

CHAPTER VI

Audiovisual Production Contract

Article 68. Under an audiovisual production contract, the authors or owners of the economic rights, as the case may be, grant the producer exclusive ownership of

合同应当载明授予的权利是否具有专有性，并在适当情况下明确导演或表演的条件和特点。

第 62 条　作品公开表演的期限如未在舞台表演合同中明确的，应当理解为一年。

第 63 条　主办方应承担下列义务：

(i)确保公开表演按照约定的条件开展；

(ii)保证作者、经济权利的所有人及其代理人可以无偿获取表演；

(iii)向经济权利所有人支付约定的报酬。

第 64 条　除非另有约定，作者和主办方签署的舞台演出合同应授权后者在墨西哥共和国全境演出。

第 65 条　在不违反本章规定的情况下，文学作品出版合同的规定适用于舞台演出合同。

第五章
广播合同

第 66 条　根据广播合同，作者和经济权利的所有人(视情况而定)授权广播组织广播作品。

适用于这类组织之广播的规定应酌情适用于受电缆、光纤、电磁波、卫星或任何其他与向公众提供受保护作品的远程通信相当的媒介之影响的广播。

第 67 条　文学作品出版合同的规定应当适用于广播合同，但不得与本章规定相抵触。

第六章
视听制作合同

第 68 条　除非另有约定，根据视听制作合同，作者或经济权利的所有人(视情况而定)授予制作者对视听作品复制、发行、向公众传播和制作字幕的专

the economic rights of reproduction, distribution, communication to the public and subtitling of the audiovisual works, unless otherwise agreed. The foregoing shall not apply to musical works.

Article 69. Where an author's contribution is not completed for reasons of force majeure, the producer may use the part already completed, subject to respect for the rights of the said author in that part, including the right of anonymity, and without prejudice to any indemnification that might be appropriate.

Article 70. The effects of the production contract shall lapse as of right if the making of the audiovisual work does not start within the period specified by the parties or for reasons of force majeure.

Article 71. The audiovisual work shall be considered completed when the final version has been achieved in accordance with the agreement between the director or maker on the one hand and the producer on the other.

Article 72. The provisions on publishing contracts for literary works shall apply to audiovisual production contracts in so far as they are not at variance with the provisions of this Chapter.

CHAPTER VII
Advertising Contracts

Article 73. Advertising contracts are those whose purpose is the exploitation of literary or artistic works for promotional or identification purposes in advertising or commercial announcements in any medium of communication.

Article 74. Advertising or commercial announcements may be disseminated for a period not exceeding six months following the first communication. After that time limit communication shall be for payment for each additional period of six months, even if it is effected only for fractions of such a period, with a minimum payment of at least that originally contracted for. After three years have elapsed following the first communication, use shall require the permission of the authors of the work used and the owners of the neighboring rights therein.

Article 75. In the case of advertising in printed media, the contract shall specify the physical medium or media in which the work is to be reproduced and, in the case of pamphlets or media other than periodical publications, the number of copies constituting the print-run. There shall be an express agreement for every

有权利。前述内容不适用于音乐作品。

第 69 条　如果作者因不可抗力原因未完成，制片人可以使用已完成的部分，但须尊重该作者在该部分的权利，包括匿名权，也不得影响作者获得任何适当的赔偿。

第 70 条　如果视听作品的制作未在当事人规定的期限内开始或由于不可抗力未开始，则制作合同依法失效。

第 71 条　当视听作品的最终版本按照导演或制作者与制片人之间的协议完成时，视听作品应被视为完成。

第 72 条　只要不违反本章的规定，关于文学作品出版合同的规定适用于视听制作合同。

第七章
广告合同

第 73 条　广告合同是指在通过任何传播媒介进行的广告或商业公告中，为了促销或识别目的利用文学或艺术作品的合同。

第 74 条　广告或商业公告可在首次播出后六个月内传播。在此期限之后，传播每增加六个月需再付款，即使只在六个月中的部分时间传播，且至少应支付最初合同规定的最低款项。首次播出满三年后，使用广告或商业公告应获得所使用作品的作者和相关邻接权人的许可。

第 75 条　就印刷媒体广告而言，合同应规定作品复制的物理媒介或媒体，且在涉及小册子或除期刊出版物以外的媒体时，还应规定本次印刷的份数。对于每一个增印批次，都应订立明确的协议。

additional print-run.

Article 76. The provisions on publishing contracts for literary works or musical works and those on audiovisual production contracts shall apply to advertising contracts in so far as they are not at variance with the provisions of this Chapter. [...]

TITLE IV

Protection of Copyright

[...]

CHAPTER III

Cinematographic and Audiovisual Works

Article 94. Audiovisual works means those expressed as a sequence of associated images, with or without incorporated sound, that are made perceptible by mechanical means and produce an impression of movement.

Article 95. Without prejudice to the rights of the authors of the works adapted for or included in it, the audiovisual work shall be protected as an original work.

Article 96. The owners of economic rights may use their contributions to the audiovisual work for exploitation in their own right, provided that the normal exploitation of the said work is not thereby prejudiced.

Article 97. The following are the authors of an audiovisual work:

(i) the director or maker;

(ii) the authors of the plot, adaptation, screenplay or dialogue;

(iii) the authors of the musical compositions;

(iv) the photographer;

(v) the authors of cartoons and animated pictures.

Unless otherwise agreed, the producer shall be considered the owner of the economic rights in the whole work.

Article 98. The producer of the audiovisual work is the person, whether natural person or legal entity, who takes the initiative for the making of a work, coordinates it and assumes responsibility for it, or who sponsors it.

Article 99. Unless otherwise agreed, the contract concluded between the author or the owners of the economic rights, as the case may be, and the producer shall not imply unlimited, exclusive assignment to the latter of the economic rights in the audiovisual work.

第 76 条　只要不违反本章的规定，关于文学作品、音乐作品出版合同和视听制作合同的规定适用于广告合同。……

第四部分

保护版权

……

第三章

电影和视听作品

第 94 条　视听作品是指通过机械手段使人感知并产生动态效果，不论是否伴有声音的一系列相关联的图像。

第 95 条　在不损害其所改编或所包含作品之作者的权利的情况下，视听作品应作为独创作品受到保护。

第 96 条　经济权利所有人可在其权利范围内利用其对视听作品所贡献的部分，但不得因此损害对该作品的正常利用。

第 97 条　以下是视听作品的作者：

（i）导演或制作者；

（ii）情节、改编、剧本或对话的作者；

（iii）音乐作品的作者；

（iv）摄影师；

（v）卡通和动画片的作者。

除非另有约定，制片人应被视为整个作品经济权利的所有人。

第 98 条　视听作品的制片人（无论是自然人还是法人）是指发起作品的制作、进行协调并承担责任的人，或者为作品提供赞助的人。

第 99 条　除非另有约定，作者或经济权利所有人（视情况而定）与制片人订立的合同不得暗示将视听作品中的经济权利无限、专有地转让给后者。

Once the authors of owners of economic rights have undertaken to make their contributions to the making of the audiovisual work, they may not object to the reproduction, distribution, public performance, cable distribution, broadcasting, communication to the public or subtitling and dubbing of the texts of the said work.

Without prejudice to the rights of the authors, the producer may perform all such acts as are necessary for the exploitation of the audiovisual work.

Article 100. The provisions contained in this Chapter shall apply as appropriate to broadcast works.

[...]

TITLE V

Neighboring Rights

CHAPTER I

General Provisions

Article 115. The protection provided for in this Title shall leave intact and in no way affect the protection of the copyright in literary and artistic works. Consequently, none of the provisions of this Title may be interpreted in a manner that detracts from that protection.

CHAPTER II

Performers

Article 116. Performer means the actor, narrator, speaker, singer, musician, dancer or any other person who performs a literary or artistic work or an expression of folklore or who engages in a similar activity, even though he may have no preexisting text to guide his performance. Extras and understudies are not included in this definition.

Article 117. The performer has the right to have his name associated with his performances, and also to object to any distortion or mutilation of his performance or other adverse act in relation to it that might damage his prestige or reputation.

Article 118. Performers have the right to object to:

(i) the communication of their performances to the public;

(ii) the fixing of their performances in a physical medium;

(iii) the reproduction of such a fixation of their performances.

The above rights shall be considered exhausted once the performer has

身为经济权利所有人的作者一旦承诺为制作视听作品作出贡献，就不得反对对该作品的复制、发行、公开表演、有线传播、广播、向公众传播、制作字幕或配音。

在不损害作者权利的情况下，制片人可以为利用视听作品而实施任何必要的上述行为。

第 100 条　本章所载规定应酌情适用于广播作品。

……

第五部分

邻接权

第一章

一般规定

第 115 条　本条所规定的不得触动或以任何方式影响对文学和艺术作品版权的保护。因此，本条的任何规定都不能以减损对文学艺术作品版权保护的方式加以解释。

第二章

表演者

第 116 条　表演者是指演员、解说员、演讲者、歌唱家、音乐家、舞蹈家，或者任何其他对文学、艺术作品或民间艺术表达进行表演或从事类似活动的人，尽管其可能没有事先准备的文本用以指导表演。这一定义不包括临时演员和候补演员。

第 117 条　表演者有权将他的名字与他的表演联系起来，并有权反对任何可能损害其声望或声誉的歪曲、毁损其表演的行为，或与之有关的其他不利行为。

第 118 条　表演者有权反对：

（i）向公众传播其表演；

（ii）将其表演录制在物理介质中；

（iii）复制录有其表演的录制品。

一旦表演者授权将其表演录制在视觉、声音或视听制品中，上述权利即视

authorized the incorporation of his performance in a visual, sound or audiovisual fixation.

Article 119. Performers who collectively participate in one and the same performance, like musical groups, choirs, orchestras or ballet or theater companies, shall designate a representative from among themselves for the exercise of the right of opposition referred to in the foregoing Article.

In the absence of such designation, it shall be presumed that the leader of the group or company is acting as representative.

Article 120. Performance contracts shall specify the times, periods, remuneration and other terms and procedures associated with the fixing, reproduction and communication to the public of the said performance.

Article 121. Unless otherwise agreed, the conclusion of a contract between a performer and a producer of audiovisual works with a view to the production of an audiovisual work shall include the right to fix and reproduce the performer's performances and communicate them to the public. The foregoing does not include the right to use the sounds and the images fixed in the audiovisual work separately, unless agreed otherwise.

Article 122. The duration of the protection granted to performers shall be 50 years counted from:

(i) the first fixing of the performance of a phonogram;

(ii) the first performance of works not recorded on phonograms;

(iii) the first transmission by radio, television or other medium.

[...]

CHAPTER IV

Producers of Phonograms

Article 129. A phonogram is any fixation exclusively of the sounds of a performance or other sounds, or digital representations thereof.

Article 130. A producer of phonograms is a person, whether natural person or legal entity, who first fixes the sounds of a performance or other sounds, or a digital representation thereof, and is responsible for the manufacture, production and publication of phonograms.

Article 131. Producers of phonograms have the right to authorize or prohibit:

为用尽。

第 119 条 集体参加同一演出的演出者，例如音乐团体、合唱团、管弦乐队、芭蕾舞团或剧团，应从其成员中间指定一名代表行使上述条款所述的反对权。

如无此种指定，应推定该团体或团队的领导人是代表。

第 120 条 表演合同应明确录制、复制以及向公众传播上述表演的次数、周期、报酬以及其他条款和程序。

第 121 条 除非另有约定，表演者与视听作品制作者为制作视听作品订立的合同应包括录制和复制表演者的表演并向公众传播的权利。除非另有约定，上述不包括单独使用视听作品中录制的声音和图像的权利。

第 122 条 给予表演者的保护期限为 50 年，起算点为：

(i)表演首次被录制在录音制品中；
(ii)未录制在录音制品上的作品的首次表演；
(iii)首次通过无线电、电视或其他媒体传播。

……

第四章

录音制品制作者

第 129 条 录音制品是专门录制表演的声音或其他声音，或这些声音的数字形式。

第 130 条 录音制品制作者是首先录制表演的声音或其他声音，或这些声音的数字形式，并负责录音制品的制作、生产和出版的主体(无论是自然人还是法人)。

第 131 条 录音制品制作者有权授权或禁止：

(i) the direct or indirect reproduction of all or part of their phonograms, and also the direct or indirect exploitation thereof;

(ii) the importation of copies of phonograms made without their authorization;

(iii) the distribution to the public of the original and every copy of the phonogram by sale or other means, including distribution by means of signals or broadcasts;

(iv) the adaptation or transformation of the phonogram;

(v) the commercial rental of the original phonogram or a copy thereof, even after it has been sold, provided that the authors or owners of the economic rights have not reserved it for themselves.

Article 132. Phonograms shall display the circled P symbol accompanied by a mention of the year of first publication.

Failure to meet the above requirements shall not cause the producer of the phonogram to lose his rights, but makes him liable to the sanctions provided for by law.

Producers of phonograms shall notify collective administration organizations of the particulars on the labels of their products and on the master copies that are exported, with a mention of the country in each case.

Article 133. Once the phonogram has been lawfully brought into any commercial circuit, neither the owner of the economic rights nor the performers nor the phonogram producers may object to its direct communication to the public, provided that the persons using it for profit-making purposes make the corresponding payment to them.

Article 134. The protection referred to in this Chapter shall be for 50 years following the first fixation of the sounds on the phonogram.

CHAPTER V

Producers of Videograms

Article 135. A videogram shall be taken to mean the fixation of related images, with or without incorporated sound, that give an impression of movement, or a digital representation of such images, taken from an audiovisual work or the performance of another work or of an expression of folklore, and also other images of the same kind, with or without sound.

(i)直接或间接复制其全部或部分录音制品，以及直接或间接利用该复制件；

(ii)进口未经授权制作的录音制品；

(iii)以销售或其他方式向公众发行录音制品的原件和复制件，包括通过信号或广播的方式发行；

(iv)录音制品的调试或转换；

(v)录音制品原件或复制件的商业性出租，即使已经出售，前提是作者或者经济权利所有人没有为自己保留该项权利。

第132条　录音制品应显示圆圈P符号，并注明首次出版的年份。

不符合上述要求并不会使录音制品制作者丧失权利，但会使其受到法律规定的处罚。

录音制品制作者应将其产品标签和导出的母本上的详细情况通知集体管理组织，并在每种情况下注明国家。

第133条　一旦录音制品被合法带入任何商业场合，经济权利的所有人、表演者或录音制品制作者都不得反对他人直接向公众传播该录音制品，但是以营利目的使用该录音制品的人应支付相应的款项。

第134条　本章所指的保护期限为声音首次录制在录音制品之日起50年。

第五章
录像制作者

第135条　录像是指对相关图像的录制，无论是否伴有声音，给人以动态效果，或对此类图像的数字化呈现；这些图像系从视听作品、其他作品的表演、民间文学艺术表达中获取，或其他同类的图像，无论是否伴有声音。

Article 136. The producer of videograms is the person, whether natural person or legal entity, who first fixes related images, with or without incorporated sound, that give an impression of movement, or a digital representation of such images, whether constituting or not constituting an audiovisual work.

Article 137. The producer shall enjoy with respect to his videograms the right to authorize or prohibit their reproduction, distribution and communication to the public.

Article 138. The term of the rights provided for in this Chapter shall be 50 years from the first fixing of the images on the videogram.

CHAPTER VI
Broadcasting Organizations

Article 139. For the purposes of this Law, an entity holding a concession or license that is capable of emitting sound or visual signals or both that may be received by a public of more than one person shall be considered a broadcasting organization.

Article 140. Broadcasting or transmission means the communication of works, sounds or sounds and images by means of electromagnetic waves, cable, optic fiber or other comparable media. The concept of broadcasting likewise includes the sending of signals from a terrestrial station towards a satellite for subsequent broadcasting.

Article 141. Retransmission is the simultaneous transmission by one broadcasting organization of a broadcast from another such organization.

Article 142. An ephemeral recording is a recording made by a broadcasting organization where, for technical or scheduling reasons, and for the purposes of a single subsequent broadcast, it has to record or fix, in its own studios, the image, sound or both of musical selections of parts thereof, working papers, lectures or scientific studies, literary, dramatic, choreographic and dramatico-musical works, computer programs and, generally, any work suitable for broadcasting.

Article 143. Signals may be:

(i) in terms of their accessibility to the public:

(a) coded, enciphered or encrypted: those that have been altered with a view to being received and decrypted solely and exclusively by those who have previously

第 136 条　录像制品制作者（无论是自然人还是法人）是首次录制相关图像的人，无论是否伴有声音，给人以动态效果，或者首次录制这些图像的数字化呈现的人，无论是否构成视听作品。

第 137 条　制作者享有授权或禁止其复制、发行和向公众传播其录像制品的权利。

第 138 条　本章规定的权利期限为把图像首次录制在录像制品之日起 50 年。

第六章
广播组织

第 139 条　就本法而言，持有特许或许可证、能够发出一人以上公众接收到的声音或 / 和视觉信号的实体，应视为广播组织。

第 140 条　广播或传输是指通过电磁波、电缆、光纤或其他相当的媒介传播作品、声音或带声音的图像。同样地，广播的概念包括从地面站向卫星发送信号以便后续进行广播。

第 141 条　转播是一个广播组织从另一个广播组织同步传输一个广播。

第 142 条　临时录制是一种广播组织由于技术或时间安排的原因，为一个单次后续广播的目的所作的录音，广播组织必须在自己的工作室中录制或录制图像、声音或部分音乐作品的选曲、工作文件、演讲或科学研究、文学、戏剧、编舞和戏剧音乐作品、计算机程序，以及任何适合广播的作品。

第 143 条　信号可能是：

（i）就公众利用而言：

（a）被编码的、加密的：经过改变，以便只由先前已从发出这些信息的广播组织获得这一权利的人接收和解密的信息；

acquired that right from the broadcasting organization that emitted them;

(b) free: those that may be received by means of any apparatus suitable for receiving the signals;

(ii) in terms of their time of emission:

(a) direct: those that carry live programs or events;

(b) deferred: those that carry prerecorded programs or events.

Article 144. Broadcasting organizations have the right to authorize or prohibit the following in relation to their broadcasts:

(i) retransmission;

(ii) deferred transmission;

(iii) simultaneous or deferred distribution by cable or any other system;

(iv) fixation in a material medium;

(v) reproduction of fixations;

(vi) communication to the public by any means and in any form for direct profit-making purposes.

Article 145. That person shall be liable for damages and prejudice who, without the permission of the lawful distributor of the signal:

(i) decrypts a coded program-carrying satellite signal;

(ii) receives and distributes a coded program-carrying satellite signal that has been unlawfully decrypted;

(iii) participates or assists in the manufacture, importation, sale or rental of, or in the performance of any act serving to supply, a device or system that substantially aids in the decrypting of a coded program-carrying satellite signal.

Article 146. The rights of broadcasting organizations referred to in this Chapter shall have a term of 25 years as from the first original broadcasting or transmission of the program.

NORWAY

According to the Norwegian copyright act (12 May 1961 No. 2), section 42, a performer enjoys a right to authorize the fixation of his/her performance. The performer further enjoys a right ot authorize reproduction of copies of such a fixation, including audiovisual fixations, as well as a distribution right. The distribution right is exhausted after the first sale of a copy of the audiovisual fixation

(b)可自由获得的：可用任何适合接收信号的装置接收的；

(ii)就发射时间而言：
(a)直接发送：播放现场节目或活动；
(b)延迟发送：播放预录节目或活动。
第144条　广播组织有权授权或禁止其广播的：

(i)转播；
(ii)延迟传输；
(iii)通过有线电缆或任何其他系统同步或延迟发送；
(iv)录制在物质媒介中；
(v)录制品的复制；
(vi)以直接营利为目的以任何方式和任何形式向公众传播。

第145条　未经信号的合法发布者许可实施下列行为的，应承担损害赔偿责任：
(i)解密已加密的节目卫星信号；
(ii)接收和分发被非法解密的节目卫星信号；

(iii)参与或协助制造、进口、销售或出租，或实施任何为供应主要用于解密已加密节目卫星信号的设备或系统。

第146条　本章所称广播组织权利的期限，自节目首次播出或传输之日起25年。

挪威

根据挪威版权法(1961年5月12日第2号)第42条，表演者享有授权录制其表演的权利。表演者还享有授权复制这种录制品(包括视听录制品)的权利以及发行权。在EEA地区内首次出售视听制品的复制件后，发行权用尽。这意味着，录制表演的视听制品的复制件存在区域性的发行权用尽。然而，出租权没有用尽。当表演者同意将他的表演纳入视听录制品中时，法律推定该种

within the EEA-area. This means that there is regional exhaustion of the distribution right regarding copies of audiovisual fixations of performances. However, there is no exhaustion of the rental right. When a performer has consented to the incorporation of his performance in an audiovisual fixation, there is a statutory presumption for such a consent to include the transfer of his rental right.

We do not possess any relevant information on the contractual practices between performers and e. g. producers of films... According to our legislative tradition, we do not have statutory regulations of the transfer of rights from employee to employer in such situations.

These questions are governed by traditional contractual principles...

As regards statistics, we are not quite sure of the nature of information requested. To our knowledge, there are no official, national statistics on e. g. remuneration levels, contractual practices or other information on the exercise of rights in audiovisual performances.

REPUBLIC OF MOLDOVA

The rights of performers are protected by the Law on Copyright and Neighboring Rights which is effective in the Republic of Moldova from the day of its publication (March 2, 1995). Under Article 27, a performer has the right to use his performance in any form, including the right to receive remuneration for every kind of use of the performance.

We shall touch upon the question dealing with the protection of the performance included into the audiovisual work. In the narrow meaning of the word, an audiovisual work (Art. 12, Law of the RM) means film. The rights of the role performers (economic rights) are not protected. In the broad meaning of the word, an audiovisual work means any "work which consists of a number of interconnected images (with sound accompaniment or without it) creating an impression of movement, and which can be perceived by means of hearing or sight" (Art. 3 of the Law). Those are videograms and TV programs which contain, as a rule, a great number of performances.

The legislation of the Republic of Moldova protects the performances of the works of "small forms," including those fixed in the material carriers of audio and video. Article 3 of the Decree of the Parliament of the Republic of Moldova, entitled

同意包含其出租权的转移。

我们没有任何关于表演者和例如电影制作人之间的合同惯例的相关信息。……根据我们的立法传统，我们没有此种情形下将权利从雇员转移到雇主的法律规定。

这些问题受传统合同原则的制约……

关于统计数据，我们不太确定所要求的资料的性质。据我们所知，没有官方的关于行使视听表演相关权利的薪酬水平、合同惯例或其他信息的国家统计数据。

摩尔多瓦共和国

表演者权受《版权和邻接权法》保护，该法自公布之日（1995年3月2日）生效。根据该法第27条，表演者有权以任何形式使用其表演，且有权就表演的各种使用获得报酬。

我们应讨论关于保护视听作品中的表演的问题。在狭义上，视听作品（我国法律第12条）是指电影。角色表演者的权利（经济权利）不受保护。在广义上，视听作品是指任何“由许多相互关联的图像组成的（不论是否伴有声音）形成运动印象、可以通过听觉或视觉来感知的作品”（该法第3条）。它们通常是包含大量表演的录像和电视节目。

摩尔多瓦共和国的立法保护“小型”作品的表演，包括录制在物质载体上的音频和视频。摩尔多瓦共和国议会题为“关于《版权和邻接权法》生效”的法令（1994年11月21日第294-XIII号）第3条规定了该法第33条（邻接权

"On Entering into force of the Law on Copyright and Neighboring Rights" (No. 294-XIII of November 21, 1994), specifies the application procedure for Article 33 of the Law (validity term of the neighboring rights): "The rights of the authors of the earlier created audiovisual works, performers whose performances were fixed in phonograms as well as producers of phonograms and broadcasting organizations shall be protected during the period of time left till the expiration of 50 years computed from the day of their first lawful publication or till the expiration of 50 years computed from the day of their creation if they have not been published."

The Decree No. 713 of the Government of the Republic of Moldova, dated October 23, 1995, entitled "On Authors' Remuneration for the Use of the Copyright and Neighboring Rights in the Republic of Moldova" sets up the minimum tariff rates of authors' remuneration for the use of phonograms and videograms. Due to the fact that before contracts did not envisage the payment of authors' fee to the performers for the use of the fixed works, the following system of the distribution of royalties, established by the Law (Art. 20, par. 4) is applied: authors-40%, performers-30% and producers of phonograms (videograms)-30%. The absolute majority of the producers of new phonograms and videograms confirm, when registering new fixations in the Agency [the State Copyright Agency of the Republic of Moldova], such approach to the distribution of royalties for the use of the copyright and neighboring rights.

On TV, one minute of the broadcasting time is recognized as a measurement unit. Unfortunately, the quality of the program is not yet taken into consideration when determining the amount of the authors' remuneration. The Decree of the Government established the minimum tariff rates of the authors' fee for the use of phonograms (videograms) during 60 minutes-two minimum wages earned in the Republic as of the day of the use (at present time it makes 36 leus or 8 dollars).

The Agency is authorized for the collective management of the economic rights. It has concluded agreements with authors and performers (over 1 200 people) and grant licenses for the use of the fixed performances which are registered in the Agency. The problem of distribution of royalties for the performers, members of performing collective bodies, turned out to be the most difficult. Besides the individual contracts with every performer, the Agency signed contracts with 17

的有效期）的适用程序："早期创作的视听作品的作者、其表演被录制在录音制品中的表演者以及录音制品制作者和广播组织的权利，在剩余的时间内应受到保护，直到从其首次合法发表之日起计算的 50 年期满为止，如果尚未发表，则直到从其创作之日起计算的 50 年期满为止。"

摩尔多瓦共和国政府 1995 年 10 月 23 日题为"关于摩尔多瓦共和国作者就他人使用版权和邻接权的报酬问题"的第 713 号法令规定了作者就他人使用其录音制品和录像制品的最低报酬率。由于以前的合同没有规定向使用已录制作品的表演者支付作者费，因此适用该法（第 20 条第 4 段）规定的以下版税分配制度：作者 –40%，表演者 –30% 和录音（录像）制作者 –30%。绝大多数新录音制品和录像制品的制作者在向版权局［摩尔多瓦共和国国家版权局］登记新的制品时，都确认了这种分配版权和邻接权使用费的方法。

在电视上，以一分钟为公认的广播时间计量单位。遗憾的是，在确定作者的报酬数额时，尚未考虑到节目的质量。《政府法令》规定了在 60 分钟内使用录音制品（录像制品）的作者费的最低费率，即使用当天共和国最低工资的两倍（目前为 36 列伊或 8 美元）。

版权局经授权对经济权利进行集体管理。它已与（超过 1200 位）作者和表演者签订了协议，并为使用在版权局登记的已录制的表演颁发许可证。在演出者、集体表演团体成员中分配版税是最困难的问题。除了与每个表演者签订的单个的合同外，版权局还与 17 个专业表演集体组织签订了合同。这些集体组织任命了它们的代表，版权局在储蓄银行开设账户，并将应支付给版权局的报酬转入这些账户。集体组织的代表起草酬劳单，从银行领取并支付许可使用

professional performing collective bodies. The collective bodies appointed their representatives, and the Agency opened them accounts in saving banks and transfers to these accounts the remuneration due to the said bodies. The representatives of the collective bodies draft payrolls, receive from the bank and pay royalties, and return the payrolls to the accounting service of the Agency. On one hand, it is a form to control that the royalties do reach the performers, and, on the other, the Agency is entitled, if necessary, to issue certificates to the social security authorities to determine the amount of pensions and other benefits.

The brief experience in payment of... remuneration to performers stimulated the performers of the "big forms" works to demand the revision of their status in respect of the use of the fixed performances. We think that the International Bureau will also take these opinions into consideration when preparing proposals concerning modernization of the performers' rights protection system. In this context the phrase "fixed in phonograms" in Article 7 of the WIPO Performances and Phonograms Treaty would be closer to the aspirations of the performers in the wording "fixed in any means." The same applies to Art. 8, par. 1; Art. 9, par. 1 and Art. 10 of the above-said WIPO Treaty.

SWITZERLAND

The Swiss Law on Copyright and Neighboring Rights (LDA) entered into force on July 1, 1993. In the field of neighboring rights, it protects performers, producers of phonograms and videograms and broadcasting organizations in both the audiovisual and the audio field. As these rights were introduced quite recently, their implementation is still in its early stages, and we do not have any statistics.

URUGUAY

Protection of Performers in Relation to Audiovisual Performances

Contractual practices recognize this protection in the form of current contracts with public and cable television.

There is no express provision from the legal point of view, but in fact, thanks to some favorable case law in cassation appeals, protection is also recognized in the hotel trade, derived from the general principles of law enshrined in the Copyright Law and the Civil and Procedural Law.

In practice, a number of users who make use of public or cable television, even

费，并将酬劳单交给版权局的会计部门。一方面，这是确保许可使用费确实支付给表演者的一种方式；另一方面，版权局有权在必要时向社会保障当局颁出具证明，以确定养老金和其他福利的数额。

在向表演者支付报酬方面的短暂实践刺激了“大型”作品的表演者要求改变他们在已录制表演使用方面的地位。我们认为，国际局在编制有关表演者权利保护制度现代化的提案时也会考虑这些意见。在这一背景下，WPPT 第 7 条中的“录制在录音制品中”这一短语使用“以任何方式录制”的措辞将更接近表演者的愿望。这也同样适用于上述条约的第 8 条第 1 段、第 9 条第 1 段和第 10 条。

瑞士

《瑞士著作权和邻接权法》(LDA)于 1993 年 7 月 1 日生效。在邻接权领域，该法保护表演者、录音和录像制作者以及视听和音频领域的广播组织。由于这些权利是最近才有法律规定，其实施仍处于早期阶段，我们没有任何统计数据。

乌拉圭

对视听表演相关表演者的保护

合同惯例以目前与公共和有线电视签订的合同形式认可这种保护。

从法律角度看，没有明确的规定，但事实上，由于撤销原判上诉中的一些有利判例，从《版权法》和《民事和诉讼法》所规定的一般法律原则出发，酒店业也承认保护。

在实践中，一些使用公共或有线电视的用户(如餐馆、酒吧、购物中心等)

without a contract, provide protection (such as restaurants, bars, shopping centers, etc).

Performers involved in audiovisual performances receive from their collecting society, the Uruguayan Performers' Society, royalties that are collected and distributed according to the system approved by that body. Distribution takes place only among national performers where type B contracts exist with associated societies, which do not provide for cash refunds between them.

There are no official statistics.

[End of Annex and of document]

即使没有合同也提供保护。

视听表演的表演者从其集体协会(乌拉圭表演者协会)获得依照该协会批准的制度收取和分配的许可使用费。只有在与该协会签订了 B 类合同的本国表演者之间才会进行分配,这些协会之间没有现金退款的规定。

没有官方统计数据。

(附件和文件结束)

1.3 Report Adopted by Committee of Experts on a Protocol Concerning Audiovisual Performances

Document Code: AP/CE/1/4
Language: English
URL: https://www.wipo.int/edocs/mdocs/copyright/en/ap_ce_i/ap_ce_i_4.pdf

Chinese Translation: Not Available.
URL: N/A

COMMITTEE OF EXPERTS
ON A PROTOCOL
CONCERNING AUDIOVISUAL PERFORMANCES
Geneva, September 15, 16 and 19, 1997

REPORT

adopted by the Committee

I. INTRODUCTION.

1. In pursuance of the decision taken by the Governing Bodies of the World Intellectual Property Organization (WIPO) and the Unions administered by WIPO at the thirtieth Series of Meetings in Geneva, on March 20 and 21, 1997 (see document AB/XXX/4, items 3 and 4), the Director General of WIPO convened a Committee of Experts on a Protocol concerning Audiovisual Performances (hereinafter referred to as “the Committee”) at the headquarters of WIPO, in Geneva, on September 15, 16 and 19, 1997.

1.3 视听表演议定书专家委员会报告

文件编号：AP/CE/1/4
文件语言：英语
文件链接：https://www.wipo.int/edocs/mdocs/copyright/en/ap_ce_i/ap_ce_i_4.pdf
中文文本：无
文件链接：无

视听表演议定书

专家委员会

1997 年 9 月 15 日、16 日和 19 日，日内瓦

报告

由专家委员会通过

一、介绍

1. 根据世界知识产权组织（WIPO）主管理事机构和世界知识产权组织管理的各联盟于 1997 年 3 月 20 日和 21 日在日内瓦举行的第三十次系列会议上作出的决定（见 AB/XXX/4 号文件，项目 3 和项目 4），世界知识产权组织总干事于 1997 年 9 月 15 日、16 日和 19 日在世界知识产权组织日内瓦总部召开了视听表演议定书专家委员会（以下简称专家委员会）会议。

2. Experts of the following 91 States and one intergovernmental organization, members of the Committee, attended the meeting: Algeria, Angola, Argentina, Armenia, Australia, Austria, Azerbaijan, Belarus, Belgium, Bolivia, Brazil, Brunei Darussalam, Bulgaria, Burkina Faso, Cameroon, Canada, Chile, China, Colombia, Costa Rica, Côte d'Ivoire, Croatia, Cuba, Czech Republic, Democratic People's Republic of Korea, Denmark, Ecuador, Egypt, Eritrea, Estonia, Finland, France, Gambia, Germany, Ghana, Greece, Guatemala, Honduras, Hungary, India, Indonesia, Ireland, Italy, Jamaica, Japan, Jordan, Kazakstan, Kenya, Kyrgyzstan, Lesotho, Lithuania, Luxembourg, Malawi, Malaysia, Malta, Mexico, Mongolia, Morocco, Netherlands, Nigeria, Norway, Pakistan, Panama, Peru, Philippines, Portugal, Republic of Korea, Republic of Moldova, Romania, Russian Federation, Senegal, Singapore, Slovakia, South Africa, Spain, Sri Lanka, Sudan, Sweden, Switzerland, Tajikistan, Thailand, Togo, Trinidad and Tobago, Tunisia, United Arab Emirates, United Kingdom, United States of America, Uruguay, Uzbekistan, Venezuela, Viet Nam, and the Commission of the European Communities.

3. Representatives of the following five intergovernmental organizations attended the meeting in observer capacity: International Labour Organization (ILO), International Telecommunication Union (ITU), Agency for Cultural and Technical Cooperation (AGECOP), Organization of African Unity (OAU), and World Trade Organization (WTO).

4. Representatives of the following 38 non-governmental organizations attended the meeting in observer capacity: Agence pour la protection des programmes (APP), American Bar Association (ABA), American Federation of Television and Radio Artists (AFTRA), American Film Marketing Association (AFMA), Asia-Pacific Broadcasting Union (ABU), Association of Commercial Television in Europe (ACT), Association of European Performers' Organisations (AEPO), Association for the International Collective Management of Audiovisual Works (AGICOA), Caribbean Broadcasting Union (CBU), Comité "Actores, Intérpretes" (CSAI), Conseil francophone de la chanson (CFC), Copyright Research and Information Center (CRIC), European Broadcasting Union (EBU), European Project-Digital Video Broadcasting (DVB), Groupement européen représentant les organismes de gestion collective des droits des artistes interprètes ou exécutants

2. 下列91个国家和1个政府间组织、专家委员会成员出席了会议：阿尔及利亚、安哥拉、阿根廷、亚美尼亚、澳大利亚、奥地利、阿塞拜疆、白俄罗斯、比利时、玻利维亚、巴西、文莱、保加利亚、布基纳法索、喀麦隆、加拿大、智利、中国、哥伦比亚、哥斯达黎加、科特迪瓦、克罗地亚、古巴、捷克共和国、朝鲜、丹麦、厄瓜多尔、埃及、厄立特里亚、爱沙尼亚、芬兰、法国、冈比亚、德国、加纳、希腊、危地马拉、洪都拉斯、匈牙利、印度、印度尼西亚、爱尔兰、意大利、牙买加、日本、约旦、哈萨克斯坦、肯尼亚、吉尔吉斯斯坦、莱索托、立陶宛、卢森堡、马拉维、马来西亚、马耳他、墨西哥、蒙古国、摩洛哥、荷兰、尼日利亚、挪威、巴基斯坦、巴拿马、秘鲁、菲律宾、葡萄牙、韩国、摩尔多瓦共和国、罗马尼亚、俄罗斯联邦、塞内加尔、新加坡、斯洛伐克、南非、西班牙、斯里兰卡、苏丹、瑞典、瑞士、塔吉克斯坦、泰国、多哥、特立尼达和多巴哥、突尼斯、阿拉伯联合酋长国、大不列颠和北爱尔兰联合王国、美国、乌拉圭、乌兹别克斯坦、委内瑞拉、越南和欧洲共同体委员会。

3. 下列五个政府间组织的代表以观察员身份出席了会议：国际劳工组织（ILO）、国际电信联盟（ITU）、文化和技术合作机构（AGECOP）、非洲统一组织（OAU）和世界贸易组织（WTO）。

4. 下列38个非政府组织的代表以观察员身份出席了会议：保护节目局（APP）、美国律师协会（ABA）、美国电视和广播艺术家联合会（AFTRA）、美国电影销售协会（AFMA）、亚太广播联盟（ABU）、欧洲商业电视协会（ACT）、欧洲表演者组织协会（AEPO）、国际视听作品集体管理协会（AGICOA）、加勒比广播联盟（CBU）、“演员、口译”委员会（CSAI），法语国家委员会（CFC）、版权研究和信息中心（CRIC）、欧洲广播联盟（EBU）、欧洲项目－数字视频广播（DVB）、欧洲演员和口译者权利集体管理组织（ARTIS GEIE）、伊比利亚－拉丁美洲表演者联合会（FILAIE）、信息产业协会（IIA）、美国信息技术协会（ITAA）、美洲版权研究所（IIDA）、作家协会国际联合会（IAWG）、国际管弦乐协会联盟（IAOA），国际广播协会（IAB）、国际律师协会（IBA）、国际作家和作曲家协会联合会（CISAC）、国际科学联合会理事会（ICSU）、国际演员联合会（FIA）、国际电影发行者协会联合会（FIAD）、国际电影制作人协会联合会（FIAPF）、国际

(ARTIS GEIE), Ibero-Latin-American Federation of Performers (FILAIE), Information Industry Association (IIA), Information Technology Association of America (ITAA), Interamerican Copyright Institute (IIDA), International Affiliation of Writers Guilds (IAWG), International Alliance of Orchestra Associations (IAOA), International Association of Broadcasting (IAB), International Bar Association (IBA), International Confederation of Societies of Authors and Composers (CISAC), International Council of Scientific Unions (ICSU), International Federation of Actors (FIA), International Federation of Associations of Film Distributors (FIAD), International Federation of Film Producers Associations (FIAPF), International Federation of Musicians (FIM), International Federation of Reproduction Rights Organizations (IFRRO), International Federation of the Phonographic Industry (IFPI), International Intellectual Property Alliance (IIPA), International Publishers Association (IPA), Max-Planck-Institute for Foreign and International Patent, Copyright and Competition Law (MPI), Performing Arts Employers Associations League Europe (PEARLE), Union of Industrial and Employers' Confederations of Europe (UNICE), Union of National Radio and Television Organizations of Africa (URTNA) and World Federation of Music Schools (WFMS).

5. The list of participants is attached to this report.

Ⅱ. OPENING OF THE MEETING

6. A representative of the International Bureau of WIPO welcomed the participants and opened the meeting.

Ⅲ. ELECTION OF OFFICERS

7. Mr. Jukka Liedes (Finland) was unanimously elected Chairman, and Mrs. Hilda Retondo (Argentina) and Mr. Shen Rengan (China) were unanimously elected Vice-Chairmen of the Committee.

IV. EXAMINATION OF QUESTIONS RELATED TO A PROTOCOL CONCERNING AUDIOVISUAL PERFORMANCES

8. Discussions were based on the memoranda prepared by the International Bureau of WIPO, in accordance with the decision mentioned in paragraph 1, entitled:

- Existing national and regional legislation concerning audiovisual performances (document AP/CE/I/2); and

音乐家联合会（FIM）、国际复制权利组织联合会（IFRRO）、国际录音制品业联合会（IFPI）、国际知识产权联盟（IIPA）、国际出版商协会（IPA）、马克斯－普朗克外国和国际专利、版权和竞争法研究所（MPI）、欧洲表演艺术雇主协会联盟（PEARLE）、欧洲工业和雇主联合会联盟（UNICE）、非洲国家广播电视组织联盟（URTNA）和世界音乐学校联合会（WFMS）。

5. 参会人员名单见本报告附件。

二、会议开幕

6. 世界知识产权组织国际局的一名代表欢迎与会者并宣布会议开幕。

三、选举主席团成员

7. Jukka Liedes 先生（芬兰）被一致推选为主席，Hilda Retondo 夫人（阿根廷）和沈仁干先生（中国）被一致推选为委员会副主席。

四、审查与视听表演议定书有关的问题

8. 讨论的基础是世界知识产权组织国际局根据第 1 段所述决定编写的备忘录，题为：

– 当前各国和地区立法中关于视听表演的规定（AP/CE/I/2 号文件）；以及

- Information received from Member States of WIPO and from the European Community concerning audiovisual performances (documents AP/CE/I/3 and 3 Add).

9. The Secretariat noted the interventions made and recorded on tape. The statements made during the debate are reflected in the Annex to this report.

10. The Chairman summarized the general discussion in the following way: The discussion had been very useful. Many delegations had expressed regret that protection of performers with respect to audiovisual performances was not included in the WIPO Performances and Phonograms Treaty (WPPT).

All delegations had reaffirmed that the work on a Protocol addressing this issue should continue in the framework of WIPO. Specific aspects that delegations had mentioned were, in particular: the possible scope of the protection, the specific rights to be granted to performers, the aspect of moral as well as of economic rights, the objective of obtaining protection for performers as much in parallel as possible with the protection of authors, the desire to do away with discrimination of audiovisual performers in respect of their legal protection.

On the other hand, it had also been pointed out that the Berne Convention contained specific rules on cinematographic works. The need for a flexible treaty had been underlined, namely that it should be adapted to divergent concepts in national legislations and to the realities, i. e., contractual practices, collective bargaining and collective management of rights. Further elements mentioned had been the principle of national treatment and the issues of transferability of rights and applicable law.

A pragmatic approach had been felt suitable. To take the WPPT as a starting point, would simplify the further debate. The Protocol should be of a complementary nature, in relation to the WPPT. The appropriate maxim for the forthcoming negotiations should be: compromise and commitment.

11. The Chairman noted that the memoranda prepared by the International Bureau for the current meeting had been useful. As far as amendments or additions to the memoranda requested by some delegations were concerned, it was agreed that the Secretariat would duly reflect their contents in the annex to this report mentioned in paragraph 9.

– 世界知识产权组织成员国提交的关于视听表演的信息(文件 AP/CE/I/3 和附件 3)。

9. 秘书处注意到所作的发言,并将其记录在案。讨论期间的发言载于本报告附件。

10. 主席对一般性讨论作了如下总结:讨论非常有用。许多代表团对《世界知识产权组织表演和录音制品条约》(WPPT)没有列入对表演者关于视听表演的保护表示遗憾。

所有代表团都重申,应在世界知识产权组织的框架内继续就解决这一问题的议定书开展工作。各代表团提到的具体方面特别包括:保护的可能范围、给予表演者的具体权利、精神权利和经济权利的方面、尽可能在保护作者的同时为表演者提供保护的目标、在法律保护方面消除对视听表演者的歧视的愿望。

另一方面,也有人指出,《伯尔尼公约》中包含关于电影作品的具体规则,同时他们强调需要制定一项灵活的条约,该条约应适应国家立法中不同的概念和现实,即合同惯例、集体谈判和权利集体管理。提到的其他要素有国民待遇原则和权利可转让性问题以及法律适用问题。

有人认为采取务实的办法是合适的,以 WPPT 为出发点,将简化进一步的讨论。议定书应与 WPPT 具有互补性,即将进行的谈判的适当准则应该是:妥协和承诺。

11. 主席指出,国际局为本次会议编写的备忘录是有用的。至于一些代表团要求对备忘录作出的修正或补充,会议商定,秘书处将在第 9 段提到的本报告附件中适当反映其内容。

V. FUTURE WORK

12. The Committee adopted the following decision:

(i) the second session of the Committee should take place in the period of May-June 1998, but not later than during the week starting June 8, 1998; it is recommended that the Governing Bodies of WIPO take a decision about the dates of the second session during their September-October 1997 series of meetings;

(ii) the International Bureau should invite the Governments of WIPO Member States and the European Community to submit by January 15, 1998, proposals, preferably in treaty language, concerning a protocol to the WIPO Performances and Phonograms Treaty on audiovisual performances;

(iii) the International Bureau should distribute the proposals, together with comparative tables, if appropriate, by the end of February 1998, to those invited to the second session of the Committee who should be the same as those invited to the first session;

(iv) regional consultation meetings should be organized by WIPO in consultation with the representatives of the regional groups in March-April 1998; it is recommended that the Governing Bodies of WIPO take a decision about the financing of the participation of the representatives of the regional groups, during the September-October 1997 series of meetings of the Governing Bodies.

13. The Delegation of Côte d'Ivoire, on behalf of the African Group, the Delegation of Ecuador, on behalf of the Group of Latin American and the Caribbean countries, and the Delegation of Singapore, on behalf of the Asian Group, and supported by the Delegation of China, underlined the need for financial support by WIPO for the participation of representatives of countries from these regional groups in the regional consultation meetings. Those Delegations referred to the way in which participation in the regional consultation meetings, that had been held in the autumn of 1996 in preparation of the WIPO Diplomatic Conference on Certain Copyright and Neighboring Rights Questions (December 1996), had been financially supported by WIPO, and indicated that the number of participants financed for each of those regions should be similar.

14. The Delegation of the Russian Federation requested that a consultation meeting be organized by WIPO also for those Member States of WIPO which

五、未来的工作

12. 委员会通过了以下决定：

（i）委员会第二届会议应于 1998 年 5 月至 6 月举行，但不迟于 1998 年 6 月 8 日开始的一周；建议世界知识产权组织主管理事机构在 1997 年 9 月至 10 月系列会议期间就第二届会议的日期作出决定；

（ii）国际局应请世界知识产权组织成员国政府和欧洲共同体在 1998 年 1 月 15 日之前提出关于《世界知识产权组织表演和录音制品条约》视听表演议定书的建议，最好以条约语言提出；

（iii）如果合适的话，国际局应在 1998 年 2 月底之前将提案连同比较表发给应邀参加委员会第二届会议的人，这些人应与应邀参加第一届会议的人相同；

（iv）区域协商会议应由世界知识产权组织在 1998 年 3 月至 4 月期间与各区域小组的代表协商安排；建议世界知识产权组织主管理事机构在 1997 年 9 月至 10 月的理事机构系列会议期间就资助各区域小组的代表参加会议作出决定。

13. 科特迪瓦代表团（代表非洲小组）、厄瓜多尔代表团（代表拉丁美洲和加勒比国家小组）和新加坡代表团（代表亚洲小组）在中国代表团的支持下，强调世界知识产权组织需要为这些区域小组的国家代表参加区域协商会议提供财政支持。这些代表团提到 1996 年秋季为筹备世界知识产权组织关于版权和邻接权若干问题的外交会议（1996 年 12 月）而举行的区域协商会议的参与方式得到了世界知识产权组织的财政支持，并指出，为这些区域中的每一个区域提供资金的与会者人数应相似。

14. 俄罗斯联邦代表团要求世界知识产权组织也为属于独立国家联合体成员的世界知识产权组织成员国组织一次协商会议，世界知识产权组织向除俄罗

are members of the Commonwealth of Independent States and that WIPO lend its financial support to participation of representatives of those States, except the Russian Federation.

VI. ADOPTION OF THE REPORT AND CLOSING OF THE MEETING

15. The present report was unanimously adopted by the Committee.

16. The Chairman closed the meeting.

[Annex follows]

斯联邦以外的这些国家的代表提供财政支助。

六、通过报告并结束会议

15. 委员会一致通过了本报告。

16. 主席宣布会议闭幕。

（后接附件）

2.
Committee of Experts on a Protocol Concerning Audiovisual Performances (June, 1998)

Meeting code: AP/CE/2
Date: June 8 to June 12, 1998
venue: Geneva, Switzerland
Meeting Documents URL: https://www.wipo.int/meetings/en/details.jsp?meeting_id=3453

2.

视听表演议定书专家委员会会议

（1998年6月）

会议代码：AP/CE/2

会议日期：1998年6月8—12日

会议地点：瑞士日内瓦

会议文件链接：https://www.wipo.int/meetings/en/details.jsp?meeting_id=3453

2.1 Proposals and Other Submissions Received from WIPO Member States and the European Community

Document Code: AP/CE/2/2
Language: English
URL: https://www.wipo.int/edocs/mdocs/copyright/en/ap_ce_2/ap_ce_2_2.pdf
Chinese Translation: Not Available.
URL: N/A

COMMITTEE OF EXPERTS
ON A PROTOCOL
CONCERNING AUDIOVISUAL PERFORMANCES
Second Session
GENEVA, JUNE 8 TO 12, 1998

proposals and other submissions received from WIPO member states and the European community

Memorandum prepared by the International Bureau

Ⅰ. INTRODUCTION

1. The Committee of Experts on a Protocol concerning Audiovisual Performances, during its first session, on September 19, 1997, adopted the following recommendation:

"(i) the second session of the Committee should take place in the period of

2.1 世界知识产权组织成员国和欧洲共同体提交的提案和其他材料

文件编号：AP/CE/2/2
文件语言：英语
文件链接：https://www.wipo.int/edocs/mdocs/copyright/en/ap_ce_2/ap_ce_2_2.pdf
中文文本：无
文件链接：无

视听表演议定书专家委员会

第二届会议
1998年6月8日至12日，日内瓦

世界知识产权组织成员国和欧共体提交的提案和其他材料

国际局编写的备忘录

一、介绍

1. 视听表演议定书专家委员会在1997年9月19日第一届会议上通过了以下建议：

"(i)委员会第二届会议将于1998年6月5日开始举行，但不迟于1998年

May-June 1998, but not later than during the week starting June 8, 1998; it is recommended that the Governing Bodies of WIPO take a decision about the dates of the second session during their September-October 1997 series of meetings;

(ii) the International Bureau should invite the Governments of WIPO Member States and the European Community to submit by January 15, 1998, proposals, preferably in treaty language, concerning a protocol to the WIPO Performances and Phonograms Treaty on audiovisual performances;

(iii) the International Bureau should distribute the proposals, together with comparative tables, if appropriate, by the end of February 1998, to those invited to the second session of the Committee who should be the same as those invited to the first session…" (see document AP/CE/I/4, paragraph 12).

The WIPO General Assembly approved this recommendation during its twenty-first session (see document WO/GA/XXI/13, paragraph 205).

2. On October 24, 1997, the International Bureau sent a circular letter to WIPO Member States and the European Community inviting them to submit proposals as indicated in item (ii) of the above-quoted decision.

3. This memorandum contains, in Annex I, the texts of the proposals that the International Bureau has received by January 15, 1998, namely from Argentina, Colombia, the European Community and its Member States, and Ghana, as well as information received from Australia and suggestions for discussion received from Japan, in alphabetical order.

4. In Annex II of the memorandum, a comparative table of the four above-mentioned proposals is contained. Footnotes in Annex II refer to related suggestions for discussion made by Japan.

[Annex I follows]

6月8日开始的一周；建议世界知识产权组织主管理事机构在1997年9月至10月系列会议期间就第二届会议的日期作出决定；

（ii）国际局应请世界知识产权组织成员国和欧共体成员国于1998年1月15日之前提交WPPT关于视听表演的议定书的提案，提案最好以条约的语言提出；

（iii）国际局应在1998年2月底之前将提案连同比较表分发给应邀参加委员会第二届会议的成员，这些成员应与应邀参加第一届会议的成员相同……”（见AP/CE/I/4号文件，第12段）。

世界知识产权组织大会第二十一届会议核准了该项建议（见WO/GA/XXI/13号文件，第205段）。

2. 1997年10月24日，国际局致函世界知识产权组织成员国和欧共体成员国，请它们按照上述决定第（2）项的规定递交提案。

3. 本备忘录附件一载有国际局于1998年1月15日前收到的提案案文（按字母顺序），即阿根廷、哥伦比亚、欧共体成员国和加纳的提案案文，以及澳大利亚提供的资料和日本提出的讨论建议。

4. 本备忘录附件二载有上述四项提案的比较表，附件二的脚注系关于日本提出的供讨论的相关建议。

（后接附件一）

ANNEX I
TEXTS OF THE PROPOSALS AND OTHER SUBMISSIONS RECEIVED FROM WIPO MEMBER STATES AND THE EUROPEAN COMMUNITY

ARGENTINA
PROTOCOL CONCERNING AUDIOVISUAL PERFORMANCES

Art. 1

1. Nothing in this Treaty shall derogate from the existing obligations that Contracting Parties have to each other under the International Convention for the Protection of Performers, Producers of Phonograms and Broadcasting Organizations done in Rome on October 26, 1961 (hereinafter "the Rome Convention").

2. Protection granted under this Treaty shall leave intact and shall in no way affect the protection of copyright in literary and artistic works. Consequently, no provision of this Treaty may be interpreted as prejudicing such protection.

3. This Treaty shall not have any connection with, nor shall it prejudice any rights and obligations under, any another treaties.

Art. 2: Definitions

For the purposes of this Treaty:

a)"performers" are actors, singers, musicians, dancers and other persons who act, sing, deliver, play in, interpret or otherwise perform literary or artistic works or expressions of folklore;

b)"audiovisual fixation" means the incorporation of sounds and images, or a representation thereof, from which they may be perceived, reproduced or communicated by means of a device;

c)"publication" means the offering to the public of copies of a performance fixed in an audiovisual work with the consent of the owners of the rights therein, provided that such copies are offered to the public in sufficient quantity;

d)"broadcasting" means the transmission by wireless means, for public reception, of sounds or of images and sounds, or representations thereof; such transmission by satellite is also "broadcasting;" the transmission of encrypted

附件一
从世界知识产权组织及欧共体成员国收到的提案和其他材料的案文

阿根廷
关于视听表演的协议书

第 1 条

1. 本条约的任何内容均不得减损缔约方相互之间依照 1961 年 10 月 26 日在罗马签订的《保护表演者、录音制品制作者和广播组织国际公约》(以下简称《罗马公约》)已承担的现有义务。

2. 依本条约给予的保护不得触动或以任何方式影响对文学和艺术作品版权的保护。因此,本条约的任何内容均不得被解释为损害此种保护。

3. 本条约不得与任何其他条约有任何关联,亦不得损害任何其他条约所规定的任何权利和义务。

第 2 条:定义

在本条约中:

a)"表演者"是指演员、歌唱家、音乐家、舞蹈家以及对文学或艺术作品或民间文学艺术表达进行表演、歌唱、演说、朗诵、演奏、表现或以其他方式进行表演的其他人员;

b)"视听录制品"是指声音和图像的融合物,或其表现物,从中通过某种装置可感觉、复制或传播该活动图像;

c)"发表"是指经视听作品的所有者同意,向公众提供表演活动的视听作品的复制件,且这些复制件必须以足够数量提供给公众;

d)"广播"是指以无线方式向公众传输声音,或图像和声音,或图像和声音的表现物的过程;通过卫星进行的此种传输亦为"广播";如果通过广播组织或经广播组织同意向公众提供解密信号的手段,则加密信号的传输属于"广播";

signals is "broadcasting" where the means of decrypting the signals are made available to the public by the broadcasting organization or with its consent;

e)"communication to the public" means the transmission to the public, by any means other than broadcasting, of the sounds and images of a performance.

Art. 3: Beneficiaries of protection under this Treaty

1. Contracting Parties shall accord the protection provided for in this Treaty to performers who are nationals of other Contracting Parties.

2. Nationals of other Contracting Parties shall be understood to be those performers who would meet the criteria of eligibility for protection provided for in the Rome Convention if all the Contracting Parties to this Treaty were Contracting States of the said Convention. With respect to those eligibility criteria, Contracting Parties shall apply the relevant definitions in Article 2 of this Treaty.

Any Contracting Party availing itself, mutatis mutandis, of the possibilities provided for in Article 5(3) of the Berne Convention or, for the purposes of Article 5 of the same Convention, Article 17 thereof shall make a notification as provided in those provisions to the Director General of the World Intellectual Property Organization (WIPO).

Art. 4: National treatment

Each Contracting Party shall accord to nationals of other Contracting Parties, as defined in Article 3(2), the treatment that it accords to its own nationals with regard to the exclusive rights specifically granted in this Treaty.

Art. 5: Moral rights

The performer shall have the following rights in relation to his performances in audiovisual works:

1. to be identified by the mention of his name or pseudonym, except where its omission is dictated by the manner in which the performance is to be used;

2. to object to any distortion of his performance that would be prejudicial to his professional standing.

The performer may authorize the making of changes to his performance. Such authorization shall only be valid when it is given in writing.

The rights accorded to the performer in the foregoing paragraphs shall be maintained, after his death, at least until the expiry of his economic rights, and shall

e)“向公众传播”是指以广播以外的任何方式向公众传播表演的声音和图像。

第 3 条：本条约保护的受益者

1. 缔约方应向其他缔约方国民的表演提供本条约规定的保护。

2. 如果本条约的所有缔约方都是《罗马公约》的缔约国，其他缔约方的国民应被理解为符合《罗马公约》所规定的保护资格标准的表演者。关于这些资格标准，缔约方应适用本条约第 2 条中的有关定义。

任何缔约方应比照利用《伯尔尼公约》第 5 条第（3）款提供的可能性，或为同一公约第 5 条、第 17 条的目的，向世界知识产权组织总干事发出通知。

第 4 条：国民待遇

按照本条约第 3 条第（2）款的规定，在本条约所专门授予的专有权方面，每一缔约方均应将其给予本国国民的待遇给予其他缔约方的国民。

第 5 条：精神权利

表演者对视听作品中的表演享有下列权利：

1. 通过提及其姓名或化名来确定其身份，除非因表演的使用方式而必须不提及；

2. 反对对其表演进行任何有损于其专业地位的歪曲。

表演者可以授权修改其表演，有效授权须以书面形式作出。

根据上述各款授予表演者的权利在其死亡后应继续保留，至少到其经济权利期满为止，并应由被要求提供保护的缔约方立法所授权的个人或机构行使。

be exercisable by the persons or institutions authorized by the legislation of the Contracting Party in which protection is claimed.

Art. 6: Economic rights

1. Economic rights of performers in their unfixed performances

Performers shall enjoy the exclusive right to authorize the following in relation to their unfixed performances:

a) the broadcasting and communication to the public of their unfixed performances, except where the performance is already a broadcast performance;

b) the fixation of their unfixed performances.

2. Economic rights of performers in their performances fixed in audiovisual works

Performers shall have the exclusive right to authorize the following in relation to their performances fixed in audiovisual works:

a) Reproduction:

the direct or indirect reproduction of their performances in any manner or form.

b) Distribution:

the making available to the public of copies of their performances by sale or other transfer of ownership.

Nothing in this Treaty shall affect the freedom of Contracting Parties to determine the conditions under which exhaustion of the right under subparagraph (b) applies after the first sale or other transfer of ownership of the original or a copy of the performance fixed with the performer's authorization.

c) Rental:

the commercial rental to the public of copies of their performances as provided in the national legislation of Contracting Parties, even after distribution effected by the performer or with his authorization.

d) Broadcasting and communication to the public:

the broadcasting and communication to the public of their performances.

Unless otherwise agreed, consent given for the fixing of the performance in an audiovisual work shall constitute authorization of broadcasting and communication to the public by means of subscription systems.

第6条：经济权利

1. 表演者对其尚未录制的表演的经济权利

表演者对其尚未录制的表演应享有专有权，授权下列行为：

a）广播和向公众传播其尚未录制的表演，除非该表演本身已属广播表演；

b）录制其尚未录制的表演。

2. 表演者对其以视听作品录制的表演的经济权利

表演者对其以视听作品录制的表演享有专有权，授权下列行为：

a）复制：

以任何方式或形式对其以视听作品录制的表演直接或间接地进行复制。

b）发行：

通过销售或其他转让所有权的形式向公众提供其以视听作品录制的表演的复制件。

对于已录制表演的原件或复制件经表演者授权被首次销售或以其他形式转让所有权之后适用（b）项中权利的用尽所依据的条件（如有此种条件），本条约的任何内容均不得影响缔约方确定该条件的自由。

c）出租：

根据缔约国的国家法律规定向公众出租其表演的复制件，即使该复制件已由表演者发行或经表演者授权发行。

d）广播和向公众传播：

广播和向公众传播其以视听作品录制的表演。

除非另有约定，表演者同意以视听作品录制其表演的，即构成对通过订阅系统广播和向公众传播之授权。

e) Interactive services:

the making available to the public of their performances, by wire or wireless means, in such a way that members of the public may access them from a place and at a time individually chosen by them.

In the absence of specific provisions in individual contracts, the economic rights provided for in this Article shall apply.

Art. 7: Limitations and exceptions

1. Contracting Parties may provide the same kinds of limitation on or exception to the protection of performers as they provide at present in connection with the protection of copyright in literary and artistic works.

2. The Contracting Parties shall confine any limitation of or exceptions to the rights provided for in this Treaty to certain special cases that do not conflict with the normal exploitation of the performance fixed in audiovisual works or unreasonably prejudice the legitimate interests of the performer.

3. The term of protection to be granted to performers under this Treaty shall be at least 50years, calculated from the end of the year in which the performance was fixed.

4. Contracting Parties shall apply the provisions of Article 18 of the Berne Convention, *mutatis mutandis*, to the rights of performers provided for in this Treaty.

5. This Treaty shall not prejudice any rights acquired in any Contracting Party prior to the date of its entry into force for that Party.

6. A Contracting Party shall not be obliged to apply the provisions of this Treaty to performances given or audiovisual fixations made prior to its entry into force for that Party.

Art. 8: Obligations concerning technological measures

Contracting Parties shall provide adequate legal protection and effective legal remedies against the circumvention of effective technological measures that are used by performers in connection with the exercise of their rights under this Treaty and that restrict acts, in relation to their performances fixed in audiovisual works, that have not been authorized by the performers concerned or are not permitted by law.

e）交互式服务：

以有线或无线方式向公众提供其表演，使公众可以在个人选择的时间和地点获得其表演。

合同无具体规定的，适用本条规定的经济权利。

第7条：限制与例外

1. 缔约各方可给予表演者与其现行立法中给予文学和艺术作品的版权保护相同种类的限制或例外。

2. 缔约各方应使本条约中所规定权利的任何限制或例外仅限于某些不与表演的正常利用相冲突，也不致不合理地损害表演者合法利益的特殊情况。

3. 依本条约给予表演者的保护期，应自表演录制之年年终算起，至少持续到50年期满为止。

4. 缔约方应比照适用《伯尔尼公约》第18条关于表演者权利的规定。

5. 本条约不得损害任何缔约国在条约对其生效之日前获得的任何权利。

6. 缔约各方没有义务将本条约的规定适用于本条约在该缔约方生效之前所作出的表演或者视听录制品中。

第8条：关于技术措施的义务

缔约国应提供充分的法律保护和有效的法律补救措施，防止表演者在行使本条约规定的权利时规避有效的技术措施，限制未经有关表演者授权或法律不允许的与视听作品中的表演有关的行为。

Art. 9: Obligations concerning rights management information

1. Contracting Parties shall provide adequate and effective legal remedies against any person who deliberately commits any of the following acts knowing, or with respect to civil remedies having reasonable grounds to know, that it will induce, enable, facilitate or conceal an infringement of any right covered by this Treaty:

i) removes or alters any rights management information without authority;

ii) distributes, imports for distribution, broadcasts, communicates or makes available to the public, without authority, performances or copies thereof knowing that electronic rights management information has been removed or altered without authority.

2. As used in this Article, “rights management information” means information that identifies the performer, his performance or the audiovisual producer, or information on the terms and conditions of use of the performance fixed in an audiovisual work.

Art. 10: Formalities

The enjoyment and exercise of the rights provided for in this Treaty shall not be subject to any formality.

Art. 11: Provisions on enforcement of rights

1. Contracting Parties undertake to adopt, in accordance with their legal systems, the measures necessary to ensure the application of this Treaty.

2. Contracting Parties shall ensure that enforcement procedures are available under their law so as to permit effective action against any act of infringement of rights covered by this Treaty, and in addition prevent further infringements from being committed.

AUSTRALIA

The Australian Government is currently determining its position on a Protocol to the WPPT on Audiovisual Performances, and on the issue of providing for greater performers’ rights in sound recordings, modeled on those in the WPPT. Consequently, the Government is not able to submit a proposal to the International Bureau by January 15, 1998, as invited.

The Australian Government is committed to giving careful consideration to

第 9 条：关于权利管理信息的义务

1. 缔约各方应规定适当和有效的法律补救办法，制止任何人明知、或就民事补救而言有合理根据知道其行为会诱使、促成、便利或包庇对本条约所涵盖的任何权利的侵犯而故意从事以下行为：

（i）未经许可去除或改变任何权利管理的电子信息；

（ii）未经许可发行、为发行目的进口、广播、向公众传播或提供明知已被未经许可去除或改变权利管理电子信息的表演或其复制件。

2. 在本条中，“权利管理信息”系指识能够别表演者、表演者的表演或视听制作者的信息，或关于视听作品中录制表演的使用条款和条件的信息。

第 10 条：手续

享有和行使本议定书所规定的权利无须履行任何手续。

第 11 条：关于权利行使的条款

1. 缔约方承诺根据其法律制度采取必要的措施，以确保本条约的适用。

2. 缔约方应确保根据其法律规定执法程序，以便对任何侵犯本条约所述权利的行为采取有效行动，并防止发生进一步的侵权行为。

澳大利亚

澳大利亚政府目前正在确定其对 WPPT 关于视听表演的议定书的立场，以及“依照 WPPT 相关规定允许表演者对录音制品享有更大权利”这一问题的立场。因此，澳大利亚政府不能应邀在 1998 年 1 月 15 日之前向国际局提交提案。

澳大利亚政府正在认真考虑视听表演相关问题，以及“依照 WPPT 相关

the issue of audiovisual performances, in addition to greater rights for performers in sound recordings based on the WPPT. As part of determining our position on these issues, I am pleased to note that the Australian Government has recently released a discussion paper, "Performers' Intellectual Property Rights," to solicit the views of domestic interests. That discussion paper is available at http://law.gov.au/publications/performers.htm.

Australia looks forward to participating in the next session of the Committee of Experts on a Protocol concerning Audiovisual Performances. By that time, we hope that views received and consultations carried out, following on from the release of the discussion paper, will enable us to contribute substantively to the Committee's discussions.

COLOMBIA

PROTOCOL TO THE WIPO PERFORMANCES AND PHONOGRAMS TREATY CONCERNING AUDIOVISUAL PERFORMANCES

Safeguarding of copyright

Protection provided for in this Protocol shall leave intact and in no way affect the protection of copyright in literary and artistic works. Consequently, none of the provisions of this Protocol shall be interpreted as prejudicing such protection.

Definitions

- Performer
- Audiovisual work
- Fixation
- Publication
- Rental
- Broadcasting
- Communication to the public

(This proposal refers to the concepts to be defined, but does not define them).

Moral rights of performers

The performer shall have the following rights in relation to his audiovisual performances:

(a) to demand that his name appear in connection with or be associated with every performance that takes place;

规定允许表演者对录音制品享有更大权利”这一问题。值得注意的是，在确定相关立场的过程中，澳大利亚政府最近发表了一份题为“表演者的知识产权”的讨论文件，以征求国内利益主体的意见，该讨论文件可在 http://law.gov.au/publications/performers.htm. 网站中获得。

澳大利亚期待参加视听表演议定书专家委员会的下届会议。届时，我们希望在讨论文件发布后收到的意见和进行的协商能够使我们为委员会的讨论作出实质性贡献。

哥伦比亚
关于 WPPT 视听表演的议定书

版权保护

依本议定书给予的保护不得触动或以任何方式影响对文学和艺术作品版权的保护。因此，本条约的任何内容均不得被解释为损害此种保护。

定义

- 表演者
- 视听作品
- 录制
- 发行
- 出租
- 广播
- 向公众传播

（本提案提到了有待定义的概念，但没有对其进行定义）

表演者的精神权利

表演者对其视听表演享有下列权利：

a）要求自己的名字出现在每场表演中或与表演相联系；

(b) to object to any distortion, mutilation or other violation of his performance that might damage his standing or reputation.

Term of moral rights

The rights accorded to the performer under the foregoing Article shall be maintained, after his death, at least until the expiry of his economic rights, and shall be exercisable by the persons or institutions authorized by the legislation of the Contracting Party in which protection is claimed.

Economic rights of performers in their unfixed performances

Performers shall enjoy the exclusive right to authorize:

a) the broadcasting and communication to the public of their unfixed performances, except where the performance is already a broadcast performance;

b) the fixation of their unfixed performances.

Right of reproduction

Performers shall enjoy the exclusive right to authorize the direct or indirect, permanent or temporary reproduction, in any manner or form, of their performances fixed in any medium.

Right of distribution

Performers shall enjoy the exclusive right to authorize the making available to the public, by sale or other transfer of ownership, of the original and copies of their performances fixed in any medium.

Nothing in this Protocol shall affect the right of Contracting Parties to determine the conditions, if any, on which the exhaustion of rights applies after the first sale or other transfer of ownership of the original or a copy of a performance fixed in any medium.

Right of rental

Performers shall enjoy the exclusive right to authorize the rental of the original and copies of their performances fixed in any medium, even after distribution thereof by the performer or with his authorization.

Right of making available of fixed performances

Performers shall enjoy the exclusive right to authorize the making available of their performances fixed in any medium, by wire or wireless means, in such a way that members of the public may access them from a place and at a time individually

b）禁止任何可能损害其地位或名誉的歪曲、篡改或其他侵犯其表演的行为。

精神权利条款

根据上述条款授予表演者的权利在其死亡后应继续保留，至少到其经济权利期满为止，并由被要求提供保护的缔约方立法所授权的个人或机构行使。

表演者对其尚未录制的表演的经济权利

表演者应当享有专有权：

a）广播和向公众传播其尚未录制的表演，除非该表演本身已属广播表演；

b）录制其尚未录制的表演。

复制权

表演者应享有授权对其录制在任何媒介上的表演，直接或间接地进行永久性或临时性复制的专有权。

发行权

表演者应享有授权他人以销售或其他转让所有权的形式向公众提供其录制在任何媒介上的表演的原件或复制件的专有权。

无论表演被录制在何种媒介上，在该录制件的原件或者复制件被首次销售或者以其他方式转让了所有权之后，该录制件上的权利用尽。本议定书的任何规定均不影响缔约国（在国内法上）对权利用尽施加限制条件的权力。

出租权

表演者应享有专有权，以授权将其录制在任何媒介上的表演的原件和复制件向公众进行出租，即使该原件或复制件已由表演者发行或经表演者授权发行。

提供已录制表演的权利

表演者应享有专有权，以授权通过有线或无线的方式向公众提供其录制在任何媒介上的表演，使该表演可为公众中的成员在其个人选定的地点和时间获得。

chosen by them.

Limitations and exceptions

Contracting Parties may, in their national legislation, provide the same kinds of limitation on or exception to the protection of performers as they provide at present in connection with the protection of copyright in literary and artistic works.

Contracting Parties shall confine any limitation of or exceptions to rights provided for in this Protocol to certain special cases that do not conflict with the normal exploitation of the performance or unreasonably prejudice the legitimate interests of the performer.

Term of protection of economic rights

The economic rights accorded to performers shall have a term of 50 years following the date of audiovisual fixation.

Obligations concerning technological measures

Contracting Parties shall provide adequate legal protection and effective legal remedies against the circumvention of effective technological measures that are used by performers in connection with the exercise of their rights under this Protocol.

Obligations concerning rights management information

Contracting Parties shall provide adequate and effective legal remedies against any person who deliberately commits any of the following acts knowing, or with respect to civil remedies having reasonable grounds to know, that it will induce, enable, facilitate or conceal an infringement of any right covered by this Protocol:

- removes or alters any electronic rights management information without authority;

- distributes, imports for distribution, broadcasts, communicates or makes available to the public, without authority, performances or copies of fixed performances knowing that the electronic rights management information has been removed or altered without authority.

- "Rights management information" means information that identifies the performer, his performance, the fixation of the performance and the owner of any right in the performance or fixation, or information on the terms and conditions of use of the performance or fixation, and any numbers or codes representing that information where any of those items of information is attached to a copy of a fixed

限制与例外

缔约各方可以在其国内立法中，给予表演者与其国内关于文学和艺术作品的版权保护相同种类的限制或例外的保护规定。

缔约各方应使本议定书中所规定权利的任何限制或例外仅限于某些不与表演的正常利用相冲突，也不致不合理地损害表演者合法利益的特殊情况。

经济权利保护期限

给予表演者经济权利的期限为视听录制品被录制之日起 50 年。

关于技术措施的义务

缔约各方应规定适当的法律保护和有效的法律补救办法，制止规避由表演者为行使本条约所规定的权利而使用并限制对其表演实施未经该有关表演者许可的或法律不允许的行为的有效技术措施。

有关权利管理信息的义务

缔约各方应规定适当和有效的法律补救办法，制止任何人明知、或就民事补救而言有合理根据知道其行为会诱使、促成、便利或包庇对本条约所涵盖的任何权利的侵犯而故意从事以下行为：

– 未经许可去除或改变任何权利管理的电子信息；

– 未经许可发行、为发行目的进口、广播、向公众传播或提供明知已被未经许可去除或改变权利管理电子信息的表演或其复制件。

– “权利管理信息”是指能够识别表演者、表演者的表演、表演的录制品、对表演或表演的录制品拥有任何权利的所有人的信息，或有关使用表演或表演的录制品的条款和条件的信息，以及代表此种信息的任何数字或代码，各该项信息均附在已录制表演的复制件上，或在向公众传播时或向公众提供已录制表演时出现。

performance or appears in connection with the communication or making available to the public of a fixed performance.

Formalities and independence of protection

The enjoyment and exercise of the rights provided for in this Protocol shall not be subject to any formality.

Such enjoyment and exercise shall be independent of the existence of protection in the country of origin of the performance.

Reservations

No reservations to this Protocol shall be permitted.

Application in time

Contracting Parties shall not apply the provisions of this Protocol to performances that have taken place prior to the date of its entry into force.

EUROPEAN COMMUNITY AND ITS MEMBER STATES

PROTOCOL TO THE WIPO PERFORMANCES AND PHONOGRAMS TREATY, CONCERNING AUDIOVISUAL PERFORMANCES

Preamble

The Contracting Parties

Wishing to ensure an adequate level of protection for audiovisual performances, especially in the digital environment;

Noting that the WIPO Performances and Phonograms Treaty does not cover the rights of performers in the audiovisual fixation of their unfixed performances, nor the exploitation of their audiovisually fixed performances;

Referring to the resolution concerning audiovisual performances adopted by the Diplomatic Conference on Certain Copyright and Neighboring Rights Questions on December 20, 1996;

Have agreed as follows:

CHAPTER I

GENERAL PROVISIONS

Article 1

Relation to Other Conventions

(1) This Treaty constitutes a Protocol to the WIPO Performances and Phonograms Treaty done in Geneva, 20 December 1996 (hereinafter the "WIPO

手续和保护的独立性

享有和行使本议定书所规定的权利无须履行任何手续。

权利的享有和行使应独立于表演的起源国是否存在保护。

保留

本议定书不得作出任何保留。

适用的时限

缔约各方不得将本议定书的规定适用于本条约对该缔约方生效之前进行的表演。

欧共体成员国
关于 WPPT 视听表演的议定书

序言

缔约方

为确保对视听表演，特别是在数字环境中的视听表演提供足够的保护；

注意到《WIPO 表演和录音制品条约》对表演者的保护并未延伸到对其尚未录制的表演进行视听录制的权利，也未涵盖对其已录制的视听表演进行利用的权利；

提及 1996 年 12 月 20 日关于版权和邻接权若干问题的外交会议通过的《关于视听表演的决议》；

达成协议如下：

第一章
一般条款

第 1 条

与其他公约的关系

(1)该条约系 1996 年 12 月 20 日在日内瓦签订的《世界知识产权组织表演和录音制品条约》(以下简称 WIPO 条约)的议定书。

Treaty").

(2) Nothing in this Protocol shall derogate from existing obligations that Contracting Parties have to each other under the WIPO Treaty.

(3) Protection granted under this protocol shall leave intact and shall in no way affect the protection of copyright in literary and artistic works. Consequently, no provisions of this protocol may be interpreted as prejudicing such protection.

Article 2

Definitions

(1) The Contracting Parties shall apply, *mutatis mutandis*, the definitions set out in Article 2 paragraphs (a), (e), (f) and (g) of the WIPO Treaty in connection with the protection granted under this Protocol.

(2) For the purposes of this Protocol, "audiovisual fixation" means the embodiment of moving images, whether or not accompanied by sound, or the representations thereof, from which they can be perceived, reproduced or communicated through a device.

Article 3

Beneficiaries of protection under this protocol

The Contracting Parties shall accord the protection provided under this protocol to performers who are nationals of other Contracting Parties.

CHAPTER II

RIGHTS OF PERFORMERS IN THEIR AUDIOVISUAL PERFORMANCES

Article 4

Rights of performers in their unfixed audiovisual performances

The Contracting Parties shall accord, mutatis mutandis, to performers, as regards their unfixed audiovisual performances, whether or not accompanied by sound, the same rights as those granted under the WIPO Treaty to performers as regards their live aural performances, namely the rights provided under Article 5 (Moral Rights) and Article 6 (Economic rights of Performers in their unfixed performances).

Article 5

Rights of performers in audiovisual fixations of their performances

The Contracting Parties shall accord, mutatis mutandis, to performers, as regards the use of audiovisual fixations of their performances, the same rights as

(2)本议定书的任何规定均不得减损缔约方根据 WIPO 条约彼此承担的现有义务。

(3)依本议定书给予的保护不得触动或以任何方式影响对文学和艺术作品版权的保护。因此,本条约的任何内容均不得被解释为损害此种保护。

第 2 条

定义

(1)缔约各方应比照适用 WIPO 条约第 2 条(a)、(e)、(f)和(g)款中关于本议定书所给予保护的定义。

(2)在本议定书中,"视听录制品"系指活动图像的体现物,不论是否伴有声音或声音表现物,从中通过某种装置可感知、复制或传播该活动图像。

第 3 条

本议定书保护的受益者

缔约各方应向其他缔约方国民的表演者提供本议定书规定的保护。

第二章
表演者在视听表演中的权利

第 4 条

表演者对其尚未录制的表演的权利

缔约各方应比照适用 WIPO 条约第 5 条(精神权利)和第 6 条(表演者在尚未录制表演中的经济权利)所赋予的权利,授予表演者对其现场表演和尚未录制表演的权利,无论其是否伴有声音。

第 5 条

表演者对其表演的视听录制品享有的权利

缔约各方在使用表演者的视听录制品时,应比照适用 WIPO 条约第 5 条(精神权利)、第 7 条(复制权)、第 8 条(发行权)、第 9 条(出租权)和第 10 条

those granted under the WIPO Treaty to performers as regards the use of their performances fixed in phonograms, namely the rights provided under Articles 5(Moral Rights), 7 (Right of Reproduction),8 (Right of Distribution), 9 (Right of Rental) and 10 (Right of Making Available of Fixed Performances) of the WIPO Treaty.

Article 6

Application of certain substantive provisions of the WIPO Treaty

The Contracting Parties shall apply, *mutatis mutandis*, in respect of protection granted under this Protocol, the provisions of Articles 4 (National Treatment), 16 (Limitations and Exceptions), 17 (Term of Protection), 18 (Obligations concerning Technological Measures), 19 (Obligations concerning Rights Management Information), 20 (Formalities),22 (Application in Time) and 23 (Provisions on Enforcement of Rights) of the WIPO Treaty.

Article 7

Reservations

No reservations to this Protocol shall be permitted.

CHAPTER III

ADMINISTRATIVE AND FINAL CLAUSES

Article 8

Application of certain administrative provisions

The Contracting Parties shall have an Assembly. This Assembly shall be the same as the one created by the WIPO Treaty and its functioning shall be governed, *mutatis mutandis*, by Article 24 of the WIPO Treaty.

Article 9

Eligibility for becoming party to the Treaty

Any party to the WIPO Treaty may become party to this Protocol.

Article 10

Signature of the Protocol

This Protocol shall be open for signature until... by any Member State of WIPO and by the European Community.

（提供权）规定中授予表演者对其已录制表演的权利相同的权利。

第 6 条

WIPO 条约某些实质性条款的适用

对于根据本议定书给予的保护，缔约各方应比照适用 WIPO 条约第 4 条（国民待遇）、第 16 条（限制与例外）、第 17 条（保护期限）、第 18 条（有关技术措施的义务）、第 19 条（有关权利管理信息的义务）、第 20 条（手续）、第 22 条（适用的时限）和第 23 条（关于权利行使的条款）的规定。

第 7 条

保留

本议定书不得作出任何保留。

第三章

行政和最后条款

第 8 条

某些行政性规定的适用

缔约方应设大会，大会应与 WIPO 条约设立的大会相同，其运作比照适用 WIPO 条约第 24 条的规定。

第 9 条

加入条约的资格

WIPO 条约的任何缔约方都可以加入本议定书。

第 10 条

议定书的签署

本议定书开放以供任何世界知识产权组织成员国和欧共体成员国签署，直至……

Article 11

Entry into force of the Protocol

This Protocol shall enter into force, following the date of entry into force of the WIPO Treaty, three months after 5 instruments of ratification or accession by States have been deposited with the Director General of WIPO.

Article 12

Final clauses

The provisions of Articles 25 (International Bureau), 27 (Rights and Obligations under the Treaty), 30 (Effective Date of Becoming Party of the Treaty), 31 (Denunciation of the Treaty), 32 (Languages of the Treaty) and 33 (Depository) of the WIPO Treaty shall apply, *mutatis mutandis*.

GHANA

PROTOCOL TO THE WIPO PERFORMANCES AND PHONOGRAMS TREATY (WPPT) FOR THE PROTECTION OF AUDIOVISUAL PERFORMANCES AND PRODUCERS

I. RIGHTS OF PRODUCERS OF AUDIOVISUAL WORKS

1. Right of reproduction

Producers shall enjoy the exclusive right to authorize the direct or indirect reproductionof their works in any manner or form.

2. Right of distribution

Producers shall enjoy the exclusive right to authorize the availability of the original and copies of their works to the public through sale or other transfer of ownership.

3. Right of rental

Producers shall enjoy the exclusive right to authorize commercial rental of the original and copies of their works to the public, except, if such commercial rental has led to widespread copying of the works which materially impairs the exclusive right of reproduction.

Notwithstanding the above provisions:

a) Both parties i. e. the producers and performers of audiovisual works may by contract determine the extent to which the rights granted to the performers if any are to be exercised in a particular performance.

第 11 条

议定书生效

本议定书自 WIPO 条约生效之日起生效，即自各国向世界知识产权组织总干事交存 5 份法律文本或加入书之日起 3 个月后生效。

第 12 条

最后条款

本议定书比照适用 WIPO 条约第 25 条（国际局）、第 27 条（条约规定的权利和义务）、第 30 条（成为条约缔约方的生效日期）、第 31 条（退约）、第 32 条（条约的语文）和第 33 条（保存人）的规定。

加纳

关于视听表演的 WPPT 议定书

Ⅰ. 视听作品制作者的权利

1. 复制权

制作者应享有授权以任何方式或形式对其作品直接或间接地进行复制的专有权。

2. 发行权

制作者享有授权通过销售或其他所有权转让形式向公众提供其作品原件或复制件的专有权。

3. 出租权

制作者应享有授权将其作品原件和复制件向公众进行商业性出租的专有权，除非商业性出租已导致作品的广泛复制，从而严重损害表演者的专有复制权。

虽有上述规定：

a）双方，即视听作品的制作者和表演者，可以通过合同约定在某一特定表演中行使给予表演者的权利的程度。

b) In order to ensure that the exploitation of the work is not unnecessarily stifled, the producer may exercise the rights of reproduction, distribution and rental granted to the performer on such conditions as the producer and performer may agree upon.

4. Right of communication to the public of audiovisual productions

(1) Producers shall enjoy the exclusive right to authorize the availability of their works by wire or wireless means, to the public in such a way that members of the public may access them from a place and at a time individually chosen by them.

(2) Nothing in this Treaty shall exclude Contracting Parties from authorizing the exercise of the rights in paragraph 4(1) by a system of Collective Administration for and on behalf of the Contracting Parties.

II. RIGHTS IN AUDIOVISUAL PERFORMANCES

1. Right of reproduction

Performers shall enjoy the exclusive right to authorize the direct or indirect reproduction of their audiovisual performances fixed in any manner or form.

2. Right of distribution

Performers shall enjoy the exclusive right to authorize the availability of the original and copies of their works to the public through sale or other transfer of ownership.

3. Right of rental

Performers shall enjoy the exclusive right to authorize the commercial rental of the original and copies of performances to the public, except, if the commercial rental has led to widespread copying of the works which materially impairs the exclusive right of reproduction. Notwithstanding the above provisions:

a) Both parties i. e. the producers and performers of audiovisual works may by contract determine the extent to which the rights granted to the performers if any are to be exercised in a particular performance.

b) In order to ensure that the exploitation of the work is not unnecessarily stifled, the producer may exercise the rights of reproduction, distribution and rental granted to the performer on such conditions as the producer and performer may agree upon.

b）为使确保作品的利用不受到损害，制作者可在与表演者约定的情况下行使授予给表演者的复制权、发行权和出租权。

4. 就视听制品享有的向公众传播权

（1）制作者应享有授权以有线或无线方式向公众提供其作品，其提供方式使公众能够在其个人选定的时间和地点获得作品。

（2）但本条约的任何规定均不得排除缔约方授权集体管理组织为了缔约方和代表缔约方行使第4条第（1）款所规定的权利。

II. 视听表演中的权利

1. 复制权

表演者应享有授权直接或间接复制其以任何方式或形式录制的视听表演的专有权。

2. 发行权

表演者应享有通过出售或以其他方式转让所有权的方式授权向公众提供其作品的原件和复制件的专有权。

3. 出租权

表演者应享有授权向公众商业出租其表演的原件和复制件的专有权，但如果商业性出租导致作品被广泛复制，从而严重损害了复制权，则不在此列。

尽管有上述规定，但：

a）双方，即视听作品的制作者和表演者，可以通过合同确定授予表演者的权利在特定的表演中的行使范围。

b）为了确保作品的利用不受到不必要的限制，制作人可以按照制作人和表演者商定的条件行使授予表演者的复制、发行和出租的权利。

4. Right of communication to the public of audiovisual productions

(1) Performers shall enjoy the exclusive right to authorize the availability of their works to the public by wire or wireless means, in such a way that members of the public may access them from a place and at a time individually chosen by them.

(2) But nothing in this Treaty shall exclude Contracting Parties from authorizing the exercise of the rights in paragraph 4(1) by a system of Collective Administration for and on behalf of the Contracting Parties.

JAPAN

With a view to exploring an appropriate national system concerning audiovisual performances which could encourage creation of performances as well as use of such performances in the age of new media, the Government of Japan has established an *ad hoc* Committee comprised of interested circles, lawyers and scholars in November 1997. While the discussions of this Committee on possible new rights and measures for use, which would be reflected in Japan's position for a Protocol concerning Audiovisual Performances, still continue, the Government of Japan would like at this stage to suggest with background explanation the following three issues to be discussed for the Protocol. Such suggestions are not exhaustive and Japan reserves the right to make further suggestions reflecting the discussions of the Committee in the future.

1. Right of Making Available of Unfixed Performances

<explanation>

Wire/wireless transmission of works, performances, etc., to the public can be categorized by the following two types of acts:

(1) wire/wireless broadcasting (in which members of the public *cannot* control the act of transmission);

(2) wire/wireless interactive transmission (in which members of the public *can* control the act of transmission by their "access" from a place and at a time individually chosen by them).

The most typical example of type (2) is transmission to the public through the Internet.

Although the majority of "home pages" in web site are still composed of non-moving images and/or texts, fixed/unfixed moving images are increasing in

4. 向公众传播视听作品的权利

（1）表演者应享有授权通过有线或无线方式向公众提供其作品，使公众可以从某一地点和某一时间获得这些作品的专有权。

（2）但本条约中的任何内容都不应排除缔约国授权一个为了缔约国并代表缔约国的集体行政系统行使第 4 条第（1）款中的权利。

日本

为了探索合理的视听表演制度，以鼓励新媒体时代创作和对表演的利用，日本政府于 1997 年 11 月设立了一个由有关人士、律师和学者组成的特设委员会。虽然本委员会关于可能使用的新权利和措施的讨论仍在继续，这将反映在日本对《视听表演议定书》的立场上，但日本政府希望在现阶段就以下三个问题的背景进行解释以供《议定书》讨论。这些建议并非详尽无遗，日本保留提出反映委员会今后讨论情况的进一步建议的权利。

1. 提供尚未录制的表演的权利

<解释>

通过有线 / 无线方式传输作品、表演的情形可分为以下两类：

（1）有线 / 无线广播（公众无法控制的传输行为）；

（2）有线 / 无线交互式传输（公众可以通过在个人选定的时间和地点进行“访问”来控制传输行为）。

类型（2）最典型的例子是通过互联网向公众传播。

虽然网站中的大多数“主页”仍然由非动态图像和 / 或文本组成，但录制 / 非录制的动态图像数量在交互式传输中正在增加。

interactive transmissions.

If *unfixed* performances are transmitted through the Internet (to only those who have accessed it), this act is not covered by the right of wire/wireless broadcasting as provided for in Article 6(i) of the WPPT, because transmission through the Internet belongs to type (2) rather than (1).

Therefore, with a view to adequately coping with the expanding use of live performances through the Internet, the right of making available through type (2) transmission for unfixed performances should be discussed.

2. Right of Fixation of Unfixed Performances

<explanation>

Japan's understanding is that during the discussions at the Diplomatic Conference, the term "musical" was deleted from Article 6 of the basic proposal for the WPPT which enabled Article 6(ii) to be interpreted to cover an act of fixing their unfixed audiovisual performances.

Although there seems to be another interpretation which excludes audiovisual performances from the scope of Article 6(ii) in the light of Article 2(c) which defines the term "fixation" as embodiment of sounds, or of the representation thereof as is taken by the International Bureau, it should be noted that the term "fixation" in Article 6(ii) means an "act," and therefore, the scope of Article 6(ii) seems to have nothing to do with Article 2(c) which defines the "fixation" clearly as a "thing" rather than an "act."

Therefore, a provision should be discussed to declare that performers enjoy the exclusive right to authorize fixing their unfixed performances.

3. Non-retroactivity

<explanation>

The retroactive protection of all audiovisual performances already fixed in the past would be extremely difficult and cause trouble to smooth transaction unless effective right clearance systems are established by relevant performers' organizations.

[End of Annex I, Annex II follows]

如果尚未录制表演是通过互联网传输的（仅向那些访问过它的人），这一行为不包括在 WPPT 第 6 条第（1）款规定的有线 / 无线广播权范围内，因为通过互联网进行传输属于第（2）种情形，而非第（1）种情形。

因此，为了充分应对通过互联网扩大对现场表演的使用问题，应讨论以下问题，即授予通过第（2）种方式传输尚未录制的表演的行为权利。

2. 录制尚未录制的表演的权利

< 解释 >

日本的理解是，在外交会议的讨论中，WPPT 基本提案第 6 条中删除了“音乐剧”一词，使第 6 条第（2）款能够被解释为包括录制尚未录制的视听表演的行为。

虽然似乎有另一种解释将视听表演排除在第 6 条第（2）款的范围之外，因为第 2 条（c）项将“录制”一词定义为声音的体现物，或国际局所采取的代表物，但应该指出，第 6 条第（2）款中的“录制”一词是指“行为”，因此，第 6 条第（2）款的范围似乎与第 2 条（c）项无关，后者将“录制”明确定义为“事物”，而不是“行为”。

因此，应讨论一项规定，宣布表演者享有授权对其尚未录制的表演进行录制的专有权。

3. 不溯及既往

< 解释 >

为已被录制的所有视听表演进行追溯并提供保护是极其困难的，而且会影响交易的顺利进行，除非相关表演者组织已建立有效的权利许可制度。

（附件一末，后接附件二）

ANNEX II
COMPARATIVE TABLE OF THE PROPOSALS RECEIVED FROM WIPO MEMBER STATES AND THE EUROPEAN COMMUNITY CONTENTS

page

附件二
世界知识产权组织成员国和欧共体成员国提案内容的比较表目录

页码

I. Title

ARGENTINA

Protocol concerning audiovisual performances.

COLOMBIA

Protocol to the WIPO Performances and Phonograms Treaty concerning audiovisual performance.

EUROPEAN COMMUNITY AND ITS MEMBER STATES

Protocol to the WIPO Performances and Phonograms Treaty, concerning audiovisual performances.

GHANA

Protocol to the WIPO Performances and Phonograms Treaty (WPPT) for the protection of audiovisual performances and producers.

II. Preamble

EUROPEAN COMMUNITY

The Contracting Parties

Wishing to ensure an adequate level of protection for audiovisual performances, especially in the digital environment;

Noting that the WIPO Performances and Phonograms Treaty does not cover the rights of performers in the audiovisual fixation of their unfixed performances, nor the exploitation of their audiovisually fixed performances;

Referring to the resolution concerning audiovisual performances adopted by the Diplomatic Conference on Certain Copyright and Neighboring Rights Questions on December 20, 1996;

Have agreed as follows:

III. Relation to other conventions and treaties; relation to copyright

ARGENTINA

Art. 1

1. No provision of this Treaty shall detract from the mutual obligations of Contracting Parties under the International Convention for the Protection of Performers, Producers of Phonograms and Broadcasting Organizations, done at Rome on October 26, 1961 (hereinafter referred to as "the Rome

I. 标题

阿根廷

视听表演议定书

哥伦比亚

WPPT 关于视听表演的议定书

欧共体成员国

WPPT 关于视听表演的议定书

加纳

WPPT 关于视听表演和制作者的议定书

II. 序言

欧共体

缔约各方

为确保对视听表演，特别是在数字环境中的视听表演提供足够的保护；

注意到《世界知识产权组织表演和录音制品条约》对表演者的保护并未延伸到对其尚未录制的表演进行视听录制的权利，也未涵盖对其已录制的视听表演进行利用的权利；

提及关于版权和邻接权若干问题的外交会议于 1996 年 12 月 20 日通过的《关于视听表演的决议》；

达成协议如下：

III. 与其他公约和条约的关系；与版权的关系

阿根廷

第 1 条

1. 本条约的任何规定均不得减损缔约各方之间依照 1961 年 10 月 26 日在罗马签订的《保护表演者、录音制品制作者和广播组织国际公约》(《罗马公约》)承担的相互义务。

Convention").

2. The protection granted under this Treaty shall leave intact and in no way affect the protection of the copyright in literary and artistic works. Consequently, no provision of this Treaty may be interpreted to the detriment of that protection.

3. This Treaty shall have no connection with and shall not prejudice any right or obligation under another Treaty.

COLOMBIA

Safeguarding of copyright

The protection provided for in this Protocol shall leave intact and in no way affect the protection of the copyright in literary and artistic works. Consequently, none of the provisions of this Protocol may be interpreted in a manner detrimental to that protection.

EUROPEAN COMMUNITY AND ITS MEMBER STATES

Article 1

Relation to Other Conventions

(1) This Treaty constitutes a Protocol to the WIPO Performances and Phonograms Treaty done in Geneva, 20 December 1996 (hereinafter the "WIPO Treaty").

(2) Nothing in this Protocol shall derogate from existing obligations that Contracting Parties have to each other under the WIPO Treaty.

(3) Protection granted under this protocol shall leave intact and shall in no way affect the protection of copyright in literary and artistic works. Consequently, no provisions of this protocol may be interpreted as prejudicing such protection.

IV. Definitions

ARGENTINA

Art. 2: Definitions

For the purposes of this Treaty:

a) "Performers" means all actors, singers, musicians, dancers or other persons who act a part, sing, recite, declaim or in any way perform literary or artistic works or expressions of folklore.

b) "Audiovisual fixation" means the incorporation of sounds and images, or a representation thereof, from which they may be perceived, reproduced or communicated with an appropriate device.

2. 依本条约给予的保护不得触动或以任何方式影响对文学和艺术作品版权的保护。因此，本条约的任何内容均不得被解释为损害此种保护。

3. 本条约不得与任何其他条约有任何关联，亦不得损害任何其他条约所规定的任何权利和义务。

哥伦比亚

版权保护

依本议定书给予的保护不得触动或以任何方式影响对文学和艺术作品版权的保护。因此，本条约的任何内容均不得被解释为损害此种保护。

欧共体成员国

第 1 条

与其他公约的关系

（1）该条约是 1996 年 12 月 20 日在日内瓦缔结的《世界知识产权组织表演和录音制品条约议定书》(以下简称 WIPO 条约)。

（2）本议定书的任何内容均不得减损缔约方相互之间依照 WIPO 条约已承担的现有义务。

（3）根据本议定书给予的保护不得触动或以任何方式影响对文学和艺术作品版权的保护。因此，本议定书的任何内容均不得被解释为损害此种保护。

IV. 定义

阿根廷

第 2 条：定义

在本条约中：

a)“表演者”系指演员、歌唱家、音乐家、舞蹈家以及对文学或艺术作品或民间文学艺术表达进行表演、歌唱、背诵、朗诵或以其他方式进行表演的其他人员。

b)“视听录制品”系指声音和图像的体现物或其表现物，从中通过某种装置可感知、复制或传播。

c) "Publication" is the offering to the public of copies of a performance fixed in an audiovisual work with the consent of the owners of the rights concerned, provided that the said copies are offered to the public in sufficient quantity.

d) "Broadcasting" means the wireless transmission of sounds or images and sounds, or representations thereof, for reception by the public; such transmission by satellite is also "broadcasting;" the transmission of coded signals shall be "broadcasting" where the means of decoding the signals are offered to the public by the broadcasting organization or with its consent.

e) "Communication to the public" is the transmission to the public by any medium other than broadcasting of the sounds and images of a performance.

COLOMBIA

Definitions

- Performer
- Audiovisual work
- Fixation
- Publication
- Rental
- Broadcasting
- Communication to the public

(This proposal refers to concepts to be defined, but does not define them).

EUROPEAN COMMUNITY AND ITS MEMBER STATES

Article 2

Definitions

(1) The Contracting Parties shall apply, *mutatis mutandis*, the definitions set out in Article 2 paragraphs (a), (f) and (g) of the WIPO Treaty in connection with the protection granted under this Protocol.

(2) For the purposes of this Protocol, "audiovisual fixation" means the embodiment of moving images, whether or not accompanied by sound, or the representations thereof, from which they can be perceived, reproduced or communicated through a device.

c)“发行”系指在有关权利所有人同意下，向公众提供录制在视听作品中的表演复制件，但须向公众提供足够数量的上述复制件。

d)“广播”系指以无线方式的传送，使公众能接收声音或图像，或图像和声音，或图像和声音的表现物；通过卫星进行的此种传送亦为“广播”；传送密码信号，只要广播组织或经其同意向公众提供了解码的手段，即为“广播”。

e)“向公众传播”系指通过除广播以外的任何媒界向公众传送表演的声音和图像。

哥伦比亚

定义

- 表演者
- 视听作品
- 录制
- 发行
- 出租
- 广播
- 向公众传播

(这项提案的“定义”是指要界定但尚未界定的概念)。

欧共体成员国

第 2 条

定义

(1)缔约各方应比照适用《世界知识产权组织条约》第 2 条(a)、(f)和(g)款中关于本议定书所给予保护的定义。

(2)在本议定书中，“视听录制品”系指活动图像的体现物，且从中可通过某种装置感觉、复制或传播该活动图像，不论是否伴有声音或声音的表现物。

V. Beneficiaries of protection

ARGENTINA

Art. 3: Beneficiaries of protection under this Treaty

1. The Contracting Parties shall grant the protection provided for under this Treaty to performers who are nationals of other Contracting Parties.

2. Nationals of other Contracting Parties means those performers who meet the criteria of eligibility for protection provided for under the Rome Convention where all the Contracting Parties to this Treaty are Contracting States of the said Convention. The Contracting Parties shall apply to those eligibility criteria the relevant definitions contained in Article 2 of this Treaty.

Any Contracting Party may have recourse, *mutatis mutandis*, to the options provided for in Article 5(3) or, for the purposes of the provisions of Article 5, to Article 17, all of them of the Rome Convention, and shall give notice thereof to the Director General of the World Intellectual Property Organization (WIPO) as provided in those provisions.

EUROPEAN COMMUNITY AND ITS MEMBER STATES

Article 3

Beneficiaries of protection under this protocol

The Contracting Parties shall accord the protection provided under this protocol to performers who are nationals of other Contracting Parties.

VI. National treatment

ARGENTINA

Art. 4: National treatment

Every Contracting Party shall grant to the nationals of other Contracting Parties, as defined in Article 3(2), the treatment that it grants to its own nationals with respect to the exclusive rights accorded specifically in this Treaty.

EUROPEAN COMMUNITY AND ITS MEMBER STATES

Article 6

Application of certain substantive provisions of the WIPO Treaty

The Contracting Parties shall apply, *mutatis mutandis*, in respect of protection granted under this Protocol, the provisions of Articles 4 (National Treatment)... of the WIPO Treaty.

V. 保护的受益者

阿根廷

第 3 条：本条约保护的受益者

1. 缔约方应向其他缔约方国民的表演者提供本条约规定的保护。

2. 其他缔约方的国民是指符合《罗马公约》规定的保护资格标准的表演者，而本条约的所有缔约方都是该公约的缔约国。关于这些资格标准，缔约方应适用本条约第 2 条中的有关定义。

任何缔约方应比照利用《伯尔尼公约》第 5 条第（3）款提供的可能性，或为同一公约第 5 条、第 17 条的目的，向世界知识产权组织总干事发出通知。

欧共体成员国

第 3 条

本议定书保护的受益者

缔约各方应向其他缔约方国民的表演者提供本议定书规定的保护。

VI. 国民待遇

阿根廷

第 4 条：国民待遇

缔约各方应按照第 3 条第（2）款的规定，将其给予本国国民在专有权方面的待遇给予其他缔约方的国民。

欧共体成员国

第 6 条

《世界知识产权组织条约》（WIPO 条约）某些实质性条款的适用

对于根据本议定书给予的保护，缔约各方应比照适用 WIPO 条约第 4 条（国民待遇）的规定。

VII. Formalities; independence from protection in country of origin

ARGENTINA

Art. 10: Formalities

The enjoyment of exercise of the rights provided for in this Treaty shall not be subject to any formality.

COLOMBIA

Formalities and independence of protection

The enjoyment and exercise of the rights provided for in this Protocol shall not be subject to any formality.

The said enjoyment and exercise shall be independent of the existence of protection in the country of origin of the performance.

EUROPEAN COMMUNITY AND ITS MEMBER STATES

Article 6

Application of certain substantive provisions of the WIPO Treaty

The Contracting Parties shall apply, *mutatis mutandis*, in respect of protection granted under this Protocol, the provisions of Articles… 20 (Formalities)… of the WIPO Treaty.

VIII. Moral rights of performers

ARGENTINA

Art. 5: Moral rights

The performer shall have the following rights in his performances in audiovisual works:

1. to be identified by the mention of his name or pseudonym, except where the omission thereof is dictated by the manner in which the performance is used;

2. to object to any distortion of his performance that would prejudice his professional standing.

The performer may authorize the making of changes to his performance. Such authorization shall be valid only if it is given in writing.

The rights accorded to the performer in the foregoing paragraphs shall remain valid after his death at least until the expiration of his economic rights, and shall be exercised by the persons or institutions authorized by the legislation of the Contracting Party in which protection is claimed.

VII. 手续；独立于原籍国提供的保护

阿根廷

第 10 条：手续

行使本条约规定的权利无须履行任何手续。

哥伦比亚

手续和保护的独立性

享有和行使本议定书所规定的权利无须履行任何手续。

上述权利的享有和行使独立于原籍国对表演提供的保护。

欧共体成员国

第 6 条

《世界知识产权组织条约》(WIPO 条约)某些实质性条款的适用

对于根据本议定书给予的保护，缔约方应比照适用 WIPO 条约第 20 条(手续)的规定。

VIII. 表演者的精神权利

阿根廷

第 5 条：精神权利

表演者对表演的视听作品享有下列权利：

1. 以提及其姓名或化名的方式被确认表演者身份，但因使用表演方式而决定可省略不提及的除外；
2. 反对任何对其表演进行的将有损其声誉的歪曲。

表演者可授权修改他的表演，但授权须以书面形式才有效。

根据上述条款授予表演者的权利在其死亡后应继续保留，至少到其经济权利期满为止，并可由被要求提供保护的缔约方立法所授权的个人或机构行使。

COLOMBIA

Moral rights of performers

The performer shall have the following rights in relation to his audiovisual performances:

a) to demand that his name appears in connection with or is associated with every performance that takes place;

b) to object to any distortion, mutilation or any other violation of his performance that might damage his standing or reputation.

Term of moral rights

The rights accorded to the performer under the foregoing Article shall be maintained, after his death, at least until the expiry of his economic rights, and shall be exercisable by the persons or institutions authorized by the legislation of the Contracting Party in which protection is claimed.

EUROPEAN COMMUNITY AND ITS MEMBER STATES

Article 4

Rights of performers in their unfixed audiovisual performances

The Contracting Parties shall accord, *mutatis mutandis*, to performers, as regards their unfixed audiovisual performances, whether or not accompanied by sound, the same rights as those granted under the WIPO Treaty to performers as regards their live aural performances, namely the rights provided under Article 5 (Moral Rights)...

Article 5

Rights of performers in audiovisual fixations of their performances

The Contracting Parties shall accord, *mutatis mutandis*, to performers, as regards the use of audiovisual fixations of their performances, the same rights as those granted under the WIPO Treaty to performers as regards the use of their performances fixed in phonograms, namely the rights provided under Articles 5 (Moral Rights), of the WIPO Treaty.

IX. Rights of performers in their unfixed performances

ARGENTINA

Art. 6: Economic rights

1. Economic rights of performers in their unfixed performances.

哥伦比亚

表演者的精神权利

表演者对其视听表演享有下列权利：

a）要求自己的名字出现在每场表演中或与表演相联系；

b）反对任何对其表演进行的将有损其声誉的歪曲、篡改或其他侵权行为。

精神权利条款

授予表演者的权利在其死亡后应继续保留，至少到其经济权利期满为止，并可由被要求提供保护的缔约方立法所授权的个人或机构行使。

欧共体成员国

第 4 条

表演者对其尚未录制表演的权利

缔约方应比照适用 WIPO 条约第 5 条（精神权利）的规定，给予表演者对其尚未录制表演与现场表演相同的权利。

第 5 条

表演者对其表演的视听录制品的权利

缔约各方在使用表演者的视听录制品时，应比照适用 WIPO 条约第 5 条（精神权利）的规定，授予表演者对使用其录制在录音制品上的表演的相同权利。

IX. 表演者在尚未录制表演中的权利

阿根廷

第 6 条：经济权利

1. 表演者对其尚未录制的表演的经济权利。

Performers shall enjoy the exclusive right to authorize the following in relation to their unfixed performances:

a) broadcasting and communication to the public of their unfixed performances, except where the performance is in itself a broadcast performance;

b) fixation of their unfixed performances.

COLOMBIA

Economic rights of performers in their unfixed performances

Performers shall enjoy the exclusive right to authorize:

a) the broadcasting and communication to the public of their unfixed performances, except where the performance is in itself a broadcast performance;

b) fixation of their unfixed performances.

EUROPEAN COMMUNITY AND ITS MEMBER STATES

Article 4

Rights of performers in their unfixed audiovisual performances

The Contracting Parties shall accord, *mutatis mutandis*, to performers, as regards their unfixed audiovisual performances, whether or not accompanied by sound, the same rights as those granted under the WIPO Treaty to performers as regards their live aural performances, namely the rights provided under Article… 6 (Economic rights of Performers in their unfixed performances).

X. Rights of performers in audiovisual fixations

1. right of reproduction

ARGENTINA

Art 6.2: Performers shall have the exclusive right to authorize the following in relation to their performances fixed in audiovisual works:

a) Reproduction:

direct or indirect reproduction of their performances by any process or in any form.

COLOMBIA

Right of reproduction

Performers shall enjoy the exclusive right to authorize the direct or indirect, permanent or temporary reproduction, by any process or in any form, of their performances fixed in any medium.

表演者应对以下与其尚未录制的表演相关授权享有专有权：

a）广播和向公众传播其尚未录制的表演，除非该表演本身已属广播表演；

b）录制其尚未录制的表演。

哥伦比亚

表演者对其尚未录制的表演的经济权利

表演者应享有专有权，授权：

a）广播和向公众传播其尚未录制的表演，除非该表演本身已属广播表演；

b）录制其尚未录制的表演。

欧共体成员国

第 4 条

表演者对其尚未录制的表演的权利

缔约各方应比照适用 WIPO 条约第 6 条（表演者对其尚未录制的表演的经济权利）给予表演者对其现场表演享有的权利，授予表演者就其尚未录制的视听表演以相同的权利，无论是否有伴音。

X. 表演者就视听录制品享有的权利

1. 复制权

阿根廷

第 6 条第 2 款：表演者对其以视听作品录制的表演享有专有权，授权：

a）复制：

以任何方式或形式对其表演直接或间接地进行复制。

哥伦比亚

复制权

表演者应享有授权以任何方式或形式对其录制在任何媒介上的表演直接或间接、永久或临时地进行复制的专有权。

EUROPEAN COMMUNITY AND ITS MEMBER STATES

Article 5

Rights of performers in audiovisual fixations of their performances

The Contracting Parties shall accord, *mutatis mutandis*, to performers, as regards the use of audiovisual fixations of their performances, the same rights as those granted under the WIPO Treaty to performers as regards the use of their performances fixed in phonograms, namely the rights provided under Articles... 7 (Right of Reproduction)... of the WIPO Treaty.

GHANA

1. Right of reproduction

Performers shall enjoy the exclusive right to authorize the direct or indirect reproduction of their audiovisual performances fixed in any manner or form.

2. Right of distribution

ARGENTINA

Art. 6.2: Performers shall have the exclusive right to authorize the following in relation to their performances fixed in audiovisual works:

……

b) Distribution:

the making available to the public of the copies of their performances by sale or other transfer of ownership.

Nothing in this Treaty shall affect the right of the Contracting Parties to determine the conditions of application of the exhaustion of the right under paragraph (b) after the first sale or other transfer of ownership of the original or a copy of the performance fixed with the performer's consent.

COLOMBIA

Right of distribution

Performers shall enjoy the exclusive right to authorize the making available to the public of the original and copies of their performances fixed in any medium by means of sale or other transfer of ownership.

Nothing in this Protocol shall affect the right of Contracting Parties to determine the conditions of application, if any, of the exhaustion of rights after first sale or other transfer for ownership of the original or a copy of the performance

欧共体成员国

第5条

表演者对其表演的视听录制品的权利

缔约各方应比照适用WIPO条约第7条（复制权）的规定，将给予表演者对其表演的录音制品的权利，授予给表演者对他人使用其表演的视听录制品进行控制的相同权利。

加纳

1.复制权

表演者应享有授权以任何方式或形式对其以任何形式录制的视听表演直接或间接地进行复制的专有权。

2.发行权

阿根廷

第6条第2款：表演者对其以视听作品录制的表演享有专有权，授权：

……

b)发行：

通过销售或其他所有权转让形式向公众提供其表演的复制件。

对于已录制表演的原件或复制件经表演者授权被首次销售或以其他形式转让所有权之后适用（b）项中权利的用尽所依据的条件（如有此种条件），本条约的任何内容均不得影响缔约方确定该条件的自由。

哥伦比亚

发行权

表演者应享有授权通过销售或其他所有权转让形式向公众提供其录制在任何媒介上的表演的原件和复制件的专有权。

对于已录制表演的原件或复制件，经表演者授权被首次销售或其他所有权转让之后适用权利的用尽所依据的条件，本议定书的任何内容均不得影响缔约各方确定该条件的权利。

fixed in any medium.

EUROPEAN COMMUNITY AND ITS MEMBER STATES

Article 5

Rights of performers in audiovisual fixations of their performances

The Contracting Parties shall accord, *mutatis mutandis*, to performers, as regards the use of audiovisual fixations of their performances, the same rights as those granted under the WIPO Treaty to performers as regards the use of their performances fixed in phonograms, namely the rights provided under Articles… 8 (Right of Distribution)… of the WIPO Treaty.

GHANA

2. Right of distribution

Performers shall enjoy the exclusive right to authorize the availability of the original and copies of their works to the public through sale or other transfer of ownership.

3. Right of rental

ARGENTINA

Art. 6.2: Performers shall have the exclusive right to authorize the following in relation to their performances fixed in audiovisual works:

……

c) Rental:

the commercial rental to the public of the copies of their performances, as provided in the national legislation of Contracting Parties, including after distribution effected by the performer or with his consent.

COLOMBIA

Right of rental

Performers shall enjoy the exclusive right to authorize the rental of the original and copies of their performances fixed in any medium, including after distribution effected by the performer or with his consent.

EUROPEAN COMMUNITY AND ITS MEMBER STATES

Article 5

Rights of performers in audiovisual fixations of their performances

The Contracting Parties shall accord, *mutatis mutandis*, to performers, as

欧共体成员国

第 5 条

表演者对其表演的视听录制品的权利

缔约各方应比照适用《世界知识产权组织条约》(WIPO 条约)第 8 条(发行权)的规定,将给予表演者对其表演的录音制品的权利,授予给表演者对他人使用其表演的视听录制品进行控制的相同权利。

加纳

2. 发行权

表演者应享有授权通过销售或其他所有权转让形式向公众提供其作品的原件和复制件的专有权。

3. 出租权

阿根廷

第 6 条第 2 款:表演者对其以视听作品录制的表演享有专有权,授权:

……

c)出租

按缔约各方国内法中的规定将其表演的复制件向公众进行商业性出租的专有权,由表演者发行或经表演者授权发行。

哥伦比亚

出租权

表演者应享有授权按缔约各方国内法中的规定将其表演的复制件向公众进行商业性出租的专有权,包括由表演者发行或经表演者授权发行。

欧共体成员国

第 5 条

表演者对其表演的视听录制品的权利

缔约方应比照适用《世界知识产权组织条约》第 9 条(出租权)规定的权

regards the use of audiovisual fixations of their performances, the same rights as those granted under the WIPO Treaty to performers as regards the use of their performances fixed in phonograms, namely the rights provided under Articles... 9 (Right of Rental)... of the WIPO Treaty.

GHANA

3. Right of rental

Performers shall enjoy the exclusive right to authorize the commercial rental of the original and copies of performances to the public, except, if the commercial rental has led to widespread copying of the works which materially impairs the exclusive right of reproduction.

4. Right of making available

ARGENTINA

Art. 6.2: Performers shall enjoy the exclusive right to authorize the following in relation to their performances fixed in audiovisual works:

......

e) Interactive Services:

the making available to the public of their performances, by either wire or wireless means, in such a way that the members of the public may have access to them from a place and at a time of their choosing.

COLOMBIA

Right to make fixed performances available

Performers shall enjoy the exclusive right to authorize the making available of their performances fixed in any medium, whether by wire or wireless means, in such a way that the members of the public may have access to them from a place and at a time of their choosing.

EUROPEAN COMMUNITY AND ITS MEMBER STATES

Article 5

Rights of performers in audiovisual fixations of their performances

The Contracting Parties shall accord, *mutatis mutandis*, to performers, as regards the use of audiovisual fixations of their performances, the same rights as those granted under the WIPO Treaty to performers as regards the use of their performances fixed in phonograms, namely the rights provided under Articles... 10

利，即表演者对使用其表演的录音制品的权利，授予表演者对其表演的视听录制品相同的权利。

加纳

3. 出租权

表演者应享有授权将其表演的原件和复制件向公众进行商业性出租的专有权，除非商业性出租已导致此种作品的广泛复制，从而严重损害专有复制权。

4. 提供权

阿根廷

第6条第2款：表演者对其以视听作品录制的表演享有专有权，授权：

……

e）交互式服务：

以有线或无线方式向公众提供其表演，使该表演可由公众在个人选择的时间和地点获得。

哥伦比亚

提供已录制表演的权利

表演者应享有专有权，以授权通过有线或无线的方式向公众提供其录制在任何媒介中的表演，使该表演可为公众中的成员在其个人选定的地点和时间获得。

欧共体成员国

第5条

表演者对其以视听录制品录制的表演的权利

缔约方应比照适用《世界知识产权组织条约》（WIPO条约）第10条（提供已录制表演的权利）规定的权利，即表演者对使用其表演的录音制品的权利，授予表演者对其表演的视听录制品相同的权利。

(Right of Making Available of Fixed Performances)… of the WIPO Treaty.

GHANA

4. Right of communication to the public of audiovisual productions

(1) Performers shall enjoy the exclusive right to authorize the availability of their works to the public by wire or wireless means, in such a way that members of the public may access them from a place and at a time individually chosen by them.

(2) But nothing in this Treaty shall exclude Contracting Parties from authorizing the exercise of the rights in paragraph 4(1) by a system of Collective Administration for and on behalf of the Contracting Parties.

5. Right of broadcasting and communication to the public

ARGENTINA

Art. 6.2: Performers shall have the exclusive right to authorize the following in relation to their performances fixed in audiovisual works:

……

d) Broadcasting and communication to the public: the broadcasting and communication to the public of their performances. Unless otherwise agreed, consent given for the fixing of the performance in an audiovisual work constitutes authorization of broadcasting and communication to the public by means of subscription systems.

XI. Rights of producers of audiovisual works

GHANA

1. Right of reproduction

Producers shall enjoy the exclusive right to authorize the direct or indirect reproduction of their works in any manner or form.

2. Right of distribution

Producers shall enjoy the exclusive right to authorize the availability of the original and copies of their works to the public through sale or other transfer of ownership.

3. Right of rental

Producers shall enjoy the exclusive right to authorize commercial rental of the original and copies of their works to the public, except, if such commercial rental has led to widespread copying of the works which materially impairs the exclusive

加纳

4. 就视听制品享有的向公众传播权

（1）表演者应享有专有权，以授权通过有线或无线的方式向公众提供其以作品，使该作品可为公众中的成员在其个人选定的地点和时间获得。

（2）但本条约的任何规定均不得排除缔约方授权集体管理组织为了缔约方和代表缔约方行使第4条第（1）款所规定的权利。

5. 广播权和向公众传播权

阿根廷

第6条第2款：表演者对其以视听作品录制的表演享有专有权，授权：

……

d）广播和向公众传播：

向公众广播和向公众传播其表演。

除非另有约定，为在视听作品中录制其表演而给予的同意，构成对通过订阅系统向公众广播和传播的授权。

XI. 制作者对视听作品的权利

加纳

1. 复制权

制作者应享有授权以任何方式或形式对其作品直接或间接地进行复制的专有权。

2. 发行权

制作者应享有通过销售或其他所有权转让形式，授权向公众提供其作品的原件和复制件的专有权。

3. 出租权

制作者应享有授权将其作品的原件和复制件向公众进行商业性出租的专有权，除非商业性出租已导致此种作品的广泛复制，从而严重损害其专有复制权。

right of reproduction.

4. Right of communication to the public of audiovisual productions

(1) Producers shall enjoy the exclusive right to authorize the availability of their works by wire or wireless means, to the public in such a way that members of the public may access them from a place and at a time individually chosen by them.

(2) Nothing in this Treaty shall exclude Contracting Parties from authorizing the exercise of the rights in paragraph 4(1) by a system of Collective Administration for and on behalf of the Contracting Parties.

XII. Limitations and exceptions

ARGENTINA

Art. 7: Limitations and exceptions

1. The Contracting Parties may provide in their national legislation for the same types of limitations and exceptions for the protection of performers as it contains at present with respect to the protection of the copyright in literary and artistic works.

2. The Contracting Parties shall confine any limitation or exception imposed on the rights provided for in this Treaty to certain special cases that do not adversely affect the normal exploitation of the performance fixed in audiovisual works, or unjustifiably prejudice the legitimate interests of the performer.

COLOMBIA

Limitations and exceptions

The Contracting Parties may provide in their national legislation for the same types of limitation or exception imposed on protection of performers as it contains at present with respect to the protection of the copyright in literary and artistic works.

The Contracting Parties shall confine any limitation or exception imposed on the rights provided for in this Protocol to certain special cases that do not adversely affect the normal exploitation of the performance or unjustifiably prejudice the legitimate interests of the performer.

EUROPEAN COMMUNITY AND ITS MEMBER STATES

Article 6

Application of certain substantive provisions of the WIPO Treaty

The Contracting Parties shall apply, *mutatis mutandis*, in respect of protection granted under this Protocol, the provisions of Articles… 16 (Limitations and

4. 就视听制品享有的向公众传播权

（1）制作者应享有专有权，以授权通过有线或无线的方式向公众提供其以作品，使该作品可为公众中的成员在其个人选定的地点和时间获得。

（2）本条约的任何规定均不得排除缔约方授权集体管理组织为了缔约方和代表缔约方行使第 4 条第（1）款所规定的权利。

XII. 限制与例外

阿根廷

第 7 条：限制与例外

1. 缔约各方可以在其国内立法中，对给予表演者的保护规定与其国内立法给予文学和艺术作品的版权保护相同种类的限制或例外。

2. 缔约各方应使本条约中所规定权利的任何限制或例外仅限于某些不与录制在视听作品中表演的正常利用相抵触、也不致不合理地损害表演者合法利益的特殊情况。

哥伦比亚

限制与例外

缔约各方可以在其国内立法中，对给予表演者的保护规定与其国内立法给予文学和艺术作品的版权保护相同种类的限制或例外。

缔约各方应使本议定书中所规定权利的任何限制或例外仅限于某些不与表演的正常利用相抵触、也不致不合理地损害表演者合法利益的特殊情况。

欧共体成员国

第 6 条

《世界知识产权组织条约》（WIPO 条约）某些实质性条款的适用

对于根据本议定书给予的保护，缔约方应比照适用 WIPO 条约第 16 条（限制与例外）的规定。

Exceptions)... of the WIPO Treaty.

XIII. Contractual arrangements concerning rights of performers

ARGENTINA

Art. 6, last sentence: In the absence of specific provisions on particular contracts, the economic rights laid down in this Article shall apply.

GHANA

Notwithstanding the above provisions:

a) Both parties i. e. the producers and performers of audiovisual works may by contract determine the extent to which the rights granted to the performers if any are to be exercised in a particular performance.

b) In order to ensure that the exploitation of the work is not unnecessarily stifled, the producer may exercise the rights of reproduction, distribution and rental granted to the performer on such conditions as the producer and performer may agree upon.

XIV. Duration of economic rights of performers

ARGENTINA

Art. 7.3: The duration of the protection granted to performers under this Treaty may not be less than 50 years, calculated as from the end of the year in which the performance was fixed.

COLOMBIA

Duration of the protection of economic rights

The economic rights accorded to performers shall have a duration of fifty (50) years as from the date of audiovisual fixation.

EUROPEAN COMMUNITY AND ITS MEMBER STATES

Article 6

Application of certain substantive provisions of the WIPO Treaty

The Contracting Parties shall apply, *mutatis mutandis*, in respect of protection granted under this Protocol, the provisions of Articles... 17 (Term of Protection)... of the WIPO Treaty.

XV. Obligations concerning technological measures

ARGENTINA

Art. 8: Obligations concerning technological measures

The Contracting Parties shall provide adequate legal protection and effective

XIII. 关于表演者权利的合同安排

阿根廷

第 6 条最后一句：在无合同的特别条款情况下，适用本条规定的经济权利。

加纳

虽有上述规定：

a）双方，即视听作品的制作者和表演者，可以通过合同约定在某一特定表演中行使给予表演者的权利的程度。

b）为使确保作品的利用不受到损害，制作者可在与表演者约定的情况下行使授予给表演者的复制权、发行权和出租权。

XIV. 表演者经济权利的期限

阿根廷

第 7 条第 3 款：依本条约给予表演者的保护期，应自表演录制之年年终起算，至少持续到 50 年期满为止。

哥伦比亚

经济权利保护期限

表演者就视听录制品的经济权利的保护期限为 50 年。

欧共体成员国

第 6 条

《世界知识产权组织条约》（WIPO 条约）某些实质性条款的适用

对于根据本议定书给予的保护，缔约方应比照适用 WIPO 条约第 17 条（保护期限）的规定。

XV. 关于技术措施的义务

阿根廷

第 8 条：关于技术措施的义务

缔约各方应规定适当的法律保护和有效的法律补救办法，制止规避由表演

legal remedies against any action to circumvent effective technological measures that are used by performers in connection with the exercise of their rights under this Treaty and which restrict acts in relation to their performances fixed in audiovisual works that are not authorized by the performers concerned or permitted by the law.

COLOMBIA

Obligations concerning technological measures

The Contracting Parties shall provide adequate legal protection and effective legal remedies against action to circumvent effective technological measures that are used by performers in connection with the exercise of their rights under this Protocol.

EUROPEAN COMMUNITY AND ITS MEMBER STATES

Article 6

Application of certain substantive provisions of the WIPO Treaty

The Contracting Parties shall apply, *mutatis mutandis*, in respect of protection granted under this Protocol, the provisions of Articles... 18 (Obligations concerning Technological Measures)... of the WIPO Treaty.

XVI. Obligations concerning rights management information

ARGENTINA

Art. 9: Obligations concerning rights management information

1. The Contracting Parties shall provide adequate and effective legal remedies against any person who deliberately engages in any of the following acts in the knowledge or, with respect to civil remedies, having reasonable grounds to know that it causes, permits, facilitates or conceals an infringement of any of the rights provided for in this Treaty:

i) without authorization deletes or alters any electronic information on rights management;

ii) without authorization distributes, imports for distribution or broadcasts performances or copies thereof or communicates them or makes them available to the public, in the knowledge that the electronic rights management information has been deleted or altered without authorization.

2. For the purposes of this Article, “rights management information” means the information identifying the performer, his performance and the audiovisual

者为行使本条约所规定的权利而使用并限制对其表演实施未经该有关表演者许可的或法律不允许的行为的有效技术措施。

哥伦比亚

关于技术措施的义务

缔约各方应规定适当的法律保护和有效的法律补救办法，防止表演者为行使本议定书所规定权利而采取的有效技术措施被规避。

欧共体成员国

第 6 条

《世界知识产权组织条约》(WIPO 条约)某些实质性条款的适用

对于根据本议定书给予的保护，缔约方应比照适用 WIPO 条约第 18 条(技术措施义务)的规定。

XVI. 有关权利管理信息的义务

阿根廷

第 9 条：权利管理信息义务

1. 缔约各方应规定适当和有效的法律补救办法，制止任何人明知、或就民事补救而言有合理根据知道其行为会诱使、促成、便利或包庇对本条约所涵盖的任何权利的侵犯而故意从事以下行为：

i)未经许可去除或改变任何权利管理的电子信息；

ii)未经许可发行、为发行目的进口、广播、向公众传播或提供明知已被未经许可去除或改变权利管理电子信息的表演或其复制件。

2. 就本条而言，“权利管理信息”是指识别识别表演者、表演者的表演、视听制作人的信息，或关于使用视听作品中录制表演的条款和条件的信息。

producer, or information on the clauses and conditions governing the use of the performance fixed in audiovisual work.

COLOMBIA

Obligations concerning rights management information

The Contracting Parties shall provide adequate and effective legal remedies against any person who deliberately engages in any of the following acts in the knowledge or, with respect to civil remedies, having reasonable grounds to know that it causes, permits, facilitates or conceals an infringement of any of the rights provided for in this Protocol:

- without authorization removes or alters any electronic rights management information;

- without authorization distributes, imports for distribution or broadcasts performances or copies of fixed performances, or communicates them or makes them available to the public, in the knowledge that the electronic information on rights management has been removed or altered without authorization.

- "Rights management information" means the information identifying the performer, his performance, the fixation of the performance and the owner of any right in the performance or fixation, or information on the clauses and conditions governing the use of the performance or fixation, and any number or code representing that information, where any of those information elements is affixed to a copy of a fixed performance or appears in connection with the communication or making available to the public of a fixed performance.

EUROPEAN COMMUNITY AND ITS MEMBER STATES

Article 6

Application of certain substantive provisions of the WIPO Treaty

The Contracting Parties shall apply, *mutatis mutandis*, in respect of protection granted under this Protocol, the provisions of Articles… 19 (Obligations concerning Rights Management Information)… of the WIPO Treaty.

XVII. Reservations

COLOMBIA

Reservations

No reservations to this Protocol shall be permitted.

哥伦比亚

有关权利管理信息的义务

缔约各方应规定适当和有效的法律补救办法，制止任何人明知或就民事补救而言有合理根据知道其行为会诱使、促成、便利或包庇对本条约所涵盖的任何权利的侵犯而故意从事以下行为：

– 未经许可去除或改变任何权利管理的电子信息；

– 未经许可发行、为发行目的进口、广播、向公众传播或提供明知已被未经许可去除或改变权利管理电子信息的表演或其复制件。

– "权利管理信息"系指识别表演者、表演者的表演、表演的录制品或对表演拥有任何权利的所有人的信息，或有关使用表演的条款和条件的信息，以及代表此种信息的任何数字或代码，各该项信息均附于以视听录制品录制的表演上。

欧共体成员国

第 6 条

《世界知识产权组织条约》（WIPO 条约）某些实质性条款的适用

对于根据本议定书给予的保护，缔约方应比照适用 WIPO 条约第 19 条（关于权利管理信息的义务）的规定。

XVII. 保留

哥伦比亚

保留

本议定书不得作出任何保留。

EUROPEAN COMMUNITY AND ITS MEMBER STATES

Article 7

Reservations

No reservations to this Protocol shall be permitted.

XVIII. Application in Time

ARGENTINA

Art. 7

4. The Contracting Parties shall apply the provisions of Article 18 of the Berne Convention, *mutatis mutandis*, to the rights of the performers provided for in this Treaty.

5. This Treaty shall not detract from the rights acquired in any Contracting Party prior to the date of entry into force of this Treaty in that party.

A Contracting Party shall not be obliged to apply the provisions of this Treaty to performances given or to audiovisual fixations made prior to its entry into force in that party.

COLOMBIA

Application in time

The Contracting Parties shall not apply the provisions of this Protocol to performances that have taken place prior to the date of entry into force of this Protocol.

EUROPEAN COMMUNITY AND ITS MEMBER STATES

Article 6

Application of certain substantive provisions of the WIPO Treaty

The Contracting Parties shall apply, *mutatis mutandis*, in respect of protection granted under this Protocol, the provisions of Articles… 22 (Application in Time)… of the WIPO Treaty.

XIX. Provisions on enforcement of rights

ARGENTINA

Art. 11: Provisions on enforcement of rights

1. The Contracting Parties undertake to adopt, in accordance with their legal systems, the measures necessary to ensure the application of this Treaty.

2. The Contracting Parties shall ensure that such procedures for the

欧共体成员国

第 7 条

保留

本议定书不得作出任何保留。

XVIII. 适用的时限

阿根廷

第 7 条

4. 缔约方应比照适用《伯尔尼公约》第 18 条关于公约授予表演者的权利的规定。

5. 本条约不得减损任何缔约方在本条约对该缔约方生效之日之前取得的权利。

缔约一方无义务将本条约的规定适用于在其在该方生效之前所作的表演或视听录制品。

哥伦比亚

适用的时限

缔约各方不得将本议定书的规定适用于本条约对该缔约方生效之前进行的表演。

欧共体成员国

第 6 条

《世界知识产权组织条约》(WIPO 条约)某些实质性条款的适用

对于根据本议定书给予的保护,缔约方应比照适用 WIPO 条约第 22 条(适用的时限)的规定。

XIX. 权利行使条款

阿根廷

第 11 条:权利行使条款

1. 缔约各方承诺根据其法律制度采取必要的措施,以确保本条约的适用。

2. 缔约各方应确保依照其法律可以提供执法程序,以便能够对侵犯本条约

enforcement of rights are introduced in their legislation as will permit the institution of effective measures against any action infringing the rights referred to in this Treaty, and in addition that the commission of new infringements is prevented.

EUROPEAN COMMUNITY AND ITS MEMBER STATES

Article 6

Application of certain substantive provisions of the WIPO Treaty

The Contracting Parties shall apply, *mutatis mutandis*, in respect of protection granted under this Protocol, the provisions of Articles... 23 (Enforcement of Rights)... of the WIPO Treaty.

XX. Administrative and final clauses

EUROPEAN COMMUNITY AND ITS MEMBER STATES

Article 8

Application of certain administrative provisions

The Contracting Parties shall have an Assembly. This Assembly shall be the same as the one created by the WIPO Treaty and its functioning shall be governed, *mutatis mutandis*, by Article 24 of the WIPO Treaty.

Article 9

Eligibility for becoming party to the Treaty

Any party to the WIPO Treaty may become party to this Protocol.

Article 10

Signature of the Protocol

This Protocol shall be open for signature until... by any Member State of WIPO and by the European Community.

Article 11

Entry into force of the Protocol

This Protocol shall enter into force, following the date of entry into force of the WIPO Treaty, three months after 5 instruments of ratification or accession by States have been deposited with the Director General of WIPO.

Article 12

Final clause

The provisions of Articles 25 (International Bureau), 27 (Rights and Obligations under the Treaty), 30 (Effective Date of Becoming Party of the Treaty),

所述权利的任何行为采取有效措施，此外，还应防止发生新的侵权行为。

欧共体成员国

第 6 条

《世界知识产权组织条约》（WIPO 条约）某些实质性条款的适用

对于根据本议定书给予的保护，缔约方应比照适用 WIPO 条约第 23 条（权利的行使）的规定。

XX. 行政条款和最后条款

欧共体成员国

第 8 条

某些行政性规定的适用

缔约各方应设大会，大会应与《世界知识产权组织条约》（WIPO 条约）所设大会相同，大会的运作应比照适用 WIPO 条约第 24 条的规定。

第 9 条

成为本条约缔约方的资格

WIPO 条约的任何缔约方均可加入本议定书。

第 10 条

议定书的签署

本议定书开放以供任何世界知识产权组织成员国和欧共体成员国签署，直至……

第 11 条

议定书的生效

本议定书自 WIPO 条约生效之日起生效，即自各国向世界知识产权组织总干事交存 5 份法律文本或加入书 3 个月后生效。

第 12 条

最后条款

其他应比照适用 WIPO 条约第 25 条（国际局）、第 27 条（条约规定的权利和义务）、第 30 条（成为条约缔约方的生效日期）、第 31 条（退约）、第 32 条（条

31 (Denunciation of the Treaty), 32 (Languages of the Treaty) and 33 (Depository) of the WIPO Treaty shall apply, *mutatis mutandis*.

[End of Annex II and of document]

约的语文）和第 33 条（保存人）的规定。

（附件二和文件完）

2.2 Proposal from the Republic of Korea

Document Code: AP/CE/2/3
Language: English
URL: https://www.wipo.int/edocs/mdocs/copyright/en/ap_ce_2/ap_ce_2_3.pdf
Chinese Translation: Not Available.
URL: N/A

COMMITTEE OF EXPERTS
ON A PROTOCOL
CONCERNING AUDIOVISUAL PERFORMANCES
Second Session
Geneva, June 8 to 12, 1998

PROPOSAL FROM THE REPUBLIC OF KOREA

PROPOSAL OF THE GOVERNMENT OF THE REPUBLIC OF KOREA CONCERNING A PROTOCOL TO THE WIPO PERFORMANCES AND PHONOGRAMS TREATY ON AUDIOVISUAL PERFORMANCES

"The Government of the Republic of Korea would like to make the following contribution on the issues of audiovisual performances, although it admits that further considerations are necessary during the negotiation process. The Republic of Korea's proposals are not definitive, and we reserve the right to make further proposals.

1. Audiovisual performances shall be protected in line with the WIPO

2.2 韩国的提案

文件编号：AP/CE/2/3
文件语言：英语
文件链接：https://www.wipo.int/edocs/mdocs/copyright/en/ap_ce_2/ap_ce_2_3.pdf
中文文本：无
文件链接：无

视听表演议定书专家委员会

第二届会议
1998年6月8日至12日，日内瓦

韩国的提案

韩国政府关于世界知识产权组织表演和录音制品的视听表演条约议定书的提案

“韩国政府愿意就视听表演问题作出以下贡献，尽管它承认在谈判过程中需要进一步考虑。韩国的以下提案并非最终确定，我们保留进一步提议的权利。

1. 视听表演应按照保护听觉表演的《知识产权组织表演和录音制品条约》

Performances and Phonograms Treaty (hereinafter referred to as WPPT) in which aural performances are protected.

2. However, we should respect special conditions surrounding audiovisual performances in each country such as contractual practices in the audiovisual industry and should take into account the purpose of the relevant provisions of the Rome Convention and the Berne Convention.

3. Performers shall enjoy the following exclusive rights of authorizing their unfixed audiovisual performances:

(a) fixation;

(b) broadcasting and communication to the public.

4. Performers shall enjoy the following rights of their fixed audiovisual performances:

(a) the exclusive right to authorize the reproduction;

(b) the exclusive right of making available to the public, equivalent to the right given in the WPPT;

(c) the right to remuneration for broadcasting and communication to the public.

5. Concerning the right to remuneration for broadcasting and communication to the public of fixed performances, reservation on national treatment should be permitted in this protocol in the manner as provided in the WPPT.

6. We are also in favor of the provisions on the obligations concerning technological measures and rights management information included in the Protocol as those provided for in the WPPT.

"We have so far studied but could not work out a concrete position on the issues of moral rights, the right of distribution, and retroactive protection of audiovisual performances. These issues require further consultations with the interested parties in the Republic of Korea."

[End of document]

（以下简称 WPPT）加以保护。

2. 然而，我们应尊重每个国家视听表演的特殊条件，如视听行业的契约惯例，并应考虑到《罗马公约》和《伯尔尼公约》相关条款的目的。

3. 表演者对其尚未录制的视听表演享有以下专有权：

（a）录制；
（b）广播和向公众传播。
4. 表演者对其录制的视听表演享有下列权利：

（a）授权复制的专有权；
（b）向公众提供的专有权，该权利与 WPPT 规定的权利相同；

（c）基于广播和向公众传播而获得报酬的权利。
5. 基于对录制表演的广播和向公众传播而享有的获酬权，本议定书应允许以 WPPT 规定的方式保留国民待遇。

6. 我们还赞成与 WPPT 所规定的关于技术措施和权利管理信息义务的相关条款。

"到目前为止，我们已经研究过，但未能就精神权利、发行权和追溯保护视听表演等问题确定我们的立场。这些问题需要与韩国有关各方进一步协商。"

（文件完）

2.3 Proposal from the United States of America

Document Code: AP/CE/2/4
Language: English
URL: https://www.wipo.int/edocs/mdocs/copyright/en/ap_ce_2/ap_ce_2_4.pdf
Chinese Translation: Not Available.
URL: N/A

COMMITTEE OF EXPERTS
ON A PROTOCOL
CONCERNING AUDIOVISUAL PERFORMANCES

Second Session
GENEVA, JUNE 8 TO 12, 1998

PROPOSAL FROM THE UNITED STATES OF AMERICA

SUBSTANTIVE PROVISIONS OF A TREATY FOR THE PROTECTION OF PERFORMERS IN AUDIOVISUAL WORKS

Preamble

The Contracting Parties,

Noting that the development and convergence of new information and communicationtechnologies will allow for a rapid growth of audiovisual services and that this will increase the opportunities for performing artists to exploit their performances;

2.3 美国的提案

文件编号：AP/CE/2/4
文件语言：英语
文件链接：https://www.wipo.int/edocs/mdocs/copyright/en/ap_ce_2/ap_ce_2_4.pdf
中文文本：无
文件链接：无

视听表演议定书专家委员会

第二届会议

1998年6月8日至12日，日内瓦

美国的提案

保护视听作品表演者条约的实质性条款

序言

缔约各方

注意到新的信息和通信技术的发展和融合将使视听服务迅速增长，这将增加表演艺术家利用其表演的机会；

Recognizing the great importance of ensuring an adequate level of protection for these performances, in particular when they are exploited in the new digital environment;

Recognizing that the WIPO Performances and Phonograms Treaty (WPPT) does not cover the rights of performers in the audiovisual fixations of their performances, but that many provisions of the WPPT can be used or adapted as the basis for a new treaty protecting performers with respect to their audiovisual performances.

Have agreed as follows:

CHAPTER I
GENERAL PROVISIONS

Article 1
Relation to Other Conventions

(1) Nothing in this Treaty shall derogate from existing obligations that Contracting Parties have to each other under the International Convention for the Protection of Performers, Producers of Phonograms and Broadcasting Organizations done in Rome, October 26, 1961.

(2) Protection granted under this Treaty shall leave intact and shall in no way affect the protection of copyright in literary and artistic works. Consequently, no provision of this Treaty may be interpreted as prejudicing such protection.

This Treaty shall not have any connection with, nor shall it prejudice any rights and obligations under any other treaties.

Article 2
Definitions

For the purposes of this Treaty:

(a) “performers” are actors, singers, musicians, dancers, and other persons who act, sing, deliver, declaim, play in, interpret, or otherwise perform literary or artistic works or expressions of folklore, but not including extra performers or background performers;

(b) “fixation” means the embodiment of images, or of images and sounds, or of the representations thereof, from which they can be perceived, reproduced, or communicated through a device;

(c) “broadcasting” means the transmission by wireless means for public reception of images, or of images and sounds, or the representations thereof; such

意识到充分保护这些表演的重要性，特别是在新的数字环境中对其加以利用时；

认识到《世界知识产权组织表演和录音制品条约》（以下简称 WPPT）并未涵盖表演者对其表演的视听录制品方面的权利，但 WPPT 的许多条款可作为基础供保护表演者的视听表演新条约采纳或使用。

达成协议如下：

第一章
一般规定

第 1 条
与其他公约的关系

（1）本条约的任何内容均不得减损缔约方相互之间依照 1961 年 10 月 26 日在罗马签订的《保护表演者、录音制品制作者和广播组织国际公约》已承担的现有义务。

（2）依本议定书给予的保护不得触动或以任何方式影响对文学和艺术作品版权的保护。因此，本条约的任何内容均不得被解释为损害此种保护。

本条约不得与任何其他条约有任何关联，亦不得损害任何其他条约所规定的任何权利和义务。

第 2 条
定义

在本条约中：

（a）“表演者”是指演员、歌唱家、音乐家、舞蹈家以及对文学或艺术作品或民间文学艺术表达进行表演、歌唱、演说、朗诵、演奏、演绎或以其他方式进行表演的其他人员，但不包括临时演员或背景表演者；

（b）“录制品”是指图像、图像和声音或其体现物，通过装置可以被感觉、复制或传播；

（c）“广播”是指以无线方式的传送，使公众能接收声音或图像，或图像和声音，或图像和声音的表现物；通过卫星进行的此种传送亦为“广播”；传送密

transmission by satellite is also "broadcasting;" transmission of encrypted signals is "broadcasting" where the means for decrypting are provided to the public by the broadcasting organization or with its consent;

(d) "communication to the public" means the transmission to the public by any medium, otherwise than by broadcasting, of the images, or the sounds and images, or the representations thereof, comprised in an unfixed performance or in a fixed performance;

(e) an "audiovisual work" is a work consisting of a series of related images that are intended to be shown by the use of a device, together with any accompanying sounds.

Article 3

Beneficiaries of Protection

(1) Contracting Parties shall accord the protection provided under this Treaty to performers of other Contracting Parties as defined in paragraph (2) of this Article.

(2) Performers of other Contracting Parties shall be understood to be performers who meet any of the following conditions:

(a) those performers who are nationals of another Contracting Party and whose performance is unfixed or is fixed in an audiovisual work;

(b) those performers whose unfixed performance takes place on the territory of another Contracting Party;

(c) those performers whose performance is first fixed in an audiovisual work on the territory of another Contracting Party.

Article 4

National Treatment

With respect to performances for which they are protected under this Treaty as provided in Article 3, performers shall enjoy, in other Contracting Parties, the treatment that the laws of such parties do now or may hereafter grant to their own nationals, as well as the rights specifically granted by this Treaty.

CHAPTER II

RIGHTS OF PERFORMERS

Article 5

Moral Rights of Performers

(1) Independently of a performer's economic rights, and even after the transfer

码信号，只要广播组织或经其同意向公众提供了解码的手段；

(d)“向公众传播”是指通过除广播以外的任何媒介向公众传送图像、图像和声音或其体现物，尚未录制的表演或以视听录制品录制的表演；

(e)“视听作品”是指由一系列相关的图像组成，旨在通过使用设备进行显示，并且伴随声音的作品。

第3条

保护的受益人

(1)缔约各方应当对根据本条第(2)款所界定的其他缔约方的表演者进行保护。

(2)其他缔约方的表演者应被理解为符合下列条件：

(a)表演者是另一缔约方的国民，其表演已录制或尚未录制在视听作品中；

(b)尚未录制的表演发生在另一缔约方领土上的表演者；

(c)其表演在另一缔约方领土上首次被录制在视听作品中的表演者。

第4条

国民待遇

对于按照第3条规定受本条约保护的表演，表演者在其他缔约国应享有这些缔约国的法律现在或将来给予本国国民的待遇，以及本条约特别授予的权利。

第二章
表演者的权利

第5条

表演者的精神权利

(1)独立于表演者的经济权利，甚至在这些权利转让之后，表演者仍应对

of those rights, the performer shall, as regards his or her live performances or performances fixed in an audiovisual work, have the right to claim to be identified as the performer of such performances, except where omission is dictated by the manner of the use of the performance, and to object to any distortion, mutilation, or other modification of his or her performance that would be seriously prejudicial to the performer's reputation, where such modification is not part of the normal exploitation of an audiovisual work by the producer of the work or its successors in interest, pursuant to the exercise of rights of authorization acquired by the producer in the performance.

(2) The rights granted to a performer in accordance with paragraph (1) shall, after the said performer's death, be maintained, at least until the expiry of the rights of authorization set forth in Articles 6 through 10, and shall be exercisable by the persons or institutions authorized by the legislation of the Contracting Party where protection is claimed. However, those Contracting Parties whose legislation, at the moment of their ratification of or accession to this Treaty, does not provide for protection after the death of the performer of all rights set out in the preceding paragraph, may provide that some of these rights will, after the performer's death, cease to be maintained.

(3) The means of redress for safeguarding the rights granted under this Article shall be governed by the legislation of the Contracting Party where protection is claimed.

(4) The "normal exploitation of an audiovisual work" shall include the use of new or changed technology, media, formats and/or methods of distribution, dissemination, making available or communication to the public. A performer shall give reasonable consideration to the interests of the other performers in and creative authors of an audiovisual work when exercising the above described rights with respect to such work.

Article 6

Economic Rights of Performers in their Unfixed Performances

Performers shall enjoy the exclusive right of authorizing, as regards their performances:

(i) the broadcasting and communication to the public of their unfixed

于其现场表演或以视听录制品录制的表演享有权利：要求承认其系表演的表演者，除非因使用表演的方式而决定可省略不提其系表演者；反对任何对其表演进行的将有损其声誉的歪曲、篡改或其他修改，且这种修改不是作品制作者或其利益继承人根据制片人在演出中获得的授权对视听作品进行正常利用的一部分。

（2）根据第（1）款给予表演者的权利在其死亡后应继续保留，至少在第 6 条至第 10 条规定的权利期满为止，并可由被要求提供保护的缔约方立法所授权的个人或机构行使。但批准或加入本条约时其立法尚未规定在表演者死亡后保护上款所述全部权利的国家，则可规定其中部分权利在表演者死亡后不再保留。

（3）为保障本条所授予的权利而采取的救济措施应由被要求提供保护的缔约方立法规定。

（4）“视听作品的正常利用”应包括使用新的或经改变的技术、媒介、格式和 / 或发行、传播、向公众提供或传播的方法。表演者在行使上述作品权利时，应当合理考虑视听作品的其他表演者和创作者的利益。

第 6 条

表演者对其尚未录制的表演的经济权利

表演者应享有对其表演授权专有权利：

（i）广播和向公众传播其尚未录制的表演，除非该表演本身已属广播或向

performances, except where the performance is already a broadcast or a publicly communicated performance; and

(ii) the fixation of their unfixed performances.

Article 7

Right of Reproduction

Performers shall enjoy the exclusive right of authorizing the direct or indirect reproduction of their fixed performances in any manner or form.

Article 8

Right of Distribution

(1) Performers shall enjoy the exclusive right of authorizing the making available to the public of the original and copies of their fixed performances through sale or other transfer of ownership.

(2) Nothing in this Treaty shall affect the freedom of Contracting Parties to determine the conditions, if any, under which the exhaustion of the right in paragraph (1) applies after the first sale or other transfer of ownership of the original or a copy of the fixed performance with the authorization of the performer.

Article 9

Right of Making Available

Performers shall enjoy the exclusive right of authorizing the making available to the public of their fixed performances, by wire or wireless means, in such a way that members of the public may access them from a place and at a time individually chosen by them.

Article 10

Right of Broadcasting and Communication to the Public

(1) Except for conditions on the exercise of the right that would be permissible for audiovisual works under Article 11*bis* of the Berne Convention for the Protection of Literary and Artistic Works, performers shall enjoy the exclusive right of authorizing, as regards their performances fixed in audiovisual works, the broadcasting and communication to the public of such performances, except where such a performance is already a broadcast or a publicly communicated performance.

(2) Any Contracting Party may, in a notification deposited with the Director General of WIPO, declare that it will limit the right set forth in paragraph (1) to a

公众传播的表演；和

（ii）录制其尚未录制的表演。

第 7 条

复制权

表演者应享有授权以任何方式或形式对其已录制表演直接或间接地进行复制的专有权。

第 8 条

发行权

（1）表演者应享有授权通过销售或其他转让所有权的形式向公众提供其已录制表演的原件或复制件的专有权。

（2）对于已录制表演的原件或复制件经表演者授权被首次销售或以其他方式转让所有权之后适用本条第（1）款中权利用尽所依据的条件（如有此种条件），本条约的任何内容均不得影响缔约各方确定该条件的自由。

第 9 条

提供权

表演者应享有专有权，以授权通过有线或无线的方式向公众提供其已录制表演，使该表演可为公众在其个人选定的地点和时间获得。

第 10 条

广播权和向公众传播权

（1）除了《伯尔尼保护文学和艺术作品公约》第 11 条之二所允许的视听作品行使权利的条件外，表演者应享有授权广播和向公众传播其以视听录制品录制的表演的专有权，除非这类表演已经是广播或已公开传播的表演。

（2）缔约各方可以在向世界知识产权组织总干事交存的通知书中声明，第（1）款规定的权利仅限于获酬权。

right to remuneration only.

CHAPTER III
ADDITIONAL PROVISIONS

Article 11
Transfer of rights

Once a performer has consented to the fixation of his or her performance in an audiovisual work, he or she shall be deemed to have transferred all exclusive rights of authorization granted under this Treaty with respect to that particular audiovisual work to the producer of that work and its successors in interest, subject to contractual clauses to the contrary. The foregoing sentence shall not apply to any rights of remuneration a performer may have under the law of any Contracting Party, nor shall it require a Contracting Party to establish any such rights of remuneration.

Article 12
Limitations and Exceptions

(1) Contracting Parties may, in their national legislation, provide for the same kinds of limitations or exceptions with regard to the protection of performers as they provide for, in their national legislation, in connection with the protection of copyright in literary and artistic works.

(2) Contracting Parties shall confine any limitations of or exceptions to rights provided for in this Treaty to certain special cases which do not conflict with a normal exploitation of the performance and do not unreasonably prejudice the legitimate interests of the performer.

Article 13
Term of Protection

The term of protection to be granted to performers under this Treaty shall last, at least, until the end of a period of 50 years from the end of the year in which the performance was fixed.

Article 14
Implementation

Each Contracting Party may determine the means by which it will give effect to the provisions of this Treaty, including by means of the grant of a copyright or

第三章
补充规定

第 11 条
权利转让

表演者一旦同意将其表演录制于视听录制品中，应被视为将根据本条约授予的关于该特定视听作品的专有权转让给该作品的制作者及其利益继承人，但订立有任何相反合同者除外。上句不应适用于表演者根据任何缔约方的法律可能享有的任何报酬权，也不应要求缔约方确立任何此类报酬权。

第 12 条
限制与例外

（1）缔约方可以在其国内立法中规定有关保护表演者的限制或例外，正如它们在其国家立法中规定的有关保护文学和艺术作品的版权的限制或例外一样。

（2）缔约方应使本条约中所规定的任何权利限制或例外仅限于某些不与表演的正常利用相抵触、也不致不合理地损害表演者合法利益的特殊情况。

第 13 条
保护期限

根据本条约给予表演者的保护期，应自表演录制之年年终算起，至少持续到 50 年期满为止。

第 14 条
权利行使

每个缔约方可决定以何种方式落实本条约的规定，包括通过授予版权或其他相关权利的方式。

other related right.

Article 15

Obligations concerning Technological Measures

Contracting Parties shall provide adequate legal protection and effective legal remedies against the circumvention of effective technological measures that are used by performers or their transferees in connection with the exercise of their rights under this Treaty and that restrict acts, in respect of their performances, that are not authorized by the performers or that are not permitted by law.

Article 16

Obligations concerning Rights Management Information

(1) Contracting Parties shall provide adequate and effective legal remedies against any person knowingly performing any of the following acts knowing, or with respect to civil remedies having reasonable grounds to know, that it will induce, enable, facilitate, or conceal an infringement of any right covered by this Treaty:

(i) to remove or alter any electronic rights management information without authority;

(ii) to distribute, import for distribution, broadcast, communicate or make available to the public, without authority, performances or copies of fixed performances knowing that electronic rights management information has been removed or altered without authority.

(2) As used in this Article, “rights management information” means information that identifies the performer, the performance of the performer, or the owner of any right in the performance, or information about the terms and conditions of use of the performance, and any numbers or codes that represent such information, when any of these items of information is attached to a copy of a fixed performance or appears in connection with the broadcast, public communication, or making available to the public of a fixed performance.

Article 17

Formalities

The enjoyment and exercise of the rights provided for in this Treaty shall not be subject to any formality.

第 15 条

有关技术措施的义务

缔约各方应规定适当的法律保护和有效的法律补救办法，制止规避表演者或其受让人在行使本条约规定的权利时使用的、限制未经表演者授权或法律不允许的表演的有效技术措施。

第 16 条

有关权利管理信息义务

（1）缔约各方应规定适当和有效的法律补救办法，制止任何人明知、或就民事补救而言有合理根据知道其行为会诱使、促成、便利或包庇对本条约所涵盖的任何权利的侵犯而故意从事以下行为：

（i）未经许可去除或改变任何权利管理的电子信息；

（ii）未经许可发行、为发行目的进口、广播、向公众传播或提供明知已被未经许可去除或改变权利管理电子信息的表演或已录制表演的复制件。

（2）本条中的用语“权利管理信息”系指识别表演者、表演者的表演或对表演拥有任何权利的所有人的信息，或有关使用表演的条款和条件的信息，以及代表此种信息的任何数字或代码，各该项信息均附于已录制表演的复制件上，或者出现在广播、向公众传播或向公众提供的已录制表演上。

第 17 条

手续

享有和行使本议定书所规定的权利无须履行任何手续。

Article 18

Reservations

Subject to the provisions of Article 10(2), no reservations to this Treaty shall be permitted.

Article 19

Application in Time

(1) Contracting Parties shall apply the provisions of Article 18 of the Berne Convention, *mutatis mutandis*, to the rights of performers provided for in this Treaty.

(2) Notwithstanding paragraph (1), a Contracting Party may limit the application of Article 5 of this Treaty to performances that occurred after the entry into force of this Treaty for that Party.

Article 20

Provisions on Enforcement of Rights

(1) Contracting Parties undertake to adopt, in accordance with their legal systems, the measures necessary to ensure the application of this Treaty.

(2) Contracting Parties shall ensure that enforcement procedures are available under their law so as to permit effective action against any act of infringement of rights covered by this Treaty, including expeditious remedies to prevent infringement and remedies which constitute a deterrent to further infringements.

[End of document]

第 18 条

保留

在不违反第 10 条第（2）款规定的情况下，不得对本条约作出任何保留。

第 19 条

适用的时限

（1）缔约方应比照适用《伯尔尼公约》第 18 条关于表演者权利的规定。

（2）尽管有第（1）款的规定，缔约方可将本条约第 5 条的适用范围限于本条约对其生效后发生的表演。

第 20 条

权利行使条款

（1）缔约方承诺根据其法律制度采取必要的措施，以确保本条约的适用。

（2）缔约各方应确保依照其法律可以提供执法程序，以便能采取制止对本条约所涵盖权利的任何侵犯行为的有效行动，包括防止侵权的快速补救和为遏制进一步侵权的补救。

（文件完）

2.4 Proposal from Algeria, Burkina Faso, Cameroon, Ghana, Kenya, Malawi, Mali, Morocco, Namibia, Nigeria, Senegal, South Africa, Sudan, Togo and Zambia

Document Code: AP/CE/2/5
Language: English
URL: https://www.wipo.int/edocs/mdocs/copyright/en/ap_ce_2/ap_ce_2_5.pdf
Chinese Translation: Not Available.
URL: N/A

COMMITTEE OF EXPERTS
ON A PROTOCOL
CONCERNING AUDIOVISUAL PERFORMANCES
Second Session
GENEVA, JUNE 8 TO 12, 1998

PROPOSAL FROM ALGERIA, BURKINA FASO, CAMEROON, GHANA, KENYA, MALAWI, MALI, MOROCCO, NAMIBIA, NIGERIA, SENEGAL, SOUTH AFRICA, SUDAN, TOGO AND ZAMBIA

2.4 阿尔及利亚、布基纳法索、喀麦隆、加纳、肯尼亚、马拉维、马里、摩洛哥、纳米比亚、尼日利亚、塞内加尔、南非、苏丹、多哥和赞比亚的提案

文件编号：AP/CE/2/5
文件语言：英语
文件链接：https://www.wipo.int/edocs/mdocs/copyright/en/ap_ce_2/ap_ce_2_5.pdf
中文文本：无
文件链接：无

视听表演议定书专家委员会

第二届会议
1998年6月8日至12日，日内瓦

阿尔及利亚、布基纳法索、喀麦隆、加纳、肯尼亚、马拉维、马里、摩洛哥、纳米比亚、尼日利亚、塞内加尔、南非、苏丹、多哥和赞比亚的提案

PROTOCOL TO THE WIPO PERFORMANCES AND PHONOGRAMS TREATY, CONCERNING AUDIOVISUAL PERFORMANCES

The Contracting Parties,

Wishing to ensure an adequate level of protection for audiovisual performances, especially in the digital environment;

Noting that the WIPO Performances and Phonograms Treaty does not cover the moral or economic rights of performers in the audiovisual fixation of their unfixed performances, nor these rights in their audiovisually fixed performances;

Referring to the resolution concerning audiovisual performances adopted by the Diplomatic Conference on Certain Copyright and Neighboring Rights Questions on December 20, 1996;

Have agreed as follows:

Article 1

Relation to Other Conventions

(1) This Treaty constitutes a protocol to the WIPO Performances and Phonograms Treaty (hereinafter the "WPPT").

(2) Nothing in this Protocol shall derogate from existing obligations that Contracting Parties have to each other under the WPPT.

(3) Protection granted under this Protocol shall leave intact and shall in no way affect the protection of copyright in literary and artistic works. Consequently, no provision of this Protocol may be interpreted to prejudice such protection.

Article 2

Definitions

For the purposes of this Protocol:

(a) "performers" means actors, singers, musicians, dancers, and other persons who act, sing, deliver, declaim, play in, interpret, or otherwise perform literary or artistic works, or expressions of folklore;

(b) "audiovisual fixation" means the embodiment of moving images, whether or not accompanied by sound, or the representations thereof, from which they can

WPPT关于视听表演的议定书

缔约各方

为确保对视听表演，特别是在数字环境中的视听表演提供足够的保护；

注意到《世界知识产权组织表演和录音制品条约》对表演者的保护并未延伸到对其尚未录制的表演进行视听录制的权利，也未涵盖对其音频性录制表演进行利用的权利；

提及关于版权和邻接权若干问题的外交会议于 1996 年 12 月 20 日通过的《关于视听表演的决议》；

达成协议如下：

第 1 条

与其他公约的关系

（1）该条约为《世界知识产权组织表演和录音制品条约》（WPPT）的一项议定书。

（2）本议定书的任何规定均不得减损缔约方根据 WPPT 彼此承担的现有义务。

（3）依本议定书给予的保护不得触动或以任何方式影响对文学和艺术作品版权的保护。因此，本条约的任何内容均不得被解释为损害此种保护。

第 2 条

定义

在本条约中：

（a）“表演者”系指演员、歌唱家、音乐家、舞蹈家以及对文学或艺术作品或民间文学艺术表达进行表演、歌唱、演说、朗诵、演奏、演绎或以其他方式进行表演的其他人员；

（b）“视听录制品”系指活动图像的体现物，不论其是否伴有声音或声音表现物，它们可以通过某种装置被感知、复制或传播。

be perceived, reproduced, or communicated through a device.

Article 3

Beneficiaries of Protection under this Protocol

The Contracting Parties shall accord the protection granted under this Protocol to performers who are nationals of other Contracting Parties.

Article 4

National Treatment

(1) Each Contracting Party shall accord to nationals of other Contracting Parties, in respect of the subject matter protected under this Protocol:

(a) the rights specifically granted by this Protocol; and

(b) such additional rights as it accords to its own nationals.

(2) A Contracting Party shall be entitled, in respect of nationals of any other Contracting Party, to limit the protection provided for in subparagraph (b) of paragraph (1) to the extent to which, and to the term for which, the latter Contracting Party grants such rights to the nationals of the former Contracting Party.

Article 5

Moral Rights of Performers

(1) Independently of a performer's economic rights, and even after the transfer of those rights, a performer shall, as regards his performances, whether live of embodied in audiovisual fixations, have the right:

(a) to be identified as the performer of his performances, except where omission is dictated by the manner of the use of the performance; and

(b) to object to any distortion, mutilation, or other modification of his performances that would be prejudicial to his reputation.

(2) The rights granted to a performer in accordance with paragraph (1) shall, after his death, be maintained, at least until the expiry of the economic rights, and shall be exercisable by the person or institutions authorized by the legislation of the Contracting Party where protection is claimed. However, those Contracting Parties whose legislation, at the moment of their ratification of this Protocol, does not provide for protection after the death of the performer ofall rights set out in the

第3条

本议定书保护的受益者

缔约方应向其他缔约方国民的表演者提供本条约规定的保护。

第4条

国民待遇

（1）在本议定书所保护的客体方面，每一缔约方均应将其给予本国国民的待遇给予其他缔约方的国民：

（a）本议定书具体授予的权利；

（b）授予本国国民的额外权利。

（2）对于任何其他缔约方的国民，缔约一方有权将第（1）款（b）项规定的保护限制在其本国国民在该另一缔约方享有的权利的范围和期限之内。

第5条

表演者的精神权利

（1）独立于表演者的经济权利，甚至在这些权利转让之后，表演者仍应对于其现场表演或以视听录制品录制的表演享有权利：

（a）承认其系表演的表演者，除非因使用表演的方式而决定可省略不提其系表演者；以及

（b）反对任何对其表演进行的将有损其声誉的歪曲、篡改或其他修改。

（2）根据第（1）款授予表演者的权利在其死亡后应继续保留，至少到其经济权利期满为止，并可由被要求提供保护的缔约方立法所授权的个人或机构行使。但批准本议定书时其立法尚未规定在表演者死亡后保护上款所述全部权利的国家，则可规定其中部分权利在表演者死亡后不再保留。

preceding paragraph may provide that some of these rights will, after his death, cease to be maintained.

(3) The means of redress for safeguarding the rights granted under this Article shall be governed by the legislation of the Contracting Party where protection is claimed.

Article 6

Right of Fixation of Unfixed Performances

Performers shall enjoy the exclusive right of authorizing the audiovisual fixation of their unfixed performances.

Article 7

Right of Reproduction

Performers shall enjoy the exclusive right of authorizing the direct or indirect reproduction, in any manner or form, of audiovisual fixations of their performances.

Article 8

Right of Distribution

(1) Performers shall enjoy the exclusive right of authorizing the making available to the public of the original and copies of the audiovisual fixations of their performances through sale or other transfer of ownership.

(2) Nothing in this Protocol shall affect the freedom of Contracting Parties to determine the conditions, if any, under which the exhaustion of the right in paragraph (1) applies after the first sale or other transfer of ownership of the original or a copy of the fixed performance with the authorization of the performer.

Article 9

Right of Rental

Performers shall enjoy the exclusive right of authorizing the commercial rental to the public of the original and copies of the audiovisual fixations of their performances. Contracting Parties are exempt from this obligation unless the commercial rental has led to widespread copying of the works which materially impairs the exclusive right of reproduction.

Article 10

Right of Making Available of Fixed Performances

Performers shall enjoy the exclusive right of authorizing the making available to the public of audiovisual fixations of their performances, by wire or wireless

（3）为保障本条所授予的权利而采取的补救方法应由被要求提供保护的缔约方立法规定。

第 6 条

录制尚未录制的表演的权利

表演者享有专有权，授权对其尚未录制的表演进行视听录制。

第 7 条

复制权

表演者应享有授权以任何方式或形式对其以视听录制品录制的表演直接或间接地进行复制的专有权。

第 8 条

发行权

（1）表演者应享有授权通过销售或其他转让所有权的形式向公众提供其以视听录制品录制的表演的原件或复制件的专有权。

（2）对于已录制表演的原件或复制件经表演者授权被首次销售或以其他形式转让所有权之后适用本条第（1）款中权利的用尽所依据的条件（如有此种条件），本议定书的任何内容均不得影响缔约方确定该条件的自由。

第 9 条

出租权

表演者应享有授权将其以视听录制品录制的表演的原件和复制件向公众进行商业性出租的专有权。除非商业性出租已导致此种录制品的广泛复制，从而严重损害表演者的专有复制权，缔约各方才能免除此义务。

第 10 条

提供已录制表演的权利

表演者应享有专有权，以授权通过有线或无线的方式向公众提供其以视听录制品录制的表演，使该表演可为公众在其个人选定的地点和时间获得。

means, in such a way that members of the public may access them from a place and at a time individually chosen by them.

Article 11

Reservations

No reservations to this Protocol shall be permitted.

Article 12

Application of Certain Substantive Provisions of the WPPT

The Contracting Parties shall apply, mutatis mutandis, in respect of the protection granted under this Protocol, the provisions of Articles 16 (Limitations and Exceptions),17 (Term of Protection), 18 (Obligations concerning Technological Measures), 19 (Obligations concerning the Rights Management Information), 20 (Formalities), 22 (Application in Time) and 23 (Provisions on Enforcement of Rights) of the WPPT.

Article 13

Assembly

(1) The Contracting Parties shall have an Assembly.

(2) This Assembly shall be the same as the one created by the WPPT. Its functioning shall be governed, *mutatis mutandis*, by Article 24 of the WPPT.

Article 14

Eligibility for Becoming Party to the Protocol

Any party to the WPPT may become party to this Protocol.

Article 15

Signature of the Protocol

This Protocol shall be open for signature until... by any party eligible under Article 14.

Article 16

Final Clauses

The provisions of Articles 25 (International Bureau), 27 (Rights and Obligations under the Treaty), 29 (Entry into Force of the Treaty), 30 (Effective Date of Becoming Party to the Treaty), 31 (Denunciation of the Treaty), 32 (Languages of the Treaty) and 33 (Depository) of the WPPT shall apply, *mutatis mutandis*.

[End of document]

第 11 条

保留

本议定书不得作出任何保留。

第 12 条

WPPT 某些实质性条款的适用

缔约方应比照适用 WPPT 第 16 条（限制与例外）、第 17 条（保护期限）、第 18 条（与技术措施有关的义务）、第 19 条（与权利管理信息有关的义务）、第 20 条（手续）、第 22 条（适用的时限）、第 23 条（权利行使条款）的规定。

第 13 条

大会

（1）缔约方应设大会。

（2）大会应与根据 WPPT 设立的大会相同，其运作比照适用 WPPT 第 24 条的规定。

第 14 条

加入议定书的资格

WPPT 的任何缔约方均可成为本议定书的缔约方。

第 15 条

议定书的签署

本议定书开放以供任何符合本议定书第 14 条规定的缔约方签署，直至……

第 16 条

最后条款

其他应比照适用 WPPT 第 25 条（国际局）、第 27 条（本条约规定的权利和义务）、第 29 条（本条约的生效）、第 30 条（成为本条约缔约方的生效日期）、第 31 条（退约）、第 32 条（本条约的语文）和第 33 条（保存人）的规定。

（文件完）

2.5 Report of the Regional Consultation Meeting for Latin America and the Caribbean, Held in Quito from May 4 to 6, 1998

Document Code: AP/CE/2/6
Language: English
URL: https://www.wipo.int/edocs/mdocs/copyright/en/ap_ce_2/ap_ce_2_6.pdf
Chinese Translation: Not Available.
URL: N/A

COMMITTEE OF EXPERTS
ON A PROTOCOL
CONCERNING AUDIOVISUAL PERFORMANCES
Second Session
GENEVA, JUNE 8 TO 12, 1998

REPORT OF THE REGIONAL CONSULTATION MEETING FOR LATIN AMERICA AND THE CARIBBEAN, HELD IN QUITO FROM MAY 4 TO 6, 1998

submitted on behalf of Argentina, Brazil, Colombia, Costa Rica, Cuba, Ecuador, Guyana, Jamaica, Mexico, Panama, Paraguay, Peru, Trinidad and Tobago, Uruguay and Venezuela

2.5 1998 年 5 月 4 日至 6 日在基多举行的拉丁美洲和加勒比区域协商会议的报告

文件编号：AP/CE/2/6
文件语言：英语
文件链接：https://www.wipo.int/edocs/mdocs/copyright/en/ap_ce_2/ap_ce_2_6.pdf
中文文本：无
文件链接：无

视听表演议定书专家委员会

第二届会议
1998 年 6 月 8 日至 12 日，日内瓦

1998年5月4日至6日在基多举行的拉丁美洲和加勒比区域协商会议的报告

由代表阿根廷、巴西、哥伦比亚、哥斯达黎加、古巴、厄瓜多尔、圭亚那、牙买加、墨西哥、巴拿马、巴拉圭、秘鲁、特立尼达和多巴哥、乌拉圭和委内瑞拉提交

REPORT ON THE REGIONAL CONSULTATION MEETING FOR LATIN AMERICAN AND CARIBBEAN COUNTRIES ON A PROTOCOL CONCERNING AUDIOVISUAL PERFORMANCES AND OTHER NEW INTERNATIONAL NORMS CONCERNING THE PROTECTION OF COPYRIGHT AND RELATED RIGHTS

Quito, May 4 to 6, 1998

In the city of Quito, Ecuador, from May 4 to 6, 1998, the Regional Consultation Meeting of Latin American and Caribbean Countries on a Protocol concerning Audiovisual Performances and Other New International Norms concerning the Protection of Copyright and Related Rights took place. Dr. Carlos Játiva (Ecuador) was elected Chairman and Ms. Dianne Daley (Jamaica) was elected Vice-Chairman of the Consultation Meeting. The list of participants is attached.

The discussions were based on documents AP/CE/2/2 and AP/CE/2/3, prepared by WIPO, and on the proposal presented by Peru.

Consensus was reached on the following points:

I. Title

Protocol to the WIPO Performances and Phonograms Treaty concerning Audiovisual Performances.

II. Preamble

The Contracting Parties

Noting that the WIPO Performances and Phonograms Treaty does not cover the rights ofperformers in the audiovisual fixation of their unfixed performances, nor the exploitation of their audiovisually fixed performances;

Referring to the resolution concerning audiovisual performances adopted by theDiplomatic Conference on Certain Copyright and Neighboring Rights Questions on December 20, 1996;

拉丁美洲和加勒比地区国家关于视听表演议定书和其他有关版权和邻接权保护的新国际规范区域协商会议的报告

1998年5月4日至6日，基多

1998 年 5 月 4 日至 6 日在厄瓜多尔基多市举行了拉丁美洲和加勒比地区国家关于视听表演议定书和其他有关版权和邻接权保护的新国际规范区域协商会议。Carlos Játiva 博士（厄瓜多尔）当选为主席，Dianne Daley 女士（牙买加）当选为会议副主席，参会人员名单见附件。

讨论以世界知识产权组织编写的 AP/CE/2/2 号文件、AP/CE/2/3 号文件以及秘鲁的提案为基础。

会议就下列事项达成了共识：

I. 标题

《世界知识产权组织表演和录音制品条约》关于视听表演的议定书

II. 序言

缔约各方

注意到《世界知识产权组织表演和录音制品条约》对表演者的保护并未延伸到对其尚未录制的表演进行视听录制的权利，也未涵盖对其音频性录制表演进行利用的权利；

提及关于版权和邻接权若干问题的外交会议于 1996 年 12 月 20 日通过的《关于视听表演的决议》；

Wishing to ensure an adequate level of protection for audiovisual performances, especially in the digital environment;

Have agreed as follows:

III. Relation to other Conventions; Relation with copyright

1. This treaty constitutes a Protocol to the WIPO Performances and Phonograms Treaty done in Geneva on December 20, 1996 (hereinafter "the WIPO Treaty").

2. No provision of this Protocol shall detract from the mutual obligations of Contracting Parties under the International Convention for the Protection of Performers, Producers of Phonograms and Broadcasting Organizations, done at Rome on October 26, 1961 ("the Rome Convention").

3. The protection granted under this Protocol shall leave intact and in no way affect the protection of copyright in literary and artistic works. Consequently, no provision of this Treaty may be interpreted as prejudicing such protection.

4. This Protocol shall have no connection with, and shall not prejudice any right or obligation under, any treaty other than the WIPO Treaty.

IV. Definitions

1. The Contracting Parties shall apply, *mutatis mutandis*, the definitions set out in Article 2 paragraphs (a), (e), (f) and (g) of the WIPO Treaty in connection with the protection granted under this Protocol.

2. For the purposes of this Protocol, "audiovisual fixation" means the embodiment of moving images, whether or not accompanied by sound, or the representations thereof, from which they can be perceived, reproduced or communicated through a device.

3. There was consensus that the definition of the term "performer" should not extend to persons whose contributions to a performance cannot be identified individually, such as the so-called extras.

V. Beneficiaries of protection

The Contracting Parties shall accord the protection provided under this Protocol:

a) to the performers who are nationals of other Contracting Parties, and/or

b) in case where a performance is fixed in another Contracting Party.

希望确保对视听表演，特别是在数字环境中的视听表演提供足够的保护；

达成协议如下：

III. 与其他公约的关系；与版权的关系

1. 该条约系 1996 年 12 月 20 日在日内瓦签订的《世界知识产权组织表演和录音制品条约》（以下简称 WIPO 条约）的一项议定书的组成部分。

2. 本议定书的任何规定均不得减损缔约各方之间依照 1961 年 10 月 26 日在罗马签订的《保护表演者、录音制品制作者和广播组织国际公约》（《罗马公约》）承担的相互义务。

3. 依本议定书给予的保护不得触动或以任何方式影响对文学和艺术作品版权的保护。因此，本条约的任何内容均不得被解释为损害此种保护。

4. 除 WIPO 条约之外，本议定书不得与任何其他条约有任何关联，亦不得损害任何其他条约所规定的任何权利和义务。

IV. 定义

1. 缔约各方应比照适用 WIPO 条约第 2 条（a）、（e）、（f）和（g）款中关于本议定书所给予保护的定义。

2. 在本议定书中，"视听录制品" 系指活动图像的体现物，无论其是否伴有声音或声音表现物，它们可以通过某种装置被感知、复制或传播。

3. 与会者一致认为，"表演者" 一词的定义不应扩大到那些对表演的贡献无法单独确定的人，如所谓的临时演员。

V. 保护的受益者

缔约各方应将本议定书规定的保护给予：

a）属于其他缔约方国民的表演者，和 / 或

b）其表演在另一缔约方国内被录制的表演者。

VI. National treatment

The issue is left for further consultations during the June 1998 session of the Committee of Experts.

VII. Formalities

The enjoyment and exercise of the rights provided for in this Protocol shall not be subject to any formality.

VIII. Moral rights of performers

(1) Independently of a performer's economic rights, and even after the transfer of those rights, the performer shall, as regards his live audiovisual performances, with or without sounds, or performances included in audiovisual fixations, have the right to claim to be identified as the performer of his performances, except where omission is dictated by the manner of the use of the performance (and to object to any distortion, mutilation or other modification of his performances that would be prejudicial to his reputation, on the understanding, however, that the producer of the audiovisual fixation may make modifications necessary to facilitate the normal exploitations of the fixations).

(2) The rights granted to a performer in accordance with paragraph (1) shall, after his death, be maintained, at least until the expiry of the economic rights, and shall be exercisable by the persons or institutions authorized by the legislation of the Contracting Party where protection is claimed. However, those Contracting Parties whose legislation, at the moment of their ratification of, or accession to, this Treaty, does not provide for protection after the death of the performer of all rights set out in the preceding paragraph may provide that some of these rights will, after his death, cease to be maintained.

(3) The means of redress for safeguarding the rights granted under this Article shall be governed by the legislation of the Contracting Party where protection is claimed.

Note: In paragraph (1), the phrase included in square brackets will be subject of further consultations.

IX. Economic rights of performers in their unfixed performances

The Contracting Parties shall accord, *mutatis mutandis*, to performers, as

VI. 国民待遇

这个问题留待专家委员会于 1998 年 6 月的会议上进一步协商。

VII. 手续

享有和行使本议定书所规定的权利无须履行任何手续。

VIII. 表演者的精神权利

（1）独立于表演者的经济权利，甚至在这些权利转让之后，表演者仍应对于其现场表演（无论是否伴有声音）或以视听录制品录制的表演享有权利：要求承认其系表演的表演者，除非因使用表演的方式而决定可省略不提其系表演者；（反对任何对其表演进行的将有损其声誉的歪曲、篡改或其他修改，且这种修改不是作品制作者或其利益继承人根据制片人在演出中获得的授权对视听作品进行正常利用的一部分）。

（2）根据本条第（1）款授予表演者的权利在其死亡后应继续保留，至少到其经济权利期满为止，并可由被要求提供保护的缔约各方立法所授权的个人或机构行使。但批准或加入本条约时其立法尚未规定在表演者死亡后保护上款所述全部权利的缔约方，则可规定其中部分权利在表演者死亡后不再保留。

（3）为保障本条所授予的权利而采取的救济措施应由被要求提供保护的缔约方立法规定。

注：在本条第（1）款中，方括号中的短语有待于进一步协商。

IX. 表演者对其尚未录制的表演的经济权利

缔约各方应比照适用 WIPO 条约第 6 条（表演者在尚未录制表演中的经济

regards their unfixed audiovisual performances, whether or not accompanied by sound, the same rights as those granted under Article 6 (Economic rights of performers in their unfixed performances) of the WIPO Treaty.

X. Economic rights of performers concerning audiovisual fixations

1. Right of reproduction

The Contracting Parties shall accord, *mutatis mutandis*, to performers, as regards the use of audiovisual fixations of their performances, the same rights as those granted under Article 7 (Right of reproduction) of the WIPO Treaty.

2. Right of distribution

The Contracting Parties shall accord, *mutatis mutandis*, to performers, as regards the use of audiovisual fixations of their performances, the same rights as those granted under Article 8 (Right of distribution) of the WIPO Treaty.

3. Right of rental

The Contracting Parties shall accord, *mutatis mutandis*, to performers, as regards the use of audiovisual fixations of their performances, the same rights as those granted under Article 9 (Right of rental) of the WIPO Treaty.

4. Right of making available

The Contracting Parties shall accord, *mutatis mutandis*, to performers, as regards the use of audiovisual fixations of their performances, the same rights as those granted under Article 10 (Right of making available of fixed performances) of the WIPO Treaty.

5. Right of broadcasting and communication to the public

Performers shall enjoy the exclusive rights of authorizing the broadcasting and other communication to the public of their performances fixed in audiovisual fixations.

In respect of broadcasting of audiovisual fixations, the Contracting Parties may apply *mutatis mutandis*, the provision of Article 11*bis*(2) of the Berne Convention.

The Delegation of Brazil declared that, with respect to point 5, it was not in the position to express its opinion, since, in its country, there were still consultations in preparation of the June 8 to 12, 1998, session of the Committee of Experts.

The Delegation of Uruguay declared that, with respect to the entire contents of title X, it was not in a position to express its opinion, since, in its country, there were

权利）所赋予的权利，授予表演者对其尚未录制的表演经济权利，无论其是否伴有声音。

X. 表演者对视听录制品的经济权利

1. 复制权

缔约各方在使用表演者的视听录制品时，应比照适用 WIPO 条约第 7 条（复制权）所赋予的权利，授予表演者相同的权利。

2. 发行权

缔约各方在使用表演者的视听录制品时，应比照适用 WIPO 条约第 8 条（发行权）所赋予的权利，授予表演者相同的权利。

3. 出租权

缔约各方在使用表演者的视听录制品时，应比照适用 WIPO 条约第 9 条（出租权）所赋予的权利，授予表演者相同的权利。

4. 提供权

缔约各方在使用表演者的视听录制品时，应比照适用 WIPO 条约第 10 条（提供已录制表演的权利）所赋予的权利，授予表演者相同的权利。

5. 广播权和向公众传播权

表演者应享有授权进行广播和向公众传播其以视听录制品录制的表演的专有权。

关于视听录制品的广播，缔约各方可比照适用《伯尔尼公约》第 11 条第（2）款的规定。

巴西代表团表示，其对本条第 5 点不发表意见。因为巴西仍在为筹备 1998 年 6 月 8 日至 12 日的专家委员会届会进行协商。

乌拉圭代表团表示，其对本条全部内容不发表意见，因为乌拉圭仍在为筹备 1998 年 6 月 8 日至 12 日的专家委员会届会进行协商。

still consultations in preparation of the June 8 to 12, 1998, session of the Committee of Experts.

XI. Limitations and exceptions

The Contracting Parties shall apply, *mutatis mutandis*, in respect of the protection granted under this Protocol, the provisions of Article 16 (Limitations and exceptions) of the WIPO Treaty.

XII. Contractual arrangements concerning the rights of performers

In the case where a performer authorizes the inclusion of his performance in an audiovisual fixation, the Contracting Parties shall apply, *mutatis mutandis*, the provision of Article 14*bis*(2)(b) of the Berne Convention.

The Delegation of Brazil declared that, with respect to the entire contents of title XII, it was not in the position to express its opinion, since, in its country, there were still consultations in preparation of the June 8 to 12, 1998, session of the Committee of Experts.

XIII. Term of protection

The term of protection to be granted under this Protocol shall last, at least, until the end of a period of 50 years computed from the end of the year in which the performance was fixed.

XIV. Obligations concerning technological measures

The Contracting Parties shall apply, *mutatis mutandis*, in respect of protection granted under this Protocol, the provisions of Article 18 (Obligations concerning technological measures) of the WIPO Treaty.

XV. Obligations concerning rights management information

The Contracting Parties shall apply, *mutatis mutandis*, in respect of protection granted under this Protocol, the provisions of Article 19 (Obligations concerning rights management information) of the WIPO Treaty.

XVI. Reservations

No reservations to this Protocol shall be permitted.

XVII. Application in time

1. The Contracting Parties shall apply the provisions of Article 18 of the Berne Convention, *mutatis mutandis*, to the rights of the performers provided for in this

XI. 限制与例外

对于根据本议定书给予的保护，缔约各方应比照适用 WIPO 条约第 16 条（限制与例外）的规定。

XII. 关于表演者权利的合同安排

如果表演者授权将其表演录制成视听录制品，缔约各方应比照适用《伯尔尼公约》第 14 条之二（2）（b）款的规定。

巴西代表团表示，其对本条的全部内容不发表意见。因为巴西仍在为筹备 1998 年 6 月 8 日至 12 日的专家委员会届会进行协商。

XIII. 保护期

根据本议定书授予的保护期限，应自表演被录制之年年终算起，至少持续到 50 年期满为止。

XIV. 关于技术措施的义务

对于根据本议定书给予的保护，缔约各方应比照适用 WIPO 条约第 18 条（有关技术措施的义务）的规定。

XV. 关于权利管理信息的义务

对于根据本议定书给予的保护，缔约各方应比照适用 WIPO 条约第 19 条（关于权利管理信息的义务）的规定。

XVI. 保留

不得对本议定书作出任何保留。

XVII. 适用的时限

1. 对于根据本议定书给予的表演者权利，缔约各方应比照适用《伯尔尼公约》第 18 条的规定。

Protocol.

2. This Protocol shall not detract from the rights acquired in any Contracting Party prior to the date of entry into force of this Protocol in that Party.

3. A Contracting Party shall not be obliged to apply the provisions of this Protocol toperformances given, or to audiovisual fixations made, prior to its entry into force in that Party.

XVIII. Provisions on enforcement of rights

The Contracting Parties shall apply, *mutatis mutandis*, in respect of protection granted under this Protocol, the provisions of Article 23 (Enforcement of rights) of the WIPO Treaty.

XIX. Administrative provisions and final clauses

1. Assembly

The Contracting Parties shall have an Assembly. This Assembly shall be the same as the one created by the WIPO Treaty.

2. Eligibility for becoming party to the Protocol

Any party to the WIPO Treaty may become party to this Protocol.

3. Signature of the Protocol

This Protocol shall be open for signature until... by any Member State of WIPO and by the European Community.

4. Entry into force of the Protocol

This Protocol shall enter into force, following the date of entry into force of the WIPO Treaty, three months after 20 instruments of ratification or accession by States have been deposited with the Director General of WIPO.

5. Final clauses

The provisions of Articles 25 (International Bureau), 27 (Rights and obligations under the Treaty), 30 (Effective date of becoming party of the Treaty), 31 (Denunciation of the Treaty), 32 (Languages of the Treaty) and 33 (Depository) of the WIPO Treaty shall apply, mutatis mutandis.

[End of document]

2. 本议定书规定的保护不得损害本议定书对每一缔约方生效之前取得的任何权利。

3. 缔约各方没有义务将本议定书的规定适用于本议定书在该缔约方生效之前所作出的表演或者视听录制品中。

XVIII. 权利行使条款

对于根据本议定书给予的保护，缔约方应比照适用WIPO条约第23条（权利的行使）的规定。

XIX. 行政性规定和最后条款

1. 大会

缔约方应设大会，大会应与WIPO条约设立的大会相同。

2. 成为本议定书缔约方的资格

WIPO条约的任何缔约方都可以加入本议定书。

3. 议定书的签署

本议定书开放以供任何世界知识产权组织成员国和欧共体成员国签署，直至……

4. 议定书的生效

本议定书自WIPO条约生效之日起生效，即自各国向世界知识产权组织总干事交存20份批准书或加入书之日起3个月后生效。

5. 最后条款

本议定书比照适用WIPO条约第25条（国际局）、第27条（本条约规定的权利和义务）、第30条（成为本条约缔约方的生效日期）、第31条（退约）、第32条（本条约的语文）和第33条（保存人）的规定。

（文件完）

2.6 Comparative Table of Proposals Received by June 3, 1998

Document Code: AP/CE/2/7
Language: English
URL: https://www.wipo.int/edocs/mdocs/copyright/en/ap_ce_2/ap_ce_2_7.pdf
Chinese Translation: Not Available.
URL: N/A

COMMITTEE OF EXPERTS
ON A PROTOCOL
CONCERNING AUDIOVISUAL PERFORMANCES
Second Session
GENEVA, JUNE 8 TO 12, 1998

COMPARATIVE TABLE OF PROPOSALS RECEIVED BY JUNE 3, 1998

prepared by the International Bureau

Introductory note

The Comparative Table of Proposals presented in the Annex of this document is an updated version of Annex II of document AP/CE/2/2. In addition to the contents of that first comparative table, the new comparative table takes also into account all submissions from WIPO Member States received after the deadline of January 15,1998, namely from:

- the Republic of Korea(document AP/CE/2/3);

2.6 截至 1998 年 6 月 3 日收到的提案比较表

文件编号：AP/CE/2/7
文件语言：英语
文件链接：https://www.wipo.int/edocs/mdocs/copyright/en/ap_ce_2/ap_ce_2_7.pdf
中文文本：无
文件链接：无

视听表演议定书专家委员会

第二届会议
1998 年 6 月 8 日至 12 日，日内瓦

截至1998年6月3日收到的提案比较表

由国际局编写

介绍性说明

本文件附件所载提案比较表是 AP/CE/2/2 号会议文件附件二的更新版本。除了第一个比较表的内容外，新的比较表还考虑到 1998 年 1 月 15 日截止日期之后从世界知识产权组织成员国收到的所有材料，包括：

– 韩国（AP/CE/2/3 号文件）；

- the United States of America(documents AP/CE/2/4 and AP/CE/2/4 Corr.);

- Algeria, Burkina Faso, Cameroon, Ghana, Kenya, Malawi, Mali, Morocco, Namibia, Nigeria, Senegal, South Africa, Sudan, Togo and Zambia(hereinafter referred to as "Certain States of Africa"(document AP/CE/2/5));

- Argentina, Brazil, Colombia, Costa Rica, Cuba, Ecuador, Guyana, Jamaica, Mexico, Panama, Paraguay, Peru, Trinidad and Tobago, Uruguay and Venezuela(hereinafter referred to as "Certain States of Latin America and the Caribbean"(document AP/CE/2/6)).

The new Comparative Table of Proposals does not contain any more the individual proposals from Argentina, Colombia and Ghana(see document AP/CE/2/2), as these countries have later joined the common proposals contained in document AP/CE/2/5 and AP/CE/2/6, respectively.

[The Comparative Table of Proposals is limited to proposals for a Protocol or a Treaty. Therefore, it does not contain other suggestions or elements of information, as were submitted by Australia and Japan(document AP/CE/2/2), but also, in conjunction with their proposals, by the Republic of Korea(document AP/CE/2/3) and Certain States of Latin America and the Caribbean(document AP/CE/2/6)].

[Annex follows]

– 美国（AP/CE/2/4 号文件和 AP/CE/2/4 号文件修正案）；

– 阿尔及利亚、布基纳法索、喀麦隆、加纳、肯尼亚、马拉维、马里、摩洛哥、纳米比亚、尼日利亚、塞内加尔、南非、苏丹、多哥和赞比亚（以下简称某些非洲国家）（AP/CE/2/5 号文件）；

– 阿根廷、巴西、哥伦比亚、哥斯达黎加、古巴、厄瓜多尔、圭亚那、牙买加、墨西哥、巴拿马、巴拉圭、秘鲁、特立尼达和多巴哥、乌拉圭和委内瑞拉（以下简称拉丁美洲和加勒比某些国家）（AP/CE/2/6 号文件）。

新的提案比较表不再包含阿根廷、哥伦比亚和加纳的单独提案（见 AP/CE/2/2 号文件），因为这些国家后来分别加入了 AP/CE/2/5 号文件和 AP/CE/2/6 号文件所载的共同提案。

［提案比较表仅限于议定书或条约提案，因此不包含澳大利亚和日本提交的其他建议或信息的要点（AP/CE/2/2 号文件），也不包含韩国（AP/CE/2/3 号文件）和拉丁美洲和加勒比某些国家（AP/CE/2/6 号文件）的建议］。

（后接附件）

COMPARATIVE TABLE OF THE PROPOSALS RECEIVED FROM WIPO MEMBER STATES AND THE EUROPEAN COMMUNITYCONTENTS

(page)

从世界知识产权组织成员国和欧共体成员国收到的提案比较表

（页码）

I. Title

CERTAIN STATES OF AFRICA

Protocol to the WIPO Performances and Phonograms Treaty, concerning Audiovisual Performances.

CERTAIN STATES OF LATIN AMERICA AND THE CARIBBEAN

Protocol to the WIPO Performances and Phonograms Treaty concerning Audiovisual Performances.

EUROPEAN COMMUNITY AND ITS MEMBER STATES

Protocol to the WIPO Performances and Phonograms Treaty, concerning Audiovisual Performances.

UNITED STATES OF AMERICA

Substantive Provisions of a Treaty for the Protection of Performers in Audiovisual Works.

II. Preamble

CERTAIN STATES OF AFRICA

The Contracting Parties,

Wishing to ensure an adequate level of protection for audiovisual performances, especially in the digital environment;

Noting that the WIPO Performances and Phonograms Treaty does not cover the moral or economic rights of performers in the audiovisual fixation of their unfixed performances, nor these rights in their audiovisually fixed performances;

Referring to the resolution concerning audiovisual performances adopted by the Diplomatic Conference on Certain Copyright and Neighboring Rights Questions on December 20, 1996;

Have agreed as follows:

CERTAIN STATES OF LATIN AMERICA AND THE CARIBBEAN

The Contracting Parties

Noting that the WIPO Performances and Phonograms Treaty does not cover the rights of performers in the audiovisual fixation of their unfixed performances, nor the exploitation of their audiovisually fixed performances;

Referring to the resolution concerning audiovisual performances adopted by the Diplomatic Conference on Certain Copyright and Neighboring Rights Questions

I. 标题

非洲的某些国家

《WPPT 关于视听表演的议定书》

拉丁美洲和加勒比地区的某些国家

《WWPT 关于视听表演的议定书》

欧共体及其成员国

《WPPT 关于视听表演的议定书》

美国

《视听作品表演者保护条约》的实质性条款

II. 序言

非洲的某些国家

各缔约方

为确保对视听表演，特别是在数字环境中的视听表演提供足够的保护；

注意到《世界知识产权组织表演和录音制品条约》对表演者的保护并未延伸到对其尚未录制的表演进行视听录制的权利，也未涵盖对其音频性录制表演进行利用的权利；

根据关于版权和邻接权若干问题的外交会议于 1996 年 12 月 20 日通过的《视听表演的决议》；

达成协议如下：

拉丁美洲和加勒比地区的某些国家

各缔约方

注意到《世界知识产权组织表演和录音制品条约》对表演者的保护并未延伸到对其尚未录制的表演进行视听录制的权利，也未涵盖对其音频性录制表演进行利用的权利；

根据关于版权和邻接权若干问题的外交会议于 1996 年 12 月 20 日通过的《关于视听表演的决议》；

on December 20, 1996;

Wishing to ensure an adequate level of protection for audiovisual performances, especially in the digital environment;

Have agreed as follows:

EUROPEAN COMMUNITY AND ITS MEMBER STATES

The Contracting Parties

Wishing to ensure an adequate level of protection for audiovisual performances, especially in the digital environment;

Noting that the WIPO Performances and Phonograms Treaty does not cover the rights of performers in the audiovisual fixation of their unfixed performances, nor the exploitation of their audiovisually fixed performances;

Referring to the resolution concerning audiovisual performances adopted by the Diplomatic Conference on Certain Copyright and Neighboring Rights Questions on December 20, 1996;

Have agreed as follows:

UNITED STATES OF AMERICA

The Contracting Parties,

Noting that the development and convergence of new information and communication technologies will allow for a rapid growth of audiovisual services and that this will increase the opportunities for performing artists to exploit their performances;

Recognizing the great importance of ensuring an adequate level of protection for these performances, in particular when they are exploited in the new digital environment;

Recognizing that the WIPO Performances and Phonograms Treaty (WPPT) does not cover the rights of performers in the audiovisual fixations of their performances, but that many provisions of the WPPT can be used or adapted as the basis for a new treaty protecting performers with respect to their audiovisual performances;

Have agreed as follows:

为确保对视听表演，特别是在数字环境中的视听表演提供足够的保护；

达成协议如下：

欧共体及其成员国

各缔约方

为确保对视听表演，特别是在数字环境中的视听表演提供足够的保护；

注意到《世界知识产权组织表演和录音制品条约》对表演者的保护并未延伸到对其尚未录制的表演进行视听录制的权利，也未涵盖对其音频性录制表演进行利用的权利；

根据关于版权和邻接权若干问题的外交会议于 1996 年 12 月 20 日通过的《关于视听表演的决议》；

达成协议如下：

美国

各缔约方

注意到新的信息和通信技术的发展和融合将使视听服务迅速增长，这将增加表演艺术家利用其表演的机会；

意识到充分保护这些表演的重要性，特别是在新的数字环境中对其加以利用时；

认识到《世界知识产权组织表演和录音制品条约》（以下简称 WPPT）并未涵盖表演者对其表演的视听录制品方面的权利，但 WPPT 的许多条款可作为基础供保护表演者的视听表演新条约采纳或使用；

达成协议如下：

III. Relation to other conventions and treaties; relation to copyright

CERTAIN STATES OF AFRICA

Article 1

Relation to Other Conventions

(1) This Treaty constitutes a protocol to the WIPO Performances and Phonograms Treaty (hereinafter the "WPPT").

(2) Nothing in this Protocol shall derogate from existing obligations that Contracting Parties have to each other under the WPPT.

(3) Protection granted under this Protocol shall leave intact and shall in no way affect the protection of copyright in literary and artistic works. Consequently, no provision of this Protocol may be interpreted to prejudice such protection.

CERTAIN STATES OF LATIN AMERICA AND THE CARIBBEAN

Relation to other Conventions; Relation with copyright

1. This treaty constitutes a Protocol to the WIPO Performances and Phonograms Treaty done in Geneva on December 20, 1996 (hereinafter "the WIPO Treaty").

2. No provision of this Protocol shall detract from the mutual obligations of Contracting Parties under the International Convention for the Protection of Performers, Producers of Phonograms and Broadcasting Organizations, done at Rome on October 26, 1961 ("the Rome Convention").

3. The protection granted under this Protocol shall leave intact and in no way affect the protection of copyright in literary and artistic works. Consequently, no provision of this Treaty may be interpreted as prejudicing such protection.

4. This Protocol shall have no connection with, and shall not prejudice any right or obligation under, any treaty other than the WIPO Treaty.

EUROPEAN COMMUNITY AND ITS MEMBER STATES

Article 1

Relation to Other Conventions

(1) This Treaty constitutes a Protocol to the WIPO Performances and Phonograms Treaty done in Geneva, 20 December 1996 (hereinafter the "WIPO Treaty").

(2) Nothing in this Protocol shall derogate from existing obligations that

III. 与其他公约和条约的关系；与版权的关系

非洲的某些国家

第 1 条

与其他公约的关系

（1）本条约系《世界知识产权组织表演和录音制品条约》(WPPT)的议定书。

（2）本议定书的任何规定均不得减损缔约各方之间根据 WPPT 承担的现有义务。

（3）根据本议定书给予的保护不得触动或以任何方式影响对文学和艺术作品版权的保护。因此，本议定书的任何内容均不得被解释为损害此种保护。

拉丁美洲和加勒比地区的某些国家

与其他公约的关系；与版权的关系

1. 该条约系 1996 年 12 月 20 日在日内瓦签订的《世界知识产权组织表演和录音制品条约》(以下简称 WIPO 条约)的议定书。

2. 本议定书的任何规定均不得减损缔约各方之间依照 1961 年 10 月 26 日在罗马签订的《保护表演者、录音制品制作者和广播组织国际公约》(《罗马公约》)承担的相互义务。

3. 本议定书给予的保护不得触动或以任何方式影响对文学和艺术作品版权的保护。因此，本议定书的任何内容均不得被解释为损害此种保护。

4. 本议定书不应与 WIPO 条约以外的任何条约有任何联系，也不应损害条约规定的任何权利或义务。

欧共体及其成员国

第 1 条

与其他公约的关系

（1）该条约是 1996 年 12 月 20 日在日内瓦缔结的《世界知识产权组织表演和录音制品条约》(以下简称 WIPO 条约)的议定书。

（2）本议定书的任何规定均不得减损缔约方根据 WIPO 条约彼此承担的现

Contracting Parties have to each other under the WIPO Treaty.

(3) Protection granted under this protocol shall leave intact and shall in no way affect the protection of copyright in literary and artistic works. Consequently, no provisions of this protocol may be interpreted as prejudicing such protection.

UNITED STATES OF AMERICA

Article 1

Relation to Other Conventions

(1) Nothing in this Treaty shall derogate from existing obligations that Contracting Parties have to each other under the International Convention for the Protection of Performers, Producers of Phonograms and Broadcasting Organizations done in Rome, October 26, 1961.

(2) Protection granted under this Treaty shall leave intact and shall in no way affect the protection of copyright in literary and artistic works. Consequently, no provision of this Treaty may be interpreted as prejudicing such protection.

(3) This Treaty shall not have any connection with, nor shall it prejudice any rights and obligations under any other treaties.

IV. Definitions

CERTAIN STATES OF AFRICA

Article 2

Definitions

For the purposes of this Protocol:

(a)"performers" means actors, singers, musicians, dancers, and other persons who act, sing, deliver, declaim, play in, interpret, or otherwise perform literary or artistic works, or expressions of folklore;

(b)"audiovisual fixation" means the embodiment of moving images, whether or not accompanied by sound, or the representations thereof, from which they can be perceived, reproduced, or communicated through a device.

CERTAIN STATES OF LATIN AMERICA AND THE CARIBBEAN

Definitions

1. The Contracting Parties shall apply, *mutatis mutandis*, the definitions set out in Article 2 paragraphs (a), (e), (f) and (g) of the WIPO Treaty in connection with the protection granted under this Protocol.

有义务。

（3）依本议定书给予的保护不得触动或以任何方式影响对文学和艺术作品版权的保护。因此，本条约的任何内容均不得被解释为损害此种保护。

美国

第 1 条

与其他公约的关系

（1）本条约的任何规定均不得减损缔约各方之间依照 1961 年 10 月 26 日在罗马签订的《保护表演者、录音制品制作者和广播组织国际公约》承担的相互义务。

（2）依本条约给予的保护不得触动或以任何方式影响对文学和艺术作品版权的保护。因此，本条约的任何内容均不得被解释为损害此种保护。

（3）本条约不得与任何其他条约有任何关联，亦不得损害任何其他条约所规定的任何权利和义务。

IV. 定义

非洲的某些国家

第 2 条

定义

在本条约中：

（a）"表演者" 系指演员、歌唱家、音乐家、舞蹈家以及对文学或艺术作品或民间文学艺术表达进行表演、歌唱、演说、朗诵、演奏、演绎或以其他方式进行表演的其他人员；

（b）"视听录制品" 系指声音和图像的体现物或其表现物，无论其是否有伴音，它们可以通过某种装置被感知、复制或传播。

拉丁美洲和加勒比地区的某些国家

定义

1. 缔约各方应比照适用 WIPO 条约第 2 条第（a）、（e）、（f）和（g）款中关于本议定书所给予保护的定义。

2. For the purposes of this Protocol, “audiovisual fixation” means the embodiment of moving images, whether or not accompanied by sound, or the representations thereof, from which they can be perceived, reproduced or communicated through a device.

3. There was consensus that the definition of the term “performer” should not extend to persons whose contributions to a performance cannot be identified individually, such as the so-called extras.

EUROPEAN COMMUNITY AND ITS MEMBER STATES

Article 2

Definitions

(1) The Contracting Parties shall apply, *mutatis mutandis*, the definitions set out in Article 2 paragraphs (a), (f) and (g) of the WIPO Treaty in connection with the protection granted under this Protocol.

(2) For the purposes of this Protocol, “audiovisual fixation” means the embodiment of moving images, whether or not accompanied by sound, or the representations thereof, from which they can be perceived, reproduced or communicated through a device.

UNITED STATES OF AMERICA

Article 2

Definitions

For the purposes of this Treaty:

(a) “performers” are actors, singers, musicians, dancers, and other persons who act, sing, deliver, declaim, play in, interpret, or otherwise perform literary or artistic works or expressions of folklore, but not including extra performers or background performers;

(b) “fixation” means the embodiment of images, or of images and sounds, or of the representations thereof, from which they can be perceived, reproduced, or communicated through a device;

(c) “broadcasting” means the transmission by wireless means for public reception of images, or of images and sounds, or the representations thereof; such transmission by satellite is also “broadcasting”; transmission of encrypted signals is “broadcasting” where the means for decrypting are provided to the public by the

2. 在本条约中，“视听录制品”系指声音和图像的体现物或其表现物，无论其是否有伴音，它们可以通过某种装置被感知、复制或传播。

3. 与会者一致认为，“表演者”一词的定义不应扩大到对表演的贡献不能单独确定的人，比如临时演员。

欧共体及其成员国

第2条

定义

（1）缔约各方应比照适用WIPO条约第2条第（a）、（f）和（g）款中关于本议定书所给予保护的定义。

（2）在本条约中，“视听录制品”系指声音和图像的体现物或其表现物，无论是否伴随着声音，它们可以通过某种装置被感知、复制或传播。

美国

第2条

定义

在本条约中：

（a）“表演者”是指演员、歌唱家、音乐家、舞蹈家以及对文学或艺术作品或民间文学艺术表达进行表演、歌唱、演说、朗诵、演奏、演绎或以其他方式进行表演的其他人员，但不包括临时演员或背景演员；

（b）“录制品”是指图像、图像和声音的体现物，或其表现物，它们可以通过某种装置被感知、复制或传播；

（c）“广播”系指以无线方式的传送，使公众能接收声音或图像，或图像和声音，或图像和声音的表现物；通过卫星进行的此种传送亦为“广播”；传送密码信号，只要广播组织或经其同意向公众提供了解码的手段，即为“广播”；

broadcasting organization or with its consent;

(d) "communication to the public" means the transmission to the public by any medium, otherwise than by broadcasting, of the images, or the sounds and images, or the representations thereof, comprised in an unfixed performance or in a fixed performance;

(e) an "audiovisual work" is a work consisting of a series of related images that are intended to be shown by the use of a device, together with any accompanying sounds.

V. Beneficiaries of protection

CERTAIN STATES OF AFRICA

Article 3

Beneficiaries of Protection under this Protocol

The Contracting Parties shall accord the protection granted under this Protocol to performers who are nationals of other Contracting Parties.

CERTAIN STATES OF LATIN AMERICA AND THE CARIBBEAN

Beneficiaries of protection

The Contracting Parties shall accord the protection provided under this Protocol:

a) to the performers who are nationals of other Contracting Parties, and/or

b) in case where a performance is fixed in another Contracting Party.

EUROPEAN COMMUNITY AND ITS MEMBER STATES

Article 3

Beneficiaries of protection under this protocol

The Contracting Parties shall accord the protection provided under this protocol to performers who are nationals of other Contracting Parties.

UNITED STATES OF AMERICA

Article 3

Beneficiaries of Protection

(1) Contracting Parties shall accord the protection provided under this Treaty to performers of other Contracting Parties as defined in paragraph (2) of this Article.

(2) Performers of other Contracting Parties shall be understood to be performers who meet any of the following conditions:

(d)“向公众传播”是指通过除广播以外的任何媒体向公众传送表演的声音和图像，或其表现物，包括已录制的或者尚未录制的表演；

(e)“视听作品”是由一系列旨在通过使用设备显示的相关图像以及任何伴随的声音组成的作品。

V. 保护的受益人

非洲的某些国家

第3条

本议定书保护的受益人

缔约各方应向作为其他缔约方国民的表演者提供本议定书规定的保护。

拉丁美洲和加勒比地区的某些国家

保护的受益人

缔约各方应将本议定书规定的保护给予：

a)属于其他缔约方国民的表演者，和/或

b)其表演在另一缔约方国内被录制的表演者。

欧共体及其成员国

第3条

本议定书保护的受益人

缔约各方应向作为其他缔约方国民的表演者提供本议定书规定的保护。

美国

第3条

保护的受益人

(1)缔约各方应当对根据本条第(2)款所界定的其他缔约方的表演者进行保护。

(2)其他缔约方的表演者应被理解为符合下列条件：

(a) those performers who are nationals of another Contracting Party and whose performance is unfixed or is fixed in an audiovisual work;

(b) those performers whose unfixed performance takes place on the territory of another Contracting Party;

(c) those performers whose performance is first fixed in an audiovisual work on the territory of another Contracting Party.

VI. National treatment

CERTAIN STATES OF AFRICA

Article 4

National Treatment

(1) Each Contracting Party shall accord to nationals of other Contracting Parties, in respect of the subject matter protected under this Protocol:

(a) the rights specifically granted by this Protocol; and

(b) such additional rights as it accords to its own nationals.

(2) A Contracting Party shall be entitled, in respect of nationals of any other Contracting Party, to limit the protection provided for in subparagraph (b) of paragraph (1) to the extent to which, and to the term for which, the latter Contracting Party grants such rights to the nationals of the former Contracting Party.

EUROPEAN COMMUNITY AND ITS MEMBER STATES

Article 6

Application of certain substantive provisions of the WIPO Treaty

The Contracting Parties shall apply, *mutatis mutandis*, in respect of protection granted under this Protocol, the provisions of Articles 4 (National Treatment)... of the WIPO Treaty.

REPUBLIC OF KOREA

5. Concerning the right to remuneration for broadcasting and communication to the public of fixed performances, reservation on national treatment should be permitted in this protocol in the manner as provided in the WPPT.

UNITED STATES OF AMERICA

Article 4

National Treatment

With respect to performances for which they are protected under this Treaty

（a）表演者是另一缔约方的国民，其表演已录制或尚未录制在视听作品中；

（b）尚未录制的表演发生在另一缔约方领土上的表演者；

（c）其表演在另一缔约方领土上首次被录制在视听作品中的表演者。

VI. 国民待遇

非洲的某些国家

第 4 条

国民待遇

（1）在本议定书所保护的客体方面，每一缔约方均应将其给予本国国民的待遇给予其他缔约方的国民：

（a）本议定书具体授予的权利；和

（b）授予本国国民的额外权利。

（2）对于任何其他缔约方的国民，缔约一方有权将第（1）款（b）项规定的保护限制在其本国国民在该另一缔约方享有的权利的范围和期限之内。

欧共体及其成员国

第 6 条

WIPO 条约某些实质性条款的适用

对于根据本议定书给予的保护，缔约各方应比照适用 WIPO 条约第 4 条（国民待遇）的规定。

韩国

5. 基于对录制表演的广播和向公众传播而享有的获酬权，本议定书应允许以 WPPT 规定的方式保留国民待遇。

美国

第 4 条

国民待遇

对于按照第 3 条规定受本条约保护的表演，表演者在其他缔约国应享有这

as provided in Article 3, performers shall enjoy, in other Contracting Parties, the treatment that the laws of such parties do now or may hereafter grant to their own nationals, as well as the rights specifically granted by this Treaty.

VII. Formalities; independence from protection in country of origin

CERTAIN STATES OF AFRICA

Article 12

Application of Certain Substantive Provisions of the WPPT

The Contracting Parties shall apply, *mutatis mutandis*, in respect of the protection granted under this Protocol, the provisions of Articles... 20 (Formalities)... of the WPPT.

CERTAIN STATES OF LATIN AMERICA AND THE CARIBBEAN

Formalities

The enjoyment and exercise of the rights provided for in this Protocol shall not be subject to any formality.

EUROPEAN COMMUNITY AND ITS MEMBER STATES

Article 6

Application of certain substantive provisions of the WIPO Treaty

The Contracting Parties shall apply, *mutatis mutandis*, in respect of protection granted under this Protocol, the provisions of Articles... 20 (Formalities)... of the WIPO Treaty.

UNITED STATES OF AMERICA

Article 17

Formalities

The enjoyment and exercise of the rights provided for in this Treaty shall not be subject to any formality.

VIII. Moral rights of performers

CERTAIN STATES OF AFRICA

Article 5

Moral Rights of Performers

(1) Independently of a performer's economic rights, and even after the transfer of those rights, a performer shall, as regards his performances, whether live of embodied in audiovisual fixations, have the right:

些缔约国的法律现在或将来给予本国国民的待遇，以及本条约特别授予的权利。

VII. 手续；独立于原籍国提供的保护

非洲的某些国家

第 12 条

WPPT 某些实质性条款的适用

关于根据本议定书给予的保护，缔约方应比照适用 WPPT 第 20 条（手续）的规定。

拉丁美洲和加勒比地区的某些国家

手续

享有和行使本议定书所规定的权利无须履行任何手续。

欧共体及其成员国

第 6 条

WIPO Treaty 某些实质性条款的适用

对于根据本议定书给予的保护，缔约方应比照适用 WIPO 条约第 20 条（手续）的规定。

美国

第 17 条

手续

享有和行使本议定书所规定的权利无须履行任何手续。

VIII. 表演者的精神权利

非洲的某些国家

第 5 条

表演者的精神权利

（1）独立于表演者的经济权利，甚至在这些权利转让之后，表演者仍应对于其现场表演或以视听录制品录制的表演享有权利：

(a) to be identified as the performer of his performances, except where omission is dictated by the manner of the use of the performance; and

(b) to object to any distortion, mutilation, or other modification of his performances that would be prejudicial to his reputation.

(2) The rights granted to a performer in accordance with paragraph (1) shall, after his death, be maintained, at least until the expiry of the economic rights, and shall be exercisable by the person or institutions authorized by the legislation of the Contracting Party where protection is claimed. However, those Contracting Parties whose legislation, at the moment of their ratification of this Protocol, does not provide for protection after the death of the performer of all rights set out in the preceding paragraph may provide that some of these rights will, after his death, cease to be maintained.

(3) The means of redress for safeguarding the rights granted under this Article shall be governed by the legislation of the Contracting Party where protection is claimed.

CERTAIN STATES OF LATIN AMERICA AND THE CARIBBEAN

Moral rights of performers

(1) Independently of a performer's economic rights, and even after the transfer of those rights, the performer shall, as regards his live audiovisual performances, with or without sounds, or performances included in audiovisual fixations, have the right to claim to be identified as the performer of his performances, except where omission is dictated by the manner of the use of the performance [, and to object to any distortion, mutilation or other modification of his performances that would be prejudicial to his reputation, on the understanding, however, that the producer of the audiovisual fixation may make modifications necessary to facilitate the normal exploitations of the fixations].

(2) The rights granted to a performer in accordance with paragraph (1) shall, after his death, be maintained, at least until the expiry of the economic rights, and shall be exercisable by the persons or institutions authorized by the legislation of the Contracting Party where protection is claimed. However, those Contracting Parties whose legislation, at the moment of their ratification of, or accession to, this Treaty, does not provide for protection after the death of the performer of all rights set out

（a）承认其系表演的表演者，除非因使用表演的方式而决定可省略不提其系表演者；以及

（b）反对任何对其表演进行的将有损其声誉的歪曲、篡改或其他修改。

（2）根据第（1）款授予表演者的权利在其死亡后应继续保留，至少到其经济权利期满为止，并可由被要求提供保护的缔约方立法所授权的个人或机构行使。但批准本议定书时其立法尚未规定在表演者死亡后保护上款所述全部权利的国家，则可规定其中部分权利在表演者死亡后不再保留。

（3）为保障本条所授予的权利而采取的补救方法应由被要求提供保护的缔约方立法规定。

拉丁美洲和加勒比地区的某些国家

表演者的精神权利

（1）独立于表演者的经济权利，甚至在这些权利转让之后，表演者仍应对于其现场表演（无论是否伴有声音）或以视听录制品录制的表演享有权利：要求承认其系表演的表演者，除非因使用表演的方式而决定可省略不提其系表演者；（反对任何对其表演进行的将有损其声誉的歪曲、篡改或其他修改，且这种修改不是作品制作者或其利益继承人根据制片人在演出中获得的授权对视听作品进行正常利用的一部分）。

（2）根据本条第（1）款授予表演者的权利在其死亡后应继续保留，至少到其经济权利期满为止，并可由被要求提供保护的缔约各方立法所授权的个人或机构行使。但批准或加入本条约时其立法尚未规定在表演者死亡后保护上款所述全部权利的缔约方，则可规定其中部分权利在表演者死亡后不再保留。

in the preceding paragraph may provide that some of these rights will, after his death, cease to be maintained.

(3) The means of redress for safeguarding the rights granted under this Article shall be governed by the legislation of the Contracting Party where protection is claimed.

EUROPEAN COMMUNITY AND ITS MEMBER STATES

Article 4

Rights of performers in their unfixed audiovisual performances

The Contracting Parties shall accord, *mutatis mutandis*, to performers, as regards their unfixed audiovisual performances, whether or not accompanied by sound, the same rights as those granted under the WIPO Treaty to performers as regards their live aural performances, namely the rights provided under Article 5 (Moral Rights)…

Article 5

Rights of performers in audiovisual fixations of their performances

The Contracting Parties shall accord, *mutatis mutandis*, to performers, as regards the use of audiovisual fixations of their performances, the same rights as those granted under the WIPO Treaty to performers as regards the use of their performances fixed in phonograms, namely the rights provided under Articles 5 (Moral Rights)… of the WIPO Treaty.

UNITED STATES OF AMERICA

Article 5

Moral Rights of Performers

(1) Independently of a performer's economic rights, and even after the transfer of those rights, the performer shall, as regards his or her live performances or performances fixed in an audiovisual work, have the right to claim to be identified as the performer of such performances, except where omission is dictated by the manner of the use of the performance, and to object to any distortion, mutilation, or other modification of his or her performance that would be seriously prejudicial to the performer's reputation, where such modification is not part of the normal exploitation of an audiovisual work by the producer of the work or its successors in interest, pursuant to the exercise of rights of authorization acquired by the producer

（3）为保障本条所授予的权利而采取的救济措施应由被要求提供保护的缔约方立法规定。

欧共体及其成员国

第 4 条

表演者对其尚未录制的表演的权利

缔约各方应比照适用 WIPO 条约第 6 条（表演者在尚未录制表演中的经济权利）所赋予的权利，授予表演者对其现场表演和尚未录制表演的权利，无论其是否伴有声音。

第 5 条

表演者对其表演的视听录制品的权利

缔约各方在使用表演者的视听录制品时，应比照适用 WIPO 条约第 7 条（复制权）规定中授予表演者对其已录制表演的权利相同的权利。

美国

第 5 条

表演者的精神权利

（1）独立于表演者的经济权利，甚至在这些权利转让之后，表演者仍应对于其现场表演或以视听录制品录制的表演享有权利：要求承认其系表演的表演者，除非因使用表演的方式而决定可省略不提其系表演者；反对任何对其表演进行的将有损其声誉的歪曲、篡改或其他修改，且这种修改不是作品制作者或其利益继承人根据制片人在演出中获得的授权对视听作品进行正常利用的一部分。

in the performance.

(2) The rights granted to a performer in accordance with paragraph (1) shall, after the said performer's death, be maintained, at least until the expiry of the rights of authorization set forth in Articles 6 through 10, and shall be exercisable by the persons or institutions authorized by the legislation of the Contracting Party where protection is claimed. However, those Contracting Parties whose legislation, at the moment of their ratification of or accession to this Treaty, does not provide for protection after the death of the performer of all rights set out in the preceding paragraph, may provide that some of these rights will, after the performer's death, cease to be maintained.

(3) The means of redress for safeguarding the rights granted under this Article shall be governed by the legislation of the Contracting Party where protection is claimed.

(4) The "normal exploitation of an audiovisual work" shall include the use of new or changed technology, media, formats and/or methods of distribution, dissemination, making available or communication to the public. A performer shall give reasonable consideration to the interests of the other performers in and creative authors of an audiovisual work when exercising the above described rights with respect to such work.

IX. Rights of performers in their unfixed performances

CERTAIN STATES OF AFRICA

Article 6

Right of Fixation of Unfixed Performances

Performers shall enjoy the exclusive right of authorizing the audiovisual fixation of their unfixed performances.

CERTAIN STATES OF LATIN AMERICA AND THE CARIBBEAN

Economic rights of performers in their unfixed performances

The Contracting Parties shall accord, *mutatis mutandis*, to performers, as regards their unfixed audiovisual performances, whether or not accompanied by sound, the same rights as those granted under Article 6 (Economic rights of performers in their unfixed performances) of the WIPO Treaty.

(2) 根据第(1)款给予表演者的权利在其死亡后应继续保留，至少在第 6 条至第 10 条规定的权利期满为止，并可由被要求提供保护的缔约方立法所授权的个人或机构行使。但批准或加入本条约时其立法尚未规定在表演者死亡后保护上款所述全部权利的国家，则可规定其中部分权利在表演者死亡后不再保留。

(3) 为保障本条所授予的权利而采取的救济措施应由被要求提供保护的缔约方立法规定。

(4)"视听作品的正常利用"应包括使用新的或经改变的技术、媒介、格式和 / 或发行、传播、向公众提供或传播的方法。表演者在行使上述作品权利时，应当合理考虑视听作品的其他表演者和创作者的利益。

IX. 表演者在尚未录制表演中的权利

非洲的某些国家

第 6 条

录制尚未录制的表演的权利

表演者享有授权对其尚未录制的表演进行视听录制的专有权。

拉丁美洲和加勒比地区的某些国家

表演者在尚未录制的表演中的经济权利

缔约各方应比照 WIPO 条约第 6 条(表演者在尚未录制表演中的经济权利)所赋予的权利，给予表演者不录制的视听表演，不论其是否伴有声音。

EUROPEAN COMMUNITY AND ITS MEMBER STATES

Article 4

Rights of performers in their unfixed audiovisual performances

The Contracting Parties shall accord, *mutatis mutandis*, to performers, as regards their unfixed audiovisual performances, whether or not accompanied by sound, the same rights as those granted under the WIPO Treaty to performers as regards their live aural performances, namely the rights provided under Article… 6 (Economic rights of Performers in their unfixed performances).

REPUBLIC OF KOREA

3. Performers shall enjoy the following exclusive rights of authorizing their unfixed audiovisual performances:

(a) fixation;

(b) broadcasting and communication to the public.

UNITED STATES OF AMERICA

Article 6

Economic Rights of Performers in their Unfixed Performances

Performers shall enjoy the exclusive right of authorizing, as regards their performances:

(i) the broadcasting and communication to the public of their unfixed performances, except where the performance is already a broadcast or a publicly communicated performance; and

(ii) the fixation of their unfixed performances.

X. Rights of performers in audiovisual fixations

1. Right of reproduction

CERTAIN STATES OF AFRICA

Article 7

Right of Reproduction

Performers shall enjoy the exclusive right of authorizing the direct or indirect reproduction, in any manner or form, of audiovisual fixations of their performances.

CERTAIN STATES OF LATIN AMERICA AND THE CARIBBEAN

Right of reproduction

The Contracting Parties shall accord, *mutatis mutandis*, to performers, as regards the use of audiovisual fixations of their performances, the same rights as

欧共体及其成员国

第 4 条

表演者在尚未录制的视听表演中的权利

缔约各方应比照适用 WIPO 条约第 6 条(表演者在尚未录制表演中的经济权利)所赋予的权利,授予表演者对其现场表演和尚未录制表演的权利,无论其是否伴有声音。

韩国

3. 表演者对其尚未录制的视听表演享有以下专有权:

(a)录制;

(b)广播和向公众传播。

美国

第 6 条

表演者对其尚未录制的表演的经济权利

表演者应享有对其表演进行授权的专有权利:

(i)广播和向公众传播其尚未录制的表演,除非该表演本身已属广播或向公众传播的表演;和

(ii)录制其尚未录制的表演。

X. 表演者对视听录制品的权利

1. 复制权

非洲的某些国家

第 7 条

复制权

表演者应享有授权以任何方式或形式对其以视听录制品录制的表演直接或间接地进行复制的专有权。

拉丁美洲和加勒比地区的某些国家

复制权

缔约各方在使用表演的视听录制品时,应比照适用 WIPO 条约第 7 条(复制权)的规定赋予表演者相同的权利。

those granted under Article 7 (Right of reproduction) of the WIPO Treaty.

EUROPEAN COMMUNITY AND ITS MEMBER STATES

Article 5

Rights of performers in audiovisual fixations of their performances

The Contracting Parties shall accord, *mutatis mutandis*, to performers, as regards the use of audiovisual fixations of their performances, the same rights as those granted under the WIPO Treaty to performers as regards the use of their performances fixed in phonograms, namely the rights provided under Articles... 7 (Right of Reproduction)... of the WIPO Treaty.

REPUBLIC OF KOREA

4. Performers shall enjoy the following rights of their fixed audiovisual performances:

(a) the exclusive right to authorize the reproduction;

UNITED STATES OF AMERICA

Article 7

Right of Reproduction

Performers shall enjoy the exclusive right of authorizing the direct or indirect reproduction of their fixed performances in any manner or form.

2. Right of distribution

CERTAIN STATES OF AFRICA

Article 8

Right of Distribution

(1) Performers shall enjoy the exclusive right of authorizing the making available to the public of the original and copies of the audiovisual fixations of their performances through sale or other transfer of ownership.

(2) Nothing in this Protocol shall affect the freedom of Contracting Parties to determine the conditions, if any, under which the exhaustion of the right in paragraph (1) applies after the first sale or other transfer of ownership of the original or a copy of the fixed performance with the authorization of the performer.

CERTAIN STATES OF LATIN AMERICA AND THE CARIBBEAN

Right of distribution

The Contracting Parties shall accord, *mutatis mutandis*, to performers, as

欧共体及其成员国

第 5 条

表演者对其表演的视听录制品的权利

缔约方应比照适用 WIPO 条约第 7 条(复制权)的规定,给予表演者使用其表演的视听录制品的权利。

韩国

4. 表演者对其已经录制的视听表演享有下列权利:

(a)授权复制的专有权;

美国

第 7 条

复制权

表演者享有以任何方式或形式授权直接或间接对已录制表演进行复制的专有权。

2. 发行权

非洲的某些国家

第 8 条

发行权

(1)表演者应享有授权通过销售或其他转让所有权的形式向公众提供其以视听录制品录制的表演的原件或复制件的专有权。

(2)对于已录制表演的原件或复制件经表演者授权被首次销售或以其他形式转让所有权之后适用本条第(1)款中权利的用尽所依据的条件(如有此种条件),本议定书的任何内容均不得影响缔约方确定该条件的自由。

拉丁美洲和加勒比地区的某些国家

发行权

缔约各方在使用表演的视听录制品时,应比照适用 WIPO 条约第 8 条(发

regards the use of audiovisual fixations of their performances, the same rights as those granted under Article 8 (Right of distribution) of the WIPO Treaty.

EUROPEAN COMMUNITY AND ITS MEMBER STATES

Article 5

Rights of performers in audiovisual fixations of their performances

The Contracting Parties shall accord, *mutatis mutandis*, to performers, as regards the use of audiovisual fixations of their performances, the same rights as those granted under the WIPO Treaty to performers as regards the use of their performances fixed in phonograms, namely the rights provided under Articles… 8 (Right of Distribution)… of the WIPO Treaty.

UNITED STATES OF AMERICA

Article 8

Right of Distribution

(1) Performers shall enjoy the exclusive right of authorizing the making available to the public of the original and copies of their fixed performances through sale or other transfer of ownership.

(2) Nothing in this Treaty shall affect the freedom of Contracting Parties to determine the conditions, if any, under which the exhaustion of the right in paragraph (1) applies after the first sale or other transfer of ownership of the original or a copy of the fixed performance with the authorization of the performer.

3. Right of rental

CERTAIN STATES OF AFRICA

Article 9

Right of Rental

Performers shall enjoy the exclusive right of authorizing the commercial rental to the public of the original and copies of the audiovisual fixations of their performances. Contracting Parties are exempt from this obligation unless the commercial rental has led to widespread copying of the works which materially impairs the exclusive right of reproduction.

CERTAIN STATES OF LATIN AMERICA AND THE CARIBBEAN

Right of rental

The Contracting Parties shall accord, *mutatis mutandis*, to performers, as

行权）的规定，赋予表演者相同的权利。

欧共体及其成员国

第5条

表演者对其表演的视听录制品的权利

缔约方在使用表演者的视听录制品时，应比照适用WIPO条约第8条（发行权）的规定中授予表演者对其已录制表演的权利相同的权利。

美国

第8条

发行权

（1）表演者应享有授权通过销售或其他转让所有权的形式向公众提供其已录制表演的原件或复制件的专有权。

（2）对于已录制表演的原件或复制件经表演者授权被首次销售或以其他形式转让所有权之后适用本条第（1）款中权利的用尽所依据的条件（如有此种条件），本议定书的任何内容均不得影响缔约方确定该条件的自由。

3. 出租权

非洲的某些国家

第9条

出租权

表演者应享有授权将其以视听录制品录制的表演的原件和复制件向公众进行商业性出租的专有权。除非商业性出租已导致此种录制品的广泛复制，从而严重损害表演者的专有复制权，缔约各方才能免除此义务。

拉丁美洲和加勒比地区的某些国家

出租权

缔约各方在使用表演者的视听录制品时，应比照适用WIPO条约第9条

regards the use of audiovisual fixations of their performances, the same rights as those granted under Article 9 (Right of rental) of the WIPO Treaty.

EUROPEAN COMMUNITY AND ITS MEMBER STATES

Article 5

Rights of performers in audiovisual fixations of their performances

The Contracting Parties shall accord, *mutatis mutandis*, to performers, as regards the use of audiovisual fixations of their performances, the same rights as those granted under the WIPO Treaty to performers as regards the use of their performances fixed in phonograms, namely the rights provided under Articles... 9 (Right of Rental)... of the WIPO Treaty.

4. Right of making available

CERTAIN STATES OF AFRICA

Article 10

Right of Making Available of Fixed Performances

Performers shall enjoy the exclusive right of authorizing the making available to the public of audiovisual fixations of their performances, by wire or wireless means, in such a way that members of the public may access them from a place and at a time individually chosen by them.

CERTAIN STATES OF LATIN AMERICA AND THE CARIBBEAN

Right of making available

The Contracting Parties shall accord, *mutatis mutandis*, to performers, as regards the use of audiovisual fixations of their performances, the same rights as those granted under Article 10 (Right of making available of fixed performances) of the WIPO Treaty.

EUROPEAN COMMUNITY AND ITS MEMBER STATES

Article 5

Rights of performers in audiovisual fixations of their performances

The Contracting Parties shall accord, *mutatis mutandis*, to performers, as regards the use of audiovisual fixations of their performances, the same rights as those granted under the WIPO Treaty to performers as regards the use of their performances fixed in phonograms, namely the rights provided under Articles... 10 (Right of Making Available of Fixed Performances)... of the WIPO Treaty.

（出租权）所赋予的权利，授予表演者相同的权利。

欧共体及其成员国

第5条

表演者对其表演的视听录制品的权利

缔约方在使用表演者的视听录制品时，应比照适用WIPO条约第9条（出租权）的规定授予表演者对其已录制表演的权利相同的权利。

4. 提供权

非洲的某些国家

第10条

提供已录制表演的权利

表演者应享有专有权，以授权通过有线或无线的方式向公众提供其以视听录制品录制的表演，使该表演可为公众在其个人选定的地点和时间获得。

拉丁美洲和加勒比地区的某些国家

提供权

缔约各方在使用表演的视听录制品时，应比照适用WIPO条约第10条（提供已录制表演的权利）的规定，给予表演者相同的权利。

欧共体及其成员国

第5条

表演者对其表演的视听录制品的权利

缔约方在使用表演者的视听录制品时，应比照适用WIPO条约第10条（提供已录制表演的权利）的规定授予表演者对其已录制表演的权利相同的权利。

REPUBLIC OF KOREA

4. Performers shall enjoy the following rights of their fixed audiovisual performances:

(b) the exclusive right of making available to the public, equivalent to the right given in the WPPT;

UNITED STATES OF AMERICA

Article 9

Right of Making Available

Performers shall enjoy the exclusive right of authorizing the making available to the public of their fixed performances, by wire or wireless means, in such a way that members of the public may access them from a place and at a time individually chosen by them.

5. Right of broadcasting and communication to the public

CERTAIN STATES OF LATIN AMERICA AND THE CARIBBEAN

Right of broadcasting and communication to the public

Performers shall enjoy the exclusive rights of authorizing the broadcasting and other communication to the public of their performances fixed in audiovisual fixations.

In respect of broadcasting of audiovisual fixations, the Contracting Parties may apply *mutatis mutandis*, the provision of Article 11*bis*(2) of the Berne Convention.

[The Delegation of Brazil declared that, with respect to point 5, it was not in the position to express its opinion, since, in its country, there were still consultations in preparation of the June 8 to 12, 1998, session of the Committee of Experts.

The Delegation of Uruguay declared that, with respect to the entire contents of title X, it was not in a position to express its opinion, since, in its country, there were still consultations in preparation of the June 8 to 12, 1998, session of the Committee of Experts.]

REPUBLIC OF KOREA

4. Performers shall enjoy the following rights of their fixed audiovisual performances:

(c) the right to remuneration for broadcasting and communication to the public.

5. Concerning the right to remuneration for broadcasting and communication

韩国

4. 表演者对其录制的视听表演享有下列权利：

(b)向公众提供的专有权，该权利与 WPPT 规定的权利相同；

美国

第 9 条

提供权

表演者应享有专有权，以授权通过有线或无线的方式向公众提供其已录制表演，使该表演可为公众在其个人选定的地点和时间获得。

5. 广播权和向公众传播权

拉丁美洲和加勒比地区的某些国家

广播权和向公众传播权

表演者应享有授权进行广播和向公众传播其以视听录制品录制的表演的专有权。

关于视听录制品的广播，缔约各方可比照适用《伯尔尼公约》第 11 条之二第(2)款的规定。

(巴西代表团表示，其对本条第 5 点不发表意见。因为巴西仍在为筹备 1998 年 6 月 8 日至 12 日的专家委员会届会进行协商。

乌拉圭代表团表示，其对本条全部内容不发表意见，因为乌拉圭仍在为筹备 1998 年 6 月 8 日至 12 日的专家委员会届会进行协商。)

韩国

4. 表演者对其录制的视听表演，享有以下权利：

(c)基于广播和向公众传播而获得报酬的权利。

5. 基于对录制表演的广播和向公众传播而享有的获酬权，本议定书应允许

to the public of fixed performances, reservation on national treatment should be permitted in this protocol in the manner as provided in the WPPT.

UNITED STATES OF AMERICA

Article 10

Right of Broadcasting and Communication to the Public

(1) Except for conditions on the exercise of the right that would be permissible for audiovisual works under Article 11*bis* of the Berne Convention for the Protection of Literary and Artistic Works, performers shall enjoy the exclusive right of authorizing, as regards their performances fixed in audiovisual works, the broadcasting and communication to the public of such performances, except where such a performance is already a broadcast or a publicly communicated performance.

(2) Any Contracting Party may, in a notification deposited with the Director General of WIPO, declare that it will limit the right set forth in paragraph (1) to a right to remuneration only.

XI. Limitations and exceptions

CERTAIN STATES OF AFRICA

Article 12

Application of Certain Substantive Provisions of the WPPT

The Contracting Parties shall apply, *mutatis mutandis*, in respect of the protection granted under this Protocol, the provisions of Articles 16 (Limitations and Exceptions)… of the WPPT.

CERTAIN STATES OF LATIN AMERICA AND THE CARIBBEAN

Limitations and exceptions

The Contracting Parties shall apply, *mutatis mutandis*, in respect of the protection granted under this Protocol, the provisions of Article 16 (Limitations and exceptions) of the WIPO Treaty.

EUROPEAN COMMUNITY AND ITS MEMBER STATES

Article 6

Application of certain substantive provisions of the WIPO Treaty

The Contracting Parties shall apply, *mutatis mutandis*, in respect of protection granted under this Protocol, the provisions of Articles… 16 (Limitations and Exceptions)… of the WIPO Treaty.

以 WPPT 规定的方式保留国民待遇。

美国

第 10 条

广播权和向公众传播权

（1）除了《伯尔尼保护文学和艺术作品公约》第 11 条之二所允许的视听作品行使权利的条件外，表演者应享有授权广播和向公众传播其以视听录制品录制的表演的专有权，除非这类表演已经是广播或已公开传播的表演。

（2）缔约各方可以在向世界知识产权组织总干事交存的通知书中声明，第（1）款规定的权利仅限于获酬权。

XI. 限制与例外

非洲的某些国家

第 12 条

WPPT 某些实质性条款的适用

缔约方应比照适用 WPPT 第 16 条（限制与例外）的规定，以提供根据本议定书给予的保护。

拉丁美洲和加勒比地区的某些国家

限制与例外

对于根据本议定书给予的保护，缔约各方应比照适用 WIPO 条约第 16 条（限制与例外）的规定。

欧共体及其成员国

第 6 条

WIPO 条约某些实质性条款的适用

对于根据本议定书给予的保护，缔约方应比照适用 WIPO 条约第 16 条（限制与例外）的规定。

UNITED STATES OF AMERICA

Article 12

Limitations and Exceptions

(1) Contracting Parties may, in their national legislation, provide for the same kinds of limitations or exceptions with regard to the protection of performers as they provide for, in their national legislation, in connection with the protection of copyright in literary and artistic works.

(2) Contracting Parties shall confine any limitations of or exceptions to rights provided for in this Treaty to certain special cases which do not conflict with a normal exploitation of the performance and do not unreasonably prejudice the legitimate interests of the performer.

XII. Contractual arrangements concerning rights of performers

CERTAIN STATES OF LATIN AMERICA AND THE CARIBBEAN

Contractual arrangements concerning the rights of performers

In the case where a performer authorizes the inclusion of his performance in an audiovisual fixation, the Contracting Parties shall apply, *mutatis mutandis*, the provision of Article 14*bis*(2)(b) of the Berne Convention.

[The Delegation of Brazil declared that, with respect to the entire contents of title XII, it was not in the position to express its opinion, since, in its country, there were still consultations in preparation of the June 8 to 12, 1998, session of the Committee of Experts.]

UNITED STATES OF AMERICA

Article 11

Transfer of rights

Once a performer has consented to the fixation of his or her performance in an audiovisual work, he or she shall be deemed to have transferred all exclusive rights of authorization granted under this Treaty with respect to that particular audiovisual work to the producer of that work and its successors in interest, subject to written contractual clauses to the contrary. The foregoing sentence shall not apply to any rights of remuneration a performer may have under the law of any Contracting Party, nor shall it require a Contracting Party to establish any such rights of remuneration.

美国

第 12 条

限制与例外

（1）缔约方可以在其国内立法中规定有关保护表演者的限制或例外，正如它们在其国家立法中规定的有关保护文学和艺术作品的版权的限制或例外一样。

（2）缔约方应使本条约中所规定的任何权利限制或例外仅限于某些不与表演的正常利用相抵触、也不致不合理地损害表演者合法利益的特殊情况。

XII. 关于表演者权利的合同安排

拉丁美洲和加勒比地区的某些国家

关于表演者权利的合同安排

如果表演者授权将其表演录制成视听录制品，缔约各方应比照适用《伯尔尼公约》第 14 条第（2）款（b）项的规定。

（巴西代表团表示，其对本条的全部内容不发表意见。因为巴西仍在为筹备 1998 年 6 月 8 日至 12 日的专家委员会届会进行协商。）

美国

第 11 条

权利的转让

表演者一旦同意将其表演录制于视听录制品中，应被视为将根据本条约授予的关于该特定视听作品的专有权转让给该作品的制作者及其利益继承人，但订立有任何相反合同者除外。上句不应适用于表演者根据任何缔约方的法律可能享有的任何报酬权，也不应要求缔约方确立任何此类报酬权。

XIII. Duration of economic rights of performers

CERTAIN STATES OF AFRICA

Article 12

Application of Certain Substantive Provisions of the WPPT

The Contracting Parties shall apply, *mutatis mutandis*, in respect of the protection granted under this Protocol, the provisions of Articles... 17 (Term of Protection),... of the WPPT.

CERTAIN STATES OF LATIN AMERICA AND THE CARIBBEAN

Term of protection

The term of protection to be granted under this Protocol shall last, at least, until the end of a period of 50 years computed from the end of the year in which the performance was fixed.

EUROPEAN COMMUNITY AND ITS MEMBER STATES

Article 6

Application of certain substantive provisions of the WIPO Treaty

The Contracting Parties shall apply, *mutatis mutandis*, in respect of protection granted under this Protocol, the provisions of Articles... 17 (Term of Protection)... of the WIPO Treaty.

UNITED STATES OF AMERICA

Article 13

Term of Protection

The term of protection to be granted to performers under this Treaty shall last, at least, until the end of a period of 50 years from the end of the year in which the performance was fixed.

XIV. Obligations concerning technological measures

CERTAIN STATES OF AFRICA

Article 12

Application of Certain Substantive Provisions of the WPPT

The Contracting Parties shall apply, *mutatis mutandis*, in respect of the protection granted under this Protocol, the provisions of Articles... 18 (Obligations concerning Technological Measures)... of the WPPT.

XIII. 表演者经济权利期限

非洲的某些国家

第 12 条

WPPT 某些实质性条款的适用

关于根据本议定书给予的保护，缔约方应比照适用 WPPT 第 17 条（保护期限）的规定。

拉丁美洲和加勒比地区的某些国家

保护期

根据本议定书授予的保护期限，应自表演被录制之年年终算起，至少持续到 50 年期满为止。

欧共体及其成员国

第 6 条

WIPO 条约某些实质性条款的适用

对于根据本议定书给予的保护，缔约方应比照适用 WIPO 条约第 17 条（保护期限）的规定。

美国

第 13 条

保护期限

根据本条约给予表演者的保护期，应自表演录制之年年终算起，至少持续到 50 年期满为止。

XIV. 有关技术措施的义务

非洲的某些国家

第 12 条

WPPT 某些实质性条款的适用

对于根据本议定书给予的保护，缔约方应比照适用 WPPT 第 18 条（有关技术措施的义务）的规定。

CERTAIN STATES OF LATIN AMERICA AND THE CARIBBEAN

Obligations concerning technological measures

The Contracting Parties shall apply, *mutatis mutandis*, in respect of protection granted under this Protocol, the provisions of Article 18 (Obligations concerning technological measures) of the WIPO Treaty.

EUROPEAN COMMUNITY AND ITS MEMBER STATES

Article 6

Application of certain substantive provisions of the WIPO Treaty

The Contracting Parties shall apply, *mutatis mutandis*, in respect of protection granted under this Protocol, the provisions of Articles… 18 (Obligations concerning Technological Measures)… of the WIPO Treaty.

REPUBLIC OF KOREA

6. We are also in favor of the provisions on the obligations concerning technological measures and rights management information included in the Protocol as those provided for in the WPPT.

UNITED STATES OF AMERICA

Article 15

Obligations concerning Technological Measures

Contracting Parties shall provide adequate legal protection and effective legal remedies against the circumvention of effective technological measures that are used by performers or their transferees in connection with the exercise of their rights under this Treaty and that restrict acts, in respect of their performances, that are not authorized by the performers or that are not permitted by law.

XV. Obligations concerning rights management information

CERTAIN STATES OF AFRICA

Article 12

Application of Certain Substantive Provisions of the WPPT

The Contracting Parties shall apply, *mutatis mutandis*, in respect of the protection granted under this Protocol, the provisions of Articles… 19 (Obligations concerning the Rights Management Information),… of the WPPT.

拉丁美洲和加勒比地区的某些国家

关于技术措施的义务

对于根据本议定书给予的保护，缔约各方应比照适用 WIPO 条约第 18 条（关于权利管理信息的义务）的规定。

欧共体及其成员国

第 6 条

WIPO 条约某些实质性条款的适用

对于根据本议定书给予的保护，缔约方应比照适用 WIPO 条约第 18 条（技术措施义务）的规定。

韩国

6. 我们还赞成与 WPPT 所规定的关于技术措施和权利管理信息义务的相关条款。

美国

第 15 条

有关技术措施的义务

缔约各方应规定适当的法律保护和有效的法律补救办法，制止规避表演者或其受让人在行使本条约规定的权利时使用的、限制未经表演者授权或法律不允许的表演的有效技术措施。

XV. 有关权利管理信息的义务

非洲的某些国家

第 12 条

WPPT 某些实质性条款的适用

对于根据本议定书给予的保护，缔约方应比照适用 WPPT 第 19 条（关于权利管理信息的义务）的规定。

CERTAIN STATES OF LATIN AMERICA AND THE CARIBBEAN

Obligations concerning rights management information

The Contracting Parties shall apply, *mutatis mutandis*, in respect of protection granted under this Protocol, the provisions of Article 19 (Obligations concerning rights management information) of the WIPO Treaty.

EUROPEAN COMMUNITY AND ITS MEMBER STATES

Article 6

Application of certain substantive provisions of the WIPO Treaty

The Contracting Parties shall apply, *mutatis mutandis*, in respect of protection granted under this Protocol, the provisions of Articles… 19 (Obligations concerning Rights Management Information)… of the WIPO Treaty.

REPUBLIC OF KOREA

6. We are also in favor of the provisions on the obligations concerning technological measures and rights management information included in the Protocol as those provided for in the WPPT.

UNITED STATES OF AMERICA

Article 16

Obligations concerning Rights Management Information

(1) Contracting Parties shall provide adequate and effective legal remedies against any person knowingly performing any of the following acts knowing, or with respect to civil remedies having reasonable grounds to know, that it will induce, enable, facilitate, or conceal an infringement of any right covered by this Treaty:

(i) to remove or alter any electronic rights management information without authority;

(ii) to distribute, import for distribution, broadcast, communicate or make available to the public, without authority, performances or copies of fixed performances knowing that electronic rights management information has been removed or altered without authority.

(2) As used in this Article, "rights management information" means information that identifies the performer, the performance of the performer, or the owner of any right in the performance, or information about the terms and conditions of use of the

拉丁美洲和加勒比地区的某些国家

有关权利管理信息的义务

对于根据本议定书给予的保护，缔约各方应比照适用 WIPO 条约第 19 条（关于权利管理信息的义务）的规定。

欧共体及其成员国

第 6 条

WIPO 条约某些实质性条款的适用

对于根据本议定书给予的保护，缔约方应比照适用 WIPO 条约第 19 条（关于权利管理信息的义务）的规定。

韩国

6. 我们还赞成与 WPPT 所规定的关于技术措施和权利管理信息义务的相关条款。

美国

第 16 条

权利管理信息义务

（1）缔约各方应规定适当和有效的法律补救办法，制止任何人明知或就民事补救而言有合理根据知道其行为会诱使、促成、便利或包庇对本条约所涵盖的任何权利的侵犯而故意从事以下行为：

（i）未经许可去除或改变任何权利管理的电子信息；

（ii）未经许可发行、为发行目的进口、广播、向公众传播或提供明知已被未经许可去除或改变权利管理电子信息的表演或已录制表演的复制件。

（2）本条中的用语"权利管理信息"系指识别表演者、表演者的表演或对表演拥有任何权利的所有人的信息，或有关使用表演的条款和条件的信息，以及代表此种信息的任何数字或代码，各该项信息均附于已录制表演的复制件上，

performance, and any numbers or codes that represent such information, when any of these items of information is attached to a copy of a fixed performance or appears in connection with the broadcast, public communication, or making available to the public of a fixed performance.

XVI. Reservations

CERTAIN STATES OF AFRICA

Article 11

Reservations

No reservations to this Protocol shall be permitted.

CERTAIN STATES OF LATIN AMERICA AND THE CARIBBEAN

Reservations

No reservations to this Protocol shall be permitted.

EUROPEAN COMMUNITY AND ITS MEMBER STATES

Article 7

Reservations

No reservations to this Protocol shall be permitted.

UNITED STATES OF AMERICA

Article 18

Reservations

Subject to the provisions of Article 10(2), no reservations to this Treaty shall be permitted.

XVII. Application in time

CERTAIN STATES OF AFRICA

Article 12

Application of Certain Substantive Provisions of the WPPT

The Contracting Parties shall apply, *mutatis mutandis*, in respect of the protection granted under this Protocol, the provisions of Articles… 22 (Application in Time)… of the WPPT.

CERTAIN STATES OF LATIN AMERICA AND THE CARIBBEAN

Application in time

1. The Contracting Parties shall apply the provisions of Article 18 of the Berne Convention, *mutatis mutandis*, to the rights of the performers provided for in this

或者出现在广播、向公众传播或向公众提供的已录制表演上。

XVI. 保留

非洲的某些国家

第 11 条

保留

本议定书不得作出任何保留。

拉丁美洲和加勒比地区的某些国家

保留

本议定书不得作出任何保留。

欧共体及其成员国

第 7 条

保留

本议定书不得作出任何保留。

美国

第 18 条

保留

在不违反第 10 条第(2)款规定的情况下，本议定书不得作出任何保留。

XVII. 适用的时限

非洲的某些国家

第 12 条

WPPT 某些实质性条款的适用

对于根据本议定书给予的保护，缔约方应比照适用 WPPT 第 22 条（适用的时限）的规定。

拉丁美洲和加勒比地区的某些国家

适用的时限

1. 对于根据本议定书给予的表演者权利，缔约各方应比照适用《伯尔尼公约》第 18 条的规定。

Protocol.

2. This Protocol shall not detract from the rights acquired in any Contracting Party prior to the date of entry into force of this Protocol in that Party.

3. A Contracting Party shall not be obliged to apply the provisions of this Protocol to performances given, or to audiovisual fixations made, prior to its entry into force in that Party.

EUROPEAN COMMUNITY AND ITS MEMBER STATES

Article 6

Application of certain substantive provisions of the WIPO Treaty

The Contracting Parties shall apply, *mutatis mutandis*, in respect of protection granted under this Protocol, the provisions of Articles... 22 (Application in Time)... of the WIPO Treaty.

UNITED STATES OF AMERICA

Article 19

Application in Time

(1) Contracting Parties shall apply the provisions of Article 18 of the Berne Convention, *mutatis mutandis*, to the rights of performers provided for in this Treaty.

(2) Notwithstanding paragraph (1), a Contracting Party may limit the application of Article 5 of this Treaty to performances that occurred after the entry into force of this Treaty for that Party.

XVIII. Provisions on enforcement of rights

CERTAIN STATES OF AFRICA

Article 12

Application of Certain Substantive Provisions of the WPPT

The Contracting Parties shall apply, *mutatis mutandis*, in respect of the protection granted under this Protocol, the provisions of Articles... 23 (Provisions on Enforcement of Rights) of the WPPT.

CERTAIN STATES OF LATIN AMERICA AND THE CARIBBEAN

Provisions on enforcement of rights

The Contracting Parties shall apply, *mutatis mutandis*, in respect of protection granted under this Protocol, the provisions of Article 23 (Enforcement of rights) of the WIPO Treaty.

2. 本议定书规定的保护不得损害本议定书对每一缔约方生效之前取得的任何权利。

3. 缔约各方没有义务将本议定书的规定适用于本议定书在该缔约方生效之前所作出的表演或者视听录制品中。

欧共体及其成员国

第 6 条

WIPO 条约某些实质性条款的适用

对于根据本议定书给予的保护，缔约方应比照适用 WIPO 条约第 22 条（适用的时限）的规定。

美国

第 19 条

适用的时限

（1）缔约方应比照适用《伯尔尼公约》第 18 条关于表演者权利的规定。

（2）尽管有第（1）款的规定，缔约方可将本条约第 5 条的适用范围限于本条约对其生效后发生的表演。

XVIII. 权利行使条款

非洲的某些国家

第 12 条

WPPT 某些实质性条款的适用

对于根据本议定书给予的保护，缔约方应比照适用 WPPT 第 23 条（权利行使条款）的规定。

拉丁美洲和加勒比地区的某些国家

权利行使条款

对于根据本议定书给予的保护，缔约方应比照适用 WIPO 条约第 23 条（权利的行使）的规定。

EUROPEAN COMMUNITY AND ITS MEMBER STATES

Article 6

Application of certain substantive provisions of the WIPO Treaty

The Contracting Parties shall apply, *mutatis mutandis*, in respect of protection granted under this Protocol, the provisions of Articles... 23 (Enforcement of Rights)... of the WIPO Treaty.

UNITED STATES OF AMERICA

Article 20

Provisions on Enforcement of Rights

(1) Contracting Parties undertake to adopt, in accordance with their legal systems, the measures necessary to ensure the application of this Treaty.

(2) Contracting Parties shall ensure that enforcement procedures are available under their law so as to permit effective action against any act of infringement of rights covered by this Treaty, including expeditious remedies to prevent infringement and remedies which constitute a deterrent to further infringements.

XIX. Implementation

UNITED STATES OF AMERICA

Article 14

Implementation

Each Contracting Party may determine the means by which it will give effect to the provisions of this Treaty, including by means of the grant of a copyright or other related right.

XX. Administrative and final clauses

CERTAIN STATES OF AFRICA

Article 13

Assembly

(1) The Contracting Parties shall have an Assembly.

(2) This Assembly shall be the same as the one created by the WPPT. Its functioning shall be governed, *mutatis mutandis*, by Article 24 of the WPPT.

Article 14

Eligibility for Becoming Party to the Protocol

Any party to the WPPT may become party to this Protocol.

欧共体及其成员国

第 6 条

WIPO 条约某些实质性条款的适用

对于根据本议定书给予的保护，缔约方应比照适用 WIPO 条约第 23 条（权利的行使）的规定。

美国

第 20 条

权利行使条款

（1）缔约方承诺根据其法律制度采取必要的措施，以确保本条约的适用。

（2）缔约各方应确保依照其法律可以提供执法程序，以便能采取制止对本条约所涵盖权利的任何侵犯行为的有效行动，包括防止侵权的快速补救和为遏制进一步侵权的补救。

XIX. 权利行使

美国

第 14 条

权利行使

每个缔约方可决定以何种方式落实本条约的规定，包括通过授予版权或其他相关权利的方式。

XX. 行政条款和最后条款

非洲的某些国家

第 13 条

大会

（1）缔约方应设大会。

（2）大会应与根据 WPPT 设立的大会相同，其运作比照适用 WPPT 第 24 条的规定。

第 14 条

加入议定书的资格

WPPT 的任何缔约方均可成为本议定书的缔约方。

Article 15

Signature of the Protocol

This Protocol shall be open for signature until... by any party eligible under Article 14.

Article 16

Final Clauses

The provisions of Articles 25 (International Bureau), 27 (Rights and Obligations under the Treaty), 29 (Entry into Force of the Treaty), 30 (Effective Date of Becoming Party to the Treaty), 31 (Denunciation of the Treaty), 32 (Languages of the Treaty) and 33 (Depository) of the WPPT shall apply, *mutatis mutandis*.

CERTAIN STATES OF LATIN AMERICA AND THE CARIBBEAN

1. Assembly

The Contracting Parties shall have an Assembly. This Assembly shall be the same as the one created by the WIPO Treaty.

2. Eligibility for becoming party to the Protocol

Any party to the WIPO Treaty may become party to this Protocol.

3. Signature of the Protocol

This Protocol shall be open for signature until... by any Member State of WIPO and by the European Community.

4. Entry into force of the Protocol

This Protocol shall enter into force, following the date of entry into force of the WIPO Treaty, three months after 20 instruments of ratification or accession by States have been deposited with the Director General of WIPO.

5. Final clauses

The provisions of Articles 25 (International Bureau), 27 (Rights and obligations under the Treaty), 30 (Effective date of becoming party of the Treaty), 31 (Denunciation of the Treaty), 32 (Languages of the Treaty) and 33 (Depository) of the WIPO Treaty shall apply, *mutatis mutandis*.

EUROPEAN COMMUNITY AND ITS MEMBER STATES

Article 8

Application of certain administrative provisions

The Contracting Parties shall have an Assembly. This Assembly shall be the

第 15 条

议定书的签署

本议定书开放以供任何符合本议定书第 14 条规定的缔约方签署，直至……

第 16 条

最后条款

其他应比照适用 WPPT 第 25 条（国际局）、第 27 条（本条约规定的权利和义务）、第 29 条（本条约的生效）、第 30 条（成为本条约缔约方的生效日期）、第 31 条（退约）、第 32 条（本条约的语文）和第 33 条（保存人）的规定。

拉丁美洲和加勒比地区的某些国家

1. 大会

缔约方应设大会，大会应与 WIPO 条约设立的大会相同。

2. 成为本议定书缔约方的资格

WIPO 条约的任何缔约方都可以加入本议定书。

3. 议定书的签署

本议定书开放以供任何世界知识产权组织成员国和欧共体成员国签署，直至……

4. 议定书的生效

本议定书自 WIPO 条约生效之日起生效，即自各国向世界知识产权组织总干事交存 20 份批准书或加入书之日起 3 个月后生效。

5. 最后条款

本议定书比照适用 WIPO 条约第 25 条（国际局）、第 27 条（本条约规定的权利和义务）、第 30 条（成为本条约缔约方的生效日期）、第 31 条（退约）、第 32 条（本条约的语文）和第 33 条（保存人）的规定。

欧共体成员

第 8 条

某些行政性规定的适用

缔约方应设大会，大会应与 WIPO 条约设立的大会相同，其运作比照适用

same as the one created by the WIPO Treaty and its functioning shall be governed, *mutatis mutandis*, by Article 24 of the WIPO Treaty.

Article 9

Eligibility for becoming party to the Treaty

Any party to the WIPO Treaty may become party to this Protocol.

Article 10

Signature of the Protocol

This Protocol shall be open for signature until... by any Member State of WIPO and by the European Community.

Article 11

Entry into force of the Protocol

This Protocol shall enter into force, following the date of entry into force of the WIPO Treaty, three months after 5 instruments of ratification or accession by States have been deposited with the Director General of WIPO.

Article 12

Final clause

The provisions of Articles 25 (International Bureau), 27 (Rights and Obligations under the Treaty), 30 (Effective Date of Becoming Party of the Treaty), 31 (Denunciation of the Treaty), 32 (Languages of the Treaty) and 33 (Depository) of the WIPO Treaty shall apply, *mutatis mutandis*.

[End of Annex and of document]

WIPO 条约第 24 条的规定。

第 9 条

加入条约的资格

WIPO 条约的任何缔约方都可以加入本议定书。

第 10 条

议定书的签署

本议定书开放以供任何世界知识产权组织成员国和欧共体成员国签署，直至……

第 11 条

议定书生效

本议定书自 WIPO 条约生效之日起生效，即自各国向世界知识产权组织总干事交存 5 份法律文本或加入书之日起 3 个月后生效。

第 12 条

最后条款

本议定书比照适用 WIPO 条约第 25 条（国际局）、第 27 条（条约规定的权利和义务）、第 30 条（成为条约缔约方的生效日期）、第 31 条（退约）、第 32 条（条约的语文）和第 33 条（保存人）的规定。

（附件和文件完）

2.7 Report of the Regional Consultation Meeting for Asia and the Pacific, Held in New Delhi from May 20 to 22, 1998

Document Code: AP/CE/2/8
Language: English
URL: https://www.wipo.int/edocs/mdocs/copyright/en/ap_ce_2/ap_ce_2_8.pdf
Chinese Translation: Not Available.
URL: N/A

COMMITTEE OF EXPERTS
ON A PROTOCOL
CONCERNING AUDIOVISUAL PERFORMANCES
Second Session
GENEVA, JUNE 8 TO 12, 1998

Report of the Regional Consultation Meeting for Asia and the Pacific, Held in New Delhi from May 20 to 22, 1998

submitted on behalf of Bangladesh, Brunei Darussalam, India, Indonesia, Malaysia, Mongolia, Pakistan, Philippines, Qatar, Republic of Korea, Singapore, Thailand and the United Arab Emirates

2.7 1998年5月20日至22日在新德里举行的亚洲及太平洋区域协商会议的报告

文件编号：AP/CE/2/8
文件语言：英语
文件链接：https://www.wipo.int/edocs/mdocs/copyright/en/ap_ce_2/ap_ce_2_8.pdf
中文文本：无
文件链接：无

视听表演议定书专家委员会

第二届会议
1998年6月8日至12日，日内瓦

1998年5月20日至22日在新德里举行的亚洲及太平洋区域协商会议的报告

由代表孟加拉国、文莱、印度、
印度尼西亚、马来西亚、蒙古国、巴基斯坦、菲律宾、卡塔尔、
韩国、新加坡、泰国和阿拉伯联合酋长国提交

REPORT OF THE REGIONAL CONSULTATION MEETING FOR COUNTRIES OF ASIA AND THE PACIFIC ON A PROTOCOL CONCERNING AUDIOVISUAL PERFORMANCES

New Delhi, May 20 to 22,1998

The Regional Consultation Meeting for Countries of Asia and the Pacific on a Protocol Concerning Audiovisual Performances was held in New Delhi from May 20 to 22, 1998. India was elected Chairman of the meeting.

The discussion was based on the WIPO document No. AP/CE/2/2 (Proposals and other Submissions received from WIPO Member States and European Community). The participating countries had also before them the proposals of the United States of America and those of the Republic of Korea(WIPO document No. AP/CE/2/3).

Consensus was reached on the following:

The context of extending performers' rights to audiovisual performances is not uniform. For example, it may differ in developing countries in view of the special industrial practices existing in the film industry. Administration of copyright and related rights needs to be developed much in these countries. In the absence of a well-developed collective administration system, provision of new rights to performers in their audiovisual performances may not help the performers. It is also necessary to wait for the results of the rights given to performers in their audio performances. In this scenario, several participants felt that it was necessary not to hasten with a new Protocol.

The Group went through the proposals submitted by different countries and held detailed discussions amongst others on the following issues:

- Definitions
- National Treatment
- Moral rights of performers
- Economic rights of performers, particularly right of rental, rights of

亚洲和太平洋地区国家关于视听表演议定书区域协商会议的报告

1998年5月20日至22日，新德里

亚洲和太平洋地区国家就视听表演议定书召开的区域协商会议于1998年5月20日至22日在新德里举行。印度当选为会议主席国。

本次会议的讨论以世界知识产权组织第AP/CE/2/2号文件（世界知识产权组织成员国和欧洲共同体的提案和其他材料）为基础。与会国还就美国和韩国的提案（世界知识产权组织第AP/CE/2/3号文件）进行了审议。

会议就下列事项达成共识：

将表演者扩展至视听表演的背景并不统一。例如，在不同的发展中国家中，电影产业的特殊惯例就会有所不同。这些国家的版权和邻接权的管理仍有待发展，而在缺乏完善的集体管理制度的情况下，规定表演者就视听表演享有新权利可能无助于表演者。同时有必要等待授予表演者就其视听表演享有权利的条约实施的结果。在这种情况下，部分与会国认为，没有必要匆忙制定新的议定书。

工作组审议了各国的提案，并就下列问题进行了详细讨论：

- 定义
- 国民待遇
- 表演者的精神权利
- 表演者的经济权利，特别是出租权、广播权和向公众传播权

broadcasting and communication to the public

- Transfer of rights

Pursuant to the discussion, the following broad positions have emerged:

- Considering the special nature of the audiovisual industry, the Group expressed the need to consider exclusion of certain categories of performers, whose performances are casual or incidental, from the definition of performers, but felt it necessary to discuss the issue further.

- The Group also noted the differences in the definitions of "fixations" and "audiovisual works" in the various proposals.

- On the questions of Beneficiaries to the Protocol and National Treatment the Group discussed the Berne Convention and Rome Convention approaches and decided to take a stand only after the substantive provisions of the Protocol were finalized.

- Considering the changes in technology and adaptations required to facilitate commercial exploitation of films by producers, the Group felt the need to incorporate appropriate exceptions in the moral rights. The extent and scope of exceptions will be spelt out after discussions in their respective countries.

- On the question of the economic rights of the audiovisual performers, the Group discussed the right of reproduction, the right of distribution and the right of making available the performance and agreed to follow generally the principles adopted in WIPO Performances and Phonograms Treaty(WPPT) including those contained in the Agreed Statements appearing as footnotes thereto.

- Regarding rental rights, the Group considered the implications of recognizing it as a separate right but reserved their positions for further study and discussion on whether to follow the TRIPS Agreement approach or the WPPT approach or any other approach.

- Regarding rights of broadcasting and communication to the public, the Group decided to look into their implications for domestic law and come out with a position later.

- Regarding transfer of rights, the rebuttable presumption clause incorporated in some proposals was found to be deserving merit.

- Regarding limitations and exceptions, obligations concerning technological

– 权利的转让

经过讨论，确定了以下立场：

– 考虑到视听行业的特殊性，工作组表示需要考虑将某些类别的表演者（表演具有随意性或偶然性）排除在表演者的定义之外，但认为有必要对该问题进行进一步讨论。

– 工作组还注意不同提案中对“录制品”和“视听作品”的定义存在差异。

– 关于议定书的受益者和国民待遇问题，工作组讨论了《伯尔尼公约》和《罗马公约》的做法，并决定在议定书的实质性条款最终确定后再表态。

– 考虑到制片人在促进电影商业开发时所采用的技术和改编手段会发生变化，工作组认为有必要在精神权利规定中设置适当的例外规定。例外规定的程度和范围将在各国家自行讨论后加以说明。

– 关于视听表演者的经济权利问题，工作组讨论了复制权、发行权和提供表演的权利，并商定一般按照《世界知识产权组织表演和录音制品条约》（WPPT）及脚注部分《议定声明》所载的原则解决有关问题。

– 关于出租权，工作组审议了将其作为一项单独权利的影响，但保留了进一步研究和讨论是否遵循《与贸易有关的知识产权协议》或 WPPT 的做法或任何其他做法的立场。

– 关于广播权和向公众传播权，工作组决定在研究这些权利对国内法的影响后表态。

– 关于权利的转让，一些提案中建议的可推翻权利转让推定的条款被认为值得采纳。

– 关于限制与例外、关于技术措施的义务、关于权利管理信息的义务以及

measures, obligations concerning rights management information, provisions on enforcement of rights and formalities, it was agreed to follow generally the WPPT approach.

- Regarding application in time, the Group wanted to look into its implications further.

- The Group felt that the clause regarding reservations needs to be considered after the substantive provisions are agreed upon.

- There was a general consensus that the number of signatories must be the same as that of WPPT.

The participating countries reserved their rights to examine the issues afresh in the light of new proposals that may be presented in future and their implications to the domestic situations and laws.

关于权利行使和手续的规定，会议同意一般应遵循 WPPT 的做法。

– 关于适用的时限，工作组希望能够进一步研究其影响。

– 工作组认为，保留条款需要在实体规范商定之后再进行审议。

– 与会国普遍认为，议定书中规定的签署方数量必须与 WPPT 中签署方数量相同。

与会国保留根据今后可能提出的新提案及其对国内情况和法律的影响重新审查这些问题的权利。

（文件完）

2.8 Report Adopted by Committee of Experts on a Protocol Concerning Audiovisual Performance

Document Code: AP/CE/2/9
Language: English
URL: https://www.wipo.int/edocs/mdocs/copyright/en/ap_ce_2/ap_ce_2_9.pdf
Chinese Translation: Not Available.
URL: N/A

COMMITTEE OF EXPERTS
ON A PROTOCOL
CONCERNING AUDIOVISUAL PERFORMANCES
Second Session
GENEVA, JUNE 8 TO 12, 1998

Report Adopted by Committee of Experts on a Protocol Concerning Audiovisual Performance

adopted by the Committee

2.8 视听表演议定书专家委员会报告

文件编号：AP/CE/2/9
文件语言：英语
文件链接：https://www.wipo.int/edocs/mdocs/copyright/en/ap_ce_2/ap_ce_2_9.pdf
中文文本：无
文件链接：无

视听表演议定书专家委员会

第二届会议
1998年6月8日至12日，日内瓦

视听表演议定书专家委员会报告

由委员会通过

REPORT

adopted by the Committee

Ⅰ. INTRODUCTION

1. In pursuance of the decision taken by the WIPO General Assembly during its twenty-first session (see document WO/GA/XXI/13, paragraph 205), the Director General of WIPO convened the second session of the Committee of Experts on a Protocol concerning Audiovisual Performances (hereinafter referred to as "the Committee") at the headquarters of WIPO, in Geneva, from June 8 to 12, 1998.

2. Experts of the following ninety-three States and one intergovernmental organization, members of the Committee, attended the meeting: Algeria, Argentina, Australia, Austria, Azerbaijan, Bahrain, Bangladesh, Belarus, Belgium, Brazil, Brunei Darussalam, Burkina Faso, Cameroon, Canada, Chile, China, Colombia, Costa Rica, Côte d'Ivoire, Croatia, Cuba, Czech Republic, Denmark, Dominican Republic, Ecuador, Egypt, El Salvador, Finland, France, Germany, Ghana, Greece, Guyana, Hungary, India, Indonesia, Ireland, Israel, Italy, Jamaica, Japan, Jordan, Kazakstan, Kenya, Kyrgyzstan, Latvia, Libya, Luxembourg, Malawi, Malaysia, Mali, Malta, Mauritius, Mexico, Mongolia, Morocco, Namibia, Netherlands, New Zealand, Nigeria, Norway, Pakistan, Paraguay, Peru, Philippines, Portugal, Qatar, Republic of Korea, Republic of Moldova, Romania, Russian Federation, Senegal, Singapore, Slovakia, Slovenia, South Africa, Spain, Sri Lanka, Sudan, Sweden, Switzerland, Thailand, The Former Yugoslav Republic of Macedonia, Trinidad and Tobago, Ukraine, United Arab Emirates, United Kingdom, United States of America, Uruguay, Uzbekistan, Venezuela, Viet Nam, Zambia and the European Community.

3. Representatives of the following seven intergovernmental organizations attended the meeting in observer capacity: International Labour Organization (ILO), United Nations Educational, Scientific and Cultural Organization (UNESCO), World Meteorological Organization (WMO), World Trade Organization (WTO), League of Arab States (LAS), Organization of African Unity (OAU) and Organization of the Islamic Conference (OIC).

报告

由委员会通过

Ⅰ. 介绍

1. 根据世界知识产权组织大会第二十一届会议作出的决定（见 WO/GA/XXI/13 号文件第 205 段），世界知识产权组织总干事于 1998 年 6 月 8 日至 12 日在世界知识产权组织日内瓦总部召开了关于视听表演议定书的专家委员会第二届会议（以下简称委员会）。

2. 下列 93 个国家派出的专家和一个政府间组织的专家，委员会成员出席了会议：阿尔及利亚、阿根廷、澳大利亚、奥地利、阿塞拜疆、巴林、孟加拉国、白俄罗斯、比利时、巴西、文莱、布基纳法索、喀麦隆、加拿大、智利、中国、哥伦比亚、哥斯达黎加、科特迪瓦、克罗地亚、古巴、捷克共和国、丹麦、多米尼加共和国、厄瓜多尔、埃及、萨尔瓦多、芬兰、法国、德国、加纳、希腊、圭亚那、匈牙利、印度、印度尼西亚、爱尔兰、以色列、意大利、牙买加、日本、约旦、哈萨克斯坦、肯尼亚、吉尔吉斯斯坦、拉脱维亚、利比亚、卢森堡、马拉维、马来西亚、马里、马耳他、毛里求斯、墨西哥、蒙古国、摩洛哥、纳米比亚、荷兰、新西兰、尼日利亚、挪威、巴基斯坦、巴拉圭、秘鲁、菲律宾、葡萄牙、卡塔尔、韩国、摩尔多瓦共和国、罗马尼亚、俄罗斯联邦、塞内加尔、新加坡、斯洛伐克、斯洛文尼亚、南非、西班牙、斯里兰卡、苏丹、瑞典、瑞士、泰国、前南斯拉夫马其顿共和国、特立尼达和多巴哥、乌克兰、阿拉伯联合酋长国、英国、美国、乌拉圭、乌兹别克斯坦、委内瑞拉、越南、赞比亚、欧共体。

3. 下列七个政府间组织的代表以观察员身份出席了会议：国际劳工组织（ILO）、联合国教育、科学及文化组织（UNESCO）、世界气象组织（WMO）、世界贸易组织（WTO）、阿拉伯国家联盟（LAS）、非洲统一组织（OAU）和伊斯兰合作组织（OIC）。

4. Representatives of the following forty-one non-governmental organizations attended the meeting in observer capacity: Agence pour la protection des programmes (APP), American Bar Association (ABA), American Federation of Television and Radio Artists (AFTRA), American Intellectual Property Law Association (AIPLA), American Film Marketing Association (AFMA), Asia-Pacific Broadcasting Union (ABU), Association of Commercial Television in Europe (ACT), Association of European Performers' Organizations (AEPO), Association for the International Collective Management of Audiovisual Works (AGICOA), Comité "Actores, Intérpretes" (CSAI), Copyright Research and Information Center (CRIC), European Broadcasting Union (EBU), European Federation of Joint Management Societies of Producers for Private Audiovisual Copying (EUROCOPYA), Groupement européen représentant les organismes de gestion collective des droits des artistes interprètes ou exécutants (ARTIS GEIE), Ibero-American Television Organization (OTI), Ibero-Latin-American Federation of Performers (FILAIE), Intellectual Property Owners (IPO), Interamerican Copyright Institute (IIDA), International Affiliation of Writers Guilds (IAWG), International Association of Broadcasting (IAB), International Association for the Protection of Industrial Property (AIPPI), International Chamber of Commerce (ICC), International Confederation of Societies of Authors and Composers (CISAC), International DOI Foundation (IDF), International Federation of Actors (FIA), International Federation of Associations of Film Distributors (FIAD), International Federation of Film Producers Associations (FIAPF), International Federation of Musicians (FIM), International Federation of Reproduction Rights Organizations (IFRRO), International Federation of the Phonographic Industry (IFPI), International Intellectual Property Alliance (IIPA), International League of Competition Law (LIDC), International Literary and Artistic Association (ALAI), International Video Federation (IVF), Latin American Institute for Advanced Technology, Computer Science and Law (ILATID), Max-Planck-Institute for Foreign and International Patent, Copyright and Competition Law (MPI), Media and Entertainment International (MEI), National Association of Broadcasters (NAB), National Association of Commercial Broadcasters in Japan (NAB-Japan), Union of National Radio and Television Organizations of Africa (URTNA), and World Federation of

4. 下列41个非政府组织的代表以观察员身份出席了会议：节目保护组织（APP）、美国律师协会（ABA）、美国电视和广播艺术家联合会（AFTRA）、美国知识产权法协会（AIPLA）、美国电影营销协会（AFMA）、亚洲－太平洋广播联盟（ABU）、欧洲商业电视协会（ACT）、欧洲表演者组织协会（AEPO）、国际视听作品集体管理协会（AGICOA）、Comité "Actores, Intérpretes"（CSAI）、著作权研究和信息中心（CRIC）、欧洲广播联盟（EBU）、欧洲个人视听复制制作者联合管理协会联合会（EUROCOPYA）、欧洲表演者权集体管理组织代表团体（ARTIS GEIE）、伊比利亚－美洲电视组织（OTI）、西语拉丁美洲表演者联合会（FILAIE）、知识产权所有者协会（IPO）、美洲国家间版权机构（IIDA）、国际作家协会联盟（IAWG）、国际广播协会（IAB）、国际工业产权保护协会（AIPPI）、国际商会（ICC）、国际作者和作曲家协会联合会（CISAC）、国际数字对象识别符基金会（IDF）、国际演员联合会（FIA）、国际电影发行者协会联合会（FIAD）、国际电影制片人协会（FIAPF）、国际音乐家联合会（FIM）、国际复制权利组织联盟（IFRRO）、国际唱片业协会（IFPI）、国际知识产权联盟（IIPA）、国际竞争法联盟（LIDC）、国际文学艺术协会（ALAI）、国际影像联合会（IVF）、拉丁美洲先进技术、计算机科学与法律研究所（ILATID）、马克斯·普朗克外国与国际专利、著作权和竞争法研究所（MPI）、国际媒体和娱乐协会（MEI）、全美广播事业者联盟（NAB）、日本民间放送联盟（NAB-Japan）、非洲国家广播电视组织联盟（URTNA）、世界音乐学校联合会（WFMS）。

Music Schools (WFMS).

5. The list of participants (Annex) is attached to this report.

II. OPENING OF THE MEETING

6. A representative of the International Bureau of WIPO welcomed the participants and opened the meeting on behalf of the Director General of WIPO.

III. ELECTION OF OFFICERS

7. Mr. Jukka Liedes (Finland) was unanimously elected Chairman, and Mrs. Hilda Retondo (Argentina) and Mr. Chang Cheng (China) were unanimously elected Vice-Chairmen of the Committee.

IV. CONSIDERATION OF QUESTIONS RELATED TO A PROTOCOL CONCERNING AUDIOVISUAL PERFORMANCES

Basis of discussions and work plan

8. Discussions were based on the following documents:

- proposals and other submissions received from WIPO Member States and the European Community (document AP/CE/2/2);

- proposal from the Republic of Korea (document AP/CE/2/3);

- proposal from the United States of America (document AP/CE/2/4), with Corrigendum to document AP/CE/2/4 (document AP/CE/2/4 Corr.);

- proposal from Algeria, Burkina Faso, Cameroon, Ghana, Kenya, Malawi, Mali, Morocco, Namibia, Nigeria, Senegal, South Africa, Sudan, Togo and Zambia (document AP/CE/2/5);

- report of the Regional Consultation Meeting for Latin America and the Caribbean, submitted by Argentina, Brazil, Colombia, Costa Rica, Cuba, Ecuador, Guyana, Jamaica, Mexico, Panama, Paraguay, Peru, Trinidad and Tobago, Uruguay and Venezuela (document AP/CE/2/6);

- comparative table of Proposals received by June 3, 1998 (document AP/CE/2/7); and

- report of the Regional Consultation Meeting for Asia and the Pacific, submitted by Bangladesh, Brunei Darussalam, India, Indonesia, Malaysia, Mongolia, Pakistan, Philippines, Qatar, Republic of Korea, Singapore, Thailand and the United Arab Emirates (document AP/CE/2/8).

9. The Chairman proposed the following proceedings: first, Delegations which

5. 参会人员名单（附件）附于本报告之后。

II. 会议开幕

6. 世界知识产权组织国际局的一名代表欢迎与会者并代表世界知识产权组织总干事宣布会议开幕。

III. 选举主席团成员

7. 经一致同意，尤卡·利德斯（Jukka Liedes）先生（芬兰）被推选为主席，希尔达·雷东多（Hilda Retondo）女士（阿根廷）和常城（Chang Cheng）先生（中国）被推选为副主席。

IV. 审议与视听表演议定书有关的问题

讨论基础和工作计划

8. 讨论以下列文件为基础：

– 世界知识产权组织成员国和欧洲共同体提交的提案和其他材料（AP/CE/2/2 号文件）；

– 韩国的提案（AP/CE/2/3 号文件）；

– 美国的提案（AP/CE/2/4 号文件），以及 AP/CE/2/4 号修正案（AP/CE/2/4 Corr）；

– 阿尔及利亚、布基纳法索、喀麦隆、加纳、肯尼亚、马拉维、马里、摩洛哥、纳米比亚、尼日利亚、塞内加尔、南非、苏丹、多哥和赞比亚的提案（AP/CE/2/5 号文件）；

– 阿根廷、巴西、哥伦比亚、哥斯达黎加、古巴、厄瓜多尔、圭亚那、牙买加、墨西哥、巴拿马、巴拉圭、秘鲁、特立尼达和多巴哥、乌拉圭和委内瑞拉提交的拉丁美洲和加勒比区域协商会议报告（AP/CE/2/6 号文件）；

– 截至 1998 年 6 月 3 日收到的提案比较表（AP/CE/2/7 号文件）；以及

– 孟加拉国、文莱、印度、印度尼西亚、马来西亚、蒙古国、巴基斯坦、菲律宾、卡塔尔、韩国、新加坡、泰国和阿拉伯联合酋长国提交的亚洲及太平洋地区区域协商会议报告（AP/CE/2/8 号文件）。

9. 主席建议会议议程如下：第一，已提交建议的代表团就其提案进行报告，

had made proposals would present them; other Delegations might, in a general statement, inform about new developments; second, selected items would be discussed, leaving out those where a high degree of convergence already existed; third, conclusions would be drawn, concerning the future work.

Presentation of proposals and general comments

10. The Delegation of Bangladesh, on behalf of the Asian Group, introduced the Report of the Group's Regional Consultation Meeting (document AP/CE/2/8) and underlined the positions taken therein. It concluded that the Asian Group looked forward to a meaningful discussion in the light of new proposals that might be submitted in the current session. The Asian Group believed that the discussion in this session would ultimately lead to the conclusion of a new Protocol on Audiovisual Performances, on the basis of consensus so that it could be acceptable to and beneficial for all the Member States.

11. The Delegation of Côte d'Ivoire said that the proposal from African States contained in document AP/CE/2/5 should be considered to have been made on behalf of Côte d'Ivoire, too.

12. The Delegation of China said that it regretted the lack of interpretation and translation of documents into Chinese and Arabic languages.

13. The Delegation of the European Community recalled the background of the proposal from the European Community and its Member States (document AP/CE/2/2), and presented it. The European Community and its Member States had before and at the Diplomatic Conference of 1996, proposed the full inclusion of audiovisual performances and then, as a compromise, approved the WPPT and the Resolution of the Conference on Audiovisual Performances. The main thrust of their current proposal was on a meaningful protection for audiovisual performances. The borderline between aural and audiovisual performances was becoming more and more blurred, for instance as regards videoclips and certain multimedia products. The proposal did not neglect the particular features of film production. In the European Union, performers were already protected on an equal footing in respect of aural and audiovisual performances, and these rules were operated also to the benefit of the film industries. The structure of the proposal was to maintain the principle of a Protocol to the WPPT, in line with the Resolution. The membership

其他代表团可在一般性发言中通报相关领域新发展情况；第二，讨论选定项目，将已经达成高度一致意见的项目排除在讨论范围之外；第三，就后续工作得出结论。

提案报告和一般性意见

10. 孟加拉国代表团代表亚洲介绍了该区域协商会议的报告（AP/CE/2/8 号文件），并强调了该报告确定的立场。会议的结论是，亚洲期待着根据可能在本届会议上提出的新提案进行有意义的讨论。亚洲相信本届会议的讨论将最终缔结一项新的视听表演议定书，当然这应当是以协商一致为基础的，这样才能让所有成员国都能接受该议定书并从中受益。

11. 科特迪瓦代表团称，AP/CE/2/5 号文件中的非洲国家提案也应被视为代表科特迪瓦提出。

12. 中国代表团对没有将有关文件译成中文和阿拉伯文感到遗憾。

13. 欧共体代表团回顾了欧共体及其成员国提出的提案（AP/CE/2/2 号文件）的背景，并作了介绍。欧共体及其成员国在 1996 年外交会议之前和会议上曾提议将视听表演全面纳入保护范围之中，随后作为一项妥协，批准了 WPPT 和视听表演会议决议。欧共体及其成员国目前提案的着眼点是为视听表演提供有意义的保护。有声表演和视听表演之间的界限越来越模糊，例如短视频和其他某些多媒体制品。这项提案也没有忽视电影制作的特点。在欧盟，无论是视听表演的表演者还是有声表演的表演者都已得到平等保护，而且有关规则的制定实施也有利于维护电影产业的利益。该提案的结构原则上以 WPPT 议定书的形式将视听表演纳入 WPPT 的保护范围中，这也与视听表演会议的决议相一致。同时，议定书的成员国应当以 WPPT 的缔约国为限。而提案第 3 条的目的是鼓励遵守议定书；总的来说，该提案在强调 WPPT 解决方案充分性的基础上作了一些适当的修改。

in the Protocol should be reserved to Contracting Parties of the WPPT. Article 3 of the Proposal was meant as an incentive to adhere to the Protocol; on the whole, the proposal underlined the adequacy of the solutions of the WPPT with some appropriate modifications.

14. The Delegation of Australia explained that it had not made a proposal because consultations on the issue had been going on, and were still continuing, in its country, but that it would actively participate in the discussions.

15. The Delegation of Japan, recalling its contribution contained in document AP/CE/2/2, said that the ad hoc Committee mentioned therein still had not concluded its discussions. Therefore, the Delegation did not yet feel in a position to make proposals, but would actively contribute to the further discussions.

16. The Delegation of the Republic of Korea, presenting its proposal (document AP/CE/2/3), underlined the importance of the transferability of economic rights. Special consideration should be given to the questions of beneficiaries and of national treatment. While it agreed to granting the right of fixation and the right of broadcasting and the communication to the public of unfixed performances, and the right of reproduction and the right of making available of fixed performances as envisaged in the WPPT, the Delegation opposed moral rights, the rental right and retroactive protection.

17. The Delegation of the United States of America, explaining its proposal (documents AP/CE/2/4 and AP/CE/2/4 Corr.), said that the Government had been working, with the US film industry and performers unions, on a proposal aimed at meeting needs of both groups. The proposal was a milestone in US copyright policy; the first time a full and affirmative proposal, containing moral and economic rights, was made. It differed from the WPPT in several ways: Moral rights should not conflict with a normal exploitation of the film production; normal exploitation was meant to include use of new technology and new media formats. The rebuttable presumption of transfer of rights of performers to the producers should apply to all exclusive rights of authorization, but not to remuneration rights nor to moral rights.

18. The Delegation of South Africa, on behalf of certain States of Africa, outlined three characteristic elements of the proposal from these States (document AP/CE/2/5): Firstly, in Article 4, the point of departure was a strong national

14. 澳大利亚代表团解释说，其之所以未提交提案是因为该国一直在就这一问题进行商讨，而该等商讨仍在继续，但其将积极参与本届会议的讨论。

15. 日本代表团回顾了其在 AP/CE/2/2 号文件中所作的贡献，该代表团称由于该文件中提到的特设委员会讨论尚在进行中，因此其目前无法提出建议，但日本代表团将积极推动进一步的讨论。

16. 韩国代表团在介绍其提案（AP/CE/2/3 号文件）时强调了经济权利可转让性的重要性，同时，其认为应特别考虑受益人和国民待遇问题。虽然该代表团同意按照 WPPT 的设想，授予表演者录制权、现场直播和向公众传播其尚未录制的表演的权利、复制权和提供已录制表演的权利，但其反对授予表演者精神权利、出租权和溯及既往的保护。

17. 美国代表团在解释其提案（AP/CE/2/4 和 AP/CE/2/4 号修正文件）时表示，该国政府一直在与美国电影业和演员工会合作，以制定一项能够满足两者需求的提案。该提案是美国版权政策中的一个里程碑，它首次提供了精神和经济权利两方面的全面和正向保护。它与 WPPT 在几个方面有所不同：精神权利的行使不应与电影制作的正常利用相冲突；正常利用包括电影制作中使用的新技术和新媒体格式。表演者所有授权专有权推定转让给制作者，但该推定是可以被推翻的，且不适用于报酬权或精神权利。

18. 南非代表团代表某些非洲国家概述了这些国家的提案（AP/CE/2/5 号文件），其总结的三个特征如下：第一，提案的第 4 条旨在设置一项如《伯尔尼公约》一样强有力的国民待遇条款，但该条第（2）款使得缔约方有权在互惠基础

treatment provision, like in the Berne Convention, but paragraph (2) gave Contracting Parties the right to limit that obligation on the basis of reciprocity, similar to Article 16 of the Rome Convention. Secondly, the rental right was conceived in a way similar to Article 11 of the TRIPS Agreement. Thirdly, the absence of a right of broadcasting and of communication to the public only meant that it had been decided to defer the matter until further consultations at regional or national level have taken place.

19. The Delegation of Ghana confirmed that it now subscribed to the proposal in document AP/CE/2/5. The Delegation said that in its national consultations the producers were opposed to granting rights to performers. The producers suggested that contracts and agreements should govern the protection of performers in order that normal exploitation of the work is not unreasonably stifled by the performers. However, at the African Regional Consultation Meeting, it was decided that the issue be left to national legislation.

20. The Delegation of Jamaica introduced the report of the Regional Consultation Meeting for Latin America and the Caribbean (document AP/CE/2/6) on behalf of the 15 countries represented there. The proposals contained in the report were a common position of those countries. The Delegation expressed the hope that the meeting would lead closer to the adoption of a Protocol.

21. The Delegation of Uruguay referred to the reservations expressed by its country's representative at Quito regarding the contents of Title X of the report, and said that it was not yet in a position to pronounce on the subject for want of a national consensus, basically on account of the concern shown by certain interest groups that there should be an investigation of whether the proposals might not constitute the recognition of economic rights potentially stronger than those of authors.

22. The Delegation of Argentina explained that the representative of Argentina had also spoken in favor of granting the right of broadcasting and communication to the public at Quito, but that it had not yet been possible to achieve full agreement. The Delegation added that it preferred to have the Protocol formulate explicit provisions without resorting to the expedient of " mutatis mutandis" references. Finally, it considered that the content of the proposal put forward by the United

上限制国民待遇义务履行，这类似于《罗马公约》第16条的规定。第二，出租权的构想方式类似于《与贸易有关的知识产权协定》第11条。第三，提案中没有规定广播权和向公众传播权，但这只意味着有关国家决定待该项事宜经区域级别或国家级别的协商进一步讨论后再行处理。

19. 加纳代表团确认，其目前同意AP/CE/2/5号文件中的提案。该代表团说，在其国内协商过程中，该国制作者反对赋予表演者权利。制作者建议，应当根据合同和协议来保护表演者的利益，以免表演者不合理地阻碍对作品的正常利用。然而，非洲区域协商会议决定将这一问题留给各国立法处理。

20. 牙买加代表团代表出席拉丁美洲和加勒比区域间协商会议的15个国家介绍了该会议的报告（AP/CE/2/6号文件）。报告中的建议是这些国家的共同立场。该代表团表示，希望本次会议能够推动议定书的通过。

21. 乌拉圭代表团提到该国代表在基多举行的上述区域间协商会议上对会议报告第十章的内容表示保留，因该国尚无法就这一问题达成一致，而这主要是因为某些利益集团的反对所导致的，他们认为应调查相关建议是否可能导致对表演者经济权利的保护水平高于对作者的保护水平。

22. 阿根廷代表团解释说，该国代表在基多会议上也表达了倾向于授予表演者广播权和向公众传播权的意见，但与会国尚未就此达成完全一致意见。该代表团还补充说，其倾向于在议定书中通过制定明确条款的方式将相关事宜确定下来，而不采取“比照适用”的权宜之计。最后，代表团认为美国提出的提案的内容是一项重要贡献。

States of America was an important contribution.

23. The Delegation of Colombia, endorsing the findings of the Quito meeting, said that it was very interested in the proposals by the United States of America on economic rights. It also thought that moral rights should be studied specially.

24. The Delegation of Brazil, referring to the report of the GRULAC Regional Consultation Meeting, said that the questions of moral rights and national treatment, among others, required particular attention, and reserved its position regarding the substantive debate.

25. The Delegation of Mexico said that it was necessary to direct efforts towards the successful drafting of a Protocol Concerning Audiovisual Performances, and that its country was fully prepared to participate.

26. The Delegation of Chile said that Chile had not been represented at Quito, but that it subscribed to the proposals contained in document AP/CE/2/6, with the exception however of subjects on which there had been no consensus.

27. The Delegation of India said that most of its views and concerns had been expressed by the Delegation of Bangladesh, presenting the outcome of the Regional Consultation Meeting that took place in New Delhi. It recalled that India had a huge film industry, which currently was subject to various new developments like the recent liberalization of the economy and institutional financing, and insurance becoming available to the film industry in the wake of the film business having been accorded the status of an "industry." The interests of performers had always been protected in India and the relationship between producers and performers was based on mutual trust and agreement. India wanted to go very steady on the question of extending performers' rights to new categories of works. The question of implementing the provisions of the WPPT still had to be considered by India. It would like to watch how the rights of performers in audio fixations worked in practice before venturing into extending rights to performers in audiovisual works. In order to reap the benefits of a legislation extending rights to performers, there was a need to have strong collecting societies in the field of performers' audiovisual rights. In India, like in many other developing countries, the concept of collective management of rights was yet to take roots. Therefore, the speed of progress in moving towards a Diplomatic Conference needed to be limited.

23. 哥伦比亚代表团赞同基多会议的结论，该国对美国关于经济权利的建议非常感兴趣，其还认为应对精神权利进行特别研究。

24. 巴西代表团在提到拉加组区域间协商会议的报告时称需要特别注意精神权利和国民待遇等问题，并表示其对实质性争论持保留态度。

25. 墨西哥代表团说，有必要集中力量推动《视听表演议定书》草案的形成，墨西哥已经为参加会议做好了充分准备。

26. 智利代表团说，智利没有派代表出席基多会议，但其同意 AP/CE/2/6 号文件中除未达成一致意见主题以外的建议。

27. 印度代表团称，孟加拉国代表团对新德里区域间协商会议的成果介绍已经表述了其大部分意见和关注点。其回顾说，印度有一个规模庞大的电影产业，目前该产业正在经历各种新的发展，如最近的经济和融资机构自由化，并且在获得“产业”地位后，电影行业可以通过保险获得保障。表演者的利益在印度一直受到保护并且制作者和表演者之间的关系是建立在相互信任和协议的基础上的。印度希望将表演者的权利扩大到新的作品类别的进程能够稳步进行。印度仍需要考虑 WPPT 条款的执行问题。在冒险将表演者权利扩大到视听作品之前，印度希望能够观察到录音制品中表演者权是如何在实践中运作的。为了获得扩张表演者权所带来的利益，在表演者视听权利领域需要建立起强有力的收费团体，然而同许多其他发展中国家一样，在印度，权利的集体惯例概念尚未深入人心。因此，在召开外交会议方面的进展速度必须有所限制。

28. The representative of the International Labour Organization (ILO) said that recent studies commissioned by ILO as well as a meeting on multimedia convergence held by ILO had focused on the impact of converging information and communication technologies and the internationalization of the media and entertainment industries on the labor and social conditions of performers. On the one hand, findings pointed to both increasing and decreasing employment opportunities. On the other hand, there was increasing precariousness in contractual arrangements for performers. This gave rise to lower levels of social security protection and to difficulties for collective representation by trade unions or other organizations to protect the interests of performers, especially in developing countries, in relation to remuneration, hours of work, training, and safety and health concerns. This situation undoubtedly engendered risks for the protection of the cultural heritage and creators' rights in the long term. Therefore, ILO welcomed any steps that would increase the level of protection of performers in audiovisual performances. The protection of the rights and working conditions of performers was essential as their talent and creativity represented a precious resource in the world of today, where entertainment played an increasingly important role in the lives of millions in many countries. The ILO was deeply interested in the Committee's deliberations and wished for a successful outcome.

29. The representative of the United Nations Educational, Scientific and Cultural Organization (UNESCO) recalled that his Organization had expressed the wish at the 1996 Diplomatic Conference that audiovisual performances might be included in the WPPT. He noted with great satisfaction that his wish was shared and had evolved further in the various proposals put to the Committee. He saw that as an emerging consensus in favor of international protection for performers, which would contribute to an improvement in their circumstances in all forms of exploitation of audiovisual fixations. He declared himself confident that a balanced agreement could be achieved.

30. An observer from the International Federation of Actors (FIA) stressed that her organization had worked on these issues for many years. She recognized that audiovisual performers had to contribute to the practical functioning of their rights, in particular by establishing collective management systems, but they also

28. 国际劳工组织（ILO）的代表说，该组织最近委托进行的研究以及举行的多媒体融合会议，聚焦于信息和通信技术的融合以及媒体和娱乐产业的国际化给表演者的劳动和社会条件带来的影响。一方面，研究结果指出，就业机会同时出现了增加和减少的现象。另一方面，表演者合同安排的不确定性逐渐提升，这导致表演者社会保障水平的降低，同时工会或其他组织难以通过集体代表的方式保护表演者在薪酬、工作时间、培训以及安全和健康等方面的利益，这些现象在发展中国家尤为突出。这种局面从长远来看无疑会给文化遗产的保护和创作者的权利带来风险。因此，国际劳工组织欢迎采取任何措施以加强对视听表演表演者的保护。在该组织看来，保护表演者的权利以及提升其工作条件至关重要，因为表演者的才华和创造力是当今世界的宝贵资源，而他们所处的娱乐产业当下在众多国家人民的生活中发挥着越来越重要的作用。国际劳工组织对委员会的审议深感兴趣，并希望讨论能够取得成功。

29. 联合国教育、科学及文化组织（UNESCO）的代表回顾说，该组织曾在1996 年外交会议上表示希望将视听表演纳入 WPPT 的保护范围。他非常满意地注意到，该组织的愿望得到了赞同，并在向委员会提出的各项提案中得到了进一步发展。他认为这代表了各方在为表演者提供国际保护方面达成了新的共识，而这将有助于改善表演者在处理他人以各种形式利用视听录制品问题时的处境。该代表宣称自己对能够达成一项平衡的协议怀有信心。

30. 来自国际演员联合会（FIA）的一名观察员强调，该组织多年来一直致力于解决视听表演保护问题。该观察员承认视听表演者必须为其权利的实际运作作出贡献，特别是通过建立集体管理制度，但他们也需要在国际法中占据一席之地并且在数字环境下利用视听表演的协商中拥有发言权。她还特别指

needed a standing in international law and a voice in the dialogue concerning the use of audiovisual performances in the digital environment. She particularly pointed at the need for appropriate protection in terms of moral rights, broadcasting and communication to the public. She recognized that existing national systems regarding the rights of audiovisual performers varied, necessitating harmonization, and that this had led to different positions even among the performers themselves which they were attempting to resolve. She stressed that there was no disagreement about the need to raise the level of protection of performers internationally without undermining high levels that had been achieved in some countries.

31. An observer from the International Federation of Film Producers Associations (FIAPF) pointed out that, for both legal and economical reasons, one should not look at audiovisual performances merely as a sub-category of sound performances. Audiovisual works were works in their own right with their own copyright protection under the Berne Convention. Audiovisual performances were an integrated part of that whole, more than just a fixation of a performance. Economically, the investments in audiovisual works were much higher than in phonograms and they involved thousands of jobs and millions of dollars in investments. He also warned against rules that would entail incompatibilities between the protection of copyright and related rights. Concerning the transfer of rights, he pointed at the tradition of concentrating all rights in the hand of the producer who can then represent them towards users.

32. An observer from the Ibero-Latin-American Federation of Performers (FILAIE) tended to prefer a Protocol to the WPPT rather than a separate treaty, since that would be in harmony with the decision of the Diplomatic Conference of December 1996 and it would simplify the preparatory work and the ratification procedures. He also pointed to the similarities in regard of the substance of the subject matter in question. He emphasized that a strong protection in the field was functioning well in the European Union, and he stressed that it would be essential for the Protocol to cover moral rights, also because of the weak bargaining power of many performers.

33. An observer from the International Federation of Musicians (FIM) felt that the Protocol should protect performers rather than performances. Because

出，在精神权利、广播和向公众传播方面需要给予表演者适当保护。该观察员承认，各国保护视听表演者权利的现有制度各不相同，亟待统一，而这些制度上的差异甚至导致了表演者之间在解决有关问题时的不同立场。她还强调，在提高表演者国际保护水平的同时而不降低某些国家已经为表演者提供的高水平保护的立场方面，各方不存在意见分歧。

31. 国际电影制片人协会（FIAPF）的一名观察员指出，出于法律和经济两方面的原因，人们不应仅仅将视听表演视为声音表演的一个子类。视听作品是在《伯尔尼公约》中受到独立保护的一类作品。视听表演是相关产业一个组成部分，而不仅仅涉及表演的录制。从经济上来说，制作视听作品所需投资远远高于录音制品，该产业牵涉成千上万个就业机会和成百上千万美元的投资。他还警告称其反对导致版权保护和邻接权保护不相适应的规则。在权利的转让问题上，他指出立法传统上是将有关权利集中授予制作者，这样便于制作者代表参与创作者授权给使用者。

32. 西语拉丁美洲表演者联合会（FILAIE）的一名观察员倾向于通过制定WPPT 议定书的形式保护视听表演而不是单独制定条约，这也与 1996 年 12 月举行的外交会议的决议相一致，并将有助于简化筹备工作和批准程序。他还指出了有关主题事项实质内容的相似之处。该观察员强调，欧盟在视听表演保护方面建立的强有力的保护制度在实践中运作良好，并且他还强调，议定书中必须规定保护表演者的精神权利，这也是考虑到许多表演者在利用视听表演的协商中缺少谈判资本的现实状况。

33. 国际音乐家联合会（FIM）的一名观察员认为议定书保护的应该是表演者而不是表演。考虑到录音制品和视听录制品之间在法律上的区别在实践中

a legal distinction between audio and audiovisual fixation was more and more artificial in practice, he preferred the elaboration of a Protocol to the WPPT rather than a separate treaty. His organization supported the proposal from the European Community and its Member States and those proposals that followed the same principles, although it had certain reservations. It considered it useless to include a separate definition of "performer," because such a definition already existed in the WPPT, and it was opposed to the granting of moral rights that were weaker than those granted in that Treaty. It also had reservations regarding the clauses in that proposal on rights to broadcasting and communication to the public. Intellectual Property Rights development ought to really assist performers to benefit from their rights so that their socio-economical position, which generally has deteriorated during recent years, could improve.

34. An observer from the Max-Planck-Institute for Foreign and International Patent, Copyright and Competition Law (MPI) recommended the adoption of a Protocol to the WPPT, which should follow the WPPT as closely as possible, rather than a separate treaty because otherwise the already difficult borderline between audiovisual and other performances would be even more blurred. She considered moral rights important, but she feared that the reservation regarding the normal exploitation of audiovisual works could take the essential contents out of such rights. She stressed that the protection under Article 6(i) of the proposal from the United States of America would grant a level of protection even lower than that under the Rome Convention, and presumptions of transfer of rights would in many countries mean a weakening of the position of performers and therefore should not be an obligatory content of a Protocol. Regarding national treatment, she pointed at the increasing political awareness of economic consequences of legislation on related rights, and she felt it difficult to go further than in the WPPT. She said that remuneration rights should be granted for broadcasting and communication to the public of fixations of audiovisual performances upon the model of the WPPT. She felt that the flexibility of implementation as proposed under Article 14 of the proposal from the US would contradict the obligation to provide exclusive rights and would not make sufficiently clear the nature of protection which foreign performers could enjoy under the Protocol.

更多是人为干涉的结果，他倾向于通过制定 WPPT 议定书的形式保护视听表演而不是单独制定条约。该组织支持欧共体及其成员国的提案及其他遵循同样原则的提案，尽管该组织对上述提案在某些方面持保留意见。该组织认为议定书中没有必要对"表演者"的概念进行单独定义，因为 WPPT 已经对"表演者"进行了定义，并且该组织反对对视听表演者精神权利的保护低于 WPPT 要求的水平，其还对该提案中关于广播和向公众传播权的条款持保留意见。该组织认为，知识产权的发展应该真正帮助表演者从其权利中获益，以便改善他们近年来普遍降低的社会经济地位。

34. 一位来自马克斯·普朗克外国与国际专利、著作权和竞争法研究所（MPI）的观察员建议通过一项 WPPT 议定书来保护视听表演，该议定书应尽可能遵循 WPPT，而无须单独制定一项条约，因为视听表演和其他类型的表演之间的界限将变得越来越模糊。该观察员认为对精神权利的保护很重要，但其担心如果允许在对视听作品正常利用的情况下对精神权利予以保留，可能会使这些权利的保护徒有其表。她强调，美国提案中第 6 条（i）项所提供的保护甚至低于《罗马公约》所要求的保护水平，而权利转让的推定在许多国家则意味着表演者地位的削弱，因此该推定不应成为议定书的强制性内容。关于国民待遇的规定，该观察员指出，由于各国对邻接权立法带来的经济影响在政治层面上的意识日益提高，她感到有关规定很难在 WPPT 的基础上更进一步。她说应赋予表演者向通过广播和向公众传播其已录制视听表演的使用者获取报酬的权利，该获酬权的规定应采用 WPPT 的模式。该观察员认为，美国提案中第 14 条所建议的执行灵活性过大，这将与提供专有权保护的义务相矛盾，并且会使得外国表演者根据议定书所享有的保护的性质变得模糊。

35. An observer from the Comité de Seguimiento "Actores, Intérpretes" (CSAI) stressed that a treaty should be based on exclusive rights because such rights would offer the best basis for negotiations between the parties, but other models could in certain cases also be considered. As an example, he mentioned the law of Spain, where the producer obtained all rights, but performers kept a right of remuneration. Otherwise, exclusive rights would remain empty words without practical impact. He also supported the introduction of moral rights in the field.

36. An observer from the Copyright Research and Information Center (CRIC), speaking on behalf of the Japan Council of Performers' Organizations (GEIDANKYO), proposed that the definition of performers in the WPPT apply mutatis mutandis, however with the words added: "including similar acts not involving the performance of a work which have the nature of public entertainment." Regarding economic rights, he proposed exclusive rights in fixation, broadcasting, communication to the public and in making available to the public for unfixed performances, and rights of reproduction, broadcasting, communication to the public, distribution, rental and making available to the public for fixed performances. He pointed at the immense impact of digitization on the exploitation of performances, and stressed that performances should enjoy a protection equal to that of literary and artistic works.

37. An observer from the Groupement européen représentant les organismes de gestion collective des droits des artistes interprètes ou exécutants (ARTIS GEIE) welcomed the work of the Committee. He said that his organization did not support national treatment without modifications, and preferred the models that had been developed in this respect in existing treaties on related rights. He appealed to the Delegation of the United States of America to approach the level of the WPPT regarding the scope of the economic rights. He deplored that audiovisual performers remained without protection at the international level, and he called for a coherence between the WPPT and the Protocol.

38. An observer from the International Literary and Artistic Association (ALAI) said that his organization could not agree to any provision that would allow producers to make any distortion or mutilation of a performance that would be seriously prejudicial to the performer's reputation. He called for rights of first

35. 来自演员与口译家协会(CSAI)的一位观察员强调,条约提供的保护应以专有权为基础,因为只有专有权才能为表演者与使用者之间的谈判提供最佳基础,但在某些情况下,其他保护模式也可考虑。例如,根据西班牙法律的规定,虽然视听录制品的制作者获得了对该录制品的所有权利,但表演者保留了获酬权。如若不然,即便规定了专有权,对表演者来说将仍然是一纸空文,不会产生实际影响。该观察员还支持在视听表演领域引入对精神权利保护的规定。

36. 著作权研究和信息中心(CRIC)的一名观察员代表日本艺术表演家团体协会(GEIDANKYO)发言。在发言中,该观察员提议比照适用 WPPT 中对表演者的定义,但加上如下内容:“包括对具有公共娱乐性质的作品表演以外的其他类似表演。”就经济权利的规定而言,他建议为表演者规定录制、广播、向公众传播和向公众提供尚未录制的表演的专有权利,以及复制、广播、向公众传播、发行、出租和向公众提供已录制表演的权利。他指出,数字化对表演的利用产生了巨大影响,并强调表演活动应当获得与文学艺术作品同等的保护。

37. 来自欧洲表演者权利集体管理组织(ARTIS GEIE)的观察员对委员会的工作表示欢迎。他说该组织认为应当对国民待遇的规定进行修改,并倾向于采取在现有的邻接权条约有关规定的基础上发展而来的模式。他呼吁美国代表团将其提案中规定的经济权利的范围扩大到 WPPT 要求的保护水平。他为视听表演者仍然得不到国际层面的保护而感到遗憾,并且他呼吁 WPPT 和议定书之间应当协调一致。

38. 国际文学艺术协会(ALAI)一位观察员说,该组织反对任何条款允许制作者对表演进行严重损害表演者声誉的歪曲或篡改。他呼吁赋予表演者首次录制权、复制权、发行权和向公众提供权,他建议议定书采用 WPPT 第 9 条关于出租权的规定。该观察员还表示,该组织不赞成授予表演者广播或向公众传

fixation, reproduction, distribution and of making the performance available to the public, and he suggested that the formula regarding rental rights in Article 9 of the WPPT should be used in the Protocol. He also indicated that his organization would not endorse an exclusive right of broadcasting or communication to the public, but could live with the application, mutatis mutandis, of the provisions of Article 15 of the WPPT regarding broadcasting and communication to the public.

39. An observer from the International Association of Broadcasting (AIR) pronounced himself against the extension, mutatis mutandis, of the rights in phonograms to cover audiovisual performances, because he saw decisive legal and economic differences, as also recognized in Article 14bis of the Berne Convention. He also opposed that performers have a stronger position than authors, and he called on the authors' organizations to pronounce themselves on that issue.

40. An observer from the National Association of Commercial Broadcasters in Japan (NAB-Japan) stated that his Association did not have an unanimous view on the questions relating to the Protocol, but in his personal opinion an international agreement could entail a settlement on a particular form of payment which would be the maximum that could be accepted, provided that acceptable details and rules could be agreed on. He stressed that national treatment should fall into the pattern of the Rome Convention and that no-retroactivity is very important for broadcasters.

41. An observer from the European Federation of Joint Management Societies of Producers for Private Audiovisual Copying (EUROCOPYA) pointed out that the audiovisual sector was based on well-established procedures, and, therefore, a Protocol could not be drawn directly from the provisions of the WPPT. A central question was that of transfer of rights where detailed provisions in Article 14bis of the Berne Convention already regulated the status of authors contributing to audiovisual works. He also pointed out that a possible retroactive protection would pose problems for a normal exploitation of audiovisual works.

42. An observer from the American Film Marketing Association (AFMA) stressed the danger of creating a situation where the recoupment of the investments in audiovisual works were hindered. In his view, the only way of maintaining or increasing levels of film production was by keeping control of all rights with the producers. He was opposed to enacting a retroactive protection for existing

播的专有权，但接受议定书比照适用 WPPT 第 15 条关于广播和向公众传播的规定。

39. 国际广播协会（IAB）的一名观察员宣布，他反对将对录音制品享有的权利比照适用于视听表演，因为这两种形式的表演之间存在着明显的法律和经济差异，这也为《伯尔尼公约》第 14 条之二所承认。他还反对为表演者提供的保护强于对作者的保护，并且呼吁作者组织在这个问题上表态。

40. 日本民间放送联盟（NAB-Japan）的一名观察员说，该联盟尚未就议定书的有关问题达成一致意见，但他个人认为，一项国际协议可以为一种特定的支付方式找到解决方案，而如果各方能够就其中的细节和规则达成一致意见，那么这种支付方式就在最大限度上使得各方可以接受。他还强调，国民待遇的规定应当遵循《罗马公约》的要求，且不溯及既往条款对广播组织而言是非常重要的。

41. 欧洲个人视听复制制作者联合管理协会联合会（EUROCOPYA）的一名观察员指出，视听产业有其既定的产业流程，因此，关于视听表演的议定书不能直接照搬照抄 WPPT 的条款。问题的核心在于，就权利转让而言，《伯尔尼公约》第 14 条之二已经对视听作品作者的地位作出了详细规定。他还指出，如果议定书提供溯及既往的保护可能会妨碍视听作品的正常利用。

42. 美国电影营销协会（AFMA）的一名观察员强调，对视听表演的保护可能导致收回视听作品的投资受到阻碍。他认为，保持或提高电影制作水平的唯一办法就是让制作者控制与视听作品有关的一切权利。他反对为现有的视听作品提供溯及既往的保护，因为这将对这些作品的未来利用造成混乱。

audiovisual works, because that would create confusion regarding their future exploitation.

43. An observer from the Interamerican Copyright Institute (IIDA) pointed out that, regarding moral rights, there were already differences between the Berne Convention and the WPPT, and now an even lower level of protection was proposed to be introduced. He stressed the possibility that the provisions of the Protocol could promote negotiations between the parties, and that related rights were different from copyright which was reflected in the important differences in national legislation. He also mentioned that a more nuanced regulation of related rights might be useful in that it would encourage countries to increase their level of protection.

44. An observer from the Latin American Institute for Advanced Technology, Computer Science and Law (ILATID) was of the view that audiovisual performances were quite different from phonograms, and this was of decisive importance for their protection and the future development in that field. For this reason, he preferred a new treaty rather than a Protocol. He also indicated interest in the proposal from the United States of America to include a definition of audiovisual works.

Definitions

45. The Chairman pointed at the differences between the proposals regarding how many definitions were included, but he considered this to be more a drafting question than a substantial one. In his view, there were mainly two questions that needed discussion and analysis at this stage, namely, first, the question whether "extra performers" and "background performers" should be excluded, as indicated in the proposal by the United States of America and as also suggested, with other words, in the proposal by certain countries in Latin America and the Caribbean, second, and the question of whether there should be definitions of "audiovisual fixation" and/or "audiovisual work" and if so, how these should be worded.

General questions regarding definitions

46. The Delegation of Singapore, supported by the Delegation of Australia, pointed out that the application of a definition, mutatis mutandis, was sometimes quite complicated, because it meant that one first had to find the substantial meaning of the clause, and then find a way to implement that meaning in national legislation.

47. The Delegation of the European Community was of the opinion that at

43. 美洲国家间版权机构（IIDA）的一名观察员指出，在精神权利方面，《伯尔尼公约》和 WPPT 的规定之间已经存在着差异，而该机构建议为表演者提供精神权利保护的水平应当低于前述条约的要求。他强调，议定书相关条款的规定可能促进各方之间的谈判；而邻接权不同于版权，这一点从各国版权和邻接权立法的重大差异中就可以看出。他还提到对邻接权进行更为细致的规定是有益的，因为这将鼓励各国提高其保护水平。

44. 拉丁美洲先进技术、计算机科学与法律研究所（ILATID）的一名观察员认为，视听表演与录音制品有很大的不同，这对其保护和该领域未来的发展具有关键性的重要作用。因此，他更倾向于通过单独的条约而不是 WPPT 议定书的形式来保护视听表演。他还对美国将视听作品定义纳入提案中的做法表示了兴趣。

定义

45. 主席指出，关于将多少定义纳入议定书之中，不同提案之间存在着分歧，但他认为这更多地是一个起草问题，而不是一个实质性问题。他认为，现阶段主要有两个问题需要讨论和分析。第一，是否应将“临时演员”和“背景演员”排除在保护范围之外的问题，这在美国的提案中有指出，并且拉丁美洲和加勒比地区某些国家的提案也以不同的表述方式提及。第二，议定书中是否应该有“视听录制品”和/或“视听作品”的定义的问题，如果有的话，那么又该如何进行表述。

关于定义的一般问题

46. 新加坡代表团指出定义的比照适用有时相当复杂，因为这意味着必须首先确定该条款的实质含义，然后通过各国国内立法规定来落实这一含义。该意见也得到了澳大利亚代表团的支持。

47. 欧共体代表团认为只有确有必要性的定义才适合在国际层面予以规

the international level there should only be such definitions that were absolutely necessary. It considered the definitions of the WPPT a valid starting point, even if they were not all needed in this context. It stressed that, at the international level, definitions had to be wide and leave sufficient scope for their implementation in national law and contracts. It warned against having different definitions of the same concepts in various international treaties, because that, as well as adding more undefined elements to definitions, would create unnecessary uncertainty.

48. The Delegation of China pointed out that the contents of possible definitions would depend on the contents of the corresponding substantial provisions. It was generally of the opinion that it would be advisable to follow the definitions in the WPPT, but it accepted that exceptions in certain cases might be warranted.

The definition of "performers"

49. At the request of the Chairman, the Delegation of the United States of America explained that the exclusion of "extra performers" and "background performers" was an important addition in order not to upset industry practice. Such performers had no speaking roles, but, for example, filled out crowds, were sitting at tables in restaurants as mere background to the acting, were marching soldiers and in other ways participated in filling out the picture without being listed in the credits normally given by the end of the film.

50. The Delegations of India, Israel, Kenya, Morocco, Nigeria, Philippines, Senegal, Singapore and South Africa, speaking on behalf of the African Group, as well as the observer from the National Association of Broadcasters (NAB), supported the view that "extra performers" and "background performers" participating in audiovisual fixations should be excluded from the definition of the term "performer." The Delegation of India also mentioned that dubbers, dummies and stunts should be excluded. The Delegation of South Africa, speaking on behalf of the African Group, supported by the Delegations of Kenya, Nigeria and Senegal, pointed out that the question of how possible exclusions should be done should be left to national legislation, and the Delegation of Nigeria added that the remuneration of these participants should be dealt with in contracts. An observer from the International Federation of Actors (FIA) said that she supported

定。该代表团认为 WPPT 中的定义提供了一个有效的考虑角度，即使并非其中的全部定义都是本议定书所必须规定的。其强调，在国际层面的规定中，定义必须足够宽泛，并为在各国国内立法和合同落实这些定义留有足够的余地。欧共体代表团警告称，不要在不同国际条约中对同一概念进行不同的定义，也不要在定义中增加未确定的要素，这都会给定义带来不必要的不确定性。

48. 中国代表团指出，可能的定义的内容将取决于相应的实质性条款的内容。该代表团认为一般而言应遵循 WPPT 中对相关概念的定义，但其同意在某些情况下可作出与之不同的定义。

"表演者"的定义

49. 应主席的要求，美国代表团解释说，将"临时演员"和"背景演员"排除在保护范围之外是对其提案的一个重要的补充，这一做法将有利于维护行业惯例。这些表演者在视听作品中并无台词，只是起到了组成人群的作用，例如，仅为了构成表演背景而坐在餐馆的桌子旁，或者扮演行军士兵以及通过其他方式填充画面，这些表演者的名字也不会被列入通常出现在影片结尾的表演者名单中。

50. 印度、以色列、肯尼亚、摩洛哥、尼日利亚、菲律宾、塞内加尔、新加坡代表团和代表非洲小组发言的南非代表团，以及全美广播事业者联盟（NAB）观察员支持这样的观点，即参与视听录制品制作的"临时演员"和"背景演员"应排除在"表演者"一词的定义之外。印度代表团还提到，配音演员、人偶演员和特技演员也应当排除。南非代表团在代表非洲小组发言时指出，应当将排除问题留给各国国内立法决定。该观点得到了肯尼亚、尼日利亚以及塞内加尔代表团的支持。尼日利亚代表团补充说，这些排除在保护范围之外的表演者的薪酬问题应当通过合同来解决。国际演员联合会（FIA）的一名观察员说，其支持将临时演员排除在保护范围之外，但背景演员仍应当予以保护。该观察员进一步指出其倾向于将表演者的定义扩展到马戏演员和综艺演员。

the exclusion of extras, but not of background performers. She further favored the extension of the definition to circus and variety artists.

51. The Delegations of Finland, Greece and Norway were of the opinion that the existing definitions in the Rome Convention and the WPPT already excluded those groups of participants, because of the condition that a performer "perform a literary or artistic work." The Delegation of Canada noted that such groups would be excluded if they were not performing literary and artistic works. The Delegation added that countries which protected such participants could encounter problems with any possible retroactive protection. The Delegation of Finland pointed out that the question of musicians was quite different and should be considered separately, and the Delegation of Norway mentioned that the explicit exclusion of certain groups might create conflicts with the delimitation already practiced in some countries, such as its own.

52. The Delegations of France and the European Community pointed out that the definition in the Rome Convention already covered audiovisual performers and emphasized that sufficient flexibility in the application should be given to national law. The Delegation of France also stressed that new definitions needed to be consistent with definitions in existing treaties, in order to avoid legal uncertainty. Supported by the Delegation of China, it also warned against introducing definitions that implied qualitative distinctions. The Delegation of Greece, pointing out that the definition of the WPPT was partly a tautology, also emphasized the need for flexibility in the national implementation.

53. The observers from the Association of European Performers' Organizations (AEPO), the International Literary and Artistic Association (ALAI), the International Confederation of Societies of Authors and Composers (CISAC) and the International Federation of Musicians (FIM) said that no exclusion of certain categories from the definition of performers, as recognized in the existing international instruments, should be formulated in the Protocol. The observer from the International Federation of Film Producers' Associations (FIAPF) said that, whatever the wording of the exception for extras, background performers, dummies and the like, which were concepts determined by professional practice, the terms did not require detailed definition in the Treaty; it added however that a certain

51. 芬兰、希腊和挪威代表团认为,《罗马公约》和WPPT中的定义已经排除了上述类型的表演者,因为只有"表演文学或艺术作品"才能构成符合要求的"表演者"。加拿大代表团指出,只要上述类型的表演者并未从事"表演文学或艺术作品"的活动,就会被排除在保护范围之外。该代表团还指出保护这类表演者的国家也许会在可能的追溯保护方面遇到问题。芬兰代表团指出,音乐家的保护问题则大不相同,应当单独审议。挪威代表团提到,将某些表演者群体排除在保护范围之外可能会与一些国家(如挪威)的已有实践界定产生冲突。

52. 法国和欧共体代表团指出,《罗马公约》中的表演者定义已经包含了视听表演者,并强调议定书的定义应当为各国国内法的适用提供足够灵活性。法国代表团还强调,新的定义必须与现有条约中的定义保持一致,以避免带来法律上的不确定性。其还警告称不要引入含有定性区别的定义。该观点也得到了中国代表团的支持。希腊代表团指出,WPPT的定义在一定程度上是一种赘述,其还强调各国立法在适用定义时需要保持灵活性。

53. 欧洲表演者组织协会(AEPO)、国际文学艺术协会(ALAI)、国际作者和作曲家协会联合会(CISAC)和国际音乐家联合会(FIM)的观察员说,议定书不应将某些类别的表演者排除在现有国际法律文本承认的表演者定义之外。来自国际电影制片人协会(FIAPF)的观察员说,无论如何表述需要被排除的临时演员、背景演员、人偶演员以及其他类似演员的定义,这些概念都已在专业实践中确定,无须在条约中作详细定义。但该观察员补充说,要想作为表演者受到条约的保护也需要符合某种最低限度的要求。

minimum was necessary to qualify for the status of performer.

54. The Delegations of Australia, Israel, Nigeria, the Philippines and Sudan discussed various groups that could raise questions of interpretation, such as storytellers, skating artists, gymnasts, acrobats, football players and session musicians. It was pointed out that storytellers are already covered by the definition of the WPPT, and that Article 9 of the Rome Convention allowed, on a national basis, the extension of protection to such artists that did not perform works. The Delegation of South Africa, speaking on behalf of the African Group, and the Delegation of Australia emphasized that participants in sports events should not be covered by the protection under the Protocol.

55. The Delegation of China stated that it could not support a definition that explicitly excluded certain participants, and called for a more detailed analysis of the need for such an exclusion.

The definitions of "audiovisual fixation" and "audiovisual work"

56. The Delegation of Brazil, referring to the definition of audiovisual fixation in the proposal by certain Latin American and Caribbean countries, said that it understood fixation to be done frame by frame and not by incorporating moving pictures. In that respect it said that it would be more appropriate to provide separate definitions for "fixation" and "audiovisual work." Finally, it referred to the definition of audiovisual work in the proposal by the United States of America, to which the element of movement could be added. In respect of the element of movement, this statement was supported by the Delegations of Australia and the Philippines. The latter Delegation considered also necessary that the images be related.

57. The Delegations of Côte d'Ivoire and the European Community expressed, with support from the Delegations of Australia, China and Morocco, reservations regarding the need for a separate definition of the term "audiovisual work," and asked for clarification why such a definition had been proposed. The Delegation of the United States of America responded that this was because in its proposal there was a need to separate the work and its embodiment, and because the term "audiovisual work" was used in certain provisions in the proposal.

58. The Delegation of Australia pointed at the contradiction in having in the

54. 澳大利亚、以色列、尼日利亚、菲律宾和苏丹代表团讨论了在概念解释方面可能存在问题的各种类型的表演者，如说故事的人、滑冰艺术家、体操运动员、杂技演员、足球运动员和临时乐师。有人指出，WPPT 的定义已经涵盖了讲故事的人，而《罗马公约》第 9 条允许缔约方在其国内立法中不为此类未表演作品的从艺人员提供保护。代表非洲小组发言的南非代表团和澳大利亚代表团均强调，体育活动参与者不应受到议定书提供的保护。

55. 中国代表团表示其无法支持将某类表演者明确排除在保护范围之外的定义，还呼吁对做出此种排除的必要性进行更详细的分析。

“视听录制品”和“视听作品”的定义

56. 巴西代表团在提到某些拉丁美洲和加勒比地区国家提案中关于视听录制品的定义时说，其理解的录制应该是逐帧完成的，而不是通过添加动态图像。因此，该代表团认为将“录制品”和“视听作品”分别定义更为合适。最后，该代表团指出美国提案关于视听作品的定义中可以加入对动态要素的要求。澳大利亚和菲律宾代表团支持巴西代表团的这一建议。菲律宾代表团认为还有必要在定义中要求画面之间必须相互关联。

57. 科特迪瓦和欧共体代表团表示其对“视听作品”一词进行单独定义的做法持保留意见，该立场得到了澳大利亚、中国和摩洛哥代表团的支持。这两个代表团还要求澄清为何提议这样的定义。美国代表团回应称，根据其提案的要求，有必要将作品和其载体进行区分，同时这也是由于该国提案的某些条款使用了“视听作品”一词。

58. 澳大利亚代表团指出，在“视听”的定义中使用“有无伴音”这个词是

definition of "audiovisual" works the words "with or without sound," and referred to the formulation in the Rome Convention, Article 19-"visual or audiovisual fixation."

59. Observers from the International Confederation of Societies of Authors and Composers (CISAC), the Ibero-Latin-American Federation of Performers (FILAIE) and the International Federation of Film Producers Associations (FIAPF), spoke in favor of a definition of "audiovisual fixation," and the observer from the Association of European Performers' Organizations (AEPO) supported the proposal from the European Community in this respect, but all these, except the observer from the International Federation of Film Producers Associations (FIAPF), were against the need to define "audiovisual work."

Moral rights

60. The Chairman noted that almost all proposals included provisions on moral rights for audiovisual performers, and that they all included the two basic elements also found in the Berne Convention and the WPPT, namely the right of being identified and the right to oppose prejudicial distortions, etc. Also, the clauses concerning the term and exercise of those rights and those concerning the means of redress had substantial similarities. He asked the Committee to address only those issues where substantial differences existed, notably the qualifications which were introduced in certain proposals.

61. At the invitation of the Chairman, the Delegation of the United States of America explained that the intention of its proposal was to ensure the balance between the performers' need for moral rights protection and the producers' need to control the rights necessary for a meaningful exploitation of the audiovisual fixation.

62. The Delegations of Argentina, Burkina Faso, France, Ghana, Greece, Ireland, Italy, Russian Federation, Senegal, South Africa, speaking on behalf of the African Group, Spain, Sudan and the European Community supported the inclusion of provisions on moral rights without the qualifications indicated in the proposal from the United States of America and, in square brackets, in the proposal from certain countries in Latin America and the Caribbean. The Delegation of the Russian Federation indicated its national administration was still analyzing the

矛盾的，并提到《罗马公约》第 19 条中的用语是“视觉或视听录制品”。

59. 国际作者和作曲家协会联合会（CISAC）、西语拉丁美洲表演者联合会（FILAIE）和国际电影制片人协会（FIAPF）的观察员赞成对“视听录制品”的概念进行定义，欧洲表演者组织协会（AEPO）的观察员支持欧共体在此方面的建议，但除国际电影制片人协会（FIAPF）的观察员外，其他所有观察员都认为没有必要对“视听作品”进行定义。

精神权利

60. 主席指出，几乎所有提案都包括关于视听表演者精神权利的条款，且都将《伯尔尼公约》和 WPPT 中规定的两种精神权利纳入其中，即表明表演者身份权和保护表演完整权等。此外，各提案中有关术语、权利行使以及权利救济途径的条款都存在着实质性相似之处。因此，他要求委员会只处理存在实质性分歧的问题，特别是某些提案中有关限定条件的规定。

61. 应主席邀请，美国代表团对其提案的意图进行了解释，该代表团称其提案能够确保在保护表演者精神权利的需要与满足制作者控制正常利用视听录制品权利的需求之间保持平衡。

62. 阿根廷、布基纳法索、法国、加纳、希腊、爱尔兰、意大利、俄罗斯联邦、塞内加尔、代表非洲小组的南非、西班牙、苏丹和欧共体代表团支持加入关于保护表演者精神权利的条款，但是他们认为不应当采纳美国和某些拉丁美洲及加勒比地区国家提案中对精神权利限定条件的规定。俄罗斯联邦代表团表示该国立法机关仍在对相关建议进行分析审议。欧共体代表团则提到其成员国之间就相关问题持不同的立场。该代表团还表示应当首先进一步明确对视听录制品可能存在的特殊考虑，然后才能考虑将 WPPT 要求之外的限定条件加以

proposals, and the Delegation of the European Community referred to the existence of differing positions among its member States. The latter Delegation, supported by the Delegation of Ireland, stated that possible special considerations regarding audiovisual fixations should be clarified further before it could be considered to include any qualifications beyond those in the WPPT. It also stated that there was a need for flexibility in the national implementation of the right. The Delegations of the European Community and France indicated that it was not desirable to introduce such qualifications because they would be very difficult to interpret and apply in practice, and the Delegation of Italy pointed out that, if an exploitation were prejudicial to the reputation of a performer, it could not be considered normal. The Delegation of South Africa saw a risk in introducing the producers as beneficiaries under the Protocol, without defining them in more detail. The Delegation of Greece questioned whether an international legal text could validly deprive performers of rights relating to future uses that were not, and could not be, known. The Delegation of Argentina accepted that the producers should be secured the possibility of a normal exploitation of audiovisual fixations.

63. The Delegation of the United Kingdom expressed interest in the proposals of the United States of America and of certain countries in Latin America and the Caribbean and stated that there were differences between audio and audiovisual fixations that made it difficult to apply directly the provisions on moral rights in the WPPT. It had, however, reservations concerning the concept of "normal exploitation" which it considered difficult to interpret.

64. The Delegation of Singapore expressed its opinion that moral rights should not create hindrances for the development of digital uses of performances, including use in multimedia contexts and it therefore found that the qualifications suggested by certain countries merited further discussions. It indicated that the qualification "seriously prejudicial" in the proposal from the United States of America might be more difficult than just "prejudicial," and it asked for clarification of the intended connotation of the "normal exploitation" of an audiovisual work.

65. The Delegation of Israel expressed the view that the proposal of the United States of America went a long way towards achieving the reasonable balance emphasized by the Delegation of Singapore. It proposed the deletion of the word

规定。该观点也得到了爱尔兰代表团的支持。该代表团还指出，国际层面的规定应当为各国落实相关权留下灵活操作的空间。欧共体和法国代表团表示，不宜为精神权利规定上述限定条件，因为在实践中很难对其进行解释和适用。意大利代表团则指出，如果利用行为损害了表演者的声誉，就不能将其称为正常利用。南非代表团认为，在没有对制作者进行细致定义的情况下，将制作者作为议定书的受益人是有风险的。希腊代表团质疑，一项国际法律文本是否有权剥夺表演者享有未来才出现的利用表演行为的权利，这些利用方式是当前并不存在也不可能得知的。阿根廷代表团赞同对表演者精神权利的保护不应当与制作者正常利用视听录制品的需要相冲突。

63. 英国代表团对美国以及拉丁美洲和加勒比地区某些国家的提案表示了兴趣，该代表团指出录音制品和视听录制品两者之间的差异导致难以直接通过 WPPT 中的有关规定来保护表演者的精神权利。但是，考虑到难以对"正常利用"的概念进行解释，因此其对该用语持保留意见。

64. 新加坡代表团认为，对表演者精神权利的保护不应阻碍对表演的包括多媒体在内的数字化利用方式的发展，因此，其认为某些国家提出的限定条件要求值得进一步讨论。其表示，美国提案中"造成严重损害"的限定条件带来的解释难度可能远高于单纯规定"造成损害"时的难度，并且该代表团要求澄清对视听作品进行"正常利用"的内涵。

65. 以色列代表团认为，美国提案中的有关规定十分有助于实现新加坡代表团强调的合理平衡。该代表团建议删除"对其表演进行修改"之前的"其他"一词，在该代表团看来，这样有利于体现出歪曲和篡改之间的区别，有些修

"other" before the words "modification of his or her performance," in order to reflect what, in the opinion of the Israel Delegation, was the distinction between distortion and mutilation, which were prima facie prejudicial, and modification, which might have positive and beneficial connotations regarding normal exploitation. It also proposed that consideration be given to the replacement of the words "normal exploitation" by the words "commercial exploitation."

66. The Delegation of China pointed out that its national legislation provided for moral rights for audiovisual performers and it was of the opinion that it would rather be the exercise than the existence of moral rights that could pose practical problems, and it suggested that Article 5 of the WPPT should be applied, mutatis mutandis, to performers as regards their audiovisual performances, and that a presumption could be added, namely: "unless the parties have otherwise stipulated in contracts, performers are presumed to have consented to exercise their moral rights in such a way as not to prejudice the normal exploitation of the audiovisual work." The member of the Delegation from the Hong Kong Special Administrative Region mentioned that that Region had a large film industry, for which it was indispensable to guarantee that the normal exploitation of their productions could be safeguarded.

67. The Delegation of Brazil, referring to the proposal from certain countries in Latin America and the Caribbean, pointed out that the consultations between those countries had not been conclusive. It proposed that, in the Spanish language version of that proposal, the words "prestigio profesional" be replaced by "reputación" and that, after that word, the qualification "subject to the producer being allowed to abridge, condense, edit or dub the work, without however distorting the performer's contribution" be added.

68. The Delegation of Canada pointed out that the use of the pronoun "it" for the producer in the proposal from the United States of America could cause problems in its country, because under its law the producer could be a natural person. It also suggested that the proposal be clarified regarding the possible difference between the producer and the owner of copyright in the audiovisual work, because it would not be certain that they would be identical. It asked for examples of moral rights for live performances.

改虽然表面上看起来造成了损害，但其可能有利于对表演的正常利用。以色列代表团还建议考虑用“商业利用”一词来替换“正常利用”的用语。

66. 中国代表团指出其国内立法已为视听表演者提供了精神权利方面的保护，该代表团认为问题的实质并不在于是否规定精神权利，而在于如何对精神权利的行使进行规定。中国代表团建议，应比照适用 WPPT 第 5 条的规定对表演者进行保护，并可在该条内容的基础上增加一款规定，即“除非当事人在合同中另有约定，否则推定表演者同意以不影响视听作品正常利用的方式行使其精神权利”。来自中国香港特别行政区代表团的成员提到，其辖区内电影产业规模庞大，因此对其来说，保障相关成果能为该产业正常利用是必不可少的条件。

67. 巴西代表团在提到某些拉丁美洲和加勒比地区国家的提案时指出，这些国家之间的协商尚未得出结论。其建议，将该提案西班牙语版本中的“职业声望”(prestigio profesional)一词替换成“名声”(reputación)，并且在该用语之后增加限定条件的规定，即“允许制作者在不歪曲表演者的表演的情况下，对该表演进行删减、压缩、剪辑或配音”。

68. 加拿大代表团指出，美国提案中使用代词“它”来指称制作者可能会在加拿大遇到的问题，因为根据其法律，制作者可以是自然人。该代表团建议提案澄清视听作品版权人和制作者之间可能存在的区别，因为两者之间可能会出现主体不一致的情况，其还要求举例说明表演者对其现场表演享有的精神权利。

69. The Delegation of Australia mentioned that this could occur, for example, when commercials were inserted on the screen, during the live broadcast of the performance. Regarding the proposal from the United States of America, it asked for clarification of what the term "creative authors" meant, and why the words "pursuant to the exercise of rights of authorization acquired by the producer in the performance" were necessary. It also asked for clarification of the legal effect of the second sentence in Article 5(4) of that proposal.

70. The Delegation of South Africa, speaking on behalf of the African Group, asked for clarification from the Delegation of the United States of America, why it was considered necessary to add "seriously" before "prejudicial," and what was the intended scope of the reference to the normal exploitation of the audiovisual work.

71. The Delegation of the United States of America stressed that this was the first time that its country had proposed norms concerning this issue and that its proposal intended to bridge very different positions within the relevant groups by finding a balance between the performers' need for protection against Internet pirates and unscrupulous producers and the producers' need to be able to make the adaptations necessary for the use of audiovisual works in various media, such as reformatting and inserting of breaks for commercials. The term "creative authors" referred to the situation under its national law where the author could be deemed to be somebody else that the actual creator, and the words "pursuant to the exercise of rights of authorization acquired by the producer in the performance" aimed at clarifying that the use needed to be covered by a license, and that the economic exploitation was authorized; they did not aim at a waiver of the moral rights. The language in Article 5(4) of its proposal followed similar provisions in other countries, such as Germany, dealing with the possible abuse of moral rights detrimental to the legitimate interests of other parties, such as authors or other performers. The word "seriously" had been inserted before "prejudicial" because the audiovisual sector operated differently from the audio sector, and the proposal recognized in this way that adaptations are a part of the routine preparation of an audiovisual work. The word "other" before "modification of his or her performance" followed the texts of the Berne Convention and the WPPT and it was necessary because the terms "distortion" and "mutilation" normally in themselves also implied

69. 澳大利亚代表团提到，这种情况在对表演进行现场直播时也可能会出现，例如在屏幕上穿插广告的情况。就美国的提案而言，该代表团要求澄清“创造性作者”一词的含义，并说明为何有必要限定“在制作者行使其就演出所获授权的范围内”。其还要求澄清该提案第 5 条第(4)项第二句的法律效力。

70. 南非代表团在代表非洲小组发言时要求美国代表团澄清为何其认为有必要在“损害”之前加上“严重”二字，以及提及对视听作品进行正常利用的预期范围是什么。

71. 美国代表团强调，这是该国首次就视听表演保护的标准提出建议，该代表团称该国提案为了试图通过在表演者打击互联网盗版以及不诚信制作者的需要，与制作者对各种媒介上的视听作品进行修改(如转换格式或插入广告)以实现对该作品正常利用的需要之间寻求平衡，来衔接各个相关团体所持的截然不同的立场。“创造性作者”一词针对的是有些国家立法将实际创作者以外的其他主体视为作者的情况，而“在制作者行使其就演出所获授权的范围内”的用语旨在澄清该条所提到的使用行为必须是经过许可的，该对表演进行经济上利用的行为是获得授权了的，使用上述用语的目的均不在于让表演者放弃精神权利。其提案第 5 条第(4)项的规定与德国等其他国家的相关规定类似，该项针对的是可能的滥用精神权利的行为，该行为会损害作者或其他表演者等其他各方的合法利益。在“损害”之前加上“严重”二词是因为考虑到视听行业的运作不同于音频行业，在制作视听作品时通常需要对视听表演进行修改。在“对其表演进行修改”之前增加“其他”一词则是遵循《伯尔尼公约》和 WPPT 文本的结果，而这一增加是有必要的，因为“歪曲”和“篡改”通常本身也包含有修改的含义。

a modification.

72. Article 5 of the proposal from the United States of America was supported by the observers from the National Association of Broadcasters (NAB) and the International Federation of Film Producers Associations (FIAPF), while observers from the Association of European Performers' Organizations (AEPO), the International Literary and Artistic Association (ALAI), the Ibero-Latin-American Federation of Performers (FILAIE), the International Federation of Musicians (FIM) and the International Confederation of Societies of Authors and Composers (CISAC) supported the proposals based on Article 5 of the WPPT.

73. The Chairman concluded that the discussion had highlighted most of the relevant questions and that the issue could be considered further in the next generation of working documents.

Economic rights concerning unfixed performances

74. The Chairman pointed out that the existing proposals showed a high degree of convergence in this field. He stated that subsisting differences were not such that the Committee needed a discussion at this session. For further discussion at a next step, he recalled the contribution made by Japan, concerning the right of making available (interactive transmission) of live performances (document AP/CE/2/2, Annex I).

75. The Delegation of the United Kingdom questioned whether the last-mentioned right was somewhat different in character from the interactive transmission right in the WCT and the WPPT, as in the case of accessing a live performance there was no individual choice possible in respect of the time of transmission of a particular performance.

76. The Delegation of Canada recalled its request, already made in the Diplomatic Conference of 1996, concerning the right to prevent certain uses, like broadcasting, of an unauthorized recording of a live performance and the right to claim damages or compensation in case of such uses.

77. The Delegation of Australia reminded the Committee of the potential overlap between the WPPT and the Protocol, as regards rights in live performances.

78. The Chairman stated that these points might be noted without further discussion for future deliberations concerning rights in unfixed performances.

72. 美国提案中的第5条得到了来自全美广播事业者联盟（NAB）和国际电影制片人协会（FIAPF）观察员的支持，而来自欧洲表演者组织协会（AEPO）、国际文学艺术协会（ALAI）、西语拉丁美洲表演者联合会（FILAIE）、国际音乐家联合会（FIM）、国际作者和作曲家协会联合会（CISAC）的观察员则对采用WPPT第5条的规定表示了支持。

73. 主席总结称，讨论中大多数相关问题都得到了强调，下一次工作文件中可就该议题进行进一步审议。

与未录制表演有关的经济权利

74. 主席指出，目前各提案在此方面的规定高度趋同。他说勉强可以称之为分歧之处，也无须由委员会在本届会议上进行讨论。而就下一步进行深入讨论的问题而言，他回顾了日本在提供现场表演权（交互式传播）领域所作的贡献（AP/CE/2/2号文件，附件一）。

75. 英国代表团质疑，该权利在性质上是否与WCT和WPPT规定的交互式传播权有所不同，因为在收看现场表演时，用户无法就特定表演的传输时间作出个人选择。

76. 加拿大代表团提及其在1996年外交会议上就已经要求授予表演者控制某些利用表演行为的权利，如对未经授权录制的现场表演进行广播，以及相关的损害赔偿请求权或要求补偿的权利。

77. 澳大利亚代表团提醒委员会，WPPT与议定书在现场表演方面的权利规定可能存在重叠。

78. 主席称，可能需要对未录制的表演的权利问题有所关注，但无须在今后予以深入讨论。

Economic rights in audiovisual fixations

Right of reproduction, right of distribution, right of making available

79. The Chairman stressed that the existing proposals, building on certain elements settled in the WPPT, were very close to each other in recognizing the rights of reproduction, distribution and making available. Consequently, in this field again, there was no need for a discussion at this stage.

80. The Delegations of Singapore and India referred to the Agreed Statements of the Diplomatic Conference of 1996 concerning the right of reproduction and the right of distribution. These results of the Diplomatic Conference should, in their view, also be taken over for the corresponding rights in the Protocol.

Rental right

81. The Delegation of the European Community spoke in favor of a full rental right, as provided in the WPPT, and without the so-called impairment test exception. It was supported by the Delegations of Germany and India, as well as by the observer from the Copyright Research and Information Center (CRIC). The Delegation of Argentina supported the rental right, together with the impairment test exception.

82. The Delegation of Australia stressed that the proposal from the European Community referred to Article 9 of the WPPT, containing the wording "as determined in the national law of Contracting Parties," and questioned what that meant for a country becoming a Party to the Protocol at a time when its legislation did not provide for a rental right of performers in audiovisual fixations.

83. The Delegation of South Africa explained that the background of the proposal from certain States of Africa was Article 11 of the TRIPS Agreement, where the rental right of authors of cinematographic works was subject to the impairment test exception. The idea was that performers should not have stronger rights than authors. The Delegation of Singapore stated that, if a rental right was to be provided for, it should be along the lines of Article 11 of the TRIPS Agreement. The Delegation of the United States of America expressed interest in the African proposal.

84. The Delegation of Brazil also stressed the importance of balancing the rights of performers in the Protocol against the rights of authors in other

视听录制品的经济权利

复制权、发行权、提供权

79. 主席强调，现有的提案以 WPPT 中的相关规定为基础，因此在复制权、发行权和提供权方面彼此之间的规定非常接近。因此现阶段无须在此领域进行讨论。

80. 新加坡和印度代表团提到了 1996 年外交会议就复制权和发行权所作的议定声明。他们认为，外交会议的这些成果也应为议定书中的相应权利的规定所采纳。

出租权

81. 欧共体代表团赞成按照 WPPT 中规定对出租权进行充分保护，而不规定所谓的实质性减损例外。该观点得到了德国代表团、印度代表团以及著作权研究和信息中心（CRIC）观察员的支持。阿根廷代表团则支持损害测试例外的规定。

82. 澳大利亚代表团强调说，欧共体提案参照 WPPT 第 9 条的规定采用了"应按缔约各方国内法中的规定"的措辞，该代表团因此质疑一国在其国内立法未向视听表演者提供出租权保护的情况下，将对该国成为议定书缔约方意味着什么。

83. 南非代表团解释说，某些非洲国家的提案是以《与贸易有关的知识产权协定》第 11 条为背景的，该条规定对电影作品作者出租权的保护是以其利益受到实质性减损为前提的。这些国家之所以在提案中作如此规定是考虑到表演者不应该拥有比作者更强的权利。新加坡代表团也认为，如果要规定出租权，则该规定应符合《与贸易有关的知识产权协定》第 11 条的要求。美国代表团对非洲提案表示了兴趣。

84. 巴西代表团还强调，必须平衡议定书中表演者的权利与其他国际文书中作者的权利。因此，该代表团建议为议定书中的出租权设定与其他文书为电

international instruments. Consequently, the Delegation proposed the same exception from the rental right in the Protocol as contained in other instruments for authors of cinematographic works.

Right of broadcasting, right of communication to the public

85. The Delegation of the United States of America spoke in favor of a broad exclusive right of broadcasting and communication to the public. Performers needed a valuable right in the digital era, on a basis comparable with authors' rights, as provided for in Article 11 bis of the Berne Convention. Consequently, Article 10(2) of the proposal submitted by the United States of America allowed Contracting Parties to limit the right to a remuneration right only.

86. The Delegation of Argentina also considered that the Protocol should provide for exclusive rights in this area. In the case where a Contracting Party, in conformity with the proposal from the United States, chose the option of a right to remuneration, the question was in which way the remuneration was collected.

87. The Delegation of the Republic of Korea, explaining its proposal, said that the rights level provided was intended to be comparable with the protection granted to aural performers in the Rome Convention and the WPPT, but that the Delegation did not insist on this element becoming part of the Protocol. The Delegation of Singapore also considered that the WPPT might serve as a model.

88. The Delegation of India said that it refrained from commenting on the proposals, but stressed that the meaning of the notion of communication to the public should be clarified. The Delegations of Japan and of the Republic of Korea agreed with this.

89. The Delegation of the European Community recalled that in the Diplomatic Conference of 1996 it had been considered that the issue of rights in this area had not been ripe yet for being resolved, and said that still that was the situation. It questioned therefore whether the Protocol was the right place for this subject. The proposals that had been presented were not sufficiently clear; in particular, it was doubtful whether the rights provided therein covered simultaneous cable retransmission of broadcasts and whether the proposals would also be maintained if presumptions of transfer of rights in favor of the producer were not linked to them. The Delegations of Denmark and Germany supported these statements. The

影作品作者出租权规定的相同的例外。

广播权，向公众传播权

85. 美国代表团发言赞成为表演者规定一项宽泛的广播和向公众传播的专有权。在数字时代，表演者应当获得一项有价值的权利，该权利要与作者根据《伯尔尼公约》第 11 条之二的规定享有的权利相匹配。因此，美国提案中的第 10 条第（2）款允许缔约方将表演者的权利限定为获酬权。

86. 阿根廷代表团也认为议定书应授予表演者广播和向公众传播的专有权。并且该代表团还赞同采纳美国提案的建议，允许缔约方仅规定获酬权，但问题在于如何收取该方面的报酬。

87. 韩国代表团解释称，其提案所提供的相关权保护水平旨在与《罗马公约》和 WPPT 中给予音频表演者的保护相一致，但该代表团并未坚持必须以该立场来制定成为议定书。新加坡代表团也认为可以将 WPPT 的相关规定作为参照。

88. 印度代表团说其对相关建议不予置评，但强调应澄清“向公众传播”这一概念的含义。日本和韩国代表团表示赞成。

89. 欧共体代表团回顾说，在 1996 年的外交会议上，该代表团就认为解决广播和向公众传播权问题的时机尚未成熟，并且其当下仍坚持此判断。因此，其对通过议定书来解决相关问题的适当性提出质疑。该代表团认为目前相关的建议都不够明确，尤其是该权利是否包含对广播的同步有线转播的情形？在不存在有利于制作者的权利转让推定的情况下，各个提案是否仍可适用？这些问题有关建议都未加以考虑，因此都是存在疑问的。丹麦和德国代表团赞同上述观点。丹麦代表团特别强调，其中一些建议似乎对有线同步转播广播提供了非常深入的保护，而某建议是否涵盖了这种情形则令人有些怀疑。总的来说，该代表团认为，在全世界范围内统一对广播和向公众传播权进行规定的时机尚

Danish Delegation, in particular, underlined that some of the proposals seemed to give a very far reaching protection for simultaneous cable retransmission of broadcasts, and for one proposal it seemed doubtful whether the proposal covered such retransmission. In general, the Delegation considered that the time was not ripe for harmonizing this area of rights at a worldwide level and that the implications, specially in conjunction with the question of national treatment, had to be looked into carefully.

90. The proposals for exclusive rights of performers in this area were supported by observers from the Association of European Performers' Organizations (AEPO), the Groupement européen représentant les organismes de gestion collective des droits des artistes interprètes ou exécutants (ARTIS GEIE), the International Federation of Musicians (FIM) and the International Federation of Actors (FIA), and rejected by observers from the Asia-Pacific Broadcasting Union (ABU), the Association of Commercial Television in Europe (ACT), the International Association of Broadcasting (IAB) and the National Association of Broadcasters (NAB), whereas the observer of the European Broadcasting Union (EBU) considered that the issue of rights in this area was too complicated to solve in the context of this Protocol or Treaty. The observer from the Ibero-Latin-American Federation of Performers (FILAIE) said that a balance between producers and performers was necessary, as to granting exclusive rights. The observer from the Comité "Actores, Intérpretes" (CSAI) advocated that exclusive rights should be subject to contractual transfer, but that in any case the performer should retain a right of remuneration which he could not renounce and which had to be exercised through collective management.

91. The Chairman, summarizing the debate, said that convergence of opinions allowed to take along the right of reproduction, the right of distribution and the right of making available, whereas there was still reason to continue discussions of the right of rental and of the rights of broadcasting and communication to the public. As regards the latter issue, clarification was still sought from those who had proposed granting these rights.

<u>Beneficiaries of Protection</u>

92. The Chairman noted that the issue of beneficiaries of protection, or points

未成熟，因此必须对相关问题进行周密思考，特别是在结合国民待遇问题进行考虑的情况下更是如此。

90. 欧洲表演者组织协会（AEPO）、欧洲表演者权利集体管理组织（ARTISGEIE）、国际音乐家联合会（FIM）、国际演员联合会（FIA）的观察员表示支持授予视听表演者广播和向公众传播的专有权的建议，而亚洲－太平洋广播联盟（ABU）、欧洲商业电视协会（ACT）、国际广播协会（IAB）以及全美广播事业者联盟（NAB）表示反对。同时，来自欧洲广播联盟（EBU）的观察员认为，有关该权利的问题太过复杂，无法通过本协定书或条约来解决。西语拉丁美洲表演者联合会（FILAIE）的观察员表示，如果要授予该项专有权，那么有必要保持制作者和表演者之间的平衡。国际作者和作曲家协会联合会（CISAC）的观察员则提议规定相关专有权可通过合同约定转让，在这种情况下，表演者保留获酬权，该权利不得放弃且必须通过集体管理的方式行使。

91. 主席在对讨论进行总结时说，各方在为表演者规定复制权、发行权以及提供权方面的意见趋于一致，但就出租权、广播和向公众传播权而言仍有继续讨论的必要。同时关于广播和向公众传播权的问题，提议规定该权利的有关各方需要进行说明澄清。

保护的受益人

92. 主席指出，有四项提案提到了保护的受益人问题或者说连接点问题，且

of attachment, had been addressed in four proposals which had the nationality of the performer as common ground. Two other points of attachment were also proposed, namely the place of the fixation and the place of the performance. He felt that it would be interesting to get information about the reasons behind the two latter points of attachment. He noted that the points of attachment regarding performers and producers of phonograms in the Rome Convention had been used also in the TRIPS Agreement and in the WPPT, but because of the special nature of audiovisual performances it seemed advisable to look at the matter with a fresh mind.

93. The Delegation of Israel pointed out that the existing rules in this respect merited reconsideration in the different context of audiovisual performances. The Delegation suggested that the domicile of the performer be considered as an additional point of attachment. The Delegation of the United States of America expressed interest in that proposal. The Delegation of the European Community expressed reservations, because it found that the domicile would be more difficult to determine and it might more often vary over time, or there might even be more simultaneous domiciles for the same person.

94. The Delegation of Australia recalled that it had had reservations regarding the points of attachment in the WPPT, and said that it would support a clearer and simpler solution. It asked for clarification why Article 3(2)(b) in the proposal of the United States of America was confined to unfixed performances. Referring to the suggestion of domicile, as another point of attachment, the Delegation noted that the notion of habitual residence was also effectively made a point of attachment under Article 3(2) of the Berne Convention.

95. The Delegation of China, in the presentation of its member representing the Hong Kong Special Administrative Region, suggested that also an "open system," protecting everybody, without points of attachment and without demand for reciprocity, as it existed in that region, might also be considered.

96. The Delegation of the United States of America explained that the proposal of its country reflected the realities of the entertainment industries. Article 3(2)(b) in that proposal was limited to unfixed performances, because the intention was to cover both fixed and unfixed performances, and in paragraph (2)(c) the country of first fixation was established as a separate point. The observer from the International

它们均将表演者国籍作为连接点。此外，有的提案也将录制地点和表演地点作为连接点，他有兴趣了解此等提议的理由等信息。主席提示说，《罗马公约》就表演者和录音制品制作者所作的连接点规定也为《与贸易有关的知识产权协定》和 WPPT 所采纳，但考虑到视听表演的特殊性，他建议各方就此问题进行重新考虑。

93. 以色列代表团指出，由于视听表演的不同特点，应当从现有规定出发重新考虑连接点的问题。该代表团建议将表演者的住所作为国籍之外的另一连接点。美国代表团对该建议表示了兴趣。欧共体代表团则持保留意见，因为该代表团认为表演者的住所更难以确定，对表演者来说，其住所可能会随着时间的推移而发生改变，或者可能同时拥有多个住所。

94. 澳大利亚代表团回顾说其早就对 WPPT 中连接点的规定提出保留，并称其将支持一个更明确和更简单的解决方案。该代表团要求澄清美国提案中第 3 条第（2）款（b）项规定仅针对未录制的表演的原因。至于将住所作为另一个连接点的建议，该代表团指出，《伯尔尼公约》第 3 条第（2）款也是将惯常居所作为一个连接点规定下来。

95. 中国代表团的一个代表香港特别行政区的成员在发言中建议，也可以考虑建立一个“开放制度”，该制度不对连接点作出要求，也不要求以互惠为基础，从而达到保护每个表演者的效果，该特别行政区的有关法律就是这样规定的。

96. 美国代表团解释说该国提案反映了娱乐产业的现实状况。该提案第 3 条第（2）款（b）项之所以仅针对未录制的表演是因为其意在同时涵盖已录制的表演和未录制的表演两种情况，而在该条第（2）款（c）项中则将首次录制所在国作为另一个连接点进行了规定。来自国际演员联合会（FIA）的观察员支持该提案中关于连接点的所有规定。

Federation of Actors (FIA) supported all points of attachment in this proposal.

97. The Delegation of the European Community stated that it wished to simplify the rules. Audiovisual works could be shot in several countries which sometimes could be difficult to determine later. It could also be difficult to identify the places of different performances. Nationality was much simpler and would create a high degree of legal certainty. That criterion would also encourage countries to become party to the protocol, because that would be the appropriate way their nationals could be protected under it, wherever the performance took place or the film was fixed.

98. The Chairman noted that much depended on the structure of the industry and its practices. It was also a question of the level at which one wished to harmonize and a question of fairness towards the involved parties. In practical terms, it was a question of how easily one could determine the status of a fixation, but there was also the issue of avoiding "back door protection", in order to create an incentive for countries to join the protocol. He stated that the question would be brought forward to the next round of discussions.

Contractual arrangements

99. The Chairman noted that the proposals of certain countries of Latin America and the Caribbean and of the United States of America addressed the issue, and that the report of the Regional Consultation Meeting for Asia and the Pacific indicated that those clauses were found to be deserving merit.

100. The Delegation of the United States of America stated that the proposed presumption was a key element in its proposal as a whole, because it was closely connected to the decision to grant wide-ranging exclusive rights. It considered it essential to ensure producers of audiovisual works the business certainty that they could exploit those works globally. The proposal did not include the rule concerning choice of law that was found in the proposal of its country at the 1996 Diplomatic Conference, but without assurances that their contracts would be respected worldwide, it would be very difficult for the producers to do business. The proposal had won the acceptance of the audiovisual performers' organizations in its country, and it represented distinct changes from the earlier position of the United States of America, in that the presumption was rebuttable; it covered only rights of

97. 欧共体代表团称其希望简化连接点的规定。视听作品可能在几个国家拍摄制作，有时候很难确定首次录制所在国，也可能很难确定不同表演发生的地点。采用国籍标准则要简单得多。该标准不仅有助于实现高度的法律确定性，还能鼓励各国加入议定书，因为该标准不考虑表演的发生地以及电影的录制地，而这才是使其国民获得议定书保护的适当方式。

98. 主席指出，连接点的规定在很大程度上取决于相关产业的结构及其一贯做法，它涉及各方希望在何种层面统一保护视听表演规定的问题，同时也涉及公平对待相关各方的问题。从实践角度来看，这又是一个如何简单确定录制品状态的问题，但也要考虑到避免“变相保护”问题的产生，这样才能激励各国加入协议。主席称将在下一轮讨论中继续商议连接点问题。

合同安排

99. 主席指出，拉丁美洲和加勒比地区某些国家以及美国的提案就该问题作出了规定，亚洲及太平洋地区区域间协商会议的报告则指出，上述提案中的有关条款有可取之处。

100. 美国代表团指出，其建议的推定权利转让条款是其整个提案的一个关键要素，因为它与授予广泛的专有权利的决定密切相关。该代表团认为，必须保障视听作品制作者在全球范围内利用这些作品的商业确定性。该提案没有将该国在 1996 年外交会议上提出的关于法律选择规定的建议包含在内，但如果制作者无法确信其合同能在世界范围内得到尊重，制作者从业难度就会大大增加。该代表团表示，该提案获得了本国视听表演者组织的接受，同时它也体现了美国在该问题上立场的转变，因为该推定是可以被推翻的，同时它只涉及表演者授权专有权，获酬权和精神权利则被排除在外，而且该推定只适用于合同约定的特定作品，也不允许制作者以外的第三方进行使用。

authorization, not remuneration rights or moral rights; it covered only the particular work that was subject to the agreement; and it did not allow uses by third parties.

101. The Delegation of Brazil declared that it was now in a position to support the proposal of certain countries of Latin America and the Caribbean, with respect to contractual arrangements.

102. The Delegation of India found the proposal of the United States of America acceptable. India "did not want to kill producers and thereby murder performers."

103. The Delegation of China supported the inclusion of specific provisions on the issue, the latter Delegation with reference to the massive investments and many contributors that were involved in the making of an audiovisual work. That Delegation also pointed out that the provision in Article 14bis of the Berne Convention established a presumption of legitimation for the producers, rather than a presumption of transfer. The Delegation supported that approach, and also pointed at the possibility of letting audiovisual performers be entitled to a right to remuneration exercisable through collective management organizations. The Delegation of Australia agreed that the very inclusion of Article 14bis(2) in the Berne Convention demonstrated recognition that the film industry was a special case.

104. The Delegation of the European Community, supported by the Delegation of Hungary, was of the opinion in this respect sufficient flexibility should be left to national legislation, court decisions and contracts, and it saw no need to state that the rights were transferable since they are obviously transferable. The Delegation noted that the presumption proposed by the United States of America was rebuttable, but in its mandatory form it would be less flexible than the provision in Article 19 of the Rome Convention, and the Delegation could not support that. It questioned why it should be necessary to limit the freedom of performers to assign their rights to collective management organizations or others. Regarding the proposal of certain countries in Latin America and the Caribbean, the Delegation stated its interest and asked for clarification why there was no reference to Article 14bis(3) of the Berne Convention.

105. The Delegation of Argentina stated that in the report of the regional

101. 巴西代表团表示，目前其支持拉丁美洲和加勒比地区某些国家关于合同安排的建议。

102. 印度代表团认为美国的建议是可以接受的。印度称“不想杀死制作者，从而谋杀表演者”。

103. 中国代表团提到视听作品的制作需要耗费大量的投资，同时也需要众多贡献者的参与，因此其支持对该议题进行具体规定。该代表团还指出，《伯尔尼公约》第 14 条之二规定的是对制作者合法地位的推定，而不是权利转让的推定，该代表团支持采用该做法，其还指出授予视听表演者一项通过集体管理组织行使的获酬权也是一种可能的解决方案。澳大利亚代表团则赞同《伯尔尼公约》第 14 条之二第(2)款的规定本身就是对电影业特殊地位的认可。

104. 欧共体代表团认为，就该问题所作的规定应当给各国国内立法、法院裁判和合同约定留下充分的灵活操作的空间，其还认为没有必要规定这些权利是可转让的，因为它们本来就是可转让的。该代表团的观点也得到了匈牙利代表团的支持。欧共体代表团指出，虽然美国建议的推定是可以被推翻的，但该推定却又是强制性的，这点不如《罗马公约》第 19 条的规定灵活，因此该代表团无法支持这一规定。其还质疑限制表演者将其权利授权给集体管理组织或其他组织的自由的必要性。而对拉丁美洲和加勒比地区某些国家的建议，该代表团则表示了兴趣，并要求澄清说明相关建议没有提到《伯尔尼公约》第 14 条之二第(3)款的理由。

105. 阿根廷代表团指出，拉丁美洲和加勒比地区区域间协商会议的报告提

consultations for Latin America and the Caribbean a reference to Article 14bis(2)(b) of the Berne Convention had been proposed in order not to grant performers a stronger position than that of authors. Article 14bis(3) should not apply to performers, because it was related to the special situation of certain specific authors.

106. The Delegation of Singapore stated that the relationship between producers and performers might be different in various countries. It suggested that, in the proposal of the United States of America, the words "subject to written contractual clauses to the contrary" be replaced by the words "subject to contrary provisions in national legislation." That would allow each country to let its legislation reflect the national situation.

107. The Delegation of Senegal, supported by the Delegation of Sudan, stated that the African Group had wished to leave the issue to national legislation, and it had in this respect particularly the remuneration aspect in mind. It recognized the need of producers to get a reasonable return on their investments, but also performers had a reasonable claim for remuneration. The Delegation felt that more time was needed to consider all aspects of the issue.

108. The Delegation of Australia said that the application, mutatis mutandis, of Article 14bis might be difficult to carry out. It asked for clarification whether the second sentence of the proposal of the United States of America was a qualification of the first sentence, or only a clarification. It also wished to know what the words "nor shall it require a Contracting Party to establish any such rights of remuneration" were aiming at.

109. The Delegation of Canada declared that its country had not taken a definite position, but questioned whether, if such a provision were to be included, it should refer to the first owner of copyright rather than the producer, since they may not be the same person. If such a provision were to be included, it suggested the possibility that it might be an optional provision under which, if the presumption were used by a Contracting State, it would imply that the transfer should be accepted in all other Contracting States.

110. The Delegation of the United States of America found the suggestion by the Delegation of Canada interesting, and confirmed that the second sentence of its proposal was a clarification of the first sentence. It stated that the second half of that

及了《伯尔尼公约》第 14 条之二第(2)款(b)项的规定，这样可以避免给予表演者比作者更强的地位。同时第 14 条之二第(3)款不应适用于表演者，因为它只适用于某些特定作者的特殊情况。

106. 新加坡代表团指出，制作者和表演者之间的关系在不同国家可能有所不同，因此其建议将美国提案中的“书面合同条款有相反规定的除外”改为“国家立法条款有相反规定的除外”。这样各国可以制定与其国情相适应的法律规定。

107. 塞内加尔代表团表示，非洲小组希望将这一问题留给各国国内立法处理。这一意见也得到了苏丹代表团的支持。塞内加尔代表团在这一方面特别注意到了获酬问题，其承认制作者有就其投资获得合理回报的需要，但表演者同样也有权要求对方支付合理报酬。该代表团认为需要更多的时间来全面审议该议题。

108. 澳大利亚代表团说，比照适用《伯尔尼公约》第 14 条之二规定可能存在实施方面的困难。该代表团要求澄清美国提案中相关规定的第二句话是对第一句的限定还是只是进一步的说明，其还想知道“也不应要求缔约方规定任何此种获酬权”这句话的目的是什么。

109. 加拿大代表团表示，就该议题，加拿大没有明确的立场，但其质疑如果作出了相关规定，是否应用版权原始取得者而不是制作者来指称受让方，因为这两者可能不是同一个主体。同时其还建议在做出相关规定的情况下，可以将有关条款确定为任择条款，这样一来，如果一个缔约方采用了这一推定，则意味着这种权利转让的效果应为其他所有缔约方承认。

110. 美国代表团认为加拿大代表团的建议很有意思，其还确认了其提案中的第二句话是对第一句话的澄清。该代表团称之所以加入第二句话是因为该国认为在该条中解决获酬问题并不合适。

sentence had been included because its country did not consider it appropriate to deal with the remuneration question in this context.

111. The Delegation of Jamaica, speaking on behalf of the group of countries in Latin America and the Caribbean, declared that, in the light of new information, it needed more time for consultations within the group on the proposals in respect of which some Delegations had indicated an interest and had asked questions.

112. Observers from the International Federation of Film Producers Associations (FIAPF), the International Video Federation (IVF) and the National Association of Broadcasters (NAB) said that a provision providing for a presumption of transfer of rights, as contained in the proposal from the United States of America, was essential. The observer from the International Video Federation (IVF) said that it should apply in favor of the producer or its successor in title. Observers from the Association of European Performers' Organizations (AEPO), the Ibero-Latin-American Federation of Performers (FILAIE), the International Federation of Musicians (FIM) and the International Confederation of Societies of Authors and Composers (CISAC) opposed such a provision. The observer from the International Federation of Actors (FIA) said that the provision in the United States of America proposal was not acceptable in its current form, although she noted that it was not the wish of performers to frustrate the ability of the producer to exploit the audiovisual work to the mutual benefit of the producer and the performers. She also rejected the provision in the proposal of certain States of Latin America and the Caribbean.

113. The Chairman noted that the discussions had showed that there was no convergence yet. Some delegations had supported the inclusions of rules, and some had argued for flexibility at the level of national legislation. There had also been reference to a possible optional rule with a specified legal effect. He concluded that continued work on the issue was needed.

<u>Application in time</u>

114. The Chairman noted that all four proposals containing a provision on this issue referred mutatis mutandis to Article 18 of the Berne Convention, either directly or through referring to Article 22 of the WPPT.

115. The Delegation of Australia questioned the relationship between paragraph

111. 牙买加代表团在代表拉丁美洲和加勒比地区国家小组发言时宣布，由于新信息的出现，该国需要更多的时间与该小组成员国就某些代表团表示兴趣、提出问题的建议进行协商。

112. 来自国际电影制片人协会（FIAPF）、国际影像联合会（IVF）和全美广播事业者联盟（NAB）的观察员说，美国提案中的推定权利转让条款至关重要。国际影像联合会（IVF）的观察员说，该条在适用上应有利于制作者或其合法继承者。欧洲表演者组织协会（AEPO）、西语拉丁美洲表演者联合会（FILAIE）、国际音乐家联合会（FIM）、国际作者和作曲家协会联合会（CISAC）的观察员则反对这一规定。国际演员联合会（FIA）的观察员说，美国提案中有关条款目前的规定是不可接受的，虽然该观察员也称表演者不希望损害制作者利用视听作品的能力，也只有这样才能实现制作者和表演者互惠互利的局面，她还对某些拉丁美洲和加勒比地区国家提案中的规定表示了反对。

113. 主席指出，讨论结果表明各方尚未就此议题达成一致意见。一些代表团支持采用相关规定，一些代表团主张应为各国国内立法留下灵活操作的空间，还有代表团提到了可以将该规定确定为一项具有特定法律效力的任择规则。主席总结说就这一议题仍须进一步开展工作。

适用的时限

114. 主席指出，四项包含该议题条款的提案都比照适用了《伯尔尼公约》第 18 条的规定，它们要么直接提及该条，要么间接地通过提及 WPPT 第 22 条来比照适用该条。

115. 澳大利亚代表团对拉丁美洲和加勒比地区某些国家提案中有关条款

(1) and paragraph (3) of the proposal from Certain States of Latin America and the Caribbean, since paragraph (3) seemed to largely negate the effect of paragraph (1). The observer from the Ibero-Latin-American Federation of Performers (FILAIE) joined the Delegation in that criticism.

116. The Chairman noted that no Delegations wished to take the floor, and said that it seemed to reflect that further consideration of this issue was needed.

Implementation

117. The Chairman noted that only in the proposal from the United States of America (document AP/CE/2/4) there was a provision on implementation, and invited that Delegation to explain it.

118. The Delegation of the United States of America said that the purpose of the proposed provision was to make it clear that Contracting Parties could implement the obligation to grant exclusive rights to performers through various bodies of law, including copyright, neighboring rights or other legislative areas, such as labor law, in accordance with their domestic legal system.

119. The Chairman, noting that no questions were asked by other delegations, stated that the explanation given seemed to have been satisfactory.

Nature of the instrument/Relations to other Conventions

120. The Chairman pointed out that these two questions were closely linked with each other. In both respects, there was a clear distinction between the proposal from the United States of America and the other proposals.

121. The Delegation of the United States of America said that an independent treaty was proposed because the audiovisual industry had developed quite differently from the phonographic industry. In its view, this solution seemed to be clearer, cleaner and simpler.

122. While no other delegation took the floor on this subject, the observer from the International Federation of the Phonographic Industry (IFPI) expressed preference for the option taken in the proposal from the United States of America, for the same reasons as expressed by the Delegation.

National Treatment

123. The Chairman noted that the solution of this issue depended so much on the substantive clauses of the future instrument that it was clearly a question to be

中第(1)段和第(3)段之间的关系产生了疑问,因为第(3)段的规定似乎基本上否定了第(1)段的效力。西语拉丁美洲表演者联合会(FILAIE)的观察员也赞同该批评意见。

116. 主席指出没有任何代表团希望就此议题进行发言,他还说,这似乎反映出需要进一步审议这一议题。

权利行使

117. 主席指出,只有美国的提案(AP/CE/2/4 号文件)包含了议定书如何落地实施的条款,因此他邀请该代表团解释这一规定。

118 美国代表团说,拟议条款的目的是明确缔约方可以根据其国内法律制度,选择通过各种部门法律完成向表演者授予专有权利的义务,包括版权、邻接权或其他领域的立法,如劳动法。

119. 主席指出,其他代表团没有提出任何问题,这说明美国代表团所作的解释似乎令人满意。

法律文本的性质 / 与其他公约的关系

120. 主席指出,这两个问题密切相关。就这两个问题,美国的提案与其他提案之间存在明显的区别。

121. 美国代表团说之所以建议单独制定一项条约,是因为视听产业的发展与录音产业有很大不同。其认为,这一解决办法似乎更明确、更清晰,也更简单。

122. 虽然没有其他代表团就这一议题进行发言,但国际唱片业协会(IFPI)的观察员表示赞成美国提案的选择,理由与该代表团所表示的相同。

国民待遇

123. 主席指出,这一议题的解决方案在很大程度上取决于未来法律文本的实质性条款,因此这显然是一个有待以后协商的问题。

negotiated at a later stage.

Ⅴ. CONCLUSIONS

124. The Chairman noted that regarding the substantial issues concerning the protection of audiovisual performances, the Committee had made notable progress. As many of the proposals discussed in this meeting had come quite late and could not have been studied before the session, further time was required for examination of these proposals. Although very clearly the process had gained momentum in this session, the prevailing feeling among delegations was that still some discussions at experts level was needed. Conclusions, in concrete terms, on the future work program, beyond the experts level, would only be possible after the summer.

125. A representative of the International Bureau informed the Committee that the next opportunity for continuing the work at experts level would be the first session of the newly formed Standing Committee on Copyright and Related Rights, scheduled from November 2 to 10, 1998. The intention of the International Bureau was to include in the draft agenda of that session the issue of the Protocol, as well as the issues of the protection of databases and rights of broadcasting organizations.

126. On a comment made by the Delegation of Nigeria, on the need for one more regional consultation meeting for the African Group prior to the session of the Standing Committee, a representative of the International Bureau said that the Program and Budget of WIPO for the 1998-1999 biennium provided for financing of one or two series of regional consultations, of which one series had taken place. Thus, in principle, a new consultation was possible. The venue, the timing of the meeting and the financial implications should be discussed between the representatives of the Group and the International Bureau. In respect of the financial implications, it should also be considered that, with the financing of participation of representatives of developing countries and countries in transition in the present session of the Committee, certain unforeseen costs had emerged, but also that all the financial implications might be discussed at the sessions of the Assemblies of the Member States of WIPO scheduled from September 7 to 15, 1998, when, following the decision of the Assemblies taken at their March 1998 sessions, also the question of the use of the financial surplus of WIPO would be on the agenda.

127. On the proposal of the Chairman, the Committee drew then the following

V. 结论

124. 主席指出，在视听表演保护的实质性议题方面，委员会已经取得了显著进展。本次会议上所讨论的提案提交的时间很晚，因此无法在会议之前进行研究，这就导致需要更多的时间来审查这些提案。虽然在本届会议上相关工作明显取得了重大进展，但各代表团普遍认为，仍需要举行专家级别的讨论。而在今后超出专家级别的工作计划中得出关于具体条款的结论，可能只有在夏季之后才有可能进行。

125. 国际局的一名代表告知委员会，下一次在专家级别继续就相关议题展开工作的机会是新成立的版权及相关权常设委员会的第一届会议，会议定于1998 年 11 月 2 日至 10 日举行。国际局打算将与议定书有关的议题以及保护数据库和广播组织权问题列入该届会议的议程草案。

126. 尼日利亚代表团建议在常设委员会会议举行之前，非洲小组需要再举行一次区域间协商会议，对此，国际局的一名代表说，世界知识产权组织1998～1999 年两年期计划和预算规定为一个或两个系列的区域间协商提供经费，目前其中一个系列的协商已经举行。因此，原则上可以举行一个新系列的协商。该小组和国际局的代表应就会议地点、时间和财政负担问题进行讨论。关于财政负担问题，还应考虑到在资助发展中国家和转型期国家代表参加委员会本届委员会会议的时候，产生了某些不可预见的费用的情况，但大会 1998 年3 月的会议所作决议，所有财政负担问题也可在 1998 年 9 月 7 日至 15 日举行的世界知识产权组织成员国大会会议上进行讨论，而关于利用世界知识产权组织的盈余收入问题也将列入大会议程。

127. 根据主席的提议，委员会得出以下结论：

conclusions:

- the further substantial discussions on the Protocol will take place at the first session of the Standing Committee on Copyright and Related Rights in November 1998, where this issue should be given a proper priority.

- any new proposals or amendments to the proposals currently existing, or any other submissions of delegations, should, preferably in treaty language, reach the International Bureau by the end of September 1998, for the purpose of translation and circulation prior to the session of the Standing Committee.

- only after the substantial discussion on the Protocol at the first session of the Standing Committee in November 1998 will have come the moment to consider recommendations on a possible diplomatic conference, its date and venue and any further preparatory steps.

VI. ADOPTION OF THE REPORT AND CLOSING OF THE MEETING

128. The Committee unanimously adopted the report.

129. The Delegation of Bangladesh, speaking on behalf of the Asian group, said that the proposed Protocol was very important for some countries of Asia, and that the Group strongly supported the views expressed by the Delegation of Nigeria, concerning the need for one more regional consultation. The Delegation proposed that such second regional consultation for the Asian countries be held after the session of the Assemblies of the Member States of WIPO in September 1998. The Group looked forward to continuing the discussion on the Protocol in the first session of the Standing Committee in November 1998. It felt that, in the interest of continuity, full understanding of the issue and meaningful discussion in the Standing Committee, the experts from developing countries whose travel had been financed by WIPO for participation in the current meeting should again receive financial support from WIPO for attending the session of the Standing Committee in November. The Delegation of Jamaica, speaking on behalf of the Group of countries in Latin America and the Caribbean, associated itself with the intervention made by the Delegation of Nigeria. Bearing in mind cost considerations, it suggested, supported by the Delegation of Senegal, that such a meeting of regional groups be held at WIPO headquarters in Geneva, two or three days before the meeting of the

– 对《议定书》进一步的实质性讨论将在 1998 年 11 月举行的版权及相关权常设委员会第一届会议上进行，并且该会议将对此议题进行适当优先讨论。

– 在现有提案基础上提交任何新提案或修正案，或各代表团提交的任何其他建议，最好以条约文字的形式在 1998 年 9 月底之前送交国际局，以便在常设委员会本届会议之前对其进行翻译和分发。

– 只有在 1998 年 11 月常设委员会第一届会议对议定书进行实质性讨论之后，才会对召开外交会议的可能性、会议的日期和地点以及任何进一步的筹备步骤的建议进行审议。

VI. 通过报告及会议闭幕

128. 委员会一致通过该报告。

129. 孟加拉国代表团代表亚洲小组发言时称，拟议的议定书对亚洲一些国家非常重要，且该小组对尼日利亚代表团认为需要再进行一次区域间协商的意见表示强烈支持。尼日利亚代表团建议在 1998 年 9 月世界知识产权组织成员国大会之后举行第二次亚洲国家区域间协商。亚洲小组期待在 1998 年 11 月举行的常设委员会第一届会议上对该议定书继续进行讨论。其认为，为了保持讨论的连续性，实现对该议题的充分理解以及便于常设委员会进行有意义的讨论，受世界知识产权组织资助而参加本次会议的发展中国家的专家应再次得到世界知识产权组织的财政资助，以便他们接着出席常设委员会 11 月的会议。牙买加代表团在代表拉丁美洲和加勒比地区国家小组发言时称赞同尼日利亚代表团的发言。出于节省费用方面的考虑，其建议在举行常设委员会会议之前两三天在位于日内瓦的世界知识产权组织总部举行这样一次区域小组会议，各方专家根据通常规定参加前述会议。

Standing Committee, with the usual provisions for the participation of experts.

130. The Chairman, noting that the purpose of the meeting on this day had been the adoption of the report only, closed the meeting.

[Annex follows]

130. 主席指出，今天的会议只是为了通过报告并宣布会议闭幕。

（后接附件）

3.
Standing Committee on Copyright and Related Rights: First Session

Meeting code: SCCR/1
Date: November 2 to 10, 1998
venue: Geneva, Switzerland
Meeting Documents URL: https://www.wipo.int/meetings/en/details.jsp?meeting_id=3598

3.

版权及相关权常设委员会：第一届会议

会议代码：SCCR/1
会议日期：1998 年 11 月 2—10 日
会议地点：瑞士日内瓦
会议文件链接：https://www.wipo.int/meetings/en/details.jsp?meeting_id=3598

3.1 Submissions Received from Member States of WIPO by September 30, 1998

Document Code: SCCR/1/4
Language: English
URL: https://www.wipo.int/edocs/mdocs/copyright/en/sccr_1/sccr_1_4.pdf

Chinese Translation: Not Available.
URL: N/A

STANDING COMMITTEE ON COPYRIGHT
AND RELATED RIGHTS
First Session
Geneva, November 2 to 10, 1998

AGENDA ITEM 5: PROTECTION OF AUDIOVISUAL PERFORMANCES

SUBMISSIONS RECEIVED FROM MEMBER STATES
OF WIPO BY SEPTEMBER 30, 1998

Document prepared by the International Bureau

Introductory note

The Committee of Experts on a Protocol concerning Audiovisual Performances, at the end of its second session, which took place in Geneva from June 8 to 12,1998, drew the conclusions that:

3.1 截至 1998 年 9 月 30 日收到的世界知识产权组织成员国提交的材料

文件编号：SCCR/1/4
文件语言：英语
文件链接：https://www.wipo.int/edocs/mdocs/copyright/en/sccr_1/sccr_1_4.pdf
中文文本：无
文件链接：无

版权及相关权常设委员会

第一届会议

1998 年 11 月 2 日至 10 日，日内瓦

议程项目五：保护视听表演

截至 1998 年 9 月 30 日收到的世界知识产权组织成员国提交的材料

由国际局编制的文件

介绍说明

1998 年 6 月 8 日至 12 日在日内瓦举行的第二届会议结束时，专家委员会对视听表演议定书得出结论：

- the further substantial discussions on the Protocol concerning Audiovisual Performances would take place at the first session of the Standing Committee on Copyright and Related Rights(SCCR);and that

- any new proposals or amendments to the proposals already existing, or any other submissions of delegations, should, preferably in treaty language, reach the International Bureau by the end of September 1998.

The Annex of this document contains all submissions received by that date, namely, a proposal from Japan, a report submitted on behalf of Argentina, Brazil, Colombia, Costa Rica, Cuba, Ecuador, Guyana, Jamaica, Mexico, Panama, Paraguay, Peru, Trinidad and Tobago, Uruguay and Venezuela, and a revised proposal, accompanied by a commentary, from the United States of America.

(It is recalled that the proposals existing at the second session of the Committee of Experts are contained in document AP/CE/2/7.)

[Annex follows]

– 关于视听表演议定书的进一步实质性讨论将在版权及邻接权常务委员会第一届会议上举行；

– 任何新的提案或对已提案的修正，或代表团提出的任何其他意见，应在1998年9月底之前，以条约语言递交国际局。

本文件附件载有截至该日收到的所有材料，包括一项来自日本的提案，一份代表阿根廷、巴西、哥伦比亚、哥斯达黎加、古巴、厄瓜多尔、圭亚那、牙买加、墨西哥、巴拿马、巴拉圭、秘鲁、特立尼达和多巴哥、乌拉圭和委内瑞拉提交的报告，以及一份来自美国的附有批注的修订提案。

（应当指出，专家委员会第二届会议上的提案载于AP/CE/2/7号文件。）

（附件附后）

ANNEX

JAPAN

PROTOCOL TO THE WIPO PERFORMANCES AND PHONOGRAMS TREATY CONCERNING AUDIOVISUAL PERFORMANCES

Article 1

Relation to Other Conventions

(1) This Treaty constitutes a Protocol to the WIPO Performances and Phonograms Treaty(hereinafter the "WPPT").

(2) Nothing in this Protocol shall derogate from existing obligations that Contracting Parties have to each other under the International Convention for the Protection of Performers, Producers of Phonograms and Broadcasting Organization done in Rome, October 26,1961.

(3) Protection granted under this Protocol shall leave intact and shall in no way affect the protection of copyright in literary and artistic works. Consequently, no provision of this Protocol may be interpreted as prejudicing such protection.

(4) This Protocol shall not prejudice any rights and obligations under any other treaties.

Article 2

Definitions

(1) Contracting Parties shall apply, *mutatis mutandis*, the definitions set out in paragraphs(a),(f) and(g) of Article 2 of the WPPT in connection with the protection granted under this Protocol.

(2) For the purposes of this Protocol, "audiovisual fixation" means the embodiment of moving images, whether or not accompanied by sound, or of the representations thereof, from which they can be perceived, reproduced or communicated through a device.

Article 3

Beneficiaries of Protection under this Protocol

Contracting Parties shall accord the protection granted under this Protocol to the performers who are nationals of other Contracting Parties.

附件

日本
WPPT 关于视听表演的议定书

第 1 条

与其他公约的关系

（1）本条约构成《世界知识产权组织表演和录音制品条约》（以下简称WPPT）的议定书。

（2）本议定书的任何规定均不得减损各缔约方根据 1961 年 10 月 26 日在罗马签订的《保护表演者、唱片制作者和广播组织国际公约》对彼此承担的现有义务。

（3）依本条约给予的保护不得触动或以任何方式影响对文学和艺术作品版权的保护。因此，本条约的任何内容均不得被解释为损害此种保护。

（4）本议定书不得减损任何其他条约规定的任何权利和义务。

第 2 条

定义

（1）关于本议定书提供的保护，缔约各方应比照适用 WPPT 第 2 条第（a）、（f）及（g）款中的定义。

（2）在本条约中，"视听录制品"系指活动图像的体现物，且从中可通过某种装置感觉、复制或传播该活动图像，不论是否伴有声音或声音的表现物。

第 3 条

本议定书的保护受益人

缔约方应向其他缔约方的表演者提供本议定书给予的保护。

Article 4

National Treatment

(1) Each Contracting Party shall accord to nationals of other Contracting Parties the treatment it accords to its own nationals with regard to exclusive rights specifically granted in this Protocol, and to the right to equitable remuneration provided for in Article 10 of this Protocol.

(2) Notwithstanding the provisions of paragraph(1), any Contracting Party may, as regards performers who are nationals of another Contracting Party, limit the protection provided for in Article 10 to the extent to which, and to the term for which, the latter Contracting Party grants protection to performers who are nationals of the former Contracting Party.

Article 5

Formalities

Contracting Parties shall apply, *mutatis mutandis*, in respect of the protection granted under this Protocol, the provisions of Article 20(Formalities) of the WPPT.

Article 6

Moral Rights of Performers

(There is no proposal at this stage).

Article 7

Economic Rights of Performers in their Unfixed Performances

Contracting Parties shall accord, *mutatis mutandis*, to performers, as regards their unfixed audiovisual performances, whether or not accompanied by sound, the same rights as those provided for in Article 6(Economic Rights of Performers in their Unfixed Performances) of the WPPT.

Article 8

Economic Rights of Performers in their Performances fixed in Audiovisual Fixations

(1) Contracting Parties shall accord, *mutatis mutandis*, to performers, as regards the exploitation of their performances fixed in audiovisual fixations, the same rights as those provided for in Articles 7(Right of Reproduction),8(Right of Distribution) and 10(Right of Making Available of Fixed Performances) of the WPPT.

(2) Contracting Parties shall accord to performers the exclusive right of

第4条

国民待遇

（1）每一缔约方应给予其他缔约方的国民在本议定书具体赋予的专有权和本议定书第10条规定的公平获酬权方面的待遇。

（2）尽管有第（1）款的规定，任何缔约方均可对属于另一缔约方国民的表演者限制第10条规定的保护，其范围和期限为后者向属于前一缔约方国民的表演者提供保护为限。

第5条

手续

缔约方应比照适用WPPT第20条（手续）的规定。

第6条

表演者的精神权利

（暂无提案）

第7条

表演者对其尚未录制的表演的经济权利

缔约方对表演者的尚未录制的视听表演，无论是否伴有声音，都应比照WPPT第6条（表演者对其尚未录制的表演的经济权利）的规定，给予其相同的权利。

第8条

表演者对其已录制在视听录制品上的表演的经济权利

（1）对于利用其已录制在视听录制品中的表演的行为，缔约方应比照给予表演者与WPPT第7条（复制权）、第8条（发行权）和第10条（提供录制表演的权利）所规定的相同权利。

（2）缔约方应给予表演者授权向公众商业出租其表演的视听录制品原件和

authorizing the commercial rental to the public of the original and copies of their performances fixed in audiovisual fixations, even after distribution of them by or pursuant to authorization by the performer. A Contracting Party shall be excepted from this obligation unless such rental has led to widespread copying of such performances fixed in audiovisual fixations which is materially impairing the exclusive right of reproduction conferred in that Contracting Party on performers and their successors in title.

Article 9

Contractual Arrangements

(1) A performer who has undertaken to bring contributions to the making of an audiovisual fixation of his performance may not, in the absence of any contrary or special contract, object to the reproduction, distribution, rental and making available of his performance fixed in the audiovisual fixation.

(2) Notwithstanding the provisions of Article 4(1), any Contracting Party may, as regards performers who are nationals of such Contracting Party, establish national legislation which does not contain rules providing for the application of paragraph(1). Such Contracting Party shall notify the Director General of WIPO by means of a written declaration, which will be immediately communicated by him to all the other parties of this Protocol.

Article 10

Right to Remuneration of Performers in their Performances fixed in Audiovisual Fixations

Contracting Parties may establish in their national legislation the right to equitable remuneration of performers for the exploitation of their performances fixed in audiovisual fixations.

Article 11

Limitations and Exceptions

Contracting Parties shall apply, *mutatis mutandis*, in respect of the protection granted under this Protocol, the provisions of Article 16(Limitations and Exceptions) of the WPPT.

复制件的专有权利，即使是在表演者发行了这些原件或经表演者授权后也是如此。如果这种出租导致了对录制在视听录制品中的表演的广泛复制，从而导致该缔约方赋予表演者及其所有权继承人的专有复制权受到严重损害，缔约方应被排除在这一义务之外。

第 9 条

合同安排

（1）在没有任何相反或特殊合同的情况下，承诺对其表演制作视听录制品作出贡献的表演者，不得反对复制、发行、出租和提供录制在视听录制品中的表演。

（2）尽管有第 4 条第（1）款的规定，任何缔约方均可就该缔约方国民的表演者制定不包含规定第（1）款适用规则的国内法案。该缔约方应以书面声明的方式通知世界知识产权组织总干事，并由其立即通知本议定书的所有其他缔约方。

第 10 条

表演者对录制在视听录制品上表演的获酬权

缔约各方可在本国立法中规定表演者享有对录制在视听录制品上表演的公平获酬权。

第 11 条

限制与例外

缔约方应比照适用 WPPT 第 16 条（限制与例外）的规定。

Article 12

Term of Protection

Contracting Parties shall apply, *mutatis mutandis*, in respect of the protection granted under this Protocol, the provisions of Article 17(Term of Protection) (1) of the WPPT.

Article 13

Obligations concerning Technological Measures

Contracting Parties shall apply, *mutatis mutandis*, in respect of the protection granted under this Protocol, the provisions of Article 18(Obligations concerning Technological Measures) of the WPPT.

Article 14

Obligations concerning Rights Management Information

Contracting Parties shall apply, *mutatis mutandis*, in respect of the protection granted under this Protocol, the provisions of Article 19(Obligations concerning Rights Management Information) of the WPPT.

Article 15

Reservations

Subject to the provisions of Article 4(2) and Article 9(2), no reservations to this Protocol shall be permitted.

Article 16

Application in Time

(1) Contracting Parties shall apply, *mutatis mutandis*, in respect of the protection granted under this Protocol, the provisions of Article 22(Application in Time) (1) of the WPPT.

(2) The provisions of paragraph(1) do not apply to the right to equitable remuneration of performers provided for in Article 10 of this Protocol.

Article 17

Enforcement of Rights

Contracting Parties shall apply, *mutatis mutandis*, in respect of the protection granted under this Protocol, the provisions of Article 23(Enforcement of Rights) of the WPPT.

第 12 条

保护期限

缔约方应比照适用 WPPT 第 17 条(保护期限)第(1)款的规定。

第 13 条

关于技术措施的义务

缔约方应比照适用 WPPT 第 18 条(有关技术措施的义务)的规定。

第 14 条

关于权利管理信息的义务

缔约方应比照适用 WPPT 第 19 条(关于权利管理信息的义务)的规定。

第 15 条

保留

除了第 4 条第(2)款和第 9 条第(2)款规定的情况外,不得对本议定书作出任何保留。

第 16 条

适用的时限

(1)缔约方应比照适用 WPPT 第 22 条(适用的时限)第(1)款中的规定。

(2)前款(1)中的内容,不适用于本条约第 10 条关于表演者公平获酬权的规定。

第 17 条

权利的行使

缔约方应比照适用 WPPT 第 23 条(权利的行使)的规定。

Article 18

Assembly

Contracting Parties shall have an Assembly. This Assembly shall be the same as the one created by the WPPT and its functioning shall be governed, *mutatis mutandis*, by Article 24 of the WPPT.

Article 19

Eligibility for Becoming Party to the Protocol

Any party to the WPPT may become party to this Protocol.

Article 20

Signature of the Protocol

This Protocol shall be open for signature until… by any party to the WPPT.

Article 21

Entry into Force of the Protocol

This Protocol shall enter into force three months after 30 instruments of ratification or accession by States have been deposited with the Director General of WIPO.

Article 22

Final Clauses

The provisions of Article 25 (International Bureau), 27 (Rights and Obligations under the Treaty), 30 (Effective Date of Becoming Party to the Treaty), 31 (Denunciation of the Treaty), 32 (Languages of the Treaty) and 33 (Depository) of the WPPT shall apply, *mutatis mutandis*.

第 18 条

大会

缔约方应设置大会。大会应与 WPPT 所设大会相同，其运作应比照 WPPT 第 24 条的规定。

第 19 条

加入议定书的资格

WPPT 的任何缔约方均可成为本议定书的缔约方。

第 20 条

议定书的签署

本议定书应开放供 WPPT 的任何缔约方签署，直至……

第 21 条

议定书的生效

本议定书应在各国向世界知识产权组织总干事交存 30 份法律文本或加入书 3 个月后生效。

第 22 条

最后条款

应比照适用 WPPT 第 25 条（国际局）、第 27 条（本条约规定的权利和义务）、第 30 条（成为本条约缔约方的生效日期）、第 31 条（退约）、第 32 条（本条约的语文）和第 33 条（保存人）的规定。

ARGENTINA, BRAZIL, COLOMBIA, COSTARICA, CUBA, ECUADOR, GUYANA, JAMAICA, MEXICO, PANAMA, PARAGUAY, PERU, TRINIDAD AND TOBAGO, URUGUAY, VENEZUELA
REPORT ON THE REGIONAL CONSULTATION MEETING FOR LATIN AMERICA AND CARIBBEAN COUNTRIES ON A PROTOCOL CONCERNING AUDIOVISUAL PERFORMANCES AND OTHER NEW INTERNATIONAL PROVISIONS CONCERNING THE PROTECTION OF INTELLECTUAL PROPERTY
Geneva, June 12,1998

A Regional Consultation Meeting of Latin American and Caribbean Countries on a Protocol Concerning Audiovisual Performances and Other New International Provisions on Intellectual Property took place in Geneva, Switzerland, on June 12,1998. The meeting was presided over by Mr. Franz Hall(Jamaica).

The discussions were based on documents AP/CE/2/2, AP/CE/2/4, AP/CE/2/4 Corr. and AP/CE/2/6, presented by WIPO.

Consensus was reached on the following points:

I. Title

Protocol to the WIPO Performances and Phonograms Treaty Concerning Audiovisual Performances.

II. Preamble

The Contracting Parties,

Wishing to ensure an adequate level of protection for performances in audiovisual works, owing to the fact that the development and convergence of new information and communication technology will bring about a rapid broadening of the range of audiovisual services and also an increase in the opportunities for performers to exploit their performances;

Referring to the Resolution Concerning Audiovisual Performances adopted by the Diplomatic Conference on Certain Copyright and Neighboring Rights Questions on December 20,1996;

Have agreed as follows:

III. Relation to Other Conventions;Relation to Copyright

1. This treaty constitutes a Protocol to the WIPO Performances and

阿根廷、巴西、哥伦比亚、哥斯达黎加、古巴、厄瓜多尔、圭亚那、牙买加、墨西哥、巴拿马、巴拉圭、秘鲁、特立尼达和多巴哥、乌拉圭、维也纳拉丁美洲和加勒比国家的区域协商会议关于视听表演议定书和其他新的知识产权国际规定的报告 1998年6月12日，日内瓦

1998年6月12日在瑞士日内瓦举行了拉丁美洲和加勒比国家关于视听表演议定书和其他新的知识产权国际规定的区域协商会议。会议由Franz Hall先生(牙买加)主持。

讨论以世界知识产权组织提交的AP/CE/2/2、AP/CE/2/4、AP/CE/2/4Corr以及AP/CE/2/6号文件为基础。

就以下几点达成了共识：

一、标题

《世界知识产权组织表演和录音制品条约》视听表演议定书。

二、序言

各缔约方：

由于新的信息和通信技术的发展和融合将迅速扩大视听服务的范围，并增加表演者利用其表演的机会，希望能够对视听作品中的表演提供适当的保护；

参照1996年12月20日某些版权和邻接权问题外交会议通过的关于视听表演的决议；

达成如下协议：

三、与其他公约的关系；与版权的关系

1. 该条约构成1996年12月20日在日内瓦签订的《世界知识产权组织表

Phonograms Treaty done in Geneva on December 20,1996(hereinafter "the WIPO Treaty").

2. No provision of this Protocol shall detract from the mutual obligations of Contracting Parties under the International Convention for the Protection of Performers, Producers of Phonograms and Broadcasting Organizations, done at Rome on October 26,1961(hereinafter "the Rome Convention").

3. The protection granted under this Protocol shall leave intact and in no way affect the protection of copyright in literary and artistic works. Consequently no provision of this Treaty may be interpreted as prejudicing such protection.

4. This Protocol shall have no connection with, and shall not prejudice any right or obligation under, any treaty other than the WIPO Treaty.

IV. Definitions

1. The Contracting Parties shall apply, *mutatis mutandis*, the definitions set out in Article(a),(e),(f) and(g) of the WIPO Treaty in connection with the protection granted under this Protocol.

2. For the purposes of this Protocol, "audiovisual fixation" means the embodiment of moving images, whether or not accompanied by sound, or the representations thereof, from which they can be perceived, reproduced or communicated through a device.

3. For the purposes of this Protocol, "performers" means all actors, singers, musicians, dancers or other persons who interpret a role, sing, recite, declaim or in any way perform literary or artistic works or expressions of folklore, with the exception of extras.

4. *The Delegation of Brazil proposes that the audiovisual work should be defined, and will submit a text for the purpose.*

V. Beneficiaries of Protection

The Contracting Parties shall accord the protection provided under this Protocol to performers who are nationals of other Contracting Parties.

VI. National Treatment

Each Contracting Party shall accord to the nationals of other Contracting Parties the same treatment as it accords to its own nationals with respect to the exclusive rights specifically granted in this Protocol.

演和录音制品条约》(以下简称 WIPO 条约)的议定书。

2. 本议定书的任何规定均不得减损 1961 年 10 月 26 日在罗马签订的《保护表演者、唱片制作者和广播组织国际公约》(以下简称《罗马公约》)所规定的缔约方的相互义务。

3. 本议定书给予的保护不得触动或以任何方式影响对文学和艺术作品版权的保护。因此,本条的任何规定都不能以减损对文学艺术作品版权保护的方式加以解释。

4. 本议定书不应与 WIPO 条约以外的任何条约有任何联系,也不应损害条约规定的任何权利或义务。

四、定义

1. 缔约方应比照适用 WIPO 条约第(a)、(e)、(f)和(g)条中与本议定书给予的保护有关规定所列之定义。

2. 在本条约中,“视听录制品”系指活动图像的体现物,且从中可通过某种装置感觉、复制或传播该活动图像,不论是否伴有声音或声音的表现物。

3. 在本条约中,“表演者”是指所有演员、歌手、音乐家、舞蹈家以及对文学或艺术作品或民间文学艺术表达进行表演、歌唱、背诵、朗诵或以其他方式进行表演的其他人员,但临时演员除外。

4. 巴西代表团建议定义视听作品,并为此目的提交一份案文。

五、保护的受益者

缔约方应向其他缔约方的表演者提供本议定书规定的保护。

六、国民待遇

在本议定书具体赋予的专有权利方面,每一缔约方均应给予其他缔约方的国民与其本国国民相同的待遇。

VII. Formalities

The enjoyment and exercise of the rights provided for in this Protocol shall not be subject to any formality.

VIII. Moral Rights of Performers

1) Independently of the performer's economic rights, and even after the transfer of those rights, the performer shall, as regards his live audiovisual performances, with or without sounds, or performances included in audiovisual fixations, have the right to claim to be identified as the performer of his performances, except where omission is dictated by the manner of the use of the performance, and to object to any distortion, mutilation or other modification of his performances that would be prejudicial to his reputation.

The Delegation of Argentina proposed adding the following:

"The performer may authorize the making of modifications to his performance, but such authorization shall be valid only where it has been given in writing."

2) The rights granted to the performer in accordance with the foregoing paragraph shall, after his death, be maintained, at least until the expiry of his economic rights, and shall be exercisable by the persons or institutions authorized by the legislation of the Contracting Party where protection is claimed. However, those Contracting Parties whose legislation, at the moment of their ratification of or accession to this Treaty does not provide for protection after the death of the performer of all rights set out in the preceding paragraph may provide that some of those rights will, after his death, cease to be maintained.

3) The means of redress for safeguarding the rights granted under this Article shall be governed by the legislation of the Contracting Party where protection is claimed.

IX. Economic Rights of Performers in their Unfixed Performances

Performers shall enjoy the exclusive right to authorize the following in relation to their unfixed performances:

i) broadcasting and communication to the public of their unfixed performances, except where the performance constitutes a broadcast performance in itself;

ii) fixation of their unfixed performances.

The Delegation of Venezuela was of the opinion that, as the present document

七、手续

享有和行使本条约所规定的权利无须履行任何手续。

八、表演者的精神权利

1）独立于表演者的经济权利，甚至在这些权利转让之后，表演者仍应对于其现场表（无论是否伴有声音）或以视听录制品录制的表演享有权利：要求承认其系表演的表演者，除非因使用表演的方式而决定可省略不提其系表演者；反对任何对其表演进行的将有损其声誉的歪曲、篡改或其他修改。

阿根廷代表团提议增加以下内容：

"表演者可以授权对其表演进行修改，但这种授权只有在书面授权的情况下才有效。"

2）根据上款给予表演者的权利，在其死亡后，应予以保留，至少到其经济权利期满为止，并应由主张保护的缔约国立法授权的个人或机构行使。但是，那些在批准或加入本条约时未规定在表演者去世后对前款所规定的所有权利的保护的缔约方，可以规定其中某些权利将在表演者死亡后不再保留。

3）为保障本条所赋予的权利而采取的补救办法，应由被要求提供保护的缔约国之法律管辖。

九、表演者对其尚未录制的表演的经济权利

表演者应享有专有权，对于其尚未录制的表演授权：

i）广播和向公众传播其尚未录制的表演，除非该表演本身已属广播表演；

ii）录制其尚未录制的表演。

委内瑞拉代表团认为，由于本文件本身就是上述《条约》的一项议定书，而

was itself a Protocol to the above-mentioned Treaty, and as the wording of Article IX was identical to Article 6 of the WPPT, there was no point in repeating it and that it could be removed, but a number of delegations did not share that opinion.

X. Economic Rights of Performers Concerning Audiovisual Fixations

1. Right of reproduction

Performers shall enjoy the exclusive right to authorize the direct or indirect reproduction of their performances fixed in audiovisual works in any manner or form.

2. Right of distribution

1) Performers shall enjoy the exclusive right to authorize the making available to the public of the original and copies of their performances fixed in audiovisual works through sale or other transfer of ownership.

2) Nothing in this Protocol shall affect the freedom of Contracting Parties to determine the conditions, if any, under which the exhaustion of the right in paragraph(1) applies after the first sale or other transfer of ownership of the original or a copy of the fixed performance with the authorization of the performer.

3. Right of rental

Performers shall enjoy the exclusive right to authorize the commercial rental to the public of copies of their performances fixed in audiovisual works on the terms laid down in the national law of the Contracting Parties, even after distribution effected with the authorization of the performer.

The Delegations of Argentina, Brazil, Colombia and Uruguay proposed the following wording:

1) Performers shall enjoy the exclusive right to authorize the commercial rental to the public of copies of their performances fixed in audiovisual works.

2) Paragraph(1) shall not be applicable in the case of an audiovisual work except where the said commercial rental has given rise to widespread copying of the work which considerably detracts from the performer's exclusive rights of reproduction.

4. Right of making available

Performers shall enjoy the exclusive right to authorize the making available to the public of their performances fixed in audiovisual works, by wire or wireless

且第9条的措辞与《世界知识产权组织表演和录音制品条约》第6条相同，因此没有必要重复该条，可以删除该条，但一些代表团不同意这一意见。

十、表演者在视听录制品方面的经济权利

1. 复制权

表演者应享有授权以任何方式或形式对其录制在视听作品上的表演直接或间接地进行复制的专有权。

2. 发行权

1）表演者应享有授权通过销售或其他所有权转让形式向公众提供其录制在视听作品上的表演的原件或复制件的专有权。

2）对于已录制表演的原件或复制件经表演者授权被首次销售或其他所有权转让之后适用本条第1款中的权利穷竭所依据的条件（如有此种条件），本条约的任何内容均不得影响缔约各方确定该条件的自由。

3. 出租权

表演者应享有授权按缔约各方国内法中的规定将其录制在视听作品上的表演的原件和复制件向公众进行商业性出租的专有权，即使该原件或复制件已由表演者发行或经表演者授权发行。

阿根廷、巴西、哥伦比亚和乌拉圭代表团提议采用以下措辞：

1）表演者享有将其录制在视听作品中的表演复制件出租给公众的专有权。

2）第（1）款不适用于视听作品，除非该商业性出租导致广泛复制该作品，从而大大减损表演者的专有复制权。

4. 提供权

表演者应享有专有权，以授权通过有线或无线的方式向公众提供其录制在视听作品上的表演，使该表演可为公众中的一员在其个人选定的地点和时

means, in such a way that members of the public may access them from a place and at a time individually chosen by them.

5. Right of broadcasting and communication to the public

Performers shall enjoy the exclusive right to authorize the broadcasting and the communication to the public of their performances fixed in audiovisual works.

With regard to the broadcasting of audiovisual fixations, the Contracting Parties may apply *mutatis mutandis* the provisions of Article 11*bis*(2) of the Berne Convention.

The Delegation of Brazil said that, with respect to point 5, it preferred an agreed statement and would make a submission on the subject prior to the meeting of the Committee of Experts to be held in Geneva from November 2 to 10,1998.

The Delegation of Uruguay said that, with regard to the same point 5, it was not in a position to pronounce on it, owing to the fact that consultations were still going on with a view to the taking of a position for the purposes of the meeting of the Committee of Experts to be held in Geneva from November 2 to 10,1998.

The Delegation of Argentina proposed the following text:

"Performers shall enjoy the exclusive right to authorize the broadcasting and the communication to the public of their performances fixed in audiovisual works."

"Consent given for the fixing of the performance in an audiovisual work shall include the authorization of broadcasting and communication to the public by means of subscription systems, unless otherwise agreed."

The Argentine Delegation was considering the possibility of drawing up an agreed statement in the event of the foregoing text not being accepted.

XI. Limitations and Exceptions

1) The Contracting Parties may, in their national legislation, provide for the same kinds of limitation or exception with regard to the protection of performers as they provide for, in their national legislation, in connection with the protection of the copyright in literary and artistic works.

2) The Contracting Parties shall confine any limitation on or exception to rights provided for in this Protocol to certain special cases that do not conflict with a normal exploitation of the performance fixed in audiovisual works or unreasonably prejudice the legitimate interests of the performer or of the audiovisual producer.

间获得。

5. 广播权和向公众传播权

表演者应享有授权广播和向公众传播其录制在视听作品上之表演的专有权。

关于视听录制品的广播问题，缔约方可参照适用《伯尔尼公约》第 11 条之二第（2）款的规定。

巴西代表团说，关于第 5 点，他们赞成已经商定的并将在 1998 年 11 月 2 日至 10 日在日内瓦举行的专家委员会会议之前就此问题提交一份文件。

乌拉圭代表团认为，关于第 5 点，他们无法就此发表意见，因为目前仍在进行协商，以便为 1998 年 11 月 2 日至 10 日在日内瓦举行的专家委员会会议确定立场。

阿根廷代表团提出以下案文：

“表演者享有授权广播和向公众传播其录制在视听作品中的表演的专有权。”

“对确定视听作品表演的同意应包括通过订阅系统向公众广播和通信的授权，除非另有协议。”

阿根廷代表团正考虑在上述案文未获接受的情况下起草一份议定声明的可能性。

十一、限制与例外

1）缔约各方可以在其国内立法中，对给予表演者的保护规定与其国内立法给予文学和艺术作品的版权保护相同种类的限制或例外。

2）缔约各方应使本条约中所规定权利的任何限制或例外，仅限于某些不与录制在视听作品上的表演的正常利用相抵触、也不致不合理地损害表演者或视听录制者合法利益的特殊情况。

XII. Contractual Arrangements Concerning the Rights of Performers

Where a performer authorizes the inclusion of his performance in an audiovisual fixation, the Contracting Parties shall apply, *mutatis mutandis*, the provisions of Article 14*bis*(2)(b) of the Berne Convention *The Delegation of Argentina drew attention, for consideration, to the fact that Article 14bis(2)(b) of the Berne Convention contained no reference to the right of rental.*

The Delegation of Brazil said that, with regard to the whole of Title XII, it was not in a position to pronounce on it owing to the fact that consultations were still going on with a view to the taking of a position for the purposes of the meeting of the Committee of Experts to be held in Geneva from November 2 to 10,1998.

XIII. Term of Protection of the Economic Rights of Performers

The term of protection to be granted to performers under this Protocol shall last, at least, until the end of a period of 50 years counted from the end of the year in which the performance was fixed.

XIV. Obligations Concerning Technological Measures

1) The Contracting Parties shall provide effective remedies against any person knowingly performing any of the following acts knowing, or with respect to civil remedies having reasonable grounds to know, that it will induce, enable, facilitate or conceal an infringement of any of the rights provided for in this Protocol:

(i) removing or altering any electronic information rights management information without authority;

(ii) distributing, importing for distribution, broadcasting, communicating or otherwise making available to the public, without authority, performances, copies of fixed performances or audiovisual works knowing that electronic rights management information has been removed or altered without authority.

2) As used in this Article, "rights management information" means information that identifies the performer, his performance, the audiovisual producer or the audiovisual work, or information on the terms and conditions governing the use of the performance fixed in an audiovisual work.

XV. Obligations Concerning Rights Management Information

1) Contracting Parties shall provide adequate and effective legal remedies against any person knowingly performing any of the following acts knowing,

十二、关于表演者权的合同安排

如果表演者授权将其表演纳入视听录制品，缔约方应参照适用《伯尔尼公约》第 14 条之二第（2）款（b）项的规定。

巴西代表团表示，关于第十二编的全部内容，由于仍在进行协商，以期为 1998 年 11 月 2 日至 10 日在日内瓦举行的专家委员会会议确定立场，巴西无法就此发表意见。

十三、表演者经济权利的保护期限

依本条约给予表演者的保护期，应自表演录制之年年终算起，至少持续到 50 年期满为止。

十四、关于技术措施的义务

1）缔约各方应规定适当和有效的法律补救办法，制止任何人明知或就民事补救而言有合理根据知道其行为会诱使、促成、便利或包庇对本条约所涵盖的任何权利的侵犯而故意从事以下行为：

（i）未经许可去除或改变任何权利管理的电子信息；

（ii）未经许可发行、为发行目的进口、广播、向公众传播或提供明知已被未经许可去除或改变权利管理电子信息的表演或录制在视听作品上的的表演的复制件。

2）如本条所用，“权利管理信息”系指识别表演者、表演者的表演、视听制作人或视听作品的信息，或有关使用视听作品中的表演的条款和条件的信息。

十五、关于权利管理信息的义务

1）缔约各方应规定适当和有效的法律补救办法，制止任何人明知或就民事补救而言有合理根据知道其行为会诱使、促成、便利或包庇对本条约所涵盖的

or with respect to civil remedies having reasonable grounds to know, that it will induce, enable, facilitate or conceal an infringement of any right covered by this Protocol:

(i) removing or altering any electronic rights management information without authority;

(ii) distributing, importing for distribution, broadcasting, communicating or otherwise making available to the public, without authority, performances, copies of fixed performances or audiovisual works knowing that electronic rights management information has been removed or altered without authority.

2) As used in this Article, "rights management information" means information that identifies the performer, his performance, the audiovisual producer or the audiovisual work, or information about the terms and conditions governing the use of the performance of the audiovisual work, and any numbers or codes that represent such information, when any of those items of information is attached to a copy of a fixed performance or to an audiovisual work or appears in connection with the communication or making available to the public of a performance fixed in an audiovisual work.

XVI. Reservations

No reservations to this Protocol shall be permitted.

The Delegations of Brazil and Argentina undertook to confirm whether they wished to include a reservation, in which case they would provide the appropriate text.

XVII. Application in Time

1) The Contracting Parties shall apply the provisions of Article 18 of the Berne Convention, *mutatis mutandis*, to the rights of the performers provided for in this Protocol.

2) This Protocol shall not detract from the rights acquired in any Contracting Party prior to the date of entry into force of this Protocol in that Party.

The Delegation of Argentina proposed the substitution of the following text for the above point 1:

"The provisions of this Protocol shall not apply to performances given or audiovisual fixations made prior to the entry into force of this Protocol."

任何权利的侵犯而故意从事以下行为：

（i）未经许可去除或改变任何权利管理的电子信息；

（ii）未经许可发行、为发行目的进口、广播、向公众传播或提供明知已被未经许可去除或改变权利管理电子信息的表演或以视听录制品录制的表演的复制件。

2）本条中的用语“权利管理信息”系指识别表演者、表演者的表演、视听制作人或视听作品的信息，或有关使用视听作品中的表演的条款和条件的信息，和代表此种信息的任何数字或代码，各该项信息均附于录制的表演的每件复制件上或视听作品上，或在已录制在视听作品中的表演向公众提供时出现。

十六、保留

不得对本议定书作出任何保留。

巴西和阿根廷代表团承诺确认是否希望列入保留，在这种情况下，它们将提供适当的案文。

十七、适用的时限

1）缔约方应比照适用《伯尔尼公约》第 18 条的规定，适用于本议定书规定的履约者的权利。

2）本议定书不得减损任何缔约方在本议定书对该缔约方生效日之前取得的权利。

阿根廷代表团提议用以下案文取代上述第 1 点：

“本议定书的规定不适用于本议定书生效前所作的表演或视听录制品。”

XVIII. Provisions on Enforcement of Rights

1) The Contracting Parties undertake to adopt, in accordance with their legal systems, the measures necessary to ensure the application of this Protocol.

2) The Contracting Parties shall ensure that enforcement procedures are available under their law so as to permit effective action against any act of infringement of rights covered by this Protocol, including expeditious remedies to prevent infringement and remedies that constitute a deterrent to further infringements.

XIX. Administrative Provisions and Final Clauses

1. The Assembly

The Contracting Parties shall have an Assembly. That Assembly shall be the same as the one created by the WIPO Treaty.

2. Eligibility for Becoming Party to the Protocol

Any party to the WIPO Treaty may become party to this Protocol.

3. Signature of the Protocol

This Protocol shall be open for signature until... by any Member State of WIPO and by the European Community.

4. Entry into Force of the Protocol

This Protocol shall enter into force, following the date of entry into force of the WIPO Treaty, three months after 20 instruments of ratification or accession by States have been deposited with the Director General of WIPO.

5. Final Clauses

The provisions of Articles 25(International Bureau), 27(Rights and Obligations under the Treaty), 30(Effective Date of Becoming Party to the Treaty), 31(Denunciation of the Treaty), 32(Languages of the Treaty) and 33(Depositary) of the WIPO Treaty shall apply *mutatis mutandis*.

十八、关于权利行使的条款

1)缔约各方承诺根据其法律制度采取必要的措施，以确保本条约的适用。

2)缔约各方应确保依照其法律可以提供执法程序，以便能采取制止对本条约所涵盖权利的任何侵犯行为的有效行动，包括防止侵权的快速补救和为遏制进一步侵权的补救。

十九、行政条款及最后条款

1. 大会

缔约各方应有一个大会。该大会应与 WIPO 条约设立的大会相同。

2. 加入议定书的资格

WIPO 条约的任何缔约国都可以加入本议定书。

3. 签署议定书

本议定书开放供签署，直至 WIPO 条约的任何成员国和欧洲共同体签署。

4. 议定书生效

本议定书自 WIPO 条约生效之日起生效，各国已向世界知识产权组织总干事交存 20 份法律文本或加入书 3 个月后生效。

5. 最后条款

应比照适用 WIPO 条约第 25 条(国际局)、第 27 条(本条约规定的权利和义务)、第 30 条(成为本条约缔约方的生效日期)、第 31 条(退约)、第 32 条(本条约的语文)和第 33 条(保存人)的规定。

UNITED STATES OF AMERICA
SUBSTANTIVE PROVISIONS OF A TREATY FOR THE PROTECTION OF PERFORMERS IN AUDIOVISUAL WORKS

Preamble

The Contracting Parties,

Noting that the development and convergence of new information and communication technologies will allow for a rapid growth of audiovisual services and that this will increase the opportunities for performing artists to exploit their performances;

Recognizing the great importance of ensuring an adequate level of protection for these performances, in particular when they are exploited in the new digital environment;

Recognizing that the WIPO Performances and Phonograms Treaty(WPPT) does not cover the rights of performers in the audiovisual fixations of their performances, but that many provisions of the WPPT can be used or adapted as the basis for a new treaty protecting performers with respect to their audiovisual performances;

Have agreed as follows:

CHAPTER I
GENERAL PROVISIONS

Article 1
Relation to Other Conventions

(1) Nothing in this Treaty shall derogate from existing obligations that Contracting Parties have to each other under the International Convention for the Protection of Performers, Producers of Phonograms and Broadcasting Organizations done in Rome, October 26,1961.

(2) Protection granted under this Treaty shall leave intact and shall in no way affect the protection of copyright in literary and artistic works. Consequently, no provision of this Treaty may be interpreted as prejudicing such protection.

(3) This Treaty shall not have any connection with, nor shall it prejudice any rights and obligations under any other treaties.

美国
《关于保护视听作品表演者条约的实质性条款》

序言

各缔约方：

注意到新的信息和通信技术的发展和融合将使视听服务迅速增长，这将增加表演艺术家利用其表演的机会；

认识到必须确保对这些表演提供适当程度的保护，特别是在新的数字环境中加以利用时；

认识到《世界知识产权组织表演和录音制品条约》（WPPT）并未涵盖表演者在其表演的视听录制品方面的权利，但 WPPT 的许多条款可作为保护表演者视听表演的新条约的基础加以使用或修改；

达成如下共识：

第一章
一般规定

第 1 条

与其他公约的关系

（1）本条约的任何规定均不得减损各缔约国根据 1961 年 10 月 26 日在罗马签订的《保护表演者、唱片制作者和广播组织国际公约》相互承担的现有义务。

（2）根据本条约给予的保护不得触动或以任何方式影响对文学和艺术作品版权的保护。因此，本条约的任何内容均不得被解释为损害此种保护。

（3）条约不得与任何其他条约有任何联系，也不得减损任何其他条约规定的权利和义务。

Article 2

Definitions

For the purposes of this Treaty:

(1) “performers” are actors, singers, musicians, dancers, and other persons who act, sing, deliver, declaim, play in, interpret, or otherwise perform literary or artistic works or expressions of folklore, but not including ancillary performers considered such by professional practice;

(2) “fixation” means the embodiment of images, or of images and sounds, or of the representations thereof, from which they can be perceived, reproduced, or communicated through a device;

(3) “broadcasting” means the transmission by wireless means for public reception of images, or of images and sounds, or the representations thereof;such transmission by satellite is also “broadcasting;” transmission of encrypted signals is “broadcasting” where the means for decrypting are provided to the public by the broadcasting organization or with its consent;

(4) “communication to the public” means the transmission to the public by any medium, otherwise than by broadcasting, of the images, or the sounds and images, or the representations thereof, comprised in an unfixed performance or in a fixed performance;

(5) an “audiovisual work” is a work consisting of a series of related images that impart an impression of motion and are intended to be shown by the use of a device, together with any accompanying sounds.

Article 3

Beneficiaries of Protection

(1) Contracting Parties shall accord the protection provided under this Treaty to performers of other Contracting Parties as defined in paragraph(2) of this Article.

(2) Performers of other Contracting Parties shall be understood to be performers who meet any of the following conditions:

(a) those performers who are nationals of another Contracting Party and whose performance is unfixed or is fixed in an audiovisual work;

(b) those performers whose unfixed performance takes place on the territory of

第 2 条

定义

在本条约中：

（1）“表演者”是指演员、歌手、音乐家、舞蹈演员和其他演员，以及对文学或艺术作品或民间文学艺术表达进行表演、歌唱、演说、朗诵、演奏、演绎或以其他方式进行表演的人员，但不包括专业实践认为的辅助表演者；

（2）“录制”是指活动图像的体现物，且从中可通过某种装置感觉、复制或传播该活动图像，不论是否伴有声音或声音的表现物；

（3）“广播”是指以无线方式的传送，使公众能接收声音或图像，或图像和声音，或图像和声音的表现物；通过卫星进行的此种传送亦为“广播”；传送密码信号，只要广播组织或经其同意向公众提供了解码的手段，即为“广播”；

（4）“向公众传播”是指以广播以外的任何媒介向公众传送未录制的表演或者以视听录制品的表演，包括图像、或声音和图像，或其表现物；

（5）“视听作品”是由一系列旨在通过使用设备显示的相关图像以及任何伴随的声音组成的作品。

第 3 条

保护的受益者

（1）缔约国应给予本条第（2）款所界定的其他缔约国的履约者以本条约规定的保护。

（2）其他缔约方的表演者应被理解为符合下列任何条件的表演者：

（a）表演者是另一缔约方的国民，其表演尚未录制的或已录制在视听作品中；

（b）在另一缔约方领土上进行尚未录制表演的表演者；

another Contracting Party;

(c) those performers whose performance is first fixed in an audiovisual work on the territory of another Contracting Party.

(3) Performers who are not nationals of one of the Contracting Parties but who have their habitual residence in one of them shall, for the purposes of this Treaty, be assimilated to nationals of that Contracting Party.

Article 4

National Treatment

With respect to performances for which they are protected under this Treaty as provided in Article 3, performers shall enjoy, in other Contracting Parties, the treatment that the laws of such parties do now or may hereafter grant to their own nationals, as well as the rights specifically granted by this Treaty.

CHAPTER II

RIGHTS OF PERFORMERS

Article 5

Moral Rights of Performers

(1) Independently of a performer's economic rights, and even after the transfer of those rights, the performer shall, as regards his or her live performances or performances fixed in an audiovisual fixation, have the right to claim to be identified as the performer of such performances, except where omission is dictated by the manner of the use of the performance, and to object to any distortion, mutilation, or other modification of his or her performance that would be seriously prejudicial to the performer's reputation. Modifications consistent with the normal exploitation of an audiovisual work undertaken by the producer of the work or the producer's successors in interest, pursuant to the exercise of rights of authorization acquired by the producer in the performance, shall not be considered seriously prejudicial to the performer's reputation.

(2) The rights granted to a performer in accordance with paragraph(1) shall, after the said performer's death, be maintained, at least until the expiry of the rights of authorization set forth in Articles 6 through 10, and shall be exercisable by the persons or institutions authorized by the legislation of the Contracting Party where protection is claimed. However, those Contracting Parties whose legislation, at

(c)其表演首先在另一缔约方领土录制到视听作品中的表演者。

(3)非缔约方国民但在一个缔约方境内有惯常居所的表演者，在本条约中视同该缔约方的国民。

第4条

国民待遇

关于第3条规定的受本条约保护的表演，表演者应在其他缔约国享有这些缔约国的法律现在或以后给予本国国民的待遇，以及本条约具体赋予的权利。

第二章
表演者权

第5条

表演者的精神权利

(1)独立于表演者的经济权利，甚至在这些权利转让之后，表演者仍应对于其现场表演(无论是否伴有声音)或以视听录制品录制的表演享有权利：要求承认其系表演的表演者，除非因使用表演的方式而决定可省略不提其系表演者；反对任何对其表演进行的严重有损其声誉的歪曲、篡改或其他修改。根据制片人在表演中获得的授权，作品制作者或其利益继承人对视听作品正常利用进行的修改，不应被视为严重损害表演者的声誉。

(2)根据第(1)款给予表演者的权利，应在该表演者死亡后予以维持，至少在第6条至第10条规定的授权期满之前，并应由主张保护的缔约方立法授权的个人或机构行使。然而，那些在批准或加入本条约时其立法未规定在执行方死亡后保护上一款所列所有权利的缔约国可规定，在执行方死亡后，其中一些权利将停止维持。

the moment of their ratification of or accession to this Treaty, does not provide for protection after the death of the performer of all rights set out in the preceding paragraph, may provide that some of these rights will, after the performer's death, cease to be maintained.

(3) The means of redress for safeguarding the rights granted under this Article shall be governed by the legislation of the Contracting Party where protection is claimed.

(4) The "normal exploitation of an audiovisual work" shall include the use of new or changed technology, media, formats and/or methods of distribution, dissemination, making available or communication to the public. A performer shall give reasonable consideration to the interests of the other performers in the work, the writers of scenarios, dialogues or musical works created for the work, and the principal director of the work when seeking to exercise the above described rights with respect to such work.

Article 6

Economic Rights of Performers in their Unfixed Performances

Performers shall enjoy the exclusive right of authorizing, as regards their performances:

(i) the broadcasting and communication to the public of their unfixed performances, except where the performance is already a broadcast performance;and

(ii) the fixation of their unfixed performances.

Article 7

Right of Reproduction

Performers shall enjoy the exclusive right of authorizing the direct or indirect reproduction of their fixed performances in any manner or form.

Article 8

Right of Distribution

(1) Performers shall enjoy the exclusive right of authorizing the making available to the public of the original and copies of their fixed performances through sale or other transfer of ownership.

(2) Nothing in this Treaty shall affect the freedom of Contracting Parties to determine the conditions, if any, under which the exhaustion of the right in paragraph(1) applies after the first sale or other transfer of ownership of the original

(3)为保障本条所赋予的权利而采取的补救办法，应受要求保护的缔约国法律管辖。

(4)“视听作品的正常利用”应包括使用新的或经改变的技术、媒介、格式和/或发行、传播、向公众提供或传播的方法。表演者在谋求对作品行使上述权利时，应合理考虑作品中其他表演者、为作品创作的情景、对话或音乐作品的作者以及作品的主要导演的利益。

第6条

表演者对其尚未录制的表演的经济权利

表演者应享有专有权，对于其表演授权：

(i)广播和向公众传播其尚未录制的表演，除非该表演本身已属广播表演；和

(ii)录制其尚未录制的表演。

第7条

复制权

表演者享有以任何方式或形式授权直接或间接复制其录制表演的专有权。

第8条

发行权

(1)表演者应享有授权通过销售或其他所有权转让形式向公众提供其以视听录制品录制的表演的原件或复制件的专有权。

(2)对于已录制表演的原件或复制件，经表演者授权被首次销售或其他所有权转让之后，适用本条第一款中权利的穷竭所依据的条件(如有此种条件)，本条约的任何内容均不得影响缔约各方确定该条件的自由。

or a copy of the fixed performance with the authorization of the performer.

Article 9

Right of Making Available

Performers shall enjoy the exclusive right of authorizing the making available to the public of their fixed performances, by wire or wireless means, in such a way that members of the public may access them from a place and at a time individually chosen by them.

Article 10

Right of Broadcasting and Communication to the Public

Except for conditions on the exercise of the right that would be permissible for audiovisual works under Article 11*bis* of the Berne Convention for the Protection of Literary and Artistic Works, performers shall enjoy the exclusive right of authorizing, as regards their performances fixed in audiovisual works, the broadcasting and communication to the public of such performances, except where such a performance is already a broadcast performance.

CHAPTER III

ADDITIONAL PROVISIONS

Article 11

Transfer of Rights

Once a performer has consented to the fixation of his or her performance in an audiovisual work, he or she shall be deemed to have transferred all exclusive rights of authorization granted under this Treaty with respect to that particular audiovisual work to the producer of that work and its successors in interest, subject to written contractual clauses to the contrary. The foregoing sentence shall not apply to any rights of remuneration a performer may have under the law of any Contracting Party, nor shall it require a Contracting Party to establish any such rights of remuneration.

Article 12

Limitations and Exceptions

(1) Contracting Parties may, in their national legislation, for the same kinds of limitations or exceptions with regard to the protection of performers as they provide for, in their national legislation, in connection with the protection of copyright in

第 9 条

提供权

表演者享有专有权，授权以有线或无线方式向公众提供其录制表演，使该表演可为公众中的成员在其个人选定的地点和时间获得。

第 10 条

广播权和向公众传播权

除了《伯尔尼保护文学和艺术作品公约》第 11 条之二所允许的视听作品行使权利的条件外，表演者应享有在录制在视听作品中的表演，授权广播和向公众传播这种表演的专有权，但这种表演已经是广播表演的除外。

第三章
附加条款

第 11 条

权利的转让

一旦表演者同意将其表演录制在视听作品中，他或她应被视为，根据本条约授予的与该特定视听作品有关的所有专有权，转让给该作品的生产者及其感兴趣的继承者，但须遵守相反的书面合同条款。上述决议不适用于表演者根据任一缔约方的法律可能享有的任何获酬权，也不要求一缔约方确立任何此种获酬权。

第 12 条

限制与例外

（1）缔约各方可以在其国内立法中，对给予表演者的保护规定与其国内立法给予文学和艺术作品的版权保护相同种类的限制或例外。

literary and artistic works.

(2) Contracting Parties shall confine any limitations of or exceptions to rights provided for in this Treaty to certain special cases which do not conflict with a normal exploitation of the performance and do not unreasonably prejudice the legitimate interests of the performer.

Article 13

Term of Protection

The term of protection to be granted to performers under this Treaty shall last, at least, until the end of a period of 50 years from the end of the year in which the performance was fixed.

Article 14

Obligations concerning Technological Measures

Contracting Parties shall provide adequate legal protection and effective legal remedies against the circumvention of effective technological measures that are used by performers or their transferees in connection with the exercise of their rights under this Treaty and that restrict acts, in respect of their performances, that are not authorized by the performers or that are not permitted by law.

Article 15

Obligations concerning Rights Management Information

(1) Contracting Parties shall provide adequate and effective legal remedies against any person knowingly performing any of the following acts knowing, or with respect to civil remedies having reasonable grounds to know, that it will induce, enable, facilitate, or conceal an infringement of any right covered by this Treaty:

(i) to remove or alter any electronic rights management information without authority;

(ii) to distribute, import for distribution, broadcast, communicate or make available to the public, without authority, performances or copies of fixed performances knowing that electronic rights management information has been removed or altered without authority.

(2) As used in this Article, "rights management information" means information that identifies the performer, the performance of the performer, or the owner of any

（2）缔约各方应使本条约中所规定权利的任何限制或例外仅限于某些不与表演的正常利用相抵触、也不致不合理地损害表演者合法利益的特殊情况。

第 13 条

保护期限

依本条约给予表演者的保护期，应自表演录制之年的年底算起，至少持续到 50 年期满为止。

第 14 条

关于技术措施的义务

缔约各方应规定适当的法律保护和有效的法律补救办法，防止表演者及其受让人为行使本议定书所规定权利而采取的有效技术措施被规避，且就其表演而言，限制未经表演者授权或法律不允许的行为。

第 15 条

关于权利管理信息的义务

（1）缔约各方应规定适当和有效的法律补救办法，制止任何人明知或就民事补救而言有合理根据知道其行为会诱使、促成、便利或包庇对本条约所涵盖的任何权利的侵犯而故意从事以下行为：

（i）未经许可去除或改变任何权利管理的电子信息；

（ii）未经许可发行、为发行目的进口、广播、向公众传播或提供明知已被未经许可去除或改变权利管理电子信息的表演或以视听录制品录制的表演的复制件。

（2）本条中的用语“权利管理信息”系指识别表演者、表演者的表演、视听制作人或视听作品的信息，或有关使用视听作品中的表演的条款和条件的信

right in the performance, or information about the terms and conditions of use of the performance, and any numbers or codes that represent such information, when any of these items of information is attached to a copy of a fixed performance or appears in connection with the broadcast, public communication, or making available to the public of a fixed performance.

Article 16

Formalities

The enjoyment and exercise of the rights provided for in this Treaty shall not be subject to any formality.

Article 17

Reservations

No reservations to this Treaty shall be permitted.

Article 18

Application in Time

(1) Contracting Parties shall apply the provisions of Article 18 of the Berne Convention, *mutatis mutandis,* to the rights of performers provided for in this Treaty.

(2) Notwithstanding paragraph(1), a Contracting Party may limit the application of Article 5 of this Treaty to performances that occurred after the entry into force of this Treaty for that Party.

Article 19

Provisions on Enforcement of Rights

(1) Contracting Parties undertake to adopt, in accordance with their legal systems, the measures necessary to ensure the application of this Treaty.

(2) Contracting Parties shall ensure that enforcement procedures are available under their law so as to permit effective action against any act of infringement of rights covered by this Treaty, including expeditious remedies to prevent infringement and remedies which constitute a deterrent to further infringements.

息，和代表此种信息的任何数字或代码，各该项信息均附于录制的表演的每件复制件上或视听作品上，或在已录制在视听作品中的表演向公众提供时出现。

第 16 条

手续

享有和行使本条约所规定的权利无须履行任何手续。

第 17 条

保留

不得对本条约作出任何保留。

第 18 条

适用的时限

（1）缔约国应将《伯尔尼公约》第 18 条的规定比照适用于本条约所规定的表演者的权利。

（2）尽管有第（1）款的规定，缔约方可将本条约第 5 条的适用限于本条约对该缔约方生效后发生的履约行为。

第 19 条

关于权利行使的规定

（1）缔约各方承诺根据其法律制度采取必要的措施，以确保本条约的适用。

（2）缔约各方应确保依照其法律可以提供执法程序，以便能采取制止对本条约所涵盖权利的任何侵犯行为的有效行动，包括防止侵权的快速补救和为遏制进一步侵权的补救。

COMMENTARY ON THE REVISED U. S. PROPOSAL FOR A TREATY FOR THE PROTECTION OF PERFORMERS IN AUDIOVISUAL WORKS

Introduction

At the closing session of the Committee of Experts on June 12,1998, the Chair asked that new recommendations or revisions with respect to the proposed WIPO Audiovisual Performers Treaty be sent to the Secretariat before the end of September. Based on the discussions at that meeting, the United States has concluded that the U. S. proposal of May 18,1998(AP/CE/2/4, May 18,1998 and AP/CE/2/4 Corr., May 27,1998, hereinafter the "May 18 U. S. Proposal") could be improved by:(i) certain revisions prompted by suggestions or questions raised at the June 1998 Committee of Experts meeting, and(ii) other clarifications or simplifications in language. These revisions and clarifications do not alter the principles upon which the May 18 U. S. Proposal was based. These changes are explained below:

Article 2

Definitions

1. Article 2(a):"performers"

The May 18 U. S. Proposal excluded "extra performers and background performers" from the definition of performers. We now propose that this language be replaced by the exclusion of "ancillary performers, considered such by professional practice." In response to the concerns raised at the June meeting about the scope of "extra performers" and "background performers," the revised language, which comes directly from the WIPO English translation of the French copyright statute, seeks to provide greater clarity. Further, it is sufficient to cover the basic concept while providing flexibility for national interpretation.

2. Article 2(e):"audiovisual work"

At the June meeting a number of delegates urged that the concept of motion be added to the definition of audiovisual work. In view of this concern, we have revised the language accordingly to read:

"... a work consisting of a series of related images that impart an impression of motion and are intended to be shown by the use of a device, together with any

对美国修订的关于在今后工作中保护视听作品表演者的条约提案的评论

说明

在1998年6月12日专家委员会闭幕会议上，主席要求在9月底之前向秘书处提出关于拟议的世界知识产权组织视听表演者条约的新建议或修订。根据该次会议的讨论，美国的结论是，美国1998年5月18日的提案（AP/CE/2/4，1998年5月18日和AP/CE/2/4Corr，1998年5月27日，以下简称5月18日美国提案）可以通过以下方式加以改进：（一）根据1998年6月专家委员会会议上提出的建议或问题作出的某些修订，以及（二）其他语言上的澄清或简化。这些修改和澄清并没有改变5月18日美国提案所依据的原则。这些变化解释如下：

第2条

定义

1. 第2(a)条："表演者"

5月18日美国提案将"临时演员和背景表演者"排除在表演者的定义之外。我们现在建议将这种语言改为排除"被专业实践认为的辅助表演者"。针对6月会议上提出的关于"临时演员"和"背景表演者"范围的关切，修订后的语言直接来自世界知识产权组织对法国版权法规的英文翻译，旨在提供更大的清晰度。此外，它足以涵盖基本概念，同时为国家解释提供灵活性。

2. 第2(e)条："视听作品"

在6月的会议上，一些代表敦促在视听工作的定义中加入运动的概念。鉴于这一关切，我们对措辞作了相应修改，改为：

"……一种由一系列相关图像组成的作品，这些图像赋予运动的印象，并打算通过使用设备来显示，同时还伴随着任何一些声音。"

accompanying sounds."

Article 3

Beneficiaries of Protection

During the June meeting, it was suggested that the points of attachment under the proposed treaty be enlarged to include domicile or habitual residence. This would expand, to some extent, the body of performers(including stateless persons) eligible for the benefits of the proposed treaty and is consistent with the philosophy of broad protection underlying Article 3 of the May 18 U. S. Proposal.

Therefore, we propose adding a new paragraph(3) to Article 3, adapted from Article 3(2) of the Berne Convention, as follows:

"Performers who are not nationals of one of the Contracting Parties but who have their habitual residence in one of them shall, for the purposes of this Treaty, be assimilated to nationals of that Contracting Party."

Article 5

Moral Rights

The changes proposed in this article are not designed to expand or narrow the intended scope of the provision as put forward by the United States in its May 18 Proposal. Rather, these revisions are meant to make the language more precise and to answer some justifiable criticisms of the earlier drafting.

a. In the opening of paragraph(1), the phrase "as regards his or her live performances or performances fixed in an audiovisual work" would be changed to read "as regards his or her live performances or performances fixed in an audiovisual fixation…". The purpose of this revision is to make clear that a performer's moral rights extend not only to violations with respect to a performance as integrated into the final version of an audiovisual work, but also to violations with respect to any audiovisual fixation of the performance. This revision does not provide that performers have a moral right with respect to the editing(i. e. the selection and order of fixed performances) of an audiovisual work by the director or producer, or subsequent editing consistent with the normal exploitation of the audiovisual work.

b. A number of interventions at the June meeting suggested that the language of the May 18 U. S. Proposal was being read to mean that any modification made

第 3 条

保护的受益者

在 6 月的会议上，有人建议扩大拟议条约的附加范围，以包括住所或经常居住地。这将在某种程度上扩大有资格享受拟议《公约》所列福利的表演人员（包括无国籍人）的人数，并符合 5 月 18 日美国提案第 3 条所依据的广泛保护理念。

因此，为适应《伯尔尼公约》第 3 条第（2）款，我们建议在第 3 条中增加一个新的第（3）款，规定如下：

“为本条约的目的，非缔约国之一的国民但在其中一个缔约国有惯常居所的表演者应被视同为该缔约国的国民。”

第 5 条

精神权利

本条提出的修改并不是为了扩大或缩小美国在其 5 月 18 日提案中提出的该条款的预期范围。相反，这些修改的目的是使语言更加精确，并回答一些有道理的对早先的措辞提出的一些合理批评。

a. 在第（1）款的开头，“关于他或她在视听作品中录制的现场表演或表演”一语将改为“关于他或她在视听录制品中录制的现场表演或表演……”这一修订是为了明确表演者的精神权利不仅包括与视听作品最终版本相结合的表演有关的侵犯，也包括与任何视听录制品表演有关的侵犯。这一修订没有规定表演者在编辑方面有精神权利（即导演或制片人对视听作品的选择和顺序），或随后与视听作品的正常利用相一致的编辑。

b. 6 月会议上的一些发言表明，5 月 18 日美国提案的措辞被解读为，在“作为一部分”的背景下对视听作品的正常利用所做的任何修改都将不受表演

in the context of-"as part of"-the normal exploitation of an audiovisual work would be exempt from the performer's moral right, no matter how prejudicial. This was not the intention of the May 18 U. S. Proposal. Rather, the United States recognizes that commercial exploitation of an audiovisual work necessitates certain changes or modifications for different methods of distribution and to meet market realities. Such changes, when made pursuant to the authorized exercise of economic rights, are not considered to be distortions or mutilations that seriously prejudice the reputation of performers. Hence the end of Paragraph (1) has been revised to read as follows:

"Modifications consistent with the normal exploitation of an audiovisual work undertaken by the producer of the work or the producer's successors in interest, pursuant to the exercise of rights of authorization acquired by the producer in the performance, shall not be considered seriously prejudicial to the performer's reputation."

c. Several delegations at the June meeting raised questions about the meaning of the phrase "creative authors" in Article 5(4). This language, which sought to identify the body of other individual contributors whose rights must be considered by performers when seeking to assert moral rights in audiovisual works, should be clarified. The proposed revision adapts language from Article 14*bis*(3) of the Berne Convention:"other performers in the work, the writers of scenarios, dialogues or musical works created for the work, and the principal director of the work."

Articles 6 and 10

Economic Rights of Broadcasting and Public Communication

The May 18 U. S. Proposal for Article 6(unfixed performances) represented an effort to clarify the language taken from Article 6 of the WIPO Performances and Phonograms Treaty("WPPT"):"The broadcasting or communication to the public of their unfixed performances except where the performance is already a broadcast performance." The May 18 U. S. Proposal added "or a publicly communicated performance," and made the same change in Article 10. As was pointed out at the meeting, these additions are not only unclear but also could have unintended consequences. Hence, the previously added language in both articles has been

者的精神权利的约束，无论这种权利有多大的偏见。这不是5月18日美国提案的意图。相反，美国认识到，对视听作品的商业开发需要对不同的发行方法进行某些改变或修改，并满足市场现实。根据经济权利的授权行使而作出的这种改变不被视为严重损害表演者声誉的歪曲或篡改。因此，第（1）款的结尾修改如下：

“作品制作者或制作者的利益继承人根据制作者在表演中行使获得的授权权利而对视听作品进行的符合正常利用的修改，不应视为严重损害表演者的名誉。”

c. 几个代表团在6月的会议上对第5条第（4）款中“创造性作者”一词的含义提出了问题。“创造性作者”一词的含义须被明确，即当表演者从试听作品中主张精神权利时，其他对表演有贡献的个体的权利需要获得认可。拟议的修订调整了《伯尔尼公约》第14条之二第（3）款的措辞：“作品中的其他表演者、为作品创作的情景、对话或音乐作品的作者以及作品的主要导演。”

第6条和第10条

广播权和向公共传播的经济权利

5月18日美国关于第6条（尚未录制的表演）的提案是为了澄清《世界知识产权组织表演和录音制品条约》（WPPT）第6条中的措辞：“向公众广播或传播其未录制的表演，除非该表演已经是广播表演。”5月18日美国提案中还增加了“或者已公开传播的表演”这一表述，并在第10条中进行了同样的改动。正如会议上指出的那样，这些增加不仅不清楚，而且可能产生意想不到的后果。因此，这两条中先前增加的措辞已被删除，使条约提案与WPPT一致。

dropped, leaving the treaty proposal consistent with the WPPT.

Article 10

Right of Broadcasting and Communication to the Public

In the May 18 U. S. Proposal, Article 10(2) provided that Contracting Parties could provide a right of remuneration rather than an exclusive right. However, Article 10(1) of that Proposal incorporates the standards of Article 11*bis* of the Berne Convention by reference, which allows Contracting Parties to limit the right to a right of remuneration. Hence, as was made clear at the June meeting, Article 10(2) is redundant and confusing. It is therefore deleted.

Article 14

Implementation

This article, which was based on the U. S. proposal concerning audiovisual performers made at the 1996 Diplomatic Conference(CRNR/DC/34, December 11,1996) raised a number of concerns at the Committee of Experts meeting. It is not necessary in the context of the present draft and therefore is deleted.

Article 18

Reservations(now Article 17)

The May 18 U. S. Proposal would have made the prohibition against reservations subject to Article 10(2). Since the revised proposal deletes Article 10(2), the prohibition against reservations should be stated without qualification.

Article 19

Application in Time(now Article 18)

The United States takes serious note of the Chair's recommendation for further consideration and study of this provision. We are continuing to study this provision and may come forward with recommended changes at a future date.

第 10 条

广播权和向公众传播权

在 5 月 18 日的美国提案中，第 10 条第（2）款规定，缔约方可提供获酬权，而不是专有权。然而，该提案第 10 条第（1）款以提及方式纳入了《伯尔尼公约》第 11 条之二的标准，该标准允许缔约方限制获酬权。因此，正如在 6 月会议上明确指出的那样，第 10 条第（2）款是多余和令人困惑的。因此予以删除。

第 14 条

权利行使

该条是根据美国在 1996 年外交会议上关于视听表演者的建议（CRNR/DC/34，1996 年 12 月 11 日）提出的，在专家委员会会议上提出了一些关切。在本草案中没有必要，因此删除。

第 18 条

保留（现为第 17 条）

美国 5 月 18 日的提案本应使禁止保留受到第 10 条第（2）款的约束。由于修订后的提案删除了第 10 条第（2）款，应无条件地说明禁止保留的情况。

第 19 条

适用的时限（现为第 18 条）

美国认真注意到主席关于进一步审议和研究这一条款的建议。我们正在继续研究这一条款，并可能在今后提出修改建议。

3.2 Report of the Regional Consultation Meeting for Asia and the Pacific, Held in Shanghai, from October 14 to 16, 1998

Document Code: SCCR/1/5
Language: English
URL: https://www.wipo.int/edocs/mdocs/copyright/en/sccr_1/sccr_1_5.pdf

Chinese Translation: Not Available.
URL: N/A

STANDING COMMITTEE ON COPYRIGHT
AND RELATED RIGHTS
First Session
Geneva, November 2 to 10, 1998

AGENDA ITEM 5: PROTECTION OF AUDIOVISUAL PERFORMANCES

REPORT OF THE REGIONAL CONSULTATION MEETING
FOR ASIA AND THE PACIFIC, HELD IN SHANGHAI,
FROM OCTOBER 14 TO 16, 1998

Document prepared by the International Bureau

3.2 1998年10月14日至16日在上海举行的亚洲及太平洋区域协商会议的报告

文件编号：SCCR/1/5
文件语言：英语
文件链接：https://www.wipo.int/edocs/mdocs/copyright/en/sccr_1/sccr_1_5.pdf
中文文本：无
文件链接：无

版权及相关权常设委员会

第一届会议
1998年11月2日至10日，日内瓦

议程项目五：保护视听表演

1998年10月14日至16日在上海举行的亚洲及太平洋区域协商会议的报告

由国际局编制的文件

REPORT OF THE WIPO REGIONAL CONSULTATION MEETING FOR ASIA AND THE PACIFIC CONCERNING A PROTOCOL ON AUDIOVISUAL PERFORMANCES AND RELATED ISSUES, SHANGHAI (OCTOBER 14 TO 16, 1998)[1]

1. The WIPO Regional Consultation Meeting for Asia and the Pacific concerning a Protocol on Audiovisual Performances and Related Issues was held in Shanghai, People's Republic of China, from October 14 to 16, 1998.

2. The following countries participated in the Meeting: Bangladesh, Brunei Darussalam, Fiji, Indonesia, Malaysia, Mongolia, Nepal, Pakistan, Philippines, Republic of Korea, Singapore, Sri Lanka, Thailand and the People's Republic of China.

3. Mr. S. Tiwari from Singapore was elected as the Chairman of the Meeting. Mr. Zheng Cheng-si from the People's Republic of China and Mr. Asaduzzaman Bhuiyan from Bangladesh were elected as Vice-Chairmen.

4. The discussion was based on the WIPO documents SCCR/1/2 (Organizational and Procedural Matters and Overview of Substantive Issues), AP/CE/2/7 (Comparative Table of the Proposals received from WIPO Member States and the European Community), SCCR/1/4 (Protection of Audiovisual Performances-Submissions received from Member States of WIPO).

PROTECTION OF AUDIOVISUAL PERFORMANCES

5. Three points were agreed upon as an overview to the discussions. First, it was felt that the special industry practices in the film industries in the developing countries may differ. Second, these countries needed to further develop the administration of copyright and related rights. Third, it was necessary to have a properly developed collective administration system in the countries to enable performers to benefit from the new rights.

1 This report was submitted to the International Bureau on behalf of the States mentioned in paragraph 2.

世界知识产权组织亚洲及太平洋区域协商会议关于视听表演和有关问题的报告（1998年10月14日至16日于上海）[1]

1. 世界知识产权组织亚洲及太平洋区域关于视听表演和相关问题议定书的协商会议于 1998 年 10 月 14 至 16 日在中国上海举办。

2. 以下国家参加了会议：孟加拉国，文莱，斐济，印度尼西亚，马来西亚，蒙古国，尼泊尔，巴基斯坦，菲律宾，韩国，新加坡，斯里兰卡，泰国，中华人民共和国。

3. 新加坡的 S.Tiwari 先生当选为会议主席。中国的郑成思先生和孟加拉国的 Asaduzzaman Bhuiyan 先生当选为副主席。

4. 讨论依据的是世界知识产权组织文件 SCCR/1/2（组织和程序事项以及实质性问题概述），AP/CE/2/7（从世界知识产权组织成员国和欧洲共同体收到的提案比较表），SCCR/1/4（世界知识产权组织成员国提交的关于视听表演保护的材料）。

保护视听表演

5. 商定了三点共识作为讨论的大纲。第一，人们认为发展中国家电影业的独特工业实践可能有所不同。第二，这些国家需要进一步发展版权和相关权的管理。第三，有必要在这些国家建立一个适当发展的集体管理制度，以使表演者能够从新权利中受益。

1　本报告由国际局代表第二段所记录的各成员国所提交。

6. The Meeting considered the relevant documents listed above. In this connection, the Meeting also studied a new proposal by Japan, a revised proposal by the United States of America and a general summary (provided by the WIPO representative) of the amended proposal of the GRULAC.

7. Representatives from the United States and Japan made a presentation of their proposals; the European Community drew attention to the salient points of its existing proposal. Australia offered certain clarifications to enable a better understanding of the various proposals.

Definitions

8. The Meeting exchanged views on the desirability or otherwise of having a specific exclusion of certain categories of performers or to follow the formulation in Article 2 of the WPPT and leave it to national legislation to provide the necessary exclusions based on the criterion of creativity. In this connection, views were also expressed whether the amended suggestion of the United States was ambiguous. The Meeting agreed to study the issue further.

Beneficiaries of protection

9. The Meeting generally felt that the protection granted to performers under the Protocol should be restricted to nationals of Contracting Parties to the instrument.

National Treatment

10. There was a useful discussion on the question of national treatment and the possible approaches. It was felt that the issue also tied up with the substantive provisions. This being the case, the Meeting decided to defer the question, pending further development of the substantive provisions of the Protocol.

Moral Rights of Performers

11. There was an extensive discussion of the issue. The Meeting agreed that moral rights needed to be qualified to allow for development in technology and to facilitate commercial exploitation of films by producers.

12. Misgivings were expressed about the use of the word “seriously” in the revised Article 5 of the US Proposal. The Meeting agreed to discuss the question of the scope of the qualification further domestically before finalizing its position.

6. 会议审议了上述有关文件。在这方面，会议还研究了日本的一项新提案，美国的一项修订提案以及拉丁美洲和加勒比地区国家修订提案的总摘要（由世界知识产权组织代表提供）。

7. 美国和日本的代表介绍了他们的提案；欧洲共同体提请注意其现有提案的重点。澳大利亚提供了清晰说明，以使人们更好地理解各种提案。

定义

8. 会议就是否应将某些特定类别的表演者排除在外或遵循 WPPT 第 2 条的规定，以创造力为标准通过国家立法进行必要的排除，交换了看法。在这方面，也有人表示美国的修改建议是否模棱两可。会议同意进一步研究该问题。

9. 保护的受益人

会议普遍认为，根据议定书给予表演者的保护应限于缔约国的国民。

国民待遇

10. 就国民待遇问题和可行的做法进行了有益的讨论。有人认为，这个问题也与实质性条款有关。在这种情况下，会议决定在议定书的实质性条款达成进一步共识之前推迟这个问题的讨论。

表演者的精神权利

11. 会议对这个问题进行了广泛的讨论。会议一致认为，精神权利必须受到限制，以便于技术的发展和促进制片人对电影的商业利用。

12. 有代表对美国提案中修订的第 5 条中使用“严重”一词表示疑虑。会议同意在确定其立场之前，在国内进一步讨论该限定的范围问题。

Economic Rights of Performers in their Unfixed Performances and in relation to Fixed Performances (Right of Reproduction, Right of Distribution and Right of Making Available) Agreed Statements

13. The Meeting agreed that the principles adopted in the WIPO Performances and Phonograms Treaty, including those incorporated in the Agreed Statements reproduced in the footnotes to the WPPT, should be followed in relation to these rights.

Right of Rental

14. The Meeting felt that a case had not been made out, at this stage, for a right of rental for audiovisual performances. However, the Meeting remained open to further consideration of the issue.

Right of Broadcasting and Communication to the Public

15. The Meeting explored the various options to deal with the issue: (a) not to have such a right in view of the fact that the Berne Convention had provided this right to authors of cinematographic works (which would generally be exercised by producers) and as providing them such a right would give an even stronger protection than that provided to authors; (b) to follow Article 15 of the WPPT; or (c) to follow Article 10 of the revised US proposal. In light of the flexibility provided under Article 15(3) of the WPPT, the Meeting felt that this would be a better option to follow.

Transfer of Rights/Contractual Arrangements

16. The Meeting considered the differing practice in the film industry of the larger film-producing countries. The Meeting considered Article 9 of the Japanese proposal, Article 11 of the US proposal and a suggestion whether the issue could be dealt with by reference to Article 14bis of the Berne Convention. Members were not entirely clear as to the operation of the Japanese proposal. It was agreed to study the issue further in the light of discussions that will take place in Geneva in November 98.

Limitations and Exceptions, Obligations concerning Technological Measures, Obligations concerning Rights Management Information, Provisions on Enforcement of Rights and Formalities

17. The Meeting agreed to follow the WPPT approach in relation to these areas.

表演者对其尚未录制的表演和已录制表演有关的经济权利（复制权、发行权和提供权）

13. 会议一致认为，在这些权利方面应遵循《世界知识产权组织表演和录音制品条约》中所采用的原则，包括 WPPT 脚注中所包含的议定声明。

出租权

14. 会议认为，在目前阶段，还没有提出关于出租视听表演的权利的理由。但是，会议仍有可能进一步审议这个问题。

广播权和向公众传播权

15. 会议探讨了解决该问题的各种方案：(a)不设立该项权利是基于《伯尔尼公约》已向电影作品的作者（通常由制片人行使）提供了该权利保护的事实，一旦提供这样的权利保护，将使他们获得比电影作品作者更强的保护；(b)遵循 WPPT 第 15 条；或(c)遵循美国修订提案的第 10 条。鉴于 WPPT 第 15 条第(3)款规定的灵活性，会议认为这将是一个更好的选择。

权利转让 / 合同安排

16. 会议审议了较大的电影制作国电影业的不同做法。会议审议了日本提案的第 9 条，美国提案的第 11 条以及是否可以参考《伯尔尼公约》第 14 条之二处理该问题的建议。成员们对日本提案的执行情况并不完全清楚。会议同意根据将于 1998 年 11 月在日内瓦举行的讨论进一步研究这个问题。

限制与例外，关于技术措施的义务，关于权利管理信息的义务，关于权利行使和手续的规定

17. 会议商定在这些领域遵循 WPPT 的规定。

Application in Time

18. The difficulties of retroactive application were referred to. Some members were not in favor of applying Article 18 of the Berne Convention. The Meeting felt that the issue should be looked into further.

Reservations

19. It was felt that the position on reservations was best considered after the substantive provisions of the Protocol had been agreed upon.

Entry into Force

20. The Meeting felt that the number of instruments of ratification or accession required for entry into force of the Protocol should be the same as the WPPT, i. e., 30 instruments.

Position on any new Proposals

21. Participating countries reserved their right to examine afresh the matters dealt with in the event that new proposals may be presented in the future.

22. As the host country of the Meeting, the People's Republic of China appreciates the efforts taken by the countries of the Asian and the Pacific Group in this Meeting. It can go along with the positions of the Group indicated above and will continue to study further those unsettled questions.

[End of document]

适用的时限

18. 会议提到了溯及既往适用的困难。一些成员不赞成适用《伯尔尼公约》第18条。会议认为应该进一步研究这个问题。

保留

19. 有与会成员认为，在商定议定书的实质性条款后，再考虑适用保留的问题。

生效

20. 会议认为，议定书生效所需的批准书或加入书数量应与WPPT相同，即30份文书。

对任何新提案的立场

21. 如果将来可能提出新的提案，与会各国保留重新审查所处理事项的权利。

22. 作为会议的东道国，中国赞赏亚洲及太平洋小组国家在本次会议上所作的努力。中国将与上述小组国家的立场保持一致，并将继续进一步研究那些尚未解决的问题。

（文件完）

3.3 Submission by Brazil Relating to the Report on the Regional Consultation Meeting for Latin America and the Caribbean

Document Code: SCCR/1/6
Language: English
URL: https://www.wipo.int/edocs/mdocs/copyright/en/sccr_1/sccr_1_6.pdf

Chinese Translation: Not Available.
URL: N/A

STANDING COMMITTEE ON COPYRIGHT
AND RELATED RIGHTS
First Session
Geneva, November 2 to 10, 1998

AGENDA ITEM 5: PROTECTION OF AUDIOVISUAL PERFORMANCES

SUBMISSION BY BRAZIL[1] RELATING TO THE REPORT ON THE REGIONAL CONSULTATION MEETING FOR LATIN AMERICA AND THE CARIBBEAN (DOCUMENT SCCR/1/4)

Document prepared by the International Bureau

1 Received by the International Bureau of WIPO on October 20, 1998.

3.3 巴西提交的关于拉丁美洲和加勒比区域协商会议报告的材料

文件编号：SCCR/1/6
文件语言：英语
文件链接：https://www.wipo.int/edocs/mdocs/copyright/en/sccr_1/sccr_1_6.pdf
中文文本：无
文件链接：无

版权及相关权常设委员会

第一届会议
1998 年 11 月 2 日至 10 日，日内瓦

议程项目五：保护视听表演

巴西提交的关于拉丁美洲和加勒比区域协商会议报告的材料[1]

由国际局编制的文件

1　世界知识产权组织国际局于 1998 年 10 月 20 日收到。

The Permanent Mission of Brazil to the United Nations Office and other International Organizations in Geneva has submitted the following comments, so as to accurately reflect the views of the Brazilian Government.

COMMENTS BY BRAZIL ON THE REPORT OF THE REGIONAL MEETING FOR LATIN AMERICAN AND CARIBBEAN COUNTRIES (DOCUMENT SCCR/1/4)

Article IV (Definitions)

Include the following in paragraph (2): "The Delegation of Brazil understands that audiovisual fixation takes place in an individual (non-sequential) manner, and does not involve the incorporation of moving images."

Article VIII (Moral rights)

With regard to paragraph (1), include the following text: "The Delegation of Brazil proposes the addition, at the end of the paragraph, of "the audiovisual producer being free to abridge, condense, edit or dub the work, but without distorting the performer's participation."

Article X (Rights of performers concerning audiovisual fixations)

Delete the passage referring to Brazil under 5 (Right of broadcasting and communication to the public). The following paragraph should start as follows: "The Delegations of Brazil and Uruguay said that, with regard to the same point 5…"

Article XII (Contractual arrangements concerning the rights of performers)

Delete the passage referring to Brazil.

Article XIV (Obligations concerning technological measures)

In the opinion of the Delegation of Brazil, the wording of this Article should correspond to that of Article 18 of the WPPT, which also refers to technological measures, instead of being based on Article 19 of the same instrument, which has to do with the collective management of rights.

巴西常驻联合国日内瓦办事处和其他国际组织代表团已提出以下评论，以准确反映巴西政府的意见。

巴西对拉丁美洲和加勒比国家区域会议报告的评论（文件SCCR/1/4）

第四条（定义）

在第（2）款中包括以下内容："巴西代表团认为，视听录制品是以单独（非连续）的方式进行的，不涉及移动图像的纳入。"

第八条（精神权利）

关于第（1）款，请包括以下内容："巴西代表团建议在该款末尾处增加"视听制作人可以自由地对作品进行删减、压缩、编辑或配音，但又不歪曲表演者的参与。"

第十条（与视听录制品有关的表演者权利）

删除第5项中提及巴西的段落（广播权和向公众传播权）。以下段落应以如下开头："巴西和乌拉圭代表团认为，关于同一点5……"

第十二条（关于表演者权利的合同安排）

删除提及巴西的段落。

第十四条（有关技术措施的义务）

巴西代表团认为，该条的措辞应与WPPT第18条的措辞一致，该条也提到了技术措施，而不是以同一文件的第19条（该条涉及权利的集体管理）为基础。

Article XV (Obligations concerning rights management information)

In paragraph (1)(i), the Delegation of Brazil proposes the following wording:

[The proposal concerns the Spanish text only].

In addition, the Delegation of Brazil expresses concern regarding the inclusion in the text of certain references to the terms "audiovisual producer" and "audiovisual work," as they are already dealt with in the WCT.

Article XVII (application in time).

Add Brazil to the sentence starting "The Delegation of Argentina proposes replacing...," so that the wording would be: "The Delegations of Argentina and Brazil propose..."

[End of document]

第十五条（有关权利管理信息的义务）

巴西代表团在第（1）(i)款中建议以下措词：

（该提案仅涉及西班牙文本）。

此外，巴西代表团对在案文中提及“视听制作者”和“视听作品”这两个术语表示关切，因为WCT中已经涉及这些术语。

第十七条（适用的时限）

在“阿根廷代表团提议替换……”这样的措词就会是：“阿根廷和巴西代表团提议……”

（文件完）

3.4 Report on the Regional Consultation Meeting for Latin American and Caribbean Countries, Geneva, October 29 and 30, 1998

Document Code: SCCR/1/7
Language: English
URL: https://www.wipo.int/edocs/mdocs/copyright/en/sccr_1/sccr_1_7.pdf

Chinese Translation: Not Available.
URL: N/A

STANDING COMMITTEE ON COPYRIGHT
AND RELATED RIGHTS
First Session
Geneva, November 2 to 10, 1998

AGENDA ITEM 5: PROTECTION OF AUDIOVISUAL PERFORMANCES

REPORT ON THE REGIONAL CONSULTATION MEETING
FOR LATIN AMERICAN AND CARIBBEAN COUNTRIES,
GENEVA, OCTOBER 29 AND 30, 1998

Document prepared by the International Bureau

3.4 关于1998年10月29日和30日在日内瓦举行的拉丁美洲和加勒比国家区域协商会议的报告

文件编号：SCCR/1/7
文件语言：英语
文件链接：https://www.wipo.int/edocs/mdocs/copyright/en/sccr_1/sccr_1_7.pdf
中文文本：无
文件链接：无

版权及相关权常设委员会

第一届会议
1998年11月2日至10日，日内瓦

议程项目五：保护视听表演

关于1998年10月29日、30日在日内瓦举行的拉丁美洲和加勒比国家区域协商会议的报告

由国际局编制的文件

ARGENTINA, BRAZIL, COLOMBIA, COSTA RICA, CUBA, DOMINICAN REPUBLIC, ECUADOR, GUYANA, JAMAICA, MEXICO, PANAMA, PARAGUAY, PERU, TRINIDAD AND TOBAGO, URUGUAY, VENEZUELA

REPORT ON THE REGIONAL CONSULTATION MEETING FOR LATIN AMERICA AND CARIBBEAN COUNTRIES ON A PROTOCOL CONCERNING AUDIOVISUAL PERFORMANCES AND OTHER NEW INTERNATIONAL PROVISIONS CONCERNING THE PROTECTION OF INTELLECTUAL PROPERTY

Geneva, October 29 and 30, 1998

A Regional Consultation Meeting of Latin American and Caribbean Countries on a Protocol Concerning Audiovisual Performances and Other New International Provisions on Intellectual Property took place in Geneva, Switzerland, on October 29 and 30, 1998. The meeting was presided over by Mr. Arturo Hernández Basave (Mexico).

The discussions were based on documents AP/CE/2/7 and SCCR/1/4, presented by WIPO.

Consensus was reached on the following points:

I. Title

Protocol to the WIPO Performances and Phonograms Treaty Concerning Audiovisual Performances.

II. Preamble

The Contracting Parties,

Wishing to ensure an adequate level of protection for performances in audiovisual works, owing to the fact that the development and convergence of new

阿根廷、巴西、哥伦比亚、哥斯达黎加、古巴、多米尼加共和国、厄瓜多尔、圭亚那、牙买加、墨西哥、巴拿马、巴拉圭、秘鲁、特立尼达和多巴哥共和国、乌拉圭、委内瑞拉

拉丁美洲和加勒比国家关于视听表演的议定书及关于保护知识产权的其他新国际条款的区域协商会议的报告

1998年10月29日、30日 日内瓦

1998 年 10 月 29 日至 30 日在瑞士日内瓦举行了拉丁美洲和加勒比国家关于视听表演和其他新的国际知识产权条约的区域协商会议。会议由 Arturo Hernández Basave 先生主持(墨西哥)。

讨论依据的是世界知识产权组织提交的 AP/CE/2/7 号文件和 SCCR/1/4 号文件。

会议就以下几点已经达成共识:

一、标题

WPPT 关于视听表演的议定书

二、序言

缔约方,

希望确保对视听作品中的表演给予适当的保护,因为新信息和通信技术的发展和融合将带来视听服务范围的迅速扩大,并增加表演者利用他们的表演的

information and communication technology will bring about a rapid broadening of the range of audiovisual services and also an increase in the opportunities for performers to exploit their performances;

Referring to the Resolution Concerning Audiovisual Performances adopted by the Diplomatic Conference on Certain Copyright and Neighboring Rights Questions on December 20, 1996;

Have agreed as follows:

III. Relation to Other Conventions; Relation to Copyright

(1) This instrument constitutes a Protocol to the WIPO Performances and Phonograms Treaty done in Geneva on December 20, 1996 (hereinafter "the WIPO Treaty").

(2) No provision of this Protocol shall detract from the mutual obligations of Contracting Parties under the International Convention for the Protection of Performers, Producers of Phonograms and Broadcasting Organizations, done at Rome on October 26, 1961.

(3) The protection granted under this Protocol shall leave intact and in no way affect the protection of copyright in literary and artistic works. Consequently no provision of this Treaty may be interpreted as prejudicing such protection.

(4) This Protocol shall have no connection with, and shall not prejudice any right or obligation under, any treaty other than the WIPO Treaty.

IV. Definitions

(1) The Contracting Parties shall apply, *mutatis mutandis*, the definitions set out in Article 2 (a), (e), (f) and (g) of the WIPO Treaty in connection with the protection granted under this Protocol.

(2) For the purposes of this Protocol, "fixation" means the embodiment of images, whether or not accompanied by sound, or the representation thereof, from which they can be perceived, reproduced or communicated through a technical device.

(3) For the purposes of this Protocol, "performers" means all actors, singers, musicians, dancers or other persons who interpret a role, sing, recite, declaim or in any way perform literary or artistic works or expressions of folklore, with the exception of extras.

机会；

提及 1996 年 12 月 20 日召开的版权和邻接权若干问题外交会议通过的《关于视听表演的决议》；

达成如下协议：

三、与其他公约的关系；与版权的关系

（1）本文书构成了 1996 年 12 月 20 日在日内瓦签订的《世界知识产权组织表演和录音制品条约》（以下简称 WIPO 条约）的议定书。

（2）本议定书的任何规定均不得损害缔约方 1961 年 10 月 26 日在罗马订立的《保护表演者、录音制品制作者和广播组织国际公约》规定的相互义务。

（3）根据本议定书给予的保护不得触动或以任何方式影响对文学和艺术作品版权的保护。因此，本条的任何规定都不能以减损对文学艺术作品版权保护的方式加以解释。

（4）本议定书应与《WIPO 条约》以外的其他条约没有任何关系，也不得损害该其他条约下的任何权利或义务。

四、定义

（1）缔约方应比照适用《WIPO 条约》第 2 条（a）、（e）、（f）、（g）项中与本议定书所给予的保护有关的定义。

（2）就本议定书而言，“录制品”是指图像的体现物，且从中可通过某种装置感知、复制或传播该活动图像，不论是否伴有声音或声音的表现物。

（3）就本议定书而言，“表演者”是指所有演员、歌唱家、音乐家舞蹈家，或其他演绎角色、歌唱、背诵、朗诵，或以其他方式进行表演的其他人员，但临时演员除外。

(4) For the purpose of this Protocol "audiovisual work" means a creation consisting of a sequence of images with or without accompanying sound, or the representation thereof, so interrelated as to give an impression of movement regardless of the medium in which they are incorporated, and intended to be perceived, reproduced or communicated by means of any technical device.

V. Beneficiaries of Protection

The Contracting Parties shall accord the protection provided under this Protocol to performers who are nationals of other Contracting Parties.

VI. National Treatment

Each Contracting Party shall accord to the nationals of other Contracting Parties the same treatment as it accords to its own nationals with respect to the rights specifically granted in this Protocol.

VII. Formalities

The enjoyment and exercise of the rights provided for in this Protocol shall not be subject to any formality.

VIII. Moral Rights of Performers

(1) Independently of the performer's economic rights, and even after the transfer of those rights, the performer shall, as regards his live audiovisual performances, with or without sounds, or performances included in audiovisual fixations, have the right to claim to be identified as the performer of his performances, except where omission is dictated by the manner of the use of the performance, and to object to any distortion, mutilation or other modification of his performances that would be prejudicial to his reputation, provided that the audiovisual producer may abridge, condense, edit or dub the work, but without thereby distorting the performance of a performer.

(2) The rights granted to the performer in accordance with the foregoing paragraph shall, after his death, be maintained, at least until the expiry of his economic rights, and shall be exercisable by the persons or institutions authorized by the legislation of the Contracting Party where protection is claimed. However, those Contracting Parties whose legislation, at the moment of their ratification of or accession to this Treaty does not provide for protection after the death of the performer of all rights set out in the preceding paragraph may provide that some of

(4)就本议定书而言,“视听作品”是指由一系列有或无伴音的图像组成的创作,或其表现形式,这些图像相互关联,给人以运动的印象,而不论其包含在何种媒介中,并打算通过任何技术设备进行感知、复制或传播。

五、保护的受益人

缔约方应将本议定书所规定的保护给予具有其他缔约方国民身份的表演者。

六、国民待遇

在本议定书专门授予的专有权方面,每一缔约方应将给予本国国民的待遇同等地给予其他缔约方国民。

七、手续

享有和行使本议定书所规定的权利无须任何手续。

八、表演者精神权利

(1)独立于表演者的经济权利,甚至在这些权利转让之后,表演者仍应对于其现场表(无论是否伴有声音)或以视听录制品录制的表演享有权利:要求承认其系表演的表演者,除非因使用表演的方式而决定可省略不提其系表演者;反对任何对其表演进行的将有损其声誉的歪曲、篡改或其他修改,视听制作人可以对作品进行删减、压缩、编辑或配音,但不得歪曲表演者的表演。

(2)表演者去世后,依前款授予表演者的权利应继续保留至少到其经济权利期满之前,并应由被要求提供保护的缔约方的立法授权的个人或机构行使。但是,在缔约方批准或加入本条约之时其立法者尚未规定在表演者去世后保护前款所述的全部权利的,可以规定其中部分权利在表演者去世后不再保留。

those rights will, after his death, cease to be maintained.

(3) The means of redress for safeguarding the rights granted under this Article shall be governed by the legislation of the Contracting Party where protection is claimed.

IX. Economic Rights of Performers in their Unfixed Performances

Performers shall enjoy the exclusive right to authorize the following in relation to their unfixed performances:

(i) broadcasting and communication to the public of their unfixed performances, except where the performance constitutes a broadcast performance in itself;

(ii) fixation of their unfixed performances.

X. Economic Rights of Performers Concerning Audiovisual Fixations

1. Right of reproduction

Performers shall enjoy the exclusive right to authorize the direct or indirect reproduction of their performances fixed in audiovisual works in any manner or form.

2. Right of distribution

(i) Performers shall enjoy the exclusive right to authorize the making available to the public of the original and copies of their performances fixed in audiovisual works through sale or other transfer of ownership.

(ii) Nothing in this Protocol shall affect the freedom of Contracting Parties to determine the conditions, if any, under which the exhaustion of the right in paragraph (1) applies after the first sale or other transfer of ownership of the original or a copy of the fixed performance with the authorization of the performer.

3. Right of rental

(1) Performers shall enjoy the exclusive right to authorize the commercial rental to the public of copies of their performances fixed in audiovisual works.

(2) Paragraph (1) shall not be applicable in the case of an audiovisual work except where the said commercial rental has given rise to widespread copying of the work which considerably detracts from the performer's exclusive rights of reproduction.

4. Right of making available

Performers shall enjoy the exclusive right to authorize the making available

（3）为维护根据本条授予的权利而采取的救济手段，应由受要求保护的缔约方的法律管辖。

九、表演者对其未录制表演的经济权利

表演者应享有对其未录制表演授权以下内容的专有权：

（i）广播和向公众传播其未录制的表演，除非该表演本身属于广播表演；

（ii）录制其尚未录制的表演。

十、表演者对视听录制品的经济权利

1. 复制权

表演者应享有授权以任何方式或形式录制在视听作品中的表演直接或间接进行复制的专有权。

2. 发行权

（i）表演者应享有授权通过出售或其他转让所有权的方式向公众提供其录制在视听作品中的表演原件和复制件的专有权。

（ii）对于已录制表演的原件或复制件经表演者授权被首次销售或以其他形式转让所有权之后适用本条第（1）款中权利的用尽所依据的条件（如有此种条件），本议定书的任何内容均不得影响缔约方确定该条件的自由。

3. 出租权

（1）表演者享有授权将其录制在视听作品中的表演复制件出租给公众的专有权。

（2）第（1）款不应适用于视听作品，除非上述商业性出租引起了对作品的广泛复制，从而在很大程度上减损了表演者的专有复制权。

4. 提供权

表演者享有专有权，以有线或无线方式向公众提供其录制在视听作品中的

to the public of their performances fixed in audiovisual works, by wire or wireless means, in such a way that members of the public may access them from a place and at a time individually chosen by them.

5. Right of broadcasting and communication to the public

Performers shall enjoy the exclusive right to authorize the broadcasting and the communication to the public of their performances fixed in audiovisual works.

With regard to the broadcasting of audiovisual fixations, the Contracting Parties may apply, *mutatis mutandis,* the provisions of Article 11*bis*(2) of the Berne Convention.

The Delegation of Brazil and Uruguay said that, with regard to the same point 5, it was not in a position to pronounce on it, owing to the fact that consultations were still going on with a view to the taking of a position for the purposes of the meeting of the Committee of Experts to be held in Geneva from November 2 to 10, 1998.

The Delegation of Argentina proposes the following text:

"Performers shall enjoy the exclusive right to authorize the broadcasting and the communication to the public of their performances fixed in audiovisual works."

"Consent given for the fixing of the performance in an audiovisual work shall include the authorization of broadcasting and communication to the public by means of subscription systems, unless otherwise agreed."

XI. Limitations and Exceptions

(1) The Contracting Parties may, in their national legislation, provide for the same kinds of limitation or exception with regard to the protection of performers as they provide for, in their national legislation, in connection with the protection of the copyright in literary and artistic works.

(2) The Contracting Parties shall confine any limitation on or exception to rights provided for in this Protocol to certain special cases that do not conflict with a normal exploitation of the performance fixed in audiovisual works or unreasonably prejudice the legitimate interests of the performer or of the audiovisual producer.

XII. Contractual Arrangements Concerning the Rights of Performers

Where a performer authorizes the inclusion of his performance in an audiovisual fixation, the Contracting Parties shall apply, *mutatis mutandis*, the provisions of Article 14*bis*(2)(b) of the Berne Convention, it being understood that

表演，以便公众成员可以在其个人选择的地点和时间获得这些表演。

5. 广播权和向公众传播权

表演者享有授权广播、向公众传播其录制在视听作品中的表演的专有权。

关于广播视听录制品，缔约方可比照适用《伯尔尼公约》第 11 条第（2）款的规定。

巴西和乌拉圭代表团表示，对于同样的第 5 点，他们不能就此发表意见，因为协商仍在进行中，以便为定于 1998 年 11 月 2 日至 10 日在日内瓦举行的专家委员会会议采取立场。

阿根廷代表团提议以下案文：

"表演者应享有授权广播和向公众传播其录制在视听作品中的表演的专有权。"

"为在视听作品中已录制的表演而给予的同意应包括授权通过订阅系统向公众广播和传播，另有约定除外。"

十一、限制与例外

（1）缔约方可以在其本国法律中就保护表演者作出与其本国法律中保护文学和艺术作品的版权所规定的相同种类的限制或例外的规定。

（2）缔约方应将对本议定书所规定的权利的任何限制或例外仅限于某些不与录制在视听作品中的表演的正常利用相冲突、也不至不合理损害表演者或视听制作人的合法利益的特殊情况。

十二、关于表演者权利的合同安排

如果表演者授权将其表演纳入视听录制品，则缔约方应比照适用《伯尔尼公约》第 14 条之二第（2）款（b）项的规定，应理解为，上述规定同样适用关于本议定书第 10 条的规定。

the said provisions shall likewise be applicable in relation to those of Article X of this Protocol.

XIII. Term of Protection of the Economic Rights of Performers

The term of protection to be granted to performers under this Protocol shall last, at least, until the end of a period of 50 years counted from the end of the year in which the performance was fixed.

XIV. Obligations Concerning Technological Measures

The Contracting Parties shall provide adequate legal protection and effective legal remedies against the circumvention of effective technological measures that are used by performers in connection with the exercise of their rights under this Protocol and which restrict acts, in respect of their performances, that are not authorized by the performers concerned or permitted by law.

XV. Obligations Concerning Rights Management Information

(1) Contracting Parties shall provide adequate and effective legal remedies against any person knowingly performing any of the following acts knowing, or with respect to civil remedies having reasonable grounds to know, that it will induce, enable, facilitate or conceal an infringement of any right covered by this Protocol:

(i) removing or altering any electronic rights management information without authority;

(ii) distributing, importing for distribution, broadcasting, communicating or otherwise making available to the public, without authority, performances, copies of fixed performances or audiovisual works knowing that electronic rights management information has been removed or altered without authority.

(2) As used in this Article, "rights management information" means information that identifies the performer, his performance, the audiovisual producer or the audiovisual work, or information about the terms and conditions governing the use of the performance of the audiovisual work, and any numbers or codes that represent such information, when any of those items of information is attached to a copy of a fixed performance or to an audiovisual work or appears in connection with the communication or making available to the public of a performance fixed in an audiovisual work.

十三、表演者经济权利的保护期限

根据本议定书给予表演者的保护期限，应自表演录制之年的年终起算，至少持续到50年期满为止。

十四、有关技术措施的义务

缔约方应规定适当的法律保护和有效的法律补救办法，防止表演者为行使本议定书所规定的权利以及为了限制未经有关表演者授权或法律不允许的行为而采取的有效技术措施被规避。

十五、有关权利管理信息的义务

（1）缔约各方应规定适当和有效的法律补救办法，制止任何人明知或就民事补救而言有合理根据知道其行为会诱使、促成、便利或包庇对本条约所涵盖的任何权利的侵犯而故意从事以下行为：

（i）未经许可去除或改变任何权利管理的电子信息；

（ii）未经许可发行、为发行目的进口、广播、向公众传播或提供明知已被未经许可去除或改变权利管理电子信息的表演或者以视听录制的表演的复制件。

（2）在本条中，“权利管理信息”系指识别表演者、表演者的表演、视听制作人或视听作品的信息，或有关使用视听作品中的表演的条款和条件的信息，和代表此种信息的任何数字或代码，各该项信息均附于录制的表演的每件复制件上或视听作品上，或在已录制在视听作品中的表演向公众提供时出现。

XVI. Reservations

GRULAC will pronounce on this matter after the articles concerning the various rights have been put in final form.

XVII. Application in Time

(1) The Contracting Parties shall apply the provisions of Article 18 of the Berne Convention, *mutatis mutandis*, to the rights of the performers provided for in this Protocol.

(2) This Protocol shall not detract from the rights acquired in any Contracting Party prior to the date of entry into force of this Protocol in that Party.

The Delegation of Brazil proposes the substitution of the following text for the above point 1:

"The provisions of this Protocol shall not apply to performances given or audiovisual fixations made prior to the entry into force of this Protocol."

The Delegations of Argentina, Bolivia, Colombia and Paraguay announced in connection with this matter that they were not able to take a position for as long as consultations were still going on with a view to the adoption of a stance for the meeting to be held in Geneva from November 2 to 10, 1998.

XVIII. Provisions on Enforcement of Rights

(1) The Contracting Parties undertake to adopt, in accordance with their legal systems, the measures necessary to ensure the application of this Protocol.

(2) The Contracting Parties shall ensure that enforcement procedures are available under their law so as to permit effective action against any act of infringement of rights covered by this Protocol, including expeditious remedies to prevent infringement and remedies that constitute a deterrent to further infringements.

XIX. Administrative Provisions and Final Clauses

1. Assembly

The Contracting Parties shall have an Assembly. That Assembly shall be the same as the one created by the WIPO Treaty.

2. Eligibility to Become Party to the Protocol

Any party to the WIPO Treaty may become party to this Protocol.

十六、保留

在各种权利的条款以最终形式确定之后，拉丁美洲和加勒比国家小组将就此发表声明。

十七、适用的时限

（1）缔约方应就本议定书所规定的表演者的权利比照适用《伯尔尼公约》第 18 条的规定。

（2）本议定书规定的保护不得减损任何缔约方在本议定书对该缔约方生效前获得的权利。

巴西代表团建议用以下案文代替上述观点：

“本议定书的规定不适用于在本议定书生效之前进行的表演或制作的视听录制品。”

阿根廷、玻利维亚和巴拉圭代表团宣布，只要仍在进行协商，以便在 1998 年 11 月 2 日至 10 日于日内瓦举行的会议上采取立场，他们就无法发表意见。

十八、权利行使规定

（1）缔约方承诺根据其法律制度采取必要措施，以确保本议定书的适用。

（2）缔约方应确保根据其法律可采用执行程序，以便针对本议定书所涵盖的任何侵权行为采取有效行动，包括为防止侵权而迅速采取的救济措施以及对进一步侵权构成威慑作用的救济措施。

十九、行政条款和最后条款

1. 大会

缔约方应举行大会。该大会应与《WIPO 条约》设立的大会相同。

2. 成为议定书缔约方的资格

《WIPO 条约》的任何缔约方均可成为本议定书的缔约方。

3. Signature of the Protocol

This Protocol shall be open for signature until… by any Member State of WIPO and by the European Community.

4. Entry into Force of the Protocol

This Protocol shall enter into force, following the date of entry into force of the WIPO Treaty, three months after 20 instruments of ratification or accession by States have been deposited with the Director General of WIPO.

[End of document]

3. 议定书的签署

本议定书应开放供世界知识产权组织任何成员国和欧洲共同体签署，直到……

4. 议定书生效

本议定书应自《WIPO条约》生效之日起，在将二十份国家批准或加入书交存WIPO总干事后三个月生效。

（文件完）

3.5 Submission by Canada

Document Code: SCCR/1/8
Language: English
URL: https://www.wipo.int/edocs/mdocs/copyright/en/sccr_1/sccr_1_8.pdf

Chinese Translation: Not Available.
URL: N/A

STANDING COMMITTEE ON COPYRIGHT
AND RELATED RIGHTS
First Session
Geneva, November 2 to 10, 1998

AGENDA ITEM 5: PROTECTION OF AUDIOVISUAL PERFORMANCES

Submission by Canada[1]

Document prepared by the International Bureau

EXPLANATORY NOTE

Transfer of Rights

At the June 1998 meeting of the WIPO Committee of Experts on a Protocol Concerning Audiovisual Performances, the Canadian delegation made a verbal proposal concerning a possible transfer of rights provision. A number of representatives at the meeting expressed an interest in seeing a written version of

1 Received by the International Bureau of WIPO on October 30, 1998.

3.5 加拿大提交的材料

文件编号：SCCR/1/8
文件语言：英语
文件链接：https://www.wipo.int/edocs/mdocs/copyright/en/sccr_1/sccr_1_8.pdf
中文文本：无
文件链接：无

版权及相关权常设委员会

第一届会议

1998 年 11 月 2 日至 10 日，日内瓦

议程项目五：保护视听表演

加拿大提交的材料[1]

由国际局编制的文件

介绍说明

权利的转让

在 1998 年 6 月世界知识产权组织视听表演议定书专家委员会的会议上，加拿大代表团就可能的权利转让条款提出了口头建议。出席会议的一些代表表示有兴趣看到该建议的书面文本。作为对这些要求的回应，我们提出这份文本是为了促进对这一问题的进一步讨论。

1　世界知识产权组织国际局于 1998 年 10 月 30 日收到。

that proposal. In response to those requests, we are submitting this text as a means of promoting further discussion of this issue.

Canada would be opposed to any provision that required countries to amend their domestic legislation to create a deemed or presumed transfer of rights with respect to performers in audiovisual works made by nationals of that country. However, we would be open to considering a provision which required countries to recognize such transfers made in other Contracting Parties. In order to recognize such a transfer, it would be essential that it be done by a voluntary contract or, if done by operation of law, that the performer have the right to opt out of it.

Throughout this proposed text we have used the term "[author]/[producer]/[first owner of copyright]". The main reason for this is that the Canadian *Copyright Act* is completely silent on the substantive rights of the producer of an audiovisual work. If there is a provision in the final instrument which requires Contracting Parties to recognize such transfers which occurred in other Contracting Parties, it would be inappropriate to limit it to one type of transferee.

PROPOSAL

I. Transfer of Rights

Option A

At the time of ratifying or acceding to this [Protocol]/[Treaty] or at any subsequent time a Contracting Party may declare by an instrument deposited with the Director General that once a performer [who is a national of [that]/[any] Contracting Party]/[regardless of nationality] has consented to the fixation of his or her performance in an audiovisual work by a national of that Contracting Party, he or she shall be deemed to have transferred all exclusive rights of authorization granted under this [Protocol]/[Treaty] with respect to that particular audiovisual work to the [author]/[producer]/[first owner of copyright] of that work [provided such [author]/[producer]/[first owner of copyright] is a national of a Contracting Party] and [his, hers or] its successors in interest subject to any written [contractual [clause]/[provision]]/[agreement] to the contrary. The foregoing sentence shall not apply to any rights of remuneration a performer may have under the law of any Contracting Party, nor shall it require a Contracting Party to establish any such rights of remuneration.

加拿大将反对任何要求各国修改其国内立法，以建立一个被视为或推定的与知识产权转让的条款。但是，我们愿意考虑要求各国承认在其他缔约方进行的这种转让的规定。为了认可这种转让，必须通过自愿的合同约定，或者，如果通过法律规定实施，则表演者有权选择排除适用。

在整个建议的案文中，我们使用了“（作者）/（制作者）/（版权的第一所有人）”一词。这样做的主要原因是，加拿大《版权法》对视听作品的制作者的实质权利完全没有提及。如果最终文书中有一项规定要求缔约方承认在其他缔约方中发生的这种转让，则将其限于一种类型的受让人是不合适的。

提案

一、<u>权利的转让</u>

选项 A

在批准或加入本（议定书）/（条约）时或在随后的任何时间，缔约方可通过交存于总干事的文书宣布，表演者［其是（该）/（任何）缔约方国民］/（不论国籍）已同意将该缔约方的国民的表演录制为视听作品，则应视同他/她已转让所有专有权，其是根据本［关于该作品的（作者）/（制作者）/（版权的第一所有人）的特定视听作品的议定书］/（条约）授权，其［提供于在该缔约方的国民为（作者）/（制作者）/（版权的第一所有人）］及［其本人或其继承人］的利益受任何相反的书面［合同（条款）/（规定）］/［协议］的约束。前述句子不适用于表演者根据任何缔约方的法律可能享有的任何获酬权，也不应要求缔约方确立任何这种获酬权。

Where a Contracting Party makes such a declaration it shall apply [and be binding] in all other Contracting Parties of this [Protocol]/[Treaty].

For purposes of this article the term "an audiovisual work by a national of that Contracting Party" means an audiovisual work where the [author]/[producer]/[first owner of copyright] is a national of the Contracting Party which made the declaration [regardless of the place of fixation or publication of the audiovisual work].

[[For purposes of this article] "producer" shall include both individuals and legal entities [and the identity of the producer shall be determined by the law of the Contracting Party which made the declaration]].

A declaration made under this article may be revoked at any time.

*Option*al

Where a declaration under this article is made subsequent to the time of a Contracting Party ratifying or acceding to this [Protocol]/[Treaty], it shall apply effective January 1 of the year immediately following the date of deposit.

Option B

No transfer of rights provision.

II. Term of Protection

Option C

The term of protection to be granted to performers under this [Protocol]/[Treaty] shall last, at least, until the end of a period of 50 years from the end of the year in which the performance was fixed.

Option D

The term of protection to be granted to performers under this [Protocol]/[Treaty] shall last until the end of the term of protection of the audiovisual work in which it is fixed.

Option D. 1

[Notwithstanding [Option D] no act done with respect to the audio portion of an audiovisual work shall be an infringement of any rights under this [Protocol]/[Treaty] if that act occurred more than 50 years after the end of the year in which the performance was fixed.]

缔约方作出此种声明的，应在本（议定书）/（条约）的所有其他缔约方中适用（并具有约束力）。

就本条而言，术语“该缔约方国民的视听作品”是指其中（作者）/（制作者）/（版权的第一所有人）是作出声明的缔约方的国民的视听作品（无论视听作品的录制或出版地点）。

[（就本条而言）“制作者”应包括个人和法人实体（制作者的身份应由作出声明的缔约方的法律确定）]。

根据本条作出的声明可以随时撤销。

可选的

在缔约方批准或加入本（议定书）/（条约）之后，根据本条作出声明的，该声明应自交存之日起第二年的1月1日起生效。

选项B

没有权利转让条款。

二、保护期限

选项C

根据本（协议）/（条约）授予表演者的保护期限，至少应持续到表演录制之年年底起的50年为止。

选项D

根据本（协议）/（条约）给予表演者的保护期限应持续到录制有其的视听作品的保护期限届满为止。

选择D.1

[尽管（选项D），就视听作品的音频部分所作的任何行为，如果该行为发生在录制表演的当年年底之后50年以上，均不构成对本（议定书）/（条约）项下的任何权利的侵犯。]

III. Applicable Term

The term shall be governed by the legislation of the Contracting Party where protection is claimed; however, unless the legislation of that Contracting Party otherwise provides, the term shall not exceed the term fixed in the Contracting Party of the performer's nationality.

[End of document]

三、适用时限

该期限应受被要求提供保护的缔约方的法律管辖；但是，除非该缔约方的法律另有规定，否则该期限不得超过该表演者的国籍的缔约方所确定的期限。

（文件完）

4.

Standing Committee on Copyright and Related Rights: Second Session

Meeting code: SCCR/2
Date: May 4 to May 11, 1999
venue: Geneva, Switzerland
Meeting Documents URL: https://www.wipo.int/meetings/en/details.jsp?meeting_id=3736

4.
版权及相关权常设委员会：第二届会议

会议代码：SCCR/2
会议日期：1999年5月4—11日
会议地点：瑞士日内瓦
会议文件链接：https://www.wipo.int/meetings/en/details.jsp?meeting_id=3736

4.1 Report on the Regional Consultation Meeting for Latin American and Caribbean Countries, Geneva, 6 November 1998

Document Code: SCCR/2/2
Language: English
URL: https://www.wipo.int/edocs/mdocs/copyright/en/sccr_2/sccr_2_2.pdf

Chinese Translation: Not Available.
URL: N/A

STANDING COMMITTEE ON COPYRIGHT
AND RELATED RIGHTS
Second Session
Geneva, May 4 to 11, 1999

ITEM 4 OF THE AGENDA: PROTECTION OF AUDIOVISUAL PERFORMANCES

Report on the Regional Consultation Meeting for Latin American and Caribbean Countries, Geneva, 6 November 1998[1]

Submitted on behalf of Argentina, Brazil, Colombia, Costa Rica, Cuba, the Dominican Republic, Ecuador, Guyana, Jamaica, Mexico, Panama, Paraguay, Peru, Trinidad and Tobago, Uruguay and Venezuela

1 Received on 16 February 1999.

4.1 1998年11月6日日内瓦拉丁美洲和加勒比国家区域协商会议报告

文件编号：SCCR/2/2
文件语言：英语
文件链接：https://www.wipo.int/edocs/mdocs/copyright/en/sccr_2/sccr_2_2.pdf
中文文本：无
文件链接：无

版权及相关权常设委员会

第二届会议

1999年5月4日至11日，日内瓦

议程项目四：保护视听表演

1998年11月6日日内瓦拉丁美洲和加勒比国家区域协商会议报告[1]

由代表阿根廷、巴西、哥伦比亚、哥斯达黎加、古巴、多米尼加共和国、厄瓜多尔、圭亚那、牙买加、墨西哥、巴拿马、巴拉圭、秘鲁、特立尼达和多巴哥共和国、乌拉圭、委内瑞拉提交

1　于1999年2月16日收到。

REPORT ON THE REGIONAL CONSULTATION MEETING FOR LATIN AMERICAN AND CARIBBEAN COUNTRIES ON A PROTOCOL CONCERNING AUDIOVISUAL PERFORMANCES AND OTHER NEW INTERNATIONAL PROVISIONS CONCERNING THE PROTECTION OF INTELLECTUAL PROPERTY

Geneva, 6 November 1998

A Regional Consultation Meeting of Latin American and Caribbean Countries on a Protocol Concerning Audiovisual Performances and Other New International Provisions on Intellectual Property took place in Geneva, Switzerland, on 6 November 1998. The meeting was presided over by the Delegates of Argentina and Mexico (Dr. Hilda Retondo, Mr. Arturo Hernández Basave and Mr. Fernando Serrano Migallón).

The discussions were based on documents AP/CE/2/2, AP/CE/2/4, AP/CE/2/4 Corr. and AP/CE/2/6, presented by WIPO.

Consensus was reached on the following points:

I. TITLE

Protocol to the WIPO Performances and Phonograms Treaty Concerning Audiovisual Performances.

II. PREAMBLE

The Contracting Parties,

Wishing to ensure an adequate level of protection for performances in audiovisual works, owing to the fact that the development and convergence of new information and communication technology will bring about a rapid broadening of the range of audiovisual services and also an increase in the opportunities for performers to exploit their performances;

Referring to the Resolution Concerning Audiovisual Performances adopted by

关于视听表演议定书和其他知识产权保护的新国际条约的拉丁美洲和加勒比国家区域协商会议报告

1998年11月6日，日内瓦

1998 年 11 月 6 日在瑞士日内瓦举行了拉丁美洲和加勒比国家关于视听表演的议定书和其他新的国际知识产权条约的区域协商会议。该会议由阿根廷和墨西哥代表（Hilda Retondo 博士、Arturo Hernández Basave 先生和 Fernando Serrano Migallón 先生）主持。

讨论依据世界知识产权组织提交的 AP/CE/2/2 号、AP/CE/2/4 号、AP/CE/2/4Corr 号和 AP/CE/2/6 号文件。

会议就以下几点达成共识：

一、标题

WPPT 关于视听表演的议定书

二、序言

缔约方，

希望确保对视听作品中的表演给予适当的保护，因为新信息和通信技术的发展和融合将带来视听服务范围的迅速扩大，并增加表演者利用他们表演的机会；

提及 1996 年 12 月 20 日召开的版权和邻接权若干问题外交会议通过的

the Diplomatic Conference on Certain Copyright and Neighboring Rights Questions on 20 December 1996;

Have agreed as follows:

III. RELATION TO OTHER CONVENTIONS; RELATION TO COPYRIGHT

1. This instrument constitutes a Protocol to the WIPO Performances and Phonograms Treaty done in Geneva on 20 December 1996 (hereinafter "the WIPO Treaty").

2. No provision of this Protocol shall detract from the mutual obligations of Contracting Parties under the International Convention for the Protection of Performers, Producers of Phonograms and Broadcasting Organizations, done at Rome on 26 October 1961 (hereinafter "the Rome Convention").

3. The protection granted under this Protocol shall leave intact and in no way affect the protection of copyright in literary and artistic works. Consequently no provision of this Treaty may be interpreted as prejudicing such protection.

4. This Protocol shall have no connection with, and shall not prejudice any right or obligation under, any treaty other than the WIPO Treaty.

IV. DEFINITIONS

1. The Contracting Parties shall apply, *mutatis mutandis*, the definitions set out in Article 2 (a), (e), (f) and (g) of the WIPO Treaty in connection with the protection granted under this Protocol.

2. For the purposes of this Protocol, "audiovisual fixation" means the embodiment of images, whether or not accompanied by sound, or the representation thereof, from which they can be perceived, reproduced or communicated by means of a device.

3. For the purposes of this Protocol, "performers" means all actors, singers, musicians, dancers or other persons who interpret a role, sing, recite, declaim or in any way perform literary or artistic works or expressions of folklore, with the exception of extras [the definition of the latter term being left to the legislation of each Contracting Party].

V. BENEFICIARIES OF PROTECTION

The Contracting Parties shall accord the protection provided under this Protocol:

《关于视听表演的决议》;

达成如下协议:

三、与其他公约有关;与版权的关系

1. 本文书构成了1996年12月20日在日内瓦签订的《世界知识产权组织表演和录音制品条约》(以下简称WIPO条约)的议定书。

2. 本议定书的任何规定均不得损害缔约方1961年10月26日在罗马订立的《保护表演者、录音制品制作者和广播组织国际公约》规定的相互义务。

3. 根据本议定书给予的保护不得触动或以任何方式影响对文学和艺术作品版权的保护。因此,本条的任何规定都不能以减损对文学艺术作品版权保护的方式加以解释。

4. 本议定书应与WIPO条约以外的其他条约没有任何关系,也不得损害该其他条约下的任何权利或义务。

四、定义

1. 缔约方应比照适用WIPO条约第2条(a)(e)(f)(g)项中与本议定书所给予的保护有关的定义。

2. 就本议定书而言,"视听录制品"是指图像的体现物,且从中可通过某种装置感知、复制或传播该活动图像,不论是否伴有声音或声音的表现物。

3. 就本议定书而言,"表演者"是指所有演员、歌唱家、音乐家舞蹈家或其他演绎角色、歌唱、背诵、朗诵或以其他方式进行表演的其他人员,例外情况(其定义留给每个缔约方的立法)除外。

五、保护的受益人

缔约方应将本议定书规定的保护给予:

(a) to performers who are nationals of other Contracting Parties;

(b) to performers who are not nationals of any of the Contracting Parties but are ordinarily resident in one of them, who shall be treated as nationals of the Contracting Party concerned.

VI. NATIONAL TREATMENT

Each Contracting Party shall accord to the nationals of other Contracting Parties the same treatment as it accords to its own nationals with respect to the rights specifically granted in this Protocol.

VII. FORMALITIES

The enjoyment and exercise of the rights provided for in this Protocol shall not be subject to any formality.

VIII. Moral Rights of Performers

1. Independently of the performer's economic rights, and even after the transfer of those rights, the performer shall, as regards his live audiovisual performances, with or without sounds, or performances included in audiovisual fixations, have the right to claim to be identified as the performer of his performances, except where omission is dictated by the manner of the use of the performance, and to object to any distortion, mutilation or other modification of his performances that would be prejudicial to his reputation, provided that the audiovisual producer may abridge, condense, edit or dub the work, but without thereby distorting the performance of the performer.

2. The rights granted to the performer in accordance with the foregoing paragraph shall, after his death, be maintained, at least until the expiry of his economic rights, and shall be exercisable by the persons or institutions authorized by the legislation of the Contracting Party where protection is claimed. However, those Contracting Parties whose legislation, at the moment of their ratification of or accession to this Treaty does not provide for protection after the death of the performer of all rights set out in the preceding paragraph may provide that some of those rights will, after his death, cease to be maintained.

3. The means of redress for safeguarding the rights granted under this Article shall be governed by the legislation of the Contracting Party where protection is claimed.

(a)属于其他缔约方国民的表演者；

(b)非任何缔约方的国民但在一个缔约方境内有惯常居住地的表演者，视为该缔约方的国民。

六、国民待遇

在本议定书专门授予的专有权方面，每一缔约方应给予其他缔约方国民与本国国民同等的待遇。

七、手续

享有和行使本议定书所规定的权利无须任何手续。

八、表演者的精神权利

1. 独立于表演者的经济权利，甚至在这些权利转让之后，表演者仍应对于其现场表演（无论是否伴有声音）或以视听录制品录制的表演享有权利：要求承认其系表演的表演者，除非因使用表演的方式而决定可省略不提其系表演者；反对任何对其表演进行的将有损其声誉的歪曲、篡改或其他修改，视听制作人可以对作品进行删减、压缩、编辑或配音，但不得歪曲表演者的表演。

2. 表演者去世后，依前款授予表演者的权利应继续保留至少到其经济权利期满之前，并应由被要求提供保护的缔约方的立法授权的个人或机构行使。但是，在缔约方批准或加入本条约之时其立法者尚未规定在表演者去世后保护前款所述的全部权利的，可以规定其中部分权利在表演者去世后不再保留。

3. 为维护根据本条授予的权利而采取的救济手段，应由受要求保护的缔约方的法律管辖。

IX. ECONOMIC RIGHTS OF PERFORMERS IN THEIR UNFIXED PERFORMANCES

Performers shall enjoy the exclusive right to authorize the following in relation to their unfixed performances:

(i) broadcasting and communication to the public of their unfixed performances, except where the performance constitutes a broadcast performance in itself;

(ii) fixation of their unfixed performances.

X. ECONOMIC RIGHTS OF PERFORMERS CONCERNING AUDIOVISUAL FIXATIONS

1. Right of reproduction

Performers shall enjoy the exclusive right to authorize the direct or indirect reproduction of their performances incorporated in audiovisual fixations in any manner or form.

2. Right of distribution

(a) Performers shall enjoy the exclusive right to authorize the making available to the public, through sale or other transfer of ownership, of the original and copies of their performances incorporated in audiovisual fixations.

(b) Nothing in this Protocol shall affect the freedom of Contracting Parties to determine the conditions, if any, under which the exhaustion of the right in paragraph (a) applies after the first sale or other transfer of ownership of the original or a copy of the fixed performance with the authorization of the performer.

3. Right of rental

(a) Performers shall enjoy the exclusive right to authorize the commercial rental to the public of copies of their audiovisual fixations.

(b) Paragraph (a) shall not be applicable in the case of an audiovisual work except where the said commercial rental has given rise to widespread copying thereof which considerably detracts from the performer's exclusive rights of reproduction.

4. Right of making available

Performers shall enjoy the exclusive right to authorize the making available to

九、表演者对未录制的表演的经济权利

表演者应享有对其未录制的表演授权以下内容的专有权：

（i）广播和向公众传播其未录制的表演，除非该表演本身属于广播表演；

（ii）录制其尚未录制的表演。

十、表演者对其视听录制品的经济权利

1 复制权

表演者应享有授权以任何方式或形式录制在视听作品中的表演直接或间接进行复制的专有权。

2. 发行权

（a）表演者应享有授权通过出售或其他转让所有权的方式向公众提供其结合在视听录制品中的表演原件和复制件的专有权。

（b）对于已录制表演的原件或复制件经表演者授权被首次销售或以其他形式转让所有权之后适用本条第（1）款中权利的用尽所依据的条件（如有此种条件），本条约的任何内容均不得影响缔约方确定该条件的自由。

3. 出租权

（a）表演者享有授权向公众出租其视听录制品副本的专有权。

（b）第（1）款不应适用于视听作品，除非上述商业性出租引起了对作品的广泛复制，从而在很大程度上减损了表演者的专有复制权。

4. 提供权

表演者享有专有权，以有线或无线方式向公众提供其表演的视听录制品，

the public of their performances incorporated in audiovisual fixations, by wire or wireless means, in such a way that members of the public may access them from a place and at a time individually chosen by them.

5. Right of broadcasting and communication to the public

No agreement having been reached, the discussions continue.

The Delegation of Brazil proposes omitting all provisions on the right of broadcasting or communication to the public.

XI. LIMITATIONS AND EXCEPTIONS

1. The Contracting Parties may, in their national legislation, provide for the same kinds of limitation or exception with regard to the protection of performers as they provide for, in their national legislation, in connection with the protection of the copyright in literary and artistic works.

2. The Contracting Parties shall confine any limitation on or exception to rights provided for in this Protocol to certain special cases that do not conflict with a normal exploitation of the audiovisual fixations or unreasonably prejudice the legitimate interests of the performer or of the audiovisual producer.

XII. Contractual Arrangements Concerning the Rights of Performers

Where a performer authorizes the inclusion of his performance in an audiovisual fixation, the Contracting Parties shall apply, *mutatis mutandis*, the provisions of Article 14*bis*(2)(b) of the Berne Convention, it being understood that the said provisions shall likewise be applicable to those of item 3 ofArticle X of this Protocol.

The Delegation of Brazil proposes omitting all provisions on contractual arrangements concerning the rights of performers in relation to broadcasting or communication to the public.

XIII. TERM OF PROTECTION OF THE ECONOMIC RIGHTS OF PERFORMERS

The term of protection to be granted to performers under this Protocol shall last, at least, until the end of a period of 50 years counted from the end of the year in which the performance was fixed.

XIV. OBLIGATIONS CONCERNING TECHNOLOGICAL MEASURES

The Contracting Parties shall provide adequate legal protection and effective

使公众成员可在其自行选择的地点和时间获得其表演。

5. 广播权和向公众传播权

由于没有达成协议，讨论仍在继续。

巴西代表团建议略去关于向公众广播或传播权利的所有条款。

十一、限制与例外

1. 缔约双方可在其本国法律中就保护表演者规定同在其本国法律中就保护文学和艺术作品的版权所规定的同样种类的限制或例外。

2. 缔约方应将对本议定书所规定的权利的任何限制或例外仅限于某些不与视听录制品的正常利用相冲突、也不至不合理损害表演者或视听制作人的合法利益的特殊情况。

十二、表演者权利的合同安排

如果表演者授权将其表演列入视听录制品中，缔约双方应比照适用《伯尔尼公约》第 14 条之二第（2）（b）款的规定，但有一项理解，即上述规定同样适用于本议定书第 X 条第 3 项的规定。

巴西代表团建议略去关于表演者在广播或向公众传播方面的权利的合同安排的所有条款。

十三、表演者经济权利的保护期

根据本议定书给予表演者的保护期，应自表演录制之年的年终起算，至少持续到 50 年为止。

十四、技术措施的义务

缔约方应规定适当的法律保护和有效的法律补救办法，防止表演者为行使

legal remedies against the circumvention of effective technological measures that are used by performers in connection with the exercise of their rights under this Protocol and which restrict acts, in respect of their performances, that are not authorized by the performers concerned or permitted by law.

XV. OBLIGATIONS CONCERNING RIGHTS MANAGEMENT INFORMATION

1. Contracting Parties shall provide adequate and effective legal remedies against any person knowingly performing any of the following acts knowing, or with respect to civil remedies having reasonable grounds to know, that it will induce, enable, facilitate or conceal an infringement of any right covered by this Protocol:

(i) removing or altering any electronic rights management information without authority;

(ii) distributing, importing for distribution, broadcasting, communicating or otherwise making available to the public, without authority, performances, copies of performances incorporated in audiovisual fixations knowing that electronic rights management information has been removed or altered without authority.

2. As used in this Article, "rights management information" means information that identifies the performer, his performance, the audiovisual producer or the audiovisual work, or information about the terms and conditions governing the use of the performance of the audiovisual work, and any numbers or codes that represent such information, when any of those items of information is attached to a copy of a fixed performance or appears in connection with the communication or making available to the public of a performance incorporated in an audiovisual fixation.

XVI. Reservations

GRULAC will pronounce on this matter after the articles concerning the various rights have been put in final form.

The Delegation of Brazil will propose reservations should the Protocol contain provisions on entitlement to equitable remuneration.

XVII. APPLICATION IN TIME

1. The Contracting Parties shall apply the provisions of Article 18 of the Berne Convention, *mutatis mutandis*, to the rights of the performers provided for in this Protocol.

2. This Protocol shall not detract from the rights acquired in any Contracting

本议定书所规定的权利以及为了限制未经有关表演者授权或法律不允许的行为而采取的有效技术措施被规避。

十五、关于权利管理信息的义务

1. 缔约各方应规定适当和有效的法律补救办法，制止任何人明知或就民事补救而言有合理根据知道其行为会诱使、促成、便利或包庇对本条约所涵盖的任何权利的侵犯而故意从事以下行为：

（i）未经许可去除或改变任何权利管理的电子信息；

（ii）未经许可发行、为发行目的进口、广播、向公众传播或提供明知已被未经许可去除或改变权利管理电子信息的表演或者表演的视听录制品的复制件。

2. 本条所称权利管理信息，系指识别表演者、表演者的表演、视听制作人或视听作品的信息，或有关使用视听作品中的表演的条款和条件的信息，和代表此种信息的任何数字或代码，各该项信息均附于录制的表演的每件复制件上或视听作品上，或在已录制在视听作品中的表演向公众提供时出现。

十六、保留

拉丁美洲和加勒比国家小组将在有关各项权利的条款定稿后就此事发表意见。

如果议定书载有关于应得公平的报酬的规定，巴西代表团将提出保留意见。

十七、适用的时限

1. 缔约方应对本议定书规定的表演者的权利比照适用《伯尔尼公约》第18条的规定。

2. 本条约规定的保护不得减损每一缔约方在该条约生效前获得的任何

Party prior to the date of entry into force of this Protocol in that Party.

XVIII. PROVISIONS ON ENFORCEMENT OF RIGHTS

1. The Contracting Parties undertake to adopt, in accordance with their legal systems, the measures necessary to ensure the application of this Protocol.

2. The Contracting Parties shall ensure that enforcement procedures are available under their law so as to permit effective action against any act of infringement of rights covered by this Protocol, including expeditious remedies to prevent infringement and remedies that constitute a deterrent to further infringements.

XIX. ADMINISTRATIVE PROVISIONS AND FINAL CLAUSES

1. Assembly

The Contracting Parties shall have an Assembly. That Assembly shall be the same as the one created by the WIPO Treaty.

2. Eligibility to Become Party to the Protocol

Any party to the WIPO Treaty may become party to this Protocol.

3. Signature of the Protocol

This Protocol shall be open for signature until... by any Member State of WIPO and by the European Community.

4. Entry into Force of the Protocol

This Protocol shall enter into force, following the date of entry into force of the WIPO Treaty, three months after 20 instruments of ratification or accession by States have been deposited with the Director General of WIPO.

5. Final Clauses

The provisions of Articles 25 (International Bureau), 27 (Rights and obligations under the Treaty), 30 (Effective Date of Becoming Party to the Treaty), 31 (Denunciation of the Treaty), 32 (Languages of the Treaty) and 33 (Depositary) of the WIPO Treaty shall apply *mutatis mutandis* to this Protocol.

Note: The Delegation of Brazil maintains that the expression "performances incorporated in audiovisual fixations" should be replaced by "audiovisual fixations" in all articles in which the former expression appears. The proposal is going through a consultation process within GRULAC.

[End of document]

权利。

十八、权利行使的规定

1. 缔约各方承诺根据其法律制度采取必要措施，确保本议定书的适用。

2. 缔约各方应确保依照其法律可以提供执法程序，以便能采取制止对本议定书所涵盖权利的任何侵犯行为的有效行动，包括防止侵权的快速补救和为遏制进一步侵权的补救。

十九、行政条款和最后条款

1. 大会

缔约双方应举行大会。该大会应与 WIPO 条约设立的大会相同。

2. 成为议定书缔约方的资格

WIPO 条约的任何缔约方均可成为本议定书的缔约方。

3. 协议的签署

本议定书开放签字，有效期至由世界知识产权组织的任何成员国和欧洲共同体提出。

4. 议定书生效

本议定书应自 WIPO 条约生效之日起，在 20 份国家批准书或加入书交存知识产权组织总干事三个月后生效。

5. 最后条款

WIPO 条约第 25 条（国际局）、第 27 条（条约项下的权利和义务）、第 30 条（成为条约缔约方的生效日期）、第 31 条（退出条约）、第 32 条（条约的语言）和第 33 条（保存人）的规定应比照适用于本议定书。

注：巴西代表团认为，“表演的视听录制品”一词应在其出现的所有条款中改为“视听录制品”。该提案正在拉丁美洲和加勒比国家小组内部进行协商。

（文件完）

4.2 Submission by the European Community and its Member States

Document Code: SCCR/2/3
Language: English
URL: https://www.wipo.int/edocs/mdocs/copyright/en/sccr_2/sccr_2_3.pdf

Chinese Translation: Not Available.
URL: N/A

STANDING COMMITTEE ON COPYRIGHT
AND RELATED RIGHTS
Second Session
Geneva, May 4 to 11, 1999

AGENDA ITEM 4: PROTECTION OF AUDIOVISUAL PERFORMANCES

SUBMISSION BY THE EUROPEAN COMMUNITY
AND ITS MEMBER STATES[1]
prepared by the International Bureau

1 Received on February 28, 1999.

4.2 欧洲共同体及其成员国提交的材料

文件编号：SCCR/2/3
文件语言：英语
文件链接：https://www.wipo.int/edocs/mdocs/copyright/en/sccr_2/sccr_2_3.pdf
中文文本：无
文件链接：无

版权及相关权常设委员会

第二届会议
1999 年 5 月 4 日至 11 日，日内瓦

议程项目四：保护视听表演

欧洲共同体及其成员国提交的材料[1]

由国际局编制

1　于 1999 年 2 月 28 日收到。

FURTHER SUBMISSION BY THE EUROPEAN COMMUNITY AND ITS MEMBER STATES ON A PROTOCOL CONCERNING AUDIOVISUAL PERFORMANCES

I. TRANSFER OF RIGHTS

1. During the last session of the Standing Committee on Copyright and Related Rights (SCCR), that took place in Geneva from 2 to 10 November 1998, the question of the transfer of rights was discussed at length. The representative of the European Community took the floor to reiterate the Community position on this point, i. e. that the protocol that is currently being discussed should target first of all the improvement of the protection of performers, and not of producers; consequently, it should leave sufficient flexibility to Contracting Parties in order to allow contractual practices established in this sector to continue, once the principles of the instrument have been implemented at national level.

2. The European Community and its Member States cannot support an international provision that would make mandatory for Contracting Parties, as foreseen by some proposals, the introduction of a provision on transfer of rights in their national legislation. In fact, it would imply in many countries major changes in contractual practices, which in different degrees are already subject to presumption of transfer. This adaptation would no doubt be controversial, and could disturb well-established and sometimes delicate balances.

3. Consequently, the European Community and its Member States still propose that the protocol discussed should leave the Contracting Parties the widest flexibility in their own domestic regulation, including the possibility to introduce and/or maintain provisions on transfer of rights, according to their legal traditions and national considerations. In a spirit of clarity, Contracting Parties should agree that it will be a matter for legislation in the Contracting Parties whether or not to provide for a transfer of rights and to determine its nature and scope.

欧洲共同体及其成员国进一步提交的关于视听表演的议定书

一、权利的转让

1. 1998 年 11 月 2 日至 10 日在日内瓦举行的版权及相关权常设委员会（SCCR）上届会议期间，会议详细讨论了权利转让的问题。欧洲共同体代表发言重申了共同体在这一点上的立场，即目前正在讨论的议定书的首要目标应是改善对表演者的保护，而不是对制作者的保护；因此，它应该给缔约方留有足够的灵活性，以便一旦该文书的原则在国家层面得到实施，该领域确立的合同惯例可以延续。

2. 欧洲共同体及其成员国不能支持这样一项国际条款，即：如某些提案所预见的那样，强制要求缔约国在其国家立法中引入有关权利转让的规定。事实上，这将意味着许多国家合同惯例的重大改变，这些做法在不同程度上已经受到推定转让的影响。强制引进该规定无疑会引起争议，可能会扰乱既成的、有时是微妙的平衡。

3. 因此，欧洲共同体及其成员国仍然建议，所讨论的议定书应使缔约方在其自身发展中具有最广泛的灵活性，包括根据其法律传统和国家考虑，引入和/或保持关于权利转让的规定的可能性。本着明确的精神，缔约各方应同意，是否规定权利转让并确定其性质和范围，将是缔约方的立法问题。

II. BROADCASTING AND COMMUNICATION TO THE PUBLIC RIGHTS

4. The right of broadcasting and communication to the public also gave rise to a lively debate during the last SCCR. On this occasion the representative of the European Community took the floor to explain that the Community position does not propose at this stage broadcasting and communication to public rights for performers in their fixed audiovisual performances. In fact, at the present stage, such a right does not form part of the "acquis communautaire." However, in the spirit of preserving the parallel with the WIPO Performances and Phonograms Treaty (WPPT), which underlies the Community proposal, he declared that the European Community was not in principle opposed to the granting of such a right, but before proposing it, wished to analyse both the possible economic effects of such a right and different solutions in order not to subvert existing balances between different actors of the market. Indeed, prior to any final conclusion on the nature and scope of such a right, it will be necessary to have regard to its possible economic effects taking account of the overall shape of the future protocol and in particular of the national treatment obligations enshrined therein.

5. If such a right were to be granted, at first sight the application *mutatis mutandis* of Article 15 of the WPPT seems difficult, as the assimilation of "phonograms published for commercial purposes" to "fixed performances, published for commercial purposes" (for instance videotapes), would greatly limit the scope of the right, given that it is rare, nowadays, for broadcasts of an audiovisual fixation, as opposed to phonograms, to take place on the basis of a carrier available on the market.

6. The European Community and its Member States consider therefore that, if such a right would prove to be necessary, it would be essential to envisage different drafting.

7. One possibility could be, on the basis of the mechanism foreseen by Article 15 of the WPPT, to adapt it to the specificity of the audiovisual sector so as to give performers the assurance of at least an equitable remuneration for the direct or indirect use of audiovisual fixations for broadcasting or for any communication to the public. The management of any right, to which the reservations provided for in Article 15(3) could be applied *mutatis mutandis*, could be entrusted to a collecting society.

[End of document]

二、广播权和向公众传播权

4. 在上一届会议中，广播权和向公众传播权也引发了激烈的讨论。在这种情况下，欧洲共同体的代表发言解释说，共同体的立场是不建议在该阶段赋予表演者在其视听录制品以广播权和向公众传播权。事实上，在目前阶段，这种权利并不构成欧共体法规的一部分。然而，本着维护作为共同体提案基础的《世界知识产权组织表演和录音制品条约》（WPPT）的精神，欧洲共同体原则上并不反对授予这种权利，但在提议之前应分析这种权利可能的经济影响和不同解决方案，以免破坏不同市场参与者之间现有的平衡。的确，在就这一权利的性质和范围得出最后结论之前，必须考虑到其可能的经济影响，同时考虑到未来议定书的总体形式，特别是其中所载的国民待遇义务。

5. 如果要授予这种权利，乍一看似乎很难比照 WPPT 第 15 条的规定，因为将“为商业目的出版的录音制品”同化为“为商业目的出版的固定表演”（如录像带），将大大限制权利的范围，因为现在很少有在市场上可以买到的载体基础上播放视听录制品，而不是录音制品的情况。

6. 因此，欧洲共同体及其成员国认为，如果这种权利被证明是必要的，则有必要设想不同的拟定方案。

7. 一种可能性是，根据 WPPT 第 15 条所设想的机制，使其适应视听领域的特殊性，从而使表演者至少能获得公平的报酬，以直接或间接用于视听录制品的广播或任何其他形式向公众传播。可以参照第 15 条第 3 款的保留条款，将这些权利的管理委托给集体管理组织。

（文件完）

4.3 Comparative Table of Proposals Received by February 28, 1999

Document Code: SCCR/2/4
Language: English
URL: https://www.wipo.int/edocs/mdocs/copyright/en/sccr_2/sccr_2_4.pdf

Chinese Translation: Not Available.
URL: N/A

STANDING COMMITTEE ON COPYRIGHT
AND RELATED RIGHTS
Second Session
Geneva, May 4 to 11, 1999

AGENDA ITEM 4: PROTECTION OF AUDIOVISUAL PERFORMANCES

COMPARATIVE TABLE OF PROPOSALS RECEIVED
BY FEBRUARY 28, 1999

prepared by the International Bureau

Introductory note

The Standing Committee on Copyright and Related Rights (SCCR), in its first session, recommended, as regards the protection of audiovisual performances, that the International Bureau prepare a comparative table of the proposals submitted by

4.3 截至 1999 年 2 月 28 日收到的提案比较表

文件编号：SCCR/2/4
文件语言：英语
文件链接：https://www.wipo.int/edocs/mdocs/copyright/en/sccr_2/sccr_2_4.pdf
中文文本：无
文件链接：无

版权及相关权常设委员会

第二届会议
1999 年 5 月 4 日至 11 日，日内瓦

议程项目四：保护视听表演

截至 1999 年 2 月 28 日收到的提案比较表

由国际局编制

介绍说明

版权及相关权常设委员会（SCCR）第一届会议提出，在保护视听表演方面，国际局应编制一份截至 1999 年 2 月 28 日各国政府和欧洲共同体提出的任何的修正提案。

Governments and the European Community as of February 28, 1999, including any revised proposal received before that date.

This comparative table is contained in the Annex. It is based on the following documents:

- SCCR/1/4, containing submissions received after the second session of the former Committee of Experts (June 1998) and by September 30, 1998.

- AP/CE/2/5, containing the proposal from Algeria, Burkina Faso, Cameroon, Ghana, Kenya, Malawi, Mali, Morocco, Namibia, Nigeria, Senegal, South Africa, Sudan, Togo and Zambia, (referred to in the Annex as "Certain States of Africa").

- SCCR/1/5, containing the Report on the Regional Consultation Meeting for Asia and the Pacific, held in Shanghai, from October 14 to 16, 1998 (referred to in the Annex as "Certain States of Asia and the Pacific").

- SCCR/1/8, containing a submission by Canada.

- AP/CE/2/2 and SCCR/2/3, containing submissions received from the European Community and its Member States.

- SCCR/2/2, containing the Report on the Regional Consultation Meeting for Countries of Latin America and the Caribbean, held in Geneva, in November 6, 1998 (referred to in the Annex as "Certain States of Latin America and the Caribbean").

- AP/CE/2/3, containing the proposal by the Republic of Korea.

The presentation follows the same organization and titling of subject matters, as used in the Comparative Table prepared for the second session of the Committee of Experts (document AP/CE/2/7), but without the former chapter "XIX. Implementation".

这份比较表载于附件。它基于以下文件:

—SCCR/1/4,载有第二次专家委员会(1998 年 6 月)之后和 1998 年 9 月 30 日之前收到的提案。

—AP/CE/2/5,载有阿尔及利亚、布基纳法索、喀麦隆、加纳、肯尼亚、马拉维、马里、摩洛哥、纳米比亚、尼日利亚、塞内加尔、南非、苏丹、多哥和赞比亚的提案(附件中称为“非洲某些国家”)。

—SCCR/1/5,载有 1998 年 10 月 14 日至 16 日在上海举行的亚洲及太平洋区域协商会议报告(附件中称为“亚洲及太平洋某些国家”)。

—SCCR/1/8,包含加拿大的提案。

—AP/CE/2/2 和 SCCR/2/3,包含从欧洲共同体及其成员国收到的提案。

—SCCR/2/2,载有 1998 年 11 月 6 日在日内瓦举行的拉丁美洲和加勒比国家区域协商会议报告(附件中称为“拉丁美洲和加勒比某些国家”)。

—AP/CE/2/3,载有韩国的提案。

本报告采用了为专家委员会第二届会议编制的比较表(AP/CE/2/7 号文件)中所使用相同的主题事项的组织,但没有以前的“第十九章 执行情况”。

COMPARATIVE TABLE OF THE PROPOSALS RECEIVED FROM WIPO MEMBER STATES AND THE EUROPEAN COMMUNITY

CONTENTS

附件
世界知识产权组织成员国和欧洲共同体的提案比较表

目录

I. TITLE

CERTAIN STATES OF AFRICA

Protocol to the WIPO Performances and Phonograms Treaty, concerning Audiovisual Performances.

CERTAIN STATES OF LATIN AMERICA AND THE CARIBBEAN

Protocol to the WIPO Performances and Phonograms Treaty Concerning Audiovisual Performances.

EUROPEAN COMMUNITY AND ITS MEMBER STATES

Protocol to the WIPO Performances and Phonograms Treaty, concerning Audiovisual Performances.

JAPAN

Protocol to the WIPO Performances and Phonograms Treaty concerning Audiovisual Performances.

UNITED STATES OF AMERICA

Substantive Provisions of a Treaty for the Protection of Performers in Audiovisual Works.

II. PREAMBLE

CERTAIN STATES OF AFRICA

The Contracting Parties,

Wishing to ensure an adequate level of protection for audiovisual performances, especially in the digital environment;

Noting that the WIPO Performances and Phonograms Treaty does not cover the moral or economic rights of performers in the audiovisual fixation of their unfixed performances, nor these rights in their audiovisually fixed performances;

Referring to the resolution concerning audiovisual performances adopted by the Diplomatic Conference on Certain Copyright and Neighboring Rights Questions on December 20, 1996;

Have agreed as follows:

CERTAIN STATES OF LATIN AMERICA AND THE CARIBBEAN

The Contracting Parties,

Wishing to ensure an adequate level of protection for performances in audiovisual works, owing to the fact that the development and convergence of new

一、标题

非洲某些国家

WPPT 关于视听表演的议定书

拉丁美洲和加勒比某些国家

WPPT 关于视听表演的议定书

欧洲共同体及其成员国

WPPT 关于视听表演的议定书

日本

WPPT 关于视听表演的议定书

美国

保护视听作品表演者条约的实质性条款

二、序言

非洲某些国家

缔约方，

希望确保对视听表演的充分保护，特别是在数字环境中；

注意到《世界知识产权组织表演和录音制品条约》既未提及表演者在未录制的视听表演中的精神或经济权利，也未提及在其录制的视听表演中的这些权利；

考虑到 1996 年 12 月 20 日关于版权及邻接权问题的外交会议通过的关于视听表演的决议；

达成协议如下：

拉丁美洲和加勒比某些国家

缔约方，

希望确保对视听表演的充分保护，由于新的信息和通信技术的发展和交汇将迅速扩大视听服务的范围，并增加表演者利用其表演的机会；

information and communication technology will bring about a rapid broadening of the range of audiovisual services and also an increase in the opportunities for performers to exploit their performances;

Referring to the Resolution Concerning Audiovisual Performances adopted by the Diplomatic Conference on Certain Copyright and Neighboring Rights Questions on December 20, 1996;

Have agreed as follows:

EUROPEAN COMMUNITY AND ITS MEMBER STATES

The Contracting Parties

Wishing to ensure an adequate level of protection for audiovisual performances, especially in the digital environment;

Noting that the WIPO Performances and Phonograms Treaty does not cover the rights of performers in the audiovisual fixation of their unfixed performances, nor the exploitation of their audiovisually fixed performances;

Referring to the resolution concerning audiovisual performances adopted by the Diplomatic Conference on Certain Copyright and Neighboring Rights Questions on December 20, 1996;

Have agreed as follows:

UNITED STATES OF AMERICA

The Contracting Parties,

Noting that the development and convergence of new information and communication technologies will allow for a rapid growth of audiovisual services and that this will increase the opportunities for performing artists to exploit their performances;

Recognizing the great importance of ensuring an adequate level of protection for these performances, in particular when they are exploited in the new digital environment;

Recognizing that the WIPO Performances and Phonograms Treaty (WPPT) does not cover the rights of performers in the audiovisual fixations of their performances, but that many provisions of the WPPT can be used or adapted as the basis for a new treaty protecting performers with respect to their audiovisual performances;

考虑到1996年12月20日关于版权及邻接权问题的外交会议通过的关于视听表演的决议；

达成协议如下：

欧洲共同体及其成员国

缔约方

希望确保对视听表演的充分保护，特别是在数字环境中；

注意到《世界知识产权组织表演和录音制品条约》既未提及表演者在未录制的视听表演中的精神或经济权利，也未提及表演者对其录制的视听表演利用的权利；

考虑到1996年12月20日关于版权及邻接权问题的外交会议通过的关于视听表演的决议；

达成协议如下：

美国

缔约方，

注意到新的信息和通信技术的发展和融合将使视听服务迅速增长，这将增加表演艺术家利用其表演的机会；

认识到确保对这些表演提供充分保护的重要性，特别是在新的数字环境中加以利用时；

认识到《世界知识产权组织表演和录音制品条约》（WPPT）没有规定表演者对未录制的视听表演的权利，但是《世界知识产权组织表演和录音制品条约》中的许多条款可以作为保护表演者的的视听表演新条约的基础；

Have agreed as follows:

III. RELATION TO OTHER CONVENTIONS AND TREATIES; RELATION TO COPYRIGHT

CERTAIN STATES OF AFRICA

Article 1

Relation to Other Conventions

(1) This Treaty constitutes a protocol to the WIPO Performances and Phonograms Treaty (hereinafter the “WPPT”).

(2) Nothing in this Protocol shall derogate from existing obligations that Contracting Parties have to each other under the WPPT.

(3) Protection granted under this Protocol shall leave intact and shall in no way affect the protection of copyright in literary and artistic works. Consequently, no provision of this Protocol may be interpreted to prejudice such protection.

CERTAIN STATES OF LATIN AMERICA AND THE CARIBBEAN

III. Relation to Other Conventions; Relation to Copyright

(1) This instrument constitutes a Protocol to the WIPO Performances and Phonograms Treaty done in Geneva on December 20, 1996 (hereinafter “the WIPO Treaty”).

(2) No provision of this Protocol shall detract from the mutual obligations of Contracting Parties under the International Convention for the Protection of Performers, Producers of Phonograms and Broadcasting Organizations, done at Rome on October 26, 1961 (hereinafter “the Rome Convention”).

(3) The protection granted under this Protocol shall leave intact and in no way affect the protection of copyright in literary and artistic works. Consequently no provision of this Treaty may be interpreted as prejudicing such protection.

(4) This Protocol shall have no connection with, and shall not prejudice any right or obligation under, any treaty other than the WIPO Treaty.

EUROPEAN COMMUNITY AND ITS MEMBER STATES

Article 1

Relation to Other Conventions

(1) This Treaty constitutes a Protocol to the WIPO Performances and Phonograms Treaty done in Geneva, 20 December 1996 (hereinafter the “WIPO

达成协议如下：

三、与其他公约、条约的关系；与版权的关系

非洲某些国家

第一条

与其他公约的关系

（1）本条约构成《世界知识产权组织表演和录音制品条约》（WPPT）的议定书。

（2）本议定书的任何内容均不得减损缔约方相互之间依照《世界知识产权组织表演和录音制品条约》已承担的现有义务。

（3）依本议定书给予的保护不得触动或以任何方式影响对文学和艺术作品版权的保护。因此，本条约的任何内容均不得被解释为损害此种保护。

拉丁美洲和加勒比某些国家

三、与其他公约、条约的关系；与版权的关系

（1）本文书构成1996年12月20日在日内瓦签订的《世界知识产权组织表演和录音制品条约》（WIPO条约）的议定书。

（2）本议定书的任何规定均不得减损缔约方根据1961年10月26日在罗马签订的《保护表演者、录音制品制作者和广播组织罗马公约》所承担的相互义务。

（3）依本议定书给予的保护不得触动或以任何方式影响对文学和艺术作品版权的保护。因此，本条约的任何内容均不得被解释为损害此种保护。

（4）除《世界知识产权组织条约》之外，本议定书与任何其他条约没有联系，也不得损害任何条约所规定的任何权利或义务。

欧洲共同体及其成员国

第一条

和其他公约的关系

（1）本条约构成1996年12月20日在日内瓦签订的《世界知识产权组织表演和录音制品条约》（WIPO条约）的议定书。

Treaty").

(2) Nothing in this Protocol shall derogate from existing obligations that Contracting Parties have to each other under the WIPO Treaty.

(3) Protection granted under this protocol shall leave intact and shall in no way affect the protection of copyright in literary and artistic works. Consequently, no provisions of this protocol may be interpreted as prejudicing such protection.

JAPAN

Article 1

Relation to Other Conventions

(1) This Treaty constitutes a Protocol to the WIPO Performances and Phonograms Treaty (hereinafter the "WPPT").

(2) Nothing in this Protocol shall derogate from existing obligations that Contracting Parties have to each other under the International Convention for the Protection of Performers, Producers of Phonograms and Broadcasting Organization done in Rome, October 26, 1961.

(3) Protection granted under this Protocol shall leave intact and shall in no way affect the protection of copyright in literary and artistic works. Consequently, no provision of this Protocol may be interpreted as prejudicing such protection.

(4) This Protocol shall not prejudice any rights and obligations under any other treaties.

UNITED STATES OF AMERICA

Article 1

Relation to Other Conventions

(1) Nothing in this Treaty shall derogate from existing obligations that Contracting Parties have to each other under the International Convention for the Protection of Performers, Producers of Phonograms and Broadcasting Organizations done in Rome, October 26, 1961.

(2) Protection granted under this Treaty shall leave intact and shall in no way affect the protection of copyright in literary and artistic works. Consequently, no provision of this Treaty may be interpreted as prejudicing such protection.

(3) This Treaty shall not have any connection with, nor shall it prejudice any rights and obligations under any other treaties.

（2）本议定书的任何规定均不得减损缔约方相互之间依照《世界知识产权组织条约》已承担的现有义务。

（3）依本议定书给予的保护不得触动或以任何方式影响对文学和艺术作品版权的保护。因此，本条约的任何内容均不得被解释为损害此种保护。

日本

第一条

和其他公约的关系

（1）本条约构成《世界知识产权组织表演和录音制品条约》（WPPT）的议定书。

（2）本议定书不得减损缔约方相互之间依照1961年10月26日在罗马签订的《保护表演者、录音制品制作者和广播组织罗马公约》已承担的现有义务。

（3）依本议定书给予的保护不得触动或以任何方式影响对文学和艺术作品版权的保护。因此，本条约的任何内容均不得被解释为损害此种保护。

（4）本议定书不损害任何其他条约规定的任何权利和义务。

美国

第一条

和其他公约的关系

（1）本条约的任何规定不得减损缔约双方相互之间根据1961年10月26日在罗马签订的《保护表演者、录音制品制作者和广播组织罗马公约》已承担的现有义务。

（2）依本议定书给予的保护不得触动或以任何方式影响对文学和艺术作品版权的保护。因此，本条约的任何内容均不得被解释为损害此种保护。

（3）本条约与其他任何条约无任何联系，也不损害任何其他条约规定的任何权利和义务。

IV. DEFINITIONS

CERTAIN STATES OF AFRICA

Article 2

Definitions

For the purposes of this Protocol:

(a) "performers" means actors, singers, musicians, dancers, and other persons who act, sing, deliver, declaim, play in, interpret, or otherwise perform literary or artistic works, or expressions of folklore;

(b) "audiovisual fixation" means the embodiment of moving images, whether or not accompanied by sound, or the representations thereof, from which they can be perceived, reproduced, or communicated through a device.

CERTAIN STATES OF LATIN AMERICA AND THE CARIBBEAN

IV. Definitions

(1) The Contracting Parties shall apply, *mutatis mutandis*, the definitions set out in Article 2 (a), (e), (f) and (g) of the WIPO Treaty in connection with the protection granted under this Protocol.

(2) For the purposes of this Protocol, "audiovisual fixation" means the embodiment of images, whether or not accompanied by sound, or the representation thereof, from which they can be perceived, reproduced or communicated by means of a device.

(3) For the purposes of this Protocol, "performers" means all actors, singers, musicians, dancers or other persons who interpret a role, sing, recite, declaim or in any way perform literary or artistic works or expressions of folklore, with the exception of extras [the definition of the latter term being left to the legislation of each Contracting Party].

EUROPEAN COMMUNITY AND ITS MEMBER STATES

Article 2

Definitions

(1) The Contracting Parties shall apply, *mutatis mutandis*, the definitions set out in Article 2 paragraphs (a), (f) and (g) of the WIPO Treaty in connection with the protection granted under this Protocol.

(2) For the purposes of this Protocol, "audiovisual fixation" means the

四、定义

非洲某些国家

第二条

定义

就本议定书而言：

（a）“表演者”是指演员、歌唱家、音乐家舞蹈家或其他演绎角色、歌唱、背诵、朗诵或以其他方式进行表演的其他人员；

（b）“视听录制品”系指活动图像的体现物，且从中可通过某种装置感觉、复制或传播该活动图像，不论是否伴有声音或声音的表现物。

拉丁美洲和加勒比某些国家

四、定义

（1）各缔约方应比照适用《世界知识产权组织条约》第2条（a）、（e）、（f）和（g）款中关于本议定书授予保护的定义。

（2）就本议定书而言，“视听录制品”系指活动图像的体现物，且从中可通过某种装置感觉、复制或传播该活动图像，不论是否伴有声音或声音的表现物。

（3）就本议定书而言，“表演者”系指演员、歌唱家、音乐家舞蹈家或其他演绎角色、歌唱、背诵、朗诵或以其他方式进行表演的其他人员；除了临时演员（后者的定义留由各缔约方的法律规定）。

欧洲共同体及其成员国

第二条

定义

（1）各缔约方应比照适用《世界知识产权组织条约》第2条（a）、（e）、（f）和（g）款中关于本议定书授予的保护的定义。

（2）就本议定书而言，“视听录制品”系指活动图像的体现物，且从中可通

embodiment of moving images, whether or not accompanied by sound, or the representations thereof, from which they can be perceived, reproduced or communicated through a device.

JAPAN

Article 2

Definitions

(1) Contracting Parties shall apply, *mutatis mutandis*, the definitions set out in paragraphs (a), (f) and (g) of Article 2 of the WPPT in connection with the protection granted under this Protocol.

(2) For the purposes of this Protocol, "audiovisual fixation" means the embodiment of moving images, whether or not accompanied by sound, or of the representations thereof, from which they can be perceived, reproduced or communicated through a device.

UNITED STATES OF AMERICA

Article 2

Definitions

For the purposes of this Treaty:

(a) "performers" are actors, singers, musicians, dancers, and other persons who act, sing, deliver, declaim, play in, interpret, or otherwise perform literary or artistic works or expressions of folklore, but not including ancillary performers considered such by professional practice;

(b) "fixation" means the embodiment of images, or of images and sounds, or of the representations thereof, from which they can be perceived, reproduced, or communicated through a device;

(c) "broadcasting" means the transmission by wireless means for public reception of images, or of images and sounds, or the representations thereof; such transmission by satellite is also "broadcasting;" transmission of encrypted signals is "broadcasting" where the means for decrypting are provided to the public by the broadcasting organization or with its consent;

(d) "communication to the public" means the transmission to the public by any medium, otherwise than by broadcasting, of the images, or the sounds and images, or the representations thereof, comprised in an unfixed performance or in a fixed

过某种装置感觉、复制或传播该活动图像，不论是否伴有声音或声音的表现物。

日本

第二条

定义

(1)各缔约方应比照适用《世界知识产权组织表演和录音制品条约》第2条(a)、(e)、(f)和(g)款中关于本议定书授予保护的定义。

(2)就本议定书而言，"视听录制品"指活动图像的体现物，且从中可通过某种装置感觉、复制或传播该活动图像，不论是否伴有声音或声音的表现物。

美国

第二条

定义

就本条约而言：

(a)"表演者"指演员、歌唱家、音乐家、舞蹈家以及对文学或艺术作品或民间文学艺术表达进行表演、歌唱、演说、朗诵、演奏、表现或以其他方式进行表演的其他人员，但不包括专业表演中的辅助表演者；

(b)"录制品"指活动图像、图像和声音或表演本身，从中通过某种装置可感觉、复制或传播该活动图像。

(c)"广播"指以无线方式向公众传送图像、图像和声音，或图像和声音的表现物；通过卫星进行的此种传送亦为"广播"；传送密码信号，只要广播组织或经其同意向公众提供了解码的手段，即为"广播"；

(d)"向公众传播"指通过广播以外的任何媒介向公众传播由未录制的表演或录制表演组成的图像、声音和图像或其表演本身；

performance;

(e) an "audiovisual work" is a work consisting of a series of related images that impart an impression of motion and are intended to be shown by the use of a device, together with any accompanying sounds.

V. BENEFICIARIES OF PROTECTION

CERTAIN STATES OF AFRICA

Article 3

Beneficiaries of Protection under this Protocol

The Contracting Parties shall accord the protection granted under this Protocol to performers who are nationals of other Contracting Parties.

CERTAIN STATES OF ASIA AND THE PACIFIC

9. The protection granted to performers under the Protocol should be restricted to nationals of Contracting Parties to the instrument.

CERTAIN STATES OF LATIN AMERICA AND THE CARIBBEAN

V. Beneficiaries of Protection

The Contracting Parties shall accord the protection provided under this Protocol:

(a) to performers who are nationals of other Contracting Parties;

(b) to performers who are not nationals of any of the Contracting Parties but are ordinarily resident in one of them, who shall be treated as nationals of the Contracting Party concerned.

EUROPEAN COMMUNITY AND ITS MEMBER STATES

Article 3

Beneficiaries of protection under this protocol

The Contracting Parties shall accord the protection provided under this protocol to performers who are nationals of other Contracting Parties.

JAPAN

Article 3

Beneficiaries of Protection under this Protocol

Contracting Parties shall accord the protection granted under this Protocol to the performers who are nationals of other Contracting Parties.

(e)“视听作品”是由一系列相关联的图像组成的作品，这些图像给人以运动的印象，并旨在通过使用设备显示的相关图像以及任何伴随的声音组成的作品。

五、保护的受益人

非洲某些国家

第三条

本议定书下保护的受益人

缔约各方应将本条约规定的保护授予系其他缔约方国民的表演者。

亚洲和太平洋地区某些国家

9. 本条约规定的对表演者的保护应限于文书缔约方的国民。

拉丁美洲和加勒比某些国家

五、保护的受益人

缔约各方应将本条约规定的保护给予：

(a)系其他缔约方国民的表演者；

(b)非缔约方国民但经常居住在其中一个缔约方的表演者，应视作该缔约方的国民。

欧洲共同体及其成员国

第三条

本议定书下保护的受益人

缔约各方应将本条约规定的保护授予系其他缔约方国民的表演者。

日本

第三条

本议定书下保护的受益人

缔约各方应将本条约规定的保护授予系其他缔约方国民的表演者。

UNITED STATES OF AMERICA

Article 3

Beneficiaries of Protection

(1) Contracting Parties shall accord the protection provided under this Treaty to performers of other Contracting Parties as defined in paragraph (2) of this Article.

(2) Performers of other Contracting Parties shall be understood to be performers who meet any of the following conditions:

(a) those performers who are nationals of another Contracting Party and whose performance is unfixed or is fixed in an audiovisual work;

(b) those performers whose unfixed performance takes place on the territory of another Contracting Party;

(c) those performers whose performance is first fixed in an audiovisual work on the territory of another Contracting Party.

(3) Performers who are not nationals of one of the Contracting Parties but who have their habitual residence in one of them shall, for the purposes of this Treaty, be assimilated to nationals of that Contracting Party.

VI. NATIONAL TREATMENT

CERTAIN STATES OF AFRICA

Article 4

National Treatment

(1) Each Contracting Party shall accord to nationals of other Contracting Parties, in respect of the subject matter protected under this Protocol:

(a) the rights specifically granted by this Protocol; and

(b) such additional rights as it accords to its own nationals.

(2) A Contracting Party shall be entitled, in respect of nationals of any other Contracting Party, to limit the protection provided for in subparagraph (b) of paragraph (1) to the extent to which, and to the term for which, the latter Contracting Party grants such rights to the nationals of the former Contracting Party.

CERTAIN STATES OF LATIN AMERICA AND THE CARIBBEAN

VI. National Treatment

Each Contracting Party shall accord to the nationals of other Contracting Parties the same treatment as it accords to its own nationals with respect to the

美国

第三条

保护的受益人

（1）缔约各方应将本条约规定的保护授予根据本条第（2）款规定的其他缔约方国民的表演者。

（2）其他缔约方国民的表演者应被视为符合下列条件之一的表演者：

（a）属于其他缔约方国民的表演者，其表演尚未录制或已录制为视听作品；

（b）在其他缔约方境内进行未录制的表演的表演者；

（c）表演第一次录制为视听作品在其他缔约方境内的表演者。

（3）非缔约方国民但在一个缔约方境内有惯常居所的表演者，在本条约中视同该缔约方的国民。

六、国民待遇

非洲某些国家

第四条

国民待遇

（1）在本条约所专门授予的权利，每一缔约方均应将其给予其他缔约方的国民：

（a）本议定书规定的权利；

（b）给予本国国民的额外的权利。

（2）缔约方有权将其依本条第（1）款第（b）项给予另一缔约方国民的保护限制在其本国国民在该缔约方享有的那些权利的范围和期限之内。

拉丁美洲和加勒比某些国家

六、国民待遇

在本条约所专门授予的专有权，每一缔约方均应将其给予本国国民的待遇给予其他缔约方的国民。

rights specifically granted in this Protocol.

EUROPEAN COMMUNITY AND ITS MEMBER STATES

Article 6

Application of certain substantive provisions of the WIPO Treaty

The Contracting Parties shall apply, *mutatis mutandis*, in respect of protection granted under this Protocol, the provisions of Articles 4 (National Treatment)... of the WIPO Treaty.

JAPAN

Article 4

National Treatment

(1) Each Contracting Party shall accord to nationals of other Contracting Parties the treatment it accords to its own nationals with regard to exclusive rights specifically granted in this Protocol, and to the right to equitable remuneration provided for in Article 10 of this Protocol.

(2) Notwithstanding the provisions of paragraph (1), any Contracting Party may, as regards performers who are nationals of another Contracting Party, limit the protection provided for in Article 10 to the extent to which, and to the term for which, the latter Contracting Party grants protection to performers who are nationals of the former Contracting Party.

REPUBLIC OF KOREA

5. Concerning the right to remuneration for broadcasting and communication to the public of fixed performances, reservation on national treatment should be permitted in this protocol in the manner as provided in the WPPT.

UNITED STATES OF AMERICA

Article 4

National Treatment

With respect to performances for which they are protected under this Treaty as provided in Article 3, performers shall enjoy, in other Contracting Parties, the treatment that the laws of such parties do now or may hereafter grant to their own nationals, as well as the rights specifically granted by this Treaty.

欧洲共同体及其成员国

第六条

WIPO 条约某些实质性条款的适用

本议定书授予的权利，缔约各方应比照适用 WIPO 条约第 4 条(国民待遇)。

日本

第四条

国民待遇

(1)本议定书授予其国民的专有权以及本议定书第 10 条规定的获得公平的报酬的权利，各缔约方应授予其他缔约方国民上述同等的权利。

(2)尽管有第(1)款的规定，缔约方可将依据第 10 条给予另一缔约方国民的表演者提供的保护限制在其本国国民在该另一缔约方获得保护的范围和期限内。

韩国

5. 关于广播和向公众传播已录制的表演获得合理报酬权利，本议定书应允许以 WPPT 规定的方式保留国民待遇。

美国

第四条

国民待遇

对于第 3 条规定的受本条约保护的表演，表演者在其他缔约方应享有该缔约方法律现在或以后给予本国国民的待遇，以及依据本条约特别授予的权利。

VII. FORMALITIES; INDEPENDENCE FROM PROTECTION IN COUNTRY OF ORIGIN

CERTAIN STATES OF AFRICA

Article 12

Application of Certain Substantive Provisions of the WPPT

The Contracting Parties shall apply, *mutatis mutandis*, in respect of the protection granted under this Protocol, the provisions of Articles... 20 (Formalities)... of the WPPT.

CERTAIN STATES OF ASIA AND THE PACIFIC

17. Follow the WPPT approach in relation to these areas.

CERTAIN STATES OF LATIN AMERICA AND THE CARIBBEAN

VII. Formalities

The enjoyment and exercise of the rights provided for in this Protocol shall not be subject to any formality.

JAPAN

Article 5

Formalities

Contracting Parties shall apply, *mutatis mutandis*, in respect of the protection granted under this Protocol, the provisions of Article 20 (Formalities) of the WPPT.

EUROPEAN COMMUNITY AND ITS MEMBER STATES

Article 6

Application of certain substantive provisions of the WIPO Treaty

The Contracting Parties shall apply, *mutatis mutandis*, in respect of protection granted under this Protocol, the provisions of Articles... 20 (Formalities)... of the WIPO Treaty.

UNITED STATES OF AMERICA

Article 16

Formalities

The enjoyment and exercise of the rights provided for in this Treaty shall not be subject to any formality.

七、手续；与本国保护无关

非洲某些国家

第 12 条

WPPT 中某些实质性条款的适用

缔约各方就本议定书给予的保护、条款的适用应比照 WPPT 第 20 条有关手续的条款。

亚洲和太平洋地区某些国家

17. 在这方面遵循 WPPT 的规定。

拉丁美洲和加勒比某些国家

七、手续

本议定书规定的权利的享有和行使无需任何手续。

日本

第 5 条

手续

缔约各方就本议定书给予的保护、条款的适用应比照 WPPT 第 20 条有关手续的条款。

欧洲共同体及其成员国

第 6 条

WIPO 条约某些实质性条款的适用

缔约各方就本议定书给予的保护、条款的适用应比照 WIPO 条约第 20 条有关手续的条款。

美国

第 16 条

手续

本条约规定的权利的享有和行使无需任何手续。

VIII. MORAL RIGHTS OF PERFORMERS

CERTAIN STATES OF AFRICA

Article 5

Moral Rights of Performers

(1) Independently of a performer's economic rights, and even after the transfer of those rights, a performer shall, as regards his performances, whether live or embodied in audiovisual fixations, have the right:

(a) to be identified as the performer of his performances, except where omission is dictated by the manner of the use of the performance; and

(b) to object to any distortion, mutilation, or other modification of his performances that would be prejudicial to his reputation.

(2) The rights granted to a performer in accordance with paragraph (1) shall, after his death, be maintained, at least until the expiry of the economic rights, and shall be exercisable by the person or institution authorized by the legislation of the Contracting Party where protection is claimed. However, those Contracting Parties whose legislation, at the moment of their ratification of this Protocol, does not provide for protection after the death of the performer of all rights set out in the preceding paragraph may provide that some of these rights will, after his death, cease to be maintained.

(3) The means of redress for safeguarding the rights granted under this Article shall be governed by the legislation of the Contracting Party where protection is claimed.

CERTAIN STATES OF ASIA AND THE PACIFIC

11. Moral rights need to be qualified to allow for development in technology and to facilitate commercial exploitation of films by producers.

CERTAIN STATES OF LATIN AMERICA AND THE CARIBBEAN

VIII. Moral Rights of Performers

(1) Independently of the performer's economic rights, and even after the transfer of those rights, the performer shall, as regards his live audiovisual performances, with or without sounds, or performances included in audiovisual fixations, have the right to claim to be identified as the performer of his performances, except where omission is dictated by the manner of the use of the

八、表演者的精神权利

非洲某些国家

第5条

表演者的精神权利

(1)独立于表演者的经济权利,甚至在这些权利转让之后,表演者仍应对于其现场表演或以视听录制品录制的表演享有权利:

(a)承认其系表演的表演者,除非因使用表演的方式而决定可省略不提其系表演者;以及

(b)反对任何对其表演进行的将有损其声誉的歪曲、篡改或其他修改。

(2)根据第(1)款授予表演者的权利在其死亡后应继续保留,至少到其经济权利期满为止,并可由被要求提供保护的缔约方立法所授权的个人或机构行使。但批准本议定书时其立法尚未规定在表演者死亡后保护上款所述全部权利的国家,则可规定其中部分权利在表演者死亡后不再保留。

(3)为保障本条所授予的权利而采取的补救方法应由被要求提供保护的缔约方立法规定。

亚洲和太平洋地区某些国家

11. 精神权利的规定应当与技术发展、促进制作人对电影的商业利用相适应。

拉丁美洲和加勒比某些国家

八、表演者的精神权利

(1)独立于表演者的经济权利,甚至在这些权利转让之后,表演者仍应对于其现场表(无论是否伴有声音)或以视听录制品录制的表演享有权利:要求承认其系表演的表演者,除非因使用表演的方式而决定可省略不提其系表演者;(反对任何对其表演进行的将有损其声誉的歪曲、篡改或其他修改,且这种修改不是作品制作者或其利益继承人根据制片人在演出中获得的授权对视听作品

performance, and to object to any distortion, mutilation or other modification of his performances that would be prejudicial to his reputation, provided that the audiovisual producer may abridge, condense, edit or dub the work, but without thereby distorting the performance of the performer.

(2) The rights granted to the performer in accordance with the foregoing paragraph shall, after his death, be maintained, at least until the expiry of his economic rights, and shall be exercisable by the persons or institutions authorized by the legislation of the Contracting Party where protection is claimed. However, those Contracting Parties whose legislation, at the moment of their ratification of or accession to this Treaty does not provide for protection after the death of the performer of all rights set out in the preceding paragraph may provide that some of those rights will, after his death, cease to be maintained.

(3) The means of redress for safeguarding the rights granted under this Article shall be governed by the legislation of the Contracting Party where protection is claimed.

EUROPEAN COMMUNITY AND ITS MEMBER STATES

Article 4

Rights of performers in their unfixed audiovisual performances

The Contracting Parties shall accord, *mutatis mutandis*, to performers, as regards their unfixed audiovisual performances, whether or not accompanied by sound, the same rights as those granted under the WIPO Treaty to performers as regards their live aural performances, namely the rights provided under Article 5 (Moral Rights)...

Article 5

Rights of performers in audiovisual fixations of their performances

The Contracting Parties shall accord, *mutatis mutandis*, to performers, as regards the use of audiovisual fixations of their performances, the same rights as those granted under the WIPO Treaty to performers as regards the use of their performances fixed in phonograms, namely the rights provided under Articles 5 (Moral Rights), ... of the WIPO Treaty.

进行正常利用的一部分)。

(2)表演者的权利在其死亡后应继续保留,至少到其经济权利期满为止,并可由被要求提供保护的缔约各方立法所授权的个人或机构行使。但批准或加入本条约时其立法尚未规定在表演者死亡后保护上款所述全部权利的缔约方,则可规定其中部分权利在表演者死亡后不再保留。

(3)为保障本条所授予的权利而采取的救济措施应由被要求提供保护的缔约方立法规定。

欧洲共同体及其成员国

第 4 条

表演者对其尚未录制的表演的权利

缔约各方应比照适用 WIPO 条约第 5 条(精神权利)所赋予的权利,授予表演者对其现场表演和尚未录制表演的权利,无论其是否伴有声音。

第 5 条

表演者对其表演的视听录制品享有的权利

缔约各方在使用表演者的视听录制品时,应比照适用 WIPO 条约第 5 条(精神权利)规定中授予表演者对其已录制表演的权利相同的权利。

UNITED STATES OF AMERICA

Article 5

Moral Rights of Performers

(1) Independently of a performer's economic rights, and even after the transfer of those rights, the performer shall, as regards his or her live performances or performances fixed in an audiovisual fixation, have the right to claim to be identified as the performer of such performances, except where omission is dictated by the manner of the use of the performance, and to object to any distortion, mutilation, or other modification of his or her performance that would be seriously prejudicial to the performer's reputation. Modifications consistent with the normal exploitation of an audiovisual work undertaken by the producer of the work or the producer's successors in interest, pursuant to the exercise of rights of authorization acquired by the producer in the performance, shall not be considered seriously prejudicial to the performer's reputation.

(2) The rights granted to a performer in accordance with paragraph (1) shall, after the said performer's death, be maintained, at least until the expiry of the rights of authorization set forth in Articles 6 through 10, and shall be exercisable by the persons or institutions authorized by the legislation of the Contracting Party where protection is claimed. However, those Contracting Parties whose legislation, at the moment of their ratification of or accession to this Treaty, does not provide for protection after the death of the performer of all rights set out in the preceding paragraph, may provide that some of these rights will, after the performer's death, cease to be maintained.

(3) The means of redress for safeguarding the rights granted under this Article shall be governed by the legislation of the Contracting Party where protection is claimed.

(4) The "normal exploitation of an audiovisual work" shall include the use of new or changed technology, media, formats and/or methods of distribution, dissemination, making available or communication to the public. A performer shall give reasonable consideration to the interests of the other performers in the work, the writers of scenarios, dialogues or musical works created for the work, and the principal director of the work when seeking to exercise the above described rights

美国

第五条

表演者的精神权利

（1）独立于表演者的经济权利，甚至在这些权利转让之后，表演者仍应对于其现场表演或以视听录制品录制的表演享有权利：要求承认其系表演的表演者，除非因使用表演的方式而决定可省略不提其系表演者；反对任何对其表演进行的将有损其声誉的歪曲、篡改或其他修改，且这种修改不是作品制作者或其利益继承人根据制片人在演出中获得的授权对视听作品进行正常利用的一部分。

（2）根据第（1）款给予表演者的权利在其死亡后应继续保留，至少在第 6 条至第 10 条规定的权利期满为止，并可由被要求提供保护的缔约方立法所授权的个人或机构行使。但批准或加入本条约时其立法尚未规定在表演者死亡后保护上款所述全部权利的国家，则可规定其中部分权利在表演者死亡后不再保留。

（3）为保障本条所授予的权利而采取的救济措施应由被要求提供保护的缔约方立法规定。

（4）“视听作品的正常利用”应包括使用新的或经改变的技术、媒介、版式和 / 或向公众发行、宣传、提供或者传播的方法。表演者在行使上述作品权利时，应当合理考虑视听作品的其他表演者和场景、对话或音乐作品的编写者以及作品的主要导演的利益。

with respect to such work.

IX. RIGHTS OF PERFORMERS IN THEIR UNFIXED PERFORMANCES

CERTAIN STATES OF AFRICA

Article 6

Right of Fixation of Unfixed Performances

Performers shall enjoy the exclusive right of authorizing the audiovisual fixation of their unfixed performances.

CERTAIN STATES OF ASIA AND THE PACIFIC

13. The principles adopted in the WIPO Performances and Phonograms Treaty, …, should be followed in relation to these rights.

CERTAIN STATES OF LATIN AMERICA AND THE CARIBBEAN

IX. Economic Rights of Performers in their Unfixed Performances

Performers shall enjoy the exclusive right to authorize the following in relation to their unfixed performances:

(i) broadcasting and communication to the public of their unfixed performances, except where the performance constitutes a broadcast performance in itself;

(ii) fixation of their unfixed performances.

EUROPEAN COMMUNITY AND ITS MEMBER STATES

Article 4

Rights of performers in their unfixed audiovisual performances

The Contracting Parties shall accord, *mutatis mutandis*, to performers, as regards their unfixed audiovisual performances, whether or not accompanied by sound, the same rights as those granted under the WIPO Treaty to performers as regards their live aural performances, namely the rights provided under Article… 6 (Economic rights of Performers in their unfixed performances).

JAPAN

Article 7

Economic Rights of Performers in their Unfixed Performances

Contracting Parties shall accord, *mutatis mutandis*, to performers, as regards their unfixed audiovisual performances, whether or not accompanied by sound, the same rights as those provided for in Article 6 (Economic Rights of Performers in

九、表演者对其尚未录制的表演的权利

非洲某些国家

第六条

对未录制表演的录制权

表演者享有授权录制其未录制的表演的专有权。

亚洲和太平洋地区某些国家

13. 这些权利,应遵循《世界知识产权组织表演和录音制品条约》规定的原则。

拉丁美洲和加勒比某些国家

九、表演者对其尚未录制的表演的经济权利

表演者享有对其未录制的表演授权的专有权:

(i)广播和向公众传播其尚未录制的表演,除非该表演本身已属广播表演;

(ii)录制其尚未录制的表演。

欧洲共同体及其成员国

第4条

表演者对其未录制的视听表演的权利

缔约方应就表演者未录制的视听表演,不论是否伴有声音,比照给予其与WIPO条约规定的给予表演者的对现场音乐表演的同样权利,即第6条规定的表演者对其未录制表演的经济权利。

日本

第7条

表演者对未录制表演的经济权利

缔约方应就表演者未录制的视听表演,不论是否伴有声音,比照给予其与WPPT第6条规定的对未录制表演的经济权利相同的权利。

their Unfixed Performances) of the WPPT.

REPUBLIC OF KOREA

3. Performers shall enjoy the following exclusive rights of authorizing their unfixed audiovisual performances:

(a) fixation;

(b) broadcasting and communication to the public.

UNITED STATES OF AMERICA

Article 6

Economic Rights of Performers in their Unfixed Performances

Performers shall enjoy the exclusive right of authorizing, as regards their performances:

(i) the broadcasting and communication to the public of their unfixed performances, except where the performance is already a broadcast performance; and

(ii) the fixation of their unfixed performances.

X. RIGHTS OF PERFORMERS IN AUDIOVISUAL FIXATIONS

1. Right of reproduction

CERTAIN STATES OF AFRICA

Article 7

Right of Reproduction

Performers shall enjoy the exclusive right of authorizing the direct or indirect reproduction, in any manner or form, of audiovisual fixations of their performances.

CERTAIN STATES OF ASIA AND THE PACIFIC

13. The principles adopted in the WIPO Performances and Phonograms Treaty, including those incorporated in the Agreed Statements reproduced in the footnotes to the WPPT, should be followed in relation to these rights.

CERTAIN STATES OF LATIN AMERICA AND THE CARIBBEAN

1. Right of reproduction

Performers shall enjoy the exclusive right to authorize the direct or indirect reproduction of their performances incorporated in audiovisual fixations in any manner or form.

韩国

3. 表演者对其未录制的视听表演享有以下排他权：

(a)录制权；

(b)广播和向公众传播权。

美国

第 6 条

表演者对其未录制表演的经济权利

表演者应享有专有权，对于其表演授权：

(i)广播和向公众传播其尚未录制的表演，除非该表演本身已属广播表演；和

(ii)录制其尚未录制的表演。

十、表演者对其视听录制品的权利

1. 复制权

非洲某些国家

第 7 条

复制权

表演者应享有授权以任何方式或形式对其表演的视听录制品录制的表演直接或间接地进行复制的专有权。

亚洲和太平洋地区某些国家

13. 这些权利，应遵循《世界知识产权组织表演和录音制品条约》所通过的原则，包括载于世界知识产权会议脚注声明的原则。

拉丁美洲和加勒比某些国家

1. 复制权

表演者应享有授权以任何方式或形式对其以视听录制品录制的表演直接或间接地进行复制的专有权。

EUROPEAN COMMUNITY AND ITS MEMBER STATES

Article 5

Rights of performers in audiovisual fixations of their performances

The Contracting Parties shall accord, *mutatis mutandis*, to performers, as regards the use of audiovisual fixations of their performances, the same rights as those granted under the WIPO Treaty to performers as regards the use of their performances fixed in phonograms, namely the rights provided under Articles… 7 (Right of Reproduction)… of the WIPO Treaty.

JAPAN

Article 8

Economic Rights of Performers in their Performances fixed in Audiovisual Fixations

Contracting Parties shall accord, *mutatis mutandis*, to performers, as regards the exploitation of their performances fixed in audiovisual fixations, the same rights as those provided for in Articles 7 (Right of Reproduction)… of the WPPT.

REPUBLIC OF KOREA

4. Performers shall enjoy the following rights of their fixed audiovisual performances:

(a) the exclusive right to authorize the reproduction;

UNITED STATES OF AMERICA

Article 7

Right of Reproduction

Performers shall enjoy the exclusive right of authorizing the direct or indirect reproduction of their fixed performances in any manner or form.

2. Right of distribution

CERTAIN STATES OF AFRICA

Article 8

Right of Distribution

(1) Performers shall enjoy the exclusive right of authorizing the making available to the public of the original and copies of the audiovisual fixations of their performances through sale or other transfer of ownership.

(2) Nothing in this Protocol shall affect the freedom of Contracting Parties

欧洲共同体及其成员国

第 5 条

表演者对其视听录制品中表演的权利

缔约方在对视听录制品的使用方面，应比照在 WIPO 条约中给予表演者的使用其录制在录音制品上的表演的权利，即 WIPO 条约第 7 条规定的复制权。

日本

第 8 条

表演者对其录制在视听录制品中的表演的经济权利

缔约方给予表演者利用其录制在视听录制品中的表演的权利，应比照 WPPT 第 7 条（复制权）规定的权利。

韩国

4. 表演者对其已录制的视听录制品享有以下权利：

（a）授权复制的专有权；

美国

第 7 条

复制权

表演者应享有授权以任何方式或形式对其以视听录制品录制的表演直接或间接地进行复制的专有权。

2. 发行权

非洲某些国家

第 8 条

发行权

（1）表演者应享有授权通过销售或其他所有权转让形式向公众提供其以视听录制品录制的表演的原件或复制件的专有权。

（2）对于已录制表演的原件或复制件经表演者授权被首次销售或以其他形

to determine the conditions, if any, under which the exhaustion of the right in paragraph (1) applies after the first sale or other transfer of ownership of the original or a copy of the fixed performance with the authorization of the performer.

CERTAIN STATES OF ASIA AND THE PACIFIC

13. The principles adopted in the WIPO Performances and Phonograms Treaty, including those incorporated in the Agreed Statements reproduced in the footnotes to the WPPT, should be followed in relation to these rights.

CERTAIN STATES OF LATIN AMERICA AND THE CARIBBEAN

2. Right of distribution

(i) Performers shall enjoy the exclusive right to authorize the making available to the public, through sale or other transfer of ownership, of the original and copies of their performances incorporated in audiovisual fixations.

(ii) Nothing in this Protocol shall affect the freedom of Contracting Parties to determine the conditions, if any, under which the exhaustion of the right in paragraph (1) applies after the first sale or other transfer of ownership of the original or a copy of the fixed performance with the authorization of the performer.

EUROPEAN COMMUNITY AND ITS MEMBER STATES

Article 5

Rights of performers in audiovisual fixations of their performances

The Contracting Parties shall accord, *mutatis mutandis*, to performers, as regards the use of audiovisual fixations of their performances, the same rights as those granted under the WIPO Treaty to performers as regards the use of their performances fixed in phonograms, namely the rights provided under Articles… 8 (Right of Distribution)… of the WIPO Treaty.

JAPAN

Article 8

Economic Rights of Performers in their Performances fixed in Audiovisual Fixations

Contracting Parties shall accord, *mutatis mutandis*, to performers, as regards the exploitation of their performances fixed in audiovisual fixations, the same rights as those provided for in Articles … 8 (Right of Distribution) … of the WPPT.

式转让所有权之后适用本条第（1）款中权利的用尽所依据的条件（如有此种条件），本条约的任何内容均不得影响缔约方确定该条件的自由。

亚洲及其太平洋地区某些国家

13. 这些权利，应遵循《世界知识产权组织表演和录音制品条约》所通过的原则，包括载于 WPPT 脚注议定声明。

拉丁美洲和加勒比某些国家

2. 发行权

（i）表演者应享有授权通过销售或其他所有权转让形式向公众提供其以视听录制品录制的表演的原件或复制件的专有权。

（ii）对于已录制表演的原件或复制件经表演者授权被首次销售或以其他形式转让所有权之后适用本条第（1）款中权利的用尽所依据的条件（如有此种条件），本条约的任何内容均不得影响缔约方确定该条件的自由。

欧洲共同体及其成员国

第 5 条

表演者对其视听录制品中表演的权利

缔约方在对其录制在视听录制品中的表演的使用，应比照 WIPO 条约给予表演者的使用其录制在录音制品上的表演的权利，即第 8 条规定的发行权。

日本

第 8 条

表演者对其录制在视听录制品中的表演的经济权利

缔约方给予表演者对其录制在视听录制品中的表演的使用的权利，应比照 WIPO 条约第 8 条规定的复制权。

UNITED STATES OF AMERICA

Article 8

Right of Distribution

(1) Performers shall enjoy the exclusive right of authorizing the making available to the public of the original and copies of their fixed performances through sale or other transfer of ownership.

(2) Nothing in this Treaty shall affect the freedom of Contracting Parties to determine the conditions, if any, under which the exhaustion of the right in paragraph (1) applies after the first sale or other transfer of ownership of the original or a copy of the fixed performance with the authorization of the performer.

3. Right of rental

CERTAIN STATES OF AFRICA

Article 9

Right of Rental

Performers shall enjoy the exclusive right of authorizing the commercial rental to the public of the original and copies of the audiovisual fixations of their performances. Contracting Parties are exempt from this obligation unless the commercial rental has led to widespread copying of the works which materially impairs the exclusive right of reproduction.

CERTAIN STATES OF LATIN AMERICA AND THE CARIBBEAN

3. Right of rental

(1) Performers shall enjoy the exclusive right to authorize the commercial rental to the public of copies of their audiovisual fixations.

(2) Paragraph (1) shall not be applicable in the case of an audiovisual work except where the said commercial rental has given rise to widespread copying thereof which considerably detracts from the performer's exclusive rights of reproduction.

EUROPEAN COMMUNITY AND ITS MEMBER STATES

Article 5

Rights of performers in audiovisual fixations of their performances

The Contracting Parties shall accord, *mutatis mutandis*, to performers, as regards the use of audiovisual fixations of their performances, the same rights as

美国

第8条

发行权

（1）表演者应享有授权通过销售或其他所有权转让形式向公众提供其以视听录制品录制的表演的原件或复制件的专有权。

（2）对于已录制表演的原件或复制件经表演者授权被首次销售或以其他形式转让所有权之后适用本条第（1）款中权利的用尽所依据的条件（如有此种条件），本条约的任何内容均不得影响缔约方确定该条件的自由。

3. 出租权

非洲其他国家

第9条

出租权

表演者享有授权将录有其表演的视听录制品原件和复制件向公众进行商业性出租的专有权。除非商业性出租已导致作品被广泛复制，从而在实质上损害了作品的专有复制权，否则缔约方不受此义务约束。

拉丁美洲和加勒比某些国家

3. 出租权

（1）表演者享有授权将其视听录制品的复制件向公众进行商业性出租的专有权。

（2）当商业性出租而造成大量复制，严重损害表演者的专有复制权时，第（1）项规定不适用于视听作品。

欧洲共同体及其成员国

第5条

表演者对视听录制品中的表演的权利

缔约方应比照WIPO条约规定的表演者使用其录制在录音制品上的表演的权利，给予表演者相同的权利使用其录制在视听录制品中的表演，即第9条

those granted under the WIPO Treaty to performers as regards the use of their performances fixed in phonograms, namely the rights provided under Articles… 9 (Right of Rental)… of the WIPO Treaty.

JAPAN

Article 8

Economic Rights of Performers in their Performances fixed in Audiovisual Fixations

…

(2) Contracting Parties shall accord to performers the exclusive right of authorizing the commercial rental to the public of the original and copies of their performances fixed in audiovisual fixations, even after distribution of them by or pursuant to authorization by the performer. A Contracting Party shall be excepted from this obligation unless such rental has led to widespread copying of such performances fixed in audiovisual fixations which is materially impairing the exclusive right of reproduction conferred in that Contracting Party on performers and their successors in title.

4. Right of making available

CERTAIN STATES OF AFRICA

Article 10

Right of Making Available of Fixed Performances

Performers shall enjoy the exclusive right of authorizing the making available to the public of audiovisual fixations of their performances, by wire or wireless means, in such a way that members of the public may access them from a place and at a time individually chosen by them.

CERTAIN STATES OF ASIA AND THE PACIFIC

13. The principles adopted in the WIPO Performances and Phonograms Treaty, including those incorporated in the Agreed Statements reproduced in the footnotes to the WPPT, should be followed in relation to these rights.

CERTAIN STATES OF LATIN AMERICA AND THE CARIBBEAN

4. Right of making available

Performers shall enjoy the exclusive right to authorize the making available to the public of their performances incorporated in audiovisual fixations, by wire or

规定的出租权。

日本

第8条

表演者对其录制在视听录制品中的表演的经济权利

……

（2）缔约方应授予表演者授权将其以视听录制品录制的表演的原件和复制件向公众进行商业性出租的专有权，即使这些原件和复制件已由表演者发行或经表演者授权发行。缔约方应免除这一义务，除非这种出租已导致此种录制在视听录制品中的表演的广泛复制，实质性损害了缔约方授予表演者及其名义继承人的专有复制权。

4. 提供权

非洲某些国家

第10条

提供已录制表演的权利

表演者应享有专有权，以授权通过有线或无线的方式向公众提供其以视听录制品录制的表演，使该表演可为公众中的成员在其个人选定的地点和时间获得。

亚洲及太平洋地区某些国家

13. 这些权利，应遵循《世界知识产权组织表演和录音制品条约》所通过的原则，包括载于WPPT脚注议定声明。

拉丁美洲和加勒比某些国家

4. 提供权

表演者应享有专有权，以授权通过有线或无线的方式向公众提供其以视听录制品录制的表演，使该表演可为公众中的成员在其个人选定的地点和时间获

wireless means, in such a way that members of the public may access them from a place and at a time individually chosen by them.

EUROPEAN COMMUNITY AND ITS MEMBER STATES

Article 5

Rights of performers in audiovisual fixations of their performances

The Contracting Parties shall accord, *mutatis mutandis*, to performers, as regards the use of audiovisual fixations of their performances, the same rights as those granted under the WIPO Treaty to performers as regards the use of their performances fixed in phonograms, namely the rights provided under Articles... 10 (Right of Making Available of Fixed Performances)... of the WIPO Treaty.

JAPAN

Article 8

Economic Rights of Performers in their Performances fixed in Audiovisual Fixations

(1) Contracting Parties shall accord, *mutatis mutandis*, to performers, as regards the exploitation of their performances fixed in audiovisual fixations, the same rights as those provided for in Articles ... 10 (Right of Making Available of Fixed Performances) of the WPPT.

REPUBLIC OF KOREA

4. Performers shall enjoy the following rights of their fixed audiovisual performances:

(b) the exclusive right of making available to the public, equivalent to the right given in the WPPT;

UNITED STATES OF AMERICA

ARTICLE 9

Right of Making Available

Performers shall enjoy the exclusive right of authorizing the making available to the public of their fixed performances, by wire or wireless means, in such a way that members of the public may access them from a place and at a time individually chosen by them.

得。

欧洲共同体及其成员国

第 5 条

表演者对视听录制品的权利

缔约方应比照 WIPO 条约第 10 条规定的提供已录制表演的权利，应给予表演者对其录制在视听录制品中的表演的使用相同的权利。

日本

第 8 条

表演者对其录制在视听录制品中的表演的经济权利

(1)缔约方应比照 WPPT 第 10 条规定的提供已录制表演的权利，应给予表演者对其录制在视听录制品中的表演的使用相同的权利。

韩国

4. 表演者对其录制的视听表演享有以下权利：

(b)向公众提供的专有权，同 WPPT 规定的权利相似；

美国

第 9 条

提供权

表演者应享有专有权，以授权通过有线或无线的方式向公众提供其以视听录制品录制的表演，使该表演可为公众中的成员在其个人选定的地点和时间获得。

5. Right of broadcasting and communication to the public

CERTAIN STATES OF ASIA AND THE PACIFIC

15. Article 15(3) of the WPPT would be a better option to follow.

CERTAIN STATES OF LATIN AMERICA AND THE CARIBBEAN

5. Right of broadcasting and communication to the public

No agreement having been reached, the discussions continue.

The Delegation of Brazil proposes omitting all provisions on the right of broadcasting or communication to the public.

EUROPEAN COMMUNITY AND ITS MEMBER STATES

II. BROADCASTING AND COMMUNICATION TO THE PUBLIC RIGHTS

"...prior to any final conclusion on the nature and scope of such a right, it will be necessary to have regard to its possible economic effects taking account of the overall shape of the future protocol and in particular of the National Treatment obligations enshrined therein.

If such a right were to be granted, at first sight the application mutatis mutandis of Article 15 of the WPPT seems difficult, as the assimilation of "phonograms published for commercial purposes" to "fixed performances, published for commercial purposes" (for instance videotapes), would greatly limit the scope of the right, given that it is rare, nowadays, for broadcasts of an audiovisual fixation, as opposed to phonograms, to take place on the basis of a carrier available on the market.

The European Community and its Member States consider therefore that, if such a right would prove to be necessary, it would be essential to envisage different drafting.

One possibility could be, on the basis of the mechanism foreseen by Article 15 of the WPPT, to adapt it to the specificity of the audiovisual sector so as to give performers the assurance of at least an equitable remuneration for the direct or indirect use of audiovisual fixations for broadcasting or for any communication to the public. The management of any right, to which the reservations provided for in Article 15 (3) could be applied mutatis mutandis, could be entrusted to a collecting society."

5. 广播权和向公众传播权

亚洲及太平洋地区某些国家

15. WPPT 第 15 条第 3 款是一个较好的参照。

拉丁美洲和加勒比某些国家

5. 广播权和向公众传播权

由于没有达成协议，讨论仍在继续。

巴西代表团建议略去关于广播和向公众传播权利的所有规定。

欧洲共同体及其成员国

2. 广播权和向公众传播权

“……在对这一权利的性质和范围作出任何最后结论之前，必须考虑到其可能的经济影响，同时考虑到未来议定书的总体形式，特别是其中所载国民待遇的义务。

如果要授予这种权利，乍一看似乎很难比照 WPPT 第 15 条的规定，因为将‘为商业目的出版的录音制品’同化为‘为商业目的出版的固定表演’（例如录像带），将大大限制权利的范围，因为现在很少有在市场上可以买到的载体基础上播放视听录制品，而不是录音制品的情况。

因此，欧洲共同体及其成员国认为，如果这种权利被证明是必要的，则有必要设想不同的拟定方案。

一种可能性是，根据 WPPT 第 15 条所设想的机制，使其适应视听领域的特殊性，从而使表演者至少能获得公平的报酬，以直接或间接用于视听录制品的广播或任何其他形式向公众传播。可以参照第 15 条第 3 款的保留条款，将这些权利的管理委托给集体管理组织。”

JAPAN

Article 10

Right to Remuneration of Performers in their Performances fixed in Audiovisual Fixations

Contracting Parties may establish in their national legislation the right to equitable remuneration of performers for the exploitation of their performances fixed in audiovisual fixations.

REPUBLIC OF KOREA

4. Performers shall enjoy the following rights of their fixed audiovisual performances:

(c) the right to remuneration for broadcasting and communication to the public.

5. Concerning the right to remuneration for broadcasting and communication to the public of fixed performances, reservation on national treatment should be permitted in this protocol in the manner as provided in the WPPT.

UNITED STATES OF AMERICA

Article 10

Right of Broadcasting and Communication to the Public

Except for conditions on the exercise of the right that would be permissible for audiovisual works under Article 11*bis* of the Berne Convention for the Protection of Literary and Artistic Works, performers shall enjoy the exclusive right of authorizing, as regards their performances fixed in audiovisual works, the broadcasting and communication to the public of such performances, except where such a performance is already a broadcast performance.

XI. LIMITATIONS AND EXCEPTIONS

CERTAIN STATES OF AFRICA

Article 12

Application of Certain Substantive Provisions of the WPPT

The Contracting Parties shall apply, *mutatis mutandis*, in respect of the protection granted under this Protocol, the provisions of Articles 16 (Limitations and Exceptions)... of the WPPT.

CERTAIN STATES OF ASIA AND THE PACIFIC

17. Follow the WPPT approach in relation to these areas.

日本

第 10 条

表演者对录制在视听录制品上的表演获得报酬的权利

缔约方应在其本国法律中规定，表演者享有利用其录制在视听录制品中的表演获得公平报酬的权利。

韩国

4. 表演者对其已录制的视听表演享有下列权利：

(c) 利用广播和向公众传播获得报酬的权利。

5. 关于利用广播和向公众传播录制表演获得报酬的权利，本议定书应按照 WPPT 规定的方式允许对国民待遇保留意见。

美国

第 10 条

广播权和向公众传播权

除《保护文学和艺术作品伯尔尼公约》第 11 条之二规定的允许对视听作品行使权利的条件外，表演者对其录制在视听作品中的表演享有授权广播和向公众传播的专有权，除非此类表演已经是广播表演。

十一、限制与例外

非洲某些国家

第 12 条

WPPT 中某些实质性条款的适用

缔约方就本议定书所给予的保护应适用 WPPT 第 16 条关于限制与例外的规定。

亚洲及其太平洋地区某些国家

17. 遵循 WPPT 中这方面的规定。

CERTAIN STATES OF LATIN AMERICA AND THE CARIBBEAN

XI. Limitations and Exceptions

(1) The Contracting Parties may, in their national legislation, provide for the same kinds of limitation or exception with regard to the protection of performers as they provide for, in their national legislation, in connection with the protection of the copyright in literary and artistic works.

(2) The Contracting Parties shall confine any limitation on or exception to rights provided for in this Protocol to certain special cases that do not conflict with a normal exploitation of the audiovisual fixations or unreasonably prejudice the legitimate interests of the performer or of the audiovisual producer.

EUROPEAN COMMUNITY AND ITS MEMBER STATES

Article 6

Application of certain substantive provisions of the WIPO Treaty

The Contracting Parties shall apply, *mutatis mutandis*, in respect of protection granted under this Protocol, the provisions of Articles... 16 (Limitations and Exceptions)... of the WIPO Treaty.

JAPAN

Article 11

Limitations and Exceptions

Contracting Parties shall apply, *mutatis mutandis*, in respect of the protection granted under this Protocol, the provisions of Article 16 (Limitations and Exceptions) of the WPPT.

UNITED STATES OF AMERICA

Article 12

Limitations and Exceptions

(1) Contracting Parties may, in their national legislation, provide for the same kinds of limitations or exceptions with regard to the protection of performers as they provide for, in their national legislation, in connection with the protection of copyright in literary and artistic works.

(2) Contracting Parties shall confine any limitations of or exceptions to rights provided for in this Treaty to certain special cases which do not conflict with a normal exploitation of the performance and do not unreasonably prejudice the

拉丁美洲和加勒比某些国家

11. 限制与例外

（1）缔约各方可以在其国内立法中，对给予表演者的保护规定与其国内立法给予文学和艺术作品的版权保护相同种类的限制或例外。

（2）缔约各方应使本议定书中所规定权利的任何限制或例外仅限于某些不与视听录制品的正常利用相抵触、也不致不合理地损害表演者或视听录制作品录制者合法利益的特殊情况。

欧洲共同体及其成员国

第 6 条

WIPO 条约某些实质性条款的适用

缔约方就本议定书所给予的保护应比照适用 WIPO 条约第 16 条关于限制与例外的规定。

日本

第 11 条

限制与例外

缔约方就本议定书所给予的保护应比照适用 WPPT 第 16 条关于限制与例外的规定。

美国

第 12 条

限制与例外

（1）缔约各方可以在其国内立法中，对给予表演者的保护规定与其国内立法给予文学和艺术作品的版权保护相同种类的限制或例外。

（2）缔约各方应使本条约中所规定权利的任何限制或例外仅限于某些不与表演的正常利用相抵触、也不致不合理地损害表演者合法利益的特殊情况。

legitimate interests of the performer.

XII. CONTRACTUAL ARRANGEMENTS CONCERNING RIGHTS OF PERFORMERS

CANADA

TRANSFER OF RIGHTS

Option A

At the time of ratifying or acceding to this [Protocol]/[Treaty] or at any subsequent time a Contracting Party may declare by an instrument deposited with the Director General that once a performer [who is a national of [that]/[any] Contracting Party]/[regardless of nationality] has consented to the fixation of his or her performance in an audiovisual work by a national of that Contracting Party, he or she shall be deemed to have transferred all exclusive rights of authorization granted under this [Protocol]/[Treaty] with respect to that particular audiovisual work to the [author]/[producer]/[first owner of copyright] of that work [provided such [author]/[producer]/[first owner of copyright] is a national of a Contracting Party] and [his, hers or] its successors in interest subject to any written [contractual [clause]/[provision]]/[agreement] to the contrary. The foregoing sentence shall not apply to any rights of remuneration a performer may have under the law of any Contracting Party, nor shall it require a Contracting Party to establish any such rights of remuneration.

Where a Contracting Party makes such a declaration it shall apply [and be binding] in all other Contracting Parties of this [Protocol]/[Treaty].

For purposes of this article the term "an audiovisual work by a national of that Contracting Party" means an audiovisual work where the [author]/[producer]/[first owner of copyright] is a national of the Contracting Party which made the declaration [regardless of the place of fixation or publication of the audiovisual work].

[[For purposes of this article] "producer" shall include both individuals and legal entities [and the identity of the producer shall be determined by the law of the Contracting Party which made the declaration]].

A declaration made under this article may be revoked at any time.

*Optiona*l

Where a declaration under this article is made subsequent to the time of a

十二、表演者权的合同安排

加拿大

权利转让

选项 A

在批准或加入本（议定书）/（条约）时或在随后的任何时间，缔约方可通过交存于总干事的文书宣布，表演者［其是（该）/（任何）缔约方国民］/（不论国籍）已同意将该缔约方的国民的表演录制为视听作品，则应视同他/她已转让所有专有权，其是根据本［关于该作品的（作者）/（制作者）/（版权的第一所有人）的特定视听作品的议定书］/（条约）授权，其（提供于在该缔约方的国民为作者）/（制作者）/（版权的第一所有人）及（其本人或其继承人）的利益受任何相反的书面［合同（条款）/（规定）］/（协议）的约束。前述句子不适用于表演者根据任何缔约方的法律可能享有的任何获酬权，也不应要求缔约方确立任何这种获酬权。

缔约方作出此种声明的，应在本（议定书）/（条约）的所有其他缔约方中适用（并具有约束力）。

就本条而言，术语"该缔约方国民的视听作品"是指其中（作者）/（制作者）/（版权的第一所有人）是作出声明的缔约方的国民的视听作品（无论视听作品的录制或出版地点）。

［（就本条而言）"制作者"应包括个人和法人实体（制作者的身份应由作出声明的缔约方的法律确定）］。

根据本条作出的声明可以随时撤销。

<u>可选的</u>

在缔约方批准或加入本（议定书）/（条约）之后，根据本条作出声明的，该

Contracting Party ratifying or acceding to this [Protocol]/[Treaty], it shall apply effective January 1 of the year immediately following the date of deposit.

Option B

No transfer of rights provision.

CERTAIN STATES OF LATIN AMERICA AND THE CARIBBEAN

XII. Contractual Arrangements Concerning the Rights of Performers

Where a performer authorizes the inclusion of his performance in an audiovisual fixation, the Contracting Parties shall apply, *mutatis mutandis*, the provisions of Article 14*bis*(2)(b) of the Berne Convention, it being understood that the said provisions shall likewise be applicable to those of item 3 of Article X of this Protocol.

The Delegation of Brazil proposes omitting all provisions on contractual arrangements concerning the rights of performers in relation to broadcasting or communication to the public.

EUROPEAN COMMUNITY AND ITS MEMBER STATES

I. Transfer of rights

...The European Community and its Member States cannot support an international provision that would make mandatory for Contracting Parties, as foreseen by some proposals, the introduction of a provision on transfer of rights in their national legislation. In fact, it would imply in many countries major changes in contractual practices, which in different degrees are already subject to presumption of transfer. This adaptation would no doubt be controversial, and could well disturb well-established and sometimes delicate balances.

Consequently, the European Community and its Member States still propose that the protocol discussed should leave the Contracting Parties the widest flexibility in their own domestic regulation, including the possibility to introduce and/or maintain provisions on transfer of rights, according to their legal traditions and national considerations. In a spirit of clarity, Contracting Parties should agree that it will be a matter for legislation in the Contracting Parties whether or not to provide for a transfer of rights and to determine its nature and scope.

声明应自交存之日起第二年的1月1日起生效。

选项B

没有权利转让条款。

拉丁美洲和加勒比某些国家

12. 表演者权的合同安排

表演者授权将其表演录制成视听录制品的，缔约各方应比照适用《伯尔尼公约》第14条之二第(2)项(b)的规定，但须理解，上述规定应同样适用于本议定书第10条第3项。

巴西代表团建议省略关于表演者在广播或向公众传播方面的权利的合同安排的所有规定。

欧洲共同体及其成员国

1. 权利的转让

……欧洲共同体及其成员国不能支持这样一项国际条款，即：如某些提案所预见的那样，强制要求缔约国在其国家立法中引入有关权利转让的规定。事实上，这将意味着许多国家合同惯例的重大改变，这些做法在不同程度上已经受到了推定转让的影响。强制引进该规定无疑会引起争议，可能会扰乱既成的、有时是微妙的平衡。

因此，欧洲共同体及其成员国仍然建议，所讨论的议定书应使缔约方在其自身发展中具有最广泛的灵活性，包括根据其法律传统和国家考虑，引入和/或保持关于权利转让的规定的可能性。本着明确的精神，缔约各方应同意，是否规定权利转让并确定其性质和范围，将是缔约方的立法问题。

JAPAN

Article 9

Contractual Arrangements

(1) A performer who has undertaken to bring contributions to the making of an audiovisual fixation of his performance may not, in the absence of any contrary or special contract, object to the reproduction, distribution, rental and making available of his performance fixed in the audiovisual fixation.

(2) Notwithstanding the provisions of Article 4(1), any Contracting Party may, as regards performers who are nationals of such Contracting Party, establish national legislation which does not contain rules providing for the application of paragraph (1). Such Contracting Party shall notify the Director General of WIPO by means of a written declaration, which will be immediately communicated by him to all the other parties of this Protocol.

UNITED STATES OF AMERICA

Article 11

Transfer of Rights

Once a performer has consented to the fixation of his or her performance in an audiovisual work, he or she shall be deemed to have transferred all exclusive rights of authorization granted under this Treaty with respect to that particular audiovisual work to the producer of that work and its successors in interest, subject to written contractual clauses to the contrary. The foregoing sentence shall not apply to any rights of remuneration a performer may have under the law of any Contracting Party, nor shall it require a Contracting Party to establish any such rights of remuneration.

XIII. DURATION OF ECONOMIC RIGHTS OF PERFORMERS

CANADA

I. Term of Protection

Option A

The term of protection to be granted to performers under this [Protocol]/[Treaty] shall last, at least, until the end of a period of 50 years from the end of the year in which the performance was fixed.

日本

第 9 条

合同规定

（1）对将其表演制作成视听录制品作出贡献的表演者，在没有相反的或者特殊的合同的情况下，不得对复制、发行、出租、提供录制有其表演的录音制品的行为提出异议。

（2）尽管有第 4 条第（1）款的规定，任何缔约方对于属于该缔约方国民的表演者，可制定国家立法，其中不包含适用第（1）款的规则。此类缔约方应以书面声明的方式通知世界知识产权组织总干事，该声明将立即由他通知本议定书的所有其他缔约方。

美国

第 11 条

权利的转让

表演者一旦同意录制其表演于视听作品，应视为已将本条约授予的关于该特定视听作品的所有专有权转让给该作品的制作人及其利益继承人，但须遵守相反的书面合同条款。上述规定不适用于表演者根据任何缔约方的法律可能享有的任何获酬权，也不得要求缔约方确立任何此类获酬权。

十三、表演者经济权利的保护期

加拿大

1. 保护期

选项 A

根据本（议定书）/（条约）给予表演者的保护期限，应自表演录制之年年终算起，至少持续到 50 年期满为止。

Option B

The term of protection to be granted to performers under this [Protocol]/[Treaty] shall last until the end of the term of protection of the audiovisual work in which it is fixed.

Option B. 1

[Notwithstanding [Option B] no act done with respect to the audio portion of an audiovisual work shall be an infringement of any rights under this [Protocol]/[Treaty] if that act occurred more than 50 years after the end of the year in which the performance was fixed.]

II. Applicable Term

The term shall be governed by the legislation of the Contracting Party where protection is claimed; however, unless the legislation of that Contracting Party otherwise provides, the term shall not exceed the term fixed in the Contracting Party of the performer's nationality.

CERTAIN STATES OF AFRICA

Article 12

Application of Certain Substantive Provisions of the WPPT

The Contracting Parties shall apply, *mutatis mutandis*, in respect of the protection granted under this Protocol, the provisions of Articles… 17 (Term of Protection),… of the WPPT.

CERTAIN STATES OF LATIN AMERICA AND THE CARIBBEAN

XIII. Term of Protection of the Economic Rights of Performers

The term of protection to be granted to performers under this Protocol shall last, at least, until the end of a period of 50 years counted from the end of the year in which the performance was fixed.

EUROPEAN COMMUNITY AND ITS MEMBER STATES

Article 6

Application of certain substantive provisions of the WIPO Treaty

The Contracting Parties shall apply, *mutatis mutandis*, in respect of protection granted under this Protocol, the provisions of Articles… 17 (Term of Protection)… of the WIPO Treaty.

选项 B

根据本（议定书）/（条约）给予表演者的保护期限应持续到录制的视听作品的保护期结束。

选项 B.1

[尽管有（选项 B）的规定，对于视听作品的音频部分所做的任何行为，如果该行为发生在该表演录制的当年年底之后 50 年以上，则不构成对本（议定书）/（条约）项下任何权利的侵犯。]

2. 适用条款

该期限应由被要求保护的缔约方的立法所规定；但是，除非该缔约方的立法另有规定，该期限不得超过行为人国籍的缔约方规定的期限。

非洲某些国家

第 12 条

WPPT 某些实质性条款的适用

缔约方就本议定书所给予的保护应比照适用 WPPT 第 17 条关于保护期的规定。

拉丁美洲和加勒比某些国家

13. 表演者经济权利的保护期

依本条约授予表演者的保护期，应自表演录制之年年终算起，至少持续到 50 年期满为止。

欧洲共同体及其成员国

第 6 条

WIPO 条约某些实质性条款的适用

缔约方就本议定书所给予的保护应比照适用 WIPO 条约第 17 条关于保护期的规定。

JAPAN

Article 12

Term of Protection

Contracting Parties shall apply, *mutatis mutandis*, in respect of the protection granted under this Protocol, the provisions of Article 17 (Term of Protection) (1) of the WPPT.

UNITED STATES OF AMERICA

Article 13

Term of Protection

The term of protection to be granted to performers under this Treaty shall last, at least, until the end of a period of 50 years from the end of the year in which the performance was fixed.

XIV. OBLIGATIONS CONCERNING TECHNOLOGICAL MEASURES

CERTAIN STATES OF AFRICA

Article 12

Application of Certain Substantive Provisions of the WPPT

The Contracting Parties shall apply, *mutatis mutandis*, in respect of the protection granted under this Protocol, the provisions of Articles… 18 (Obligations concerning Technological Measures),… of the WPPT.

CERTAIN STATES OF ASIA AND THE PACIFIC

17. Follow the WPPT approach in relation to these areas.

CERTAIN STATES OF LATIN AMERICA AND THE CARIBBEAN

XIV. Obligations Concerning Technological Measures

The Contracting Parties shall provide adequate legal protection and effective legal remedies against the circumvention of effective technological measures that are used by performers in connection with the exercise of their rights under this Protocol and which restrict acts, in respect of their performances, that are not authorized by the performers concerned or permitted by law.

EUROPEAN COMMUNITY AND ITS MEMBER STATES

Article 6

Application of certain substantive provisions of the WIPO Treaty

The Contracting Parties shall apply, *mutatis mutandis*, in respect of protection

日本

第 12 条

保护期

缔约方就本议定书所给予的保护应比照适用 WPPT 第 17 条第 1 款关于保护期的规定。

美国

第 13 条

保护期

依本条约授予表演者的保护期，应自表演录制之年年终算起，至少持续到 50 年期满为止。

十四、关于技术措施的义务

非洲某些国家

第 12 条

WPPT 某些实质性条款的适用

缔约方就本议定书所给予的保护应比照适用 WPPT 第 18 条关于技术措施的义务的规定。

亚洲及太平洋地区某些国家

17. 遵循 WPPT 中这方面的规定。

拉丁美洲和加勒比某些国家

14. 关于技术措施的义务

对于表演者为行使本议定书所规定的权利及禁止未经表演者许可或法律允许的行为所采取的有效技术措施，缔约各方应规定缔约各方应规定适当的法律保护和有效的法律补救办法，以制止相关规避行为。

欧洲共同体及其成员国

第 6 条

WIPO 条约某些实质性条款的适用

缔约方就本议定书所给予的保护应比照适用 WIPO 条约第 18 条关于技术

granted under this Protocol, the provisions of Articles… 18 (Obligations concerning Technological Measures)… of the WIPO Treaty.

JAPAN

Article 13

Obligations concerning Technological Measures

Contracting Parties shall apply, *mutatis mutandis*, in respect of the protection granted under this Protocol, the provisions of Article 18 (Obligations concerning Technological Measures) of the WPPT.

REPUBLIC OF KOREA

6. We are also in favor of the provisions on the obligations concerning technological measures and rights management information included in the Protocol as those provided for in the WPPT.

UNITED STATES OF AMERICA

Article 14

Obligations concerning Technological Measures

Contracting Parties shall provide adequate legal protection and effective legal remedies against the circumvention of effective technological measures that are used by performers or their transferees in connection with the exercise of their rights under this Treaty and that restrict acts, in respect of their performances, that are not authorized by the performers or that are not permitted by law.

XV. OBLIGATIONS CONCERNING RIGHTS MANAGEMENT INFORMATION

CERTAIN STATES OF AFRICA

Article 12

Application of Certain Substantive Provisions of the WPPT

The Contracting Parties shall apply, *mutatis mutandis*, in respect of the protection granted under this Protocol, the provisions of Articles… 19 (Obligations concerning the Rights Management Information),… of the WPPT.

CERTAIN STATES OF ASIA AND THE PACIFIC

17. Follow the WPPT approach in relation to these areas.

措施的义务的规定。

日本

第 13 条

关于技术措施的义务

缔约方就本议定书所给予的保护应比照适用 WPPT 第 18 条关于技术措施的义务的规定。

韩国

6. 我们也赞成议定书中关于技术措施和权利管理信息义务的规定，这些规定与 WPPT 中的规定一样。

美国

第 14 条

关于技术措施的义务

对于表演者或其权利受让人为行使本议定书所规定的权利及禁止未经表演者许可或法律允许的行为所采取的有效技术措施，缔约各方应规定适当的法律保护和有效的法律补救办法，以制止相关规避行为。

十五、关于权利管理信息的义务

非洲某些国家

第 12 条

WPPT 某些实质性条款的适用

缔约方就本议定书所给予的保护应比照适用 WPPT 第 19 条关于权利管理信息的义务的规定。

亚洲及太平洋地区某些国家

17. 遵循 WPPT 中这方面的规定。

CERTAIN STATES OF LATIN AMERICA AND THE CARIBBEAN

XV. Obligations Concerning Rights Management Information

(1) Contracting Parties shall provide adequate and effective legal remedies against any person knowingly performing any of the following acts knowing, or with respect to civil remedies having reasonable grounds to know, that it will induce, enable, facilitate or conceal an infringement of any right covered by this Protocol:

(i) removing or altering any electronic rights management information without authority;

(ii) distributing, importing for distribution, broadcasting, communicating or otherwise making available to the public, without authority, performances, copies of performances incorporated in audiovisual fixations knowing that electronic rights management information has been removed or altered without authority.

(2) As used in this Article, "rights management information" means information that identifies the performer, his performance, the audiovisual producer or the audiovisual work, or information about the terms and conditions governing the use of the performance of the audiovisual work, and any numbers or codes that represent such information, when any of those items of information is attached to a copy of a fixed performance or appears in connection with the communication or making available to the public of a performance incorporated in an audiovisual fixation.

EUROPEAN COMMUNITY AND ITS MEMBER STATES

Article 6

Application of certain substantive provisions of the WIPO Treaty

The Contracting Parties shall apply, *mutatis mutandis*, in respect of protection granted under this Protocol, the provisions of Articles… 19 (Obligations concerning Rights Management Information)… of the WIPO Treaty.

JAPAN

Article 14

Obligations concerning Rights Management Information

Contracting Parties shall apply, *mutatis mutandis*, in respect of the protection granted under this Protocol, the provisions of Article 19 (Obligations concerning

拉丁美洲和加勒比某些国家

15. 关于权利管理信息的义务

（1）缔约各方应规定适当和有效的法律补救办法，制止任何人明知或就民事补救而言有合理根据知道其行为会诱使、促成、便利或包庇对本条约所涵盖的任何权利的侵犯而故意从事以下行为：

（i）未经许可去除或改变任何权利管理的电子信息；

（ii）未经许可发行、为发行目的进口、广播、向公众传播或提供明知已被未经许可去除或改变权利管理电子信息的表演或以视听录制品录制的表演的复制件。

（2）本条中，“权利管理信息”系指识别表演者、表演者的表演、视听制作人或视听作品的信息，或有关使用视听作品中的表演的条款和条件的信息，和代表此种信息的任何数字或代码，各该项信息均附于录制的表演的每件复制件上或视听作品上，或在已录制在视听作品中的表演向公众提供时出现。

欧洲共同体及其成员国

第 6 条

WIPO 条约某些实质性条款的适用

缔约方就本议定书所给予的保护应比照适用 WIPO 条约第 19 条关于权利管理信息的义务的规定。

日本

第 14 条

关于技术措施的义务

缔约方就本议定书所给予的保护应比照适用 WPPT 第 19 条关于权利管理信息的义务的规定。

Rights Management Information) of the WPPT.

REPUBLIC OF KOREA

6. We are also in favor of the provisions on the obligations concerning technological measures and rights management information included in the Protocol as those provided for in the WPPT.

UNITED STATES OF AMERICA

Article 15

Obligations concerning Rights Management Information

(1) Contracting Parties shall provide adequate and effective legal remedies against any person knowingly performing any of the following acts knowing, or with respect to civil remedies having reasonable grounds to know, that it will induce, enable, facilitate, or conceal an infringement of any right covered by this Treaty:

(i) to remove or alter any electronic rights management information without authority;

(ii) to distribute, import for distribution, broadcast, communicate or make available to the public, without authority, performances or copies of fixed performances knowing that electronic rights management information has been removed or altered without authority.

(2) As used in this Article, "rights management information" means information that identifies the performer, the performance of the performer, or the owner of any right in the performance, or information about the terms and conditions of use of the performance, and any numbers or codes that represent such information, when any of these items of information is attached to a copy of a fixed performance or appears in connection with the broadcast, public communication, or making available to the public of a fixed performance.

XVI. RESERVATIONS

CERTAIN STATES OF AFRICA

Article 11

Reservations

No reservations to this Protocol shall be permitted.

韩国

6. 我们也赞成议定书中关于技术措施和权利管理信息义务的规定，这些规定与 WPPT 中规定的一样。

美国

第 15 条

关于权利管理信息的义务

（1）缔约各方应规定适当和有效的法律补救办法，制止任何人明知或就民事补救而言有合理根据知道其行为会诱使、促成、便利或包庇对本条约所涵盖的任何权利的侵犯而故意从事以下行为：

（i）未经许可去除或改变任何权利管理的电子信息；

（ii）未经许可发行、为发行目的进口、广播、向公众传播或提供明知已被未经许可去除或改变权利管理电子信息的表演或以视听录制品录制的表演的复制件。

（2）本条中，“权利管理信息”系指识别表演者、表演者的表演、视听制作人或视听作品的信息，或有关使用视听作品中的表演的条款和条件的信息，和代表此种信息的任何数字或代码，各该项信息均附于录制的表演的每件复制件或视听作品上，或在已录制在视听作品中的表演向公众提供时出现。

十六、保留

非洲某些国家

第 11 条

保留

本议定书不允许有任何保留。

CERTAIN STATES OF LATIN AMERICA AND THE CARIBBEAN

XVI. Reservations

GRULAC will pronounce on this matter after the articles concerning the various rights have been put in final form.

The Delegation of Brazil will propose reservations should the Protocol contain provisions on entitlement to equitable remuneration.

EUROPEAN COMMUNITY AND ITS MEMBER STATES

Article 7

Reservations

No reservations to this Protocol shall be permitted.

JAPAN

Article 15

Reservations

Subject to the provisions of Article 4(2) and Article 9(2), no reservations to this Protocol shall be permitted.

UNITED STATES OF AMERICA

Article 17

Reservations

No reservations to this Treaty shall be permitted.

XVII. APPLICATION IN TIME

CERTAIN STATES OF AFRICA

Article 12

Application of Certain Substantive Provisions of the WPPT

The Contracting Parties shall apply, *mutatis mutandis*, in respect of the protection granted under this Protocol, the provisions of Articles… 22 (Application in Time)… of the WPPT.

CERTAIN STATES OF ASIA AND THE PACIFIC

17. Follow the WPPT approach in relation to these areas.

CERTAIN STATES OF LATIN AMERICA AND THE CARIBBEAN

XVII. Application in Time

(1) The Contracting Parties shall apply the provisions of Article 18 of the Berne Convention, *mutatis mutandis*, to the rights of the performers provided for in

拉丁美洲和加勒比某些国家

16. 保留

拉丁美洲和加勒比国家小组将在有关各项权利的条款最后定稿后对此事发表意见。

巴西代表团将提出保留意见，如果议定书载有关于应享有公平的报酬的规定。

欧洲共同体及其成员国

第 7 条

保留

本议定书不允许有任何保留。

日本

第 15 条

保留

除第 4 条第 2 款和第 9 条第 2 款外，本议定书不允许有任何保留。

美国

第 17 条

保留

本议定书不允许有任何保留。

十七、适用的时限

非洲某些国家

第 12 条

WPPT 某些实质性条款的适用

缔约方就本议定书所给予的保护应比照适用 WPPT 第 22 条关于适用的时限的规定。

亚洲及太平洋地区某些国家

17. 遵循 WPPT 中这方面的规定。

拉丁美洲和加勒比某些国家

第 17 条　适用的时限

(1)缔约方对本议定书规定的表演者的权利，比照适用《伯尔尼公约》第 18 条的规定。

this Protocol.

(2) This Protocol shall not detract from the rights acquired in any Contracting Party prior to the date of entry into force of this Protocol in that Party.

EUROPEAN COMMUNITY AND ITS MEMBER STATES

Article 6

Application of certain substantive provisions of the WIPO Treaty

The Contracting Parties shall apply, *mutatis mutandis*, in respect of protection granted under this Protocol, the provisions of Articles… 22 (Application in Time)… of the WIPO Treaty.

JAPAN

Article 16

Application in Time

(1) Contracting Parties shall apply, *mutatis mutandis*, in respect of the protection granted under this Protocol, the provisions of Article 22 (Application in Time) (1) of the WPPT.

(2) The provisions of paragraph (1) do not apply to the right to equitable remuneration of performers provided for in Article 10 of this Protocol.

UNITED STATES OF AMERICA

Article 18

Application in Time

(1) Contracting Parties shall apply the provisions of Article 18 of the Berne Convention, *mutatis mutandis,* to the rights of performers provided for in this Treaty.

(2) Notwithstanding paragraph (1), a Contracting Party may limit the application of Article 5 of this Treaty to performances that occurred after the entry into force of this Treaty for that Party.

XVIII. PROVISIONS ON ENFORCEMENT OF RIGHTS

CERTAIN STATES OF AFRICA

Article 12

Application of Certain Substantive Provisions of the WPPT

The Contracting Parties shall apply, *mutatis mutandis*, in respect of the protection granted under this Protocol, the provisions of Articles… 23 (Provisions

(2)本议定书不得减损在本议定书在该缔约方生效之前在该缔约方取得的权利。

欧洲共同体及其成员国

第6条

WIPO条约某些实质性条款的适用

缔约方就本议定书所给予的保护应比照适用WIPO条约第22条关于适用的时限的规定。

日本

第16条

适用的时限

(1)缔约方对本议定书规定的表演者的权利,比照适用WPPT第22条关于适用的时限的规定。

(2)第(1)款的规定不适用于本议定书第10条规定的表演者获得公平报酬的权利。

美国

第18条

适用的时限

(1)缔约方应比照适用《伯尔尼公约》第18条的规定,适用于本条约规定的表演者的权利。

(2)尽管有第(1)款的规定,缔约方可以限制本条约第5条对本条约生效后发生的表演的适用。

十八、关于权利行使的条款

非洲某些国家

第12条

WPPT某些实质性条款的适用

缔约方就本议定书所给予的保护应比照适用WPPT第23条关于权利行使的规定。

on Enforcement of Rights) of the WPPT.

CERTAIN STATES OF LATIN AMERICA AND THE CARIBBEAN

XVIII. Provisions on Enforcement of Rights

(1) The Contracting Parties undertake to adopt, in accordance with their legal systems, the measures necessary to ensure the application of this Protocol.

(2) The Contracting Parties shall ensure that enforcement procedures are available under their law so as to permit effective action against any act of infringement of rights covered by this Protocol, including expeditious remedies to prevent infringement and remedies that constitute a deterrent to further infringements.

EUROPEAN COMMUNITY AND ITS MEMBER STATES

Article 6

Application of certain substantive provisions of the WIPO Treaty

The Contracting Parties shall apply, *mutatis mutandis*, in respect of protection granted under this Protocol, the provisions of Articles... 23 (Enforcement of Rights)... of the WIPO Treaty.

JAPAN

Article 17

Enforcement of Rights

Contracting Parties shall apply, *mutatis mutandis*, in respect of the protection granted under this Protocol, the provisions of Article 23 (Enforcement of Rights) of the WPPT.

UNITED STATES OF AMERICA

Article 19

Provisions on Enforcement of Rights

(1) Contracting Parties undertake to adopt, in accordance with their legal systems, the measures necessary to ensure the application of this Treaty.

(2) Contracting Parties shall ensure that enforcement procedures are available under their law so as to permit effective action against any act of infringement of rights covered by this Treaty, including expeditious remedies to prevent infringement and remedies which constitute a deterrent to further infringements.

拉丁美洲和加勒比某些国家

18. 关于权利行使的条款

（1）缔约各方承诺根据其法律制度采取必要的措施，以确保本条约的适用。

（2）缔约各方应确保依照其法律可以提供执法程序，以便能采取制止对本条约所涵盖权利的任何侵犯行为的有效行动，包括防止侵权的快速补救和为遏制进一步侵权的补救。

欧洲共同体及其成员国

第 6 条

WIPO 条约某些实质性条款的适用

缔约方就本议定书所给予的保护应比照适用 WIPO 条约第 23 条关于权利行使的规定。

日本

第 17 条

权利的行使

缔约方就本议定书所给予的保护应比照适用 WPPT 第 23 条关于权力行使的规定。

美国

第 19 条

关于权利行使的条款

（1）缔约各方承诺根据其法律制度采取必要的措施，以确保本条约的适用。

（2）缔约各方应确保依照其法律可以提供执法程序，以便能采取制止对本条约所涵盖权利的任何侵犯行为的有效行动，包括防止侵权的快速补救和为遏制进一步侵权的补救。

XIX. ADMINISTRATIVE AND FINAL CLAUSES

CERTAIN STATES OF AFRICA

Article 13

Assembly

(1) The Contracting Parties shall have an Assembly.

(2) This Assembly shall be the same as the one created by the WPPT. Its functioning shall be governed, *mutatis mutandis*, by Article 24 of the WPPT.

Article 14

Eligibility for Becoming Party to the Protocol

Any party to the WPPT may become party to this Protocol.

Article 15

Signature of the Protocol

This Protocol shall be open for signature until... by any party eligible under Article 14.

Article 16

Final Clauses

The provisions of Articles 25 (International Bureau), 27 (Rights and Obligations under the Treaty), 29 (Entry into Force of the Treaty), 30 (Effective Date of Becoming Party to the Treaty), 31 (Denunciation of the Treaty), 32 (Languages of the Treaty) and 33 (Depository) of the WPPT shall apply, *mutatis mutandis*.

CERTAIN STATES OF ASIA AND THE PACIFIC

20. The number of instruments of ratification or accession required for entry into force of the Protocol should be the same as the WPPT, i. e., 30 instruments.

CERTAIN STATES OF LATIN AMERICA AND THE CARIBBEAN

1. Assembly

The Contracting Parties shall have an Assembly. That Assembly shall be the same as the one created by the WIPO Treaty.

2. Eligibility to Become Party to the Protocol

Any party to the WIPO Treaty may become party to this Protocol.

3. Signature of the Protocol

This Protocol shall be open for signature until... by any Member State of WIPO and by the European Community.

十九、行政条款及最后条款

非洲某些国家

第 13 条

大会

(1)缔约方应设大会。

(2)大会应与 WPPT 所建立的大会相同。其运作应比照适用 WPPT 第 24 条规制。

第 14 条

成为本条约缔约方的资格

WPPT 的任何缔约方均可成为本议定书的缔约方。

第 15 条

议定书的签署

本议定书供任何符合第 14 条规定的有关方签署。

第 16 条

最后条款

本议定书比照适用 WPPT 第 25 条(国际局)、第 27 条(权利和义务)、第 29 条(条约的生效)、第 30 条(成为条约缔约方的生效日期)、第 31 条(退约)、第 32 条(条约的语言)和第 33 条(保存人)的规定。

亚洲及太平洋地区某些国家

20. 议定书生效所需的批准书或加入缔约方的数目应与 WPPT 相同,即 30 份。

拉丁美洲和加勒比某些国家

1. 大会

缔约方应设大会。大会应与 WIPO 条约所建立的大会相同。

2. 成为本条约缔约方的资格

WIPO 条约的任何缔约方都可以成为本条约的缔约方。

3. 本条约的签署

本条约对任何世界知识产权组织成员和欧洲共同体成员开放签署。

4. Entry into Force of the Protocol

This Protocol shall enter into force, following the date of entry into force of the WIPO Treaty, three months after 20 instruments of ratification or accession by States have been deposited with the Director General of WIPO.

5. Final Clauses

The provisions of Articles 25 (International Bureau), 27 (Rights and Obligations under the Treaty), 30 (Effective Date of Becoming Party of the Treaty), 31 (Denunciation of the Treaty), 32 (Languages of the Treaty) and 33 (Depository) of the WIPO Treaty shall apply, *mutatis mutandis*.

Note: The Delegation of Brazil maintains that the expression "performances incorporated in audiovisual fixations" should be replaced by "audiovisual fixations" in all articles in which the former expression appears. The proposal is going through a consultation process within GRULAC.

EUROPEAN COMMUNITY AND ITS MEMBER STATES

Article 8

Application of certain administrative provisions

The Contracting Parties shall have an Assembly. This Assembly shall be the same as the one created by the WIPO Treaty and its functioning shall be governed, *mutatis mutandis*, by Article 24 of the WIPO Treaty.

Article 9

Eligibility for becoming party to the Treaty

Any party to the WIPO Treaty may become party to this Protocol.

Article 10

Signature of the Protocol

This Protocol shall be open for signature until... by any Member State of WIPO and by the European Community.

Article 11

Entry into force of the Protocol

This Protocol shall enter into force, following the date of entry into force of the WIPO Treaty, three months after 5 instruments of ratification or accession by States have been deposited with the Director General of WIPO.

4. 本条约的生效

本条约应自 WIPO 条约生效之日起，在 20 份国家的批准书或加入书交存世界知识产权组织总干事三个月后生效。

5. 最后条款

本议定书比照适用 WIPO 条约第 25 条（国际局）、第 27 条（权利和义务）、第 30 条（成为条约缔约方的生效日期）、第 31 条（退约）、第 32 条（条约的语言）和第 33 条（保存人）的规定。

注：巴西代表团认为，“录入视听录制品的表演”一词应在其出现的所有文章中改为“视听录制品”。该提案正在拉丁美洲和加勒比国家小组内部进行协商。

欧洲共同体及其成员国

第 8 条

某些行政性条款的适用

缔约方应设大会。该本大会应与 WIPO 条约所设立的大会相同，其运作应比照适用 WIPO 条约第 24 条的规制。

第 9 条

成为本条约缔约方的资格

WIPO 条约的任何缔约方均可以成为本条约的缔约方。

第 10 条

条约的签署

本条约对任何世界知识产权组织成员和欧洲共同体成员开放签署。

第 11 条

条约的生效

本条约应自 WIPO 条约生效之日起，在 5 份国家的批准书或加入书交存世界知识产权组织总干事三个月后生效。

Article 12

Final clause

The provisions of Articles 25 (International Bureau), 27 (Rights and Obligations under the Treaty), 30 (Effective Date of Becoming Party of the Treaty), 31 (Denunciation of the Treaty), 32 (Languages of the Treaty) and 33 (Depository) of the WIPO Treaty shall apply, *mutatis mutandis*.

JAPAN

Article 18

Assembly

Contracting Parties shall have an Assembly. This Assembly shall be the same as the one created by the WPPT and its functioning shall be governed, *mutatis mutandis*, by Article 24 of the WPPT.

Article 19

Eligibility for Becoming Party to the Protocol

Any party to the WPPT may become party to this Protocol.

Article 20

Signature of the Protocol

This Protocol shall be open for signature until… by any party to the WPPT.

Article 21

Entry into Force of the Protocol

This Protocol shall enter into force three months after 30 instruments of ratification or accession by States have been deposited with the Director General of WIPO.

Article 22

Final Clauses

The provisions of Article 25 (International Bureau), 27 (Rights and Obligations under the Treaty), 30 (Effective Date of Becoming Party to the Treaty), 31 (Denunciation of the Treaty), 32 (Languages of the Treaty) and 33 (Depository) of the WPPT shall apply, *mutatis mutandis*.

[End of Annex and of document]

第 12 条

最后条款

本议定书比照适用 WIPO 条约第 25 条(国际局)、第 27 条(权利和义务)、第 30 条(成为条约缔约方的生效日期)、第 31 条(退约)、第 32 条(条约的语言)和第 33 条(保存人)的规定。

日本

第 18 条

大会

缔约方应设大会。该本大会应与 WPPT 设立的大会相同,其运作应受 WPPT 第 24 条的规制。

第 19 条

成为本条约缔约方的资格

任何 WPPT 的成员有资格加入本条约。

第 20 条

条约的签署

本条约对 WPPT 的任何成员开放签署。

第 21 条

条约的生效

本条约应自 30 份国家的批准书或加入书交存世界知识产权组织总干事三个月后生效。

第 22 条

最后条款

本议定书比照适用 WIPO 条约第 25 条(国际局)、第 27 条(权利和义务)、第 30 条(成为条约缔约方的生效日期)、第 31 条(退约)、第 32 条(条约的语言)和第 33 条(保存人)的规定。

(文件及附件完)

4.4 Protection of Audiovisual Performances Proposal by India

Document Code: SCCR/2/9
Language: English
URL: https://www.wipo.int/edocs/mdocs/copyright/en/sccr_2/sccr_2_9.pdf

Chinese Translation: Not Available.
URL: N/A

STANDING COMMITTEE ON COPYRIGHT
AND RELATED RIGHTS
Second Session
Geneva, May 4 to 11, 1999

AGENDA ITEM 4: PROTECTION OF AUDIOVISUAL PERFORMANCES

PROPOSAL BY INDIA[1]

prepared by the International Bureau

1 Received on April 27, 1999.

4.4 印度关于保护视听表演的提案

文件编号：SCCR/2/9
文件语言：英语
文件链接：https://www.wipo.int/edocs/mdocs/copyright/en/sccr_2/sccr_2_9.pdf
中文文本：无
文件链接：无

版权及相关权常设委员会

第二届会议
1999年5月4日至11日，日内瓦

议程项目四：保护视听表演

印度的提案[1]
由国际局编制的文件

1　于1999年4月27日收到。

PROPOSAL FOR A WIPO AUDIOVISUAL PERFORMANCES TREATY
(Substantive Provisions Only)

PREAMBLE

The Contracting Parties

Desiring to develop and maintain the protection of the rights of performers in audiovisual fixations in a manner as effective and uniform as possible,

Recognizing the need to introduce new international rules in order to provide adequate solutions to the questions raised by economic, social, cultural and technological developments,

Recognizing the profound impact of the development and convergence of information and communication technologies on the production and use of audiovisual performances,

Recognizing the need to maintain a balance between the rights of performers in their audiovisual fixations and the larger public interest, particularly education, research and access to information,

Recognizing the fact that the WIPO Performances and Phonograms Treaty (WPPT) has not extended the protection to performers of audiovisual fixations and considering the special features of audiovisual fixations,

Have agreed as follows

Article 1
Relation to Other Conventions

(1) Nothing in this Treaty shall derogate from existing obligations that Contracting Parties have to each other under the WPPT.

(2) Protection granted under this Treaty shall leave intact and shall in no way affect the protection of copyright in literary and artistic works. Consequently, no provision of this Treaty may be interpreted as prejudicing such protection.

(3) This Treaty shall not have any connection with, nor shall it prejudice any rights and obligation under, any other treaties.

关于世界知识产权组织视听表演条约议定书的提案（仅实质性条款）

序言

缔约方

希望以尽可能有效和统一的方式，发展和维护表演者对其视听录制品享有的权利，

认识到有必要采用新的国际规则，以充分解决经济、社会、文化和技术发展所引起的问题，

认识到信息和通信技术的发展和融合对视听表演的制作和使用产生的深远影响，

认识到必须平衡表演者在视听录制品中享有的表演者权与更广大的公众利益，特别是教育、研究和获得信息的权利，

认识到《世界知识产权组织表演和录音制品条约》（WPPT）没有将保护范围扩大到视听录制品的表演者，并考虑到视听录制品的特点，

达成协议如下

第一条
与其他公约的关系

（1）本条约的任何内容都不得减损缔约国在 WPPT 下对彼此的现有义务。

（2）本条约规定的保护应保持不变，且不影响对文学艺术作品著作权的保护。因此，本条约的任何条款均不得解释为对这种保护的损害。

（3）本条约与其他条约无任何联系，也不损害其他条约所规定的权利和义务。

Article 2
Definitions

For the purposes of this Treaty:

(a) "performers" are actors, singers, musicians, dancers, and other persons who act, sing, deliver, declaim, play in, interpret or otherwise perform literary or artistic works or expressions of folklore but does not include performers whose performances are casual or incidental in nature such as extras;

(b) "audiovisual fixation" means the embodiment of moving images or of the representation thereof, with or without sound, from which they can be perceived, reproduced or communicated through a device;

(c) "broadcasting" means the transmission by wireless means for public reception of images or of images and sounds or of the representations thereof, such transmission by satellite is also broadcasting;

(d) "communication to the public" of an audiovisual performance means the transmission to the public by any medium, otherwise than by broadcasting, of the audiovisual fixation in any medium or of the unfixed performance;

(e) "producer" means the person or the legal entity, who or which takes the initiative and has the responsibility for the first audiovisual fixation.

Article 3
Beneficiaries of Protection under this Treaty

Contracting Parties shall accord protection provided under this Treaty to performers who are nationals of other Contracting Parties.

Article 4
National Treatment

Each Contracting Party shall accord to nationals of other Contracting Parties, the same treatment it accords to its own nationals with regard to the exclusive rights specifically granted in this Treaty.

Article 5
Moral Rights of Performers

(1) Independently of a performer's economic rights, and even after the transfer of those rights, the performer shall, as regards his fixed or unfixed audiovisual performance, have

第二条
定义

为本条约的目的：

(a)“表演者”是演员、歌手、音乐家、舞蹈家和对文学或艺术作品或民间文学艺术进行表演、歌唱、演说、朗诵、演奏、演绎或以其他方式进行表演的人员，但不包括表演属偶发或附带性质的表演者，如临时演员；

(b)“视听录制品”系指活动图像的体现物，且从中可通过某种装置感觉、复制或传播该活动图像，不论是否伴有声音或声音的表现物；

(c)“广播”系指以无线方式的传送，使公众能接收声音或图像，或图像和声音，或图像和声音的表现物；通过卫星进行的此种传送亦为“广播”；

(d)“向公众传播”视听表演是指通过除广播以外的任何媒介向公众传播在任何媒介中录制的视听录制品或尚未录制的表演；

(e)“制作人”是指主动提出或负责首次录制视听作品的自然人或法人。

第三条
本条约保护的受益人

缔约各方应将本条约所规定的保护给予属于其他缔约方国民的表演者。

第四条
国民待遇

缔约一方应就本条约特别授予的专有权，给予其他缔约方国民以本国国民相同的待遇。

第五条
表演者的精神权利

(1)独立于表演者的经济权利，即使在这些权利转让后，表演者对于其录制或尚未录制视听表演也应享有：

(a) the right to claim to be identified as the performer of his performance, except where omission is dictated by the manner of the use of the performance,

(b) the right to object to any distortion, mutilation or other modification of his performance which would be prejudicial to his reputation, provided that a modification considered necessary by the producer of the audiovisual fixation for the normal exploitation of such fixation through any medium shall not be deemed to be prejudicial to the reputation of the performer.

(2) The means of redress for safeguarding the rights granted under this Article shall be governed by the legislation of the Contracting Party where protection is claimed.

Article 6

Economic Rights of the Performers in their Unfixed Performances

Performers shall enjoy the exclusive right of authorizing, as regards their audiovisual performances:

(1) the broadcasting and communication to the public of their unfixed performances except where the performance is already a broadcast performance; and

(2) the audiovisual fixation of their unfixed performances.

Article 7

Right of Reproduction

Performers shall enjoy the exclusive right of authorizing the direct or indirect reproduction of audiovisual fixations of their performances in any manner or form.

Article 8

Right of Distribution

(1) Performers shall enjoy the exclusive right of authorizing the making available to the public of the original and copies of audiovisual fixations of their performances through sale or other transfer of ownership.

(2) Nothing in this Treaty shall affect the freedom of Contracting Parties to determine the conditions, if any, under which the exhaustion of the right in paragraph (1) applies after the first sale or other transfer of ownership of the original or a copy of the fixed performance with the authorization of the performer.

(a)要求承认其系表演的表演者，除非因使用表演的方式而决定可省略不提其系表演者；

(b)反对任何对其表演进行的将有损其声誉的歪曲、篡改或其他修改，且这种修改不是作品制作者或其利益继承人根据制片人在演出中获得的授权对视听作品进行正常利用的一部分。

(2)保障本条所赋予的权利的补救方法，应由要求保护的缔约国的立法来规定。

第六条

表演者对尚未录制的表演所享有的经济权利

表演者应享有专有权，对于其表演授权：

(1)广播，向公众传播其尚未录制的表演，但该表演本身属于广播表演的除外；和

(2)录制其尚未录制的视听表演。

第七条

复制权

表演者应享有授权以任何方式或形式对其表演的视听录制品直接或者间接地进行复制的专有权利。

第八条

发行权

(1)表演者应享有授权以出售或其他转让所有权的方式向公众提供其表演的视听录制品原件和复制件的专有权。

(2)对于已录制表演的原件或复制件经表演者授权被首次销售或以其他形式转让所有权之后适用本条第(1)款中权利的用尽所依据的条件(如有此种条件)，本条约的任何内容均不得影响缔约方确定该条件的自由。

Article 9
Right of Rental

Performers shall enjoy the exclusive right of authorizing the commercial rental to the public of the original and copies of the audiovisual fixations of their performances even after the distribution of them by, or pursuant to, authorization by the performer.

Article 10
Right of Making Available of Fixed Performances

Performers shall enjoy the exclusive right of authorizing the making available to the public of audiovisual fixations of their performances, by wire or wireless means, in such a way that the members of the public may access them from a place and at a time individually chosen by them.

Article 11
Transfer of Rights

(1) In the absence of any contract to the contrary, once the performer has by written agreement consented to the audiovisual fixation of the performance, he shall not object to the enjoyment by the producer of the exclusive rights of authorization specifically granted to the performer under this Treaty in respect of such fixation, for the purpose for which such fixation was made.

(2) It is for the legislation of the Contracting Parties to determine the manner of enforcement of this provision.

Article 12
Limitations and Exceptions

(1) Contracting Parties may, in their regional legislation, provide for the same kinds of limitations or exceptions with regard to the protection of performers with regard to audiovisual fixations of their performances as they provide for, in their national legislation, in connection with the protection of copyright in literary and artistic works.

(2) Contracting Parties shall confine any limitations of or exceptions to rights provided for in this Treaty to certain special cases which do not conflict with a normal exploitation of the audiovisual fixation and do not unreasonably prejudice the legitimate interests of the performer.

第九条
出租权

表演者应享有授权向公众商业出租其表演的视听录制品的原件和复制件的专有权，即使是在表演者授权或根据其授权已经发行的情况下。

第十条
提供已录制表演的权利

表演者享有授权以有线或无线方式向公众提供其表演的视听录制品的专有权，以便公众成员可在其自行选择的地点和时间获得。

第十一条
权利转让

（1）在没有任何相反约定的情况下，一旦表演者通过书面协议同意对其表演进行视听录制，则出于该录制制作的目的，他不应反对制作人享有本条约中特别授予表演者的关于该录制享有的授权的专有权。

（2）该规定的执行方式由缔约双方的立法决定。

第十二条
限制与例外

（1）缔约各方可在其区域立法中就在表演者在其本国法中所享有的对其表演的视听录制品的保护和对文学艺术作品的版权保护规定相同种类的限制或例外。

（2）对本条约规定的权利的任何限制或例外，缔约各方应将其限定在一些特殊情况下，既不与正常使用视听录制品相冲突，且不会不合理地损害表演者的合法利益。

Article 13
Term of Protection

The term of protection to be granted to the performers under this Treaty shall last, at least, until the end of the period of fifty years computed from the end of the year in which the audiovisual fixation was made.

Article 14
Obligations concerning Technological Measures

Contracting Parties shall provide adequate legal protection and effective legal remedies against the circumvention of effective technological measures that are used by the performers or their legal representatives or assignees of their rights in connection with the exercise of the rights conferred by this Treaty and that restrict acts, in respect of their performances, which are not authorized by the performers or which are not permitted by law.

Article 15
Obligations concerning Rights Management Information

(1) Contracting Parties shall provide adequate and effective legal remedies against any person knowingly performing any of the following acts knowing, or with respect to civil remedies having reasonable grounds to know, that it will induce, enable, facilitate, or conceal an infringement of any right covered by this Treaty:

(i) to remove or alter any electronic rights management information without authority;

(ii) to distribute, import for distribution, broadcast, communicate or make available to the public, without authority, performances, or copies of fixed performances knowing that electronic rights management information has been removed or altered without authority.

(2) As used in this Article, "rights management information" means information which identifies the audiovisual performer, the performance of the performer, or the owner of any right in the performance, or the information about the terms and conditions of use of the performance, and any numbers or codes that represent such information, when any of these items of information is attached to a copy of a fixed performance or appears in connection with the broadcast, communication or making

第十三条
保护期限

本条约给予表演者的保护期限，应自视听录制品制作完成当年年末起算，至少持续到50年期满为止。

第十四条
有关技术措施的义务

缔约方应规定适当的法律保护和有效的法律补救办法，防止表演者为行使本议定书所规定的权利以及为了限制未经有关表演者授权或法律不允许的行为而采取的有效技术措施被规避。

第十五条
有关权利管理信息的义务

（1）缔约各方应规定适当和有效的法律补救办法，制止任何人明知或就民事补救而言有合理根据知道其行为会诱使、促成、便利或包庇对本条约所涵盖的任何权利的侵犯而故意从事以下行为：

（i）未经许可去除或改变任何权利管理的电子信息；

（ii）未经许可发行、为发行目的进口、广播、向公众传播或提供明知已被未经许可去除或改变权利管理电子信息的表演或视听录制的复制件。

（2）在本条中，“权利管理信息”系指识别表演者、表演者的表演、视听制作人或视听作品的信息，或有关使用视听作品中的表演的条款和条件的信息，和代表此种信息的任何数字或代码，各该项信息均附于录制的表演的每件复制件上或视听作品上，或在已录制在视听作品中的表演向公众提供时出现。

available of a fixed performance to the public.

Article 16
Formalities

The enjoyment and exercise of the rights provided for in this Treaty shall not be subject to any formality.

Article 17
Reservations

No reservations to this Treaty shall be permitted.

Article 18
Application in Time

(1) Contracting Parties shall apply the provisions of Article 18 of the Berne Convention, *mutatis mutandis,* to the rights of performers provided for in this Treaty.

(2) Notwithstanding paragraph (1), a Contracting Party may limit the application of Article 5 of this Treaty to audiovisual performances which occurred after the entry into force of this Treaty for that party.

Article 19
Provision on Enforcement of Rights

(1) Contracting Parties undertake to adopt, in accordance with their legal systems, the measures necessary to ensure the application of this Treaty.

(2) Contracting Parties shall ensure that enforcement procedures are available under their law so as to permit effective action against any act of infringement of rights covered by this Treaty, including expeditious remedies to prevent infringements and remedies which constitute a deterrent to further infringements.

[End of document]

第十六条
形式要件

享受和行使本条约规定的权利无需满足任何形式要件。

第十七条
保留

不得对本条约作出保留。

第十八条
适用的时限

（1）缔约方应比照适用《伯尔尼公约》第 18 条的规定，适用于本条约所规定的表演者权利。

（2）尽管有第（1）款的规定，缔约方可以将本条约第 5 条的适用范围限制为在本条约对该方生效之后发生的视听表演。

第十九条
权利行使条款

（1）缔约方承诺根据其法律制度采取必要的措施，以确保本条约的适用。

（2）缔约各方应确保根据其法律可采用执法程序，以便能够对侵犯本条约所述权利的任何行为采取有效措施，此外，还应防止发生新的侵权行为。

（文件完）

5.
Standing Committee on Copyright and Related Rights: Third Session

Meeting code: SCCR/3
Date: November 16 to November 20, 1999
venue: Geneva, Switzerland
Meeting Documents URL:
https://www.wipo.int/meetings/en/details.jsp##meeting_id=3912

5.
版权及相关权常设委员会：第三届会议

会议代码：SCCR/3
会议日期：1999年11月16—20日
会议地点：瑞士日内瓦
会议文件链接：
https://www.wipo.int/meetings/en/details.jsp##meeting_id=3912

5.1 Supplementary Explanation on Japan's Proposal for a Protocol to the WIPO Performances and Phonograms Treaty Concerning Audiovisual Performances

Document Code: SCCR/3/3
Language: English
URL: https://www.wipo.int/edocs/mdocs/copyright/en/sccr_3/sccr_3_3.pdf
Chinese Translation: Not Available.
URL: N/A

STANDING COMMITTEE ON COPYRIGHT

AND RELATED RIGHTS

Third Session

Geneva, November 16 to 20, 1999

AGENDA ITEM 4: PROTECTION OF AUDIOVISUAL PERFORMANCES

SUPPLEMENTARY EXPLANATION ON JAPAN'S PROPOSAL FOR A PROTOCOL TO THE WIPO PERFORMANCES AND PHONOGRAMS TREATY CONCERNING AUDIOVISUAL PERFORMANCES[1]

submitted by Japan

1 Received on July 26, 1999.

5.1 关于日本提出的《世界知识产权组织表演和录音制品条约视听表演议定书》的补充说明

文件编号：SCCR/3/3
文件语言：英语
文件链接：https://www.wipo.int/edocs/mdocs/copyright/en/sccr_3/sccr_3_3.pdf
中文文本：无
文件链接：无

版权及相关权常设委员会

第三届会议
1999 年 11 月 16 日至 20 日，日内瓦

议程项目四：保护视听表演

关于日本提出的《世界知识产权组织表演和录音制品条约视听表演议定书》的
补充说明[1]
由日本国提交

1　于 1999 年 7 月 26 日收到。

SUPPLEMENTARY EXPLANATION ON JAPAN'S PROPOSAL FOR A PROTOCOL TO THE WIPO PERFORMANCES AND PHONOGRAMS TREATY CONCERNING AUDIOVISUAL PERFORMANCES

The Government of Japan hereby submits supplementary explanation on Japan's proposal, focusing on points concerning the right of broadcasting and communication to the public, national treatment and contractual arrangements/transfer of rights.

I. BACKGROUND

1. As Japan has reiterated in the deliberations at the Standing Committee on Copyright and Related Rights (SCCR), Japan submitted a proposal which could present a flexible framework as an alternative for Contracting Parties, aiming at contributing to WIPO's efforts to realize international harmonization in this field. Japan expects that such a framework could lead up to a compromise bridging different positions and proposals.

II. NATIONAL TREATMENT AND CONTRACTUAL ARRANGEMENTS/TRANSFER OF RIGHTS

2. According to Japan's proposal, some exclusive rights (that is, right of reproduction, right of distribution, right of rental and right of making available), shall be granted as regards fixed performances (Article 8(1)(2)). These exclusive rights, however, cannot be exercised as regards performances which have been fixed in audiovisual fixations with the consent of the performer. The rights are exercisable by the performer only upon contrary or special contract (Article 9(1)).

3. In this regard, Japan proposed to make an exception to this rule so that the Contracting Parties, including those which have already granted exclusive rights (exercisable without any contrary or special contract), may grant such exclusive rights to performers that are their nationals without according national treatment to performers of other Contracting Parties (Article 9(2)). Thus, according to Article 9(2), Japan's proposal also permits Contracting Parties to be exempted from "national

日本关于《世界知识产权组织表演和录音制品条约》中视听表演方面议定书的提案的补充说明

日本政府特此对日本的提案进行补充说明，重点是关于广播和向公众传播权，国民待遇和合同安排 / 权利的转让的要点。

一、背景

1. 正如日本在版权和相关权常设委员会（SCCR）的审议中所重申的那样，日本提出了一项建议，该建议可为缔约方提供一种可选择的灵活的框架，旨在为世界知识产权组织实现这一领域的国际协调作出贡献。日本希望这样一个框架能够使得各方达成妥协，弥合不同的立场和建议。

二、国民待遇和合同安排 / 权利转让

2. 根据日本的建议，对于已录制的表演，应授予一些专有权（即复制权、发行权、出租权和提供权）[第 8 条第（1）（2）款]。但是，对于经表演者同意而录制在视听录制品中的表演，表演者不能行使这些专有权。只有在合同有相反或特殊约定的情况下，表演者才能行使权利（第 9 条第 1 款）。

3. 在这方面，日本提议对规定做一个例外，以便包括那些已取得专有权（权利可行使且无相反或特殊的合同约定）在内的所有缔约方会授予作为其国民的表演者这种专有权，而不需要根据表演者或其他缔约方的国民待遇[第 9 条第（2）款]。因此，根据第 9 条第（2）款，日本的建议还允许缔约方被免除“国民待遇”。

treatment.”

III. RIGHT OF BROADCASTING AND COMMUNICATION TO THE PUBLIC

4. According to Japan’s proposal, although an exclusive right of broadcasting and communication to the public is not granted to performers, remuneration rights can be introduced to cover such acts as broadcasting and communication to the public (Article 10).

5. Japan wishes to clarify that the establishment of remuneration rights is not obligatory and that the content of such rights can be determined at the discretion of each Contracting Party. However, once a particular Contracting Party grants such remuneration rights to performers that are its nationals, national treatment should be accorded to performers as regards nationals of other Contracting Parties on a reciprocal basis (Article 4(1)(2)).

6. Even though Article 10 of Japan’s proposal is classified into category “5. Right of broadcasting and communication to the public” in the Comparative Table prepared by the International Bureau (SCCR/2/4), Japan’s proposal on remuneration rights is not limited to the cases concerning the right of broadcasting and communication to the public.

[End of document]

三、广播权和向公众传播权

4. 根据日本的建议，虽然表演者不享有广播权和向公众传播权，但可以享有从广播和向公众传播的行为中获得报酬的权利(第10条)。

5. 日本希望澄清，确立获酬权不是强制性的，这种权利的内容可以由每一缔约方自行决定。但是，一旦某一缔约方给予作为其国民的表演者这种获酬权，则应在对等的基础上给予作为其他缔约方国民的表演者一样的国民待遇[第4条第(1)(2)款]。

6. 尽管日本提案的第10条被归类在国际局编制的比较表(SCCR/2/4)中的"5. 广播权和向公众传播权"类中，日本关于获酬权的建议不限于对广播权和向公众传播权中。

(文件完)

5.2 Protection of Audiovisual Performances; Protection of the Rights of Broadcasting Organizations (Document submitted by the United Republic of Tanzania)

Document Code: SCCR/3/5
Language: English
URL: https://www.wipo.int/edocs/mdocs/copyright/en/sccr_3/sccr_3_5.pdf
Chinese Translation: Not Available.
URL: N/A

STANDING COMMITTEE ON COPYRIGHT
AND RELATED RIGHTS
Third Session
Geneva, November 16 to 20, 1999

AGENDA ITEM 4: PROTECTION OF AUDIOVISUAL PERFORMANCES; PROTECTION OF THE RIGHTS OF BROADCASTING ORGANIZATIONS

Document submitted by the United Republic of Tanzania[1]

I. PROTECTION OF AUDIOVISUAL PERFORMANCES

The competent office in the United Republic of Tanzania, in matters relating to

1 Received on August 23, 1999.

5.2 坦桑尼亚联合共和国提交的关于保护视听表演和保护广播组织者权的文件

文件编号：SCCR/3/5
文件语言：英语
文件链接：https://www.wipo.int/edocs/mdocs/copyright/en/sccr_3/sccr_3_5.pdf
中文文本：无
文件链接：无

版权及相关权常设委员会

第三届会议

1999年11月16日至20日，日内瓦

议程项目四：保护视听表演；保护广播组织者权

坦桑尼亚联合共和国提交的关于保护视听表演和保护广播组织者权的文件[1]

一、视听表演的保护

坦桑尼亚联合共和国主管办公室与坦桑尼亚广播委员会合作，协商与版

1　于1999年8月23日收到。

copyright, in cooperation with the Tanzania Broadcasting Commission, organized and held a stakeholders get-together-meeting on June 15, 1999, to deliberate on two agenda items, currently under deliberation by the WIPO Standing Committee on Copyright and Related Rights, namely:

(a) the Protection of Audiovisual Performances,

(b) the Protection of the Rights of Broadcasting Organizations.

The purpose was, first, to sensitize the stakeholders on those issues and, second, to take stock of the stakeholders' views on those issues, to be used as country inputs in African Group consultations and where necessary, as country inputs for the country proposals to the WIPO Standing Committee on Copyright and Related Rights.

NATIONAL LEGISLATION

1. In the Copyright and Neighboring Rights Act No. 7 of Tanzania, there are general provisions which protect all performers generally. However, under section 3(3)(c) of that Act, protection of audiovisual performances is available if the performance is in a fixed form, and the producer is a national of the United Republic of Tanzania.

Audiovisual performances is also one of the works under Section 5(2)(f) in which copyright subsists and hence qualify for copyright protection under the Act.

2. Section 15(2) of the Tanzania Copyright and Neighboring Rights Act provides for copyright ownership in respect of audiovisual works.

PROPOSALS

With the mandate of stakeholders, it is proposed:

(a) that the new international instrument should be a protocol to the WIPO Performances and Phonograms Treaty (WPPT);

(b) that the definition of performers in the WPPT should apply *mutatis mutandis* to the corresponding definition in the proposed protocol;

(c) that the Contracting Parties should accord protection to performers who are nationals and those who have habitual residence in the contracting county;

(d) that a performer should, as regards to his performance, whether fixed or embodied in an audiovisual fixation, have the right:

(i) to be identified as the performer of that work, and

权有关的事宜，于1999年6月15日组织并举行了一次利益相关者会议，以商议世界知识产权组织版权及相关权常设委员会目前正在审议的两个议程项目，即：

(a)保护视听表演；

(b)保护广播组织的权利。

目的是，第一，使利益相关者关注这些问题；第二，听取利益相关者对这些问题的意见，在非洲小组协商时作为国家建议，在必要时，作为国家提案向世界知识产权组织版权和相关权常设委员会提出。

国内立法

1. 在坦桑尼亚第7号《版权和邻接权法》中，存在普遍地保护所有表演者的一般性条款。但是，根据该法案的第3条第(3)款(c)项，如果表演是录制的形式，且制作人是坦桑尼亚联合共和国的国民，则可以对视听表演进行保护。

视听表演也是第5条第(2)款(f)项规定的作品之一，其版权仍然存在，因此有资格获得该法案的版权保护。

2. 坦桑尼亚《版权和邻接权法》第15条第(2)款规定了视听作品的版权所有权归属。

提案

根据利益相关者的授权，提议：

(a)新的国际文本应为《世界知识产权组织表演和录音制品条约》(WPPT)的议定书；

(b)WPPT中表演者的定义应比照适用于拟议议定书中的相应定义；

(c)缔约方应给予身为缔约方国民和在缔约国有经常居住地的表演者保护；

(d)表演者对其被录制或体现在视听录制品中的表演，应有权：

(i)被认定为该作品表演者，并且

(ii) to object to any distortion of his performance that would be prejudicial to his reputation.

These rights should be valid even after the transfer of ownership of the copyright.

(e) That the performers enjoy the exclusive right of authorizing the commercial rental to the public of the original and copies of audiovisual fixations of their performances. However, if commercial rental has led to widespread copying of the works which materially impairs the exclusive right or reproduction, then Contracting Parties shall have an obligation to intervene.

(f) That each Contracting Party should accord to the nationals and persons who have habitual residence in the contracting party's country, the same treatment as it accords to its own nationals and habitual residents.

(g) That the performers should enjoy the exclusive right of authorizing the making available to the public of the original and copies of the audiovisual fixations of their performances through sale or other transfer of ownership.

However, nothing in the proposed protocol should affect the freedom of the Contracting Parties in determining the conditions, if any, under which the exhaustion of the right stated above, applies after the first sale or other transfer or ownership of the original or a copy of the fixed performance with authorization of the performer.

II. PROTECTION OF THE RIGHTS OF BROADCASTING ORGANIZATIONS

The competent office in the United Republic of Tanzania, in matters relating to Copyrights, in cooperation with the Tanzania Broadcasting Commission, held a stakeholders get together consultative meeting, on June 15, 1999, to deliberate on two agenda items which are currently under deliberation by the WIPO Standing Committee on Copyright and Related Rights, namely:

(a) the Protection of the Rights of Broadcasting Organizations,

(b) the Protection of the Rights of Audiovisual Performances.

The purpose of the meeting, was, first, for the officers of the competent office, to take stock of the views of the stakeholders and use such views as inputs for the country proposals in the group consultations and also as inputs to country proposals on the ongoing deliberation by the WIPO Standing Committee on Copyright and

(ii)反对任何有损其声誉的对其表演的歪曲。

这些权利即使在版权转移后也应有效。

(e)表演者享有授权向公众商业出租其表演的视听录制品的原件和复制件的专有权。但是，如果商业性出租导致对作品的广泛复制，从而严重损害专有权或复制权，则缔约方有义务介入。

(f)每个缔约方都应以给予其他缔约方国民和拥有经常居住地的居民与本国国民和拥有经常居住地的居民同等的待遇。

(g)表演者应享有授权通过出售或其他转移所有权的方式使公众获取其表演的视听录制品的原件或复制件的专有权。

但是，对于已录制表演的原件或复制件经表演者授权被首次销售或以其他形式转让所有权之后适用本条第(1)款中权利的用尽所依据的条件(如有此种条件)，拟定的议定书不得影响缔约方确定该条件的自由。

二、保护广播组织的权利

坦桑尼亚联合共和国主管办公室与坦桑尼亚广播委员会合作，协商与版权有关的事宜，于 1999 年 6 月 15 日举行了一次利益相关者共同协商会议，以商议世界知识产权组织版权及相关权常设委员会目前正在审议的两个议程项目，即：

(a)保护广播组织的权利，
(b)保护视听表演的权利。

该会议的目的是，第一，听取利益相关者对这些问题的意见，在小组磋商中作为国家提案，也作为对世界知识产权组织版权及相关权常设委员会正在审议的议程的国家提案提出；第二，使利益相关者关注这些问题。

Related Rights; second, to sensitize the stakeholders on those issues.

NATIONAL LEGISLATION

- The national Copyright and Neighboring Rights Act No. 7 of 1999 recognizes the rights of broadcasting organizations.

- Under Section 34(1) of that Act, a broadcasting organization has exclusive rights to carry out or to authorize any of the following:

(a) the rebroadcasting of its broadcast,

(b) the communication to the public of its broadcast,

(c) the fixation of its broadcast,

(d) the reproduction of a fixation of its broadcast.

- Subsection (2) of that section provides for the commencement and the span of the protection period. The protection commences immediately when the broadcasting takes place, and remains valid until the end of the fiftieth year, following the year in which the broadcast takes place.

However, Section 35 limits the protection of such rights when the subject matter of protection is used for the following purposes:

(a) using short excerpts for reporting current events to the extent justified by the purpose of providing current information;

(b) reproduction solely for scientific research;

(c) reproduction solely for the purpose of face to face teaching activities except for performances and phonograms which have been published as teaching materials;

(d) limitation of protection under Section 7(b) of the Act which limits protection of news of the day published, broadcast or publicly communicated by any other means.

PROPOSALS

1. The United Republic of Tanzania subscribes to and supports the views of the African Group, expressed by the elected spokesperson of that group, unless, on specific issues, it is otherwise expressly signified.

2. Representing the views of the stakeholders in the broadcasting industry, the United Republic of Tanzania supports all the efforts that are directed towards reviewing, with a view to modernizing and improving the current legal protection of the rights of broadcasting organizations, at an international level. The Rome

国家立法

– 1999 年的第 7 号国家版权和邻接权法案规定了广播组织的权利。

– 根据该法第 34 条第（1）款，广播组织享有实施或授权实施下列任何行为的专有权：

（a）转播其广播，

（b）向公众传播其广播，

（c）录制其广播，

（d）复制其录制的广播。

– 该条第（2）款规定了保护期的起算点及期限。该保护自广播开始之日起，直至广播开始之年后第五十年年末为止。

但第 35 条规定，当受保护的客体被用于下列用途时，将限制对该权利的保护：

（a）仅出于提供时事新闻目的，使用简短的摘要报道时事新闻；

（b）仅用于科学研究的复制；

（c）仅作为面对面教学活动的目的进行复制，但作为教材出版表演和录音制品除外；

（d）根据该法第 7 条第（b）款的规定，限制对当天发行、广播或任何形式公开传播的新闻的保护。

提案

1. 坦桑尼亚联合共和国赞同并支持该小组当选发言人所表达的非洲小组的观点，除非在具体问题上另有明确表示。

2. 坦桑尼亚联合共和国代表广播业利害关系人的意见，支持旨在审视在国际层面上对广播组织权利的现行法律保护进行现代化和改进的一切努力。考虑到广播工业技术的迅速发展，需要重新审视《罗马公约》。

Convention needs to be re-examined to take into account the rapid technological developments in the broadcasting industry.

3. The United Republic of Tanzania makes the following proposals:

- that the envisaged international instrument for the protection of the rights of broadcasting organizations should be an independent treaty;

- that the instrument should clearly define the following terms:

• broadcasting by satellite,

• cable retransmission,

• terrestrial broadcasting,

• encrypted satellite signals,

• program-carrying signals,

• digital networks.

- That the proposed instrument should address clearly the following issues:

• the balance of rights between broadcasters and the owners of broadcast contents, in cable retransmission;

• the balance of all rights owners involved, i.e. the broadcasters, authors, performers, producers of phonograms and cable operators;

• the nature of the rights accorded. It is proposed that they should not be absolute and should have clearly spelt exceptions and limitations.

[End of document]

3. 坦桑尼亚联合共和国提出以下建议：
– 所设想的保护广播组织权利的国际法律文本应成为一项独立条约；

– 该法律文本应明确定义以下术语：
• 通过卫星广播，
• 有线电视转播，
• 地面广播，
• 加密的卫星信号，
• 节目承载信号，
• 数字网络。
– 拟议法律文本应明确解决以下问题：
• 在有线电视转播中，广播公司与广播内容所有人之间的权利平衡；

• 所涉及的所有权利人之间的平衡，即广播公司、作者、表演者、录音制品制作人和有线电视运营商；

• 所授予的权利的性质。有提议认为它们不应是绝对的，且应明确规定例外和限制。

（文件完）

5.3 Submission of the United States of America

Document Code: SCCR/3/7
Language: English
URL: https://www.wipo.int/edocs/mdocs/copyright/en/sccr_3/sccr_3_7.pdf
Chinese Translation: Not Available.
URL: N/A

STANDING COMMITTEE ON COPYRIGHT
AND RELATED RIGHTS
Third Session
Geneva, November 16 to 20, 1999

AGENDA ITEM 4: PROTECTION OF AUDIOVISUAL PERFORMANCES

SUBMISSION OF THE UNITED STATES OF AMERICA[1]

SUBMISSION OF THE UNITED STATES OF AMERICA

The United States is pleased to make this, its third, substantive submission on the protection of audiovisual performers rights. In early 1998, the United States concluded that it would be appropriate to submit a proposal to further advance the discussions which had been taking place on audiovisual performers rights in

1 Received on November 2, 1999.

5.3 美国提交的文件

文件编号：SCCR/3/7
文件语言：英语
文件链接：https://www.wipo.int/edocs/mdocs/copyright/en/sccr_3/sccr_3_7.pdf
中文文本：无
文件链接：无

版权及相关权常设委员会

第三届会议
1999年11月16日至20日，日内瓦

议程项目四：保护视听表演

美国提交的文件[1]

美国提交的文件

美国很高兴提交这份有关保护视听表演者权利的第三份实质性材料。1998年初，美国认为应该提交一份提案，以进一步推动专家委员会中关于视听表演者权利的讨论。因此，我们在1998年5月18日提交了一项基本提案（1998年5月18日的AP/CE/2/4号文件和1998年5月27日的AP/CE/2/4Corr

1　于1999年11月2日收到。

the Committee of Experts. Consequently, on May, 18, 1998, we submitted a basic proposal (AP/CE/2/4, May 18, 1998 and AP/CE/2/4 Corr., May 27, 1998) which was a substantial change from the position of the United States at the end of the 1996 Diplomatic Conference. That proposal was widely discussed at the June 8-12, 1998 final meeting of the Committee of Experts on the Protection of Audiovisual Works. In November of 1998, at the first Meeting of the Standing Committee on Copyright and Related Rights, in response to concerns raised at the June Meeting and after further consideration of the issues, we amended our proposal to clarify points where drafting had been questioned and to make changes to our proposal to seek to achieve a position acceptable to a wider range of participants (SCCR/1/4). Now, we make our third submission, amending our proposal again and noting significant proposals made by others. We hope these changes stimulate further discussion and facilitate achieving a broader agreement on the objectives to be attained.

This submission of the United States is in two parts. Part 1 includes general statements regarding transfer of rights and on national treatment and Part 2 is a revised text of the U.S. Proposal which includes clarifications of language and suggestions from earlier discussions of the text. In Part 2, the newly added material is underscored and deleted text is struck out. It should be noted that the proposed changes also include the addition of a provision on a rental right and a revised provision on application in time, which we believe is a complex issue requiring further discussion.

Part 1

STATEMENT ON TRANSFER OF RIGHTS

The United States believes that the discussions to date in the Standing Committee regarding the transfer of rights have been thoughtful and productive. Several delegations, including those from Canada, India, and Japan, along with those delegations in the Latin American and Caribbean Group, have put forward proposals that recognize the need for this treaty to address the fundamental issue of transfer of rights. We also recognize the statement submitted by the International Federation of Actors (FIA) at the May 1999 Meeting of the Standing Committee concerning the need to introduce rights for performers where they do not exist while

号文件），这与美国在1996年外交会议结束时的立场有很大的变化。这份提案在1998年6月8日至12日召开的视听作品保护专家委员会最后一次会议上得到了广泛讨论。1998年11月，在版权与相关权常设委员会的第一次会议上，针对6月会议中引起进一步关注和思考的问题，我们改进了提案以澄清其中受到质疑的内容，并对于提案进行了修改，以找到更多参与者能够接受的立场（SCCR/1/4号文件）。现在，我们提交第三份材料，再次修正我们的提案，并关注其他国家提出的重要提案。我们希望这些变化能够激发进一步的讨论，并争取对所要实现的目标达成更广泛的共识。

美国提交的提案分为两部分。第一部分包括关于权利转让和国民待遇的综述，第二部分是美国提案的修订版，其中包括对表述的澄清和较早前对案文的讨论中所提出的建议。在第二部分中，新增加的材料用下划线表示，删除的文本用删除线表示。应该指出的是，拟议的修改还包括增加一项关于出租权的条款和一项关于适用时限的修订条款，我们认为这是需要进一步讨论的复杂问题。

第一部分

有关权利转让条款的声明

美国认为，到目前为止，常设委员会关于权利转让的讨论是经过深思熟虑和富有成效的。一些代表团，包括来自加拿大、印度和日本的代表团，以及拉丁美洲和加勒比区域的代表团提出了一些建议，认为有必要通过本条约来解决权利转让的根本问题。我们也认可国际演员联合会（FIA）于1999年5月在常设委员会会议上提交的声明，其中提到需要为虚拟表演者引入权利，同时在制作和发行视听作品时，维持各方在全球市场上运作的确定性。FIA关于进一步讨论转让条款的建议很有帮助。

maintaining certainty for all parties in the production and distribution of audiovisual works in a global market. FIA's suggestions for further discussion of a transfer provision are helpful.

We appreciate that a key element of some of the proposals involves the recognition and respect by Contracting Parties of appropriate transfer rules adopted by another Contracting Party. We also understand that while many countries already include a presumption of transfer in their national laws, some countries do not and would prefer not to adopt such a presumption with respect to their own nationals. The foregoing points must be balanced with the need for a simple rule that will achieve a requisite level of certainty as audiovisual production and distribution increasingly continues to cross national boundaries.

The proposed presumption set forth in the current U.S. proposal is quite limited in several important respects. First, it is rebuttable. Second, it applies only to exclusive rights of authorization; it does not apply to moral rights or to rights of remuneration that may be established under national law. Third, it accommodates various legal systems and traditions, including those based on collective agreements and those based on the establishment of equitable remuneration rights for performers. The U.S. proposal enjoys the wide support of performers, producers and distributors in the U.S. and represents a careful balance of critical interests.

While the U.S. continues to believe that its current proposal on transfer of rights provides a necessary minimum level of international harmonization, we are continuing to study the various proposals on transfer submitted by the other delegations and welcome further discussion on this issue. The United States is convinced that this essential element of the treaty can be addressed in a manner that provides adequate protection of the interests of performers and also creates certainty and clarity with respect to the production and distribution of audiovisual works.

STATEMENT ON NATIONAL TREATMENT

The United States recognizes that national treatment is a problematic issue and that striking an appropriate balance may take some time to achieve.

It is a fundamental principle that performers should be compensated for their performances. The concept of national treatment needs to accommodate the different systems by which performers are compensated, including collective bargaining

我们对一些提案中的关键要素表示赞赏，即缔约方承认和尊重另一缔约方所采纳的适当的转让规则。我们还了解到，虽然许多国家已经在其国家法律中列入了推定的转让规则，但有些国家出于对国民的尊重不进行规定，也不愿意对其本国国民适用这种推定转让规则。上述各点必须与制定一项简单规则的需要相平衡，这样一项规则应具有必要的确定性，因为视听制作和发行正日益跨越国界。

美国目前提案中所提出的推定在几个重要方面受到相当的限制。第一，它是可以推翻的。第二，它只适用于专有权的授权；它不适用于精神权利或可能由国内法所确定的获酬权。第三，它容纳了各种法律制度和传统，包括基于集体协议的法律制度和基于为表演者确立公平报酬权利的法律制度和传统。美国的提议得到了美国表演者、制作人和发行商的广泛支持，代表了关键利益之间的谨慎平衡。

虽然美国仍然认为其目前关于权利转让的提案提供了必要的最低限度的国际协调，但我们将持续研究其他代表团提出的关于转让的各种提案，并欢迎就此问题进行进一步讨论。美国相信条约这一基本内容可以通过给予表演者充分利益保障以及增加视听作品在制作和发行方面的确定性与明确性的方式去实现。

有关国民待遇的声明

美国认识到，国民待遇是一个疑难的问题，要达到适当的平衡可能需要一些时间。

表演者对其表演应该得到报酬，这是一个基本原则。国民待遇的概念需要适应给予表演者报酬的不同制度，包括集体谈判协议和公平报酬制度。

agreements and systems of equitable remuneration.

The International Federation of Actors (FIA) at the May 1999 Standing Committee Meeting submitted a statement that money that is collected on account of performances must be distributed to the individuals appearing in those performances. We agree that this is also a fundamental principle. If such distributions are not made, then collections ought not be made with respect to such performances.

Part 2
SUBSTANTIVE PROVISIONS OF A TREATY FOR THE PROTECTION OF PERFORMERS IN AUDIOVISUAL WORKS

Preamble

The Contracting Parties,

Noting that the development and convergence of new information and communication technologies will allow for rapid growth of audiovisual services and that this will increase the opportunities for performing artists to exploit their performances;

Recognizing the great importance of ensuring an adequate level of protection for these performances, in particular when they are exploited in the new digital environment;

Recognizing that the WIPO Performances and Phonograms Treaty (WPPT) does not cover the rights of performers in the audiovisual fixations of their performances, but that many provisions of the WPPT can be used or adapted as the basis for a new treaty protecting performers with respect to their audiovisual performances;

Have agreed as follows:

CHAPTER I
GENERAL PROVISIONS

Article 1
Relation to Other Conventions

(1) Nothing in this Treaty shall derogate from existing obligations that Contracting Parties have to each other under the International Convention for the Protection of Performers, Producers of Phonograms and Broadcasting Organizations

国际演员联合会（FIA）在1999年5月的常务委员会会议上提交了一份声明，其中提到因演出而收取的款项必须分配给参加演出的个人。我们同意这也是一项基本原则。如果不进行这种分配，那么就不应该对这些表演进行收款。

第二部分
保护视听作品表演者条约的实质性条款

序言

缔约各方，

提请注意到新的信息和通信技术的发展和融合将使视听服务迅速增长，并将增加表演艺术家利用其表演的机会；

认识到对这些表演提供充足的保护极为重要，特别是当这些表演在新的数字环境中被利用时；

认识到《世界知识产权组织表演和录音制品条约》（WPPT）不包括表演者在其提供表演的视听录制品中的权利，但WPPT的许多条款可作为保护表演者在其视听表演方面的依据或修改为新条约的基础；

达成协议如下：

第一章
一般规定

第1条

与其他公约的关系

（1）本条约的任何规定均不得减损缔约方根据1961年10月26日在罗马订立的《保护表演者、录音制品制作者和广播组织国际公约》对彼此承担的现有义务。

done in Rome, October 26, 1961.

(2) Protection granted under this Treaty shall leave intact and shall in no way affect the protection of copyright in literary and artistic works. Consequently, no provision of this Treaty may be interpreted as prejudicing such protection.

(3) This Treaty shall not have any connection with, nor shall it prejudice, any rights and obligations under any other treaties.

Article 2

Definitions

For the purposes of this Treaty:

(a) "performers" are actors, singers, musicians, dancers, and other persons who act, sing, deliver, declaim, play in, interpret, or otherwise perform literary or artistic works or expressions of folklore~~, but not including ancillary performers considered such by professional practice~~ <u>with the exception of extras, the definition of the latter term being left to the legislation of each Contracting Party</u>;

(b) "fixation" means the embodiment of images, or of images and sounds, or of the representations thereof, from which they can be perceived, reproduced, or communicated through a device;

(c) "broadcasting" means the transmission by wireless means for public reception of images, or of images and sounds, or the representations thereof; such transmission by satellite is also "broadcasting;" transmission of encrypted signals is "broadcasting" where the means for decrypting are provided to the public by the broadcasting organization or with its consent;

(d) "communication to the public" means the transmission to the public by any medium, otherwise than by broadcasting, of the images, or the sounds and images, or the representations thereof, comprised in an unfixed performance or in a fixed performance;

(e) an "audiovisual work" is a work consisting of a series of related images that impart an impression of motion and ~~are~~ <u>is</u> intended to be shown by the use of a device, together with any accompanying sounds.

Article 3

Beneficiaries of Protection

(1) Contracting Parties shall accord the protection provided under this Treaty to

（2）根据本条约给予的保护不得触动或以任何方式影响对文学和艺术作品版权的保护。因此，本条约的任何内容均不得被解释为损害此种保护。

（3）本条约既不应与其他条约下的任何权利和义务之间存在联系，也不应当对其造成损害。

第2条

定义

就本条约而言：

（a）“表演者”是指所有演员、歌唱家、音乐家 舞蹈家或其他演绎角色、歌唱、背诵、朗诵或以其他方式进行表演的其他人员，~~但不包括被专业实践认为是辅助表演者的人~~。临时演员除外，后一术语的定义留待各缔约国自行立法；

（b）“录制品”是指活动图像的体现物，且从中可通过某种装置感觉、复制或传播该活动图像，不论是否伴有声音或声音的表现物；

（c）“广播”是指以无线方式的传送，使公众能接收声音或图像，或图像和声音，或图像和声音的表现物；通过卫星进行的此种传送亦为“广播”；传送密码信号，只要广播组织或经其同意向公众提供了解码的手段，即为“广播”；

（d）“向公众传播”是指以广播以外的任何媒介向公众传送图像，声音和图像或其体现物的未录制的表演或以视听录制品录制的表演；

（e）“视听作品”是由一系列相关联的图像组成的作品，这些图像给人以运动的印象，并旨在通过使用设备显示的相关图像以及任何伴随的声音组成的作品。

第3条

保护的受益人

（1）缔约国应给予~~本条第（2）款界定的其他缔约国的表演者~~本条约规定的

performers of other Contracting Parties as defined in paragraph (2) of this Article.:

(2) Performers of other Contracting Parties shall be understood to be performers who meet any of the following conditions:

(a) those performers who are nationals of a Contracting Party and whose performance is unfixed or is fixed in an audiovisual work (other than in a phonogram) regardless of the place of performance or fixation;

(b) those performers whose unfixed performance takes place on the territory of a Contracting Party;

(c) those performers whose performance is first fixed in an audiovisual work (other than in a phonogram) on the territory of another Contracting Party.

(3)(2) Performers who are not nationals of one of the Contracting Parties but who have their habitual residence in one of them shall, for the purposes of this Treaty, be assimilated to nationals of that Contracting Party.

Article 4

National Treatment

With respect to performances for which they are protected under this Treaty as provided in Article 3, performers shall enjoy, in other Contracting Parties, the treatment that the laws of such parties do now or may hereafter grant to their own nationals, as well as the rights specifically granted by this Treaty.

CHAPTER II

RIGHTS OF PERFORMERS

Article 5

Moral Rights of Performers

(1) Independently of a performer's economic rights, and even after the transfer of those rights, the performer shall, as regards his or her live performances or performances fixed in an audiovisual fixation, have the right to claim to be identified as the performer of such performances, except where omission is dictated by the manner of the use of the performance, and to object to any distortion, mutilation, or other modification of his or her performance that would be seriously prejudicial to the performer's reputation. Modifications consistent with the normal exploitation of an audiovisual work undertaken by the producer of the work or the producer's successors in interest, pursuant to the exercise of rights of authorization

保护；

(2)其他缔约方的表演者应被理解为满足以下任何条件的表演者：

(a)属于其他缔约方国民的表演者和其表演未被录制或已被录制在视听作品(非录音制品)中而无论表演或录制的地点为何的表演者；

(b)其未录制的表演发生在缔约方领土上的表演者；

(c)其表演在另一缔约方领土上被首次录制在视听作品(非录音制品)中的表演者。

(3)(2)表演者不是缔约方之一的国民，但在其中一个缔约国中有经常居住地，应将其视为为该缔约方的国民。

第4条

国民待遇

对于在第3条中受本条约保护的表演，表演者应在其他缔约方中享受该缔约国法律现在或以后可能给予其本国国民的待遇，以及本条约特别授予的权利。

第二章
表演者的权利

第5条

表演者的精神权利

(1)独立于表演者的经济权利，甚至在这些权利转让之后，表演者仍应对于其现场表演(无论是否伴有声音)或以视听录制品录制的表演享有权利：要求承认其系表演的表演者，除非因使用表演的方式而决定可省略不提其系表演者；反对任何对其表演进行的将有损其声誉的歪曲、篡改或其他修改。作品制作者或者其利益继承人行使其被授权的权利，正常使用其视听作品所作的修改，不应视为严重损害表演者的声誉。

acquired by the producer in the performance, shall not be considered seriously prejudicial to the performer's reputation.

(2) The rights granted to a performer in accordance with paragraph (1) shall, after the said performer's death, be maintained, at least until the expiry of the rights of authorization set forth in Articles 6 through ~~10~~11, and shall be exercisable by the persons or institutions authorized by the legislation of the Contracting Party where protection is claimed. However, these Contracting Parties whose legislation, at the moment of their ratification of or accession to this Treaty, does not provide for protection after the death of the performer of all rights set out in the preceding paragraph, may provide that some of these rights will, after the performer's death, ceased to be maintained.

(3) The means of redress for safeguarding the rights granted under this Article shall be governed by the legislation of the Contracting Party where protection is claimed.

(4) The "normal exploitation of an audiovisual work" shall include the use of new or changed technology, media, formats, and/or methods of distribution, dissemination, making available or communication to the public. A performer shall give reasonable consideration to the interests of the other performers in the work, the writers of scenarios, dialogues or musical works created for the work, and the principal director of the work when seeking to exercise the above described rights with respect to such work.

Article 6

Economic Rights of Performers in their Unfixed Performances

Performers shall enjoy the exclusive right of authorizing, as regards their performances:

(i) the broadcasting and communication to the public of their unfixed performances, except where the performance is already a broadcast performance; and

(ii) the fixation of their unfixed performances.

Article 7

Right of Reproduction

Performers shall enjoy the exclusive right of authorizing the direct or indirect

（2）根据第（1）款授予表演者的权利，在该表演者去世后，至少在第 6 条至第 11 条规定的授权权期满之前予以保留，并且可由被授权的个人或机构进行利用。但是，某些缔约方在正式被批准加入条约前，其国内立法并未规定表演者去世后应享有前款规定的所有权利，其可能规定表演者去世后某些权利将不再保留。

（3）保障本条所赋予的权利的补救办法，应由要求保护的缔约国的立法来规定。

（4）“视听作品的正常利用”应包括使用新的或经改变的技术、媒介、版式和 / 或向公众发行、宣传、提供或者传播的方法。表演者在行使上述作品权利时，应当合理考虑视听作品的其他表演者和场景、对话或音乐作品的编写者以及作品的主要导演的利益。

第 6 条

表演者未录制表演的经济权利

表演者对其表演享有专有权：

（一）向公众广播、传播其未录制的表演，除非该表演已经是广播表演；和

（二）录制其表演。

第 7 条

复制权

表演者享有授权以任何方式或形式直接或间接复制其已录制表演的专

reproduction of their fixed performances in any manner or form.

Article 8

Right of Distribution

(1) Performers shall enjoy the exclusive right of authorizing the making available to the public of the original and copies of their fixed performances through sale or other transfer of ownership.

(2) Nothing in this Treaty shall affect the freedom of Contracting Parties to determine the conditions, if any, under which the exhaustion of the right in paragraph (1) applies after the first sale or other transfer of ownership of the original or a copy of the fixed performance with the authorization of the performer.

Article 9

Right of Making Available

Performers shall enjoy the exclusive right of authorizing the making available to the public of their fixed performances, by wire or wireless means, in such a way that members of the public may access them from a place and at a time individually chosen by them.

Article 10

Right of Broadcasting and Communication to the Public

Except for conditions on the exercise of the right that are permissible for audiovisual works under Article 11*bis* of the Berne Convention for the Protection of Literary and Artistic Works, performers shall enjoy the exclusive right of authorizing, as regards their <u>fixed</u> performances ~~fixed in audiovisual works~~, the broadcasting and communication to the public of such performances~~, except where such a performance is already a broadcast performance~~.

<u>Article 11</u>

<u>Right of Rental</u>

<u>(1) Performers shall enjoy the exclusive right of authorizing commercial rental to the public of originals or copies of their fixed performances as determined in the national law of Contracting Parties, even after distribution of them by, or pursuant to, authorization by the performer.</u>

<u>(2) Paragraph (1) shall not apply unless such commercial rental has led to widespread copying of such performances materially impairing the exclusive right</u>

有权。

第8条

发行权

（1）表演者授权通过出售或者其他转让所有权的形式向公众提供其以视听录制品录制的表演的原件或复制件的专有权。

（2）对于已录制表演的原件或复制件经表演者授权被首次销售或以其他形式转让所有权之后适用本条第（1）款中权利的用尽所依据的条件（如有此种条件），本条约的任何内容均不得影响缔约方确定该条件的自由。

第9条

提供权

表演者享有授权以有线或无线方式向公众提供其已录制表演的专有权，公众成员可在其自行选择的地点和时间访问该等表演。

第10条

广播权和向公众传播权

除了《伯尔尼公约》第11条第2款所规定的视听作品行使权利的条件外，表演者对于~~已录制在视听作品中的已录制~~表演享有广播和向公众传播的专有权~~，除非该表演已是广播表演~~。

第11条

出租权

（1）表演者应享有授权将其根据缔约方国家法律确定的其录制表演的原件或复制件向公众进行商业性出租的专有权，即使该原件或复制件已由表演者发行或经表演者授权发行。

（2）第（1）款不适用的情形仅存在于该商业性出租导致此类表演的广泛复制，从而严重损害了复制专有权。

<u>of reproduction.</u>

CHAPTER III
ADDITIONAL PROVISIONS

Article ~~11~~12
Transfer of Rights

Once a performer has consented to the fixation of his or her performance in an audiovisual work, he or she shall be deemed to have transferred all exclusive rights of authorization granted under this Treaty with respect to that particular audiovisual work to the producer of that work and its successors in interest, subject to written contractual clauses to the contrary. The foregoing sentence shall not apply to any rights of remuneration a performer may have under the law of any Contracting Party, nor shall it require a Contracting Party to establish any such rights of remuneration.

Article ~~12~~13
Limitations and Exceptions

(1) Contracting Parties may, in their national legislation, provide for the same kinds of limitations or exceptions with regard to the protection of performers as they provide for, in their national legislation, in connection with the protection of copyright in literary and artistic works.

(2) Contracting Parties shall confine any limitations of or exceptions to rights provided for in this Treaty to certain special cases which do not conflict with a normal exploitation of thee performance and do not unreasonably prejudice the legitimate interests of the performer.

Article ~~13~~14
Term of Protection

The term of protection to be granted to performers under this Treaty shall last, at least, until the end of a period of 50 years from the end of the year in which the performance was fixed.

Article ~~14~~15
Obligations concerning Technological Measures

Contracting Parties shall provide adequate legal protection and effective legal remedies against the circumvention of effective technological measures that are

第三章
其他规定

第 ~~11~~12 条
权利转让

一旦表演者同意将其表演录制在视听作品上，应视为已将其根据本条约授予的与该特定视听作品有关的所有专有权转让给该作品的制作人以及利益继承人，除非有相反的书面合同约定。前述内容不适用于表演者根据任何缔约方的法律可能享有的任何获酬权，也不应要求缔约方确立任何这种获酬权。

第 ~~12~~13 条
限制与例外

（1）缔约各方可以在其本国法律中就保护表演者提供与在其本国法律中就保护文学和艺术作品的版权所规定的相同种类的限制或例外。

（2）缔约各方应将本条约规定的权利的任何限制或例外限制在某些特殊情况下，这些特殊情况不与对表演的正常利用相抵触，也不会不合理损害表演者的合法利益。

第 ~~13~~14 条
保护期限

根据本条约给予表演者的保护期限，应自表演录制之年年终起算，至少持续到 50 年期满为止。

第 ~~14~~15 条
关于技术措施的义务

缔约各方应规定适当和有效的法律补救办法，防止表演者为行使本议定书所规定的权利以及为了限制未经有关表演者授权或法律不允许的行为而采取

used by performers or their transferees in connection with the exercise of their rights under this Treaty and that restrict acts, in respect of their performances, that are not authorized by the performers or that are not permitted by law.

Article ~~15~~16

Obligations concerning Rights Management Information

(1) Contracting Parties shall provide adequate and effective legal remedies against any person knowingly performing any of the following acts knowing, or with respect to civil remedies having reasonable grounds to know, that it will induce, enable, facilitate, or conceal an infringement of any right covered by this Treaty:

(i) to remove or alter any electronic rights management information without authority;

(ii) to distribute, import for distribution, broadcast, communicate or make available to the public, without authority, performances or copies of fixed performances knowing that electronic rights management information has been removed or altered without authority.

(2) As used in this Article, "rights management information" means information that identifies the performer, the performance of the performer, or the owner of any right in the performance, or information about the terms and conditions of use of the performance, and any numbers or codes that represent such information, when any of these items of information is attached to a copy of a fixed performance or appears in connection with the broadcast, public communication, or making available to the public of a fixed performance.

Article ~~16~~17

Formalities

The enjoyment and exercise of the rights provided for in this Treaty shall not be subject to any formality.

Article ~~17~~18

Reservations

No reservations to this Treaty shall be permitted.

Article ~~18~~19

Application in Time

~~(1) Contracting Parties shall apply the provisions of Article 18 of the Berne~~

的有效技术措施被规避。

第 ~~15~~16 条

关于权利管理信息的义务

（1）缔约各方应规定适当和有效的法律补救办法，制止任何人明知、或就民事补救而言有合理根据知道其行为会诱使、促成、便利或包庇对本条约所涵盖的任何权利的侵犯而故意从事以下行为：

（i）未经许可去除或改变任何权利管理的电子信息；

（ii）未经许可发行、为发行目的进口、广播、向公众传播或提供明知已被未经许可去除或改变权利管理电子信息的表演或已录制表演的复制件。

（2）本条款中“权利管理信息”“权利管理信息”系指识别表演者、表演者的表演、视听制作人或视听作品的信息，或有关使用视听作品中的表演的条款和条件的信息，和代表此种信息的任何数字或代码，各该项信息均附于录制的表演的每件复制件上或视听作品上，或在已录制在视听作品中的表演向公众提供时出现。

第 ~~16~~17 条

手续

享受和行使本条约规定的权利无需任何手续。

第 ~~17~~18 条

保留

对本条约不得有任何保留。

第 ~~18~~19 条

适用的时限

~~（1）缔约国应将《伯尔尼公约》第 18 条的规定比照适用于本条约中规定的~~

~~Convention, *mutatis mutandis*, to the rights of performers provided for in this Treaty.~~

~~(2) Notwithstanding paragraph (1), a Contracting Party may limit the application of Article 5 of this Treaty to performances that occurred after the entry into force of this Treaty for that Party.~~

(1) This Treaty shall not prejudice, except as noted in paragraph (3) below, rights acquired in any Contracting Party before the date of coming into force of this Treaty for that Contracting Party.

(2) No Contracting Party, except as noted in paragraph (3) below, shall apply the provisions of this Treaty to unfixed performances that took place, or to performances that were fixed, before the coming into force of this Treaty for that Contracting Party.

(3) Contracting Parties shall apply Article 5 of this Treaty to all fixed performances in existence on the date of coming into force of this Treaty where such performances were fixed no earlier than 50 years before such date, but only where the prejudicial conduct first occurs after the effective date of this Treaty.

Article ~~19~~20

Provisions on Enforcement of Rights

(1) Contracting Parties undertake to adopt, in accordance with their legal systems, the measures necessary to ensure the application of this Treaty.

(2) Contracting Parties shall ensure that enforcement procedures are available under their law so as to permit effective action against any act of infringement of rights covered by this Treaty, including expeditious remedies to prevent infringement and remedies which constitute a deterrent to further infringements.

[End of document]

~~表演者的权利~~。

~~(2)尽管有第(1)款的规定，缔约国可将本条约第 5 条的适用范围限制在本条约对该缔约国生效后发生的表演上~~。

(1)除下文第(3)款所述情况外，本条约不应妨碍在本条约对任何缔约国生效之日前在该缔约国获得的权利。

(2)除下文第(3)款所述情况外，任何缔约国均不得将本条约的规定适用于本条约对该缔约国生效前发生的未录制的表演或已录制的表演。

(3)缔约各方应将本条约第 5 条适用于在本条约生效之日前已存在的所有已录制表演，而该表演的录制日期不得早于生效日期之前 50 年，但仅在损害行为于本条约生效后第一次发生的情况下为例外。

第 ~~19~~20 条

关于权利行使的规定

(1)缔约国承诺根据其法律制度采取必要措施，确保本条约的实施。

(2)缔约各双方应确保根据其法律的有效的执法程序，以便能够对侵犯本条约所述权利的任何行为采取有效措施，此外，还应防止发生新的侵权行为。

（文件完）

5.4 Additional Proposal of Japan Concerning Moral Rights

Document Code: SCCR/3/8
Language: English
URL: https://www.wipo.int/edocs/mdocs/copyright/en/sccr_3/sccr_3_8.pdf

Chinese Translation: Not Available.
URL: N/A

STANDING COMMITTEE ON COPYRIGHT AND RELATED RIGHTS

Third Session

Geneva, November 16 to 20, 1999

AGENDA ITEM 4: PROTECTION OF AUDIOVISUAL PERFORMANCES

ADDITIONAL PROPOSAL OF JAPAN CONCERNING MORAL RIGHTS[1]

1 Received on November 10, 1999.

5.4 日本关于精神权利的补充提案

文件编号：SCCR/3/8
文件语言：英语
文件链接：https://www.wipo.int/edocs/mdocs/copyright/en/sccr_3/sccr_3_8.pdf
中文文本：无
文件链接：无

版权及相关权常设委员会

第三届会议
1999 年 11 月 16 日至 20 日，日内瓦

议程项目四：保护视听表演

日本关于精神权利的补充提案[1]

1　于 1999 年 11 月 10 日收到。

ADDITIONAL PROPOSAL OF JAPAN ON A PROTOCOL TO THE WIPO PERFORMANCES AND PHONOGRAMS TREATY CONCERNING AUDIOVISUAL PERFORMANCES

Article 6

Moral Rights of Performers

Contracting Parties shall accord, *mutatis mutandis*, to performers, as regards their unfixed audiovisual performances, whether or not accompanied by sound, or their performances fixed in audiovisual fixations, the same rights as those provided for in Article 5 (Moral Rights of Performers) of the WPPT.

Comment:

Further consideration should be given to the scope and manner of the application of Moral Rights from such a viewpoint as the normal exploitation of performances fixed in audiovisual fixations.

[End of document]

日本关于世界知识产权组织表演和录音制品公约视听表演议定书的补充提案

第 6 条

表演者的精神权利

缔约各方对于表演者的未录制的视听表演(无论是否伴有声音)或其录制在视听录制品中的表演,缔约方应比照 WPPT 第 5 条(表演者的精神权利)给予其与上述条款所规定的相同权利。

评注:

应从正常利用录制在视听录制品中的表演等角度,进一步考虑精神权利的适用范围和方式。

(文件完)

5.5 Submission of Canada

Document Code: SCCR/3/9
Language: English
URL: https://www.wipo.int/edocs/mdocs/copyright/en/sccr_3/sccr_3_9.pdf

Chinese Translation: Not Available.
URL: N/A

STANDING COMMITTEE ON COPYRIGHT
AND RELATED RIGHTS
Third Session
Geneva, November 16 to 20, 1999

AGENDA ITEM 4: PROTECTION OF AUDIOVISUAL PERFORMANCES

SUBMISSION OF CANADA[1]

SUBMISSION OF CANADA

Canada submitted a proposal to the first session of the Standing Committee in November 1998 (document SCCR/1/8)[2]. Among other issues, that submission

1 Received on November 11, 1999.

2 Also contained in Comparative Table of Proposals (document SCCR/2/4).

5.5 加拿大提交的文件

文件编号：SCCR/3/9
文件语言：英语
文件链接：https://www.wipo.int/edocs/mdocs/copyright/en/sccr_3/sccr_3_9.pdf
中文文本：无
文件链接：无

版权及相关权常设委员会

第三届会议

1999 年 11 月 16 日至 20 日，日内瓦

议程项目四：保护视听表演

加拿大提交的文件[1]

加拿大提交的文件

加拿大于 1998 年 11 月向常设委员会第一次会议提交了一项提案（SCCR/1/8 号文件[2]）。除其他问题外，该文件还涉及权利的转让 / 转让的承认。

1　于 1999 年 11 月 11 日收到。

2　同时载于提案比较表（SCCR/2/4 号文件）。

addressed transfer of rights / recognition of transfers.

That submission and the proposals below are intended to facilitate discussion. In making these proposals we are not indicating that we support any particular substantive right in the protocol/treaty. We are retaining the proposals on term of protection and applicable term from the November 1998 submission.

I. RECOGNITION OF TRANSFERS OF RIGHTS

The proposal on recognition of transfers in the November 1998 submission contained a large number of square brackets or options. We recommend that the following principles be adopted with respect to such a provision: (1) that the same rule on transfers apply to all performers in a particular audiovisual work; (2) that there be a requirement that the original consent to be in writing (although such written consent could be given indirectly on behalf of a performer, for example, by a union or the leader of a group); and (3) that the provision does not apply to moral rights. The November 1998 submission did not apply to moral rights but we have no objection to stating this explicitly in the protocol / treaty.

In its May 1999 proposal the International Federation of Actors (FIA) proposed that there be a linkage (or point of attachment) between the producer and the audiovisual work beyond the fact that the producer might be organizing or financing the production. We agree that there should be a linkage of some type between the nation making the declaration and the audiovisual work beyond the fact that the [author]/[producer]/[first owner of copyright] is from that country. We are currently examining what would be the appropriate linkage in light of the FIA proposal and other comments we have received.

The proposal above deals only with the recognition of transfers by operation of law. We believe that it is important that the final instrument also contain a provision on the recognition of transfers by contract. We are still discussing the appropriate wording of such a provision with interested parties in Canada and we welcome any comments which other delegations or representatives may have on this issue.

II. RIGHT OF BROADCASTING AND COMMUNICATION TO THE PUBLIC

We recommend that the following three alternatives be considered for the protocol/treaty:

该文件及以下提案旨在促进讨论。这些提案并不代表我们支持议定书 / 条约中任何特定的实质性权利。我们保留 1998 年 11 月提交的关于保护期和适用期限的建议。

一、权利转让的承认

1998 年 11 月提交的关于承认转让的提案包含许多方括号或备选方案。我们建议就此条款采用以下原则:(1)同一转让规则适用于特定视听作品中的所有表演者;(2)要求原始同意必须采用书面形式(尽管这种书面同意可由表演者的授权代表间接作出,例如,由工会或团体的领导者作出);(3)该条款不适用于精神权利。1998 年 11 月的意见书不适用于精神权利,但我们不反对在议定书 / 条约中对此予以明确说明。

国际演员联合会(FIA)在其 1999 年 5 月的提案中建议,制作者除了可能组织制作并为制作提供资金外,还应与视听作品存在联系(或连接点)。我们同意,除(作者)/(制作者)/(第一著作权人)来自该国外,作出声明的国家还应与视听作品存在某种联系。目前,我们正在根据国际演员联合会的提案和我们收到的其他建议,研究什么是适当的联系。

上述提案仅涉及通过法律实施来承认转让。我们认为,重要的是,最终的法律文本还应包含一项关于承认合同转让的规定。我们仍在与加拿大有关方面讨论这一规定的适当措词,我们欢迎其他代表团或代表就此问题发表意见。

二、广播权和向公众传播权

我们建议在议定书 / 条约中考虑以下三种备选方案:

1. that it remain silent on this right (i.e. the right would not be required under the protocol/treaty); or

2. that it provide a purely optional right based on the wording of Article 15 of the WIPO Performances and Phonograms Treaty; or

3. that it provide a right which could be asserted against the copyright owner of the audiovisual work but not against a broadcaster (unless the broadcaster was also the copyright owner). A provision of this type would give the performer a remedy against the copyright owner if the copyright owner authorized the broadcast or communication of the work without the consent of the performer and the performer had not waived that right.

III. APPLICATION IN TIME

1. The Contracting Parties shall apply the provisions of Article 18 of the Berne Convention, *mutatis mutandis*, to the rights of performers provided for in this [Protocol] / [Treaty].

2. Notwithstanding paragraph (1), a Contracting Party may by notice given at the time of ratification or accession to this [Protocol] / [Treaty] state that it will limit the application of this [Protocol] / [Treaty] to [performances in] fixations or audiovisual works made after of the coming into force of this [Protocol] / [Treaty] in that Contracting Party.

3. [Application in time of moral rights provision].

IV. National Treatment

(This provision would probably be in the national treatment section.)

Notwithstanding paragraph X, if a Contracting Party grants protection to performances in fixations or audiovisual works made prior to the time of the coming into force of this [Protocol] / [Treaty] in that Contracting Party, it shall not be obliged to give such protection to performers who are nationals of Contracting Parties which have made a declaration under Article Y(2).

Note

"Paragraph X" means the relevant paragraph of the article on national treatment.

[End of document]

1. 对此项权利保持沉默(即议定书 / 条约对该项权利不作要求);

2. 根据《世界知识产权组织表演和录音制品条约》第 15 条的措辞,规定一项纯粹的选择性权利;

3. 规定一项可以对视听作品的版权权利人主张,但不得对广播者主张的权利(除非广播者同时也是版权权利人)。如果版权权利人未经表演者同意授权对作品进行广播或传播,并且表演者未放弃该项权利,则此类条款将为表演者提供针对版权权利人的救济。

三、适用的时限

1. 缔约各方应将《伯尔尼公约》第 18 条的规定比照适用于本(议定书)/(条约)规定的表演者权利。

2. 尽管有第(1)款的规定,缔约方可以在批准或加入本(议定书)/(条约)时发出通知,表明本(议定书)/(条约)的适用范围仅限于本(协议)/(条约)在该缔约方生效后的(表演的)录制品或视听作品上。

3.(精神权利的适用时限条款)。

四、国民待遇

(该规定可能出现在国民待遇一节中。)

尽管有第 X 款的规定,如果缔约方对于在本(议定书)/(条约)对该缔约方生效之前制作的表演的录制品或视听作品给予保护,如果表演者是已根据第 Y(2)条作出声明的缔约方的国民,则该缔约方没有义务给予这种保护。

说明

“第 X 款”是指国民待遇条款中的有关规定。

(文件完)

6.
Standing Committee on Copyright and Related Rights: Fourth Session

Meeting code: SCCR/4
Date: April 11 to April 14, 2000
venue: Geneva, Switzerland
Meeting Documents URL:
https://www.wipo.int/meetings/en/details.jsp##meeting_id=4031

6.
版权及相关权常设委员会：第四届会议

会议代码：SCCR/4
会议日期：2000 年 4 月 11—14 日
会议地点：瑞士日内瓦
会议文件链接：
https://www.wipo.int/meetings/en/details.jsp##meeting_id=4031

6.1 Submission on Behalf of the European Community and its Member States on the Protection of Performers' Rights in their Audiovisual Performances

Document Code: SCCR/4/2
Language: English
URL: https://www.wipo.int/edocs/mdocs/copyright/en/sccr_4/sccr_4_2.pdf

Chinese Translation: Not Available.
URL: N/A

STANDING COMMITTEE ON COPYRIGHT
AND RELATED RIGHTS
Fourth Session
Geneva, April 11, 12 and 14, 2000

SUBMISSION ON BEHALF OF THE EUROPEAN COMMUNITY AND ITS MEMBER STATES ON THE PROTECTION OF PERFORMERS' RIGHTS IN THEIR AUDIOVISUAL PERFORMANCES

Submitted by the European Community and its Members States[1]

1 Received on February 4, 2000.

6.1 代表欧洲共同体及其成员国提交的关于保护表演者视听表演权利的材料

文件编号：SCCR/4/2
文件语言：英语
文件链接：https://www.wipo.int/edocs/mdocs/copyright/en/sccr_4/sccr_4_2.pdf
中文文本：无
文件链接：无

版权及相关权常设委员会

第四届会议

2000 年 4 月 11 日、12 日和 14 日，日内瓦

代表欧洲共同体及其成员国提交的关于保护表演者视听表演权利的材料

由欧洲共同体及其成员提交[1]

1　于 2000 年 2 月 4 日收到。

SUBMISSION ON BEHALF OF THE EUROPEAN COMMUNITYAND ITS MEMBER STATES ON THE PROTECTION OF PERFORMERS' RIGHTS IN THEIR AUDIOVISUAL PERFORMANCES

1. In view of the forthcoming discussions on the protection of performers' rights in their audiovisual performances that will take place in the next extraordinary session of the WIPO Standing Committee on Copyright and Related Rights (SCCR), the European Community and its Member States wish to reiterate their commitment to the protection of audiovisual performances, as expressed already in previous submissions, notably WIPO documents AP/CE/I/3 Add., AP/CE/2/2, SCCR/1/4, SCCR/2/3 and SCCR/2/4.

2. Separate views and positions have accompanied the discussions on this issue for years. These diverging views were already reflected in the basic proposal for a treaty on the protection of performances and phonogram producers tabled in the course of the preparation for the Diplomatic Conference that took place in December 1996.

3. The European Community and its Member States have always held the view that an international treaty for the protection of performers should cover all performances - both sound and audiovisual. This view has been shared by numerous countries and regions. Unfortunately it was not possible to achieve this result in the framework of the 1996 Diplomatic Conference that adopted the WIPO Performances and Phonograms Treaty (WPPT). The alternative option, according to which audio-visual performances were not to be covered by the WPPT, prevailed—to the deep regret of the European Community and its Member States, as well as many other countries and regions.

4. As a result, at the end of the Diplomatic Conference, the European Community and its Member States fully supported the unanimously adopted Resolution that called for the adoption of an Audiovisual Protocol before the end of 1998.

代表欧洲共同体及其成员国提交的关于保护表演者视听表演权利的材料

1. 鉴于即将在世界知识产权组织版权和相关权常设委员会下一届特别会议上讨论如何保护表演者在其视听表演中的权利，欧洲共同体及其成员国愿重申其对保护视听表演的承诺，这一点在以前的文件中已经表达过，特别是第AP/CE/I/3Add 号、AP/CE/2/2 号、SCCR/1/4 号、SCCR/2/3 号和 SCCR/2/4 号文件。

2. 多年来，在讨论这个问题时一直有不同的观点和立场。这些不同的意见已经反映在 1996 年 12 月举行的外交会议筹备过程中提出的关于保护表演和录音制品制作者条约的基本建议中。

3. 欧洲共同体及其成员国一直认为，保护表演者的国际条约应包括所有的表演——包括声音表演和视听表演，许多国家和地区都赞同这一观点。遗憾的是，在 1996 年通过《世界知识产权组织表演和录音制品条约》的外交会议的框架内，未能取得这一成果。根据备选方案，视听表演不包括在 WPPT 范围内，这使欧洲共同体及其成员国以及许多其他国家和地区深感遗憾。

4. 因此，在外交会议结束时，欧洲共同体及其成员国支持一项一致通过的决议，该决议要求在 1998 年年底之前制定一份视听表演议定书。

5. The European Community and its Member States continue to be of the view that the protection of audiovisual performances should be updated and modernised. The reasoning for this position has been explained on numerous occasions but is worth repeating. In our view, the Protocol has three main objectives, which are very similar to the objectives of the WPPT:

• We have to update and to strengthen the level of protection accorded by the Rome Convention for both sound and audiovisual performers' rights. Consequently, the content and scope of the rights for audiovisual performers in the Protocol should be similar to the protection sound performers enjoy under the WPPT. While the differences should not be neglected, any unjustified discrimination between these two groups of performers should be avoided.

• When doing so, the Protocol does not have to be overly complex nor should it call into question existing traditions. The consensus enshrined in the WPPT should be taken as a basis. This implies that discussions should not, without a clearly demonstrated need to do so, focus on introducing new rules, which may be alien to existing domestic and international frameworks, such as on the transfer of rights or national treatment. Simplicity and flexibility of the Protocol will in our view pave the way to success, to common understanding and to its widespread acceptance.

• Finally, the principal objective of the Protocol is to improve and update the protection of audiovisual performers - and not the protection of audiovisual producers. The Protocol is designed to improve performers' rights rather than to reduce them or to take them away for the benefit of producers.

6. The European Community and its Member States believe that we have sufficient common ground for these objectives if the Rome Convention (that has been ratified, as of now, by more that 60 countries), the WPPT and the Resolution mentioned above are taken as starting points. Moreover, and in view of the discussions over the last years, our perspectives are now clearer than ever. All relevant issues in fact appear to be on the table, they have been discussed and the views are known.

7. As already stated during the last session of the SCCR, in the view of the European Community and its Member States, four years after the adoption of the WPPT and of the Resolution, the time has come to decide on how to successfully

5. 欧洲共同体及其成员国一致认为，对视听表演的保护应予更新和现代化。这一立场的理由已在许多场合中解释过，但仍值得重申。我们认为，该议定书有三个主要目标，这些目标与WPPT的目标非常相似：

• 我们必须更新和加强《罗马公约》对声音和视听表演者权利的保护水平。因此，议定书中视听表演者权利的内容和范围应与声音表演者根据WPPT所享有的保护相似。虽然这种差异不应被忽视，但也应避免对这两类演员任何不合理的歧视。

• 这样做时，该协议不必过于复杂，也不应对现有的传统提出质疑。应以WPPT所载的共识作为基础。这意味着，在没有明确表明需要这样做的情况下，讨论不应集中于引进新的规则，这些规则可能与现有的国内和国际框架不符，例如权利转让或国民待遇。我们认为，该议定书的简单性和灵活性将为其成功、共同理解和广泛接受铺平道路。

• 最后，该议定书的主要目标是改进和更新对视听表演者的保护，而不是对视听制作者的保护。该协议旨在提高表演者的权利，而不是减少表演者的权利，或者为了制作者的利益而取消表演者的权利。

6. 欧洲共同体及其成员国认为，如果以《罗马公约》（到目前为止已有60多个国家批准）、WPPT和上述决议为出发点，我们就有足够的共同基础实现这些目标。此外，鉴于过去几年的讨论，我们的观点比以往任何时候都更加清晰。所有相关问题实际上似乎都已摆到桌面上，它们已经被讨论过，大家都知道它们的观点。

7. 正如欧洲共同体及其成员国在SCCR上届会议上已经指出的那样，在WPPT和决议通过四年之后，现在是决定如何成功地结束我们的谈判的时候了。在SCCR下一届特别会议期间，我们必须就我们采取的方向作出决定。

conclude our negotiations. During the next extraordinary session of the SCCR we will have to take a decision on the direction we take.

8. When doing so we should be guided by:

• The objectives of the negotiations, which have been described above, and to which the European Community and its Member States attach great importance;

• A constructive approach, that would bear in mind the credibility of the SCCR. It seems difficult to accept that agreement on updating the protection of other rightholders covered by the Rome Convention is possible, but not on the protection of audiovisual performers;

• The desire to accommodate the different traditions regarding the treatment of audiovisual performers without imposing choices on the international community.

9. On the basis of these objectives, this constructive approach and these guidelines, the European Community and its Member States are ready to move ahead, together with like-minded delegations, and to proceed towards a successful Diplomatic Conference in December 2000.

[End of document]

8. 在这样做的时候，我们应该遵循以下原则：

• 上文所述的，欧洲共同体及其成员国极为重视的谈判目标；

• 考虑到版权和相关权常设委员会的信誉，这是一种建设性的做法。《罗马公约》包括的对其他权利者的保护有可能达成更新的协议，但对视听表演者的保护则不可能，这似乎难以接受；

• 希望在对待视听表演者方面容纳不同的传统，而不把选择强加给国际社会。

9. 根据这些目标、建设性办法和准则，欧洲共同体及其成员国准备同有相同想法的代表团一道向前迈进，争取在 2000 年 12 月举行一次成功的外交会议。

（文件完）

6.2 Submission of the United States of America on the New Article 4

Document Code: SCCR/4/3
Language: English
URL: https://www.wipo.int/edocs/mdocs/copyright/en/sccr_4/sccr_4_3.pdf

Chinese Translation: Not Available.
URL: N/A

STANDING COMMITTEE ON COPYRIGHT AND RELATED RIGHTS

Fourth Session

Geneva, April 11, 12 and 14, 2000

SUBMISSION OF THE UNITED STATES OF AMERICA ON THE NEW ARTICLE 4

Submitted by the United States of Americ[1]

1 Submitted on February 15, 2000.

6.2 美国就新的第 4 条提交的材料

文件编号：SCCR/4/3
文件语言：英语
文件链接：https://www.wipo.int/edocs/mdocs/copyright/en/sccr_4/sccr_4_3.pdf
中文文本：无
文件链接：无

版权及相关权常设委员会

第四届会议

2000 年 4 月 11 日、12 日和 14 日，日内瓦

美国就新的第4条提交的材料

由美国提交[1]

1　于 2000 年 2 月 15 日提交。

SUBMISSION OF THE UNITED STATES OF AMERICA FOR THE APRIL 11, 12 AND 14, 2000, MEETING OF THE STANDING COMMITTEE ON COPYRIGHT AND RELATED RIGHTS

1. The United States recognizes that national treatment is a problematic issue and that it is necessary to deal with the concerns of all of the participants in this process of developing an appropriate set of principles to deal with performers rights in the digital age. As we noted in our last submission, striking an appropriate balance may take some time to achieve.

2. It is a fundamental principle that performers should be compensated for their performances and that different approaches exist in several countries and regions. The provisions on national treatment in the proposed new treaty need to take into account the different systems by which performers are compensated, including collective bargaining agreements and systems of equitable remuneration.

3. The second fundamental principle is that remuneration that is collected on account of performances must be distributed to the individuals appearing in those performances. If such distributions are not made, then collections ought not be made with respect to such performances. In order to propose an implementation of this important principle, we submit the following new Article 4 for consideration as part of the US Proposal.

Article 4

National Treatment

(1) Each Contracting Party shall accord to nationals covered in Article 3, in respect of the subject matter protected under this Treaty, the protection that it accords its own nationals in respect to:

(i) the exclusive rights provided in this Treaty;

(ii) rights which derive from any exclusive right provided in this Treaty, including but not limited to rights of remuneration; and

(iii) any other rights as to which another Contracting Party provides, under its

美国向2000年4月11日、12日和14日召开的版权及相关权常设委员会会议提交的材料

1. 美国认识到国民待遇是一个疑难问题，在制定一套适当的原则以处理数字时代的表演者权利的过程中，有必要解决所有参与者的关切。正如我们在上次提交的文件中指出的那样，要达到适当的平衡可能需要一些时间。

2. 表演者应得到补偿是一项基本原则，而在一些国家和地区存在着不同的做法。拟议的新条约中关于国民待遇的规定需要考虑到对表演者进行补偿的不同制度，包括集体谈判协议和公平报酬制度。

3. 第二个基本原则是，因演出而收取的款项必须分配给参加这些演出的个人。如果不进行这种分配，那么就不应该对这些表演进行收费。为了落实这一重要原则，我们提出了以下新的第四条，作为美方建议的一部分予以考虑。

第四条

国民待遇

（1）就本条约所保护的客体而言，每个缔约方给予第 3 条所涉及的国民以它在以下方面给予本国国民的保护：

（i）本条约规定的专有权；

（ii）源自本条约规定的任何专有权的权利，包括但不限于获酬权；以及

（iii）另一缔约方根据其本国法律为该表演提供的基本相同水平的保护。

domestic law, substantially the same level of protection for such subject matter.

(2) Any Contracting Party that, under its domestic law, provides for rights of remuneration or mandatory collective administration of exclusive rights with respect to a performance, fixed or unfixed, protected under this Treaty may provide in a Declaration to the Director General that it will not provide the benefits of such rights to nationals of another Contracting Party. The Contracting Party making such Declaration shall provide in its national law measures that preclude collection for such rights in respect of audiovisual performances by nationals of any other Contracting Party in respect of which such Declaration is made.

[End of document]

（2）任一缔约方根据其本国法律对受本条约保护的录制或者尚未录制的表演，规定了获酬权或强制性集体管理专有权，可以向总干事提交声明，表示其不会将这种权利提供给另一缔约方的国民。作出该声明的缔约方应在其本国法律措施中进行规定，以防止该声明所指向的任何其他缔约方的国民就视听表演获得此类权利。

（文件完）

6.3 Submission of the United States of America on Transfer

Document Code: SCCR/4/4
Language: English
URL: https://www.wipo.int/edocs/mdocs/copyright/en/sccr_4/sccr_4_4.pdf

Chinese Translation: Not Available.
URL: N/A

STANDING COMMITTEE ON COPYRIGHT AND RELATED RIGHTS

Fourth Session

Geneva, April 11, 12 and 14, 2000

SUBMISSION OF THE UNITED STATES OF AMERICA ON TRANSFER

Submitted by the United States of Americ[1]

TRANSFER

1. The greatest impediment to the adoption of a globally accepted WIPO Performers' Rights Treaty seems centered around the issue of when and how the

1 Submitted on April 5, 2000.

6.3 美国就转让条款提交的材料

文件编号：SCCR/4/4
文件语言：英语
文件链接：https://www.wipo.int/edocs/mdocs/copyright/en/sccr_4/sccr_4_4.pdf
中文文本：无
文件链接：无

版权及相关权常设委员会

第四届会议
2000 年 4 月 11 日、12 日和 14 日，日内瓦

美国就转让条款提交的材料

由美国提交[1]

转让

1. 通过一项全球接受的《世界知识产权组织表演者权利条约》的最大障碍，似乎集中在条约所规定的专有权何时以及如何从表演者手中转让给制作者

1　于 2000 年 4 月 5 日提交。

exclusive rights of authorization created by the Treaty are to be transferred from the performer to the producer. While a number of proposals have been made to the Standing Committee, no meaningful consensus has yet formed behind any of those proposals.

2. One of the purposes of any international treaty is to provide certainty as to the rights created by or recognized in the treaty. Unlike literary or musical works, audiovisual works involve contributions of many different individuals who may be of different nationalities. In addition, audiovisual works are increasingly produced and financed across national borders which makes consistency and certainty of transfer and rights ownership rules extremely important. The distribution of motion pictures is by necessity a global enterprise. Growing broadband internet access will increase the scope and pace of international distribution.

3. Furthermore, the rights being created by this Treaty will, in certain territories, be new rights which do not currently exist or which are not currently recognized as separate rights. With such newly created rights, where systems are not already established for dealing with those rights, it is particularly important that the Treaty which gives rise to those rights address the questions of transfer and control of those rights.

4. This paper will examine the critical elements for an effective transfer provision and analyze the current proposals in light of those elements.

A. CRITICAL ELEMENTS FOR AN EFFECTIVE TRANSFER PROVISION

5. In order to create an environment that: (i) preserves for performers the potential for bargaining for their rights and thereby encourages development of strong collective bargaining, (ii) further reserves to performers the vital income from equitable remuneration, (iii) permits adequate recovery for the uniquely significant economic investment in motion picture production, and (iv) provides certainty both for producers and performers, the following concerns need to be addressed:

(1) The transfer provision should not be applicable to rights of remuneration

6. One of the critical purposes of a performers' rights treaty is to ensure that performers have an opportunity to secure appropriate compensation for their creative contribution to motion pictures. In many countries this is accomplished by collective bargaining; in others, through legislative systems of rights of

的问题上。虽然常设委员会收到了一些建议,但任何一个建议都没有形成有意义的共识。

2. 任何国际条约的目的之一都是为条约所创设或承认的权利提供确定性。与文学或音乐作品不同,视听作品涉及许多不同个人的贡献,他们可能属于不同的国籍。此外,视听作品越来越多地跨越国界进行制作和融资。这使转让和权利所有权规则的一致性和确定性变得极为重要。电影的发行必然是一个全球性的事业。不断增长的宽带互联网接入将增加国际发行的范围和速度。

3. 此外,本条约创造的权利在某些地区将是目前不存在或目前不被承认为独立权利的新权利。对于这些新创设的权利,在尚未建立处理这些权利的制度的情况下,特别重要的是,产生这些权利的条约应解决这些权利的转让和控制问题。

4. 本文将研究有效转移条款的关键因素,并根据这些因素分析目前的提案。

A. 有效转移条款的关键因素

5. 为了创造一个环境,以:(i)为表演者保留对其权利进行谈判的可能,从而鼓励发展强有力的集体谈判,(ii)进一步为表演者保留从公平报酬中获得的重要收入,(iii)允许对在电影制作方面进行独特的重大经济投资作出适当补偿,并且(iv)为制作人和表演者提供确定性,需要解决以下问题:

(1)转让条款不适用于获酬权

6. 表演者权利条约的重要目的之一是确保表演者有机会能够通过他们对电影的创造性贡献获得合理的报酬。在许多国家,这是通过集体谈判来实现的;另外有些国家,通过立法确立获酬权制度。还有在其他一些国家,两种制度的结合也被证明是有效的。转让条款不应损害表演者目前通过法律或其他

remuneration. In still others a combination of the two systems has proven effective. The transfer provision should not undermine the protections performers currently have in law or otherwise. Excluding rights of remuneration from the scope of the transfer provision will assure that performers whose protections are based in whole or in part on legislative rights of remuneration will be secured.

(2) The transfer provision should not be applicable to moral rights

7. Moral rights preserve a performer's individual right to the integrity of his or her performance and to be identified as the performer of his or her performance. These rights, to the extent they do not impinge on the normal exploitation of a motion picture, are not relevant to the needs of producers to distribute their motion pictures. In fact, the ability of performers to enforce their rights against violators of moral rights directly, supports the integrity of the motion picture.

8. The reservation of moral rights to performers is critical in this age where performances stored digitally can be manipulated by the use of universally available consumer equipment and easily distributed on the internet. The ability of performers to earn a living is based largely on their reputation. Without such reservation, performers would be unable to protect their most important assets—their image and reputation.

(3) Any presumption of transfer of rights should be subject to rebuttal by written contract

9. A rebuttable presumption provides the opportunity for reservation of rights to the performer and for contractual negotiations. The opportunity to bargain specific terms that reflect the particular circumstances of the production is necessary to give substance to performers' rights.

(4) The transfer provision should be applicable to a particular audiovisual production

10. At the time that a performer agrees to the fixation of his or her performance, he or she is doing so for a particular audiovisual production. The performer is compensated for the fixation of such performance for use in such production and the right to distribute such production, with further compensation assured for the distribution of such production by contract, collective bargaining, legislation, or a combination of the foregoing. A transfer provision should provide

途径享有的保护。将获酬权排除在转让条款的范围之外，将确保表演者从全部或部分立法规定获得的获酬权得到保障。

（2）获酬权不适用于精神权利

7. 精神权利保留表演者的个人权利，以确保其表演的完整性，并被确定为表演者。在不影响电影正常使用的情况下，这些权利与制片人发行其电影无关。实际上，表演者直接对侵犯精神权利的人行使其权利的能力维持了电影的完整性。

8. 在这个时代，保留表演者的精神权利至关重要，因为通过使用普通的用户设备，就可以篡改以数字形式存储的表演，并很容易在互联网上传播。表演者谋生的能力很大程度上取决于他们的声誉。如果没有这种保留，表演者将无法保护他们最重要的资产——形象和声誉。

（3）任何权利转让的推定都可以通过书面合同推翻

9. 可推翻的推定为表演者保留权利和合同谈判提供了机会。为了赋予表演者权利实质内容，必须有机会就反映具体制作情况的具体条款进行谈判。

（4）转让规定应适用于特定的视听制品

10. 表演者同意录制其表演时，就是为了制作某一特定的视听制品。在视听制品中使用其被录制下来的表演以及允许他人发行这一制品，表演者获得相应报酬，并通过合同、集体谈判、立法或前述各项的组合确保了通过这种制品的发行进一步获取报酬。转让规定应为这些电影的制片人和发行人提供关于授权的确定性。但是，将这种规定扩展到其他新的使用这些表演的视听制品是不可取的，也没有必要。表演者应当有权就其被录制的表演是否能在新作品中

certainty to producers and distributors of such motion picture with respect to the rights of authorization. However, it is not desirable nor necessary to extend such provision to the inclusion of such performances in new audiovisual productions. Performers must have the right to bargain over whether their captured performances are included in new works.

(5) The transfer provision should not require countries to change their systems regarding transfers of rights from performers to producers.

11. Some countries have legal provisions that vest rights in producers, other countries do not. Some countries have well-developed collective bargaining arrangements between producers and performers, others do not. The transfer provision should not override existing legal systems and require changes in domestic laws, nor should it supercede collective bargaining agreements between performers and producers.

(6) The transfer provision should be simple and direct.

12. The transfer provision should be simple and direct. It should not give rise to uncertainty, particularly uncertainties that would have to be resolved through judicial proceedings, and should not be open to inappropriate manipulation.

(7)The transfer provision should take into consideration the increasingly complex world of productions (with co-productions, co-financing arrangements, multi-national casts, multi-national shooting locations, etc.)

13. As noted above, for an international treaty to be effective it must provide clarity; if the crucial issue of transfer of the newly created rights is left entirely to national laws, then increased confusion will result. This is particularly true for the increasing number of audiovisual works which are not the product of a single country but rather involve producers, financiers, and casts of different nationalities. It should also be kept in mind that the importance of the issue of ownership of rights in cinematographic works has been recognized in Article 14bis of the Berne Convention.

14. Also, as noted in the introduction, the rights being created by this Treaty will, in certain territories, be new rights which do not currently exist or which are not currently recognized as separate rights. With such newly created rights, where systems are not already established for dealing with such new rights, it is

被使用进行谈判。

(5)转让规定不应要求各国改变其关于权利从表演者转让到制作者的制度。

11. 一些国家有法律规定制作者应享有权利，而其他国家则没有。一些国家为制作者和表演者确立了完善的集体谈判制度，而其他国家则没有。转让规定不应凌驾于现有法律制度之上、不应改变国内立法，也不应取代表演者与制作者之间的集体谈判协议。

(6)转让规定应当简单、直接。

12. 转让规定应简单直接。它不应引起不确定性，特别是必须通过司法程序解决的不确定性，并且不应给不适当的操纵留有空间。

(7)转让规定应考虑到日益复杂的制作产业（包括联合制作，共同融资安排，多国演员，多国拍摄地点等）。

13. 如上所述，要使一项国际条约起作用，其必须具有明确性；如果将转让这些新创设的权利的关键问题完全留给国家立法来解决，将会造成更多的混乱。对于越来越多的不是单个国家而是由不同国籍的制片人、投资人和演员参与的视听制品来说，尤其如此。还应牢记，《伯尔尼公约》第 14 条已明确摄影作品中的所有权问题。

14. 另外，如导言所述，在某些领域，本条约创造的权利在某些地区将是目前不存在或目前不被承认为独立权利的新权利。对于这些新创设的权利，在尚未建立处理这些权利的制度的情况下，特别重要的是，产生这些权利的条约应解决这些权利的转让和控制问题。

particularly important that the Treaty which gives rise to those rights address the questions of transfer and control of those rights.

(8) The transfer provision should provide certainty for the distribution of audiovisual works around the world.

15. Producers and distributors of audiovisual works should be able to determine the ownership and control of the performers' rights in the work based on the provisions of the Treaty and on written agreements. Producers should not be left, under the Treaty, with the bewildering task of trying to interpret which domestic laws of which countries are applicable when the work is being distributed around the world. Without certainty, it will become far more difficult for producers to secure financing for international productions, which in turn will decrease employment opportunities for performers.

B. VARIOUS APPROACHES TO TRANSFER

16. None of the current proposals on transfer meet all of the criteria set forth above and, as a result, it has not been possible to form a consensus behind any of the proposals.

(1) Silence on transfer - *The E.U. has proposed that the Treaty remain silent on transfer, leaving the question of ownership and control of the rights created by the Treaty to the domestic law of each country. This approach does not provide the necessary certainty and predictability. Bargaining over the value of the new rights becomes impaired by an inability to ascertain the scope of these rights. This approach also fails to assure a base level of protection for performers relating to the transfer of rights, e.g., in the areas of remuneration rights and moral rights. In addition, it would result in constant disputes and uncertainty over which countries' laws are applicable to a production and how those laws are to be interpreted.*

(2) A rebuttable presumption of transfer - *The U.S. has proposed a rebuttable presumption of transfer from the performer to the producer of the exclusive rights of authorization created by the Treaty that is limited to exclusive rights of authorization with respect to a particular audiovisual work. While many countries have a presumption of transfer in their domestic laws, this approach would require some countries to change their laws, and might impose a new system of rights transfers on their domestic audiovisual production industries.*

（8）转让规定应为视听作品在世界各地的发行提供确定性。

15. 视听作品的制作者和发行者应当能够根据条约的规定和书面协议确定在作品中表演者权的归属及控制。在该条约下，制作者不应让自己承担这样一项令人困惑的任务：当作品在世界各地发行时，试图寻找应当适用哪些国家的哪些国内法。如果没有确定性，制作者将更加难以保障国际制作的融资，这也将减少表演者的就业机会。视听作品的制作者和发行者有权根据条约规定和书面协议约定在作品中明确权利归属和表演权的行使。

B. 各种转让方式

16. 目前关于转让的建议中没有一项符合上述所有标准，因此无法就任何一项建议达成一致意见。

（1）不提及转让问题——欧盟提议该条约不提及转让问题，将该条约所创设的权利的所有权和控制问题留给各国的国内法律。这种方法没有提供必要的确定性和可预测性。由于无法确定这些权利的范围，对这些新权利价值的谈判就会受到损害。这种办法也不能保证在权利转让方面（例如在获酬权和精神权利方面）为表演者提供基本的保护。此外，它还会导致就某一制作应适用哪些国家的法律以及如何解释这些法律不断产生争议和不确定性。

（2）可被推翻的转让推定——美国提议规定一个可被推翻的转让推定，即推定表演者向制作者转让该条约规定的排他性专有权，但该推定仅限于对某一特定视听作品的排他性专有权授权。尽管许多国家在其国内法中有规定推定转让，但这种做法将要求一些国家修改其法律，并可能对其国内视听制作产业强加一个新的权利转让制度。

(3) Rules of transfer determined by the country of origin of the work - *Canada has proposed that the country of origin of the audiovisual work should control whether the exclusive rights of authorization should be presumed transferred subject to rebuttal by written agreement. That is, countries may opt in or opt out for a presumption. This approach does not require any countries to change their laws for their domestic productions and insures producers that one uniform system of transfer will apply to a given work regardless of where it is exploited. The great drawback, however, is the extremely complicated question of determining the country of origin of a work, which could be subject to improper manipulation. Such a determination may have to consider nationality of the performers, the producer, the screenwriter, the underlying material, as well as the country of principal photography, etc. - and would be compounded by the fact that each of those categories may involve multiple nationalities, such as a multi-national cast. Objections were also raised to the application within one country of the differing transfer provisions of another country.*

(4) Berne Article 14bis2 approach - *GRULAC, India, Japan and others have suggested an approach based on Article 14bis2 of the Berne Convention. Concern has been expressed that this approach decreases the bargaining power of performers, since it precludes performers from objecting to the exploitation by the producer of any of the exclusive rights set forth in the Treaty. However, the Berne provision does provide for rebuttal by written contract. These proposals do have the drawback of being broad in scope, i.e., not limiting the preclusion from objection to the work for which a performer rendered services.*

Japan has suggested a variation on the Article 14bis2 approach by adding an "opt-out" provision. The addition of an "opt-in" or "opt-out" approach for nationals of the "opting" country would solve the concern about certain countries having to change the way they treat transfers of rights for national productions (for example, this might avoid overriding those systems requiring written agreements for the transfer of exclusive rights). If countries are able to select participation in the system for their own nationals, however, the result would be that the rights of performers from different nations might be treated differently in the same production.

(5) Choice of law/ Recognition of transfer arrangements - *There has been a*

（3）由作品来源国来确定转让规则——加拿大提议，应由视听作品来源国来决定是否应推定排他性专有权已转让，且可被书面协议推翻。也就是说，各国可以选择采用或不予采用这种推定。这种方法不要求任何国家改变其关于国内制片产业的立法，并能向制作者确保，无论某一特定作品在何处被使用，都将适用一种统一的转让制度。但是，最大的缺点是，确定一份作品的来源国是一个极其复杂的问题，并可能会受到不当的操纵。这样的一种确定方式必须考虑表演者、制片人、编剧等人的国籍、基本素材以及主要拍摄地点所在国家，而且这些类别中的每个类别可能涉及多个国籍，这将使情况更加复杂，例如跨国演员的情形。也有人反对在一个国家内使用另一国不同的转让规则。

（4）《伯尔尼公约》第 14 条之二的办法——拉丁美洲和加勒比国家小组、印度、日本和其他国家根据《伯尔尼公约》第 14 条之二提出了一种办法。有人表示这种做法减损了表演者的谈判能力，因为它排除了表演者反对制作者利用条约中规定的任何专有权的可能性。然而，伯尔尼条款也规定了可以通过书面合同进行推翻。这些建议的缺点是范围太广，例如，没有限制对表演者提供服务的作品提出异议的排除。

日本建议对第 14 条之二的做法进行修改，增加一项——“选择不予采用”条款。添加一个“选择采用”或“选择不予采用”的方式，“选择”国家的国民将不必再担心一些国家不得不改变其对待本国作品权利转移的态度（例如，这也许可能避免推翻那些要求通过书面协议转让专有权的权利制度）。但是，如果各国能够为本国国民选择参加这一制度，其结果将导致不同国家表演者的权利在同一作品中可能受到不同的对待。

（5）选择法律 / 转让协议的承认——尽管常设委员会还没有收到正式的建

great deal of discussion of trying to find a compromise through a choice-of-law or a recognition-of-transfer approach, although no formal proposal of that type has been made to the Standing Committee. Such a proposal might provide "In the absence of a determination by the parties as to the applicable law, an agreement by a performer to transfer of the exclusive economic rights of authorization granted under this Treaty shall be governed by the law of the Contracting Party most closely connected to this agreement." This approach has the advantages of not requiring any country to change its laws applicable to its own audio-visual productions and does not decrease the bargaining power of performers (as it has been argued that an Article 14bis2 approach might), However, this proposal raises the complicated issue of determining the country "most closely connected to the agreement."

Conclusion

17. We believe that on-going consultations are critical to progress on this important issue. Resolution on the issue of transfer is necessary if a new instrument is to be widely adopted. Based on the foregoing, governments are urged to support discussion and proposals which will lead to consensus on this issue.

[End of document]

议，但关于“试图通过选择法律或转让协议的承认的方法来寻求折衷方案”这一问题被广泛讨论。这样的提议可以规定：“在当事方未确定适用法律的情况下，表演者达成的转让本条约规定的专有经济权利的协议应受与该协议有最密切联系的缔约方法律的约束。”这种方法的优点是不需要任何国家更改适用于其本国关于视听制品的法律，并且不会降低表演者的谈判能力（因为有人认为第 14 条之二第 2 款的方法可能会降低谈判能力），但是，该提案提出了一个复杂的问题，即如何确定哪一国家“与协议有最密切联系”。

结论

17. 我们认为，不断进行的协商对在这一重要问题上取得进展至关重要。如果要广泛通过一项新的法律文书，就必须通过关于转让问题的决议。基于以上所述，我们敦促各国政府支持讨论和建议，以便就这一问题达成共识。

（文件完）

6.4 Report on the Regional Consultation of Central European and Baltic States on the Protection of the Audiovisual Performances, Held in Geneva, on April 10, 2000

Document Code: SCCR/4/5
Language: English
URL: https://www.wipo.int/edocs/mdocs/copyright/en/sccr_4/sccr_4_5.pdf
Chinese Translation: Not Available.
URL: N/A

STANDING COMMITTEE ON COPYRIGHT
AND RELATED RIGHTS
Fourth Session
Geneva, April 11, 12 and 14, 2000

AGENDA ITEM 4: PROTECTION OF AUDIOVISUAL PERFORMANCES

REPORT ON THE REGIONAL CONSULTATION OF CENTRAL EUROPEAN AND BALTIC STATES ON THE PROTECTION OF AUDIOVISUAL PERFORMANCES, HELD IN GENEVA, ON APRIL 10, 200

submitted on behalf of Bulgaria, Croatia, Estonia, Hungary, Latvia Romania, Slovakia and Slovenia[1]

1. In the Regional Consultation, the following countries were represented:

1 Received on April 11, 2000.

6.4 关于 2000 年 4 月 10 日在日内瓦举行的中欧和波罗的海国家保护视听表演区域协商会议的报告

文件编号：SCCR/4/5
文件语言：英语
文件链接：https://www.wipo.int/edocs/mdocs/copyright/en/sccr_4/sccr_4_5.pdf
中文文本：无
文件链接：无

版权及相关权常设委员会

第四届会议

2000 年 4 月 11 日、12 日和 14 日，日内瓦

议程四：保护视听表演

关于 2000 年 4 月 10 日在日内瓦举行的中欧和波罗的海国家保护视听表演区域协商会议的报告

代表保加利亚、克罗地亚、爱沙尼亚、匈牙利、拉脱维亚、罗马尼亚、斯洛伐克和斯洛文尼亚提交[1]

1. 在区域协商中，下列国家派代表参加：保加利亚，克罗地亚，爱沙尼亚，

1　于 2000 年 4 月 11 日提交。

Bulgaria, Croatia, Estonia, Hungary, Latvia, Romania, Slovakia, and Slovenia.

2. Concerning the topic of the Agenda of the fourth session of the Standing Committee on Copyright and Related Rights, which is mentioned in document SCCR/3/11, paragraph 129, subparagraph (a)(i), the country representatives reiterated their commitment to further modernization and update of the protection of audiovisual performances. According to their view, modernization and update of the protection of audiovisual performances should not be postponed again, in particular due to the fact that it has been postponed repeatedly since the adoption of the WIPO Performances and Phonograms Treaty in 1996 and due to the Resolution adopted at the end of the 1996 Diplomatic Conference, which called for the adoption of an Audiovisual Protocol before the end of 1998. It is the opinion of represented countries that immediate action is required in order to convene a Diplomatic Conference for the adoption of an international instrument on the Protection of Audiovisual Performances. In this context, represented countries expressed their readiness to proceed towards a successful Diplomatic Conference in December 2000.

3. As far as the form of the possible instrument is concerned, represented countries are of the opinion that the form of a Protocol to the WIPO Performances and Phonograms Treaty will best serve as a basis for discussions at the Diplomatic Conference, to be held in December 2000.

4. As far as the contents of the possible Protocol are concerned, the represented countries maintain their position as mentioned in document SCCR/3/10. Moreover, they generally are of the opinion that the Diplomatic Conference should be held in December 2000 and therefore, without a compelling reason, discussions should not be re-opened on those issues in respect of which the member States of the Standing Committee seem to have reached an agreement. Therefore, they would welcome further clarification from those countries which propose a solution concerning the application in time of the possible instrument in a manner different from the one used in Article 22 of the WIPO Performances and Phonograms Treaty.

[End of document]

匈牙利，拉脱维亚，罗马尼亚，斯洛伐克和斯洛文尼亚。

2. 关于 SCCR/3/11 号文件第 129 段(a)(i)项中提到的版权及相关权常设委员会第四届会议议程的主题，国家代表重申了其对进一步现代化和更新对视听表演保护的承诺。他们认为，不应再推迟对视听表演进行保护的现代化和更新工作，尤其一方面是由于自 1996 年通过《世界知识产权组织表演和录音制品条约》以来，一再地推迟了对视听表演的保护和通过的决议；另一方面是由于 1996 年外交会议结束时通过的要求在 1998 年年底之前通过视听议定书的决议。有代表国认为，必须立即采取行动，以便召集外交会议通过一项国际文书来保护视听表演。在这方面，有代表国表示愿意继续参加 2000 年 12 月成功举行的外交会议。

3. 就可能的文书形式而言，与会代表国认为，《世界知识产权组织表演和录音制品条约议定书》的形式将最适合作为 2000 年 12 月举行的外交会议讨论的基础。

4. 就可能的议定书内容而言，代表国保持其在 SCCR/3/10 号文件中提到的立场。此外，他们普遍认为外交会议应于 2000 年 12 月举行，因此，在没有令人信服的理由的情况下，不应就常务委员会成员国似乎已达成一致的议题重新展开讨论。因此，当可能的文书与《世界知识产权组织表演和录音制品条约》第 22 条所用的方式不同的时候，他们欢迎那些提出解决方案的国家进一步澄清。

（文件完）

6.5 Report prepared by the Secretariat

Document Code: SCCR/4/6
Language: English
URL: https://www.wipo.int/edocs/mdocs/copyright/en/sccr_4/sccr_4_6-main1.pdf
Chinese Translation: Not Available.
URL: N/A

STANDING COMMITTEE ON COPYRIGHT
AND RELATED RIGHTS
Fourth Session
Geneva, April 11, 12 and 14, 2000

REPORT

prepared by the Secretariat

1. The Standing Committee on Copyright and Related Rights (hereinafter referred to as the Standing Committee) held its fourth session in Geneva on April 11, 12 and 14, 2000.

2. The following States members of WIPO and/or the Berne Union for the Protection of Literary and Artistic Works were represented at the meeting: Albania, Algeria, Andorra, Argentina, Australia, Austria, Bangladesh, Belgium, Brazil, Bulgaria, Burkina Faso, Cameroon, Canada, China, Colombia, Costa Rica, Côte d'Ivoire, Croatia, Denmark, Democratic Republic of the Congo, Ecuador, Egypt, El Salvador, Estonia, Finland, France, Germany, Ghana, Greece, Guinea,

6.5 由秘书处准备的报告

文件编号：SCCR/4/6
文件语言：英语
文件链接：https://www.wipo.int/edocs/mdocs/copyright/en/sccr_4/sccr_4_6-main1.pdf
中文文本：无
文件链接：无

版权及相关权常设委员会

第四届会议

2000 年 4 月 11 日、12 日和 14 日，日内瓦

报告

由秘书处编写

1. 版权及相关权常设委员会（以下简称常设委员会）于 2000 年 4 月 11 日、12 日、14 日在日内瓦举行第四次会议。

2. 下列世界知识产权组织成员国和 / 或伯尔尼保护文学和艺术作品联盟派代表出席了会议：阿尔巴尼亚、阿尔及利亚、安道尔、阿根廷、澳大利亚、奥地利、孟加拉国、比利时、巴西、保加利亚、布基纳法索、喀麦隆、加拿大、中国、哥伦比亚、哥斯达黎加、科特迪瓦、克罗地亚、丹麦、刚果民主共和国、厄瓜多尔、埃及、萨尔瓦多、爱沙尼亚、芬兰、法国、德国、加纳、希腊、几内亚、海地、匈牙利、印度、印度尼西亚、伊拉克、爱尔兰、意大利、牙买加、日本、哈萨克斯坦、肯

Haiti, Hungary, India, Indonesia, Iraq, Ireland, Italy, Jamaica, Japan, Kazakhstan, Kenya, Latvia, Lebanon, Libyan Arab Jamahiriya, Luxembourg, Madagascar, Malaysia, Malta, Mexico, Morocco, Netherlands, New Zealand, Nigeria, Norway, Panama, Peru, Philippines, Poland, Portugal, Qatar, Republic of Korea, Romania, Russian Federation, Rwanda, Singapore, Slovakia, Slovenia, South Africa, Spain, Sweden, Switzerland, Tajikistan, Thailand, Togo, Tunisia, Uganda, Ukraine, United Kingdom, United Republic of Tanzania, United States of America, Uruguay, Venezuela and Zimbabwe.

3. The European Community also participated in the meeting in a member capacity.

4. Iran (Islamic Republic of) participated in the meeting as an observer.

5. The following intergovernmental organizations took part in the meeting in an observer capacity: International Labour Organization (ILO), United Nations Educational, Scientific and Cultural Organization (UNESCO), World Trade Organization (WTO), African Intellectual Property Organization (OAPI) and Organization of the Islamic Conference (OIC).

6. Representatives of the following international non-governmental organizations took part in the meeting as observers: Asociación Argentina de Intérpretes (AADI), Asia-Pacific Broadcasting Union (ABU), Association of Commercial Television in Europe (ACT), Association of European Performers' Organisations (AEPO), American Film Marketing Association (AFMA), International Association for the Protection of Industrial Property (AIPPI), International Literary and Artistic Association (ALAI), Agency for the Protection of Programs (APP), European Group Representing Organizations for the Collective Administration of Performers' Rights (ARTIS GEIE), Central and Eastern European Copyright Alliance (CEECA), International Confederation of Societies of Authors and Composers (CISAC), Copyright Research and Information Center (CRIC), Actors, Interpreting Artists Committee (CSAI), European Broadcasting Union (EBU), European Federation of Joint Management Societies of Producers for Private Audiovisual Copying (EUROCOPYA), International Federation of Actors (FIA), International Federation of Associations of Film Distributors (FIAD), International Federation of Film Producers Associations (FIAPF), International

尼亚、拉脱维亚、黎巴嫩、阿拉伯利比亚民众国、卢森堡、马达加斯加、马来西亚、马耳他、墨西哥、摩洛哥、荷兰、新西兰、尼日利亚、挪威、巴拿马、秘鲁、菲律宾、波兰、葡萄牙、卡塔尔、韩国、罗马尼亚、俄罗斯、卢旺达、新加坡、斯洛伐克、斯洛文尼亚、南非、西班牙、瑞典、瑞士、塔吉克斯坦、泰国、多哥、突尼斯、乌干达、乌克兰、联合王国、坦桑尼亚联合共和国、美国、乌拉圭、委内瑞拉、津巴布韦。

3. 欧洲共同体也以成员国身份参加了会议。

4. 伊朗作为观察员参加了会议。

5. 下列政府间组织以观察员身份参加了会议：国际劳工组织（ILO）、联合国教育、科学及文化组织（UNESCO）、世界贸易组织（WTO）、非洲知识产权组织（OAPI）和伊斯兰会议组织（OIC）。

6. 下列国际非政府组织的代表以观察员身份参加了会议：阿根廷演绎协会（AADI），亚太广播联盟（ABU），欧洲商业电视协会（ACT），欧洲表演者组织协会（AEPO），美国电影市场协会（AFMA），国际工业产权保护协会（AIPPI），国际文学和艺术协会（ALAI），节目保护机构（APP），欧洲表演者权集体管理组织代表团体（ARTIS GEIE），中欧和东欧版权联盟（CEECA），国际作家和作曲家协会联合会（CISAC），版权研究和信息中心（CRIC），演员、演绎艺术家委员会（CSAI），欧洲广播联盟（EBU），私人音像复制制作者联合管理协会欧洲联合会（EUROCOPYA），国际演员联合会（FIA），国际电影发行商协会联合会（FIAD），国际电影制片人协会联合会（FIAPF），国际记者联合会（FIJ），伊比利亚－拉丁美洲表演者联合会（FILAIE），国际音乐家联合会（FIM），国际翻译家联合会（FIT），国际广播协会（IAB），国际唱片业联合会（IFPI），国际知识产权联盟（IIPA），国际出版商协会（IPA），国际视频联合会（IVF），伊比利亚－美洲版权组织、马普国际专利、版权和竞争法研究所（MPI），北美广播协会（NABA），日本全国商业广播协会（NAB-Japan），欧洲视听观景台、欧洲珀尔表演艺术雇主协会联盟、欧洲工业和雇主联合会（UNICE），国际媒体和娱乐联盟网络（UNI-MEI），非洲国家广播和电视组织联盟（URTNA）。

Federation of Journalists (FIJ), Ibero-Latin-American Federation of Performers (FILAIE), International Federation of Musicians (FIM), International Federation of Translators (FIT), International Association of Broadcasting (IAB), International Federation of the Phonographic Industry (IFPI), International Intellectual Property Alliance (IIPA), International Publishers Association (IPA), International Video Federation (IVF), Organización Iberoamericana de Derechos de Autor Latinautor Inc., Max-Planck-Institute for Foreign and International Patent, Copyright and Competition Law (MPI), North American Broadcasters Association (NABA), National Association of Commercial Broadcasters in Japan (NAB-Japan), European Audiovisual Observatory, Pearle* Performing Arts Employers Associations League Europe, Union of Industrial and Employers' Confederations of Europe (UNICE), Union Network International - Media and Entertainment International (UNI-MEI), Union of National Radio and Television Organizations of Africa (URTNA).

7. The session was opened by Mr. Shozo Uemura, Deputy Director General, who welcomed the participants on behalf of Dr. Kamil Idris, Director General of WIPO.

8. The list of participants (Annex) is attached to this Report.

ELECTION OF OFFICERS

9. The Standing Committee unanimously elected Mr. Jukka Liedes (Finland) as Chair, and Mr. Carlos Teysera Rouco (Uruguay) and Mr. Shen Rengan (China) as Vice-Chair.

ADOPTION OF THE AGENDA

10. The Standing Committee unanimously adopted the agenda (document SCCR/4/1).

PROTECTION OF AUDIOVISUAL PERFORMANCES

11. The Chairman recalled that the Standing Committee, in accordance with its Conclusions drawn at its third session (documents SCCR/3/11, paragraph 129), was convened to this special session to discuss remaining substantive issues and to assess the progress of work with a view to a possible diplomatic conference to be held in December 2000. He suggested that the discussions start with presentations of the new documents (SCCR/4/2, SCCR/4/3 and SCCR/4/4), followed by reports of the regional consultation meetings held on April 10, 2000. After that, he would

7. 会议由副总干事植村昭三先生主持开幕，他代表世界知识产权组织总干事卡米尔·伊德里斯博士对与会者表示欢迎。

8. 与会者名单（附件）载于本报告。

选举主席团成员

9. 常设委员会一致选举尤卡·利德斯先生（芬兰）为主席，卡洛斯·泰塞拉·鲁科先生（乌拉圭）和沈仁干先生（中国）为副主席。

通过议程

10. 常设委员会一致通过议程（SCCR/4/1 号文件）。

保护视听表演

11. 主席回顾道，依照常设委员会第三次会议所得出的结论（SCCR/3/11 号文件，第 129 段），常设委员会被召集在此举行这一特别会议，讨论剩下的实质性问题并评估工作进程，以期在 2000 年 12 月举行一次外交会议。他提议，此次讨论应从新文件（SCCR/4/2、SCCR/4/3 和 SCCR/4/4）的提交开始，随后是 2000 年 4 月 10 日举行的区域协商会议的报告。在这之后，他将提议讨论剩余的问题，随后评估工作的进程，并可能为结论做准备。

suggest a discussion of remaining issues and subsequently, assessing progress of work with possible preparation of conclusions.

PRESENTATION OF NEW DOCUMENTS

12. The Delegation of the European Community stated that the European Community and its member States believed that the time for a diplomatic conference had come. In this respect, the Delegation referred to their latest submission (document SCCR/4/2). The Rome Convention needed to be updated and, while the WIPO Copyright Treaty (WCT) and WIPO Performances and Phonograms Treaty (WPPT) provided a level playing field of protection for some groups of rightholders, that should now also be available for audiovisual performers. A diplomatic conference had been postponed at least three times, despite the 1996 Resolution which set the time limit to 1998, and it should now be held in December 2000. No really new issues had been under discussion for quite some time, and success could be reached with political will and commitment. The international instrument should be a protocol to the WPPT with membership in the WPPT being a condition for joining it. With such a simple and flexible structure, the instrument would be straightforward with no need for elaborate administrative and final clauses. As to the contents of the protocol, it should build upon the WPPT as much as possible, and only contain the modifications absolutely necessary to accommodate the differences between sound and audiovisual performances. The key to success was simplicity, flexibility for the contracting parties and avoidance of imposing strict rules or models without clear needs to do so. The latest proposals of the United States of America on national treatment and the transfer of rights would have to be analyzed to see if they would really comply with those key elements. The diplomatic conference should focus on the main objective to improve on the rights of audiovisual performers.

13. The Delegation of the United States of America explained that, under its revised proposal on national treatment (document SCCR/4/3), three categories of rights concerning audiovisual performances protected by the treaty would be accorded national treatment: (1) under paragraph 1(i), the exclusive rights provided by the treaty would be accorded national treatment; (2) under subparagraph (ii), rights derived from exclusive rights in the treaty would also be accorded national

提交新文件

12. 欧洲共同体代表团表示，欧洲共同体及其成员国认为召开外交会议的时机已经到来。在这方面，代表团提到了他们最近提交的材料（SCCR/4/2 号文件）。《罗马公约》需要得到更新，同时《世界知识产权组织版权条约》（WCT）和《世界知识产权组织表演和录音制品条约》（WPPT）为某些权利人群体提供了一个公平竞争的保护环境，这个环境现在也应该适用于视听表演者。尽管 1996 年的决议将召开外交会议的时间限制设定在 1998 年，但该会议已经被推迟了至少 3 次，现在应该在 2000 年 12 月举行一次外交会议。很长一段时间以来都没有真正的新问题得到讨论，但只要有政治意愿和承诺就能取得成功。这份国际法律文本应该是 WPPT 的议定书，加入这份文本的条件是拥有 WPPT 的成员资格。有了这样一个简单而灵活的结构，该文本将变得简单明了，无需详细的行政和最后条款。至于议定书的内容，它应该尽可能建立在 WPPT 之上，并且只包含为适应声音和视听表演之间的差异而做出的绝对必要的修改。成功的关键是为缔约方提供简单性和灵活性，以及避免在没有明确需要的情况下强加严格的规则或模式。必须分析美国关于国民待遇和权利转让的最新提案，看它们是否真的符合这些关键要素。外交会议应侧重于改善视听表演者权利的主要目标。

13. 美国代表团解释道，依据美国关于国民待遇的修订提案（SCCR/4/3 号文件），受条约保护的与视听表演有关的三类权利将获得国民待遇：（1）根据第 1 款第（i）项条约规定的专有权将获得国民待遇；（2）根据第（ii）项，来源于条约内专有权的权利也将获得国民待遇——例如私人复制版税就将被包括在内；（3）一些缔约方在其制度中为条约的客体提供了额外的权利或保护，第（iii）项在这些缔约方之间建立了互惠的国民待遇。因此，如果一个缔约方为其本国国

treatment—this would include, for example, private copying royalties; and (3) subparagraph (iii) created reciprocal national treatment between contracting parties whose systems provided additional rights or protection concerning the subject matter of the treaty. Thus, if one contracting party provided rights or protection for the audiovisual performances of its own nationals above and beyond those required by the treaty, it should provide such additional protection for the nationals of those other contracting parties that also provided equivalent protection for their nationals. The second paragraph in that proposal allowed contracting parties to decline national treatment for rights of remuneration or mandatory collective administration of exclusive rights regarding performances covered by the treaty, and further provided that contracting parties should ensure that if benefits were collected on behalf of foreign nationals, then distributions of those benefits must be made to such foreign nationals. That proposal was intended to be responsive to concerns about the domestic economic impact of broad national treatment provisions.

14. Regarding the flow of rights between audiovisual performers and producers, a number of approaches existed, including: 1) a rebuttable presumption of transfer with or without a possibility to opt out; 2) a presumption of legitimation along the lines of Article 14bis(2) of the Berne Convention with or without possibilities to opt out or to opt in; and 3) choice of law and rules concerning recognition by one country of transfers made by contract or operation of law in another country. It had become clear that a sufficient number of countries believed that that issue had to be addressed in order that the treaty or instrument could gain the same global consensus and support as the WCT and the WPPT. The analytic paper on transfer (document SCCR/4/4) listed eight elements that appeared necessary for a provision that could achieve a wide consensus, it reviewed the current proposals, and it attempted to summarize the advantages and disadvantages of each approach. The Delegation's own proposal on this issue continued to be supported by its entire domestic audiovisual industry, including performers and producers. It was a rebuttable presumption of transfer, limited to economic rights other than remuneration rights, giving performers the ability to negotiate meaningfully with respect to their rights, and preserving systems based on statutory rights of remuneration. All the international conventions that addressed audiovisual

民的视听表演提供了超出条约要求的权利或保护，则该缔约方也应该为那些向本国国民提供同等保护的缔约方的国民提供这种额外的保护。对于条约所涵盖表演的报酬权，或是专有权的强制性集体管理，该提案的第二段允许缔约方拒绝提供国民待遇，并进一步规定，缔约方应确保如果以外国国民的名义收取利益，就必须将这些利益分配给这些外国国民。该提案旨在回应对广泛国民待遇条款影响国内经济的担忧。

14. 就视听表演者和制作者之间的权利流动存在许多种解决方案，包括：1）可推翻的转让推定，无论是否存在退出转让的可能性；2）根据《伯尔尼公约》第 14 条之二第 2 款推定转让是合法的，无论是否存在退出或加入转让的可能性；3）选择法律和规则，使一国可以承认通过合同或在另一国国内法进行的转让。已经很明显，绝大多数国家认为必须解决该问题，以便条约或法律文本能够获得与 WCT 和 WPPT 相同的全球共识和支持。关于转让的分析文件（SCCR/4/4 号文件）列出了条款为达成广泛共识所必需的八个要素，它评估了现有的提案，并试图总结每种方法的优缺点。该代表团自身就此问题提出的提案继续得到了国内整个视听行业的支持，包括表演者和制作者。转让推定是可以被推翻的，但仅限于报酬权以外的经济权利，这使得表演者能够就其权利进行有意义的谈判，建立在法定报酬权基础之上的制度也能得到保留。所有涉及视听作品的国际公约都承认此类作品的特殊性，因为此类作品是经过多个贡献者的努力才诞生的，无论是通过诸如《伯尔尼公约》第 14 条之二第 2 款的方法还是通过诸如《罗马公约》第 19 条的方法。该代表团仍然对以实质性方式处理这一问题的其他办法持开放态度。

works recognized the special nature of such works which resulted from the efforts of multiple contributors, whether by an approach such as Article 14bis(2) of the Berne Convention or Article 19 of the Rome Convention. The Delegation remained open to alternative approaches that addressed this issue in a substantive way.

15. The Delegation of Japan, pointing at the comparative table distributed as a room document, recalled that Japan's proposal (document SCCR/3/8) included a footnote concerning moral rights that was missing in the comparative table.

REPORTS OF REGIONAL CONSULTATIONS

16. The Delegation of Uganda, speaking on behalf of the African Group, underlined that the instrument for the protection of audiovisual performances should be a protocol to the WPPT. The membership to the protocol should be conditional on adherence to the WPPT. A diplomatic conference should be convened for December 2000. A provision on transfer of rights seemed to undermine the aim of improving protection of performers. The Group took note of the views of major film producing countries. The Group was open for further considerations in this respect.

17. The Delegation of Slovakia, speaking on behalf of the Group of Central European and Baltic States in the consultation of which Albania, Bulgaria, Croatia, the Czech Republic, Estonia, Hungary, Latvia, Romania, Slovenia and Slovakia had been represented, reiterated the Group's willingness to modernize the protection of audiovisual performances and expressed its support for a diplomatic conference to be held in December 2000 to establish a protocol to the WPPT. It further confirmed that the Group maintained its previously expressed position (document SCCR/3/10), and it questioned the revised proposal of the United States of America on application in time, which it found unfavorable to the performers.

18. The Delegation of the Islamic Republic of Iran, speaking on behalf of the Asian Group, reported that the Group had no objection to a diplomatic conference to be convened for December 2000, or earlier. The Group had sympathy for a protocol rather than a treaty, but it was premature to have any concrete position on national treatment. Regarding transfer of rights, there should be a common guideline, but also some margin of freedom for implementation. The Group had no position whether the assembly of the instrument should be shared with that of the WPPT, but it expressed its general interest in streamlining the organizational structures within

15. 日本代表团指出会议室中分发的文件比较表中，缺失了日本提案（SCCR/3/8 号文件）中所包含的一个关于精神权利的脚注。

区域间协商会议的报告

16. 乌干达代表团代表非洲小组发言，强调保护视听表演的法律文本应该是 WPPT 的议定书。获取该议定书的成员资格应以遵守 WPPT 为条件。各方应当在 2000 年 12 月召开一次外交会议。关于权利转让的条款似乎危及了加强表演者保护的目标。该小组注意到了主要电影制作国的观点。在这方面，该小组愿意做进一步考虑。

17. 斯洛伐克代表团，在磋商中代表中欧和波罗的海国家小组（该小组代表了阿尔巴尼亚、保加利亚、克罗地亚、捷克共和国、爱沙尼亚、匈牙利、拉脱维亚、罗马尼亚、斯洛文尼亚和斯洛伐克）发言，重申该小组愿意使视听表演的保护更加现代化，并表示支持于 2000 年 12 月召开一次外交会议，以制定 WPPT 的议定书。它进一步确认了该小组对于维持其先前表达的立场（SCCR/3/10 号文件），并质疑美国关于及时申请的修订提案，认为该提案不利于表演者。

18. 伊朗伊斯兰共和国代表团以亚洲小组的名义发言，报告称，亚洲小组不反对在 2000 年 12 月或更早举行一次外交会议。该小组赞同制定一项议定书而不是一项条约，但现在就国民待遇问题发表任何具体立场还为时过早。关于权利的转让，应该有一个共同的准则，但也应该有一定的执行自由。对于法律文本的大会是否应与 WPPT 所建立的大会共享，该小组并无立场，但它表达了对于精简 WIPO 内部组织结构的普遍兴趣。加入 WPPT 最好不要成为遵守新法律文本的条件。

WIPO. To be party to the WPPT should preferably not be a condition for adherence to the new instrument.

19. The Delegation of Peru, speaking on behalf of the Latin American and Caribbean Group, declared that various issues were still under internal discussion. The Group favored holding a diplomatic conference not later than December 2000.

20. The Delegation of China, while in agreement with the position of the African Group, the Group of Central European and Baltic States and the Latin American and Caribbean Group, concerning the convening of the diplomatic conference, stated that the matter should be resolved without further delay. It further pointed out that upon conclusion of the diplomatic conference, consideration should immediately be given to expressions of folklore, a topic of particular importance to developing countries, and the protection of databases, as well as broadcasting organizations, those subjects that had been awaiting consideration for too long.

21. The Delegation of Switzerland supported that a diplomatic conference should be held in December 2000. The new instrument could be an annex or a protocol to the WPPT, as simple and straightforward as possible, based on the consensus enshrined in the WPPT, and taking into account the specificity of the audiovisual sector.

NATURE OF THE INSTRUMENT

22. The Chairman highlighted the question whether the Committee could recommend a protocol to the WPPT, which had been suggested by many delegations, or a separate treaty, which has also some support. The nature of the instrument had an impact on the final and administrative clauses, because if the option of a protocol to the WPPT were chosen, certain clauses of that Treaty could be re-used. If there were to be an assembly for the instrument, it could be separate, or it could be a joint assembly for the WPPT and the instrument. He invited the Secretariat to present an analysis of the choices that had to be made.

23. The Secretariat recalled that the administrative and final clauses of the WIPO administered Treaties were generally in a standard form. The choice between a protocol and a treaty was, more than a question of a name, a question of the decisions that the member States might wish to take on certain issues. There was no invariable meaning of the term protocol in international law. Three

19. 秘鲁代表团以拉丁美洲和加勒比小组的名义发言，宣布各种问题仍在进行内部讨论。该小组赞成在2000年12月之前举行一次外交会议。

20. 中国代表团虽然同意非洲小组、中欧和波罗的海国家小组以及拉丁美洲和加勒比小组关于召开外交会议的立场，但指出，这一问题应立即得到解决。它进一步指出，在外交会议结束后，应立即审议民间艺术表达——这是一个对发展中国家特别重要的主题，也要审议保护数据库和广播组织——这些主题等待审议的时间太长了。

21. 瑞士代表团对于在2000年12月举行一次外交会议表示支持。新的法律文本可以是WPPT的附件或议定书，尽可能地简单和直接，以WPPT所载共识为基础，并考虑到视听部门的特殊性。

条约的性质

22. 主席强调了这样一个问题，即委员会是否可以把一项被许多代表团所提议的议定书引荐给WPPT，或提出一项单独的、同样得到一些支持的条约。该法律文本的性质影响了最后条款和行政条款，因为如果选择将其作为WPPT的一项议定书，则WPPT的某些条款就可以重新使用。如果选择为条约创立一个大会，那么它既可以是单独的，也可以是WPPT和该项条约的联合大会。他请秘书处就必须作出的选择提出分析。

23. 秘书处回顾道，WIPO管理的条约的行政条款和最后条款一般采用标准格式。议定书和条约之间的选择不仅仅是一个名称的问题，而是成员国可能希望对某些议题作出决定的问题。在国际法中，议定书一词并没有一成不变的含义。为了编写该国际法律文本的行政和最后条款草案，必须澄清三个问题：（1）要成为该法律文本的缔约国，是否有必要成为WPPT的缔约国，即它们之

issues had to be clarified in order to prepare draft administrative and final clauses for the international instrument: (1) would it be necessary to be party to the WPPT to become party to the instrument, that is, would there be a conditional relationship between them. For instance, it was not a condition to be a party to the Madrid Agreement in order to join the Madrid Protocol. In contrast, it was indeed a condition for becoming party to the Protocol to the 1960 Act of the Hague Agreement that the State be party to the Agreement; (2) what would be the administrative organ, that is, whether it should be an assembly shared between the WPPT and the instrument, for example, if there would be sufficient similarity of subject matter to justify joint meetings, or it should be separate assemblies as was the case with most WIPO administered Treaties which were separate and independent. He recalled the current constitutional reform under consideration by the member States, which aimed at a streamlining of the WIPO administrative organs; (3) as regards the remaining provisions concerning issues like entry into force, depositary functions, etc., whether those were to be repeated, and, if so, whether this should be done by adopting such provisions in full or by reference to the WPPT.

24. The Delegation of the Islamic Republic of Iran asked for clarification regarding a conditional relationship between a possible protocol and the WPPT. The question would be whether a State could perform its obligations under a protocol without being party to the treaty. If there were a strong linkage between the instrument and the WPPT, the instrument could be a Protocol, but it would be necessary to take a look at the content of the instrument in order to determine its nature.

25. The Secretariat recalled that these decisions were up to the member States to make.

26. The Delegation of Canada asked the Secretariat to clarify whether differences in definitions or terminology in a protocol compared to the underlying treaty could have implications for the interpretation of the latter. This could be relevant for moral rights or the definition of performers, as examples.

27. The Secretariat recalled that whether a protocol or an independent treaty, generally the latter in time would prevail between Contracting States that were bound by the same instruments.

间是否存在一种条件关系。例如，加入《马德里议定书》并不以成为《马德里协定》的缔约国为条件。相反，成为《海牙协定1960年法案议定书》缔约国的一个条件确实是成为《海牙协定》的缔约国；(2)什么是行政机关，也就是说，它是否应该是WPPT和该法律文本之间共享的大会组织，例如，如果主题事项有足够的相似性以证明举行联席会议是合理的；或者，它应该是单独的大会，就像WIPO管理的大多数条约一样，它们是分离且独立的。他回顾了各成员国目前正在审议的宪章改革，其目的是精简WIPO的行政机构；(3)关于涉及生效、保管职责等问题的其余条款，是否应对这些条款进行重复，如果答案为肯定，是应充分通过这些条款，还是参照WPPT来完成这一点。

24. 伊朗伊斯兰共和国代表团要求澄清可能的议定书与WPPT之间的条件关系。未来的问题是，一个国家是否可以在不成为条约缔约国的情况下履行其议定书规定的义务。如果该法律文本与WPPT之间有很强的联系，该法律文本可以是一项议定书，但有必要审查该法律文本的内容，以确定其性质。

25. 秘书处指出，这些决定应由成员国做出。

26. 加拿大代表团请秘书处澄清议定书的定义或术语与基本条约的差异是否会影响对后者的解释。例如，这可能与精神权利或表演者的定义有关。

27. 秘书处指出，无论是议定书还是独立条约，在受同一法律文本约束的缔约国之间通常以后者为准。

28. The Delegation of Singapore asked the Secretariat if it would be possible to have some variances between a protocol and the underlying treaty. If yes, it would only be a question of terminology, but if not, there would be logic in having a separate treaty. It also asked if there were examples in international law where the nature of such instruments had been dealt with differently.

29. The Secretariat stated that the only common ground was that a protocol was, in a certain way, a supplement or an amendment to a treaty. It was up to the States to decide the exact nature of the instrument, because the question was more the substantial relationship than what the instrument should be called.

30. The Delegation of the European Community noted that the nature of the instrument depended on what the Committee could agree on in substance, and it agreed that there was no common definition of a protocol in international law. When proposing a protocol, the Delegation did not intend to amend the WPPT, but to propose an annex to it, a lex specialis on the protection of audiovisual performances. There was no conflict between the WPPT and the proposed protocol, and, for instance, there was no need for a "without prejudice" clause because the protocol was confined to its own subject matter. Treaty language proposals concerning administrative and final clauses had been made by various countries and regional groups. In the view of the Delegation, there had to be a conditional relationship between the protocol and the WPPT as regards ability to become party to the protocol, and the protocol did not need a separate assembly. An example in this respect was the various revisions of the Berne Convention under only one Assembly. Not all remaining clauses had to be repeated, because the WPPT should obviously be valid. In this way, the option of having a protocol was more pragmatic and less time consuming than that of having a treaty.

31. The Delegation of Cameroon mentioned that, in order to make progress in the discussions, a working party might be set up to examine the contents of the instrument.

32. The Delegation of the United States of America continued to believe that, for many of the reasons given by the Delegation of the European Community for wanting a protocol, the instrument should be a separate treaty. However, it also believed that it was possible to draw very heavily on the experience gained in the

28. 新加坡代表团问秘书处，议定书和基本条约之间是否可能有一些差异。如果是，这只是一个术语的问题，但如果不是，就存在制定一个单独的条约的逻辑。它还问，在国际法中是否有案例对这类法律文本的性质作了不同的处理。

29. 秘书处说，唯一的共同点是议定书在某种程度上是一项条约的补充或修正。该法律文本的确切性质应由各国决定，因为问题更多在于实质关系，而不是该法律文本的名称。

30. 欧洲共同体代表团指出，该法律文本的性质取决于委员会在实质上能达成什么协议，它也同意，在国际法中没有对议定书的共同定义。在提出一项议定书时，该代表团并不打算修改 WPPT，而是在其附件中提出一项关于保护视听表演的特别法。WPPT 和提议的议定书之间不存在冲突，例如，没有必要使用“不损害”条款，因为议定书仅仅局限于它自己的主题。各国和区域小组提出了关于行政条款和最后条款的条约措词建议。该代表团认为，关于是否能够成为该议定书的缔约国，该议定书和 WPPT 之间必须存在一种条件关系，并且该议定书不需要一个单独的大会。这方面的一个例子是仅在一个大会下对《伯尔尼公约》进行的各种修订。不需要再对所有剩余的条款进行重复，因为 WPPT 显然应该是有效的。这样，缔结一项议定书的选择比缔结一项条约的选择更实际，也更节省时间。

31. 喀麦隆代表团提到，为了在讨论中取得进展，可以设立一个工作组来审查该法律文本的内容。

32. 美国代表团继续认为，鉴于欧洲共同体代表团就希望制定一项议定书提出的许多理由，该法律文本应当是一项单独的条约。但是，它也认为，大量借鉴 WCT 和 WPPT 所取得的经验是有可能的，这是为了在新条约中有非常接近但不完全相同的行政和最后条款。法律文本的性质及其与 WPPT 的联系应

WCT and WPPT, in order to have very close, but not identical, administrative and final clauses in the new treaty. The nature of the instrument, as well as its linkage to the WPPT, should be determined after settling the substance of the instrument, as it would be premature to make final decisions on many of the questions raised at the present point in time.

33. The Delegation of Switzerland emphasized that the Committee should aim for a protocol or an annex to the WPPT. It supported the views of other delegations that the instrument would not change anything as regards the substance of the WPPT, but would add protection for a new category of rightholders and for a new subject of protection. A single assembly should be sufficient for the two instruments. As regards the conditions to become party to the protocol, the Delegation questioned whether Article 9 of the proposal of the European Community was drafted correctly if that Delegation meant that a condition to become party to the protocol should be that the State had to be party to the WPPT. As regards to the final clauses, it should be sufficient to refer to the final clauses of the WPPT.

34. The Delegation of Japan stated that the instrument should be a protocol to the WPPT, as foreseen in the Resolution of 1996, at the time of the adoption of the WPPT. Many issues of a protocol could be solved by applying provisions of the WPPT, of course, taking into account the differences between audio and audiovisual performances.

35. The Chairman concluded that it was up to the States to analyze this issue further. The Committee might have to rely on, for instance, the drafting of alternative clauses for accommodating the future procedure. He presumed that the delegations which had taken the floor on this very political issue had done it on the hypothesis that there would be a continuous process in that respect.

NATIONAL TREATMENT AND TRANSFER OF RIGHTS

36. The Chairman opened the floor for discussion on the remaining substantial issues: national treatment and contractual arrangements and transfer of rights. He suggested that the Committee discuss both issues simultaneously, and recognized that the issue of national treatment could only be decided finally after the contents of the instrument had been agreed on. Delegations could also raise other substantial issues or questions that they wished to discuss.

在解决法律文本的实质内容之后确定，因为就目前提出的许多问题作出最后决定还为时过早。

33. 瑞士代表团强调，委员会的目标应该是为 WPPT 制定一项议定书或一项附件。它支持其他代表团的意见，即该法律文本不会改变 WPPT 的实质内容，但将增加对一个新的权利持有人类别的保护和对新主题的保护。一个单独的大会对于两个条约来说应该是足够的。至于成为议定书成员的条件，该代表团质疑欧洲共同体提案第 9 条的起草是否正确，如果该代表团的意思是成为议定书缔约方的条件应是该国必须成为 WPPT 的缔约方。关于最后条款，参考 WPPT 的最后条款就足够了。

34. 日本代表团指出，正如 1996 年决议在通过 WPPT 时所预见的那样，该法律文本应是 WPPT 的一项议定书。协议的许多问题可以通过应用 WPPT 的规定来解决，当然，要考虑声音和视听表演之间的差异。

35. 主席的结论是，应由各国进一步分析这个问题。例如，委员会可能不得不依靠起草变通的条款来适应未来的程序。他假定，就这一非常具有政治性的问题发言的代表团是基于这样一种假设，即在这方面将有一个持续的进程。

国民待遇和权利的转让

36. 主席开始讨论其余的实质性问题：国民待遇和合同性安排以及权利的转让。他建议委员会同时讨论这两个问题，并承认国民待遇问题只有在就法律文本的内容达成协议之后才能在最后作出决定。各代表团还可以提出他们希望讨论的其他实质性问题。

37. The Delegation of India agreed with the United States of America that a provision on transfer of rights would be inevitable, and it should not be applicable to remuneration rights or moral rights. Such a provision should apply to a particular audiovisual production taking into account their increasingly complex character, such as co-productions, co-financial arrangements, multinational casts and multinational filming locations. In any case, the transfer of rights from performers to producers should be done in such a way that the interests of performers were not affected.

38. The Delegation of the United States of America, in answer to the questions that had been put forward by the Delegation of Singapore, clarified its proposal concerning national treatment in Article 4(1)(ii) and (iii). As to which remuneration rights would exist that were not derived from exclusive rights, it noted that some countries did not regard private copying royalties as a remuneration for exploitation or transfer of performers rights. They rather considered those royalties a compensation for non-commercial private copying that was expressly permitted under their domestic law. Still, these royalties were clearly related to the right of reproduction. Regarding national treatment based on reciprocity under paragraph (1)(iii) of its proposal, it noted that some countries, such as its own, considered rental rights to be an element of the distribution right, while other countries had established it as a separate right, distinct from other rights. Supposing there would be no provisions on rental right in the final treaty, then, under paragraph (1)(iii), a country that nonetheless provided a rental right would have to provide national treatment to other countries that also provided an exclusive rental right, or a right of remuneration for rental. The provision had to be seen in connection with its proposed Article 4(2), under which there could only be collected money in respect of performances for which a performer was going to be paid.

39. In answer to the question from the Delegation of Slovakia regarding the application in time, the Delegation of the United States of America responded that there were three parts in its proposal: (1) the treaty should not prejudice rights previously acquired before the date of coming into force of the treaty, as under Article 20 of the Rome Convention; (2) the provisions on moral rights should apply to existing works in respect of any violation that may occur after the coming

37. 印度代表团同意美国的看法，即关于权利转让的规定是不可避免的，并且权利的转让不应适用于报酬权或精神权利。这种规定应适用于特定的视听录制品——考虑到这些视听录制品日益复杂的特征，例如联合制作、联合财务安排、多国演员和多国拍摄地点。在任何情况下，将表演者权转让给制作者的方式，不应影响到表演者的利益。

38. 美国代表团在回答新加坡代表团提出的问题时，澄清了它在第 4 条第（1）款（i）和（iii）项中关于国民待遇的建议。至于会存在哪些不源自专有权的报酬权，它指出，一些国家并不将私人复制版税视为利用或转让表演者权利的报酬。他们认为这些版税是对其国内法明确允许的非商业私人复制的一种补偿。然而，这些版税显然与复制权有关。关于其提案第（1）款（iii）项中基于互惠的国民待遇，它指出，一些国家，例如本国，将出租权视为发行权的一个要素，而其他国家则将其确立为单独的权利，区别于其他权利。假设最后条约中没有关于出租权的规定，那么，根据第（1）款（iii）项，一个仍然提供出租权的国家将不得不向同样提供专有出租权或出租报酬权的其他国家提供国民待遇。这一规定必须与拟议的第 4 条第（2）款联系起来看，根据这条规定，只能就表演者将获得报酬的表演收取款项。

39. 在回答斯洛伐克代表团关于适用时限的问题时，美国代表团答复说，其提案包括三个部分：（1）本条约不应损害根据《罗马公约》第 20 条规定在本条约生效日前已取得的权利；（2）对于条约生效后可能发生的任何侵权行为，有关精神权利的规定应适用于现有作品；（3）经济权利不应追溯适用，因为在许多国家，经济权利并不存在，因此追溯适用可能导致不确定性，并导致无法发行或利用现有作品。由于视听作品长期受到版权保护，因此不需要提供追溯保护。

into force of the treaty; and (3) the economic rights should not apply retroactively because in many countries they would not already exist, and retroactive application could therefore lead to uncertainty and to the inability to distribute or exploit existing works. Retroactive protection would not be necessary, due to the longstanding copyright protection of audiovisual works. The case of sound recordings was different, because in some countries they were not protected as such.

40. The Delegation of Japan pointed out that it was necessary to ensure certainty and to take into account different national legal provisions on contractual arrangements. Thus, some provisions on transfer of rights had to be included. They should be flexible enough that contracting parties could comply with them on the basis of their national provisions on contractual arrangements. Therefore, the proposal of the Delegation was based on Article 14bis of the Berne Convention, with a possibility for countries to opt out, and subject to rebuttal by contracts. It also proposed an exception for the contracting parties' nationals. It was not so complicated since there was only a distinction between their own nationals and the other nationals. National treatment should apply only to the exclusive rights specifically granted under the Protocol, in accordance with the established principles for related rights.

41. The Delegation of the Russian Federation noted that national treatment to a great extent was related to the right of communication to the public, that is, that would be an exclusive or a remuneration right. The latter one was preferable. The issue of transfer of rights should be left to domestic legislation. It asked the Delegation of the United States of America to clarify the meaning of the last sentence of its proposed Article 4(2) concerning national treatment.

42. The Delegation of the United States of America responded that the meaning of that sentence was that if a country provided a right of remuneration or an equivalent payment of royalties to performers in respect of collectively administered rights and that country chose not to provide the benefit of those rights under national treatment, then collecting agencies should not collect money in respect of use of those performances for which rightholders would not get paid.

43. The Delegation of Cameroon stated that clauses on transfer of economic rights should take into account that transfer of economic rights could paralyze

录音的情况则不同，因为在一些国家，录音并没有受到这样的保护。

40. 日本代表团指出，有必要保证法律文本的确定性，并考虑到关于合同安排的不同国家法律规定。因此，必须在法律文本中列入关于权利转让的一些规定。这些规定应具有足够的灵活性，使缔约各方能够根据本国关于合同安排的规则遵守这些规定。因此，该代表团的建议是根据《伯尔尼公约》第 14 条之二提出的，各国可以选择退出，并可通过合同予以推翻。它还提议对缔约各国国民实行例外。这个问题并不那么复杂，因为只存在本国国民和其他国民之间的区别。根据相关权利的既定原则，国民待遇应仅适用于根据议定书具体授予的专有权。

41. 俄罗斯联邦代表团指出，国民待遇在很大程度上和向公众传播的权利有关，也就是说，这将是一种排他权或报酬权。后者更可取。权利转让的问题应留给国内立法处理。它请美国代表团厘清其拟议的关于国民待遇的第 4 条第（2）款中最后一句的含义。

42. 美国的代表团回应道，这句话的意思是，如果一个国家就集体管理的权利向表演者提供了报酬或等值的特许权使用费的权利，而该国选择在国民待遇下不提供这些权利的利益，那么对于那些权利人不会获得报酬的表演，收款机构不应收取款项。

43. 喀麦隆代表团说，关于经济权利转让的条款应考虑到经济权利的转让可能使精神权利瘫痪，而精神权利在某些情况下可能因为不能转让而阻碍经济

the moral rights, and moral rights could in certain situations, because they could not be transferred, block the exercise of economic rights. The different traditions in different legal systems concerning conditions and limitations on agreements between performers and producers had to be taken into account, including the rule of destination which prevented the producer from making a use of the performance that would be alien to the object of the transfer.

44. The Delegation of Australia asked if the Delegation of the United States of America could explain the statement that the transfer provision should be applicable to a particular audiovisual production, and that it would not be desirable nor necessary to extend the provision to the inclusion of performances in other audiovisual productions.

45. The Delegation of the United States of America answered that according to Article 12 of its proposal, if a fixation were to be used in a creation of a new audiovisual work, the rights would not be transferred, and they would remain with the performer with respect to all uses of that fixation other than the particular work for which the performer had agreed to have the fixation made.

ADOPTION OF RECOMMENDATION

46. Based on a proposal submitted by the Chairman, and following informal consultations, the Standing Committee adopted the following:

RECOMMENDATIONS

The Standing Committee on Copyright and Related Rights:

considering that the Standing Committee on Copyright and Related Rights at its third session, from November 16 to 20, 1999, recommended that the present special session of the Standing Committee should be convened to discuss remaining issues and to assess progress of work with a view to a possible diplomatic conference in December 2000, which would consider an international instrument on the protection of audiovisual performances,

considering that the work at the end of the present session of the Standing Committee is sufficiently advanced, taking into account the identification and analysis of substantive issues to be addressed in the international instrument, the progress made in these substantive issues during the deliberations in the present and previous sessions of the Standing Committee; and considering that the state

权利的行使。必须考虑到不同法律制度中关于表演者和制作者之间协议的条件和限制的不同传统，包括目的地规则，该规则阻止制作者利用那些与转让对象不相符合的表演。

44. 澳大利亚代表团询问美国代表团是否可以解释关于转让条款应适用于特定视听录制品的说法，以及将这项规定扩大到包含在其他视听录制品中的表演，既不可取，也没有必要。

45. 美国代表团回答说，根据其提案第 12 条，如果录制品被用于创作新的视听作品，则关于除表演者同意为之录制的特定作品外该录制品的所有用途，权利不会转让，它们将保留在表演者手中。

采纳建议

46. 根据主席提出的一项建议，经过非正式协商，常设委员会通过了下列提案：

建议

版权及相关权常设委员会：

考虑到版权及相关权常设委员会在其 1999 年 11 月 16 日至 20 日的第三届会议上建议召开本届常委会特别会议，讨论剩余问题并评估工作进展，以期在 2000 年 12 月召开一次可能的外交会议，审议关于保护视听表演的国际法律文本，

考虑到常委会本届会议结束时的工作已有足够推进，同时考虑到对国际法律文本要处理的实质性问题的识别和分析，本次和历届常设委员会会议于审议过程中在这些实质性问题上取得的进展；并考虑到有关国际法律文本的讨论情况允许在该级别举行外交会议和进行谈判，

of discussions concerning the international instrument allows the diplomatic conference to be held and negotiation to take place at that level,

unanimously agreed on the following recommendations:

1. <u>Administrative and Final Provisions</u>

the Preparatory Committee for the WIPO Diplomatic Conference on the Protection of Audiovisual Performances, meeting in Geneva on April 12 and 14, 2000, should request the International Bureau to prepare a basic proposal for administrative and final provisions of the international instrument, containing alternative solutions for a protocol to the WIPO Performances and Phonograms Treaty and for a separate treaty building on the provisions of the WIPO Performances and Phonograms Treaty,

2. <u>Basic Proposal</u>

the basic proposal for the substantive provisions of the international instrument for the diplomatic conference will be prepared by the Chairman of the session of the Standing Committee. The Chairman will be assisted by the WIPO International Bureau, the draft texts should be published and circulated by the WIPO International Bureau to the States, intergovernmental and non-governmental organizations to be invited to the diplomatic conference by August 1, 2000,

3. <u>Regional Consultations</u>

the International Bureau should organize regional consultation meetings, in Africa, the Arab countries, Asia and the Pacific, Latin America and the Caribbean and in certain countries of Europe and Asia, during the months of September, October and November, and regional consultations meetings at the location of the diplomatic conference on December 5 and 6, 2000,

4. <u>Diplomatic Conference</u>

The diplomatic conference should be held from December 7 to 20, 2000.

47. The Delegation of South Africa, speaking on behalf of the African Group, introduced a proposal which the Group had adopted during its consultations regarding transfer of rights. The proposal will be issued as a document of the Standing Committee.

48. The Secretariat clarified that it was the intention to arrange regional consultations separately for the countries of Central Asia, Caucasus, and Eastern

一致同意下列建议：

1. 行政和最后条款

于 2000 年 4 月 12 日至 14 日在日内瓦举行会议的世界知识产权组织保护视听表演外交会议筹备委员会，应当要求国际局就国际法律文本的行政和最后条款准备一份基本提案，其中包含《世界知识产权组织表演和录音制品条约》议定书的替代解决方案，以及基于《世界知识产权组织表演和录音制品条约》条款的单独条约的替代解决方案。

2. 基本提案

外交会议的国际法律文本实质性条款的基本提案将由常设委员会会议主席拟定。主席将得到世界知识产权组织国际局的协助，草案文本应由世界知识产权组织国际局出版，并在 2000 年 8 月 1 日之前分发给受邀参加外交会议的国家、政府间组织和非政府组织。

3. 区域协商会议

国际局应在 9 月、10 月和 11 月在非洲、阿拉伯国家、亚洲和太平洋、拉丁美洲和加勒比以及欧洲和亚洲的某些国家组织区域协商会议，并在 2000 年 12 月 5 日至 6 日在外交会议的地点组织区域协商会议。

4. 外交会议

外交会议应在 2000 年 12 月 7 日至 20 日举办。

47. 南非代表团代表非洲小组发言，介绍了该小组在其关于权利转让的协商期间通过的提案。该提案将作为常设委员会文件印发。

48. 秘书处阐明，它打算分别为中亚、高加索和东欧国家以及中欧和波罗的海国家安排区域协商。一些代表团强调，基本提案应反映各方对各种问题不同

Europe and for the countries of Central Europe and the Baltic States. Several delegations stressed that the basic proposal should reflect the different levels of agreement and disagreement on the various issues. There were also calls for the basic proposal to be circulated, if possible, before the date indicated in the Recommendation, to which the Chairman remarked that circulation would take place as early as possible and, if necessary, in stages, so the treaty language text might be circulated before the explanatory notes.

49. The Delegation of Peru, speaking on behalf of the Latin American and Caribbean Group, announced that the Group had produced an agreed text to replace document SCCR/2/2. With regard to Article X.5, on the Right of Broadcasting and Communication to the Public, and Article XII, on Contractual Arrangements Concerning the Rights of Performers, of the original proposal contained in document SCCR/2/2, the members of the Group reserved the right to take a position at a later stage.

COMMENTS FROM NON-GOVERNMENTAL ORGANIZATIONS

50. An observer from the International Federation of Actors (FIA) stated that performers should be given a broad range of exclusive rights, including exclusive rights of broadcasting and communication to the public. FIA believed that moral rights in the instrument were critical in the digital environment and should be applied retrospectively, as should economic rights. FIA reiterated its opposition to the inclusion of a presumption of transfer of rights in the instrument as it would be entirely unfair to performers who were already in a weak bargaining position. The limited application of Article 14bis of the Berne Convention and the entirely different object of that Convention precluded its application mutatis mutandis. Different countries had different systems and it should not be impossible to allow for recognition of contracts made under different systems.

51. An observer from the Copyright Research and Information Center (CRIC), speaking on behalf of the Japan Council of Performers' Organizations (GEIDANKYO), stated that audiovisual performers needed economic and moral rights to assure their protection in the digital information society. GEIDANKYO retained its position, as it had expressed during the last session of this meeting in November 1999, regarding contractual arrangements and urged governments to

程度的共识和分歧。还有人呼吁尽可能在建议书所示日期之前分发基本提案，主席对此表示，将尽早分发，如有必要，分阶段分发，因此条约语言文本可能会在解释性说明之前分发。

49. 秘鲁代表团代表拉丁美洲和加勒比小组发言，宣布该小组已经制定了一份商定的文本，以取代 SCCR/2/2 号文件。关于 SCCR/2/2 号文件所载原始提案的第 X.5 条（关于向公众广播和传播的权利）和第 XII 条（关于表演者权利的合同安排），工作组成员保留在稍后阶段发表立场的权利。

非政府组织的意见

50. 国际演员联合会（FIA）的一位观察员表示，表演者应获得广泛的专有权，包括广播和向公众传播的专有权。FIA 认为，该法律文本中的精神权利在数字环境中至关重要，应获得追溯应用，经济权利也应如此。FIA 重申对于在法律文本中包含权利转让推定的反对，因为这对已经处于弱势谈判地位的表演者完全不公平。《伯尔尼公约》第 14 条之二的有限适用和该公约的目标完全不同，这就排除了其比照适用的可能性。不同的国家有不同的制度，允许承认不同制度下所订立的合同，应该并非不可能的事。

51. 版权研究和信息中心（CRIC）的一位观察员代表日本表演者组织理事会（GEIDANKYO）发言，表示视听表演者需要经济和精神权利，以确保他们在数字信息社会中得到保护。GEIDANKYO 保留了它在 1999 年 11 月本会上一次会议上所表达的关于合同安排的立场，并敦促各国政府努力寻求一种简单而灵活的解决方案，真正为全球视听表演者提供保护。

work for a simple and flexible solution with real global protection for audiovisual performers.

52. An observer from the International Federation of Musicians (FIM) said that the concept of legal certainty regarding the presumption of transfer of rights was inaccurate, because it encouraged employers not to have written contracts. The best legal certainty would come from a written contract. He informed the Standing Committee that the American Federation of Musicians had expressed its opposition to any mechanism of presumption. The instrument should grant exclusive rights of rebroadcasting and cable distribution with the possibility of using the provisions of Article 11bis(2) of the Berne Convention.

53. An observer from the Groupement européen représentant les organismes de gestion collective des droits des artistes interprètes ou exécutants (ARTIS GEIE) supported a protocol to the WPPT that improved the rights of performers in audiovisual performances and, particularly, acknowledged their moral rights. Performers should benefit from fair remuneration, proportional to the use of their performances. Single lump sum payments were not acceptable.

54. An observer from the Fédération internationale des associations de producteurs de films (FIAPF) stated that an international treaty could be truly economically effective only if it included a presumption for the producers' acquisition of rights. The choice between rebuttable or irrebutable presumption had to be left to national legislation. The issue of application in time was very delicate, and exploitation of a work produced before the entry into force should not be abusively prohibited.

55. An observer from the Ibero-Latin-American Federation of Performers (FILAIE) fully supported that the instrument should aim at the protection of performers' and not producers' rights. The only effective protection was the granting of rights of remuneration for collective management. He opposed the proposal of the United States of America regarding national treatment and expressed concern about the fate of moral rights in the treaty.

56. An observer from the International Association of Broadcasting (IAB), stressed the need to make the promotion of the rights of broadcasting organizations into a priority issue for the Standing Committee in 2001. He also pointed to the

52. 国际音乐家联合会（FIM）的一位观察员表示，关于权利转让推定的法律确定性的概念是不准确的，因为它鼓励雇主不要签订书面合同。最佳的法律确定性来自书面合同。他告知常设委员会，美国音乐家联合会已表示反对任何推定机制。该法律文本应授予转播和有线电视发行的专有权，并有可能使用《伯尔尼公约》第 11 条之二第 2 款的规定。

53. 来自欧洲表演者权集体管理组织代表团体（ARTIS GEIE）的一名观察员支持为 WPPT 制定一项议定书，该议定书改善了表演者在视听表演中的权利，特别是承认了他们的精神权利。表演者应从与其表演使用成正比的公平报酬中受益。一次性付款是不可接受的。

54. 来自国际电影制片人协会联合会（FIAPF）的一名观察员说，一项国际条约只有包括对制作者取得权利的推定，才能真正具有经济效力。在可推翻的推定和不可推翻的推定之间如何作出选择，只能由国家立法来决定。适用时限的问题是非常微妙的，对于在法律文本生效前所制作作品的利用不应随意禁止。

55. 来自伊比利亚 – 拉丁美洲表演者联合会（FILAIE）的一名观察员完全支持该法律文本应以保护表演者而不是制作者的权利为目的。唯一有效的保护是给予受集体管理的报酬权。他反对美国关于国民待遇的建议，并对条约中精神权利的命运表示关切。

56. 来自国际广播协会（IAB）的一位观察员强调，有必要把促进广播组织的权利作为 2001 年常设委员会的一个优先问题。他还指出，如果通过一项保护表演者的议定书或条约，而不承认制作和汇编视听材料的特殊性和现实情

risks of adopting a protocol or treaty for the protection of performers that did not acknowledge the peculiarities and realities of the production and compilation of audiovisual material; that could have undesirable consequences, especially on developing countries, for the audiovisual industry and the actual performers of such countries, and the ultimate consequence of developed countries being favored at the expense of developing countries.

57. An observer from the Association of European Performers' Organisations (AEPO) remarked that a protocol should aim at enhancing the performers' rights. Some proposals on moral rights constituted a total distortion of the concept of those rights. He opposed having presumptions on transfer of rights, because of the effects in countries that did not have a tradition for written contracts. National treatment should be similar to the rules of the WPPT.

58. The Delegation of Canada stated that the Canadian branch of the American Federation of Musicians had been informed of, and had not opposed, the Canadian proposals regarding the recognition of transfers of rights in foreign audiovisual works.

FUTURE WORK

59. The Standing Committee decided to invite governments to submit, before January 31, 2001, proposals in treaty language concerning the protection of broadcasting organizations. The next session of the Standing Committee would take place in the beginning of 2001, at dates to be determined by the International Bureau.

ADOPTION OF THE REPORT AND CLOSING OF THE SESSION

60. The Standing Committee unanimously adopted this report.

61. The Chairman closed the session.

[Annex follows]

况，就会有危险；这可能会产生不良后果，特别是对发展中国家，对视听产业和这些国家的实际表演者，以及发达国家以牺牲发展中国家的利益为代价而受到优待的最终后果。

57. 来自欧洲表演者组织协会（AEPO）的一名观察员说，一项议定书应以加强表演者的权利为目标。一些关于精神权利的建议完全歪曲了这些权利的概念。他反对设立权利转让的推定，因为没有书面合同之传统的国家会受到影响。国民待遇应与 WPPT 的规则相似。

58. 加拿大代表团说，美国音乐家联合会加拿大分会已获悉加拿大关于承认转让外国视听作品权利的建议，但没有表示反对。

未来的工作

59. 常设委员会决定邀请各国政府在 2001 年 1 月 31 日之前，以条约语言提交关于保护广播组织的提案。常设委员会的下一届会议将于 2001 年年初举行，日期将由国际局决定。

通过报告并结束会议

60. 常设委员会一致通过了报告。

61. 主席宣布会议闭幕。

（后接附件）

译者注：附件参会人员名单省略。

6.6 Report on the Regional Consultation Meeting For Countries of Latin America and the Caribbean

Document Code: SCCR/4/7
Language: English
URL: https://www.wipo.int/edocs/mdocs/copyright/en/sccr_4/sccr_4_7.pdf
Chinese Translation: Not Available.
URL: N/A

STANDING COMMITTEE ON COPYRIGHT
AND RELATED RIGHTS
Forth Session
Geneva, April 11,12 and 14, 2000

REPORT ON THE REGIONAL CONSULTATION MEETING FOR COUNTRIES OF LATIN AMERICA AND THE CARIBBEAN

GENEVA, APRIL 12, 2000

submitted on behalf of Argentina, Brazil, Colombia, Costa Rica, Cuba, the Dominican Republic, Ecuador, Guyana, Jamaica, Mexico, Panama, Paraguay, Peru, Trinidad and Tobago, Uruguay and Venezuela[1]

1 Received on April 13, 2000.

6.6 拉丁美洲和加勒比国家的区域协商报告

文件编号：SCCR/4/7
文件语言：英语
文件链接：https://www.wipo.int/edocs/mdocs/copyright/en/sccr_4/sccr_4_7.pdf
中文文本：无
文件链接：无

版权及相关权常设委员会

第四届会议
2000 年 4 月 11 日、12 日和 14 日，日内瓦

拉丁美洲和加勒比国家的区域协商报告

2000 年 4 月 12 日，日内瓦
由阿根廷、巴西、哥伦比亚、哥斯达黎加、
古巴、多米尼加共和国、厄瓜多尔、圭亚那、牙买加、
墨西哥、巴拿马、巴拉圭、秘鲁、特立尼达和多巴哥、
乌拉圭、委内瑞拉提交[1]

1　2000 年 4 月 13 日收到。

REPORT ON THE REGIONAL CONSULTATION MEETING FOR LATIN AMERICAN AND CARIBBEAN COUNTRIES ON A PROTOCOL CONCERNING AUDIOVISUAL PERFORMANCES

Geneva, April 12, 2000

A Regional Consultation Meeting of Latin American and Caribbean Countries on a Protocol Concerning Audiovisual Performances took place in Geneva, Switzerland, on April 12, 2000. The meeting was presided over by the Delegate of Peru, Mrs. Betty Berendson.

The discussions were based on document SCCR/2/2, presented by WIPO.

Consensus was reached on the following points:

I. TITLE

Protocol to the WIPO Performances and Phonograms Treaty Concerning Audiovisual Performances.

II. PREAMBLE

The Contracting Parties,

Wishing to ensure an adequate level of protection for performances in audiovisual works, owing to the fact that the development and convergence of new information and communication technology will bring about a rapid broadening of the range of audiovisual services and also an increase in the opportunities for performers to exploit their performances,

Referring to the Resolution Concerning Audiovisual Performances adopted by the Diplomatic Conference on Certain Copyright and Neighboring Rights Questions on December 20, 1996,

Have agreed as follows:

III. RELATION TO OTHER CONVENTIONS; RELATION TO COPYRIGHT

1. This instrument constitutes a Protocol to the WIPO Performances and Phonograms Treaty done in Geneva on December 20, 1996 (hereinafter "the WIPO Treaty").

拉丁美洲和加勒比国家关于视听表演议定书的区域协商报告

2000年4月12日，日内瓦

拉丁美洲和加勒比国家关于视听表演议定书的区域协商会议于2000年4月12日在瑞士日内瓦举行。会议由秘鲁代表Betty Berendson女士主持。

讨论以WIPO提交的SCCR/2/2号文件为基础。

会议就下列事项达成了共识：

I. 标题

《世界知识产权组织表演和录音制品条约》关于视听表演的议定书。

II. 序言

缔约各方，

希望确保对视听作品中的表演提供适当的保护，因为新的信息和通信技术的发展和融合将带来视听服务范围的迅速扩大，也将增加表演者利用其表演的机会。

提及1996年12月20日版权和邻接权若干问题外交会议通过的《关于视听表演的决议》。

达成如下协议：

III. 与其他公约的关系；与版权的关系

1. 该条约系1996年12月20日在日内瓦签订的《世界知识产权组织表演和录音制品条约》（WIPO条约）的一项议定书的组成部分。

2. No provision of this Protocol shall detract from the mutual obligations of Contracting Parties under the International Convention for the Protection of Performers, Producers of Phonograms and Broadcasting Organizations, done at Rome on October 26, 1961 (hereinafter "the Rome Convention").

3. The protection granted under this Protocol shall leave intact and in no way affect the protection of copyright in literary and artistic works. Consequently no provision of this Treaty may be interpreted as prejudicing such protection.

4. This Protocol shall have no connection with, and shall not prejudice any right or obligation under, any treaty other than the WIPO Treaty.

IV. DEFINITIONS

1. The Contracting Parties shall apply, *mutatis mutandis*, the definitions set out in Article 2 (a), (e), (f) and (g) of the WIPO Treaty in connection with the protection granted under this Protocol.

2. For the purposes of this Protocol, "audiovisual fixation" means the embodiment of images, whether or not accompanied by sound, or the representation thereof, from which they can be perceived, reproduced or communicated by means of a device.

3. For the purposes of this Protocol, "performers" means all actors, singers, musicians, dancers or other persons who interpret a role, sing, recite, declaim or in any way perform literary or artistic works or expressions of folklore, with the exception of extras [, the definition of the latter term being left to the legislation of each Contracting Party].

V. BENEFICIARIES OF PROTECTION

The Contracting Parties shall accord the protection provided under this Protocol:

(a) to performers who are nationals of other Contracting Parties;

(b) to performers who are not nationals of any of the Contracting Parties but are ordinarily resident in one of them, who shall be treated as nationals of the Contracting Party concerned.

VI. NATIONAL TREATMENT

Each Contracting Party shall accord to the nationals of other Contracting Parties the same treatment as it accords to its own nationals with respect to the

2. 本议定书的任何规定均不得减损缔约各方之间依照1961年10月26日在罗马签订的《保护表演者、录音制品制作者和广播组织国际公约》(《罗马公约》)承担的相互义务。

3. 依本议定书给予的保护不得触动或以任何方式影响对文学和艺术作品版权的保护。因此,本条约的任何内容均不得被解释为损害此种保护。

4. 除WIPO条约之外,本议定书不得与任何其他条约有任何关联,亦不得损害任何其他条约所规定的任何权利和义务。

IV. 定义

1. 缔约各方应比照适用WIPO条约第2条(a)、(e)、(f)和(g)款中关于本议定书所给予保护的定义。

2. 在本议定书中,"视听录制品"系指活动图像的体现物,无论是否伴有声音,或其表现形式,都可以通过设备来感知、复制或传播。

3. 在本议定书中,"表演者"是指所有演员、歌唱家、音乐家、舞蹈家或其他演绎角色、唱歌、朗诵、宣读或以任何方式表演文学或艺术作品或民间文学表现形式的人,但临时演员除外。(后者的定义由各缔约方的立法决定。)

V. 保护的受益者

缔约各方应将本议定书规定的保护给予:

a)属于其他缔约方国民的表演者;

b)非任何缔约方的国民但通常居住在其中一个缔约方的表演者,他们应被视为有关缔约方的国民。

VI. 国民待遇

在本议定书具体赋予的权利方面,各缔约方应给予其他缔约方的国民与本国国民相同的待遇。

rights specifically granted in this Protocol.

VII. FORMALITIES

The enjoyment and exercise of the rights provided for in this Protocol shall not be subject to any formality.

VIII. MORAL RIGHTS OF PERFORMERS

1. Independently of the performer's economic rights, and even after the transfer of those rights, the performer shall, as regards his live audiovisual performances, with or without sound, or performances included in audiovisual fixations, have the right to claim to be identified as the performer of his performances, except where omission is dictated by the manner of the use of the performance, and to object to any distortion, mutilation or other modification of his performances that would be prejudicial to his reputation, provided that the audiovisual producer may abridge, condense, edit or dub the work, but without thereby distorting the performance of the performer.

2. The rights granted to the performer in accordance with the foregoing paragraph shall, after his death, be maintained, at least until the expiry of his economic rights, and shall be exercisable by the persons or institutions authorized by the legislation of the Contracting Party where protection is claimed. However, those Contracting Parties whose legislation, at the moment of their ratification of or accession to this Treaty does not provide for protection after the death of the performer of all rights set out in the preceding paragraph may provide that some of those rights will, after his death, cease to be maintained.

3. The means of redress for safeguarding the rights granted under this Article shall be governed by the legislation of the Contracting Party where protection is claimed.

IX. ECONOMIC RIGHTS OF PERFORMERS IN THEIR UNFIXED PERFORMANCES

Performers shall enjoy the exclusive right to authorize the following in relation to their unfixed performances:

a) broadcasting and communication to the public of their unfixed performances, except where the performance constitutes a broadcast performance in itself;

b) fixation of their unfixed performances.

VII. 手续

享有和行使本议定书所规定的权利无须履行任何手续。

VIII. 表演者的精神权利

1. 独立于表演者的经济权利，甚至在这些权利转让之后，表演者对于其有声或无声的现场表演，或包含在视听录制品中的表演，均有权要求被认定为其表演的表演者，除非因使用表演的方式而决定省略，并有权反对对其表演进行任何有损其声誉的歪曲、肢解或其他修改，但视听制作人可以对作品进行删节、压缩、编辑或配音，但不得因此而歪曲表演者的表演。

2. 根据前款规定授予表演者的权利，在其死亡后应得到维护，至少在其经济权利到期之前，并应由要求保护的缔约国立法授权的个人或机构行使。但是，那些在批准或加入本条约时，其立法没有规定在表演者死后保护前款规定的所有权利的缔约国，可以规定其中一些权利在他死后将不再得到维护。

3. 保障本条规定的权利的救济措施，应由要求保护的缔约国的立法规定。

IX. 表演者对其未录制表演的经济权利

表演者对其未录制的表演授权享有以下专有权：

a）广播和向公众传播其未录制的表演，除非该表演本身属于广播表演；

b）录制其尚未录制的表演。

X. ECONOMIC RIGHTS OF PERFORMERS CONCERNING AUDIOVISUAL FIXATIONS

1. Right of reproduction

Performers shall enjoy the exclusive right to authorize the direct or indirect reproduction of their performances incorporated in audiovisual fixations in any manner or form.

2. Right of distribution

(a) Performers shall enjoy the exclusive right to authorize the making available to the public, through sale or other transfer of ownership, of the original and copies of their performances incorporated in audiovisual fixations.

(b) Nothing in this Protocol shall affect the freedom of Contracting Parties to determine the conditions, if any, under which the exhaustion of the right in paragraph (a) applies after the first sale or other transfer of ownership of the original or a copy of the fixed performance with the authorization of the performer.

3. Right of rental

(a) Performers shall enjoy the exclusive right to authorize the commercial rental to the public of copies of their audiovisual fixations.

(b) Paragraph (a) shall not be applicable in the case of an audiovisual work except where the said commercial rental has given rise to widespread copying thereof which considerably detracts from the performer's exclusive rights of reproduction.

4. Right of making available

Performers shall enjoy the exclusive right to authorize the making available to the public of their performances incorporated in audiovisual fixations, by wire or wireless means, in such a way that members of the public may access them from a place and at a time individually chosen by them.

XI. LIMITATIONS AND EXCEPTIONS

1. The Contracting Parties may, in their national legislation, provide for the same kinds of limitation or exception with regard to the protection of performers as they provide for, in their national legislation, in connection with the protection of the copyright in literary and artistic works.

2. The Contracting Parties shall confine any limitation on or exception to

X. 表演者对视听录制品的经济权利

1. 复制权

表演者应享有授权以任何方式或形式对录制在视听作品中的表演直接或间接进行复制的专有权。

2. 发行权

(a)表演者应享有授权通过出售或其他转让所有权的方式向公众提供其录制在视听作品中的表演原件和复制件的专有权。

(b)对于已录制表演的原件或复制件经表演者授权被首次销售或以其他形式转让所有权之后适用本条第(a)款中权利的用尽所依据的条件，本议定书的任何内容均不得影响缔约方确定该条件的自由。

3. 出租权

(a)表演者应享有授权向公众商业出租其音像制品复制品的专有权利。

(b)本条第(a)款不应适用于视听作品，除非上述商业性出租引起了对作品的广泛复制，很大程度上减损了表演者的专有复制权。

4. 提供权

表演者享有专有权，以有线或无线方式向公众提供其录制在视听作品中的表演，以便公众成员可以在其个人选择的地点和时间获得这些表演。

XI. 限制与例外

1. 缔约方可以在其本国法律中就保护表演者作出与其本国法律中保护文学和艺术作品的版权所规定的相同种类的限制或例外的规定。

2. 缔约方应将对本议定书所规定的权利的任何限制或例外仅限于某些特

rights provided for in this Protocol to certain special cases that do not conflict with a normal exploitation of the audiovisual fixations or unreasonably prejudice the legitimate interests of the performer or of the audiovisual producer.

XII. TERM OF PROTECTION OF THE ECONOMIC RIGHTS OF PERFORMERS

The term of protection to be granted to performers under this Protocol shall last, at least, until the end of a period of 50 years counted from the end of the year in which the performance was fixed.

XIII. OBLIGATIONS CONCERNING TECHNOLOGICAL MEASURES

The Contracting Parties shall provide adequate legal protection and effective legal remedies against the circumvention of effective technological measures that are used by performers in connection with the exercise of their rights under this Protocol and which restrict acts, in respect of their performances, that are not authorized by the performers concerned or permitted by law.

XIV. OBLIGATIONS CONCERNING RIGHTS MANAGEMENT INFORMATION

1. Contracting Parties shall provide adequate and effective legal remedies against any person knowingly performing any of the following acts knowing, or with respect to civil remedies having reasonable grounds to know, that it will induce, enable, facilitate or conceal an infringement of any right covered by this Protocol:

a) removing or altering any electronic rights management information without authority;

b) distributing, importing for distribution, broadcasting, communicating or otherwise making available to the public, without authority, performances, copies of performances incorporated in audiovisual fixations knowing that electronic rights management information has been removed or altered without authority.

2. As used in this Article, "rights management information" means information that identifies the performer, his performance, the audiovisual producer or the audiovisual work, or information about the terms and conditions governing the use of the performance of the audiovisual work, and any numbers or codes that represent such information, when any of those items of information is attached to

殊情况，例如不与视听录制品的正常利用相冲突或不合理地损害表演者或视听制作人的合法利益。

XII. 表演者经济权利的保护期限

根据本议定书给予表演者的保护期限，应自表演录制之年的年终起算，至少持续到 50 年期满为止。

XIII. 有关技术措施的义务

缔约方应规定适当的法律保护和有效的法律救济途径，防止表演者为行使本议定书所规定的权利以及为了限制未经有关表演者授权或法律不允许的行为而采取的有效技术措施被规避。

XIV. 有关权利管理信息的义务

1. 缔约各方应规定适当和有效的法律补救办法，制止任何人明知或就民事补救而言有合理根据知道其行为会诱使、促成、便利或包庇对本条约所涵盖的任何权利的侵犯而故意从事以下行为：

a）未经许可删除或更改任何电子权利管理信息；

b）在明知电子权利管理信息已被删除或更改的情况下，擅自向公众发行、为进口目的发行、广播、传播或以其他方式提供表演或包含在视听录制品中的表演的复制件。

2. 本条中“权利管理信息”系指识别表演者、表演者的表演、视听制作人或视听作品的信息，或有关使用视听作品中的表演的条款和条件的信息，和代表此种信息的任何数字或代码，各该项信息均附于录制的表演的每件复制件上或视听作品上，或在已录制在视听作品中的表演向公众提供时出现。

a copy of a fixed performance or appears in connection with the communication or making available to the public of a performance incorporated in an audiovisual fixation.

XV. RESERVATIONS

GRULAC will pronounce on this matter after the articles concerning the various rights have been put in final form.

XVI. APPLICATION IN TIME

1. The Contracting Parties shall apply the provisions of Article 18 of the Berne Convention, *mutatis mutandis*, to the rights of the performers provided for in this Protocol.

2. This Protocol shall not detract from the rights acquired in any Contracting Party prior to the date of entry into force of this Protocol in that Party.

XVII. PROVISIONS ON ENFORCEMENT OF RIGHTS

1. The Contracting Parties undertake to adopt, in accordance with their legal systems, the measures necessary to ensure the application of this Protocol.

2. The Contracting Parties shall ensure that enforcement procedures are available under their law so as to permit effective action against any act of infringement of rights covered by this Protocol, including expeditious remedies to prevent infringement and remedies that constitute a deterrent to further infringements.

XVIII. ADMINISTRATIVE PROVISIONS AND FINAL CLAUSES

1. Assembly

The Contracting Parties shall have an Assembly. That Assembly shall be the same as the one created by the WIPO Treaty.

2. Eligibility to Become Party to the Protocol

Any party to the WIPO Treaty may become party to this Protocol.

3. Signature of the Protocol

This Protocol shall be open for signature until .... by any Member State of WIPO and by the European Community.

4. Entry into Force of the Protocol

This Protocol shall enter into force, following the date of entry into force of the WIPO Treaty, three months after 20 instruments of ratification or accession by

XV. 保留

在各种权利的条款以最终形式确定之后，拉丁美洲和加勒比国家小组将就此发表声明。

XVI. 适用的时限

1. 缔约方应就本议定书所规定的表演者的权利比照适用《伯尔尼公约》第18条的规定。

2. 本议定书规定的保护不得减损任何缔约方在本议定书对该缔约方生效前获得的权利。

XVII. 权利行使规定

1. 缔约方承诺根据其法律制度采取必要措施，以确保本议定书的适用。

2. 缔约方应确保根据其法律可采用执行程序，以便针对本议定书所涵盖的任何侵权行为采取有效行动，包括为防止侵权而迅速采取的救济措施以及对进一步侵权构成威慑作用的救济措施。

XVIII. 行政条款和最后条款

1. <u>大会</u>

缔约方应举行大会。该大会应与《WIPO 条约》设立的大会相同。

2. <u>成为议定书缔约方的资格</u>

《WIPO 条约》的任何缔约方均可成为本议定书的缔约方。

3. <u>议定书的签署</u>

本议定书应开放供世界知识产权组织任何成员国和欧洲共同体签署，直到……

4. <u>议定书生效</u>

本议定书应自《WIPO 条约》生效之日起，在将二十份国家批准或加入书交存 WIPO 总干事后三个月生效。

States have been deposited with the Director General of WIPO.

5. Final Clauses

The provisions of Articles 25 (International Bureau), 27 (Rights and Obligations under the Treaty), 30 (Effective Date of Becoming Party to the Treaty), 31 (Denunciation of the Treaty), 32 (Languages of the Treaty) and 33 (Depositary) of the WIPO Treaty shall apply *mutatis mutandis* to this Protocol.

Note: With regard to Articles X(5) and XII of the original proposal contained in document SCCR/2/2, on the Right of broadcasting and communication to the public and Contractual arrangements concerning the rights of performers respectively, the member countries of GRULAC reserve the right to speak in their own names.

[End of document]

5. 最后条款

《WIPO条约》第25条(国际局)、第27条(条约项下的权利和义务)、第30条(成为条约缔约方的生效日期)、第31条(退出条约)、第32条(条约的语言)和第33条(保存人)的规定应比照适用于本议定书。

注:关于文件SCCR/2/2所载原始提案的第X(5)条和第XII条,分别涉及向公众广播和传播的权利以及关于表演者权利的合同安排,拉丁美洲和加勒比国家保留以自己名义发言的权利。

(文件完)

6.7 Proposal by Certain African Countries Relating to Transfer

Document Code: SCCR/4/8 CORR.
Language: English
URL: https://www.wipo.int/edocs/mdocs/copyright/en/sccr_4/sccr_4_8_corr.pdf
Chinese Translation: Not Available.
URL: N/A

STANDING COMMITTEE ON COPYRIGHT
AND RELATED RIGHTS
Fourth Session
Geneva, April 11, 12 and 14, 2000

PROPOSAL BY CERTAIN AFRICAN COUNTRIES RELATING TO TRANSFER

submitted on behalf of Algeria, Burkina Faso, Cameroon, Côte d'Ivoire, Ghana, Kenya, Madagascar, Morocco, Rwanda, South Africa, Togo, Tunisia, Uganda and the United Republic of Tanzania[1]

1 Received on April 12, 2000.

6.7 某些非洲国家关于转让条款的提案

文件编号：SCCR/4/8 CORR.
文件语言：英语
文件链接：https://www.wipo.int/edocs/mdocs/copyright/en/sccr_4/sccr_4_8_corr.pdf
中文文本：无
文件链接：无

版权及相关权常设委员会

第四届会议

2000 年 4 月 11 日、12 日和 14 日，日内瓦

某些非洲国家关于转让条款的提案

代表阿尔及利亚、布基纳法索、喀麦隆、科特迪瓦、加纳、
肯尼亚、马达加斯加、摩洛哥、卢旺达、南非、多哥、
突尼斯、乌干达和坦桑尼亚联合共和国提交[1]

1　于 2000 年 4 月 12 日提交。

PROPOSAL BY CERTAIN AFRICAN COUNTRIES RELATING TO TRANSFER

1. In the absence of any contrary stipulation by the parties to a contract, any transfer, by agreement or operation of law, of any of the exclusive rights of authorization granted to a performer under this [Protocol/Treaty] shall be governed by the law of the country most closely connected with the particular audiovisual work.

2. The country most closely connected with a particular audiovisual work shall be:

(a) the Contracting Party in which the maker of the particular work has his headquarters or habitual residence; or

(b) where the maker does not have his headquarters or habitual residence in a Contracting Party, or where there is more than one maker, the country in which the particular performer has his habitual residence.

[End of document]

某些非洲国家关于转让条款的提案

1. 依照本（议定书 / 条约），依协议约定或法律规定转让表演者授予的排他性权利，除缔约方有相反约定外，均应受到与系争视听作品联系最密切的国家的法律规制。

2. 与系争视听作品联系最密切的国家是指：

（a）系争作品制作者总部或经常居住地或实际经营地所在地；或

（b）制作者在缔约方中没有总部或经常居住地或实际经营地，或者存在两个以上制作者情况下，则为该表演者经常居住地所在国家。

（文件完）